1. 00

The Wordsworth Dictionary
of Pub Names

The Wordsworth Dictionary of

PUB NAMES

Wordsworth Reference

In loving memory of
MICHAEL TRAYLER
the founder of Wordsworth Editions

2

Readers who are interested in other titles from
Wordsworth Editions are invited to visit our website at
www.wordsworth-editions.com

For our latest list and a full mail-order service, contact
Bibliophile Books, 5 Thomas Road, London E14 7BN
TEL: +44 (0)20 7515 9222 FAX: +44 (0)20 7538 4115
E-MAIL: orders@bibliophilebooks.com

First published in 2006 by Wordsworth Editions Limited
8B East Street, Ware, Hertfordshire SG12 9HJ

ISBN   978 1 84022 266 1

Text © Wordsworth Editions Limited 2006

Wordsworth® is a registered trademark of
Wordsworth Editions Limited

Typeset in Great Britain by Antony Gray
Printed and bound by Clays Ltd, St Ives plc

To my dearest friends

COLIN AND CHERRY HARRINGTON

'Drive fast, take chances and have sex.'

Group entries

We have included among the individual pub-name entries brief discussions of some of the subjects dealt with on inn signs. Pub names which do not have their own entries are occasionally mentioned in these articles, eg **Bunch of Grapes** is under **Fruit and Vegetables**. If you are looking for a particular name which is not in alphabetical order as an independent entry, try a suitable group entry.

Admirals	Cricket	Number names
American states	Dog	Occupations
Apples	Famous people	Old
Archery	Fish and sea creatures	Place names
Aviation names	Flowers	Playing cards
Barrels	Football	Racehorses
Bell	Fruit and vegetables	Railway names
Bible references	Horse	Rivers and canals
Bird	Hunting	Rose
Black	It's a Man's World	Rugby
Blacksmiths	Jolly	Saint
Blood sports	Lion	Series naming
Blue	Literary references	Ship names
Boats	Local legends and	Songs
Boot	customs	Sport
Bowls	Maritime and nautical	Street names
Bridge	names	Top Twenty
Brown	Military names	Tree
Bull	Mines and mining	Women in pub names
Cat	Musical names	Ye
Combination names	New	

Abbreviations

The system of abbreviations given below is designed to match our occasionally idiosyncratic dictionary entries. We have allowed ourselves the odd light-hearted or punning entry about a pub name, since light-heartedness is something of a tradition in this field. Past writers on the subject, and indeed pub-namers themselves, have seen no reason to be over-serious. Thus we find pubs named **Square Albert**, say, in Albert Square, Manchester, and the **Pirate**, in Penzance. The puns are there in the **Hop 'n' Scotch**, Harrogate, the **Elbow Room**, Paisley, and so on. There are many examples of such names in this book. We appreciate them ourselves: we hope you do as well.

List of Abbreviations

Ant	Co Antrim	Lincs	Lincolnshire
Arm	Co Armagh	Londy	Co Londonderry
Bdrs	Borders	Loth	Lothian
Beds	Bedfordshire	Mers	Merseyside
Berks	Berkshire	M Glarn	Mid Glamorgan
Bucks	Buckinghamshire	Nflk	Norfolk
Cambs	Cambridgeshire	Northants	Northamptonshire
Ches	Cheshire	Northld	Northumberland
Clev	Cleveland	Notts	Nottinghamshire
Corn	Cornwall	N Yorks	North Yorkshire
Cumb	Cumbria	Oxon	Oxfordshire
D and G	Dumfries and Galloway	Pwys	Powys
Derbs	Derbyshire	Salop	Shropshire
Dors	Dorset	Sflk	Suffolk
Down	Co Down	S Glam	South Glamorgan
Dur	Co Durham	Shetd	Shetland
E Ssx	East Sussex	Som	Somerset
Esx	Essex	Sry	Surrey
GL	Greater London	Staffs	Staffordshire
Glos	Gloucestershire	Strath	Strathclyde
Gramp	Grampian	S Yorks	South Yorkshire
Gynd	Gwynedd	T and W	Tyne and Wear
H and W	Hereford and Worcester	Tays	Tayside
Hants	Hampshire	Warks	Warwickshire
Herts	Hertfordshire	W Glam	West Glamorgan
Hghld	Highland	Wilts	Wiltshire
Humb	Humberside	W Mids	West Midlands
IOW	Isle of Wight	W Ssx	West Sussex
Lancs	Lancashire	W Yorks	West Yorkshire
Leics	Leicestershire		

A

A1 at Lloyds Liverpool. The usual reference is to a ship which is considered by Lloyds, the insurance syndicate, to be in first-class condition. The implication is that the pub is equally first-class. There is a similar A1 Bar in Belfast.

Abadam Arms Porthyrhyd, near Carmarthen. Abadam is a Welsh surname meaning 'son of Adam'.

Abbey Darley Abbey, near Derby. The building is part of the original twelfth-century abbey, most of which was destroyed in the Dissolution by Henry VIII. The pub of this name in Paddington, London, was formerly the Fountains Abbey, referring to the famous medieval ruin not far from Ripon. Related names include Abbey Arms, West Ham; Abbey Hostel, Crowland, Lincs; Abbey Lodge, Woodhall Spa, Lincs; Abbey Vaults Birmingham; Abbey Wine Vaults, Bath.

Abbey Barn Doulting, Som. Formerly the barn where the farmers' tithe (one-tenth of the crop) was stored. The tithe was a form of local tax, which in this case contributed to the upkeep of Glastonbury Abbey. Tithe Barn is also found.

Abbot John Wheathampstead, Herts. John Bostock, who was born locally, became Abbot of St Albans in the fourteenth century.

Abbot's Fireside Elham, Kent. The pub has a huge stone fireplace, carved by a monk-mason. It belonged formerly to the abbot of the monastery at nearby Lyminge. (Monasteries have long had close associations with alcoholic beverages.) There is an Abbot's Court at St Bees, Cumbria, an Abbot's Barton at Canterbury and an Abbot's Choice in Edinburgh.

Abbotsford Edinburgh. By 1820 the novelist Sir Walter Scott (1771–1832) was at the height of his fame and fortune. He had bought the estate of Abbotsford, near Melrose, and entertained lavishly. One commentator of the time said that Abbotsford was 'like an inn', a remark which seems to have inspired this pub name. Galashiels has an Abbotsford Arms. *See also* Sir Walter Scott.

Abbot's Mitre Chilbolton, Hants. The mitre is the tall cap with a deep cleft in it, usually associated with a bishop. It is also worn by some abbots on ceremonial occasions.

Abercorn Also Abercorn Arms. *See* Duke of Abercorn.

Aberdeen Also Aberdeen's Arms. *See* Earl of Aberdeen's Arms.

Aberfeldy London E14. An indirect reference to one of the most colourful regiments of the British Army, the Black Watch (Royal Highland) Regiment. The regiment was raised at Aberfeldy in Tayside in 1739. *See also* Black Watch.

A Bit on the Side Chippenham, Wilts. This is an updated, jokey version of a name like Annexe, often used for a pub which adjoins another building, in this case a nightclub called 'Gold Diggers'.

A'board Appleby, Cumb. Larwood and Hotten (*History of Signboards*) say that this puzzling name 'is not to be confused with' the once common Board, and that it means 'to board intoxicating liquor'. There is no evidence that 'a'board' ever had such a meaning. In coastal towns this sign would presumably be taken as an invitation to 'come aboard,' i.e., come inside. It also carries a suggestion that 'board and lodging' is available. It is just possible that in some cases the need for an inn to have 'a board' suggested the name, since some inns did in fact display a blank board.

Ace of Clubs Ingoldmells, Skegness. A name which provides a convenient visual symbol, with the suggestion that here is a first-class social club where cards can be played.

Ace of Spades Oldham. *See* Playing Cards.

Acorn St Albans and elsewhere. Probably a use of a convenient visual symbol. Fanciful interpretations made by commentators have included allusions to the pub's small size, indications of the landlord's intention to grow strong from a small beginning, and even a reference to Charles II's alleged hiding-place in the oak tree at Boscobel, near Shifnal, Salop.

AD 1606 Bristol. Formerly the Hatchet, referring to woodcutters who were active in Clifton Wood in times past. Renamed in 1984 for the date which is inscribed over the pub's front entrance. The pub was first licensed in 1606.

Adam and Eve Windsor and elsewhere. Ironically adopted as the arms of the Fruiterers' Company. There was formerly a pub of this name in the Cotswold village of Paradise, but it is now a private house. At Braughing, near Ware, the original sign of the *Adam and Eve* offended the locals (or some of them). The artist was forced to provide the pair with fig leaves. Paradise House also occurs, and there is a Fruiterers' Arms at Lewes, East Sussex.

Adams Arms London W1. For a local architect of note, a Mr Adams.

Addington New Addington, Sry. Also an Addington Arms in London E3. Henry Addington, afterwards Lord Sidmouth, was born in 1756. By 1789 he was speaker of the House of Commons. He then became prime minister 1801–04, and was home secretary in 1812. He retired from public life in 1822 and died in 1844. There is a Sidmouth Arms at Upottery, Devon.

Addison Arms Glatton, Cambs. There was formerly an Addison in Newcastle-on-Tyne. After Joseph Addison (1672–1719), playwright and politician. He would have been a suitable man to meet in a pub, since Lady Mary Montagu, who claimed to have known 'all the wits', was of the opinion that 'Addison was the best company in the world'. He was a major contributor to the extremely influential publications *The Tatler* (begun by his friend Steele – *see* Sir Richard Steele) and *The Spectator*.

Adelphi Bradford. Also Adelphi Vaults at Amlwch, Anglesey, Presumably a borrowing from the famous London area of the same name, designed by the Adams brothers in 1768. *Adelphoi* is the Greek word for 'brothers'.

ADMIRALS Admirals are well represented in pub names. We have noted thirty-six individual admirals who have been honoured by having a pub named for them. Nelson has naturally been the most popular member of this group, and indeed has more pubs named after him than any other person. Admirals Rodney and Vernon are also very popular. *See also* Anson Arms, Collingwood, Earl Howe, Earl St Vincent, Hawkins Arms, Lord Howard, Sir John Borlase Warren, Sir John Franklin, Sir Richard Grenville, Sir Sidney Smith. Paul Jones Tavern possibly belongs to this group. Admiral itself occurs as a pub name at Reading and elsewhere and there is an Admiral's Bell in Edinburgh. Sheerness has an Admiral's Walk and a British Admiral; Portsmouth has an Admiral's Head and an Admiralty Tavern. *See also* General At Sea.

Admiral Beatty Gravesend and Leicester. Sir David Beatty (1871–1936) commanded the battle-cruisers at the Battle of Jutland in 1916. At the age of thirty-nine he became the youngest admiral in the Royal Navy for over a hundred years and was known as a man of great moral and physical courage. He was raised to the peerage in 1919. At Motspur Park, Sry there is an Earl Beatty.

Admiral Benbow Shrewsbury (his birthplace) and elsewhere. John Benbow (1650–1702) died after a five-day running battle with the French in the Caribbean had left him mortally wounded. He is buried in Jamaica. His bravery was made the subject of a popular ballad.

Admiral Blake London W8. Robert Blake (1599–1657) was a Puritan and republican who had a distinguished military career, at first as a general in the civil war, later at sea. There is a Blake Arms at Bridgwater, Som. (his birthplace) and a Blake in Sheffield.

Admiral Blakeney's Head London E1. William Blakeney (1672–1761) won fame as the defender of Minorca in 1756 during the Seven Years' War, though he was eventually forced to surrender to the French on honourable terms. Although at the time of the battle he was eighty-four years old, he is said not to have taken to his bed during the seventy days of fighting. There is a Blakeney's Head at London E14.

Admiral Boscawen Truro. Edward Boscawen (1711–61) is remembered mainly for his activities along the St Lawrence River in 1758. The capture of Louisburg eventually led to the taking of Canada from the French. There is a Boscawen at St Dennis, Corn., the admiral having been born in that county. He served as member of parliament for Truro from 1742.

Admiral Codrington London SW3. Another in Coventry. Sir Edward Codrington (1770–1855) led one of Nelson's squadrons at Trafalgar. In 1827, as commander-in-chief of the combined British, French and Russian fleets, he was responsible for the defeat of the Turkish and Egyptian navies at Navarino Bay, helping the Greeks in their struggle for independence. Yate, near Bristol, has Codrington Arms. In London E8 there is a Navarino.

Admiral Cunningham Bracknell and Fareham. Sir Andrew Cunningham, later Viscount Hyndhope (1883–1963), was commander-in-chief in the Mediterranean 1939–43 and was later First Sea Lord.

Admiral Drake *See* Sir Francis Drake.

Admiral Duncan Nottingham and elsewhere. Adam Duncan (1731–1804) achieved a notable victory over the Dutch near Camperdown in 1797. He later became Viscount Duncan of Camperdown. London E8 has a Lord Duncan named after him.

Admiral Hardy London SE10. Sir Thomas Masterman Hardy (1769–1839) was flag-captain to Lord Nelson aboard HMS *Victory* at Trafalgar and was held in high esteem by him. When Nelson was dying he sent for Hardy and uttered the words which have been treated irreverently ever since: 'Kiss me, Hardy'. The admiral had a destroyer named in his honour, which was sunk by enemy action in World War Two.

Admiral Harvey Dover and elsewhere. Sir Eliab Harvey (1758–1830), a descendant of the anatomist William Harvey who discovered the circulation of the blood, commanded the *Fighting Temeraire* at Trafalgar and was made admiral the same year (1805). He was later elected as member of parliament for Maldon in Essex.

Admiral Hawke Hessle, near Hull. Sir Edward Hawke (1705–81), later Lord Hawke, made his name in 1759 when the fleet he commanded defeated the French at Quiberon Bay, off the NW coast of France.

Admiral Holland Banbury. Lancelot Ernest Holland (1887–1941) went down with his ship, HMS *Hood*, when she was sunk by the German battleship *Bismarck* in 1941. *See also* Mighty Hood.

Admiral Hood Mosterton, Dors. It is not clear which member of the distinguished naval family is meant. Admiral Viscount Hood (1724–1816) had a younger brother Alexander, later Admiral Viscount Bridport (1727–1814). They were followed by Vice-admiral Sir Samuel Hood (1762–1814), Admiral Lord Hood of Avalon (1824–1901) and Rear-admiral Sir Horace Hood (d 1916). The battle-cruiser *Hood*,

named for this family, was sunk by the *Bismarck* in 1941 (*see* Mighty Hood). Other pub names are Lord Hood at Deptford and a Hood Arms at Kilve; Som. There is also an Acland Hood Arms at Stogursey in Somerset.

Admiral Jellicoe Leigh Beck, Canvey Island. Sir John (later Earl) Jellicoe (1859–1935) was commander-in-chief of the Grand Fleet at the Battle of Jutland in 1916. It was said of him at the time that he was the man 'who could lose the whole war in one afternoon' if he made the wrong decisions.

Admiral Keppel Deal, and London N1. Augustus, Viscount Keppel (1725–86) commanded the British fleet at Ushant in 1778. He was responsible for several victories against the French. As a young midshipman he had accompanied Admiral Lord Anson on his round-the-world voyage (1740–44). There is a Keppel at Rotherham, but the Keppel's Head, formerly at Devonport, was after Admiral Sir Henry Keppel (1809–94), who became commander-in-chief at Devonport in the 1870s.

Admiral Lord Nelson *See* Lord Nelson.

Admiral Lord Rodney *See* Admiral Rodney.

Admiral McBride Plymouth. John McBride was born in Ireland. He served under Admiral Rodney, but is probably commemorated in this pub name because he served as member of parliament for Plymouth (1784–90). He died in 1800.

Admiral Napier Brighton and elsewhere. Sir Charles John Napier (1786–1860) distinguished himself in several actions on behalf of foreign powers. In 1833, he commanded a Portuguese fleet against rebels and helped to restore the Queen of Portugal to her throne. In 1840 he commanded the Turkish forces in the Mediterranean against the Egyptians. He was twice elected member of parliament for Marylebone. In London E14 and elsewhere there is a Sir Charles Napier.

Admiral Nelson *See* Lord Nelson.

Admiral Rodney Wollaton, Nottingham and elsewhere. George Brydges, Lord Rodney (1719–92) had a distinguished career but is remembered especially for the victory over the French in 1782, at the 'Battle of the Saintes' in the West Indies. This led to better peace terms with the French after the American Revolution. Rodney is well represented in pub names. Variations include Lord Rodney, Keighley; Lord Rodney's Head, London E1; Rodney, Saltash; and elsewhere, Rodney Arms, Hull; Rodney's Head, Herne Bay. Sometimes he is Admiral Lord Rodney, as in Coventry and elsewhere, and he was formerly Bold Rodney in Chesterfield. In Boston he appeared in a double-act as Rodney and Hood. The admiral had several battleships named after him, although the last of these was broken up in 1948.

Admiral Vernon Dagenham and elsewhere. Edward Vernon (1684–1757) became a national hero when in 1739 he captured Porto Bello (in Panama) from the Spaniards, a feat he accomplished with only six ships. He was several times a member of parliament, firstly for Penryn in Cornwall, later for Ipswich. There is a Vernon at Portsea and Nottingham. Portobello, once a common sign, can still be found at Worcester and elsewhere.

Chartridge, Bucks, has a Portobello Arms, and in London W11 there is a Portobello Star.

Adrian's Head Newcastle-on-Tyne. This 'Adrian' is more usually known as Hadrian, properly Hadrianus. He was the Roman emperor who caused the famous Hadrian's Wall to be built between Wallsend and Carlisle in the early second century. This ran for nearly seventy-five miles and was at least sixteen feet high and eight feet thick; with fortified towers at every mile-point. It ceased to be effective in the fourth century. At Wallsend there is an Emperor Hadrian, while the village of Wall near Hexham has a Hadrian.

Adur Brighton. The Sussex river. The river name was itself coined by a seventeenth-century historian.

A E Hobbs Henley-on-Thames. Albert Edward Hobbs, born locally in 1871, was an outstanding Thames angler who took more than 800 large trout in his lifetime. Some of his mounted specimens are inside the pub: outside is his statue complete with rod and line and his customary buttonhole.

Aerodrome Waddon near Croydon, and Scone near Perth. This word originally referred to an aeroplane, but by the turn of the century it had come to mean a small airfield. At that time everything to do with flying was very new indeed, and 'aerodrome' would have had great novelty value. Airport is found at Gloucester and elsewhere.

Afton Paisley. The Scottish river, Afton Water, was made famous by Robert Burns in his poem of that name: 'Flow gently, sweet Afton, among thy green braes,/Flow gently, I'll sing thee a song in thy praise.'

Ailsa Arms Girvan, Strath. Ailsa Craig, the island-rock off the Strathclyde coast, faces this town across the Firth of Clyde. It is sometimes referred to as 'Paddy's Milestone' because it is the halfway point on the crossing between Glasgow and Belfast.

Aintree Tavern *See* Becher's Brook.

Air Balloon Abingdon and elsewhere. The first flight in a hot-air balloon occurred on 21 November 1783. Manning it were François Pilâtre de Rozier and the Marquis d'Arlandes. The balloon had been constructed by the Montgolfier brothers, Joseph and Etienne, but at no time did they leave the ground in one of their own balloons. The first flight lasted twenty-five minutes and carried the two aeronauts just over five miles. Two years later, Blanchard and Jeffries were able to fly a balloon across the English Channel. Such events were naturally much spoken about at the time, and were deservedly commemorated in pub names.

Airborne Sowood, W Yorks. The name of the racehorse which won both the Derby and the St Leger in 1946.

Airdrieonians Airdrie. The local football team plays in the Scottish League.

Airedale Bradford. The breed of large, rough-haired dogs took its name from a district in the West Riding of Yorkshire.

Airedale Heifer *See* Craven Heifer.

Air Hostess Harmondsworth, near Heathrow and Tollerton, near Nottingham. The known examples are near civil airports, but the landlady is often the only 'hostess' present.

Airport *see* Aerodrome.

Aladdin's Lamp Darlaston, W Mid. In the *Arabian Nights* tale, Aladdin's magic lamp contains a helpful genie. No doubt the pub also contains helpful spirits.

Alan Brock Edinburgh. A character who appears in *Kidnapped* and other stories by Robert Louis Stevenson. He helps Bonnie Prince Charlie avoid capture.

Albany Twickenham and elsewhere. A poetic name for Britain similar to 'Albion', and an ancient ducal title. The Grand Old Duke of York of the nursery song was actually Frederick, Duke of York and Albany, eldest brother of the Prince Regent. The youngest son of Queen Victoria, Leopold George Duncan Albert, was also Duke of Albany. The *Albany* at Thames Ditton is named after the duke who married Mary Queen of Scots, mother of James I. Also found are Albany Arms at Brentford, Albany Lodge in Gainsborough, Albany Tap in Camberwell, York and Albany in London NW1. *See also* Prince Leopold.

Albatross Bognor Regis and elsewhere. The great albatross is the largest sea-bird, and object of a superstitious belief amongst sailors: to kill the bird will bring disaster. Samuel Taylor Coleridge based his famous *Rime of the Ancient Mariner* on that theme.

Albert Also Albert Arms, Albert Dock, Albert Hall, Albert House, Albert Oak, Albert Park, Albert Vaults. *See* Prince Albert.

Albert Edward Barking, Esx. The Prince of Wales, eldest son of Queen Victoria, later Edward VII. Pubs were also named after him when he became king – *see* Edward VII.

Albert Victor Dersingham, near King's Lynn. The eldest son of Albert Edward. He died as Duke of Clarence in 1892.

Albion London W6 and elsewhere. Also Albion Mills in Ipswich, Albion Shades at Gravesend, Albion Vaults in Cheltenham. Albion is a poetic name for Britain, probably based on Latin *albus* 'white', with reference to the whiteness of the southern coastal cliffs (as shown on the sign for the Albion at Edenbridge in Kent). Many ships have been named *Albion*, including the ninety-gun frigate which was built locally and is displayed on the sign of the Old Albion at Crantock, Corn. Ships are also shown on the signs at Weymouth and Exmouth. The New Albion at Heckmondwike appears to be a reference to the territory named by Sir Francis Drake in 1579, subsequently renamed California and Oregon.

Alderman Lambeth. A co-opted member of a borough or county council, originally an 'older man', a senior citizen.

Aleppo Merchant Carno, Pwys. The man who named this pub in the 1920s had an ancestor who owned a ship called the *Aleppo Merchant*. It traded with the Levant, especially Aleppo in northern Syria. A framed picture of the ship is over the bar, though the signboard shows a merchant in eastern dress.

Ale Tester Dewsbury. This seems to be an updated form of Aleconner, the name given centuries ago to an inspector of local ale standards. Ale-taster would be more accurate.

Alfred's Nottingham. In Alfred Street. Renamed in 1982, having previously been the White Lion, and showing a modern tendency to add an 's' to the name. The namers seem to be in doubt as to whether it is a possessive 's', as here, or a plural 's', as in Fagins, etc. Nottingham even has a Blueberry's.

Alfred the Great *See* King Alfred.

Alhambra Croydon. It is not clear why this pub was named after the palace of the Moorish kings at Granada, in Spain. The Arabic word Alhambra, or more correctly *al-hamra*, means 'red (palace)'.

Alice Hawthorne Wheldrake, near York. Name of a racehorse bred locally, in the mid-nineteenth century, which was reputedly named after her owner's mistress. She won over fifty races and later became an outstanding brood mare.

Alice Lisle Rockwood, Hants. The wife of John Lisle, the regicide, born about 1614. In 1685 she was accused of harbouring in her house John Hickes, a dissenting minister, who was himself accused of treason. Tried before the notorious Judge Jeffreys she was sentenced to be burned alive. Mercy was shown because of her age, and she was beheaded in Winchester marketplace.

Allander Milngavie, near Glasgow. Allander Water is a tributary of the River Kelvin.

Allan Ramsay Edinburgh and Carlops, Loth. Ramsay (1686–1758) was a Scottish poet and bookseller. Apart from his own elegies he issued collections of old Scottish and English songs.

Allenby Arms *See* General Allenby.

Alley Cat *See* Cat.

Alleyn's Head London SE21. Edward Alleyn, or Allen (1566–1626) was a famous actor, well-known to Shakespeare. As one of the owner-managers of the Fortune Theatre in London he amassed a large fortune which he devoted to charitable works. He founded Dulwich College, 'for the benefit of the poor'.

All Labour In Vain *See* Labour in Vain.

All Nations Madeley, Salop. In a pub context this phrase means a mixture of drinks from all the unfinished bottles. Hindley, in his *Tavern Anecdotes*, may also be right in saying that unsmoked pieces of tobacco were put together and sold as 'All Nations'. The general sense of 'mixture' seems to have been lost since the early nineteenth century.

Alma London W2 and elsewhere. The name of a river in the Crimea (Ukraine). In 1854 it became the scene of the first battle won by the Allies over the Russians. The name was widely used for pubs, streets and the daughters of soldiers who had fought there. At Silsoe, Bedford there is a Battle of Alma. Sheerness has a Heights of Alma, London NW8 a Heroes of Alma. The form Alma Arms occurs at Weston Green, Sry, and Cambridge has an Alma Brewery, built on the site of the former brewery of this name. There is a Crimea at Aldershot.

Alpenstock Falmouth. Literally a 'stick' used in the Alps by walkers and climbers, but it is not known why this German word was thought suitable as a pub name. Perhaps the landlord brought one

back as a souvenir. Other pub names with a similar theme are Alpine in Torquay, Alpine Rose in Tunbridge Wells, Alpine Horn in London W5.

Altisidora Bishop Burton, Humb. The local squire staked his all on this racehorse in 1813. He renamed the village inn when the horse won the St Leger.

Amalgamation Strood, Kent. A reference to the amalgamation in 1899 of the London, Chatham and Dover Railway with the South Eastern Railway – thus forming the South Eastern and Chatham Railway. A pub in Battersea became the London, Chatham and Dover Railway Tavern, a name which was later to qualify it for an entry in *The Guinness Book of Records* as one of the longest in Britain.

Amato Epsom. The winner of the Derby in 1838.

Amazon Port Talbot. The sign shows the magnificent four-masted barque *Amazon* which was wrecked near Port Talbot.

American Portsmouth and elsewhere. In Staffordshire towns such as Burslem and Longton, this name referred to the pottery exporting trade which was once current, Americans being good customers. The pub of this name in Portsmouth appears to celebrate the birth of American independence. The sign affixed to the wall shows a patriot waving the American flag. The name White Hart is also fixed to the wall, since the pub stands on the corner of White Hart Road.

American Eagle Bristol. The reference is presumably to the American emblem, the white-headed (sometimes called bald) eagle, though there was also an American coin called an eagle. It was a ten-dollar gold coin bearing an eagle on the reverse side.

American States These are occasionally mentioned in pub names. There is an Alabama in Liverpool, a California at Belmont, near Cheam, a Vermont at Cobham, a Virginia at Bradford and elsewhere. Washington occurs in various towns, but is usually a reference to the man rather than the place. Related names include a New California in Birmingham, a Pennsylvania Castle at Portland, a Californian in Fulham and a Virginian at Maldon, Esx. *See also* Bronx, Big Apple and Keystone.

Amherst Arms *See* Sir Jeffrey Amherst.

Amsterdam Shoreham-by-Sea. A name suggested by the Dutch appearance of the pub. It has a mansard roof, where each face has two slopes, the lower one steeper than the other.

Anchor Yiewsley, Glos and else-where. This common sign was probably first used as a convenient visual symbol, especially by landlords who had connections with the sea or wished to attract seamen as customers. Specific naval references occur in Foul Anchor, Sheet Anchor and Raffled Anchor. In his *Oxford Pubs Past and Present*, Paul J Marriott provides evidence that one of the pubs of this name in Oxford had a canal rather than sea connection. The pub was especially well used by bargees from the nearby canal. They would anchor overnight while on the trip between London and the Midlands, carrying coal. A similar pub which relied on their patronage was the Navigation. Nevertheless, a ship's anchor is more usual, and a single visit by a royal personage is enough to bring about a name like Royal Anchor at Liphook.

The second meaning of 'anchor' names is symbolic and derives from the words of St Paul (Hebrews 6:19): 'We have this as a sure and steadfast anchor of the soul, a hope . . . ' This accounts for names like Anchor of Hope in Leicester, Anchor and Hope at Limehouse. The spare anchor at sea was often known as the (Last) Hope anchor. At Hope Cove, near Kingsbridge, Devon, there is a Hope and Anchor. *See also* We Anchor in Hope. Blue is the emblematic colour of hope, which accounts for the common Blue Anchor signs in London and elsewhere, with the curious Anchor Bleu variant at Horsham, W Ssx. Possible confusion with 'anker', a measure of approximately eight and a half imperial gallons, is suggested by names like Anchor Brewery Tap in Salisbury, Anchor Tap in London SE1, Anchor and Can in Hereford. The sign of the pub at Normandy, near Guildford interprets 'anchor' in other ways: one side shows a tug-of-war team with its anchor(man), the other side shows a squad of men holding down an air balloon. Anchors Weighed, formerly at Preston, was a sign suggesting the readiness of vessels to leave port. *See also* Crown and Anchor, Golden Anchor.

Anchorage Torquay. The name manages to suggest a safe retreat for customers while implying that the landlord is a retired seaman.

Anchor and Crown *See* Crown and Anchor.

Anchor and Horsehoes Guildford. Probably a combination of two pub names brought about by a licensee's changing house and retaining the previous name.

Anchor Made For Ever Bristol. This area is known locally as 'Made for ever' because of a remark made by two miners, Lewis and Fudge, who discovered a huge deposit of coal and exclaimed 'We're made for ever'. A blacksmith's forge used to stand opposite the pub and was known for the ships' anchors made there.

Ancient Briton Colchester. The apt location here is in Iceni Way. This ancient town was once a strategic Roman settlement and of sufficient importance for Boudicca to attack it with her army of Iceni tribesmen. Another pub of this name is at St Albans, while both Burslem, Staffs and Whitchurch, Salop have an Ancient Britons.

Ancient Druid Also Ancient Druids. *See* Druid.

Ancient Forester Reading. 'Ancient' in some instances seems to be used for reasons of prestige, much as 'Ye Olde' is used to confer the dignity of supposedly great age. The Ancient Order of Foresters was in fact founded in 1834. There is a similar Ancient Foresters at London SE16. Ancient Shepherd, Bolton; Ancient Shepherds, Fen Ditton, Cambs and Ancient Unicorn, Bowes, Dur are also found.

Ancient Mariner Bognor Regis and Workington. The name naturally recalls the character created by Samuel Taylor Coleridge in *The Rime of the Ancient Mariner* (1798) but in some cases no doubt indicated that the landlord had formerly been a seaman. *See also* Albatross.

Andoversford Andoversford, Glos. Of interest because the sign interprets the name amusingly. An Elizabethan courtier is shown giving a helping hand to his lady as she crosses a ford. (The place-name means 'Anna's ford'.)

Andrew Marvell Hull. Marvell (1621–78) was born in the nearby village of Winestead. He wrote poems in praise of gardens and country life, then complimentary poems to Cromwell and to Milton, whose assistant he was for a time. Later he became the local member of parliament, being renowned for his absolute integrity.

Anfield Tavern Liverpool. For the nearby football ground, home of Liverpool Football Club. In the same city is a Shanks, recalling the affectionate nickname by which a former manager of the club, Bill Shankly, was known.

Angel Ware and elsewhere. A sign in use since the Middle Ages, reflecting the early connection between religious establishments and travellers' hostels. The commonness of the name has caused some sign painters to seek alternative ways of representing it. At Birch, near Colchester, it is seen as the gold coin, the 'angel noble' which was first minted in 1465 and survived for nearly three centuries. The figure of the Archangel Michael was impressed upon it. At Sutton, Surrey, the angel has become an angelfish on the sign: at Welshpool she is a barmaid holding two foaming pints of ale. The 'little angel' on the sign at Ware is a schoolboy with a catapult, who has obviously just broken a window. At Braintree an angel holds a tankard which has a halo over it. The sign was denounced roundly by the local vicar. Other representations lead to slightly different names, such as the Angel and Harp at Great Dunmow. Angel Arms occurs, and may have some justification in that an angel appears in the crest of the

Fletchers' Company and also supports the arms of the Tallow Chandlers and Stationers. Minor variants include the Angel Gardens in Norwich, Angel Vaults in Newtown, Pwys, Angell at Kneeshall and Angell Arms in London SW2. 'Angell' was once a common spelling variant of 'angel'. The Angel and Elephant at Appleton, Ches. is presumably an amalgamation of two signs.

Angel and Crown London E2 and elsewhere. The sign of a crown supported by angels on either side was very popular in the seventeenth century, especially after the restoration of Charles II to the throne in 1660.

Angel and Royal Grantham. A medieval inn which has many royal associations dating from the thirteenth century when King John held court here. Richard III reputedly signed the death-warrant of his cousin, the Duke of Buckingham, while visiting the inn in 1483. The unfortunate Charles I also stayed here in 1633. Nevertheless the inn was known as the Angel until 1866, when it was visited by the Prince of Wales, later Edward VII.

Angel on the Bridge Henley-on-Thames. One of the cellars of this pub is built round a complete arch of an earlier Henley bridge. The original building on the site, an ancient hospice known as The Hermitage and said to date from the fourteenth century, may have inspired the choice of 'Angel'.

Angel's Reply Hitchin. Name of a pub which replaced a previous Angel, demolished in 1965 when the site was developed in spite of many protests.

Angerstein London SE10. John Julius Angerstein (1735–1823) was born in St Petersburg but came to London when he was fifteen years old. He became an eminent merchant, and was largely responsible for establishing Lloyds of London in something like its present form. Angerstein's art collection was purchased after his death by the British government and formed the basis of the National Gallery.

Anglers Watford and elsewhere. Also Anglers' Arms at Weldon Bridge and elsewhere, Anglers' Rest at Ash Vale, Sry, Anglers' Retreat at West Drayton. Popular for obvious reasons as a riverside pub name. Oakham has a Rutland Angler and Scorton, Lancs a Wyresdale Anglers. There is a corresponding group of names with 'fishermen' replacing 'anglers'.

Anglesea Arms Halnaker near Chichester. Also Anglesea Tavern in London W8. *See* Marquis of Anglesea.

Anglo-American Liverpool. Technically, an American of English descent, but this phrase sometimes refers to an English-American partnership of some kind.

Anglo-Saxon Bidford-on-Avon, Warks. An Anglo-Saxon burial ground was excavated nearby in the 1920s, yielding a mass of jewellery and the remains of some two hundred skeletons.

Anker Nuneaton. After the River Anker which flows through Warwickshire, Leicestershire and Staffordshire. The name probably means 'winding'. By coincidence, 'anker' is a liquid measure. It may be present in some pub names in the form 'anchor'. *See also* Anchor.

Anne Boleyn Rochford, Esx. Anne Boleyn or Bullen (1507–36) became a maid of honour to the first wife of Henry VIII, Catherine of Aragon, at the age of twenty. The king was captivated by her and married her privately in 1533. She gave birth to a daughter, later Queen Elizabeth I, but by 1536 she had lost the king's favour. She was accused of adultery, found guilty, and beheaded. There is a Boleyn Tavern at East Ham. Some ingenious etymologists see a reference to Anne in Bull and Butcher ('Boleyn butchered'), but this is fanciful.

Annexe Bristol and elsewhere. The Bristol pub adjoins the pavilion of the Gloucestershire County Cricket Club. Used in other instances where the pub is a supplementary building, joined to a main one.

Ansells Arms Birmingham. A well-known local brewery, Ansells, closed down in 1981.

Anson Arms Great Yarmouth. Also **Anson Tavern** in Manchester. George, Lord Anson (1697–1762) is best remembered for the voyage he made around the world between 1740–44. He later wrote about it in a book first published in 1748 and still read today: *Voyage Round the World*. Anson also won many victories at sea, rose to full admiral's rank, and became First Lord of the admiralty. The Royal Navy has named many ships for him: one of them, a battleship built locally, gave rise to the Anson sign at Wallsend-on Tyne.

Antelope Surbiton and elsewhere. This fairly common sign is usually heraldic, referring obliquely to the dukes of Bedford or Gloucester, or perhaps to Henry IV, Henry V or Henry VI. There have been ships of the Royal Navy called *Antelope* since the mid-sixteenth century. The sign at Hereford features the frigate HMS *Antelope* which was adopted by that city and was unveiled by the ship's commanding officer in 1978. In May 1982, during the Falklands conflict, the ship was sunk by Argentinian aircraft. *See* Shiny Sheff.

Antigallican London SE1. An interesting survival of a name that at one time was fairly common. The word was coined in the 1750s to mean 'one who is opposed to everything French'. There was an Antigallican Society which met to discuss ways of hindering French business interests. All this was at a time when relations between the two countries were at a low ebb. Most of the pubs of this name changed it as the situation improved.

Antiquary Edinburgh. A veiled reference to Sir Walter Scott, since the character of the Antiquary in Scott's novel of that name, published in 1816, is usually said to resemble closely the character of Scott himself. The author described the book as his 'chief favourite' amongst those he had written.

Antwerp Arms London N17. Also Antwerp Tavern at Deal, Kent. There was an Antwerp Tavern in London in the early seventeenth century near the Royal Exchange, which had been partly modelled on the similar institution in Antwerp. Modern pubs of this name seem to owe more to an award won in Antwerp in the nineteenth century at an international brewery exhibition.

Anvil Also Anvil Arms. *See* Blacksmiths.

Apollo Yeovil and elsewhere. In early use a sign derived from heraldry. Apart from representing young manhood in all its perfection, Apollo was thought by the ancient Greeks to be the god who both brought about and cured plagues. As a healer he features on the arms of the Apothecaries, at first preparers and sellers of drugs, later those who practised medicine. More recent namings have to do with the Apollo Space programme, especially with *Apollo XI* which landed on the moon in 1969 with Neil Armstrong and his crew. *See also* Man on the Moon.

Apples feature in pub names in various ways. Apple is itself the name at Lucker, Northld; at Pilton, near Glastonbury, is an Apple Tree, the sign showing a boy perched in the tree engaged in the age-old sport of scrumping (or skrimping). Kingston-on-Thames has an Apple Market. Individual varieties of apple are represented by Beauty of Bath at Sittingbourne, Bramley Apple at Southwell, Notts (more correctly 'Bramley's Seedling'), Newton Pippin at Bracknell, Berks, Wyken Pippin at Wyken, near Coventry. General terms also occur, such as Crab Apple at Clevedon, Som, Cyder Apple at Ilfracombe, Pippin at Hereford. Apples and Pears and Big Apple are treated separately.

Apples and Pears Covent Garden and elsewhere. This name had obvious point to it for a pub situated in the middle of what was at the time London's fruit and vegetable market. The other London connection is with Cockney rhyming slang. The pub in Bermondsey of this name is no doubt meant to be a reminder of this rather 'ostentatious' dialect, as Julian Franklyn referred to it in his excellent book *The Cockney*. 'Apples and pears', for 'stairs', is the kind of phrase used jokingly by non-Cockneys, or by Cockneys in the presence of innocent American tourists.

Apsley House Portsmouth. The sign shows the house of this name at Hyde Park Corner in which the Duke of Wellington once lived. It is now the Wellington Museum. The house formerly had the address 'No 1, London' but now seems to be known as '149 Piccadilly'.

Aquarium Brighton. The pub was named after the nearby aquarium, which itself was opened in 1969.

Aqueduct Froncysyllte, Clwyd. For the aqueduct built by Thomas Telford (1757–1834). This famous engineer and bridge builder is commemorated in several pub names. *See* Thomas Telford.

Arabian Horse Aberford, Leeds. The name is thought to refer to the stallion *Godolphin* from which many famous racehorses are descended.

Arboretum Nottingham and elsewhere. Robert Holford, a local squire, began to collect trees for display and study in a special garden (not called an 'arboretum' until 1838) in 1829. He founded the arboretum at Westonbirt, Glos and is remembered in the Holford Arms, at Knockdown, near Tetbury. The novelty of the idea, and the word, seems to have appealed to several pub-namers in the nineteenth century.

Archdeacon Cockerton, Darlington. For a local priest, the Venerable Michael Perry, whose portrait is

shown on the signboard. The pub
is in grounds that were formerly
owned by the Church. Named
in 1980.

Archduke Charles London SE1.
Archduke Charles of
Austria (1771–1847) was an able
commander on the Allied side in
the fight against Napoleon.
Charles defeated Napoleon at
Aspern in May 1809, though two
months later he was defeated by
him at Wagram.

Archer's Dart Harlow. One of a
number of pubs in this town
named after a moth, as here, or a
butterfly.

Archery There is an Archery Tavern
at London W2 and elsewhere.
The London pub is on a site where
the Toxophilite Society used to
meet. (The Society takes its name
from a book *Toxophilus*, published
in 1545 by Roger Ascham. The
word means 'lover of the bow'.) At
Aveley, Romford, there is an
Archer, while at Headless Cross,
near Redditch, is Archers. New
Cross has a Royal Archer.
Bowman is at Aldridge, near
Walsall. The Hampshire Bowman
is at Dunbridge, near Romsey,
while Kendal has the Kendal
Bowman. Liverpool has a Bow and
Arrow and Longbow is at
Stapleford, Cambridge and
elsewhere. Arrow occurs
at Arnold, Nottingham and
elsewhere, and New Cross has an
Arrows. Three Arrows is at
Congleton, Five Arrows at
Waddeson, near Aylesbury, Sheaf
of Arrows at Wimborne.
The Golden Arrow at Olton,
Birmingham refers however, to
the railway not archery. Further
references to the sport are found in
Buthay at Wickwar, Glos, Bull's
Eye at Sholing, near Southampton
and Butts in Walsall. Bowyer Arms

is a related name. *See also* Fletchers
Arms.

Ardwick Empire Manchester.
A reminder of the local music-hall
theatre. 'Empire' was a popular
name at one time for such
theatres.

Argo Frigate Sunderland. Since Jason
sailed in quest of the Golden
Fleece in the *Argo* (Greek *argos*
'swift'), countless ships must have
received the name. The Royal
Navy has used it at least five
times, one of the ships being
commemorated in this pub name.

Argus Butterfly Peterlee, Dur. The
reference ultimately is to Argus,
the mythological person whose
hundred eyes, after his death, were
transferred to the tail of the
peacock. The butterfly was named
in 1827.

Ark Newhaven, E Ssx. From the
name of a boat that was used for
rescue work during a nineteenth-
century flood.

Arkle Ashleworth, Glos and elsewhere. The steeplechaser which,
in a ten-year career, won nearly
every important race, although it
was never entered for the Grand
National. A famous name in the
1960s.

Ark Royal Devonport, Gosport and
Wells, Nflk. The Devonport sign
depicts the Royal Navy's aircraft-
carrier of this name on one side,
and an old sailing ship of the same
name on the other side. The older
ship would originally have been
the *Ark Ralegh*, renamed *Ark Royal*
when taken over from Sir Walter
Ralegh (or Raleigh). It was later
renamed *Anne Royal*. The first
aircraft-carrier to bear the name
was launched in 1937 and was
torpedoed in 1941. The second
aircraft-carrier *Ark Royal*, launched
in 1950, went to the breaker's yard
in 1982. The present carrier of

this name came into service during 1985.

Arkwright Arms Duckmanton, Derby. Sir Richard Arkwright (1732–92) invented the first cotton-spinning frame. In 1771 he also erected the first spinning-mill driven by water-power. He was a pioneer of the factory system.

Armada Gravelly Hill, Birmingham and elsewhere. A pub of this name in County Clare is near Spanish Point, where several Spanish galleons were wrecked. The name normally refers to the 'Invincible' Armada, as Philip II of Spain called it, which attempted unsuccessfully to invade England in 1588.

Armoury Bristol. The pub stands on the site of an armoury which was established in the early 1800s as part of a local barracks. The sign shows a coat-of-arms with two crossed épées and two crossed pistols.

Armstrong Gun Englefield Green, Sry. A particular piece of artillery made at the Woolwich Arsenal, designed by Lord Armstrong (1810–1900). Similar names are Director-General, Royal Mortar and Woolwich Infant.

Arrow(s) *See* **Archery**. The *Arrow* at Knockholt in Kent had this masterpiece on its sign: 'Charles Collins liveth here,/Sells rum, brandy, gin and beer;/I made this board a little wider,/To let you know I sell good cider.'

Arroyo Arms Harrowby near Carlisle. In 1811, at Arroyo dos Molinos, the Border Regiment played a significant part in a victory over the French during the Peninsular War. The sign here shows the regimental drummer boy. *Arroyo* in Spanish means 'stream'.

Arsenal Tavern London N4. After the Arsenal Football Club, formerly Woolwich Arsenal. Since an 'arsenal' is a place where guns and ammunition are manufactured and stored, the team naturally has the nickname The Gunners. There is also a Gunners pub in London N4.

Artesian London W9. Near the site of a long-lost artesian well. An artesian well is one in which the water rises spontaneously, as originally at Artois, in France.

Artful Dodger Chelmsley Wood, Birmingham. In Dickens's *Oliver Twist*, the nickname of Jack Dawkins, one of Fagin's more successful young thieves – although he is eventually caught and transported. The sign of this pub shows a rugby player holding a ball and giving a conspiratorial wink. The name also occurs in Edinburgh and London.

Artichoke Norwich and elsewhere. The artichoke (Italian *articiocco*) was introduced to England in the early sixteenth century. Its distinctive shape made it a useful sign, for seedsmen and gardeners as well as tavern-owners. Walter Wicks says in his *Inns and Taverns of Old Norwich* that the yard at the rear of the *Artichoke* was regularly used to sell market garden produce.

Artillery Exeter. Also Artillery Arms at London EC1, opposite the ground of the Honourable Artillery Company, which began as a guild of archers in 1537. The Company has a claim to be the oldest and most senior regiment of the British Army, though since its members are Territorials, not regular soldiers, that claim is disputed. The Royal Artillery Arms at West Huntspill in Somerset is after the Royal Regiment of Artillery. The sign shows the regimental cap badge.

Arun Pulborough, Ssx. Also Arun View in Littlehampton. The reference is to the River Arun, the river-name being a back-formation from the place-name Arundel.

Ashen Faggot Northleigh, Devon. The name refers to a bundle of ash sticks (called 'wands'). They are used in a traditional end-of-year ceremony, left over from pagan times, in which a new fire is lit from the old, to signify the birth of a new year. Ash is said to be the only wood that will burn while still green.

Assembly House London NW5. A place where stagecoach passengers once assembled before beginning their journeys.

Assize Courts Bristol and Manchester. The Bristol pub shares a building with the city's Crown Court, formerly the Assize Courts. These were originally courts which made 'assessments'.

Astolat Peasmarsh, near Guildford. Astolat is a town mentioned in the Arthurian Romances. Tennyson describes Elaine, in his *Idylls of the King*, as the 'lily maid of Astolat'. The town is generally identified with Guildford.

Astor Plymouth. Nancy, Lady Astor (1879–1964), American-born wife of Waldorf Astor, was the first woman to sit as a member of the British parliament. She represented Plymouth as Conservative MP 1919–45.

Astronaut Rainham, Esx and elsewhere. Several pubs pay tribute to the 'star-sailor' of modern times, '-naut' being from Greek *nautes*, 'sailor'. Similar pub names are Man in Space, Man on the Moon, etc.

Asylum Tavern London SE15. The reference is to the Licensed Victuallers Asylum for distressed members of the trade, or their widows. It was opened in Peckham in 1827. 'Asylum' is used in its sense of a benevolent institution offering shelter to the destitute – but not necessarily mentally deranged.

Athelstan Arms Southbourne, near Bournemouth. For one of the outstanding Anglo-Saxon kings, who came to power in 925. He was born about 895 and died in 941. Athelstan or (more correctly), Aethelstan, was a grandson of Alfred the Great.

Atlas Bath. When most trades, not just taverns, had signs over their premises, Atlas was favoured by booksellers and map-makers, or those who sold globes. The association of this Greek Titan, who was condemned to hold up the heavens on his shoulders, with a book of maps began at the end of the sixteenth century. The Flemish geographer known as Mercator (Gerhard Kremer 1512–1594) put a figure of the Greek on the title page of his father's collection of maps. The familiarity of that figure, Atlas supporting the world, presumably made it suitable for pub-sign purposes.

Atmospheric Railway Starcross, near Exeter. This was the term used by Brunel in 1836 to describe his experimental railway system built in this area. It was supposed to work on compressed air, but was not a success. *See* Brunel.

Augustus John Liverpool. The pub is within the university precincts, John having once been a lecturer there. Augustus Edwin John (1878–1961) born in Wales, was an etcher and painter, particularly known for his portraits of famous people, such as Lloyd George, George Bernard Shaw and Lawrence of Arabia.

Auld Lang Syne formerly at Oldham.

Title of the song known the world over, sung when it is time to part and accompanied by the ritual joining of hands. Robert Burns is responsible for the words as used today. The general idea of the song is to praise the 'good old times', while remembering friends who helped to make them so. The pub name literally translates as 'old long since'.

Aunties Bristol. A former landlady was always known as 'Aunty' to her regulars and is now immortalised in the pub name. The former sign showed two ladies in Victorian dress beneath a shared parasol.

Aunt Sally London E1. Said to be a reference to the simplest and oldest form of skittles, nowadays confined mainly to Oxfordshire. A team consists of eight players who use six 'sticks' or wooden clubs to throw at a target or 'dolly' perched on a pole.

Australian London SW3. Nicholson's *London Pub Guide* suggests that this name may have been inspired by the Princes Cricket Club, which used to be next door. The latter is more familiar as the Marylebone Cricket Club, which it has been since 1814. The Nicholson theory seems highly unlikely, but what the Australian link was which caused the pub-name does not seem to have been recorded.

Aviation Names Fewer pub names refer to aviation than to the sea, but still total more than sixty. Pubs which are near airports often comment on the fact, perhaps by mentioning an Air Hostess or Airman, Feltham, GL and Meppershall, Beds. Different types of aircraft are mentioned, ranging from the Canopus to the Jumbo Jet, Spitfire, Thornaby-on-Tees and Tiger Moth. The equivalent of the sailor's Anchor-type name is found in Happy Landing(s), Bristol and Heathrow, possibly helped by a Parachute. Space flights have been commemorated since they began, and Neil Armstrong's moon-walk was commemorated in Man on the Moon and similar names. The Spotted Cow that jumped over the moon was of course one of the earliest space travellers.

Avon Tavera Emscote, Warwick and elsewhere. Rivers of this name run through nine different counties, though the best-known is probably the Upper Avon which flows past Stratford-on-Avon. Amongst the pub names which refer to one of the rivers are Avon Gorge at Bristol; Avon at Pewsey, Wilts; Avon Causeway at Hurn, Hants; Avon Vale at Aberavon near Port Talbot; Avondale Arms in Devonport; Avon mouth in Avonmouth, Bristol; Avon Packet in Bristol. The last named presumably refers to a packet-boat, a small mail boat.

Axe Chester and elsewhere. Bryant Lillywhite, in his comprehensive study *London Signs*, proves that an axe was the distinctive sign of a tavern from the fifteen century. It appears on signs either as the tool or the battle-axe. It also features in various coats of arms, such as those of the Coopers and Wheelwrights. An axe frequently appears in combination with something else (see below). London E2 has Ye Olde Axe and Rusty Axe occurs at Kingsbury Episcopi, Som.

Axe and Compass Hemingford Abbots, near Huntingdon. When the area was all woodland this pub was the Foresters' Arms. Later it became the Carpenters' Arms. It now combines tools from both trades. There is a similar Axe and

Compasses at Braughing, near Buntingford. Other names of this type include Axe and Cleaver at Much Birch, near Hereford, Axe and Handsaw at Moulton, near Spalding, Axe and Saw at Carlton-cum-Willingham, near Newmarket, Axe and Square at Countesthorpe, near Leicester. The Axe and Tun at Oswaldtwistle, near Accrington, is said to convey the message that one should 'axe for beer'. That is as obscure as the rebus contained in the sign of the similarly named pub at Warbleton, E Ssx. There the axe is really the axe-like weapon called a 'bill'. It is shown inside a tun, and the whole name is meant to be interpreted as war-bill-tun, or Warbleton.

Axe and Gate London SW1. A pub of this name was in Downing Street until 1802. Number Ten now occupies its site.

B

Babes in the Wood Hanging Heaton, W Yorks. The famous children's story of the children abandoned in the wood dates from the seventeenth century. By the end of the eighteenth century the slang phrase for a criminal in the stocks or pillory was 'a babe in the wood'. The sign of this pub shows two delinquents who are 'babes in the wood' in that sense. Hindley in his *Tavern Anecdotes* says that the phrase was also 'a public-house term for dice', but Partridge does not list it in his *Dictionary of Historical Slang*.

Baby in the Hand Hailey, near Witney. This pub was the Bird in the Hand until 1984. The renaming occurred because a baby was born in the pub car-park. The mother-to-be was being taken by ambulance to Chipping Norton hospital when it became clear that the birth was imminent. The ambulance pulled into the car-park, the baby was delivered safely, and the proud parents received champagne from the pub staff to celebrate the event.

Bacchus Shoreditch and elsewhere. The Roman god of wine, more correctly called Dionysus. He is normally represented in art as a bearded man, but on tavern signs from the early eighteenth century he was transformed into a fat little infant sitting on top of a tun, or barrel. This led to a reinterpretation of the name as Boy and Barrel, as at Selby, W Yorks and elsewhere.

Baccy Jar Bristol. The name was chosen by means of a competition. It relates to a nearby tobacco factory of the Wills Company. The sign shows Sir Walter Raleigh puffing at his pipe, since he is normally credited with, or blamed for, the introduction of tobacco to Europe. *See also* Virginia Ash.

Back to Backs Great Yarmouth. The pub was originally called Backs (perhaps because a 'back', from Dutch *bak*, is a vat used by brewers). Later the pub name was changed to Prince Consort. It has now changed again, back to *Backs*. Actually it hasn't. *Back to Backs* has become the new name.

Bacon Arms *See* Friar Bacon.

Bacon Arms Newbury. Francis Bacon, Viscount St Albans (1561–1626) was an outstanding philosopher and statesman who became lord high chancellor of England, the highest civil office to which an English subject could attain at that time. In 1621 he was charged with bribery, and spent a few days in the Tower of London. He wrote mostly philosophical works, but his *Essays* were probably the most widely read. They are full of proverb-like statements, such as: 'Some books are to be tasted, others to be swallowed, and some few to be chewed and digested.'

Bader Arms *See* Sir Douglas Bader.

Badger Blandford Forum, Dors. In this instance a trade sign of a local brewery, Hall and Woodhouse. It serves well in that capacity, since it gets its name from the distinctive white 'badge' on its forehead. It is hunted by Badger Hounds (Hinderwell, Clev) and lives in a Badger's Holt (Bridgetown, Som). 'Holt' here means 'a small wood, a copse', not a 'den' as in the case of an otter's holt. The burrow of a badger is of course a 'sett'. In Londonderry there is a Badger's Place.

Badger Box Annesley, Notts. In the 1940s the publican had a pet badger, kept in a special box in the backyard. Minnie the badger became a great local favourite but eventually escaped and disappeared. Another badger, stuffed, is now kept inside the pub in a glass case.

Bag o'Nails London SW1. This was originally the sign of an ironmonger, at a time when most tradesmen displayed a street sign. Bryant Lillywhite records several early examples in his *London Signs*, and in some instances details have come down to us of the sign itself. In all cases it was, quite simply, a bag of nails, or a bag dotted with nail-heads. This will dismay those who delight in complex explanations of simple names, such as those who insist, without evidence, that this sign was originally Bacchanals, an English form of *Bacchanalia*, a Roman festival held in honour of Bacchus, god of wine. Brewer's *Dictionary of Phrase and Fable* prefers the absurd explanation that the name was originally Bagger' Nale, thus lowering the dignity of an otherwise worthy book.

Bailie Nicol Jarvie Aberfoyle, Cent. A character in Sir Walter Scott's novel *Rob Roy*. Bailie is a Scottish title for a magistrate elected by the town councillors from amongst their own number. Scott's Jarvie has been described as 'petulant, conceited, purse-proud, without tact and intensely prejudiced, but kind-hearted and sincere'.

Bailiff's Sergeant St Mary's Bay, Kent. The brewers dedicated this pub to 'the Jurats (ie municipal officers, similar to aldermen, especially of the Cinque Ports) of the Level of Romney Marsh, and to those who have worthily upheld the office of their Bailiff's Sergeant . . . to remind us of the incalculable debt the whole of Romney Marsh owes to this ancient Corporation, which since 1252, in a charter granted by Henry III to the Lords Bailiff and Jurats, has been concerned with embanking and draining the Marsh against the wash and rage of the sea'.

Baker and Basket London EC2. A nineteenth-century sign, recalling the men who carried bread from the bakehouses to the market place. In his *Tavern Anecdotes*, Charles Hindley suggests that such a pub would be used by 'loafers'.

Baker and Oven London W1. The pub has baker's ovens which are still used to produce pies for the customers. There is a similarly named pub in Twickenham. Malvern Link, H and W has a Bakery.

Bakers' Arms Dorchester and elsewhere. The arms date from the sixteenth century and show a hand holding a balance, surrounded by cornsheaves, with two anchors at the top. The sign recalls the former close connection between bakers and brewers – both trades were frequently practised by the same man. The Dorchester pub was an actual bakery until 1970. Similar names include Bakers Tavern at Windsor, Bakers Vaults at Stockport.

Baker's Dozen Bishop's Stortford. A baker's dozen, by centuries-old tradition, is thirteen. The phrase may be used to avoid referring to that number. (Bakers added a free cake, etc, when twelve were ordered.)

Bakery *See* Baker and Basket.

Bala Llanfyllin, Pwys. Lake Bala is the largest natural lake in Wales. The River Dee rises there.

Balaclava Pell Green, near Wadhurst and elsewhere. This town is a small port in the South Crimea. It was made famous by the battle in 1854 during the Crimean War, when the charge of the Light Brigade took place (celebrated in one of Lord Tennyson's best-known poems). The kindest thing that can be said about the Earl of Cardigan, who led the charge, is that he displayed a reckless courage, if little military sense. The woollen covering for the head and shoulders known as a balaclava is so-called because it was first issued to British soldiers who fought in the Crimean War.

Balance Luston, near Leominster. Perhaps named originally because of a balance, an apparatus for weighing, being there, but now interpreted on the sign in humorous fashion. Two country bumpkins are balancing on a plank which rests across a bottle. One has a hundredweight metal block concealed behind him.

Balancing Eel South Shields. Named in 1969 and referring to a verse in *Alice in Wonderland*: 'You are old,' said the youth, 'one would hardly suppose that your eye was as steady as ever;/Yet you balanced an eel on the end of your nose – what made you so awfully clever?' The sign shows a mariner displaying dexterity in similar fashion: holding onto a rope whilst at the same time balancing an eel on the end of his nose.

Bald-faced Stag Burnt Oak, Edgware. Such a stag, with a white stripe on its forehead, is said to have been caught locally. The name occurs elsewhere, especially on the outskirts of London, sometimes as Bald-face Stag. 'Bald' commonly has the meaning 'white streak' in descriptions of animals. At Lichfield there is a Bald Buck, while Chigwell, Esx, has a Bald Hind.

Baldwin Birmingham. Stanley Baldwin (1867–1947) was prime minister on three separate occasions, twice as Conservative leader, once as leader of the Coalition. He was created Earl of Bewdley on his retirement from politics. He is remembered for having broken the National Strike of 1926. He was also prime minister at the time of Edward VIII's abdication in 1936.

Bale of Hay *See* Hay Cutter.

Balfour Edinburgh. Also Balfour Arms at Woolbrook, Devon. Arthur James Balfour, later Earl Balfour (1848–1930) was Conservative prime minister from 1902–05. Later, as foreign secretary in 1914, he issued the Balfour Declaration, pledging British support for a Jewish national homeland in Palestine.

Ball Sheffield and elsewhere. The convenience of this visual symbol has made it a popular sign since the fifteenth century. Sheffield still has six pubs of this name, one of which depicts a football. Variants include Blue Ball, Golden Ball, Silver Ball, etc.

Ball and Boot Scholes, Lancs. The pub is next to Wigan's Rugby League Club ground. *See also* Drop Kick.

Ball and Wicket *See* Cricket.

Balloon Wollaton, Nottingham. Three local men made successful ascents in hot-air balloons: a Mr Sadler in 1813, his son in 1823 and a Mr Green in 1826. The latter then persuaded a goodly number of his fellow-citizens to pay half-a-guinea for the privilege of making an ascent with him. There is a Gondola pub nearby.

Ballot Box Perivale. The pub stands on the site of a nineteenth-century polling station. ('Ballot' because originally small 'balls' were placed in a box to indicate one's secret vote.) This system was first used in South Australia in 1856, followed in Britain in 1872 and in the USA in 1884.

Balmbra's Newcastle-on-Tyne. John Balmbra created a music-hall here in the mid-nineteenth century. Patrons were the first to hear *The Blaydon Races* (in 1862), which mentioned the pub in the first verse. After a change of name to the Carlton Hotel, *Balmbra*'s reverted to its original name in 1962, but is now Balmbra's Gaslight and Laser (1985).

Balmoral Castle London N1 and elsewhere. The 'Majestic Dwelling', as it is called in Gaelic, which Prince Albert bought for Queen Victoria. In 1854 she built the white granite castle which has been a private home of British monarchs ever since. The castle is near Ballater, in Grampian. Windsor Castle is a similar pub name.

Baltic Middlesbrough and elsewhere. The Baltic is the sea bounded by Denmark, Sweden, Finland, USSR, Poland and Germany. In the eighteenth century merchants who traded in that area used to meet at the Baltic Coffee House. From these meetings came the Baltic Mercantile and Shipping Exchange, which has shipowners, brokers and merchants as its members. Baltic was always a coffee-house sign until the nineteenth century, but has been extended to pubs. Newcastle has a Baltic Tavern: Baltic Fleet is found at Wapping and elsewhere.

Bandsman Rastrick, W Yorks. The local Brighouse and Rastrick band is recognised as one of the premier brass bands in Britain.

Bank Plymouth. The building was occupied originally by the Wiltshire and Dorset Bank, then taken over by Lloyds Bank in 1913. It was converted and opened as a pub in 1984, its future liquidity doubtless ensured.

Bankes Arms Corfe Castle, Dors. Sir John Bankes was lord chief justice under Charles I. His wife, as staunch a royalist as himself, was forced to defend their castle home against the Roundheads, led by Cromwell, in 1642. She was eventually tricked into surrendering, whereupon Cromwell and his men destroyed a castle which had been there for over 600 years.

Bank of England Ancoats, near Manchester, and Marlow. Explained in the former instance, at least, as a compliment to the trustworthiness of the landlord, who in all dealings was deemed to be 'as safe as the Bank of England'.

Banks of the Wear Sunderland. The River Wear runs into the North Sea at Sunderland. Ekwall, in his *English River Names*, thinks the name merely means 'water'.

Banner Cross *See* Cross.

Bannut Tree Shelwick, near Hereford. Bannut is a dialectal word for 'walnut'. A rural saying has it: 'A woman, a spaniel and a bannut tree: the more ye bate (beat) 'em, the better they be'.

Baptist's Head London EC1. The story of Salome dancing before King Herod on his birthday, pleasing him so that he said she could have whatever she wished, is told in Matthew 14. It was

Herodias, Salome's mother, who made her ask for the 'head of John the Baptist on a platter'. Herod was reluctantly obliged to grant her wish. By the fifteenth century the Baptist's head was supposed to be in Amiens Cathedral, and pilgrims travelled to see it.

Barbican Lincoln and elsewhere. A barbican was a watchtower built over the gate of a castle or of a fortified town. Such a watch tower led to the use of the name for the London area.

Bareknuckle Boys Holmfirth, Huddersfield. The 'boys' concerned fought in the yard behind the pub until 1932. Photographs of some of them are kept in the pub.

Barking Dickey *See* Kicking Cuddy.

Barking Fox *See* **Fox.**

Barking Smack Barking, Esx. The 'smack' is a single–masted sailing vessel designed for coastal use. In the 1880s Hewitts operated two hundred such vessels, which caught mackerel just off the Yarmouth beaches. Yarmouth also has a pub of this name, as well as a **Barking Fishery**, and a Short Blue (referring to Hewitts' company flag).

Barley Bree Edinburgh. Another name for malt liquor. 'Bree' is a general word for the liquor in which anything has been boiled. Malt is barley or other grain which has been steeped in water, allowed to sprout, then dried in a kiln. Nutbourne near Chichester has a **Barley Corn**, referring to the cereal plant commonly used to make malt liquors and personified as John Barleycorn.

Barley Mow Oswestry and elsewhere. 'Mow' is a stack, and a barley mow sign was meant to be a simple indication that beer was sold – barley being one of its main ingredients. Such simplicity did

not appeal to one commentator on pub signs, who derived it from French *bel amour*, 'sweetheart'. Brampton in Cumbria has a Barley Stack.

Barley Sheaf Truro and elsewhere. A variant of barley mow. Barley sheaves appear on the arms of the Worshipful Company of Brewers, granted in 1543.

Barmy Arms Twickenham. Barmy in the sense of 'mad' derives from the word 'barm' – the froth that forms on top of fermenting liquors. Barmy is therefore frothy, empty-headed. The sign of this pub is hung upside-down.

Barnaby Rudge Broadstairs, Kent. This novel by Charles Dickens was published in 1841. It deals with the Gordon anti-popery riots in 1780. Barnaby himself is rather a pathetic and impractical character, much concerned with what makes the stars shine.

Barnyard Enfield. The pub is decorated with farming implements. Dunkinfield in Cheshire has a Barn Meadow.

Baron of Beef Cambridge and elsewhere. A baron of beef is two sirloins left uncut at the backbone. Sirloins should properly be surloins, 'sur' meaning 'above'. The spelling sirloin led to a tale about 'knighting the loin', and undoubtedly suggested 'baron' as a suitable name for a double sirloin. The sign usually means that plenty of food is available. Bath has a Beef Steak, Manchester a Beef and Barley. *See also* Sirloin.

Barrels Commonly featured in pub names, though in real life they have been superseded by metal kegs. Barrel occurs at Ross-on-Wye and elsewhere. Aberdeen has a Beer Barrel, Huddersfield a Boy and Barrel, Woore, near Market Drayton, a Man and Barrel,

Birkenhead a Glass Barrel, Northwich a Blue Barrel, Nottingham a Green Barrel, Kenilworth a Red Barrel and Bagworth, Leics an Old Barrel. Seaton, Devon has a Barrel of Beer.

Baseball Tavern Derby. Adjacent to the Baseball Ground, the home of Derby County Football Club. Before the football club moved there in 1895 it was the venue for baseball games, reflecting the attempt at the end of the nineteenth century to establish baseball as an English summer game. The last–known baseball game to be played on this ground was in July 1944, when a team of Derby County players took on a representative side of the US Air Force stationed nearby. The pub sign shows a striker preparing for a big hit.

Bason Bridge East Huntspill, Som. For the bridge nearby which was rebuilt for the opening of the Glastonbury Canal. The latter came into use in 1834 but was disused after 1853.

Bass Arms Tatenhill, near Burton-on-Trent. The Bass family established their Brewery at Burton-on-Trent in 1777. Michael Thomas Bass (1799–1884) made the beer a household name. His son, Michael Arthur, became Baron Burton in 1886. There is a Bass House at Harborne, Birmingham.

Basset Hound Thingwall, Mers. For the short-legged dog that is used to unearth foxes and badgers. ('Basset' is based on French *bas* 'low'.) According to local tradition Sir Ralph Basset was a thirteenth-century lord of the manor who kept a pack of such hounds for hunting which he bred himself.

Bat and Ball Hambledon, Hants and elsewhere. The Hambledon pub is the most famous cricketing inn in the country, with a club that was founded in 1750. Between that year and 1790 Richard Nyren, landlord of the inn and captain of the club, inflicted twenty-nine defeats on an All-England XI. Whitbread's *Inns of Sport* records that one game was played for a thousand guineas, another for 'eleven pairs of white-corded dimity breeches and eleven handsome striped waistcoats'. At Leigh, Kent however, the sign shows a bat of the winged variety flying round a sphere. The sign alludes to an eighteenth-century Hell-Fire Club whose members met in a circular building and for whom the bat was an emblem of their nocturnal activities. Such clubs became a great nuisance in the early part of the century, the most notorious being that founded about 1745 by Sir Francis Dashwood, based at Medmenham Abbey near Marlow. Northampton has a Bat and Wickets.

Bat and Wickets *See* Cricket.

Bath Penzance. There was in about 1810 a salt-water public bath alongside the pub, the first of its kind to be put up on an English seafront.

Bathpool Bathpool, Som. Of interest in the way the inn-sign illustrates the place name, in this case using an incident from local history. The members of the local volunteer force are shown parading on the green outside the inn. They were held in readiness for the threatened invasion by the Spanish Armada in 1588.

Baton St Albans. The sign shows a baton, the ornamental stick used as a symbol of office, lying on a cushion.

Battle Reading. Near the Battle Hospital, which in turn is named because of a medieval connection with Battle Abbey in East Sussex.

Battleaxes Aldenham, Herts, and elsewhere. Battleaxes feature in the coats of arms of various families. The Aldenham example refers to the arms of Lord Aldenham. At Wraxhall, Avon, the reference is to the arms of the local Gibbs family, and so on.

Battledown Cheltenham. A skirmish between Cavaliers and Round-heads took place nearby during the Civil War of the early seventeenth century, caused by the conflict between Charles I and Parliament.

Battle of Alma *See* Alma.

Battle of Britain Shears Green, Kent and elsewhere. Many Kentish pubs took this name, since the fight between the German Luftwaffe and the pilots of the RAF took place in the skies above Kent. The battle occurred in 1940 and was meant to be a prelude to invasion. The outstanding bravery of 'the Few' prevented it.

Battlesteads Wark, Northld. An archaic, or old-fashioned, word meaning 'place of battle', ie the living-quarters used by troops during a battle. The troops were in this area in 1715 and again in 1745, when two Jacobite Rebellions were crushed.

Bay and Say Colchester. The sign shows a man and woman in sixteenth-century costume, each carrying a bolt of cloth. The reference is to the Flemish weavers who fled from perse-cution and came to settle in this area. 'Bay' and 'say' are two types of cloth. Bay is more familiar as baize, which derives from the plural form of the word: it is a coarse woollen cloth with a long nap. Say is a cloth of fine texture similar to serge. *See also* Flemish Weaver.

Bay Horse Totnes and elsewhere. Blood-good and Santini, in their *Horseman's Dictionary*, define 'bay' as 'horse's colour, ranging from light brown to rich mahogany, but always with black points (ie mane and tail), which distinguishes it from any variety of chestnut'. At Astley Bridge, near Bolton there is a Bay Mare. Technically a female horse is only a mare if it has reached the age of five (thoroughbred) or four (other breeds), or after it has been bred to a stallion.

Bay Malton Dunham Massey, near Altrincham. The name of a steeplechaser which was highly successful between 1764–67.

Baynard Castle London EC4. The reference is to a castle built by one Ralph Baynard, a nobleman who came to England with William the Conqueror and died in the reign of William Rufus. The castle was destroyed by King John in 1212. A second castle on the site was destroyed by the Fire of London, 1666.

Beachcomber Brean, Weston-super-Mare. The term is here used loosely to describe a holiday-maker who spends his time on the beach. Originally a beachcomber was a long wave coming in from the ocean. Later the word was used for the settlers on the Pacific Islands who lived by what they could find on the beaches or around the wharves. Beachcomber was also the name of a famous column in the *Daily Express* begun by D B Wyndham Lewis and continued by J B Morton.

Beachy Head Eastbourne. The pub is near the headland, which is almost 600 feet high. A naval battle took place there in 1690, when the French defeated a combined English and Dutch fleet.

Beacon Penrith, and elsewhere. Referring to a nearby hill on which a signal fire is lit, or on which there is a lighthouse. In Luton there is a Beacon Arms. Gillingham has a Beacon Court, Liverpool a Beacon Light, Brighton a Beacon Royal, Exmouth a Beacon Vaults. Cawsand Beacon refers to a specific beacon on Dartmoor.

Beaconsfield Tavern London W8. Also Beaconsfield Arms at Southall. The Earl of Beaconsfield, otherwise Benjamin Disraeli (1804–81), statesman and novelist, was prime minister on two occasions (Conservative), and was a gifted orator and favourite of Queen Victoria. Related pub names are the Earl of Beaconsfield, at Beaconsfield, and the Disraeli Arms at Wycombe Marsh, Bucks. The Primrose at Moorgate may also refer to Disraeli, since the flower was closely associated with him.

Beadle Stratford-on-Avon. Originally the Salmon Tail, but renamed in 1982 as a result of a competition run by Whitbreads. The sign shows Mr Fred Baker, who was town beadle and official mace-bearer for forty years.

Beagle *See* Dog.

Beam Bridge Sampford Arundel, Som. Referring to a local foot-bridge which was at one time a 'beam', or tree trunk.

Bean Also Beanstalk. *See* Fruits and Vegetables.

Bear Oxshott and elsewhere. The bear features in the arms of many noble families, but when the inn sign is of heraldic significance, the bear is normally assigned a colour – Black Bear, Brown Bear, etc. In its simple form the sign is probably a reference to the barbaric sport of bear-baiting, which was finally made illegal in 1835. Bears were chained to posts and dogs were set on them to 'bait' them. Bulls were sometimes treated in similar fashion. It is just possible that *Bear* was also thought to be suitable as a pub name because of its closeness to 'beer'. Hindley cites an instance of a publican who offered 'bear for sale', meaning that he sold ale. Minor variants of Bear include Bear's Head at Macclesfield and Bear's Paw at St Helen's, Lancs.

Bear and Baculus *See* Bear and Ragged Staff.

Bear and Bells Beccles, Sflk. A reference to a dancing bear, which would have been led around the countryside by its handler, giving performances at various stopping-places. The Bear Cross at Kinson, Bournemouth was one such place, receiving regular visits from a travelling fair.

Bear and Billet *See* Bear and Ragged Staff.

Bear and Ragged Staff Berkswell near Coventry and elsewhere. A heraldic sign, normally referring to Richard Nevil, Earl of Warwick (1428–71), known as the King-maker. In Shakespeare's *Henry VI Part Two*, Act 5, scene 1, where there is much talk of bear-baiting, Warwick says: 'Now, by my father's badge, old Nevil's crest,/ The rampant bear chain'd to the ragged staff,/This day I'll wear aloft my burgonet.' The 'burgonet' is his helmet, and the 'ragged staff' in the coat of arms is simply a branch or young tree stripped of its branches. According to legend the first earl slew a bear by strangling it. The second earl killed a giant with a 'ragged staff', which he thereupon added to his coat of arms. The pub sign sometimes becomes the Bear and Staff, as at London W1 and elsewhere. In Bristol it has become the Bear and Rugged Staff, which is a more modern form of the name with exactly the same meaning. In Warwick there was formerly another variant, the Bear and Baculus, *baculus* being the Latin word for 'stick' or 'staff'. The Bear and Billet at Chester varies it in a different way, 'billet' being used in its older sense of 'thick piece of wood used as a weapon'.

Bear Cross *See* Bear and Bells.

Bear's Head Also Bear's Paw. *See* Bear.

Beau Brummel Brighton and elsewhere. George Bryan Brummel (1778–1840) inherited a fortune and became noted for his elegant taste in dress, which led to his nickname. He was for some time a favourite of the Prince of Wales, later George IV, and was regarded as a leader of society in matters of fashion and etiquette. After a quarrel with the prince, Brummel exiled himself to France and died there in poverty. At Bridlington there is a Brummels.

Beaufort Hunt Chipping Sodbury, Glos. The Duke of Beaufort (died 1984) was Master of this hunt and unveiled the pub sign. He is commemorated again in the Duke of Beaufort at nearby Hawkesbury Upton.

Beau Geste Edinburgh and elsewhere. The hero of *Beau Geste*, the romantic adventure novel by Percival Christopher Wren (1885–1941). The book was published in 1924. Wren himself had served in the Foreign Legion, the setting for this story, and is said to have been tall, distinguished and monocled, obviously a retired army officer.

Beau Nash Tunbridge Wells. Richard Nash (1674–1762) was a man of fashion and an accomplished gambler. When he came to Bath in 1704 the spa was being badly mismanaged. After being named as Master of Ceremonies for the spa, he was largely responsible for converting it into a fashionable resort. It seems to have been left to another spa, however, to honour him on a pub sign.

Beauty of Bath *See* Apples.

Beaver Appledore, Devon and elsewhere. The Devonshire pub name is related to fur trading ships from Canada putting into port. *Beaver* has itself frequently served as a name for a Royal Navy ship.

Becher's Brook Cantley, Doncaster. Name of the famous jump on the Aintree Steeplechase Course at Liverpool. It has to be jumped twice during the Grand National, and takes its name from Captain Becher. Although he won the first Grand National in 1839 he fell at this fence. The Becher's Brook pub is in Ascot Avenue. Ascot is another famous name in the horse-racing world, though it has only to do with flat racing. In Liverpool there is an Aintree Tavern.

Bedfordshire Yeoman Luton. The County Yeomanry was formed in 1902. *See also* Recruiting Sergeant and Yeoman.

Bee *See* Busy Bee.

Beefeater Batley, W Yorks and elsewhere. The traditional nickname for a Yeoman of the Guard at the Tower of London (or for one of the Warders of the Tower). The term was originally a contemptuous reference to a servant who was obviously well-fed, an eater of beef. Most servants ate far less nourishing food.

Beehive Grantham and elsewhere. Grantham has the best-known sign of this type, the real beehive wedged in the branches of a tree outside the pub. It is always spoken of as a 'living sign', thanks to the verse beneath it which reads: 'Stop, traveller! this wondrous sign explore,/And say, when thou hast viewed it o'er,/"Grantham, now two rareties are thine:/A lofty steeple and a living sign".' Elsewhere the sign is either a painting of a beehive or a representation of a real one, as at Brentford. A Cheltenham pub of this name reminds everyone that 'By industry we live', and it is true that the beehive has long been a symbol of industry. In many cases, however, it must have appealed as a sign because of its distinctive shape.

Beer Barrel *See* Barrels.

Beer Engine Newton St Cyres, near Exeter. Properly another term for the 'beer-pump', ie a device which draws beer from the casks in the cellar to the bar. This pub sign interprets the phrase as a George Stephenson-Health Robinson locomotive, with beer froth brimming over its boiler. Bristol has a Beer Cask. The railway puns (there is a railway station nearby) continue inside the pub, where Rail Ale and Piston Bitter may be bought.

Bees–in–the–Wall *See* Busy Bee.

Bees Knees Winsford, Ches. A use of the modern slang expression, implying that the pub is excellent.

Beeswing Southam, Warks and elsewhere. In a pub context this word refers to the film formed in port and some other wines which are kept for many years. The film is thought to look like the wing of a bee. Beeswing was used with this meaning in the 1860s; by the 1870s 'Old Beeswing' had become a term of address for a genial drinker. The Southam pub, however, merely shows bees in flight. Another sign, at York, shows a racehorse of this name which was unbeaten between 1835–42.

Beetle and Wedge Moulsford, Berks. At one time logs were floated down the river from London. A beetle and wedge would have been used to split them. A 'beetle' is like an oversized mallet, with a larger, heavier head and a longer handle. It is still used in urban areas to lay paving stones.

Beggars Bush New Oscott, Sutton Coldfield. To go home by beggar's bush once meant to go to ruin. The inference was surely that one would soon be sleeping under a bush, like a beggar. The phrase was in use by the sixteenth century and was used by John Fletcher as the title of a comic drama, produced in 1622. Brewer refers to a specific tree known as Beggars' Bush. It is in fact likely that in different districts, beggars would congregate at night at a specific location, much as modern down-and-outs gather together.

Bein Glenfarg, near Perth. This Scottish word means 'comfortable, well found'. Old Norse, Latin and French origins for it have been suggested, but none of them are convincing.

Bel and the Dragon Cookham, Berks. This name relates to two separate stories, additions to the Book of Daniel. The first concerns Daniel's refusal to believe that Bel is a living Babylonian god who consumes food. He is able to prove that priests enter the sacred place by a secret door and take the food away. In the other story he kills a dragon which is supposed to be divine. Thrown to the lions for this act, the lions' mouths are closed and they are unable to harm him. Stanley Spencer R A (died 1959) painted this pub sign when he was living in Cookham.

Belisha Beacon Rainham Mark, Kent. The Belisha beacon, which indicates a pedestrian crossing with a flashing amber light, was introduced in its original form in 1934 at the suggestion of Leslie Hore-Belisha, who was at that time minister of transport. Hore-Belisha was an ex-journalist with a flair for publicity, and probably recognised in the beacon idea, when it was put to him, its publicity value as much as its potential contribution to road safety. Aptly enough, this pub faces a pedestrian crossing.

Bell It has been said of the bell that 'it speaks all languages'. Apart from its distinctive sound, it has a conveniently distinctive, yet simple, shape which has greatly appealed to sign makers through the centuries. References to bells on inn signs are especially frequent, perhaps lending proof to Handel's comment that Britain was the 'Ringing Island'. Church bells and hand bells are those mainly referred to in pub signs. Either may be specified by number, as in One Bell at Watford, Two Bells at Folkestone, Three Bells at Hordle, Hants, Four Bells at Woodborough, near Nottingham, Five Bells at Bridport Dors, Six Bells at Ruislip, Eight Bells at Saffron Walden, Ten Bells in Aldgate, Twelve Bells at Cirencester. Ring of Bells is common, and Bells occurs at Staines and elsewhere, though the simple *Bell* is of course far more common. Specific sets of bells are mentioned in Bells of Ouzeley at Old Windsor, Bells of St Mary's, Prestatyn but Bells of Peover, at Peover, Ches, refers to the family name of the pub's previous owner since 1895. A Ringers is at Bray, Bucks, a Ringers' Rest at Willingham, Cambridge, Five Ringers at Deal, Six Ringers at Leverington, Cambridge, Eight Ringers at Wells–next–the–Sea, Nflk. A bell often appears on an inn sign in combination with something else. In some cases a licensee coming from another pub to a *Bell* has added his previous sign, rather as some people on marriage hyphenate their surnames. Explanations of some other combinations are given below. *See also* Bow Bells and Dumb Bell.

Bell and Anchor London W6 and elsewhere. The bell on a sign is sometimes a ship's bell. This sign strengthens the nautical flavour.

Bell and Antelope Holywell, Clwyd. This sign may be heraldic, since both bell and antelope are to be found on coats of arms. However, it is interesting that Fabian Stedman, author of *Campanalogia* (1677), devised a peal for St Benet's which he called 'The Antelope'.

Bell and Bear Shelton near Stoke-on-Trent. Probably a reference to a dancing bear. *See* Bear and Bells.

Bell and Bottle Littlewick Green, near Maidenhead. This is one of a group of names which contain 'bell' and another element. Many of the signs are very old and could have come into being at a time when combining two signs was a fairly common practice. Other names which appear to be of this type include Bell and Bowl, Whaplode, near Spalding, Bell and Bullock, Netherby, near Carlisle, though this may also be a bullock with a bell around its neck, Bell and Castle, Derby, Bell and Cross, Holy Cross, near Stourbridge, Bell and Cuckoo, Walsall, Bell and Dyke, Stenhousemuir, Bell and Feathers, Ugley, Esx, Bell and Gate, Romford, Bell and Hare, London N17, Bell and Jorrocks, Frittenden, Kent, Bell and Lion, Sheerness, Bell and Oak, Peterborough, Bell and Shoulder of Mutton, Swindon, Bell and Sun, Ware, Bell and Talbot, Bridgnorth.

Bell and Crown Zeals, Wilts and Chard, Som. Bells have traditionally been rung on royal occasions for centuries. Many bells also have an inscription on them, sometimes repeated on the inn-sign: 'Fear God, Honour the King'. This was transformed on one sign, according to a story in the *Craftsman*, 30 September 1738, into: 'Let the King/Live long./ Dong Ding,/Ding Dong.'

Bell and Gavel Gloucester. The 'gavel' now suggests the hammer used by an auctioneer. In earlier use, now dialectal, it referred to corn which had been cut and was ready to be made into sheaves. Tom Ingram, in his *Bells in England*, says that in rural areas a bell was rung to indicate when harvesting was to begin, and again when it had ended.

Belle Isle Leeds. A small village of this name is now one of Leeds's suburbs. The best-known *Belle Isle*, however, is at Lake Windermere. It was named by its owner Isabella Curwen in 1781, linking with her own first name.

Bell Hagg Sheffield. A prominent spot in the West Riding which has nothing to do with bells. The original form of the name was Belhaye, where the Old English word *bel* refers to a 'fire' or 'beacon', while the second element means 'enclosure'.

Bell Rock Tayport, Fife. Normally for a bell which is hung on a dangerous rock, to warn ships away. There was formerly such a bell hung on the Inchcape Reef.

Bells of Ouzeley Old Windsor. 'Ouzeley' is apparently a highly corrupt form of Osney, in Oxfordshire. Osney Abbey had a famous set of bells. 'Great Tom', the bell at Christchurch, Oxford, was brought there from the abbey at the Dissolution.

Bells of Peover *See* Bell.

Bells of St Mary's *See* Bell.

Belvedere Weymouth. Originally a kind of turret constructed in a high place so as to afford a 'fine view', which is what the word means. This pub has such a view over the inner harbour. The place in Kent named Belvedere has a Belvoir pub, presumably for a similar reason.

Ben Brierley Manchester. Ben Brierley was a founder member of the Manchester Literary Club and noted journalist-author.

Bench and Bar Nottingham. The pub is close by the Shire Hall's law courts. One meaning of 'bench' is the place where justice is administered.

Bendigo Sneinton, Nottingham. William Abednego Thompson (1811–80), popularly known as Bendigo (a corruption of Abednego, name of a biblical character), was a prizefighter who retired from the ring as Champion of All England in 1850. He subsequently became a preacher and assisted General Booth at many Salvationist meetings. The Australian town of Bendigo owes its name to an admirer of Thompson who was either dubbed Bendigo by admirers or adopted the name to boost his own reputation.

Benjamin Beale Margate. Benjamin Beale is credited with the invention of the bathing-machine, a small carriage in which a bather could be carried out to a point where the water was deep enough for swimming. It was especially useful on very flat beaches when the tide was out and remained in popular usage until about 1908.

Ben Jonson Canterbury and elsewhere. Benjamin Jonson (1572–1637), poet and playwright, was a friend of all the great writers of his day, including Shakespeare, and a considerable influence on younger writers, who formed 'the tribe of Ben'. Hindley relates a story about him which may not be true, but bears repetition. Owing the landlord of an inn some money, Jonson kept away from the house. The landlord met him in the street and told him that if Jonson could answer four questions, he would cancel the debt. The questions were: What pleases God? What pleases the Devil? What pleases the world? What pleases me? Jonson's reply was: 'God is best pleased when man forsakes his sin;/The devil's best pleased when man persists therein;/The world's best pleased when you do draw good wine;/And you'll be best pleased when I pay for mine.' The landlord gave Jonson a receipt for the sum owing and presented him with a bottle of wine.

Ben Nevis Fort William and elsewhere. Ben Nevis is the highest mountain in the British Isles, at 4,406 feet. It is in Highland. (The name has been borrowed for mountains in Tasmania and Otago, New Zealand. The latter rises to 9,125 feet.)

Ben Truman Ashford, Kent. The name of a keg bitter and bottled Export from Trumans, reputed to be Britain's oldest brewery. William Truman registered as a brewer in 1613, and the brewery itself dates from 1666.

Besom Aylburton Common, Glos. A besom is a bundle of twigs tied together and used as a broom. The name seems to have been suggested by gypsy makers of such brooms who came here to sell them. At Coldstream, Bdrs, there is another pub of this name.

Bessemer Liverpool. Also Bessemer Arms, Workington, Cumb. Sir Henry Bessemer (1813–98) invented the Bessemer Process, by which steel is made from pig iron, in 1856. The city of Bessemer in Alabama USA, is also named for him.

Best o' Brass Mossley, near Ashton-under-Lyne. The former owner of this pub was a brass-band enthusiast. The name he chose was probably borrowed from the television series 'Best of Brass', adapted into the vernacular. One of the brass bands (which are popular in this area) is seen on the inn sign.

Betsy Trotwood London EC1. Betsy Trotwood is the great-aunt of David in Charles Dickens's novel *David Copperfield*. She proves to be a good friend to him. At the end of the story she is over eighty, but still able to walk six miles at a stretch in winter weather.

Bettle and Chisel Delabole, Corn. 'Bettle', is another form of 'beetle', the name of a mallet-like tool.

Together with a wide-faced chisel it is used to split slates in the nearby slate quarries.

Bible References These are now restricted mainly to the best-known biblical characters and incidents, namely Adam and Eve, Noah's Ark, Baptist's Head, Dove and Olive Branch, Good Samaritan, Jacob's Ladder, Pillar of Fire, Pillar of Salt, Rainbow and Dove, Samson (And Lion). The eagle-eyed may spot a few more, including phrases such as World Turned Upside Down, which probably have a biblical origin.

Biddy Mulligans London NW6. A name that is meant to indicate that it is a thoroughly Irish pub. 'Biddy' is a pet form of Bridget.

Bideford Stratton, Corn. This no doubt indicated the destination of coaches which picked up their passengers at the pub. Bideford, not far away, has also named several ships of the Royal Navy since the seventeenth century, two of which had the misfortune to be wrecked in the same place, off Flamborough Head. *See also* London.

Big Apple Great Yarmouth and Bristol. The reference is to New York, which is said to have received this nickname from musicians who used 'apple' in the way 'gig' is now used. Clarence Major, in his *Black Slang*, says that black jazz musicians at one time spoke of any large city in the north as a 'big apple'. The Yarmouth pub was named in order to commemorate the owner's visit to New York. Manchester has a New York and Basildon, Esx a New Yorker. *See also* Bronx.

Big Ben Liverpool. The London bell of this name hanging in the clock tower of the Houses of Parliament recalls Sir Benjamin Hall, a vast Welshman who was First Commissioner of Works in 1856, when Big Ben seems to have received its name. Hall was asking his parliamentary colleagues for ideas about what to call the bell, weighing 13 tons, when one of them suggested that it be named for him. The nickname had first come into existence, however, because of a prizefighter called Benjamin Caunt, who weighed seventeen stones. He had some particularly memorable battles with William Thompson (*see* Bendigo). Caunt fought for the last time in 1857. He was then aged forty-two. After sixty rounds the contest was declared to be drawn.

Big Bull's Head See Bull.

Big Eighteen *See* Number Names.

Big Lock Middlewich, Ches. The lock referred to is on the nearby Chester canal, built in 1772.

Big Six Halifax. For more than a century this was the nickname of this pub, which was officially the Bowling Green. The big six were prominent Halifax businessmen who regularly met in the pub, occupying the best seats in the best room. *Big Six* became the official name of the pub in 1982.

Bilbo Baggins Eastbourne. A central character in *The Hobbit* (1937) and *The Lord of the Rings* (1954–55), by J R R Tolkien (1892–1973). There is also a Hobbit at Sowerby Bridge, W Yorks. Hobbits are little people who live in burrows. They are fond of food, bright colours and tobacco and are friendly.

Bird Blackbirds, choughs, crows, cuckoos, eagles, hawks, magpies, owls, parrots, pigeons, ravens, robins, storks, swallows, wrens, are all mentioned in pub names together with at least eighty other varieties of bird. The Pelican is good for a joke, and the Harrier is not necessarily a reference to the bird.

Bird Cage London E2. The pub has several bird cages hanging from its ceiling, no doubt reflecting the interest of a licensee.

Birdham Birdham, near Chichester. Of interest because of its punning sign, which shows a large magpie squatting on a ham. The ham in the place name would originally have meant 'meadow'.

Bird in Hand Bagshot and elsewhere. The proverbial saying 'A bird in the hand is worth two in the bush' is of great antiquity and may have suggested this sign, a popular one since the seventeenth century. Traditionally it was illustrated by a mailed fist on which a falcon was perched, but the Bagshot sign shows a Regency beau with his arm around his 'bird', a young lady. At King's Lynn the sign depicts a wild duck which is being ringed. BBC staff who work at Bush House, in London WC2, have long had their own version of the proverb: a bird in Bush is worth two in the Strand. Quarrelton near Paisley has a Bird in the Hand and there are several examples (two in Wigan) of Bird i' th' Hand. Elsdon, Northld has a Bird in Bush, Littletown near Durham a Bird in the Bush and Alnwick a Bird and Bush. At Kingswood, Bristol is a Bird in View.

Birds and the Bees Stirling. This pub is a converted byre, or cow-house, and retains a dairy-farm atmosphere with its tractor seats and milk churns. The pub name is obviously not used in a literal sense, but alludes euphemistically to what parents sometimes think they should discuss with their teenage children – the attraction between the sexes and its consequences.

Bird's Nest Twickenham, GL. Opened in 1968 by Watney Mann and designed to attract a young clientele, young men and their 'dolly bird' girlfriends.

Bishop and Wolf St Mary's, Isles of Scilly. The Bishop's Rock and Wolf Rock lighthouses, which date from the nineteenth century. The sign shows a bishop holding a model lighthouse on one side, and a wolf crouching beside the lighthouse on the other.

Bishop Blaise Richmond, N Yorks. Also Bishop Blaize, Andover, Blaise at Henbury, Bristol, Blaize at Bourne End, Bucks. Blaise is the usual modern spelling of this saint's name. There is no historical evidence for the account of his torture and death, but the story of the iron combs that were said to have been used to tear his flesh caused him to become patron of woolcombers. His emblems are a large comb and two crossed candles.

Bishop Bonner London E2. On the site of Bonner's Fields, owned by the bishops of London and named for one of them. Edmund Bonner (died 1569) persecuted Catholics when Henry VIII was on the throne. Under Mary I he seems to have persecuted the Protestants, earning for himself the nickname 'Bloody Bonner'. Since at least a hundred people suffered martyrdom because of his activities, the nickname seems to have been justified.

Bishop Bridge Thorpe Hamlet, Norwich. For a nearby bridge dating from the thirteenth century. There are two places in Lincolnshire, called Bishopbridge.

Bishop John de Grandisson Bishopsteignton, Devon. The

name of a fourteenth-century Bishop of Exeter. The place name itself refers to a 'farm on the Teign river' which was owned by the Bishop of Exeter in 1086 (Domesday Book).

Bishop Lacy Chudleigh, Devon. Bishop Lacy (died 1455) was Bishop of Exeter and is buried in Exeter Cathedral.

Bishop out of Residence Kingston-on-Thames. The pub is on the site of a residence which belonged to William of Wykeham (1324–1404), Bishop of Winchester and lord chancellor. The brewers intended to name the pub Kingston Ram, after their own trademark, but Kingston already had a Ram. The present name was the winning entry in a competition they held. The sign shows a mitred bishop doing a spot of fishing in the nearby Thames.

Bishop's Finger Canterbury and London W1. A nineteenth-century term for the kind of signpost which was shaped like a finger, correctly known as a 'finger-post'. Finger-post itself became the slang term for a parson because 'he points the way to heaven, but does not necessarily follow the way himself'. *See also* St Peter's Finger.

Bit and Bridle Newry, Down. A thoroughly horsey sign, the bridle being the leather headgear worn by a horse, the bit being the mouthpiece.

Bittern Bitterne, Southampton. The place name probably means 'house on a bend', but the pub sign shows the marsh bird of the heron family.

Black A very common colour as far as pub names are concerned, occurring in at least fifty different names. Individual instances are dealt with below where

appropriate; others which occur include Black Angus, Liverpool; Black Bear, Wareham; Black Beck, Haverthwaite, Lancs; Black Bitch, Linlithgow, Loth; Black Boar, Tewkesbury; Black Brook, Ruishton, near Taunton; Black Bull, Ruislip; Black Buoy, Wivenhoe; Black Bush, Washington, near Gateshead; Black Campbell, Glasgow; Black Cock, Tipton; Black Cow, Sunderland; Black Cross, Bromsgrove; Black Dasher, Prestonpans; Black Deer. Loughton, near Epping; Black Eagle, Northfleet; Black Fox, Milland, Hants; Black Greyhound, Wincham, near Northwich; Black Griffin, Canterbury; Black Hart, Guyhirne, near Wisbech; Black House, Edmondsley; Black Knight, Dukinfield, Ches; Black Mare, Manchester; Black Mill, Barham near Canterbury; Black Mountain, Belfast; Black Ox, Llandovery; Black Pig, Staple, near Canterbury; Black Rock, Wakefield; Black Star, Stourport; Morpeth has a Black and Grey. It has been suggested that some 'black' names came about when the Gin Act of 1736 came into force, causing tavern owners to drape their signs in black velvet or add 'black' to the pub name. Perhaps in view of this colour's association with mourning and other rather dreary states of mind, it is surprising that so many names make use of it.

Blackamoor Wigton, Cumb and elsewhere. Also Black–a–Moor Head, Preston, Blackamoor's Head, Chessington and elsewhere. This word appeared in the sixteenth century and simply meant 'a black Moor', or more generally, a Negro or dark-skinned person. The reason for its use is discussed at Black Boy. There is a Blackamoor Gate at Combe Martin near Ilfracombe.

Black Bear *See* Black.

Black Beauty Bottesford, Scunthorpe. The name was made famous by Anna Sewell (1820–78) who published the children's classic *Black Beauty* in 1877. It is the autobiography of a horse of that name. The Hull Brewery transferred the name to a sweet stout and used it mainly for that reason.

Black Beck Haverthwaite, near Ulverston. After a local 'beck' or stream.

Black Bitch *See* Black.

Black Boy Caernarfon and elsewhere. Modern signs are likely to portray the black boy as a young chimney-sweep of the Dickensian kind. In the seventeenth and eighteenth centuries, when the sign was extremely common for coffee–houses as well as taverns, the reference was to the personal servant of a rich person. Negro pageboys were highly fashionable and must have been distinctive figures in the streets of London, dressed in brightly-coloured liveries as they inevitably were, as depicted on the sign at Killay, near Swansea. For this reason they were popularly known as 'tigers', their uniforms often having a striped design.

Black Boys Norwich and elsewhere. Usually related to Black Boy, but the pub in the village of Blackboys near Uckfield, E Ssx is derived from the name of a nearby estate, owned in the fourteenth century by Richard Blackboy. This fact has not prevented tales of black-faced men from an iron-foundry being responsible for the name.

Black Bull Also Black Buoy, Black Bush. *See* Black.

Black Cap London NW1. This name is applied to many species of birds which have a black area on their heads. It is thus the name of the coal-titmouse, the marsh titmouse, the great titmouse, the reed-bunting, the stonechat, the bullfinch and black-headed gull as well as the blackcap warbler. The expression applies more sinisterly to the cap worn by English judges when passing the death sentence.

Black Castle Bristol. A sham castle built as a folly in the 1760s by William Reeve, constructed mainly from the black slag which was a waste product of brass founding. Reeve himself was declared bankrupt in 1774, mainly due to his habit of building 'exotic extravagances'. This particular one, after lying empty for many years, became a pub in 1978.

Black Cat *See* Cat.

Black Cock Tipton. This is a technical description of the male of the black grouse. The female is called a grey hen.

Black Cow Also Black Cross, Black Deer. *See* Black.

Black Diamond Cotgrave, near Nottingham and elsewhere in mining areas. A reference to coal, and the prosperity that was (formerly) derived from its presence. Brewer's *Dictionary of Phrase and Fable* points out that both coal and diamonds are carbon-based, but that is probably over-subtle. At one time the phrase 'a black diamond' referred to what would be called 'a rough diamond' today, someone of good moral quality though of unpolished manners.

Black Dog Southam, near Leamington Spa. 'The Black Dog of Arden' was Guy Beauchamp, Earl of Warwick in the early fourteenth century. He was one of

those who plotted to kill Piers
Gaveston, favourite of Edward II,
in 1312. In the West Country the
sign may relate to the labrador
dog, since one of the earliest of the
breed in Britain was owned by
a Dorset innkeeper. In the
eighteenth century a 'black dog' in
slang meant a counterfeit shilling.
In the nineteenth century it came
to mean a spell of ill-humour. At
Bury, near Arundel, there is a
Black Dog and Duck.

Black Eagle Also Black Fox.
See Black.

Black Fox *See* Fox.

Black Friar London EC4. The
Dominican monks, known as black
friars from the colour of their
robes, built a monastery here in
the thirteenth century. It was
closed at the Dissolution in 1538.
The Dominicans had a reputation
for intellectual distinction, but
were also thought to be hard
drinkers.

Black Garter Newcastle–on–Tyne.
The former Black Swan and Star
and Garter were converted into
the Market Tavern, which has now
been renamed *Black Garter*.

Black Greyhound Also Black Griffin,
Black Hart. *See* Black.

Black Hat Wilstead, near Bedford.
The pub is near the birthplace of
John Bunyan (1628–88), author of
The Pilgrim's Progress. He is shown
on the pub sign in semi-cartoon
style wearing a black sugar-loaf hat
of the type strongly associated
with the Puritans.

Black Hole Kirklington, near Bedale.
A curious name for a pub, in view
of its association with the infamous
Black Hole of Calcutta. This was a
small prison in which 146 British
prisoners were confined in June,
1756, by the Nawab of Bengal.
There was one woman amongst
them, who survived, along with

twenty-two of the men. The rest
were suffocated.

Black Horse Eastcote and elsewhere.
This popular sign dates from at
least the fourteenth century. Its
use appears to be a reflection of its
convenience as a visual symbol. By
the seventeenth century the phrase
had become the nickname of the
7th Dragoon Guards, who had
black collars and cuffs on their
jackets and rode mainly black
horses. The sign was also by this
time being used by goldsmiths in
Lombard Street, London. It is
now associated with Lloyds Bank
as well as remaining a popular pub
sign. At Catford there is a Black
Horse and Harrow.

Black House *See* Black.

Black Lion Walsingham, Nflk and
elsewhere. A heraldic sign mainly
(as here) related to Queen Philippa
of Hainault, wife of Edward III,
who was from Flanders. In Wales
the reference is to Owain Glyndwr
(Owen Glendower), the celebrated
Welsh chieftain who was born
about 1350 and died in 1415, or to
his father. Madoc ap Meredith,
both of whom had black lions on
their arms. At Lampeter the name
is therefore Black Lion Royal.

Black Mare Also Black Mill.
See Black.

Blackmore Vale Marnhull, Dors. The
name of an area in the county
where cider apples are grown.

Black Ox Llandovery. This would
have made an unsuitable name in
former times, when the proverb
'the black ox had trod on his foot'
was current. It meant that a time of
sorrow had arrived.

Black Pig *See* Black.

Black Prince Princes Risborough and
elsewhere. Edward, Prince of
Wales (1330–76) was the eldest
son of Edward III. He was known
as the Black Prince because of the

colour of his armour. His death of ill health at the early age of forty-six was a distinct loss to the nation, his military skill coupled with humanity in victory having been much admired. The Royal Navy has had several warships bearing his name, the first launched in 1650.

Black Rabbit Arundel. The pub was used by bargees on the nearby Wey-Arun canal, often used to transport coal. It is therefore tempting to think of a rabbit covered with coaldust. In fact rabbits, though naturally brownish-grey, exist in black domestic varieties.

Black Raven London EC2. Formerly a common sign in London, the Black Raven has connections with Scottish coats of arms. In a London context, however, it is difficult not to relate the sign to the ravens in the Tower of London. It may be significant that Marie Stuart, in her *Old Edinburgh Taverns*, makes no mention of any 'raven' sign. Since the publication of Dickens's *Barnaby Rudge* in 1841, a reference to Barnaby's pet raven has been possible.

Black Robin Kingston, Kent. The nickname of a local highwayman of times past. He wore a black mask and rode a black horse.

Black Rock *See* Black.

Black's Head Carlton Hill, Nottingham and elsewhere. A variant of Blackamoor and similar names. *See* Black Boy.

Blacksmiths One of the commonest signs in this group is **B**lacksmiths Arms, Bideford and elsewhere. An associated name is Three Hammers, St Albans and else-where, since these appeared on the arms of the Blacksmiths Company in the late fifteenth century. Newchapel in Surrey has a Blacksmith's Head. The blacksmith was an important member of the community in former times because he made the tools in peacetime and the weapons in wartime. He was something of a rural aristocrat, and those who could ally themselves to a smith were glad to do so – hence the frequency of the surname Smith. Blacksmiths naturally feature on many inn signs, leading to names such as Smiths Arms, Dartford and elsewhere, Smithy, Tingley, near Wakefield, Smithy Arms, Rhualt, Clwyd, Hammer, Madeley, Salop, Hammer and Anvil, March, Cambs, Hammer and Pincers, Barrow-on-Soar, Leics and elsewhere, Hammer and Stithy (= 'anvil'), Ossett, near Wakefield, Hammer and Tongs, Basingstoke, Hammer in Hand, Gander's Ash, Herts, Anvil, Mansfield Woodhouse, Notts and elsewhere, Anvil Arms, Wold Newton, near Bridlington and elsewhere. Phoenix signs may sometimes refer to blacksmiths, since this fabulous bird appeared as a crest on the later arms granted to the Company. Also related are Horseshoe and Three Horseshoes signs.

Black Smock Stathe, Som. A witch who lived in this village (says a legend) always wore a white smock. She terrified local people until they joined together and chased her up the chimney of the George Inn. She emerged on the roof covered in soot and was chased over Sedgemoor until she changed herself into a hare and disappeared.

Black Squirrel Letchworth. A colony of black squirrels lives in a local woodland area. Although rare in England, black squirrels are common elsewhere, eg in Canada, where visitors to Ottawa see them on all sides.

Black Star *See* Black.

Black Swan Idridgehay, Derbs and elsewhere. The Roman satirist Juvenal jokingly referred to a 'black swan' as an example of a *rara avis*, a 'rare bird'. He did not know that such birds existed in Australia. *Black Swan* appeared as a tavern sign in the sixteenth century, at which time it may have been meant to be a signal what a *rara avis*, a remarkable person, was the landlord. Later references may well be to Australia, since a black swan is the emblem of Western Australia. A naval reference is also possible, since HMS *Black Swan* was active between 1939 and 1956.

Black Tulip Dewsbury. This appears to be a reference to the novel by Alexandre Dumas (1802–70), *La Tulipe Noire*, published in English as *The Black Tulip*. It first appeared in 1850 but was not as successful as the same author's *Three Musketeers* and *Count of Monte Cristo*. The story concerns an obsession with the growing of tulips of rare varieties which affected Europe in the 1630s. Cornelius van Baerle succeeds in growing a black tulip, thereby winning a prize of 100,000 florins.

Black Venus Challacombe, Devon. A local term for a black sheep found on nearby Exmoor which is difficult to shear and worth little for its wool.

Black Watch Aberfeldy, Tays. The Black Watch Regiment (the Black Watch (Royal Highland) Regiment, 42nd and 73rd Foot) was raised in Aberfeldy by the Earl of Crawford in 1739. They were intended to 'watch over' Edinburgh, while the dark green, blue and black tartan adopted by

the regiment led to their 'black' title.

Blackwater Tavern Sutton, Sry. The Blackwater river rises near Farnham and eventually runs into the Loddon. There is another river of the name in Essex.

Blade Bone London E2 and elsewhere. A story is told of the London pub that a murder was committed there and the body hidden in the cellar. When the crime was discovered the remains were removed, though the landlord managed to keep the shoulder blade, which he then exhibited for the benefit of his customers. At Buckleberry Common, near Reading, the bone is that of a prehistoric animal discovered nearby. A similar reason may have accounted for the London pub of this name in the seventeenth century.

Bladud Arms Lower Painswick. Also **Bladud's Head** at Larkhall. Both pubs are near the city of Bath, which this mythical English king is said to have built. He was supposed to be the father of King Lear.

Blaise Henbury, Glos. The pub is near Blaise Hamlet and Castle, and all are named from an ancient chapel that was dedicated to St Blasius, or Blaise. Very little is known about him.

Blake Also Blake Arms *See* Admiral Blake.

Blakeney's Head *See* Admiral Blakeney's Head.

Blarney Stone Bar Glasgow. The Blarney stone is set into the wall of Blarney Castle, near Cork in Ireland. Kissing it is said to confer upon a man the gift of cajolery or flattery (women have the gift in any case). The original stone is difficult to get at, so a substitute has been provided for tourists. It is said that kissing this substitute stone is just as effective as kissing the original.

Blaydon Races Blaydon-on-Tyne. The cheerful and popular song, sometimes called the Geordies' National Anthem. It tells the story of a trip to the Blaydon Races from Balmbra's on the ninth of June, 1862. The chorus runs: 'Oh lads ye should a' seen us gannin/Passing the folks upon the road/Just as they were stannin'/Thor wis lots of lads and lasses there/Aal wi' smiling faces/Ganning along the Scotswood Road/To see the Blaydon races.' *See also* **Coffy** Johnny and Cushy Butterfield.

Blazing Donkey Ramsgate and elsewhere in Kent. 'Blazing' is a dialectal equivalent of 'braying'. There is a Roaring Donkey at Holland-on-Sea, Esx, though 'roaring' is used of a horse when it breathes noisily because of malformed air passages.

Bleak House Horsell Common, Sry and elsewhere. The novel of this name by Charles Dickens, published in 1852–53, contains a satirical attack on legal procedures.

Bleeding Wolf Hale, near Altrincham and Scholar Green near Stoke-on-Trent. Traditionally a Cheshire pub name, possibly related to the killing of the last wolf in England, something which is said to have occurred in Cheshire in 1746. A misunderstanding of a heraldic sign has also been suggested, in which case the name would link with the earls of Chester or the d'Avranches family.

Blenheim Top Valley, Nottingham and elsewhere. The name of a village in Bavaria (*Blindheim* in German) near which an important battle took place in 1704. This was during the War of the Spanish Succession, and marked a victory for Marlborough and Prince Eugene, leaders of the English and Austrian troops, over the French and Bavarians. Blenheim Palace was later given to the Duke of Malborough by the nation. A pub of this name in Hampstead commemorates the Blenheim coach, which ran from Oxford to Cheltenham. At Epsom the pub name commemorates the winner of the Derby in 1930. London W11 has a Blenheim Arms. *See* Duke of Marlborough.

Blessington Carriage Derby. The licensee of this pub says that the name was chosen 'at random' from a book on coaching days. The reference is presumably to the carriage of Margaret, Countess of Blessington (1789–1849), a celebrated Irish beauty who lived at Gore House, London. She published several books, including *Conversations With Lord Byron* (1832).

Blighty's Winchester. 'Blighty', for English soldiers serving abroad, particularly in India, meant 'England'. It is thought to derive from Urdu *bilati*, though Kipling used the form *belait* which may indicate a different source. This pub has a Home Guard theme.

Blind Beggar London E1. This refers to Henry, son of Sir Simon de Montfort, who was left for dead after the battle of Evesham. Henry is said to have assumed the garb of a blind beggar in order to escape, after being nursed by a baron's daughter, who later married him. The marriage is said to have occurred at London E2, which accounts for a drama produced in 1659 called *The Blind Beggar of Bethnal Green*. Another play on the same subject was produced in the nineteenth century. The first appearance of this name, in the sixteenth century, was no doubt due to a popular ballad which began: 'The rarest ballad that ever was seen/Of the blind beggar's daughter of Bethnal Green . . . ' General Booth, of the Salvation Army, preached his first sermon at this pub in 1865.

Blink Bonny Christon Bank, Northld. The horse which won the Derby in 1857.

Blinking Owl *see* **Winking Frog.**

Blockers Arms Luton. Luton is well–known for the manufacture of hats. 'Blockers' are the people who block the hats, or shape them. They use blockheads, heads made of wood, and it is these which gave rise to the term blockhead, meaning someone with no more sense than a hat-maker's wooden head. *See also* Boater, Panama, Hat and Bonnet and Slinky Toppers. Shoreditch has a Blockmakers Arms.

Blockhouse Stoke, Devonport. Twenty-two blockhouses, or forts, were built in 1861 for the defence of Plymouth, though they were never used for that purpose. They were derisively known as Palmerston's Follies (Lord Palmerston was prime minister when they were built) because of their great cost.

Blood Sports Reference to former 'sports' which are now banned are found in names like Dog and Badger, Dog and Bear, Dog and Bull, as at Croydon, Dog and Duck, Gamecock, Hereford and elsewhere. Cock fighting was clearly widespread, to judge from the frequency of names like Fighting Cocks.

Blooming Fuchsia *See* Flowers.

Blooming Rose *See* Rose.

Blue Pub names featuring this colour often do so for the simplest of reasons – the pub has Blue Posts, a Blue Door or whatever. Several unexpected names, however, were brought about by the Manners family who lived in the Grantham area of Lincolnshire in the early nineteenth century. They bought several inns, all of which they renamed with *Blue* as a prefix to show their allegiance to the Whigs, or Liberal Party. Travellers were thus surprised to find a Blue Bull, Blue Cow, Blue Dog, Blue Fox, Blue Horse, Blue Pig, Blue Ram and even a Blue Man in the same area. There is a simple Blue Inn at Cottown, in Grampian, and a Blues Inn at Weeton, Lancs. Apart from the names mentioned individually below, there are or have been pubs called Blue Balcony, London W1; Blue Barrel, Northwich; Blue Flag, Cadmore End, Bucks; Blue Gates, Smethwick; Blue Grotto, Chatham; Blue Harbour, Grantham; Blue Mug, Leek; Blue House, Great Yarmouth and Sunderland; Blue Lagoon, Edinburgh; Blue Lamp, Aberdeen; Blue Moon, Leicester; Blue Pigeons, Worth, Kent; Blue Pudding, Hull; Blue Ship, Rudgwick near Horsham; Blue Stone, Immingham, near Grimsby; Blue Tit, Boughton, Notts. Dickens vividly imagined a Blue Dragon in *Martin Chuzzlewit*, and commented on a problem that besets all colourful inn signs: 'A faded, and an ancient dragon he was; and many a wintry storm of rain, snow, sleet, and hail, had changed his colour from a gaudy blue to a faint lack-lustre shade of grey.'

Blue Anchor *See* Anchor.

Blue Backs Warrington. This was the nickname of the Loyal Warrington Volunteers, formed at the end of the eighteenth century.

The regiment was disbanded in 1801 but continued to use this inn as the unofficial headquarters for many years afterwards.

Blue Balcony *See* Blue.

Blue Ball Dottery, near Bridport and elsewhere. At one time a sign used by various tradesmen, including fortune-tellers, as an easy way of identifying an establishment. In the West Country the sign is heraldic, relating to the Courtenays, earls of Devon.

Blue Barrel *See* Barrels.

Blue Bell North Walsham, Nflk and elsewhere. It is uncertain whether the flower, a heraldic blue bell or a real bell painted blue gave rise to this sign. It could also be from the song which is usually known as 'Bluebells of Scotland', properly 'Bluebell of Scotland'. The bluebell in Scotland is the harebell, not the wood hyacinth of the South. There is also a Blue Bells at Newton Bewley in Cleveland.

Bluebell West Hoathly, W Ssx. The pub is near the Bluebell line, the branch railway which runs from Sheffield Park to Horsted Keynes. This was closed by British Railways, then bought up and run by a society interested in preserving an especially picturesque line. The name of the line is variously explained as being so slow a service that passengers could pick bluebells, then run after the train and catch it again, or from the guard's habit of stopping the train to allow passengers to pick the flowers. The sign at this pub shows a locomotive. At Nottingham and elsewhere there is a Blue Bell.

Bluebells of Scotland Longton, Staffs. A tune arranged for piano which was extremely popular when most middle-class homes had such an instrument. Words to the tune were written by a Mrs Grant of Laggan, Hghld in 1799, to mark the departure for Europe of the Marquis of Huntly and his regiment. The first line is: 'Oh where, tell me where, is your Highland Laddie gone?', which probably led to Highland Laddie at Hull.

Blue Berry Blewbury, Oxon. This is rather similar to the Bittern sign at Bitterne. In this case the –bury of the place name probably meant 'fortified place', but the Blew was probably 'blue'.

Bluebird Plymouth. The sign shows the streamlined racing–car of this name in which Sir Malcolm Campbell (1885–1949) captured the world land-speed record in 1935. He was the first motorist to exceed 300 miles per hour.

Blue Blanket Edinburgh. This is the name of the banner of the Edinburgh craftsmen. Tytler, in his *History of Scotland* (1864) refers to 'calling out the trained bands and armed citizens beneath a banner presented to them on this occasion (1482) and denominated the Blue Blanket'.

Blue Boar Frome, Som and elsewhere. The blue boar is a heraldic reference to the Earl of Oxford. The white boar similarly refers to Richard III. It is said that after the defeat of Richard and the Yorkists at the battle of Bosworth (1485), many White Boar signs were hastily painted blue, since the Earl of Oxford was a leading supporter of the Lancastrian cause.

Blue Bowl Bristol and elsewhere. Pubs of this name are found in the Bristol/Bath region and relate to Bristol ware. The bowls were used for punch, and Punchbowl is frequently found.

Blue Boy Bristol and elsewhere. The Bristol pub (now renamed as Gainsboroughs) is in Gainsborough Square and clearly relates to the famous painting by Thomas Gainsborough (1727–88). The sign which formerly reproduced this painting is now only on view inside the pub. The painter is also remembered in the Gainsborough Tavern. The Blue Boy sign at Clapton, near Crewkerne, shows one of the orphans who attended the school established by the local vicar, John Coombs, in 1499. The pupils at the school wore a blue uniform.

Blue Boys Kippings Cross, Kent. George IV stopped here while his horses were shod. His attendants wore blue coats and caps.

Blue Brick *See* Bricklayers Arms.

Blue Bull *See* Blue.

Blue Cap Callington, Corn. This sign is usually found in Cheshire. It commemorates a famous foxhound of the 1760s. The Cornish example was in fact named by a Cheshire man who became landlord of what until then had been the New Inn. The renaming was in honour of his former 'local'.

Blue Chip Glasgow. The pub is beneath Glasgow's Stock Exchange, and the name refers to costly but good quality shares, issued by a well-established company which enjoys consider-able public confidence.

Blue Coat Boy Hertford and else-where. This was a general term for a scholar at a charity school, since such scholars always wore blue coats. Specifically the term referred to a scholar at one of Christ's Hospital schools, three of which were founded by Edward VI in 1552. The last of them moved from London to Horsham, W Ssx in 1902.

Blue Cow *See* Blue.

Blue Dog *See* Blue.

Blue Door Langley, Kent. This was the Bell until 1880. The new name came about when election fever caused the Liberals to paint the pub door in their party colour. The Liberal colour is now orange although yellow is used by the SDP.

Blue Dragon See Blue.

Blue-Eyed Maid London SE1. Homer referred to Minerva, goddess of wisdom, by this phrase. John Wolcot (1738–1819) writing as Peter Pindar, also used it in his eighteenth–century 'A Falling Minister', which caused this pub to be renamed from the Minerva, and the sign to be repainted later as a buxom dairymaid. In turn, the name was given to a well–known stagecoach, which according to Dickens' *Little Dorrit* ran between Southwark and Dover. Wolcot's work has not lasted well; his best-known couplet is: 'What rage for fame attends both great and small! Better be damned than mentioned not at all!'

Blue Flag *See* Blue.

Blue Fox *See* Blue.

Blue Gates *See* Blue.

Blue Harbour *See* Blue.

Blue Horse *See* Blue.

Blue Inn *See* Blue.

Blue Lagoon Edinburgh. *The Blue Lagoon* (1908) was the novel with which Henry de Vere Stacpoole (1863–1951) made his name. It is a romantic story set on a south-sea island.

Blue Lias Stockton, near Rugby. 'Lias' is a blue limestone rock which usually occurs in the south west counties of England. The pub is beside the Grand Union Canal, used to transport such limestone from the nearby quarry.

Blue Lion Bracknell and elsewhere. From the arms of the Royal House of Denmark, with special reference to Queen Anne (1574–1619), wife of James I and mother of Charles I.

Blue Man *See* Blue.

Blue Monkey St Budeaux, Plymouth. Named after the mascot of the Marine Regiment which was stationed nearby in the nineteenth century. It was dressed in a handsome blue monkey–jacket (the short close-fitting jacket worn by seamen).

Blue Moon *See* Blue.

Blue Peter Peterborough and elsewhere. The name of the blue flag with a white square in the centre which is hoisted twenty-four hours before a ship leaves port. The choice of this title may have been influenced in some places by the fact that a horse of this name won the Derby in 1939.

Blue Pig *See* Blue.

Blue Pigeons *See* Blue.

Blue Pits Castleton, near Rochdale. After the blue clay pits in the area, which also gave their name to a village.

Blue Posts Burton-on-Trent and elsewhere. These were normally the pillars supporting the porch, painted blue as an easy means of identification before the numbering system for houses was introduced in the eighteenth century. Blue Posts would simply have been a description of the place concerned, not its name as such. The pub of this name near Tottenham Court Road has a sign showing an older tavern which had blue posts outside the door.

Blue Pudding *See* Blue.

Blue Ram *See* Blue.

Blues Inn Weeton, near Preston. In military circles the reference is to the Royal Horse Guards. It was the Earl of Oxford who first put his troops into blue tunics, at a time when every other soldier wore scarlet. The Royal Regiment of Horse, as they were, immediately became the 'Oxford Blues'. Musically the 'blues' are the slow, sad songs which originated with the American Negroes. Ultimately the reference is to the blue devils seen when one has had too much to drink, a condition which leads to deep despondency.

Blue Stone *See* Blue.

Blue Stoops Walton and Dronfield, near Chesterfield. The 'stoops' are posts, though the word is now used only in dialect. *See* Blue Posts.

Blue Tit *See* Blue.

Blue Vinny Puddletown, Dors. The name of a cheese which was a well-known product in Dorset in the nineteenth century. It was a mature cheese, taking its name from its blue veins.

Blyth and Tyne North Shields. Blyth is a nearby town, though it gets its name from a river. The Tyne refers to the river which flows into the North Sea at Tynemouth.

Blythe Stoweby Chartley, near Stafford. The name of a local trout stream, which rises near Longton and falls into the Trent. There are streams of this name in several other counties.

Boar Moddeshall, Staffs. A boar is a male, fully-grown swine, but the reference is likely to be to Richard III, who was known as the Boar, a nickname derived from his heraldic device. The boar was also the emblem of the Roman legion which helped to build Hadrian's Wall. A stone-sculptured wild boar was found at Corbridge, Northld. Wild Boar occurs as a pub name at Crook, Cumb.

Boardroom Manchester. The pub is sited in a corner of the Greater Manchester Council's County

Hall. One meaning of 'board' is 'council meeting.'

Boar's Head Aust, Glos and elsewhere. This sign dates from the mid-fourteenth century. It links with the Christmas custom of serving a boar's head with an apple or lemon in its mouth at a feast. The custom is observed yearly at Queen's College, Oxford, where a sixteenth-century carol is also sung as the boar's head is brought into the College dining hall. The Aust sign shows the boar with a salver round its neck, an apple in one paw, a carving knife in the other. At Perry Barr near Birmingham the pub sign shows the head on a kind of totem pole. This relates to the arms of the local Gough family.

Boater Luton and Bath. Luton was for a long time the centre of the straw-plaiting industry, introduced in the reign of James I. The manufacture of straw hats (such as the boater, the hard straw hat worn by men, especially when boating) has now given way to a felt-hat industry.

Boat House Shrewsbury. The pub is beside the river Severn and has rowing photographs and oars inside.

Boats Boat and boatmen signs are fairly common, since so many pubs are beside rivers, canals or the sea. In its simplest form, Boat is found at Whittlesey, Cambridge, while simple combination names include Boat and Anchor, Huntworth, near Bridgwater, Boat and Gun, Skeldyke, near Boston, Boat and Horses, Beeston, Nottingham, Boat and Railway, Stamford, Lincs. There is a Boathouse at Kew Green and a Boat Side at Warden Bridge, near Hexham. Boatman occurs at Kings Langley, Boatman's Arms at Brighton, Boatman's Rest at Worsborough Dale, near Barnsley, Boatman's Home in Manchester. Other names in this group include the common Ferry Boat as at Stoke Bardolph, near Nottingham and individual boats such as Heanor Boat, Leicester, Tilt Boat, Foy Boat, Peter Boat, Narrow Boat, Pleasure Boat, Packet Boat. A saying connected with boats and pubs occurs in naval slang: 'to push the boat out' means to pay for a round of drinks.

Boatswain and Call Chatham. Also Bosun's Call at Dovercourt, Esx. The reference is to the shrill piping which heralds the arrival of the commanding officer or an important visitor on board a Royal Navy ship. The 'boatswain' was originally the officer in charge of a ship's sails and rigging. Both Brighton and Cardiff have a Bo'sun.

Bobbin Manchester. Also Bobbins at Long Eaton, Bobbin Mill in Aberdeen. The bobbin is a kind of reel on which thread is wound. Signs of this type refer to local cotton mills or the lace-making industry.

Bobby Shafto Newcastle-on-Tyne. The popular folksong about a young man who ran off to sea. The song is said to be based on a true incident, when a member of a well-known Northumbrian family found that he was soon to become a father.

Bobsleigh Bovingdon, Herts and elsewhere. A bobsleigh was originally one which was joined to another by some kind of coupling, used to transport logs. Later the word was applied to the long sled used for racing, containing a crew of up to four persons. The landlord of this pub was perhaps one of them.

Bod Bradford. The premises were built in 1875 and included a *bodega* below street level. This Spanish word refers to a cellar or shop where wine only is sold. Its abbreviated form led to the pub's present name, a change from the original Boar's Head.

Boffin formerly at Kirkby, Liverpool. Originally a slang word in the services that has come to have the general meaning of a research scientist employed on government work. Wilfred Granville, in *A Dictionary of Sailor's Slang*, says that in the Royal Navy the meaning is 'an officer above the age of thirty-five'.

Bogarts Southampton. This pub contains posters, etc, of films starring Humphrey Bogart (1899–1957). He usually played the role of a tough guy or gangster. He is remembered above all for *Casablanca*, a film made in 1942 which, according to Leslie Halliwell's *Filmgoer's Companion*, nearly starred Ronald Reagan and Ann Sheridan instead of Bogart and Ingrid Bergman.

Bold Dragoon *See* Dragoon.

Bold Forester Southsea. The oak trees of the nearby New Forest were used by the ship builders of former times. Nelson's *Agamemnon* was built at Buckler's Hard in 1781, then towed down the River Beaulieu to Portsmouth.

Boldon Lad Boldon Colliery, near Sunderland. A reminder of the boys and young men who worked in the pits in former times. Bonnie Pit Lad at Hetton-le-Hole,

Sunderland, Collier Lad at Hazelrigg, near Newcastle, Pit Laddie at Shirecliff, near Durham are similar names.

Bold Rodney *See* Admiral Rodney.

Boleyn Tavern *See* Anne Boleyn.

Bolly Sunbury-on-Thames. An obsolete or dialectal word for a bogy, or hobgoblin. In the sixteenth century 'bolly' could also be used to describe water over which wind was blowing, making it 'covered with bubbles'.

Bolney Stage Bolney, W Ssx. There is a stagecoach outside the pub. An informer tells that this pub has been demolished.

Bolt and Tun A rebus sign, indicating that the landlord's name was Bolton. A 'bolt' was an arrow, the kind used with a crossbow. A 'tun' was a large barrel which held two 'pipes', or four 'hogsheads' of wine, 252 gallons. Job Bolton was at the former *Bolt and Tun* in Lombard Street in the 1680s.

Bombay Grab London E3. The 'grab' is a large, two-masted vessel used in the East. The word has been used in English since the seventeenth century, and derives ultimately from Arabic *ghurab*, 'raven'. The East India Company used such vessels, and it was their function to transport ale from the Bow Brewery to Bombay for the British troops which led to the naming of this pub. The first consignment was despatched in 1734.

Bone Mill Invergordon. Bones are ground in such a mill for use as fertilizer or animal feed.

Bonnie Gem Stone, Staffs. The pub name was obviously suggested by the place name.

Bonnie Pit Lad *See* Boldon Lad.

Bonnie Prince Charlie East Kilbride. Charles Edward Stuart (1720–88) was one of the Scottish claimants to the English throne. He was known both as Bonnie Prince Charlie and the Young Pretender ('to pretend to something' means here 'to lay claim' to it). Charles lost a decisive battle against the English at Culloden Moor in 1745. Many romantic stories are told of his subsequent escape, aided by Flora Macdonald, 'over the sea to Skye' and then to France. King's Langley has a Young Pretender.

Bonny Cravat Woodchurch, near Tenterden, Kent. Of the various explanations which have been put forward for this name, the most likely is that which refers to an old song 'Jenny, come tie my bonny cravat'. Monson-Fitzjohn, in *Quaint Signs of Olde Inns*, refers to a 'carvet' or a close-cropped yew-tree hedge, said to have been the joy of a former landlord. The word 'carvet', however, is not known to the *Oxford English Dictionary*. An alternative explanation, that the name derives from the name of a ship used for smuggling, *Bonne Corvette*, is hardly to be taken seriously. A corvette would have made a particularly unsuitable ship for smugglers, in view of its slowness, and the suggested ship-name is in any case absurd.

Bookbinders Arms Oxford. A tribute to the bookbinders of the Oxford University Press and the Clarendon Press. The name dates from 1870.

Book in Hand Mablethorpe, Lincs. Probably suggested by a religious picture of a saint carrying his emblematic book. It was the usual way of indicating someone who spread the Gospel, such as the Evangelists, or who was learned, such as Ambrose, Augustine, Bede, Gregory and Jerome. In secular terms the name would be connected with Bookbinders Arms.

Boot These signs often portray the long military boot worn by the duke of Wellington, not the modern waterproof wellington but one which covered the knee at the front and was cut away behind. At Littledon, Som, the boot on the sign has a lid on, to keep the rain out. Lapworth, Warks, has a *Boot* pub which shows a fine boot and spur. In St Albans the *Boot* is on one side of the street, the Wellington on the other. Honiley, near Kenilworth, has a Honiley Boot, Nottingham an Owd Boots, Aberdeen a Welly Boot. Devil in the Boot at Winslow, Bucks, refers to the story of a thirteenth-century priest, John Schorne, who was supposed to have trapped the devil in a boot. Schorne was never made a saint, but was regarded as 'the peasants' saint' and his shrine made a place of pilgrimage. Boot and Shoe, Lancaster, Boot and Slipper, Chesham are related signs. The Boot and Ship at Bagillt, near Holywell must represent an amalgamation of two pubs. At Renishaw, Derby, there is a Bootmakers Arms. The sign of the Boot and Clogger at Woodley near Stockport shows a cobbler at his last, mending boots and clogs.

Bo-Peep St Leonards-on-Sea, E. Ssx. The sign shows the Little Bo-Peep of the nursery rhyme on one side and smugglers rowing ashore on the other. The hide-and-seek activities of the smugglers in this area resulted in a bloody battle with Excisemen in 1828.

Border Reiver Carlisle. The marauders who came from over the Scottish border at one time were the 'reivers'. The word can also be written as 'reaver' and derives from an Old English word meaning 'to rob'.

Border Terrier *See* Dog.

Borough Bodmin, Corn. The pub stands on the borough boundary. It was once a 'stop' for parties engaged in the ancient 'beating' the bounds' ceremony.

Boscawen *See* Admiral Boscawen.

Boscobel Tavern Tipton, W Mid. The oak tree at Boscobel, near Shifnal, Salop is said to have concealed Charles II from Cromwell's troops. He was escaping from them after his defeat at Worcester in 1651. The tree is also known as the Royal Oak.

Boswell Arms Auchinleck, Strath. James Boswell (1740–95) was the son of Lord Auchinleck, a Scottish judge. He is remembered especially for his biography of Dr Samuel Johnson, the writer and lexicographer.

Bosworth Leicester. The reference is to Bosworth Field, near Market Bosworth, scene of the battle in 1485 between Richard III and the Earl of Richmond, later Henry VII. The defeat of Richard brought about the end of the Wars of the Roses.

Botany Tavern Bristol. Ships sailed from Bristol to Botany Bay, the inlet on the coast of New South Wales. Captain Cook and Joseph Banks landed there in 1770. It was made the site of a penal settlement in 1788, though this was later transferred to Port Jackson.

Botolph's Bridge West Hythe, Kent. Little is known about St Botolph, who is thought to have lived in the seventh century, but he was popular in the Middle Ages. Boston is named after him (Botolph's stone). The sign of this pub depicts monks carrying Botolph's coffin across the bridge, on their way to his midnight burial. There is also a Botolph

Arms at Orton Longueville, Peterborough.

Bottle Hawkchurch, Devon and Marshwood, Dors. This name dates from the late seventeenth century, when beer in bottles was very much a novelty. As Monson-Fitzjohn remarks: 'innkeepers were very anxious to show they were up to date and to advertise their possession of such articles'. Similar names include Bottle and Glass, Gibraltar, near Aylesbury and Bottle in Hand, Kidderminster. Occold in Suffolk used to have a Bottles.

Bottle Hall Sible Hedingham, Esx. Presumably suggested as a pub name by Bottles Hall, near Elmstead, Esx. The Batayle family lived there in the thirteenth century, so the house name should have become Battle Hall.

Bottle House Penshurst, Kent. The name comes from the verse on the sign: 'From this bottle I am sure/ You'll get a glass both good and pure;/Each goodman and eke his spouse/Drink to each other and this house.'

Boulevard Nottingham. Nottingham was the first English town to copy the French boulevards (the word is related to 'bulwarks'). The Parisian boulevards date from the 1860s, Nottingham had them by the 1870s. This pub stands on the Radford Boulevard.

Boundary *See* Cricket.

Boundary House Enfield. The pub is on the Enfield side of the boundary between the boroughs of Edmonton and Enfield.

'Bout Time *See* Montgomery of Alamein.

Bounty Maryport, Cumb and elsewhere. 'Bounty' is a word of excellent meanings, such as 'kindness', 'generosity', but was tarnished by the famous mutiny on the *Bounty*. The mutiny occurred in 1789, when Fletcher Christian, then second-in-command, led a revolt against Captain Bligh on HMS *Bounty*. There have been arguments ever since as to whether the mutiny was justified. Bligh's behaviour when he was later appointed Governor of New South Wales seems to suggest that he was indeed the tyrant Christian alleged him to be. Christian was born not far from the Cumbrian pub, at Cockermouth.

Bow and Arrow *See* Archery.

Bow Bells London E3. A London Cockney is one who was born within the sound of Bow bells, ie the bells of St Mary-le-bow in Cheapside. The 'bow' in the name refers to the shape of the Norman arches which support the building. (The place name derives from a 'bow bridge', one of stone arches. There is yet another reason for Bow Street, in London, which was thought to be curved like a bow.)

Bowd Bowd Cross, near Sidmouth. The place-name element 'bowd' means a 'curved wood'.

Bowes Incline Birtley, near Hexham-on-Tyne. The pub is adjacent to an incline on the Bowes Colliery Railway. Trucks were once rope-hauled there, but it is now disused.

Bowgie West Pentire, Corn. A 'bowgie' in dialect is a young bull, but in Cornwall the term applies to a 'cow-house'. It is found in various forms – boudi, bowda, bogee, bougie, bojea, etc. This pub was converted from a cow-house.

Bowl Charing, near Ashford. In this instance said to refer to a large punch-bowl which belonged to the village. At times of national rejoicing it would be filled and the contents ladled out to all-comers. A *Bowl* inn in London was said to have been named because a bowl of ale was given to prisoners on their way to execution. However, there is some evidence that the 'bowl' was simply a variant of 'ball', since three bowls were used by pawnbrokers in former times.

Bowler Hat Burslem, near Stoke-on-Trent. The bowler hat, accompanied by a swagger-cane, makes a convenient visual symbol. The pub has an Edwardian theme.

Bowls Several pub names mention this ancient game, one of the more popular being Bowling Green as at Nottingham. The sign often shows Drake completing his game on Plymouth Hoe as the Armada approached, according to the story known to every schoolchild. Several pubs have their own greens: the one at Southampton dates from 1299. Related names include Bowlers, Paisley, Bowlers Arms, Cliftonville, Bowlers Rest, Edinburgh and Glasgow, Bowling Tavern, Sheffield; Bowl in Hand, Mansfield (another pub with its own ancient bowling green), Bowlturners Arms, Leicester, though the last could relate to a turner of bowls in a different sense, one who uses a lathe to make the kind of wooden bowl used to hold fruit. In dialectal use 'bowls' can still refer to skittles rather than the game played on grass. There is also a difference between crown-green bowling, as played in the North, and the flat-green game played in the South.

Bowman *See* Archery.

Bow Street Runner Hove, E Ssx. This term was actually applied to eight officers who were appointed in 1805 and were attached to the Bow Street Court, near Covent Garden. They were the fore-runners of the modern CID. From their red waistcoats they earned the popular name 'robin redbreasts'. It is true, however, that Bow Street Runner is now loosely applied to any early policeman.

Bowyer Arms London SW4. The Bowyers were usually makers of bows, though the term was also applied to those who traded in them, and occasionally to bowmen, users of bows. The bowyers would have been important members of society at a time when the bow was the principal weapon of warfare. Edward IV, for example, ordained that every Englishman should have a yew bow of his own height. For pub names connected with the sport, *see* Archery.

Boy and Barrel *See* Bacchus.

Brace of Pheasants Plush, near Dorchester. Slightly unusual in that the pheasants are in a glass case over the front door instead of being painted on the sign. The word 'brace' is connected with French *bras* 'arm' and originally referred to armour that covered the arms. At one time it was possible to speak of a 'brace of dogs' or other animals, but in the sense of 'pair' the word is now usually restricted to game birds.

Brace of Pistols Bockings Elm, Esx. A reference to highwaymen of the past. *See also* Cross Hands and Highwayman.

Brae Lerwick, Shetd. A 'brae' is a slope on a hill which leads down to a river.

Brahms and Liszt Newcastle-on-Tyne and elsewhere. Cockney rhyming slang for 'pissed', ie 'drunk'. This name of dubious taste was trendy in the early 1980s and is spreading.

Brain Surgery Larkhall, Bath. The Brain Brewery is across the Severn, in Cardiff. This was the first pub on the English side to sell Brain beer.

Bramley Apple *See* Apples.

Brass Cat Halifax. Originally the Golden Lion. Its nickname amongst the locals has now been made official.

Brave Nelson *See* Lord Nelson.

Bread and Cheese South Benfleet, Esx. A reference to the traditional plain fare of the ploughman. At one time the expression to 'have bread and cheese in one's head' meant 'to be drunk'. This meaning seems to have lapsed in the mid–eighteenth century. Bread and cheese is also a child's name for the young leaves of the hawthorn, wood-sorrel or cuckoo–bread. The Essex pub once had a profusion of hawthorn growing nearby. Another pub of this name is in Norwich.

Breaksper Hemel Hempstead. Also Breakspear Arms, Ruislip, Breakspeare, Abbot's Langley, near Watford, Breakspeare Arms, Lewisham. Nicholas Breakspear, who was born at Langley, near Hitchin before 1100, became Pope Adrian IV, the only Englishman ever to become pope. He died in Italy in 1159.

Brentnor Brentnor, Devon. The sign shows the thirteenth–century church of St Michael which is on top of Brentnor, the famous Dartmoor tor (high rock), rising almost 1200 feet.

Brentnor *See* Tors.

Breton Arms Plymouth. This port formerly had close links with Breton fishermen. There is a Burton Boys in the same city, an alteration of Breton Boys. The latter raided Plymouth in the fourteenth and fifteenth centuries. Until the end of the eighteenth century mock battles were fought in commemoration, but they were stopped when they became too realistic.

Brewers Arms Hemel Hempstead and elsewhere. The Brewers Company were granted arms in the fifteenth century. The sign normally shows three barrels and three pairs of crossed corn sheaves. Related names include Brewer's Cellar, Halifax, Brewer's Delight, Canterbury, Brewers' Hall, London E1 Two Brewers, Diss and elsewhere. There was formerly a Brewer's Shives at Botley Mills, Chesham, 'shives' being thin bungs or stoppers used in casks. The word could also refer to thin, flat corks used for stopping wide-mouthed bottles.

Brewery Tap London SW18. The pub is attached to Young's Brewery and is used by the brewery staff.

Brewster New Malden, Sry. Originally a woman who brewed beer and the like. The sign shows a witch brewing something less tasty in her cauldron.

Briar Rose *See* Rose.

Bricklayers Arms Marston, Oxford and elsewhere. London alone has thirty pubs of this name, though one of the signs is highly individual in that it shows two ancient Egyptians having their tea-break. The Marston sign is unique in another way – the bricklayer shown building a wall is Sir Winston Churchill.

Bricksetters Arms at Ripon shows an interesting variation in the name. Brickmakers are mentioned in Brickmakers, Norwich and Colchester, Brickmakers Arms, Slough and elsewhere, Brickmakers Delight, Aldershot. Related names include Brick Kilns, Little Plumstead, near Norwich, Brick Mould, Hedgerley, Bucks. There is a simple Brick in Leeds, and Brick and Tile at Ilkeston and elsewhere. Names like Brick Hall, Skipton, Brick House, Springfield, near Dudley, Brick Wall, Tarbock, Mers, presumably refer to brick constructions. At Brierley Hill, Staffs, there is a Blue Brick.

Brickground Arlesey, Beds. There is a large brickworks nearby.

Bridge Bridges feature in many pub names. *Bridge* itself is common, though the sign of this pub at Yatton, Som (referring to the bridge over the Bristol-Exeter railway, built in 1841), is unique in showing an 'Impulsoria'. This was a contraption (invented in 1850) with outsize wheels and a chain drive which enabled two horses to supply the power instead of the usual locomotive. Other bridge names include Dart Bridge, Buckfastleigh, Floating Bridge, Dartmouth, Fye Bridge. Norwich, Bishop Bridge, Norwich, Halfway Bridge, Lodsworth, W. Ssx, Haw Bridge, Tirley, Glos, Iron Bridge, Limehouse, Metal Bridge, Rockliffe, near Carlisle, Suspension Bridge, Great Yarmouth, Bridge of Allan, near Stirling, Bridge of Dee at Aberdeen.

Bridge on Wool Wadebridge, Corn. Referring to a bridge built across the River Camel in the fifteenth century. There had previously been a ford, as the place name indicates, but the shifting bed of the river made the crossing difficult. The local parson suggested laying down bales of wool and building bridge arches on them, a scheme which was duly put into practice. Traces of the wool were found by workmen centuries later. The inn sign shows the local Parson Lovibond and his bishop riding over the newly-built bridge.

Bridgewater Eccles. Also Bridgewater Arms, Stockport; Duke of
Bridgewater, Crewe and Long-
port, Staffs. Francis Egerton, 3rd
Duke of Bridgewater, became
known as the 'Father of British
Inland Navigation'. He was the
projector of the first canal in
England, which joined Worsley
and Manchester. It was later
bought in 1887 by the Manchester
Ship Canal Company for nearly 2
million pounds. The Duke was
later concerned with a canal which
joined Manchester and Liverpool.

Bridgwater Squib Bridgwater,
Som. For the firework, used in
the annual celebration on 5
November, though 'squib', as it
happens, was formerly a dialectal
term in the North of England for a
small quantity of strong spirits.

Bridlecutters Arms Walsall, Staffs.
After the leather workers who
fashioned bridles, or headgear for
horses.

Brief Encounter Edinburgh. From the
1946 British film starring Trevor
Howard and Celia Johnson about
two middle-aged people, both
already married, who have a
fleeting romance. David Lean
directed; script was by Noel
Coward.

Brig Falkirk. In English pub names
'brig' invariably refers to the two-
masted, square-sailed ship. The
word is short for 'brigantine', as
with the pub of this name at South
Shields. In Scotland, as in the
Cramond Brig, at Cramond Bridge,
Loth, the word is always likely to
be the Scottish form of bridge.

Brigadier Gerard Horton Heath,
Southampton. Name of a famous
racehorse which was retired to
stud in 1973 after a highly
successful career. The racehorse
itself was clearly named after
Lieutenant (later Brigadier)
Etienne Gerard, the hero of
Conan Doyle's *The Exploits of
Brigadier Gerard*, etc from 1899.

Brigands Mallwyd, Pwys. In the
sixteenth century gangs of
marauders ambushed travellers in
the nearby mountains.

Brighton Belle Winsford, Ches. This
was formerly the Railway Hotel,
but a Pullman coach from the
Brighton Belle train has been
converted into a restaurant
attached to the pub and caused the
name change. The *Brighton Belle*
service replaced the *Southern Belle*
steam-hauled service on 1 January
1933. It made the Victoria-
Brighton return journey three
times a day until the outbreak of
World War Two. The inn sign
here is rather inconsistent in
showing an LNER locomotive.

Brighton Run Brighton. There is
another at Wickford, Esx. A
reference to the annual run from
London to Brighton made by
veteran cars (pre-1905). This was
made known internationally by the
film *Genevieve*, released in 1953.

Bright Star Peters Green, near
Harpenden. Presumably a
convenient visual symbol. The
reference is often to Venus, the
morning or evening star.

Brine Baths Nantwich, Ches. This
town was formerly important in
the salt industry. It is now known
for the brine baths mentioned in
this pub name. 'Brine' is a word of
obscure origin, referring to water
(usually sea-water) which contains
a lot of salt.

Bristol and Exeter Bridgwater and
Weston-super-Mare. The
reference is to a railway line which
served those places, opened in the
1840s.

Bristol Bridge Highbridge, Som. The
sign shows the 245-foot-high
bridge over the River Avon which

opened in 1864. The place in which this pub is situated has been known as Highbridge since the fourteenth century.

Bristol Bulldog Filton, Bristol. The name of a fighter biplane used by the Royal Air Force in the 1920s and 30s.

Bristol Flyer Bristol. Named after a famous stagecoach.

Britain's Craziest Pub Hunsdon, near Ware. The 'crazy antics' of the licensee and his wife caused the pub to receive this name in the early 1960s. It was previously the Turkey Cock, *See* Turkey.

Britannia Nailsworth, Glos and Elterwater, Cumb. Britannia was the Roman name for Britain. First mention of the symbolic female figure occurs in the diaries of Samuel Pepys, and refers to a medal struck in 1665. The model for the figure was Frances Stewart, a mistress of Charles II, later Duchess of Richmond. Britannia, resting on her familiar shield, had earlier appeared on Roman coins. Some pub signs make use of the traditional coin representation, many others (such as at Nailsworth) refer in some way to a ship which has been named Britannia. The Royal Navy has been making use of the name since 1682. Since 1953 it has sometimes been shown as the royal yacht, as at Parkstone and Portland, both in Dorset. Whitbread's had a *Britannia* pub at the International Exhibition in Brussels, 1958. It contained many prints and models of ships and aircraft which had borne the name. These are now in the similarly named pub in Dover. In London NW1 the pub of this name refers to the survey of the British Isles originally published in Latin in 1586 by the antiquarian William Camden, and called *Britannia*.

British Admiral *See* Admirals.

British Flag Gloucester. The sign shows British troops forming a hollow square, with the flag held aloft in the middle.

British Grenadier *See* Grenadier.

British Lion Folkestone. A patriotic renaming during the Napoleonic War, the British lion symbolising the nation's fighting spirit.

British Oak Bowbridge, Glos. *See* Oak. The sign here shows an oak tree surmounted by the Union Jack (more properly, the Union flag).

British Queen Iceni Way, Cambridge, and elsewhere. The Cambridge example refers to Boudicca, Queen of the Iceni tribe who died in AD 62. She took poison rather than be a prisoner of the Romans after being defeated by them. Other British queens are represented on pub signs elsewhere.

Broad Acres Harrogate. A proud reminder that Yorkshire is the largest county in England by quite a margin. This remains true in spite of recent administrative boundary changes.

Broad Face Abingdon. The sign shows a man's face grinning broadly.

Broad Leys Aylesbury. 'Leys' is a dialectal variant of 'leas', referring to arable land under grass, set aside for pasture. The same word in Flemish leads to the 'loo' of names like Waterloo. In Buckinghamshire the leys are found all around Aylesbury. In Bath there is a Broadleys Vaults.

Brockley Jack London SE4. For a highwayman named Jack Law.

Brontë Liverpool. This could be for Admiral Lord Nelson, who was made Duke of Brontë by the King of Naples. It was this title which probably influenced Patrick Prunty to change his name to

Brontë He was the father of the novelist sisters Anne, Charlotte and Emily.

Bronx Luton. A trendy use of the name of the well-known area north of New York City, always referred to in the US as The Bronx. It takes its name from a Jonas Bronck who formerly had a farm there. Visitors talked of going to the Broncks when they went to see this Dutch family. The change of spelling came later and is not unusual in place–name terms. More unusual was the retention in the place name of the definite article.

Broom Tavern Broom, near Bidford-on-Avon. Of interest for its sign, which shows Shakespeare asleep amid the daisies.

Brougham Sunderland. A brougham is a one-horse closed carriage which can have two or four wheels and seat two or four people. It was named in honour of Baron Brougham and Vaux (1778–1868) in 1851.

Brown Not an inspiring colour in pub names. Manchester has a Brown Bull, Doncaster a Brown Cow. There was formerly a Brown Dog at Millom, Cumb and Wirral has a Brown Horse. The Brown Lion at Oakengates, Salop is in Lion Street, while Aghadowey, Londy, has a Brown Trout. One or two slightly more interesting names are dealt with separately.

Brown Bear Greenhithe, Kent and elsewhere. Formerly a common sign, occasionally heraldic, more often a reference to the animal which was usually mistreated by being baited or made to dance.

Brown Bull *See* Brown and Bull.

Brown Derby Birmingham. A 'theme' pub, concentrating on the theatrical world of the 1920s. The pub name is the American version

of 'bowler hat'. Norwich has a pub of the same name.

Brown Jack Wroughton, Wilts. A well-known racehorse owned by Sir Harold Wernher, winner of the Alexandra Stakes at Ascot in six successive years during its career, 1927–34. There is now a *Brown Jack Stakes* run annually at the same course. The inn sign here reproduces the painting of the horse by Sir Alfred Munnings, president of the Royal Academy 1944–49.

Brown Jug *See* Little Brown Jug.

Brownlow Arms London E8. Also **Brownlow Tavern**, Weymouth. Mr Brownlow is the benevolent old gentleman who ultimately adopts Oliver Twist as his son in Dickens's novel *Oliver Twist*. The Artful Dodger first steals Mr Brownlow's handkerchief, and Oliver is captured as the thief.

Bruce Dumfermline. The Scottish hero, Robert Bruce (1274–1329), liberator and King of Scotland. He defeated the English under Edward II at Bannockburn in 1314 and secured Scottish independence in 1328.

Bruce Arms West Tanfield, near Ripon. Named originally with reference to the story of Robert Bruce (*see* Bruce) and the spider. In 1307, when hiding from his pursuers, Bruce watched a spider trying to fix its web to the ceiling. It failed six times, as Bruce himself had failed six times. Bruce decided that the behaviour of the spider would be an omen of what was to befall him in the future. The spider tried again, and this time succeeded, Bruce himself thereupon gathered his men together and recommenced the battle, with much subsequent success. It was only after his new signboard had been painted and hung that the patriotic Scottish landlord was informed by his Yorkshire patrons that Bruce in this context was the family name of the earls of Ailesbury, who owned estates in the district.

Brummels *See* Beau Brummel

Brunel Saltash, Corn and elsewhere. Also Brunel Arms, Crewe; Isambard Brunel, Bristol. Such signs are normally for Isambard Kingdom Brunel (1806–59), an outstanding railway and steamship engineer. Occasionally the reference may be to his father Sir Marc Isambard Brunel (1769–1849), also an engineer of distinction. Many pubs commemorate particular achieve-ments, such as the building of the Great Britain, Great Eastern and Great Western steamships. At Bristol he is referred to as the Great Engineer, and some Bridge signs, such as Two Bridges at Saltash, also have him in mind.

Brunswick Dawlish. Another at Torquay. Also Brunswick Arms, London E14; Duke of Brunswick, Maidstone; Star of Brunswick, Brighton; Brunswick Tavern, Worthing. The Sussex signs tend to be for Princess Caroline, daughter of Charles William Ferdinand, Duke of Brunswick. She married the Prince of Wales, later George IV, in 1795 but was abandoned by him in 1796. She was later accused of adultery and tried before the House of Lords in 1820, though the trial was abandoned. She had strong popular support in the country throughout this time. Other signs are after the Duke of Brunswick who lived in England for several years and was killed while fighting for the British side at Waterloo.

Brush Cowley, GL. This was the Fox until 1971, when perhaps a change of image entailed a change of name. Ropsley near Grantham has a Fox's Brush.

Brushmakers Arms Upham, near Southampton. After the makers of hazel-twig brushes or brooms, now used to sweep leaves but formerly for more general purposes. The raw materials for the brushes were found in this area.

Bubble Stenson, Derbs. There is a natural spring nearby which bubbles into the Trent and Mersey Canal.

Buccaneer Brough, Humb. The sign here shows the Hawker Siddeley (originally Blackburn) aircraft of this name, manufactured nearby. It was introduced into Fleet Air Arm squadron use in 1962, and is still in operational service with the RAF. At Gunnislake, Corn, the sign is for the more traditional piratical buccaneer. The word 'buccaneer' has an extraordinary history, and was applied originally to men who hunted wild oxen, cooking its meat on a kind of gridiron called, in French, a *boucan*.

Buccleugh Kettering. The Duke of Buccleuch was the landowner here when the pub was built in 1897.

Buck Woonton, near Hereford and elsewhere. Normally a reference to the male deer, but at Honingham, near Norwich, the sign refers to John Buck, village blacksmith in the late eighteenth century. He was also referred to in Parson Woodeford's diaries as one of the best smugglers in the county, which is possibly a compliment he would have preferred to hear privately rather than publicly. Basingstoke has a Buckskin, reminding us that leather made from the skin of a buck was formerly used to make breeches. Bald Buck at Lichfield refers to white markings on the face, while Fallow Buck at Clay Hill, near Enfield is for the pale brown or reddish yellow deer, smaller than the red deer. ('Fallow' is a description of the colour). At Standish, near Wigan there is a White Buck. Ipswich has a Running Buck. Male and female deer are mentioned in the Buck and Hind, Muiredge, Fife, and Stockport has a Buck and Dog.

Bucket of Blood Phillack, Corn. Until 1980 the New Inn. The renaming links with a (legendary) tale of a former landlord who went to the well behind the pub and drew up a 'bucket of blood'. A mutilated corpse had been thrown into the well overnight.

Buckinghamshire Yeoman *See* Yeoman.

Buck in the Park Derby. An interpretation in non–heraldic mumbo–jumbo of Derby's coat–of–arms, which has a hart cumbant on a mount vert, and so on. An antlered stag is seen on a green mound surrounded by some stakes.

Buckle Seaford, E Ssx. In the French wars at the time of Edward III, Sir John Pelham is said to have captured the French king by seizing the buckle of his belt. For this act he was allowed to incorporate a buckle into his coat of arms. Tamplin's Brewery attempted to rename the pub in 1963 but bowed to public opinion in retaining the original name. There is a Buckles at Askham Richard, near York. *See also* Hawk and Buckle.

Buddle Niton, IOW. The 'buddle' is a shallow inclined vat in which ore is washed. The name recalls the fact that tin was once mined locally.

Buffalo Newborough, Staffs and elsewhere. Also Buffaloe Arms,

Liverpool, Buffalo Head Clun, Salop, Buffaloe Head, Durham, Buffalo's Head, Puckeridge, near Ware. Such signs often indicate pubs that were frequented by members of the Friendly Society calling itself the Ancient Order of Buffaloes. This society was re-established in 1822 as the Royal Antediluvian Order of Buffaloes. The animal itself is found mainly in Asia and Africa.

Buffer Stop London NW1. A pleasantly apt name for a railway terminal pub, found at Euston Station. It is no doubt used by 'old buffers' and others. At Scholes, near Leeds there is a Buffers, converted from a railway station into a railway theme pub.

Buff Orpington Orpington, Kent. A variety of farmyard fowl.

Bug and Black Bat Coventry. This pub was opened in 1984 with a name which, according to the licensee, was chosen in a purely arbitrary way, but meant to be arresting, bizarre and alliterative. Many pubs do of course have names which are all of those things but also manage to convey a meaning of local significance.

Bugatti Gretton, Glos. The Bugatti Owners' Club holds its annual meetings here and arranges speed climbs on the nearby Prescott Hill. The sign shows one of the cars. Ettore Bugatti was born in Italy, but the cars (from 1898) were built in France and Germany.

Bugle Horn Hartwell, near Aylesbury and elsewhere. A 'bugle' was a wild ox, and until the sixteenth century its horn was used as a drinking vessel. Its other use was as a hunting horn, giving rise to the modern sense of 'bugle', a musical instrument. Inn signs can show either, though the musical instrument predominates, sometimes shown as French Horn, as at Upton, near Southwell, especially in hunting districts. In some cases the reference may be to the coach horn (or post horn) which was used by the guard on a coach much as the hooter on a motor car is used. The post horn was smaller and usually made of brass instead of copper or German silver. Surprisingly, there seem to be no pubs called *Coach Horn* or *Post Horn*, although there is a Bugle at Shepperton, GL and a Bugle Tap at Cowes.

Bull Iver, Bucks and elsewhere. An ancient and widespread sign, which may well have begun by referring to a papal bull, the leaden seal attached to the pope's edicts (Latin *bulla*). This 'seal' meaning is found in the One Bull, at Bury St Edmunds. There may also be a heraldic reference in signs such as the Three Bulls' Heads, Newcastle-on-Tyne, which is said to refer to the arms of Anne Boleyn. Two bulls feature in the arms of the Butchers Company. A Bull's Head, Reigate, was introduced into the arms of Henry VIII after he had defied the papal bull of 1538. At Penny Hill, near Holbeach, Lincs is the only example of a Bull's Neck. Many *Bull* signs are reminders that bull baiting took place in a Bull Ring, Ludlow, perhaps using a Bull Dog, Ashford, GL, a sport made illegal in 1835. Signs in market towns merely comment on the significance of this animal in farming terms. Bulls are linked with many other animals and objects, as some of the entries below indicate, to create new inn signs. A bull is also frequently described in some way: Black Bull, Ruislip and elsewhere (the commonest colour); Brown Bull, Salford; Grey Bull, Penrith; Red Bull, Peckham; White Bull, Blackburn. There is even a Blue Bull (see Blue). Variations include Chained Bull, Northallerton; Flying Bull, Rake, Hants; Great Bull, Wakefield; Hereford Bull, Ledbury; Little Bull, Spalding; Pied Bull, Enfield; Spangled Bull ('speckled'), Earlsheaton; Spotted Bull, Apsley, Herts; West Bull, Cottingham, Hull; Wild Bull, Gisburn, Lancs; New Bull, Ware; New Black Bull, Padiham, Lancs; New Bull's Head, Stratford-on-Avon, Big Bull's Head, Digbeth, Birmingham; Two Bulls' Heads, Dudley; New White Bull, Old White Bull, both at Giltbrook, Notts; Old Bull, Barnet; Old Red Bull, Morpeth, Old Pied Bull, London N7 and so on. Bull has one or two connections with drinking in certain colloquial expressions. In nautical slang a bull is a small keg. In earlier times another nautical expression was to bull the cask or barrel. It meant to pour water into an empty rum cask, leave it
there for a while, then drink it. Associated names are Bullocks at Cold Norton, Esx and Shorthorn at Appleton Wiske, N Yorks.

Bull and Butcher Bridgwater. The sign here shows a butcher armed with a cleaver being hotly pursued by a bull. The sign is found in London in the eighteenth century. Despite the obvious connection between a bull and butcher, an attempt has been made to interpret the sign as 'Bullen (Anne Boleyn) butchered', referring to her beheading two centuries before the sign appeared.

Bull and Horns Gravesend. The sign shows a bull let loose in a china shop.

Bull and Last London NW5. It is claimed that coachmen would announce, when they arrived at this inn (formerly the Bull) that it was the '*Bull* and last' (stop before the centre of London.) The 'last' was therefore added to the name.

Bull and Spectacles Blithbury, Staffs. The name is said to have come about when a prize bull nearly died after eating poisoned berries. A local wag suggested that it should be fitted with spectacles in order to avoid further accidents.

Bull and Sun Bridlington. The landlord of the Rising Sun took over the Bull and formed the new name, a common practice in former times.

Bulldog Oxford and elsewhere. The Oxford sign shows one of the bowler–hatted proctor's attendants chasing a student. The 'bulldogs' at Oxford and Cambridge are concerned with student behaviour and discipline. Elsewhere, eg at Washford Bridge, near Sheffield, the name refers to the actual dogs, in this case bred by the landlord.

Bullers Arms Landrake, Saltash. Sir Redvers Buller, VC (1839–1908), a distinguished British soldier, served in many different countries and was ultimately commander-in-chief of the British forces in South Africa in 1899. He was given land in Cornwall in recognition of his services to the nation.

Bull i' th' Thorn Hurdlow, near Buxton. There is an oak carving inside the pub, which dates from the fifteenth century, showing a bull entangled in a thorn bush.

Bullnose Morris Cowley, Oxford. The popular name of a car built as from 1913 by the local Morris car company. The pub was opened in 1967, forty years after the car ceased to be manufactured.

Bull Ring *See* Bull.

Bull's Eye Sholing, Southampton. A pleasant link with the name of the street in which it stands. Butts Road, maintaining the archery theme.

Bull's Head *See* Bull.

Bull Terrier Croscombe, Som. Named after the pet dog of the landlord. A bull terrier is a cross between a bull dog (formerly used for baiting bulls) and a terrier. There is another pub of this name at Cradley Heath, W Mids, an area well-known for the breeding of the Staffordshire terriers so often used today for the illegal 'sport' of baiting badgers.

Bunch of Bluebells Dudley Wood, H and W. Appears to be an absolutely straightforward name derived from the visual image. The only hidden message of this name may lie in the 'language of flowers' – bluebells signifying constancy.

Bunch of Carrots Hampton Bishop, Hereford. Named after a rock formation in the River Wye. The pub is on the river bank.

Bunker's Hill Milford Haven. Bunker Hill, now part of Boston, Massachusetts, was the scene of the first important battle of the American Revolution (1775). The name was taken up in England in some numbers, often as a field name, usually in the form Bunker's Hill. There is a village of this name near Oxford and also in the area of Lincoln known as New York.

Bunker's Knob New Addington, Sry. William Coppin, born in 1776, became parish clerk and local constable in this area. He had a club foot which made a 'bonking' noise as he walked, earning him the nickname Bunker. He spent much of his time on the nearby hill, which in turn became known as Bunker's Knob. Such is the local story, but 'bunker' in the latter half of the nineteenth century was a slang word for 'beer', which suggests another interpretation. Simpler still is the possibility that Bunker's Knob is merely a variant of Bunker's Hill, of which three examples are recorded in Surrey.

Bun Penny Herne Bay. Also at Lee-on-Solent. The penny issued between 1860–95, showing Queen Victoria with her hair in a bun, or chignon. The word 'bun' was only used with this meaning from the 1890s, although in fact the coins of the realm featured Victoria wearing this same 'chignon' hair-styling from 1838. *See also* Old Fourpenny Shop.

Bun Shop Cambridge. Hot-cross buns were given away on Good Friday with each pint of beer sold, an advertising gimmick that began soon after the pub first opened in 1902. Another pub of this name is at Tolworth, Sry. *See* Widows Son.

Bunters Bromley, Kent. Billy Bunter, the fat little cad of Greyfriars School, a leading character in many stories of the Magnet Library series, was created by 'Frank Richards', who was actually Charles Hamilton (1875–1961). Hamilton wrote under many other names, especially Martin Clifford for 'The Gem'. The Bunter tales were begun in 1908 and continued weekly until 1940. Bunter's Bar inside this pub is decorated appropriately, with blown-up reproductions from 'The Magnet'.

Bure Great Yarmouth, Nflk. The name of the river which rises near Melton Constable and flows into the Yare at Yarmouth.

Burke and Hare Edinburgh. William Burke and William Hare satisfied the need of Dr Robert Knox, an Edinburgh surgeon, by providing him with bodies for medical research. The two men decided that the easiest way to acquire bodies for sale was to lure living people to a suitable place, then suffocate them. They had disposed of fifteen victims before being discovered in 1829 and were known thereafter as 'the Body-Snatchers'. Their activities seem to have appealed greatly to the British public, and 'burke', in the sense of killing someone by smothering, found its way into the English dictionary.

Burlington Bertie London W1. The pub is in Burlington Street. There are many pictures on the walls of music-hall stars, many of whom would have sung about 'Burlington Bertie, who rose at ten-thirty'. The song was written by William Hargreaves (1846–1919), and made famous chiefly by Vesta Tilley and Ella Shields.

Burma Star Runcorn, Ches. The name of a medal awarded to troops of the fourteenth Army who defeated the Japanese in Burma under Field-Marshal Slim. The Japanese had occupied the country 1942–45.

Burmese Cat Melton Mowbray. Such cats were bred by the brewery chairman's wife when this pub was built. The sign shows a black cat under a pagoda-style roof.

Burns London E14, John Burns (1858–1943) was a trade–union official who led the national dock strike of 1889. He was a pioneer of the Labour Movement and represented Battersea for many years in parliament.

Burns' Arms Also Burns' Cottage, Burns' Head, Burns' Howff, Burns' Tavern. *See* Robert Burns.

Burnt Oak Gillingham, Kent. After an oak which had no doubt been struck by lightning and was burnt. A similar tree gave rise to the place name at Edgware. The Kentish tree attracted tales to itself about a witch who lived in it and offered her services for a fee.

Burrator *See* Tors.

Burton Boys *See* Breton Arms.

Busby Stoop Sand Hutton, near Thirsk. After a murderer named Busby who was hanged on a 'stoop', or post, in the seventeenth century.

Bush Dorking and elsewhere. A sign of great antiquity, used by the Romans to indicate a wine-shop in the form of a bunch of evergreens. Poles decorated with evergreens such as ivy were used as signs for early alehouses. Ivy Bush occurs as a pub name, eg at Lampeter, Dyfed, and Holly Bush, Elstree and elsewhere, is even commoner. Also found are Elder Bush, Nantyfyllon, M Glam; Furze Bush (another evergreen), Hatt Common, Berks; Hawthorn Bush, West Bromwich; Haw Bush, Little Heath, Romford; Mulberry Bush, Kempston, Beds; Round Bush, Aldenham, Herts. Beggars Bush and Cuckoo Bush are treated separately.

Bush Elms *See* Elm.

Buskers London E1. To 'busk' originally meant 'to sell obscene songs and books in pubs'. A 'busker' was therefore someone who sold such songs or books, but from the mid-nineteenth century the word was applied to an itinerant actor or musician who performs in a street or other public place. The word is unknown in the USA.

Bustard South Rauceby, Lincs and elsewhere. The Great Bustard is the largest European bird, resembling an outsize turkey. It has been extinct in Britain since 1840 but attempts are being made to reintroduce it on Salisbury Plain where the only other pub of this name is to be found, at Shrewton. 'Bustard' is from Latin *avis tarda*, 'slow bird', a name which insults a bird which can run and fly swiftly.

Busy Bee Bradford. Also Bee, Seacombe, Ches and elsewhere; Bees-in-the Wall, Whittlesford, Cambridge; Queen Bee, London SE15. The busy bee is the symbol of Boddingtons, Manchester's best-known brewery. Other signs which mention this insect probably reflect bee-keeping interests of pub–owners, or the presence for any other reason of swarms or apiaries in the area.

But and Ben Bourtreehill, near Irvine, Strath. A but and ben is a two-roomed house, referring to the but, or kitchen, through which one passes to get to the inner room, the ben. In a more general sense the phrase refers to the opposite ends of a house or passage, or sometimes a small country cottage.

Butchers Arms Sheepscombe, Glos and elsewhere. The Butchers Company was granted arms in 1540. At Yatton, Somerset, the name is said to be a corruption of Bouchier's Arms, Thomas Bouchier being a former lord of the manor. The descendants of this family became the earls of Bath.

Buthay Wickwar, Glos. The name of this pub was changed in 1970 from New Inn to Buthay (pronounced Buttie). The explanation given at the time was the new name related to the archery butts at which the

English archers trained before the Battle of Crecy (1346). The La Warre family, once lords of Wickwar, distinguished themselves in that contest.

Butler's Head London EC2. Dr William Butler was physician at the court of James I. He was not actually qualified, but was known for a medicinal ale which allegedly could cure any ailment. Originally, this sign was hung outside pubs where Butler's ale was sold.

Butt Aldermaston. Also Butts in Walsall. In both cases the reference is to an archery butt rather than the wine cask. At Aldermaston the butts were formerly in the field opposite the pub. In Walsall the pub is in Butts Road.

Butt and Oyster Pin Mill, near Ipswich. Probably a reference to oysters which were packed in butts or barrels for despatch. However, 'butt' is the name for several kinds of flat fish. It is said that there were also archery butts near this inn, but that is coincidental.

Butt of Malmsey Stratford-on-Avon. Murals inside the pub relate to Shakespeare's *Richard III*. In Act 1, scene 4, there is a long discussion between George, Duke of Clarence, and the men who have come to murder him. One of them stabs him several times, then says: 'If all this will not do, I'll drown you in the malmsey butt within.' The incident is said to have occurred in reality in 1478, when George was murdered by order of his brother Richard. Malmsey is a strong sweet wine, originally from a place called Malvasia in southern Greece. The inn sign here depicts the scene referred to in a fairly light-hearted manner.

Byard's Leap Sheffield. A reference to an incident which is said to have occurred when Rinaldo, one of the great heroes of medieval romance, was riding on his horse Bayardo. A hag sprang onto the horse, but it took three immense leaps in order to unseat her. Three stones, about thirty yards apart, gave rise to this tale, which appealed to the first tenant of the pub. The sign shows the hag on the horse's back.

Byron Also Byron Arms, Byron House, Byrons. *See* Lord Byron.

C

Cabbage Liverpool. The same city has a Cabbage Hall, where the original landlord is said to have been a tailor. 'Cabbage' became the nickname of a tailor by association. The term once referred to the pieces of cloth left over when a garment was cut from a roll. There is some evidence that the word 'garbage' was corrupted into 'cabbage'.

Cabbage Patch Twickenham. A lighthearted reference to the Twickenham Rugby Football ground. The pub was renamed in 1959 when England and Wales played Scotland and Ireland in a centenary match. *See also* Twickers.

Cabinet Reed, Herts. In the sixteenth century 'cabinet' could be applied to various types of dwelling, including village houses such as this, especially if they were fairly small. The word was simply a form of 'cabin' and had not acquired too narrow a meaning. Cabinet went on to become the word for a small, private room, one in which meetings were held, hence the modern sense of the Cabinet, the body of government ministers. It had another meaning of a small room where works of art were displayed, a kind of miniature museum, and this led to its use for a piece of furniture.

Cabman's Rest Southsea, Hants. The sign shows an old-time 'cabby' wearing his voluminous cloak. Cabs (short for cabriolets) were originally one-horse carriages seating two or four people, the forerunners of the modern taxicabs.

Cabot Weston-super-Mare. John Cabot was a fifteenth-century English explorer, though born in Genoa, Italy. He sailed from Bristol in 1497 and reached the North American coast. His son Sebastian Cabot (1483–1557) was also an explorer. English claims to North America were founded on the voyages of the Cabots.

Ca'Canny Brunswick Village, Northld. This Scottish expression literally means 'call shrewdly', but its sense was 'take it easy, don't work too quickly'. Like the Slow and Easy at Lostock Gralam, Ches, it implies that there is always time for a leisurely drink.

Cadland Old Chilwell, Nottingham. The name of a racehorse owned by the duke of Rutland. It ran a dead-heat with The Colonel in the Derby of 1828, then won by a neck in the re-run. The Running Horses, Mickleham, Sry, refers to the same event.

Cafe Royal New Town, Edinburgh. The Edinburgh pub is just off the Royal Mile and is a fine example of Victorian polished mahogany. The London Cafe Royal was a meeting place for artists in the early part of the century. Later it became the restaurant much used by BBC staff and journalists.

Calder and Hebble Salterhebble, Halifax. The name of the nearby canal, which links the Calder and Hebble rivers.

Caledonian Carlisle and elsewhere. The Caledonian Railway ran from Carlisle to Glasgow and Edinburgh and served the industrial regions of Scotland before 1923, when it became part of the London, Midland and Scottish Railway. The pub of this name at Darlington shows a GWR King class locomotive in error.

California Belmont, Sry. This pub was built in the 1860s by Joe Gibbons, on his return from a successful gold-prospecting trip to California. A similar tale attaches to the pub of the same name at Darton, near Barnsley. There is also a *California* at Scratby, near Great Yarmouth.

Call Boy Gravesend. So named because it was built (in 1953) on the site of the Grand Theatre which closed in the 1930s. The sign originally showed a pageboy knocking on the dressing-room door, but when it returned after being repainted the artist had depicted a military boy trumpeter. *See also* Stage Door.

Cambridge Blue Cambridge. This was the Dewdrop until 1985, but it now has the bow of the 1984 boat suspended behind the bar. Before that year's Boat Race had begun the Cambridge cox had the misfortune to steer the boat into a barge. The barge emerged unscathed, the boat did not. The race was rowed next day, Cambridge in a borrowed boat, and Oxford added another victory to a lengthy run of wins.

Camden Great Yarmouth and elsewhere. William Camden (1551–1623), antiquary and historian, whose main work was a survey, in Latin, of the British Isles called *Britannia*. In the supplement to that work, *Remains Concerning Britain*, he was one of the first writers in English to turn his attention to names, with chapters on the origins of English first names and surnames. The Camden Society perpetuates his memory. There is a William Camden in Bexley Heath.

Camden Arms Pembury, Kent. Another at Sissinghurst. Also Lord Camden, London SE1, Marquis of Camden, London NW1. 'Charles Pratt, 1st Earl of Camden (1714–94) became lord chancellor, and his eldest son, John Jeffreys Pratt, Marquis of Camden (1759–1840). The latter was lord lieutenant of Ireland for several years and was later secretary to the colonies. It was the Pratt family who owned the land which was developed into Camden Town.

Camel London E2. Probably suggested by the camel which occurs on the armorial bearings of certain livery companies, eg the Grocers, Coopers and Merchant Taylors.

Camellia *See* Flowers.

Camelot Queen's Camel, Som. The pub was renamed in 1972 and is near Cadbury Castle, reputed to be the site of King Arthur's court. There is also a Camelots at Doncaster, a converted church.

Camp St Albans. Near the site of a Roman camp. Another pub of this name is at Eaton Bishop, near Hereford.

Camperdown Newcastle-on-Tyne. For the naval victory gained by Admiral Duncan at Camperdown, off the Dutch coast, in 1797.

Camp House Bevere, Worcester. A reference to the nearby Camp Hill, where Cromwell defeated Prince Charles in the Battle of Worcester, 1651.

Canal Wrantage, Som. The pub was established for the labourers who were excavating a tunnel for the Chard canal.

Canary Norwich. There was once a Fanciers Arms in the city, canaries having been introduced by the early Flemish settlers, and giving rise to a local breeding industry. The bird takes its name from the Canary Isles (literally 'isles of dogs', so–called by the Romans because of the large dogs found there). Canary House, formerly in London, was so-called because it sold the light sweet wine from the Canaries.

Canary and Linnet Little Fransham, Nflk. The sign shows two footballers wearing the colours of Norwich FC, known as the *Canaries* for their colours, and King's Lynn FC, known as the *Linnets* by adaptation of the place name.

Candlestick Essendon, Herts. The regulars formerly lit candles at the bar to create a cosy atmosphere.

Cannard's Grave near Shepton Mallet, Som. The pub is at a crossroads where a local innkeeper was hanged in the 1820s for his spare–time criminal activities. The sign shows his body suspended from a gibbet with a flock of sheep passing underneath.

Canning Fenton, Staffs. Also Canning Arms, Hartpury, Glos and George Canning, London SW2 and SE5. George Canning (1770–1827) was a distinguished English statesman, orator and wit. He became prime minister in 1827, a few months before his death.

Cannon Ash, near Aldershot and elsewhere. As with Gun pub names, connected heraldically to Edward VI, Queen Mary or Queen Elizabeth I. Other instances have a military connection, such as the Ash example. The sign depicts a cannon which was abandoned during the withdrawal of the North West Frontier in India (1841), but recovered forty years later.

Cann Office Llangadfan, Pwys. An ancient inn which became a staging-post on the road from Aberdyfi to Shrewsbury with the introduction of the mail service in the mid-seventeenth century. The innkeeper became the postmaster. 'Cann' = can (of ale).

Canny Lad Newcastle-upon-Tyne. A complimentary Northern expression referring to a man who is knowing, shrewd, lucky, etc, ie someone who has enough sense to use that particular pub. The landlord may also be complimenting himself. At Hanworth, Berks there is a Cannie Man.

Canopus Rochester. The name of a famous flying-boat built locally by the Short Brothers in 1936.

Canterbury Arms London SE15 and elsewhere. There is a Canterbury at Tewkesbury and a Canterbury Tales in Canterbury itself. Canterbury has been an important centre since Roman times and became a place of pilgrimage after the murder of Thomas à Becket in December, 1170. Geoffrey Chaucer's *Canterbury Tales* is a collection of stories told by a group of pilgrims as they make their way to Becket's shrine. It is commonly said that 'to canter', meaning to gallop at an easy pace, is derived from a Canterbury gallop, because of the pace adopted by pilgrims. It is perhaps more likely to be derived from Latin *cantherius*, 'gelding'.

Canute Southampton. The King of Denmark who became King of England in 1014. He was a prudent and pious man, famous for the way he rebuked the courtiers who were trying to flatter him by saying that he could do anything at all. He demonstrated that the rising tide would not turn back at

Cap and Feathers Tillingham, Esx. The sign shows an example of this ceremonial headgear.

Cap and Gown Gorleston, Nflk. A reference to the formal academic dress of a university student or teacher. The Norfolk pub was built on land acquired from Magdalene College, Cambridge. There is a similarly named pub in the university town of Reading.

Cap and Stocking Kegworth near Derby. These items were formerly of great local importance because of the woollen industry. Elizabeth I made it obligatory for all over the age of six (with certain exceptions) to wear a woollen cap on Sundays and holy days, a statute that was not repealed until 1597.

Cape Horner Swansea. The reference is to a ship which sailed around Cape Horn, at the southernmost tip of Chile, notorious for its storms and dangers.

Cape of Good Hope Warwick and elsewhere. The original cape is at the west entrance to False Bay, off the coast of South Africa. Diaz named it the Cape of Storms in 1486; Prince Henry the Navigator renamed it because it offered hope of finding a sea route to India. As a pub name it probably indicates ex-mariners who became landlords.

Captain Cook Staithes, N Yorks. Another at Barking, Esx. James Cook (1728–79) was an English explorer and navigator who circumnavigated the globe 1768–71 and mapped more than 5,000 miles of coastline around Australia and New Zealand as well as in the Antarctic and the Pacific. He was killed by Hawaiian natives who afterwards repented their action and gave him a chieftain's cremation. He worked in his youth at Staithes and was married at Barking.

Captain Coram London WC1. Thomas Coram (1668–1751) was a benevolent merchant seaman who founded in 1740 a Hospital for Exposed and Deserted Children. In 1756 parliament voted £10,000 to the institution, whereupon the number of children exposed and deserted is said to have risen very sharply.

Captain Digby Kingsgate, near Margate. Named by Lord Holland in honour of a seaman who waged war on Kentish smugglers in the early nineteenth century.

Captain Howey New Romney. The man who founded the Romney, Hythe and Dymchurch narrow-gauge railway. This is claimed to be the world's smallest ('light') public railway, and has provided a regular service along its 15-inch track every spring and summer since its opening in 1927. The journey from Hythe to New Romney is fourteen miles.

Captain Mannering Shoeburyness. A reference to the character (spelled in the cast list as Mainwaring) in the television series *Dad's Army*, played by the late Arthur Lowe. The pub was named in 1984. There is an army barracks nearby.

Captain Vancouver Gayton, Nflk. George Vancouver (1758–98) was born at nearby King's Lynn. He charted, and gave his name to, Vancouver Island in 1792. The pub sign shows him in his cabin working with a chart.

Captain Webb Wellington, Salop. Matthew Webb (1849–83) was a local man who was the first to swim the English Channel. In 1875 it took him twenty-two hours to swim a total of forty miles. He later attempted to swim the rapids at Niagara Falls and was drowned.

his command, but only at God's command. *See also* King Canute.

Captive Queen Sheffield. The pub stands opposite Manor Castle, where Mary, Queen of Scots, was once held prisoner.

Cardiff Arms Weston-super-Mare. A Welsh innkeeper was no doubt responsible for the name, which no doubt attracts the visitors from Cardiff who arrive here by boat.

Cardinal's Cap Canterbury. The Cardinal's Hat is also found, eg at Newark and Harleston, Nflk. Such signs were visually convenient and showed religious allegiance in the way that the Crown showed royal allegiance. In some cases the land on which the pub was built may have belonged to the church and come under the jurisdiction of the cardinal.

Cardinal's Error Tonbridge, Kent. Cardinal Wolsey promised the town a grammar school. He fell out of favour and died before he could keep his promise.

Cardinal Wolsey Hampton Court, GL. Thomas Wolsey (1472–1530) was a statesman and churchman who rapidly gained favour with Henry VIII. By 1514 he virtually controlled English domestic and foreign policy. He built several palaces, including the nearby Hampton Court, but lost favour when Henry decided to divorce Katharine of Aragon in favour of Anne Boleyn. Signs of the Cardinal, eg Kingston-on-Thames and elsewhere, often refer to him. There is also a Wolsey Tavern in London NW5.

Caribou Galgate, Lancaster. The largest species of reindeer found in North America, and meant to recall trade links between the Glasson Docks, Lancs and Canada.

Carlton Plume of Feathers Minehead. The licence of the former Plume of Feathers (*see* Feathers) was transferred to the Carlton Hotel, with the proviso that the new name should be a joint one.

Carnegie's Bar Glasgow. Andrew Carnegie (1835–1919), the Scottish-born philanthropist, made his fortune in the USA. He contributed some 350,000,000 dollars to the founding of nearly 3,000 libraries and other institutions.

Carnethy Penicuik, Loth. The nearby Carnethy Hill, 1890 feet, is the highest point in the Pentland Hills.

Carousel Lowestoft. This was the Spread Eagle until 1985. The landlord, who once operated a fairground ride, had the idea of giving the pub a fairground theme.

Carpenters Arms Dundry, near Bristol and elsewhere. Early examples of this sign would have shown three pairs of compasses. Modern signs tend to show different carpentry tools at the discretion of the sign-painter. This one shows a bandsaw, adze and plane. Taverns of this name have been in existence since at least the seventeenth century.

Carriage Swindon. The railway carriage sign recalls Swindon's former importance as a railway engineering town, especially in the days of the Great Western Railway.

Carriage and Pair London SE5. Also Chaise and Pair, Barkway, Herts. Signs that were no doubt intended to appeal to the 'carriage trade', the class of people who could afford to keep their own carriages and horses. 'Chaise' literally means 'chair'.

Carriers Bude. A straightforward trade description. A former landlord was also in business as a carrier of corn, timber, coal and lime.

Carronade Arms Bainsford, near Falkirk. A carronade is a short cannon with a large bore, used mainly on board a ship. It took its name from the ironworks at Carron, where it was made, not far from this pub.

Cart and Horses Kings Worthy, Hants. Another at Rickmansworth. Also Cart and Horse, Sutton-in-Ashfield, Notts. It seems that in spite of the proverb the cart *can* be put before the horse. Normally, telling someone that he is putting the cart before the horse means that he is doing things in the wrong logical order. The saying comes from Latin: *Currus bovem trahit praepostere.*

Cartoonist London EC4. The pub is just off Fleet Street and acts as host to the Cartoonists' Club of Great Britain. *See also* Giles.

Cartwheel Whitchurch, Bristol. In the mid-nineteenth century a 'cartwheel' was the slang term for any large coin, such as a crown. Cartwheel may, in turn, have become a jocular reference to a pub called the Crown. The pub at Whitsbury, Hants, has an ordinary agricultural cartwheel as its sign.

Casbah Portsmouth. In North Africa the casbah is either a fortress or the native section of the city, often a maze of narrow streets crowded with small shops or stalls. In the 1940s the phrase 'Come into the casbah' was jokingly used as an invitation to sample exotic delights.

Case is Altered Banbury and elsewhere. A phrase first used by Edmund Plowden (1518–85), a lawyer. It referred to the effect of new evidence on the case he was dealing with in court. The phrase seems to have become almost proverbial. It was taken up by Ben Jonson for his comedy *The Case is Altered*, written before 1599. As a pub name the reason for its use is a matter of local legend in each instance. Often it is said that the landlord's situation altered for some reason, perhaps in his dispute with the licensing authorities. The Banbury sign shows a courtroom scene. There is a local story about weavers winning a court victory, resulting in the Weavers Arms changing to the *Case is Altered* overnight. Amongst the various more ingenious, but almost certainly totally false, explanations of the name one may cite a) a corruption of *Casey's Altar* for the pub at Woodbridge in Suffolk; b) a corruption of *Casa Alta* for the several pubs of the name in the Harrow district. This is supposed to be because soldiers returning from the Peninsular War at the beginning of the nineteenth century had often occupied a 'house on the hill' during the battle; c) a corruption of *Casa de Saltar*, explained as 'house of dancers' where the British soldiers betook themselves. The last phrase is totally meaningless in Spanish (though *saltarina* is a dancer) and demonstrates only that in trying to explain a pub name, most people prefer to stay in the bar and invent something rather than pursue the matter properly.

Castle West Lulworth, Dors and elsewhere. This has been a common pub name for centuries. It is tempting to connect it with the saying that an 'Englishman's home is his castle', a phrase which has been in use since the seventeenth century, but it is more likely to have been used a) because of proximity to a castle, as in the West Lulworth example;

b) because a castle figured in the coat of arms of the landowner or local squire; c) because it was a simple visual sign, easy to illustrate and easy for patrons to recognise.

Castle and Falcon Newark. A heraldic reference to Catherine Parr, the last of Henry VIII's six wives.

Castle and Wheelbarrow Rous Lench, near Evesham. It is said that this name was chosen to make fun of a publican nearby, who had called his house Castle in the Air.

Castle Barge Newark. The pub is alongside the Town Wharf, and is near the ancient ruined castle.

Castle Brook Compton Dundon, Som. The castle and brook are nearby.

Castle in the Air *See* Wheelbarrow and Castle.

Castle of Comfort Porlock, Som. The sign shows Dunster castle. The name as a whole hints at a relaxing atmosphere within the pub.

Castleton's Oak Biddenden, Kent. Ebenezer Castleton was a local carpenter who made his own oak coffin thirty years before he died. The sign shows him sitting on it, and explains the pub's nickname of *The Coffin*.

CAT There is a *Cat* on Cat Hill, East Barnet and elsewhere, and a cat occurs in many combination names which follow this entry. A few others are Cat and Mutton, London E8; Cat and Tiger, Sevenoaks. There is a Cat Head at Chiselborough, Som, and Baillieston, near Glasgow, has a Cat's Eyes, a phrase which now suggests the reflectors in the middle of the roads. Other names include Alley Cat, High Spen, T and W; Black Cat, Greenock – a symbol of good luck for many people; Copy Cat, Glasgow – perhaps a reference by the owner to a rival who was copying his ideas. The phrase probably arose for purely alliterative reasons, cats being great individualists and hardly likely to copy the behaviour of others. There is a Fat Cat at Sheffield, which in modern idiom manages to suggest someone who is doing very well for himself, a Ginger Tom at Colwick, near Nottingham and an Old Cat at Wordsley, near Stourbridge. The Rampant Cat at Burford, near Oxford is no doubt a heraldic reference, unlike the Romping Kitling at Styal, near Wilmslow. References to Whittington and Cat as at London N19 and Hull and Puss in Boots are also found. *See also* Brass Cat, Burmese Cat, Cat's Whiskers, Charlton Cat, Cheshire Cat, Mad Cat, Maltese Cat, Red Cat, Romping Cat, Squinting Cat, Tabby Cat.

Cat and Bagpipes East Harlesey, N Yorks. 'Cat' here refers to the caterans, robbers from the

Highlands of Scotland who once raided border areas. In Old Gaelic *ceatharn* meant 'a band of soldiers'. The sign shows a black cat in company with a kilted piper.

Cat and Cabbage Rotherham. The sign is the cap badge of the now-disbanded York and Lancaster Regiment, actually a tiger and a cabbage rose.

Cat and Canary Henfield, W Ssx. This was a name chosen as a result of a competition in 1976, presumably with reference to the cartoon characters, Sylvester and Tweety Pie.

Cat and Cracker Isle of Grain, near Rochester. Also **Catcracker**, Sorrels, near Stanfordle-Hope, Esx. In both cases the reference is to the 'catalytic cracking plant' at the AngloIranian Oil Refinery in the Thames estuary.

Cat and Custard Pot Shipton Moyne, Wilts. Another pub of the same name is at Paddlesworth in Kent. In *Handley Cross* (1843), by Robert Surtees, it is at a tavern of this name that the hounds belonging to Mr Jorrocks regularly meet. *See also* John Jorrocks, Surtees.

Cat and Fiddle Buxton, Derbs and elsewhere. Bryant Lillywhite, in his book *London Signs*, found instances of this name in London at the very beginning of the sixteenth century. The nursery rhyme beginning: 'Hey diddle diddle,/The cat and the fiddle . . . ' is normally ascribed to a collection which appeared in the mid-eighteenth century, though clearly it had existed in oral tradition before that. A precise first-dating of the expression would make a reasonable interpretation easier than it is at present. All one can say is that the idea of a fiddling cat (the inn sign occasionally took that form) was firmly established in the public's imagination by the beginning of the sixteenth century. This makes the traditional explanations of the name impossible, because they concern later events. The name is therefore *not* a corruption of *Catherine la Fidèle*, a reference to the French wife of Peter the Great of Russia, nor is it a form of *Caton Fidèle*, referring to an English knight named Caton, active in the late sixteenth century. The pub name was formerly popular: of the inns remaining the best-known are the thatched hostelry at Hinton Admiral near the New Forest, and the isolated moorland inn at Buxton. Cheltenham has a Cat and the Fiddle, and there is a Lion and Fiddle at Hilperton, near Trowbridge.

Cat and Wheel Bristol and elsewhere. *See* Catherine Wheel.

Catchems Swadlincote, near Burton-on-Trent. Said to be named for a former landlord, who was actually Ketcham. The local joke was that he would 'catch' travellers overnight as they passed through a nearby toll-gate.

Catchem's Corner Old Basford, near Nottingham. This was the Station Hotel until 1969, though the station itself was closed in 1964. The local tramway had its terminus right outside the pub until 1929, and locals swear that a common expression until that time was: 'I'll catch 'em all ways', meaning that a traveller would be able to catch either a tram or train. Another pub of this name is at Meir, Stoke-on-Trent.

Catch 22 London NW11. Joseph Heller's celebrated novel (1961), a satirical look at the behaviour of senior air force officers during World War Two.

Catcracker *See* Cat and Cracker.

Cat Head Chiselborough, Som. Refers to the coat-of-arms of the Pulteney family of Bath.

Cathedral Salisbury. There is another in Truro. Both cities have real cathedrals, but no doubt there are locals who find it convenient to be able to say that they spend quite a lot of time in the *Cathedral*.

Catherine Wheel Egham, Sry and elsewhere. Normally a figure of a wheel with spikes projecting from its circumference, the type of wheel on which St Catherine of Alexandria is said to have been martyred. The wheel was adopted as a badge by the Knights of St Catherine of Mount Sinai, an order created in the eleventh century with a view to protecting pilgrims who journeyed to Jerusalem. Early use of the sign for taverns probably extended this idea of protection for travellers. Later namings were sometimes because of a Catherine-wheel window in the pub itself or in a nearby church. The rotating firework known as a Catherine wheel is linked with the legendary wheel of the saint, but is unlikely to have inspired any pub names. In Puritan times, when references to saints were not popular, some publicans altered their sign to Cat and Wheel. The variant Katherine Wheel, which occurs in London E1, is said to be connected with the arms of the Turners Company, which included a Catherine wheel from the mid-sixteenth century.

Cat i' th' Well Wainstalls, Halifax. Known as the *Catty Well*. St Catherine's well was the original form, Catherine being patron of all wells and watering places, including the local one.

Cats Woodham Walter, Esx. The sign shows a group of cats washing themselves. They are good lickers, and a reminder that good liquors are obtainable inside.

Cat's Whiskers Luton and Middlewich, Ches. A fairly modern slang expression similar to 'the cat's pyjamas', indicating anything that is of excellent quality. There is a Cat's Eyes at Baillieston, near Glasgow.

Catts Rotherfield, E Ssx. The licensee says that this name derives from the village squire who bought the premises in 1740.

Catworth Fox *See* **Fox.**

Cauld Lad Hylton, Sunderland. The cauld ('cold') lad of Hilton Hall was a poltergeist. The people in the house left for him at night a green cloak and hood. This, and the warmth of the kitchen fire, so pleased him that he never troubled them again. The story is told in Brewer's *Dictionary of Phrase and Fable* but the source is not mentioned.

Cauliflower *See* Fruits and Vegetables.

Cause is Altered Dover. A variant of the Case is Altered, and perhaps indicating to foreign visitors that England was no longer a Catholic country. Because the pub stands at Cowgate (the gate itself having been removed in 1776), attempts have been made to link the pub name with cows in some way. Thus a corruption of *Cows and Halter* has been suggested. Even more fanciful is the explanation that herdsmen on their way to market would call into the pub saying: 'The cows 'as 'alted – woi shouldn't oi?'

Cavalier Bestwood, Nottingham and elsewhere. For the Royalists of the seventeenth century who fought for Charles I against the Round-heads. The term was originally

meant to be a reproach. *See* Gay
Cavalier.

Caveac London EC3. A meeting
place of the Caveac Lodge of
Freemasons, named for a French
refugee of the eighteenth century.

Cavendish Nottingham and elsewhere. The family name of the
dukes of Devonshire, owners of
land in many parts of the country.
The name is especially frequent in
the area around the family seat at
Chatsworth in Derbs. Nottingham
also has a Duke of Devonshire, and
there are several pubs named
Devonshire Arms in Notts and
Derbs.

Caxton Arms *See* William Caxton.

Caxton Gibbet Caxton, Cambridge.
The pub is on the site of a gibbet,
or gallows, where a murderer was
hung in the eighteenth century.

Cayley Arms Allerston, N Yorks.
Another at nearby Brompton-on-
Sawdon. Sir George Cayley
(1773–1857), a local squire, was an
English scientific writer who wrote
much about aerial navigation. He
is reputed to have invented the
world's first man-carrying glider
and to have forced his coachman
to fly it across a small valley near
Brompton Hall in 1853. The
coachman is said to have survived
the 500 yard flight, but left his
master's service in protest.

CB Arkengarthdale, N Yorks. The
pub once served workers from the
nearby lead mines, owned by
Charles Bathurst, lord of the
manor. His initials were stamped
on every pig of lead that came
from the mine. *See also* Pig of
Lead.

Celebrity Ashington, Northld. The
sign shows a figure who is a
mixture of Champagne Charlie
and Burlington Bertie. According
to the landlord, no particular
celebrity led to the pub name.

Centaur *See* Shakespeare.

Central Commercial *See* Commercial.

Centre of England Meriden, near
Coventry. A straightforward
geographical description.

Centurion Deptford and elsewhere.
The name at Deptford, as with
Ship Centurion at Whitstable,
refers to the ship in which Anson
made his round-the-world voyage
1740–44. *See* Anson Arms.
Various other pubs which have
this name depict a Roman
centurion on the sign. He was the
officer in the Roman army in
charge of a 'century' – 100 men.
At Bicester, Oxon, the sign shows
Mars, god of war, watching a
Roman centurion flee in terror at
the approach of a Centurion tank.
Colchester, which is an army town
today as it was for the Romans, has
a sign with a Roman centurion on
one side, a Centurion tank on the
other.

Cestrian Chester. Cestrian simply
means 'pertaining to Chester or
Cheshire'.

Chafford Arms Fordcombe, near
Tunbridge Wells. The name
refers to a 'ford for calves' which
was formerly nearby: 'calf' in Old
English was *cealf*, pronounced
'chalf'.

Chained Bull *See* Bull.

Chain Locker Falmouth. Otherwise
the Marine Hotel. The pub
overlooks Falmouth harbour and
has a nautical theme. A chain
locker is used to store chain cable
on board a ship.

Chain Pier Brighton. The floating
pier was opened in 1823,
opposite the pub. It has since
been demolished.

Chair and Rocket Leamington Spa.
The sign shows an old man in a
bath-chair being carried into space
by a rocket, though the reason for
this is not clear.

Chairmakers' Arms Worlds End, near Denmead, Hants. After the makers of armchairs, no doubt.

Chaise and Pair *See* Carriage and Pair.

Chalk Drawers Olney Heath, Bucks. Also Chalkdrawers Arms, Colney Heath near St Albans. The reference is to men who worked in a local chalk pit or quarry. There is a Chalkpit at Offham, E Ssx and a Chalk Tavern at Sittingbourne.

Champagne Charlie's Edinburgh. Another in Islington. This Victorian music-hall song was made famous by George Leybourne (1824–84). Partridge thinks that the original Champagne Charlie was a wine-merchant who often gave champagne to his friends. Brewer thinks it was the 4th Marquess of Hastings, a notorious spendthrift and gambler.

Champion London W1. The pub is on the site of a wooden booth erected by Tom Figg – first champion of the British ring – and used by him to teach the nobility and gentry of his day the art of self-defence. The brewers decided that a more modern champion should be illustrated on the sign, and chose Sir Gordon Richards, the champion jockey. The Norwich pub of this name honours Daniel Mendoza, a London prizefighter who visited Norwich in 1790.

Champion Jockey Donnington, Salop. The pub is near the birthplace of Sir Gordon Richards, champion jockey twenty-six times.

Champion Shell Stevenston, near Ayr. A reference to a product of the nearby munitions factory.

Chance Guston, near Dover. The local farmer who converted a cottage into this tavern is said to have taken a chance, competing with a nearby inn.

Chandlers Arms Shearsby near Lutterworth and Epwell, near Banbury. Also **Chandlers** at Clydebank, near Glasgow. The chandlers were originally makers of candles, or sellers of them. Later the term was extended to grocers who also sold oil, soap, etc.

Chandos London WC2 and elsewhere. A reference to one or other of the barons Chandos. The first such baron was ennobled in 1554.

Changing Lights Huddersfield. The pub is near some traffic lights.

Chapel Coggeshall, Esx. Chapel House is also found, eg in London N1. Such signs can indicate that the pub is a converted chapel, as with the Old Chapel at Devonport, or is near one. The Coggeshall sign shows the interior of a printing works, since 'chapel' can also mean a printing office, or an association of the printers who work there.

Chapelhay Rodwell. Dors. The name commemorates an ancient chapel dedicated to St Nicholas. It was converted into a fort during the Civil War and subsequently demolished.

Chaplin Arms Also **Chaplin's**. *See* **Charlie Chaplin**.

Chapter Arms Chartham Hatch, near Canterbury. Originally the chapter house of a former Dean of Canterbury Cathedral. 'Chapter' in this sense refers to the body of canons of a cathedral church, presided over by a dean. At their meetings a chapter, ie a lesson, would be read.

Charles Cotton Hotel Hartington, Derb. Cotton (1630–87) was a translator and poet, but is probably best remembered for the chapter on fly fishing which he added to Walton's *Compleat Angler*.

Charles Darwin Sutton, near Shrewsbury. Charles Darwin (1809–82) was a famous English naturalist who formed a concept of evolution subsequently known as Darwinism. His theories were set out in his *Origin of Species* (1859), and later elaborated in *Descent of Man* (1871). He had earlier described his work as naturalist during a five-year cruise on the *Beagle*. The pub which bears his name is in his birthplace.

Charles Dickens Broadstairs. Another in Portsmouth. Charles Dickens (1812–70) was one of the out-standing writers of fiction of the nineteenth century, and the most popular. In a string of novels such as the *Pickwick Papers* (1836–37), *Oliver Twist* (1838), *Nicholas Nickleby* (1839), *The Old Curiosity Shop* (1841), *Barnaby Rudge* (1841), *Martin Chuzzlewit* (1843), *Dombey and Son* (1848), *David Copperfield* (1850), *Bleak House* (1853), *Hard Times* (1854), *Little Dorritt* (1857), *A Tale of Two Cities* (1859), *Great Expectations* (1861), *The Mystery of Edwin Drood* (1870) he created hundreds of memorable characters, many of whom give their names to English pubs. This is only fitting, since the English inn features strongly throughout his books. These Dickensian pub names are listed separately in this book. Here one may note that Dickens occurs at Gravesend, Southend and near the Tower of London.

Charles II Bestwood, near Nottingham and elsewhere. Charles II (1630–85) was forced to flee the country when his father, Charles I, was defeated by the Roundheads. He was recalled to England at the Restoration in 1660. He is popularly remembered for his cavalier approach to life, and for his association with Nell Gwynn (also honoured by pubs named after her, especially in the Nottingham area). Nell was only one of his many mistresses, by whom he had several children, though he had no legitimate heir. He was eventually succeeded by his brother, James II. One illegitimate son was made Duke of St Albans, and is commemorated as such by a pub in London NW5. Charles II is shown on the sign of the King's Arms at Ockley, Sry. He is shown breathing down Nell Gwynn's neck and helping himself to one of her oranges.

Charles the First London N1. Charles I (1600–49) was the unfortunate king who became embroiled in the struggle between the throne and parliament which led to the Civil War. Charles was defeated at Marston Moor (1644) and Naseby (1645). He fell into the hands of the parliamentarians, was tried and convicted by them of treason. He was beheaded in 1649.

Charles Turnbull Stannington, near Sheffield. Mr Turnbull was formerly a director of the Tetley Walker brewery.

Charles XII Heslington, near York. A locally-owned racehorse of this name won the St Leger in 1839. It went on to win seventy more races during the following six years.

Charlie Brown's London E14. The unofficial name of the Railway Tavern, commemorating the 'uncrowned king of Limehouse' who died in 1933. He was the former licensee here. The pub has a world-wide collection of curios contributed by seamen. *See also* Curiosity Vaults.

Charlie Butler London SW14. The former head horse-keeper of Young's, the Wandsworth brewers, who retired in 1966 after forty-five years with the company. Charlie collected over 5,000 prizes in show rings all over the country when he appeared with the Brewery's black shires. He died in 1981.

Charlie Chaplin London SE1. Sir Charles Chaplin (1889–1977) was probably the best-known comedian in the world for most of his life, thanks to his screen performances after 1914. He spent most of his working life in the USA. There is a Chaplin's in Edinburgh and a Chaplin Arms at Lincoln.

Charlie Parker's Edinburgh. Charlie Parker (1920–55) was an outstanding jazz musician, an alto-sax player.

Charlie's Barn Beeston, near Nottingham. This pub is a converted pet-food warehouse. It is a fun-pub offering various kinds of entertainment in the evenings for Charlies and anyone else who cares to drop in.

Charlton Cat Charlton, Wilts. The pub was earlier the Poore's Arms, with a sign which was supposed to depict a heraldic 'lion rampant'. The new name reflected local opinion of the sign-painter's efforts.

Chartist Skelmanthorpe, near Huddersfield. A reference to William Lovett or Francis Place, who drafted the *People's Charter* (1838). Chartism was a working-men's reform movement, nearly all of the reforms having since been put into effect.

Chase Newtown, Staffs. Cannock Chase is nearby. At York the pub name refers to the local racecourse.

Chaser Shipbourne, near Tonbridge. Originally the New Inn, said to have been renamed to honour a popular trainer at the Fairlawne Racing Stables.

Chaucer *See* Geoffrey Chaucer.

Chauntry Coventry. An older spelling of 'chantry', with the meaning of a small chapel endowed by a wealthy person in order that masses might be chanted there on his behalf.

Cheddar Cheese Reading. The best-known of the English cheeses, popular in pubs as elsewhere. Cheddar is a village in Somerset.

Cheddar Valley Wells. A reference to the Cheddar Valley and Yatton Railway, opened in 1860.

Cheekie Chappie London SW9. A tribute to the music-hall comedian Max Miller, who was actually Harold Sargent (1895–1963). He was universally known as 'the cheeky chappie'. The spelling of 'cheekie' was no doubt used to make a visual match with 'chappie'.

Cheese Rollers Shurdington, near Cheltenham. The sign depicts the local Whit Monday race to secure a cheese which has been rolled from the top of a hill. The race, said to date from the sixteenth century, was originally a reminder of the traditional right to graze sheep on common land. The prize is a Double Gloucester cheese together with a cash bonus.

Cheesewring Minions, Corn. A 'wring' is variously a cider-press, wine-press or cheese-press. Here the reference is not to an actual wring, but to a granite rock formation nearby, 1250 feet high, which happens to resemble one, with large rocks being held up by smaller ones.

Chelsea Potter London SW3. This was the Commercial Tavern until 1958. It was renamed in commemoration of the Chelsea potters, who made Chelsea porcelain famous in the eighteenth century.

Chequered Flag Loddington, near Kettering and elsewhere. The Loddington pub is headquarters of the Mid-Northants Car Club. No doubt other pubs of the name have connections with motor sport, the chequered flag being used to signal that drivers have completed a race.

Chequers London N17 and elsewhere. An ancient tavern sign which was probably brought to Britain by the Romans Evidence from Pompeii suggests that it was already in use there, perhaps referring to a game such as draughts played on the premises. The sign was later associated with a money-table, and indeed the word 'exchequer' originally meant a kind of chessboard. Some inns may have used the sign to indicate that they were ready to change money or act as bankers in some way. Brewer in his *Dictionary of Phrase and Fable* rightly points out a heraldic connection by remarking that the head of the Fitzwarrens, whose coat of arms showed chequered squares, had the privilege of licensing alehouses in the reign of Edward IV. In the village of Lytchett Matravers, Dors, the sign relates to the chequered battle-flag of the Duke of Arundel. At Prestwood, Bucks, the sign shows Gladstone and Disraeli, reminding us that *Chequers* has been since 1921 the country seat of the British prime minister. Neither of those men would have used it in that capacity, of course, but at least they are both former prime ministers.

Cherry Arbour Also Cherry Gardens, Cherry Grove, Cherry Orchard, Cherry Tree, Cherry Trees, Cherrymount Tavern, Cherrywood. *See* Fruits and Vegetables.

Cherry Pickers Cheriton, near Folkestone. The nickname of the 11th Hussars, attributed by them to the colour of the Regiment's breeches. It is true that they were also known as the *Cherubims* (Lord Cardigan called them the *Cherry Bums*), but the origin of *Cherry Pickers* almost certainly goes back to an embarrassing incident in which a detachment was surprised by the French cavalry while picking cherries. The bravery of these men was never in question, and it was they who charged the Russians at Balaclava in the famous Charge of the Light Brigade. The regiment was at one time stationed at Shornecliffe camp, not far from the pub.

Cherub Dartmouth. The pub has a carved wooden sign taken from a schooner which used, to export wool. It was mainly ship's timbers which were used to build the original establishment (1380).

Cherwell Oxford. The name of a local river. The sign shows a punter who is about to fall in.

Chesapeake and Shannon Todmorden, W Yorks. A reference to a naval engagement during the war between Britain and America. In 1813 the *Chesapeake* was captured outside Boston Harbour by the *Shannon* and towed to Halifax in Nova Scotia. The British kept both the name and ship. The same incident is responsible for the Shannon pub name at Buckles-ham, Suffolk. It was built by a local squire who took part in the action. The Two Ships at Rochdale also commemorates this engagement.

Cheshire Cat Ellesmere Port, Ches. The first reference to 'grinning like a Cheshire cat' was in 1770, but no-one has been able to explain why cats in Cheshire should grin more than cats elsewhere. The phrase is now usually associated with the character created by Lewis Carroll in *Alice's Adventures in Wonderland* (1865).

Cheshire Cheese Hyde and Middlewich, Ches and elsewhere. For the well-known cheese which fittingly accompanies many of the drinks on sale. The most famous pub of this name (with some justification) is now Ye Olde Cheshire Cheese in London's Fleet Street. Its historical associations, with Dr Samuel Johnson and others, make it an essential port of call on any visit to London.

Cheshire Lines Southport. After the railway branch line which ran from Cheshire to Southport. There is a similar Cheshire Midland at Hale, near Altrincham.

Cheshire Ring Hyde. Formerly the Navigation. The present name retains a link with the canal system, referring to the fact that it forms a ring around the county.

Cheshire Yeoman *See* Yeoman.

Chesser Edinburgh. John Chesser was lord provost of Edinburgh (1919–21).

Chester Cup Plymouth. A horse-racing trophy.

Chevin Near Otley, W Yorks. The Chevin Hill is a local landmark.

Chevy Chase London E15. The reference is to an ancient ballad about the Battle of Otterburn fought at the village of Otterburn in Northumberland in 1388. *Chevy Chase* is a mysterious expression which may be a corruption of French *chevauchée*, now meaning a

tournament but applied at that time to raids by the French allies on France. The word 'chivy' lives on in local dialect for a skirmish.

Chieftain Morecambe. A transferred ship name. The ship had an American Indian chief as its figurehead.

Childe of Hale Hale, Ches. John Middleton (1578–1623) was born here and grew to be nearly eight feet tall. He achieved some fame as a wrestler, being taken to the court of James I and matched against the king's own champion. Middleton won the series of bouts.

Children's Inn Hollins Moor, Ches. Unlicensed premises which are run by Girl Guides, who stay there for their holidays. It is financed by well-wishers from all over the world, but sells to its young customers nothing stronger than ginger beer. It was originally a normal pub, the Hare and Hounds. Its present sign illustrates the nursery-rhyme, *The Cat and the Fiddle. See also* Milestone.

Chiltern Hundreds Maidstone. A 'hundred' is technically a division of a county which has its own court. The Chiltern Hundreds are significant because a member of parliament who wishes to resign applies for their stewardship. The steward was originally appointed to control the robberies that were occurring in the forested Chiltern Hills. Since the Chiltern Hundreds constitute a tract of Crown land, the stewardship is held to be an office of profit under the Crown. A member of parliament who accepts such office is obliged to vacate his seat.

Chimes London E14. *The Chimes*, a moral tale by Charles Dickens similar to *The Christmas Carol*, was published in 1844, but pubs of this name may simply refer to local church bells. It was the bells of St Dunstan's which are said to have suggested the title to Dickens himself. Northwich has a Witton Chimes; the sign showing a church steeple in the area.

Chimes of Taxal Taxal, Derbs. The unusual place name makes the pub name unusual in its turn. It is said to derive from a personal name, Tatuc, a diminutive of Tata, perhaps the lady of that name who married Edwin, king of Northumbria in the seventh century.

Chimney Boy Faversham, Kent. Chimney boys were sent up into chimneys to clean them, an undertaking that was unhealthy and dangerous. After yet another death of a boy in 1875, Lord Shaftesbury finally managed to stop the exploitation of boys in this way.

Chimney Corner Kempston Hardwick, Beds. In 1981 eighteen industrial chimneys were simultaneously demolished. The event was noted in the *Guinness Book of Records* and brought about this pub name.

China Clipper West Bromwich. Also China Ship, Wapping. The clippers (ships which sailed along at a fast clip) which formerly traded between London and China.

Chindit Wolverhampton. A mythical beast, half lion, half eagle, which is often represented on Burmese pagodas. The *Chindits* were a brigade who fought behind the Japanese lines in Burma during World War Two.

Chine Shanklin, IOW. The deep, narrow ravine cut by water in soft rock and known as a 'chine' is a feature of the Hampshire area. Shanklin Chine, on the Isle of Wight, is particularly well known.

Chiswell Vaults London EC1. The pub is in Chiswell Street, which is said to have been named for a 'choice well' which was there in the twelfth century. This legend is solemnly repeated by Gillian Bebbington in her *London Street Names*, though she normally is reliable. The real origin here is Old English *ceosel*, 'gravel', and refers to stony ground.

Chocolate Poodle Littleton Pannel, Wilts. Formerly the Black Dog, but the licensee's wife bred toy poodles.

Chopper London SW11. The pub is near the heliport and the sign shows a helicopter in flight. 'Chopper' was originally an American slang term for the helicopter but is now generally used. There is a Chopper Arms at Middle Wallop, Hants, near the Army Aviation Centre.

Chosen Churchdown, Glos. Chosen Hill is nearby, but 'Chosen' is simply the traditional local pronunciation of Churchdown.

Chough Salisbury. Also Choughs, Chard, Som, Cornish Chough, Porth, near Newquay, Cornish Choughs, Treswithian, near Camborne, Three Choughs, Hendford, near Yeovil and Blandford, Dors. A name which describes several members of the crow family, but usually applied to the red-legged crow which frequents the sea-cliffs in many parts of Britain, especially Cornwall, where the bird is protected. A chough also occurs as part of the Cornish arms and in other coats of arms. The spirit of King Arthur is said to have entered into a chough after his death. The bird is also said to have been a Royalist symbol during the Civil War.

Christopher Bath. Another at Eton. The patron saint of travellers. It was commonly believed in medieval times that anyone who looked at an image of St Christopher would come to no harm that day. His picture therefore frequently adorned church walls. It is perhaps surprising that more inns were not given his name, with signs portraying him.

Church and State Denstroude, near Canterbury. A declaration of loyalty to both.

Church Elm *see* **Elm.**

Church House Stokenham, Devon. A pub name found mainly in Devon, where more than fifty still exist. Originally these were houses which lodged masons and the like who helped build church towers and belfries. Later they were communal houses used for celebrations, which the Puritans, especially, did not want to occur in the churches themselves. One of the oldest inns of this kind is at Churchstow, near Kingsbridge. It reputedly dates from 1294 and served then as a hostelry for the Benedictine monks of Buckfast Abbey.

Churchill Bamford, near Rochdale and elsewhere. *See* Sir Winston Churchill. The Churchill Arms at Paxton, Glos is for Captain Edward Spencer Churchill, local squire and bachelor cousin of Sir Winston. He lived nearby until his death in 1964.

Churchillian Portsdown Hill, Portsmouth. A pub built by Mr Frank Fitt on the South Downs overlooking Portsmouth, and named to commemorate his Churchillian struggle to obtain a full licence. He finally won through in 1969 after thirteen applications.

Church Inn Ludlow and elsewhere. There is a pub close to most churches, and perhaps nothing should be said about which has the larger congregation. *Church Inn* was especially popular in pre-war days in the north of England, where many still remain.

Church Stile Sowerby Bridge, near Halifax. Such a stile would allow people to pass but protect the church grounds from cattle. Presumably the pub was named because one was nearby.

Church Wickets Dawley, Salop. The wickets referred to are small gates or doors. A 'wicket' is properly a small door which forms part of a larger one. It allows a single person at a time to pass through while the main door remains shut.

Cinque Ports Seaford, E Ssx. Another in Hastings. Also Cinque Ports Arms, Dover and elsewhere in Kent. The Cinque Ports ('five ports') were Hastings, Romney, Hythe, Dover and Sandwich. They were chartered by Edward the Confessor to provide ships and men to defend England against invasion. Because of silting, only Hastings and Dover are still ports.

Circus Tavern Manchester. After the well-known Belle Vue Circus, based in Manchester.

Cissbury Worthing. The name of a famous earthwork, the largest in England, which is close by.

City Arms Canterbury. Another at Wells in Somerset. The Wells pub was formerly used as the city jail but has had bars of a different kind since 1841.

City Barge London W4. The original inn was granted a 500-year charter by Elizabeth I. The pub name derives from the mooring nearby of the official barge of the lord mayor of London.

City Frog Lichfield, Staffs. Formerly the City Gate. The name change was presumably influenced by the name of the street in which the pub stands, Frog Lane.

City of London Dymchurch, Kent. Commemorates a ship of this name which was wrecked here in the eighteenth century.

City of London Yeoman *See* Yeoman.

City of Quebec London W1. The pub is in Old Quebec Street, so named for the chapel built in 1787 to commemorate the battle of Quebec. It was used as an army chapel but was demolished in 1912.

City of Rome London N1. The name was no doubt suggested by the pub's address, in Roman Way. The street name commemorates a Roman fort which was there.

City of York London NW1. The pub is in York Way, beside King's Cross station. The station was built in the 1850s for the Great Northern Railway Company, formerly the London and York.

City Pride London EC2. Formerly the Marlborough, but converted in 1972 into a nineteenth-century 'Cockney palace'. At London W1 there is a similar Cockney Pride.

City Slicker Walsall. The interior of the pub focuses on the city slickers of the 1920s rather than the present day. The phrase refers to the supposedly sophisticated people who live in big cities and are always slickly dressed.

Clachan London EC4. A curious name to find in the centre of London. It derives from a Gaelic word meaning 'stone' and means, in Scotland, 'a small village'.

Clanger London EC3. The Bishopsgate fire-station was formerly nearby, and the clanging of the fire-engine bells was frequently heard. The pub's theme is the Great Fire of London. Bristol has a Clangers, which was the Bell until 1983.

Clapgate Kearby. W Yorks A local term for a toll-gate.

Clarence Staines, GL and elsewhere. Similar signs are Duke of Clarence, Derby and elsewhere. Royal Clarence, Devonport and elsewhere. Royal Midshipman, London EC1, Royal Sailor, Bath, Royal Tar, Brentford, Sailor Prince, London SW7, Nautical William, Fenn Green, Salop. All refer to William IV before he became king. He had a short naval career and briefly took his seat in the House of Lords as Duke of Clarence. *See* King William IV for further details. Some *Clarence* signs show the four-wheeled carriage which was named after him. A good example is at Colchester.

Clarence Harbour Norwich. In 1827 there was a scheme to construct a canal from Norwich to Lowestoft. The coming of the railways made the scheme unnecessary. This pub stands where the harbour would have been at the Norwich end of the proposed canal. The scheme had been given the blessing of the Duke of Clarence, and the harbour would have been named after him.

Clarendon Chale, IOW. The pub is also known as the Wight Mouse. Clarendon refers to the various earls of Clarendon. The 1st Earl, Edward Hyde (1609–74) bequeathed the copyright of his books to Oxford University, and profits from it were used to found the Clarendon Press. He was chancellor of the university 1660–67.

Claro Beagle Harrogate. The Claro beagles are a local pack of hounds. Beagles are normally used to hunt hares, the field following on foot. *See also* Trinity Foot.

Claycutters Arms Chudleigh Knighton, S Devon. There was formerly a china-clay industry in this area. Associated pub names are Mountain and White Pyramid.

Claymore Edinburgh. There is another pub of this name in Sheffield, where claymores were manufactured. Originally a claymore (from Gaelic words meaning 'great sword') was a large, one-handed, two-edged sword. In modern times the word has been applied to the basket-hilted swords worn by officers of the Highland regiments.

Clay Pigeon Chelmsford. Another at Eastcote, GL. The plate-shaped object which is thrown up into the air by a sprung trap to be shot at in the sport of clay-pigeon shooting. The only connection with pigeons, for which the latter are no doubt thankful, is that the clay discs substitute for them.

Cleave Lustleigh, Devon. The local rock formation and tourist attraction which overlooks the village.

Clem Attlee London SW6. Clement Attlee was leader of the Labour Party and became prime minister in 1945. He served in that role until 1951, and was created 1st Earl Attlee in 1955. He died in 1967.

Cleopatra Lewes. E Ssx. Cleopatra (69 BC–30 BC) was Queen of Egypt, and is one of the most romantic figures in history. She was married, according to the usual custom, to her brother, and when he was drowned, to her younger brother, but she is mainly remembered as being the mistress of Julius Caesar and later of Mark Antony. There is little doubt that Cleopatra was a most alluring woman, though she may not have been especially beautiful. The real events of her life have been rather distorted by literary treatments, notably that of Shakespeare in

Antony and Cleopatra, and by G B Shaw in *Caesar and Cleopatra*.

Cleveland Bay Eston, near Middlesborough and Redcar. Bloodgood and Santini describe this breed of horse in their *Horseman's Dictionary* as 'a heavy harness horse evolved in the North Yorkshire (Cleveland) district.' Such horses have 'Arab blood crossed with native English, Spanish and Scandinavian stock'. In earlier times the breed was known as the Chapman or Yorkshire Packhorse.

Cleveland Tontine *See* Tontine.

Clicker Weston Favell, near Northampton. A term from the local shoe-making industry, defined by Partridge as 'a foreman shoemaker apportioning leather to the workmen'. The same term is applied in the printing industry to the foreman who distributes copy to the compositors. There is a Clickers at Leicester.

Clipper Birkenhead and elsewhere. Also Clippers Arms, Walton Highway, Cambs, Clipper Way Falmouth. The clipper was the fastest type of sailing ship. It originated in the USA, especially at Baltimore. For a long time clippers dominated long-distance sea routes, often racing each other. For a while they were faster than steamships, but their days were numbered when the steamships improved their performances in the 1860s. The *Clippers Arms* pub mentioned above has a double-interpretation sign, with a fully-rigged clipper on one side and a sheep-shearing scene on the other. The *Clipper Way* refers to the voyage by Sir Francis Chichester, when he followed the old clipper route. One famous clipper was the Cutty Sark.

Clive Arms *See* Lord Clive.

Clock House London SW11. The pub has a clock on its front roof. Its dial is reproduced on the inn sign.

Clock Tower Clevedon, Som. The tower referred to was given to the town in 1897 by Sir Edmund Elton to mark the Diamond Jubilee of Queen Victoria.

Clog and Billycock Pleasington, near Blackburn. This pub was earlier the Bay Horse but now bears as its official name what was a nickname locally for thirty years. It came about because the licensee Alfred Pomfret invariably wore clogs and a billycock. The clogs were specially made and designed by his brother. A billycock is a kind of bowler hat. Clogs are something of a local feature in this area, marked by other pub names nearby such as Clog and Shawl at Rochdale and Cloggers Arms in Failsworth.

Closed Shop Walkley, near Sheffield. A humorous reminder that this pub once had to close for a short time because the licence had not been renewed.

Clothiers Arms Stroud, Glos. Many master-weavers who had fled from France in the seventeenth century settled in the area of the Cotswolds. The Stroud valley still supplies fine cloth for military and religious use.

Clothworkers Arms London N1. The Clothworkers Company has been in existence since the sixteenth century. In 1677 the Master of the Clothworkers was Samuel Pepys.

Clown Hastings. A tribute to Joseph Grimaldi (1779–1837), the most famous clown of his day.

Club Ely, Cambs. The pub was formerly a sporting club with a gymnasium for boxers and others.

Clydesdale Debden, Esx. A breed of heavy draught horse, first bred in the Clyde valley. It is usually dark brown or light bay with white blaze or stripe and white hind stockings.

Coach and Eight London SW15. The annual Oxford and Cambridge boat race begins nearby. The pub has many old prints, photographs and other mementos related to the history of rowing. There is a pub of the same name, with a sign showing a rowing eight, in the city of Durham.

Coach and Horses London and elsewhere. A common pub name in all parts of Britain since the seventeenth century. There are more than fifty in the London area. Before that there had been private coaches. The arrival of Hackney carriages, forerunners of modern taxis, and later the introduction of stagecoaches meant that there was plenty of traffic on the roads. Inns

were natural stopping places, providing refreshments for both horses and humans. Variant names include Coach and Six, Birdsall, W Yorks, and Mail Coach, Odsal at Bradford. Many inns were named after famous stage-coaches, such as the Gloucester Flying Machine, Dairy Maid, and Red Rover at Northampton.

Coach House Locking, Avon. The private coach used by Sir John Plumley, executed in 1685 for his part in the abortive Monmouth Rebellion, is still kept in the inn yard.

Coachmakers Arms London W1. The Coachmakers Company was incorporated in 1677, in the reign of Charles II.

Coachman Snainton, near Scarborough. The coachman would have been a regular caller at this inn as he travelled from Harrogate and York on his way to Scarborough. This was the last staging-post before he reached his destination.

Coach Stop London N12. The pub is next to a bus terminus.

Coal Exchange Fareham, Hants. A place where merchants met to buy and sell coal.

Coalheavers Arms *See* Coal Hole.

Coal Hole London WC2. In the early nineteenth century the pub was a popular rendezvous for the coalheavers who worked the Thames barges. Peterborough has a similar Coalheavers Arms.

Coal House Apperley, Glos. Coal was formerly brought down river from Stourport to a nearby wharf. The sign shows men carrying sacks of coal from barge to warehouse.

Coal Miners Arms Clow's Top, Bewdley. A reminder that there was once a West Worcestershire coalfield, no longer worked.

Coat and Badge *See* Doggett Coat and Badge.

Cobblers Northampton. In honour of the local shoemakers and the local football team, who are known to their fans as the Cobblers. Presumably the pub also sells the drink known as a cobbler, a mixture of sherry, sugar, lemon and ice. There is also a cobbler's punch, which is gin and water with a little treacle or vinegar added. To a Cockney 'cobblers' means 'rubbish' because of rhyming slang – cobbler's awls=balls.

Cobblestones Bridgwater. A reminder of the time when town streets and inn-yards were paved with cobblestones, allowing horses to get a surer grip. 'Cobble' is related to 'cob', and refers to the rounded shape of the stones. Also Cobden Arms, Cobden's Head. *See* Richard Cobden.

Cobham Chatham. Also Cobham Arms, Halesowen. 'The good Lord Cobham', as he was known, was Sir John Oldcastle, who was hung in chains and burned alive on Christmas Day, 1417. His religious views had given offence. Shakes-peare originally tried to call Falstaff Sir John Oldcastle, but was obliged to change. The 10th Lord Cobham was tried and convicted in 1603 of conspiring with Raleigh and others to place Arabella Stuart on the throne. He was reprieved at the scaffold, and later died in poverty. A more fortunate bearer of this name was Sir Alan Cobham, knighted in 1926 for his services to aviation.

Coble Newbiggin-by-sea, Northld. There is also a Yorkshire Coble at Redcar. The coble is a sea-fishing boat with a flat bottom, square stern and lug sail, used chiefly in the North-East of England. In Scotland the word also refers to a short, flat-bottomed rowing boat used for crossing rivers.

Cob Tree Ightham, Kent. The sign shows a cob horse – one with short legs and a broad back – beside a cob-nut tree.

Coburg Torquay and elsewhere. Also Coburg Arms, Portsmouth, Coburg Tavern, Leeds. Some of these signs show Prince Albert, who was the second son of the Duke of Saxe–Coburg–Gotha. The Torquay sign is for a later duke of that name who was port admiral at Plymouth 1890–93.

Cobweb Boscastle, Corn. The pub was formerly a wine-bottle warehouse. Some of the cobwebs from that time are preserved in the bar. The Cobwebs in Richmond, Sry, was obliged by the local magistrates in the mid-nineteenth century to remove the cobwebs from the ceiling, which had become a great tourist attraction, in the interests of hygiene. An enlarged clipping from the local newspaper of the time, relating the incident, hangs in the bar. A 'cobweb' was originally a 'copweb', 'cop' in this sense meaning 'spider'.

Cock London and elsewhere. Also Cock Tavern, London EC1. An ancient tavern sign in use since the fourteenth century. Often an indication in the past that cock-fighting took place in the yard. In the seventeenth century the sign may also have advertised the sale of cock-ale, which was 'ale mixed with the jelly of minced meat of a boiled cock, besides other ingredients'. The sign at Stroud Green, Esx depicts the Leghorn breed of fowl. Associated names, are Cock at Highbury, London N5, Cock o' Barton, near Malpas, Ches, Cock of Tupsley, near Hereford.

Cock and Bottle Great Gaddesden, Herts. This sign traditionally proclaimed that both draught and bottled beer was available. The 'cock' in this case was the spigot or peg which was used to draw off beer from the barrel. The expression 'cock-a-hoop' may be derived from it. It is said that the cock was removed from the barrel and laid on one of hoops, so that the beer could flow freely.

Cock and Lion London W1. Originally called the Lion. The *Cock* was added to the name to commemorate the cockpit which used to be outside the pub.

Cock and Pye Ipswich. Thought to be a reference to peacock pie, a medieval dish for the wealthy. Later misunderstanding may have caused it to become Cock and Magpie, as at Old Whittington, near Chesterfield. On the other hand, 'by Cock and pie' was a common oath in Elizabethan times. 'Cock' was here a euphemism for 'God', and 'pie' referred to the ordinal, or rule-book, of the Catholic Church.

Cock and Trumpet Hartshill, Stoke-on-Trent. A common association for the Elizabethan poets, the most famous instance occurring in *Hamlet*, Act 1, scene 1: 'I have heard/The cock, that is the trumpet to the morn,/Doth with his lofty and shrill-sounding throat/Awake the god of day.'

Cock Beck Leeds. The name of a river in West Yorkshire. Ekwall argues learnedly in his *English River Names* that the origin probably lies in Welsh *cog* 'cuckoo' and not cock, 'male bird'. 'Beck' is a general word for a 'brook' or 'stream'.

Cocked Hat Aspley, Nottingham. The pub sign shows two aspects of the tricorn, or three-sided hat with the brim permanently turned up On one side it is worn by an admiral, while on the other side it is worn by a general. The sign had the rare distinction of being painted by an RA, Ralph Ellis, in 1933.

Cock Horse Banbury. A reference to the traditional nursery rhyme beginning 'Ride a Cock horse to Banbury Cross'. This in turn refers to travellers who hired a horse at the Cock in Stony Stratford in order to ride to Banbury.

Cock of the North Potters Bar and elsewhere. George, 5th Duke of Gordon (1770–1836) raised the Gordon Highlanders in 1795 and commanded the regiment thereafter. The name had earlier been bestowed on Alexander Gordon, 3rd Earl of Huntly, a Highland chieftain who died in 1524.

Cock o' the North Henleaze, Bristol. Named in 1967 as a tribute to the Bristol Caledonian Society, but *see* Cock of the North.

Cockney Pride London W1 and Cardiff. The pub presents a recreation of Victorian London. The modern Cockney is indeed proud of his name, though it began as a term of abuse for a townsman.

Cockpit London EC4. Cock-fights were held here until made illegal in 1849. The pub retains its former 'viewing gallery'.

Cock Robin Sale, Ches. Another at Swindon. The name appears to refer to the nursery-rhyme character, subject of a murder investigation.

Coconut Kingston-on-Thames. There was formerly a small factory nearby which made coconut-matting. This uses the coarse hair which surrounds and protects the outside of the nut.

Codrington Arms Yates, Bristol. *See* Admiral Codrington.

Cody's Tree Farnborough. The pub was opened in 1970 and recalls by its name the aeroplane trials made at the beginning of the century by Colonel S F Cody, who died in 1913. In order to measure the thrust of his engine, Cody attached his plane to a spring balance and tied the balance to a tree, It is the gnarled remains of this tree, standing at the end of the runway at Farnborough Aerodrome, which have inspired the pub name. The tree bears a plaque which recalls that Cody 'near this spot on 16 May 1908 made the first successful officially recorded flight'.

Coeur de Lion Bath. A French expression meaning 'heart of a lion'. It was the nickname for Richard I (Richard the Lion-Heart, 1157–99), earned by his valiant deeds during the Holy Wars.

Coffee House Liverpool and elsewhere. Coffee houses were social centres in the eighteenth century, especially. Some pubs bearing this name may formerly have been such meeting places. Similar names are Coffee Tavern in Redruth, and Coffee Pot, Yardley Gobion, Bucks and Downham Market, Nflk.

Coffy Johnny Newcastle-on-Tyne. One of the characters immortalised in *The Blaydon Races. See* Blaydon Races.

Coldstreamer Gulval, near Penzance. Commemorates Captain Michael Bolitho of the Coldstream Guards, killed in July 1940 in Algeria. He was in charge of a landing party in an action against the French naval squadron based at Oran.

Colet Arms London E1. John Colet (1466–1519) was Dean of St Paul's in 1505 and founder of St Paul's School. He was an eminent scholar who published a Latin grammar and other works.

Coliseum Derby. The pub was converted from the *Coliseum* cinema in 1962. 'Coliseum' itself is a form of 'colosseum', meaning gigantic, and refers ultimately to the famous amphitheatre of Vespasian in Rome.

Coll Bradford. There is a stream nearby called the Coll Beck, which may in turn have been named for some 'hazel trees' growing near it.

Colleen Bawn London SE16. The name of a play by Dion Boucicault in 1860, meaning 'fair-haired girl'. Sir Julius Benedict (1804–85) based his opera *The Lily of Killarney* on this work. The opera was produced in London and Dublin in 1862, New York in 1868. This pub has a predominantly Irish clientele, and includes a Killarney bar.

College Arms Quinton, near Stratford-on-Avon. Another at Eton. The Quinton pub displays the arms of Magdalen College, Oxford. Henry VIII gave the inn and its environs to that college. The pub at Eton naturally refers to the famous public school.

Collier Lad *See* Boldon Lad.

Collingwood Newcastle. Another at Thornaby-on-Tees. Also Lord Collingwood, Poppleton, near York, Collingwood Arms, Chirton, near Tynemouth. Cuthbury Collingwood (1750–1810), was born in Newcastle. He had a distinguished naval career, which included leading the British fleet into battle at Trafalgar. When Lord Nelson was killed in that battle, Collingwood assumed command.

Colonel Prior Moorside, Sunderland. The chairman of Sunderland Football Club, from early 1930s until 1951.

Colonies London SW1. A colonial style pub, decorated with skins and trophies from the days of the Raj, when Britain ruled India and the Empire.

Column Shrewsbury. The local column has a statue of Lord Hill of Hawkstone on it. He was second-in-command to Wellington at the Battle of Waterloo, and was born in this area.

Combermere Wolverhampton and elsewhere. Also Lord Combermere at London E2. Viscount Combermere (1773–1865) was a distinguished English soldier. He was severely wounded at the battle of Salamanca (1812) but went on to become commander-in-chief of the army in India in 1822.

Combination Names In the *Daily Courant*, 17 November 1728, an advertisement stated: 'Whereas Thomas Blackwell has removed from the Seven Stars on Ludgate Hill to the Black Lion and Seven Stars over the way . . . ', and therein lies a typical example of a strange-looking combination pub name coming into being. When a publican changed houses, he often took his sign with him and added it to the existing sign. We have not dealt separately with all such combinations in this book. They should be considered as two separate pub names and each part should be considered on its own.

Comedian Rotherham. After Sandy Powell (1898–1983), a locally born music-hall and radio entertainer whose catch-phrase was 'Can you hear me, Mother?'

Comedy London W1. The *Comedy* theatre is a few minutes' walk away.

Comet Shrewsbury and elsewhere. A name which can have several interpretations. The Shrewsbury sign relates it to a famous stage-coach. At Croft-on-Tees, near

Darlington it commemorates a prize shorthorn bull which was long ago sold for a thousand guineas. At Hatfield, Herts the reference is to the aircraft which was built at the nearby De Havilland factory. It flew to Australia in 1934 in just under three days, at an average speed of 160 mph. De Havilland later transferred the name to the world's first jet airliner (1952), which developed metal fatigue problems.

Comfortable Gill Leigh, Lancs. The glass of wine or other drink which gives comfort. The exact quantity of a 'gill' is supposed to be a quarter of a pint, but in Lancashire and Yorkshire the term is used for half a pint.

Commercial Killay, near Swansea and elsewhere. These were pubs and hotels where the commercial travellers of former times gathered in the evenings. The Killay sign shows an immaculate, top-hatted traveller depositing his Gladstone bag on the enquiry desk as he arrives. In the centre of Liverpool there is a Central Commercial.

Commodore Basildon and elsewhere. The naval title below rear-admiral also given to the senior captain of a shipping line or a wartime convoy. Perhaps, by implication, a pub so named is the leading one in the district. In some instances proximity to a yachting club may have suggested the name, the president of such a club being known by this title.

Commonwealth Caterham, Sry. The sign shows the flags of ten nations which are members of the British Commonwealth.

Compass Taunton and elsewhere. Also Compasses, Ludlow and elsewhere. Usually a reference to the compass or compasses which

appear in the arms of the masons (one), joiners (two) or carpenters (three). The sign may interpret the name instead as the kind of compass used by a mariner to guide his ship back to port. At Chickgrove, Wilts and Broadmayne, Dors there is a tradition that the original name was house or home of Compassion. Such institutions would not be homes for old people, but were originally hospices for travellers, especially pilgrims. *See also* Goat and Compasses.

Compass Rose Newquay. The name of the ship in the novel *Cruel Sea* by the South-African-born writer Nicholas Monsarrat. It was made into a film in 1953. The novel is also commemorated in the Cruel Sea, London NW3, which Mr Monsarrat opened.

Compleat Angler Marlow, Bucks. Another at Wirksworth, Derbyshire. The title of a book published in 1653 by Isaac Walton (1593–1683). Its secondary title was 'The Contemplative Man's Recreation', which indicated Walton's own nature. There is an Isaac Walton at Brimsdown, near Enfield, also at Creeswell, near Stafford and an Izaac Walton near one of his favourite spots, Dovedale, Derbys, and also at East Meon, Hants.

Conan Doyle Edinburgh. Sir Arthur Conan Doyle (1859–1930) is best known as the author of the Sherlock Holmes stories. He was also the author of many historical and other romances, and wrote a *History of Spiritualism* (1926). His fictional detective is commemorated in the Sherlock Holmes.

Concorde Bristol and elsewhere. The first supersonic airliner, first tested in 1968. The result of an Anglo–French co-operation, it is designed to carry 136 passengers at 1450 mph.

Coney Keston, Kent. Originally a name for a fully-grown rabbit, the latter term being used for a young animal. Now largely replaced by 'rabbit' except in some dialects and in heraldry. There is a **T**hree Conies at Thorpe Mandeville, near Banbury, another at Easingwold, near York. There may be a heraldic reference, but such signs were formerly used by poulterers.

Conquered Bear Oldham. A reference to the Oldham Improvement Act of 1826, which included a clause forbidding 'any bull, bear or other animal to be baited with dogs within the said township'.

Conquered Moon Salisbury. The pub opened a few days after the landing on the moon by Neil Armstrong and Edwin Aldrin, 20 July 1969.

Conquering Hero London SE19. There is another pub of the same name at Llantysilio, near Llangollen. The phrase, applied to a soldier returning from the war, comes from a poem by Thomas Morell (1703–84); 'See, the conquering hero comes! Sound the trumpets, beat the drums!'

Conqueror Epsom. Transferred from the name of a racehorse. The pub of the same name at Hove, E Ssx refers to William the Conqueror.

Cook's Ferry London N18. The sign shows Matthew Cook, who ran the ferry here in the late nineteenth century, making a crossing accompanied, as always, by his cats. Cook was far more interested in his cats than his fare-paying passengers, whom he ignored. His surly eccentricity became legendary in the area.

Coombe Cellars Combeinteignhead, Devon. A 'coombe' is a hollow or valley, though the precise meaning changes in different parts of the country. It can refer to the steep short valley running up from the sea coast, and often it refers to a valley closed at its head.

Cooperage Newcastle-on-Tyne. Formerly *Arthur's Cooperage*, and supplier of casks for local breweries.

Coopers Arms Newbury, Berks. Also Coopers, Mansfield and Cheltenham, Coopers Rest, Edinburgh The Coopers Company dates from the beginning of the sixteenth century. The ancient craft of making barrels, casks and tubs from staves and hoops now hardly survives in the brewing industry, thanks to the introduction of metal kegs.

Coot Horsham. A name given to several diving birds originally. Later applied to the Bald Coot, which has a white plate on its forehead – hence the expression 'as bald as a coot'. Locally applied to the water-rail and water-hen.

Copcut Elm Droitwich. A tree which has had its top cut off. 'Cop' in the sense of 'top' was especially used in the past to describe the top of a hill.

Copenhagen Tavern London N7. The original building was occupied by the Danish ambassador and his family in the seventeenth century. It stands in Camden Road, and in York Way there is a New Copenhagen.

Coppa Dolla Broadhempston, Devon. The pub has borrowed a nearby place-name, which in 1660 was recorded as *Coppadaller*. This in turn goes back to an Old English *coppede alor*, referring to an alder tree which had been pollarded.

Copper London SE1. The sign shows a London policeman on one side, a copper boiler on the other. Policemen became 'coppers' because they copped hold of criminals.

Copperfield *See* David Copperfield.

Copper Hearth Burton-on-Trent. The sign shows part of the interior of the Bass Brewery. The copper in brewing is the vessel in which the wort and the hops are boiled. In modern times it tends to be a closed stainless steel tank, heated by internal steam coils. It was formerly, and on rare occasions may still be, a vessel made of copper and heated by direct firing.

Copper Horse Windsor. Referring to the copper statue of George III on horseback which is nearby. Another pub of this name is at Seamer, near Scarborough.

Copper House Hayle, Corn. A reminder that copper mines were formerly of importance in the area. In the nineteenth century the Smelting Company used this pub as their headquarters. It was then called the Commercial. Workers in copper are mentioned in **Coppermans Arms**, Swansea, and Coppersmiths Arms, Portsmouth.

Copy Cat *See* Cat.

Coracle Penlan, near Swansea. Another at Shrewsbury. This small rowing-boat, made of wickerwork covered with watertight material, was used by the ancient Britons. It is easily carried on the shoulders and is still used by fishermen in parts of Wales and Ireland. 'Coracle' derives from a Celtic word meaning 'boat'.

Cordwainers Arms London N19. Cordwain was a kind of leather which came from Cordova, in Spain. The leather-workers who turned it into shoes and the like were granted arms in the sixteenth century. The arms show the heads of three goats. There is a similar Cordwainer at Kettering. Northants, relating to the local footwear industry. *See also* Curriers Arms.

Cormorant Portchester, Hants. The large black seabird, known for its voracious appetite. A (dubious) story relates that such a bird was shot and fell to earth outside the front door of this pub, causing its name to be changed from the Swan.

Corn Cob Rubery, W Mids. A corn cob is the woody central part of an ear of maize. In former times the bowls of tobacco pipes were sometimes made from them.

Corn Dolly Cornmarket, Oxford. The female symbol of the corn spirit made from the last sheaf to be harvested, carried home ceremoniously from the fields and kept in the farm kitchen until the next harvest. The sign of this pub turns away from this traditional meaning of a straw figure and shows a 'dolly bird' with corn in her hair.

Corner House Oxford and elsewhere. A pub which is on a corner, though the sign-painter for the Oxford pub decided to show a footballer taking a corner kick.

Corner Pin London N17. A reference to the popular pub game of skittles, the 'corner pin' being the outside pin and the most difficult to knock down.

Corner Shop Manchester. The pub incorporates alcoves where various items of food and drink can be purchased.

Cornet of Horse London SW11. This was formerly the term for the lowest commissioned rank in the British Cavalry regiments. The name referred to his carrying of the cornet, the troop's standard or colours, and had nothing to do with playing the cornet. The term is no longer used.

Cornflower *see* Flowers.

Cornish Plymouth. A straightforward declaration. Cornish Arms is more common, eg Bodmin and elsewhere. *See* Fifteen Balls.

Cornish Chough Also Cornish Choughs. *See* Choughs.

Cornkist Stirling. In Scotland a cornkist is a chest containing grain in a stable. Cornkister, however, is a farm-worker's song of his life and work. The pub stands in the centre of a grain-farming area.

Cornopean Weymouth. This musical instrument, the forerunner of the cornet, is shown on the signboard. It is a treble-sounding brass valve-instrument, more tapering in shape than a trumpet.

Corn Rigg Ayr. In Scotland a corn-rig(g) is a ridge or strip of land on which oats are grown (oats being described as 'corn' in Scotland).

Cornubia Camborne and elsewhere. A Latin form of Cornwall. It gives the adjective Cornubian, 'of Cornwall'. The Camborne sign shows the arms of the Duke of Cornwall; the one at Hayle is for the locally-built *Cornubia* which sailed between Hayle and Bristol (where there is also a sign) in the late nineteenth century.

Cornucopia Southend. The cornu-copia is the horn of plenty, and presumably implies here that there is a plentiful supply of everything a customer could wish for waiting inside. *See also* Good Intent.

Cornwallis Bristol and elsewhere. Charles, 1st Marquis Cornwallis (1738–1805) was a British general who led the Carolina Campaign during the American Revolution. Later he was forced to surrender at Yorktown, which ended the fighting. He became governor general of India and viceroy to Ireland. Bethnal Green has a Marquis of Cornwallis. In London E3 there is a Marquis Cornwallis.

Cornwall's Gate St Budeaux, near Plymouth. The pub is alongside the new Tamar Bridge opened in 1982 which connects Devon and Cornwall. At nearby Millpoint is the Devon and Cornwall.

Corsair Birkenhead. Another at Luton. The 'corsair' is a pirate, though the word can also be applied to the ship he sails. The sign at Birkenhead shows a fierce-looking pirate with his cutlass raised aloft.

Corvette North Shields. In modern times, a small naval escort vessel, used during World War Two to protect convoys against submarine attacks. *See also* Compass Rose.

Cossack Sheffield. There is another at Langstock, Hants. A famous racehorse, winner of the Derby in 1847.

Costermonger Birmingham. A term usually associated with London, where the costermonger is a person who sells fruit and vegetables from a street barrow. The name arose from the selling of apples known as costards. The costers later became known as barrow men, then barrow boys.

Cotes Mill Cotes, Leics. The pub is a recent conversion from a watermill.

Cothi Bridge Pont-ar-Gothi, Dyfed. The pub is beside the river Cothi.

Cotswold Charlton Kings, near Cheltenham. Also Cotswold Arms, Burford. The Cotswolds are a range of hills in Gloucestershire, noted for their sheep pastures. There is also a special breed of long-woolled sheep named after them.

Cott Dartington, Devon. Johannes Cott was a prominent man in nearby Totnes in the fourteenth century. He regularly passed this inn, or its site, with his packhorses, transporting the produce of his mines and farms to Totnes. Daniel Defoe is said to have written *Robinson Crusoe* while staying here.

Cottage of Content Carey, near Hereford, and elsewhere. The Carey example was originally one of three cottages built for labourers by the Mynor family in the fifteenth century. It was stipulated that it should be maintained as an ale and cider parlour. The other instances are no doubt meant to conjure up a sentimental atmosphere of rural bliss.

Cottar's Howff Edinburgh. The Scottish cottar is a farm-worker who gives his labour in exchange for his cottage. The howff is a haunt or resort, so the pub name may be interpreted as 'a place where farm-labourers gather'. There is a similar Cottar Hoose at Elgin. The Cotters in Luton may well have been influenced by Robert Burns's poem *The Cotter's Saturday Night*.

Cotton Picker Manchester. A reference to the important local cotton industry. Cotton Tree at Bury is a similar name, though the cotton tree is not like the cotton plant. It bears a kind of down which is not fit for spinning.

Countess Wear Exeter. A reference to the countess's weir, built across the River Exe in the fourteenth century by Countess Isabella Courtney. City merchants had refused to pay her taxes for taking their ships into port. She owned land on both sides of the river below Exeter itself.

Countryman Chipping, Herts. The name of the pub is fully supported by the pictures of horses and dogs inside, together with gins, sickles and billhooks. A Yokel beer is also

available. Other pubs of this name at Hinckley, Newbold Verdon and Sharnford, all in Leicestershire. Shipley, W Ssx has a Countryman's Tavern.

County Ground Swindon. The pub is halfway between the town's football club ground and the county's cricket club ground, but takes its name from the County Road opposite.

County Tavern Northampton. Close to the ground of the county cricket club, also used by the local football club.

Courtenay Arms Newton Abbot. Courtenay is the family name of the earls of Devon.

Court Jester Hampton, GL. The sign shows Will Somers, who was court jester to Henry VIII. The court itself was at Hampton Court Palace, which is nearby.

Covenanter Falkland, Fife. Also Covenanters, Edinburgh. This term applies to the Scottish Presbyterians who entered into various agreements with a view to protecting their own religious interests and furthering its influence. The *Solemn League and Covenant* of 1643, for instance, pledged the Scots and the English parliamentarians to preserve Presbyterianism in Scotland and establish it in England and Ireland. Such covenants were declared unlawful in 1662 and the covenanters were persecuted. Many resisted fanatically.

Cover *See* Cricket.

Coverdale Paignton. Miles Coverdale (1488–1568) was the first man to translate the whole of the Bible into English. The work took him fifteen years. The inn sign shows him with one of the bibles which Henry VIII ordered to be chained to the lectern in every parish church.

Covered Wagon Moseley, Birmingham. A modern 'theme' pub. It has a very fine sculptured sign showing a wagon team.

Cow and Snuffers Llandaff North, near Cardiff. The sign shows a red cow with a gigantic pair of candle-snuffers at her feet. The name is said to have arisen as a result of a bet made in the eighteenth century concerned with pairing together unrelated subjects.

Cowherds Southampton. The inn was converted from cowherds' cottages in the eighteenth century.

Cowper Arms Cole Green, Herts. Also Cowper's Oak, Weston Underwood, Bucks; William Cowper, Digswell, Herts. William Cowper (1731–1800) was an English poet, subject to melancholia. His poetry was mostly religious or rural; his letters were also much admired.

Cow Roast Wigginton, Herts. The inn was formerly a drovers' halt on the road from Aylesbury to London. 'Cows' rest' is said to have been corrupted into the present name.

Crab Apple *See* Apples.

Crab Mill Preston Bagot, Warks. The mill here was a cider mill, but the crab refers not to crab-apples, but to a kind of winch known as a crab because of the way its arms project. The crab would have been used to haul up the pulp and allow it to drain off.

Crafty Cockney Darts Pub Burslem, Stoke-on-Trent. Owned by Eric Bristow, the champion darts player, whose nickname is 'the crafty Cockney'.

Crafty Fox *See* Fox.

Crag Wildboarclough, Ches. A crag is a rough rock (Welsh *craig* 'rock'). This pub is high in the moorlands.

Crane Basildon and elsewhere. A sign first seen in London in the fifteenth century. The Basildon sign shows the bird on one side and the lifting apparatus on the other. At Wandsworth the sign shows only the bird, but the River Crane is nearby. *See also* Three Cranes.

Cranford Exmouth. A simple place name used as a pub name, but it is well illustrated on the sign, with a crane standing in a ford holding an eel in its mouth.

Cranmer Arms Aslockton, Notts. Thomas Cranmer (1489–1556), Archbishop of Canterbury under Henry VIII and Edward VI, was born in this village. Cranmer supported the claim of Lady Jane Grey to the English throne, and was doomed when Mary I succeeded. He was burned at the stake on a charge of heresy.

Craven Heifer Heckmondwike and elsewhere. Several pubs in Yorkshire bear this name, which refers to a famous heifer (ie a young cow which has not borne a calf) bred in 1807 at Gargrave-in-Craven. It weighed over a ton. A picture of this heifer was used in 1817 on notes issued by the Craven Bank. When Bank of England notes replaced them, local farmers are reported to have asked for the return of those 'wi' a coo on 'em'. Other heifers which feature on northern pub signs include Airedale Heifer at Battyeford, near Mirfield, Durham Heifer at Broxton, near Chester, Wellington Heifer at Ainderby Steeple, near Northallerton, Wensleydale Heifer at West Witton, near Leyburn, White Heifer at Scorton, near Richmond. At Thornton, near Bradford there is a Rock and Heifer: there was previously a Scotch Heifer in

Manchester, now gone. Heifer itself is a pub name at Newbiggin, near Morpeth.

Craw Auchencrow, near Eyemouth. The name is a Scottish form of 'crow' and presumably relates to the place name. There is a Craw's Nest at Carnoustie.

Cremorne Nottingham. Another in Sheffield. The name of a famous racehorse, winner of the Derby in 1872.

Cribbage Hut Sutton Mandeville, Wilts. After the game of cards, still played here as it was when the former coaching inn occupied the site. The sign shows a winning hand of four cards.

Cricket Our national summer game is most often represented in pub signs by the Cricketers, as at Great Dunmow, Esx and elsewhere, and the Cricketers Arms, King's Somborne, near Winchester and elsewhere. Variant names include Cricket Ball, Sheffield; Old County Cricket Ground, Aylestone, Leicester; Cricketer. London SW15; Cricketers Rest, Norwich; Cricket Players, Norwich; Old Cricket Players, Hyson Green, Nottingham; Eleven Cricketers, Dartford and Storrington, W Ssx; Jolly Cricketers, Seers Green, Beaconsfield; Kentish Cricketers, Canterbury; Merry Cricketers, Deptford; Royal Cricketers, London E2; Surrey Cricketers, Croydon; Sussex Cricketers, Hove; Twelfth Man, Greasby, Ches. Other allusions include Ball and Wicket, Upper Hale, near Farnham; Bat and Ball, Hambledon, Hants and elsewhere; Bat and Wickets, Northampton; Boundary, Southampton; Cover, Preston; Drive, Eastbourne; Full Pitcher, Ledbury; Long Stop, Leicester and Worcester; Maiden Over. Earley, near Reading and Pelaw near Gateshead; Pavilion End, Manchester; Sticky Wicket, Redditch; Test Match, West Bridgford, Nottingham; Three Willows, Birchangar, Esx; Wickets, Wellington, Salop; Yorker, London W1 and Nottingham. Umpire, as formerly at Sheffield, can sometimes refer to a stagecoach of that name. Cricketing personalities also feature on inn signs. *See* Doctor W G Grace, Fiery Fred, Jack Hobbs, Larwood and Voce Tavern, Spofforth, Thomas Lord. Innings, at Worksop, refers to a specific innings by Ted Alletson.

Crime View Oldham. A name transferred from an ancient farmstead nearby, but the reason for the name is not known locally.

Crispin Ashover, Derbs and elsewhere. The patron saint of cobblers and shoemakers. St Crispin's Day, 25 October, was also the day on which the battle of Agincourt was fought in 1415, a fact made known to most people by the famous speech in Shakespeare's *Henry V*. The saint is said to have paid for his travels, during which he spread the gospel, by supporting himself as a cobbler. The Stafford sign shows him with his last, the model of a foot on which the shoe is put. At Woodley, Berks, the sign shows the annual ceremony in which a pair of medieval shoes is hoisted to the top of St Catherine's church in Bermondsey. This was originally a thanks-offering made by a successful apprentice in the trade. The Crispin Inn at Ashover, Derbs, has its history detailed on a board outside. Thomas Babington, lord of the manor, returned with his comrades from Agincourt. Most of those who did so looked upon St Crispin as their saviour. Two other soldiers who fought at Agincourt are said to have founded the Crispin and Crispianus pub at Strood, near Rochester. Crispianus was Crispin's brother.

Criterion Bournemouth and elsewhere. The Bournemouth sign relates the name to a boat which made trips to the Isle of Wight in the nineteenth century. At Weston-super-Mare the name is also that of a pleasure-steamer. Elsewhere the name simply implies that the pub is the standard by which all others must be judged.

Crocker's London NW8. Renamed in 1984 to commemorate Frank Crocker, landlord of the Crown, near Lord's Cricket Ground, in the nineteenth century. Local legend has it that Crocker jumped out of the window of his establishment when he learned that Marylebone Railway Station was not to be built next door. His pub then became known as Crocker's Folly to its patrons.

Crocodile Dane Hill, W Ssx. The sign shows a crocodile wearing a fez, velvet smoking jacket, yellow check trousers, bow tie and spectacles, and smoking a pipe. The local explanation of the name is that 'crocodile' referred to a large pair of tongs (presumably resembling crocodile jaws) which were used by smugglers in the eighteenth century. They hid their contraband in nearby marshland, and used the tongs to retrieve it. Sceptics are shown the tongs themselves when they visit the pub.

Crompton's Monument Bolton. Samuel Crompton (1753–1827) was the inventor of the mule spinning frame, a machine which was capable of spinning very fine yarn. The 'mule' was presumably occasioned by the fact that the machine was a kind of spinning-jenny, 'jenny' being associated with asses. It was also a mixture, of Hargreaves' wheel and Arkwright's roller. *See also* Spinning Jenny.

Cromwell Also Cromwell's Head. *See* Oliver Cromwell.

Crook Tweedsmuir. This was a former drovers' inn and the name refers to the bent staff they would carry.

Crooked Billet Symond's Green, near Stevenage and elsewhere. The 'billet' is simply a stick or piece of wood, and 'crooked' refers to its not being straight. Hanging up an oddly shaped piece of wood was a primitive but effective way of acquiring a sign in former times. The sign at Symond's Green is anything but primitive, however. It shows a peer of the realm holding a crossed pair of shepherd's crooks.

Crooked Chimney Lemsford, Herts. The pub has a red-bricked chimney shaped like a lopsided capital letter L.

Crooked House Himley, W Mid. Officially the Glynne Arms, but it is situated in a coalmining area and the ground beneath the building has subsided considerably. This in turn has produced such curious results in the interior structure that the pub has become a tourist attraction.

Crooked Spire Chesterfield. The local parish church has a curiously warped spire, about seven feet out of true perpendicular. There is a similarly named pub at Ermington, Devon.

Crook of Devon Crook of Devon, near Kinross. Devon is the name of the local river, which has a 'crook' or bend in it nearby.

Cross Maple Cross, Rickmansworth and elsewhere. Often suggested by the presence of a large public cross in the vicinity. Such crosses often lead to place names, especially with a qualifying word. Thus there is a Banner Cross at Sheffield (pub and place), though another pub of the name is found in Torquay. Tiverton has a Staplecross, where 'staple' means a pillar or post. The Old Cross at Stapleford, Notts takes its name from the ancient Saxon cross which stands opposite in St Helen's churchyard. Many early *Cross* tavern signs were changed because of Puritan disapproval.

Crossbow Falkirk. The weapon also known as an arbalest. A steel bow, fitted to a wooden shaft, is then fitted with a mechanism for drawing back the bow-string and releasing it. It was used to fire stones and metal as well as arrows. The crossbow was more powerful than the longbow, but was relatively clumsy to use. At Crécy in 1346 English longbowmen defeated the Genoese crossbowmen, who were fighting for the French.

Cross Daggers Bolton-on-Dearne, near Rotherham. The reference is to the badge of the Hallamshire Cutlers Company.

Cross Foxes Wrexham and elsewhere. From the coat of arms of the interrelated Watkin/Williams/Wynn family, who owned land extensively in North Wales. The sign at Wrexham shows one fox crossing a bridge while another passes beneath it.

Cross Hands Cheltenham. Originally a sign of unity and friendship, this sign shows a highwayman with his hands crossed, and a pistol in each. The village of Cross Hands, near Swansea takes its name from a colliery, which in turn was probably named for an inn.

Crossings Furness Vale, near Stockport. The sign shows a railway level-crossing. There is a similar Crossing Gate at Liss, Hants.

Cross-in-Hand Near Heathfield, E Ssx. The name of a village as well as its pub. The name dates from 1547 and is explained locally as a reference to Crusaders. They met here on the way to Rye for embarkation to the Holy Land. Another story is told of murderers being pursued by a mob and escaping their immediate vengeance by grasping a crucifix and turning to face them. The inventor of that tale was probably slightly befuddled at the time and had recently been watching a film about vampires.

Cross Keys Aldeburgh and elsewhere. A common sign in Christian heraldry, referring to St Peter, to whom Jesus said: 'I will give unto thee the keys of the kingdom of heaven'. The papal arms show crossed keys, and they occur again in the arms of various bishops, such as those of Exeter, Gloucester, Peterborough, Ripon and St Asaph, where the cathedral in each case is dedicated to St Peter. At Rode, near Bath the inn-sign refers to the trademark of a local brewery. At Stratford-on-Avon the sign shows a white Yorkist rose on the handle of each key, with a glove draped across the intersection. At Lydford-on-Fosse in Somerset is a Crossed Keys, which shows the arms of a former abbot of Glastonbury.

Cross Lances Hounslow. Cavalry units were formerly stationed nearby. This sign would have been meant to attract the soldiers.

Cross Rifles Bridgwater, Som. The local Rifle Volunteer Force was formed in 1859 and was complimented by this name.

Crossroads Weedon, Northants. The pub is at the junction of the A45 and A5 roads.

Cross Scythes Totley, near Sheffield. Scythes were once made in this area.

Cross Stobs Barrhead, near Paisley. 'Stob' is a Scottish form of 'stub', though it can also mean 'stake' or 'stump'. In carpentry it also means an 'awl'.

Cross Tree Byfield, near Daventry. The sign shows a group of villagers in medieval dress assembling under a tree. John Wyclif, leader of the Lollards (who wanted church reforms) was rector at nearby Lutterworth, and the gathering shown refers to a meeting which led to a small uprising.

Crossways West Huntspill, Som. A reference to the crossroads, where stagecoaches formerly picked up and dropped passengers. At Dunkerton, near Bath, the sign shows two modern hikers consulting a map.

Crowders Well London EC2. There was originally a well here with a reputation for medicinal properties. The well adjoined St Giles' Churchyard on the north-west side and was mentioned by John Stow in his *Survey of London*, (1603).

Crown Buntingford, Herts (*publishers favourite local*) and elsewhere. Well over 500 pubs of this name are listed in recent directories, reflecting the popularity of an inn sign that has been used for some six hundred years. It has in its favour the fact that it is a simple visual symbol, easy to illustrate and as easy to recognise, while at the same time it demonstrates loyalty to the reigning monarch. For the latter reason it was a sign that rapidly disappeared during Cromwell's period of power, but as rapidly reappeared with the Restoration. In combination with other objects, animals or people it often reflects a pub which added *Crown* to a previous name when the pub concerned received some kind of royal patronage. Charles Hindley, in his *Tavern Anecdotes*, quotes a 'poem' in which the word 'crown' is common to each line. It was probably composed in the bar-room of a *Crown* inn and is meant to encourage further patronage. It begins: 'Come, my lads, and crown your wishes,/With glee come crown your greatest joys;/Come to the *Crown* and drink like fishes,/Spend each a crown my jovial boys.' Many of the *Crown* 'combination' names are treated separately below. Others include Crown and Appletrees, formerly at London W1; Crown and Buckle, Grimsby; Crown and Cannon, Winlaton, near Blaydon-on-Tyne;

Crown and Castle, London E8; Crown and Chequers, formerly at Ipswich; Crown and Compasses, Cambridge; Crown and Crooked Billet, Woodford Bridge, Esx; Crown and Cross Guns, Darlaston, W Mids; Crown and Crossed Swords, Shotley Bridge, Durham; Crown and Dolphin, London, E1; Crown and Dove, Bristol; Crown and Falcon, Puckeridge, Herts; Crown and Garter, Inkpen, Berks; Crown and Grapes, London WC2; Crown and Greyhound, London SE21; Crown and Harp, Cambridge; Crown and Horses, Bolton-by-Bowland, near Clitheroe; Crown and Horseshoe, Hanham, near Bristol; Crown and Horseshoes, London N18; Crown and Kettle, Manchester; Crown and Mitre, Oldham; Crown and Pipes, Fenstanton, near Huntingdon; Crown and Plough, Long Clawson, near Melton Mowbray; Crown and Punchbowl, Horningsea, near Cambridge; Crown and Sandys Arms, Ombersley, near Droitwich; Crown and Sceptre, Ipswich; Crown and Shears, London EC3; Crown and Shuttle, London E1; Crown and Tuns, Deddington, near Banbury; Crown and Victoria, Tintinhull, near Martock, Som; Crown and Vine, Liverpool; Crown and Woolpack, London EC1. There is a Crown of Crucis at Ampney Crucis, near Cirencester.

Crown and Anchor Staines and elsewhere. The badge of the lord high admiral, also the arm badge of the Royal Navy's petty officers. Retired seamen who become licensees are fond of the name. The tune of *The Star-Spangled Banner* was composed in the *Crown and Anchor* in Arundel Street, off the Strand, in the 1790s.

Crown and Arrows Shelton Lock, near Derby. The pub is adjacent to St Edmund's church. Edmund was the last king of the East Angles, killed in 870 by the Danes. He was tied to a tree and used for archery practice. His emblem, a crown and arrows, is shown on the inn sign.

Crown and Column Devonport. Inspired by the granting of Devonport's charter, in 1824. A column was erected locally, surmounted by a sculpted lion.

Crown and Cushion Eton and elsewhere. The signs usually show a crown resting on the cushion which is used to carry it to the monarch at a coronation or similar ceremony. The pub at Minley, near Aldershot commemorates by this name the arrest in 1671 of Colonel Blood, who attempted to steal the Crown Jewels. Blood, an Irish adventurer, was imprisoned for a time but was then released by Charles II, who granted him a pension.

Crown and Glove Chester. Another at Sheffield. A reference to the gauntlet thrown down on Coronation Day by the royal champion, daring anyone to dispute the right of succession. The tradition was established by William the Conqueror and was last observed at the coronation of George IV. In modern times the champion (a member of the Dymoke family of Lincolnshire) bears the sovereign's standard.

Crown and Horns East Ilsey, Berks. The reference is to the royal charter granted to the village in the seventeenth century and to the renowned sheep fair held locally.

Crown and Leek London E1. A patriotic Welsh landlord added the 'leek' to the existing name. The Welsh say that the leek became their national emblem after St David had asked his countrymen to wear one in their caps when they fought against the Saxons. They were thus able to distinguish friend from foe.

Crown and Mitre Oldham. Symbols of the monarchy and the Church, and the sometimes decidedly uneasy relationship between them in times past.

Crown and Shuttle London E1. The 'crown' here refers to former royal landowners in this area. The 'shuttle' is for the local weaving industry, originally imported from France in the late seventeenth century with the arrival of the Huguenots.

Crown and Stirrup Clayhill, near Lyndhurst. The stirrup is the rider's footrest, attached to a horse's saddle by leather straps. The pub name as a whole refers to hunting by royal personages in the New Forest close by.

Crown and Sugarloaf London EC4. Until 1830 many small sugar refineries existed in the side streets nearby. The oldest grocers in the City, Davidson, Newman & Co, are in neighbouring Creechurch Lane. They display a sign which incorporates three conical sugar loaves and a crown, together with the date 1650. At one time their refinery produced sugar for the royal household, a fact reflected in the inn sign.

Crown and Thistle Kingston-on-Thames and elsewhere. The name also occurs as Thistle and Crown, see Thistle. A reference to the uniting of England and Scotland when James VI of Scotland became James I of England in 1603. As an emblem of Scotland, the thistle dates from the eighth century.

Crown and Tower Taunton. The town was a Royalist stronghold during the Civil War. This sign

was meant to symbolise that the crown was a tower of strength to the people.

Crown and Treaty House Uxbridge. In 1645 Charles I's commissioners and a parliamentary council met here in order to negotiate a treaty which would end the Civil War. They were unable to reach an agreement.

Crown and Trumpet Broadway, H and W. The trumpet referred to is that of the Royal Herald, seen on the occasion of a royal visit to the town.

Crown and Two Chairmen London W1. Queen Anne is said to have sat for her portrait in the studio of Sir James Thornhill, which was opposite this pub. During the sittings the two bearers of the royal sedan-chair took refreshment in the inn. *See also* Two Chairmen.

Crown Point *See* Sir Jeffrey Amherst.

Crow's Nest Bursledon, near Southampton and elsewhere. Usually for a real crow's nest. The Bursledon sign shows the naval type of crow's nest, the look-out position on the masthead of a ship.

Cruel Sea *See* Compass Rose.

Crumpled Horn Eldene, near Swindon. A name perhaps suggested by a misshapen cow's horn, or a reference by implication to a 'house that Jack built'. The phrase would certainly remind most people of the nursery rhyme and 'the maiden all forlorn/That milked the cow with the crumpled horn/That tossed the dog/That worried the cat/That killed the rat/That ate the malt/That lay in the house that Jack built.'

Crusader Clifton, Nottingham. The local squire in the twelfth century, Sir Gervas(e) Clifton died fighting during the Third Crusade. The knight's heart was brought home in a casket which is still kept in the village church.

Crystal Palace Merthyr Tydfil and elsewhere. The mainly glass building commissioned by Prince Albert to house the International Exhibition of 1851; it was designed by Sir Joseph Paxton, who is also commemorated in several pub signs. The Crystal Palace itself was destroyed by fire in 1936. The pub of this name in Bath has a composite sign which features Prince Albert, an outline of the Great Exhibition, and a cameo portrait of Lord Nelson, who happened to visit Bath after his return from the Battle of the Nile.

Cuba New Bradwell, near Milton Keynes. A former innkeeper is said to have given this name in the nineteenth century, because of his sympathy for the island's attempt to gain independence from Spain. This may have been during the Ten Years' War (1868–78), when Spain retained control, or in 1898, when Cuba finally became independent.

Cubitt Arms London E14. Thomas Cubitt (1788–1855) was an eminent English architect whose work can be seen in many parts of London, especially Belgravia. He was also employed by Queen Victoria to rebuild Osborne on the Isle of Wight.

Cuckoo Birch Mansfield, Notts. This name won an open competition arranged by the brewery when the pub was opened in 1981. There was a forest fire in 1937 in a nearby wood. A young birch tree was found to be growing within the burned-out stump of an old oak tree. It is still flourishing.

Cuckoo Bush Gotham, Notts. The original sign showed the cuckoo flying out of the bush, despite the fence built round it: the simple villagers are looking amazed as the bird makes its escape. This legendary incident is said to have happened when King John had thoughts of establishing a hunting lodge in the area. The villagers realised that it would be cripplingly expensive for them if the king and court descended on them from time to time. They therefore made sure that whenever royal representatives were around, they always saw the locals engaged in ridiculous activities. The king was told of the extreme stupidity of the people of Gotham, and changed his mind about the lodge. Gotham's reputation for stupidity spread, leading to such stories as that told in the nursery rhyme: 'Three wise men of Gotham/Went to sea in a bowl./If the bowl had been stronger/My story would have been longer.' The villagers themselves could afford to smile at such comments. Their view was that more fools passed through the village than remained there. The American writer Washington Irving subsequently referred to the inhabitants of New York as Gothamites. He meant that they concealed their wisdom behind a cloak of stupidity.

Cuckoo Pint Stubbington, Hants. The name was selected from 467 suggestions submitted in a brewery competition. The pub is situated in Cuckoo Lane. Cuckoo pint, short for Cuckoo pintle, is another name for the wild arum. ('Pint' rhymes with 'mint'.)

Cuddles St Neots, near Huntingdon. Another at Solihull. A modern renaming intended to attract young couples. Perhaps more generally an atmosphere of warmth and security is suggested.

Cumberland Stores London W1.

The pub was a store before being converted into a pub; probably a wine store.

Cumberland Wrestlers Carlisle. For two celebrated wrestlers of the late nineteenth century, George Steadham and Hexham Clarke. The pub sign shows Steadham on one side, the two men engaged in a bout on the other. In Newcastle-on-Tyne the Cumberland Wrestler refers to Clarke. *See also* Wrestlers.

Cunard Liverpool. A reference to the Cunard Steam-Ship Company, founded in 1839 by the Canadian, Sir Samuel Cunard. The **Cunarder** in London, W1 refers to one of the 'ocean greyhounds' used by the company on the Atlantic route.

Cunning Man Burghfield Bridge, near Reading. The pub sign shows an angler leaning over a stream and tickling a trout. This method of catching the fish was described by Jefferies in his *Red Deer* (1884): 'Groping for trout (or tickling) is tracing it to the stone it lies under, then rubbing it gently beneath, which causes the fish to gradually move backwards into the hand, till the fingers suddenly close in the gills'. At Wye in Kent there is a Tickled Trout.

Cupid Cupid Green, Herts. The Roman god of love is shown on an interesting set of three signs at this pub. In the first he is frowning at a couple who have quarrelled; in the second he fires his traditional arrows at their hearts; in the third he gives a thumbs-up sign as the couple embrace. The artist was D A Clark, of Watford.

Cupola House Bury St Edmunds. This seventeenth century building does have the architectural feature known as a cupola, a kind of dome. By chance it makes a fitting pub name, since *cupola* is ultimately derived from *cupa*, the Latin word for a 'cask' or 'tun'.

Curfew Bath. A sign commemorating the curfew which was imposed on Bath during the Civil War. It was in force between 9 pm and 6 am. Originally a 'curfew' was a bell rung in the evening to indicate that fires should be extinguished.

Curiosity Vaults Liverpool. Sailors used to bring curios back from their travels to this pub. The showcases with their curiosities have gone, but the name remains.

Curlers Tavern Glasgow. This is a listed building, originally the pavilion for a curling rink behind the pub. The curlers are those who take part in the sport of curling, which consists of sliding heavy smooth stones along a sheet of ice.

Curlew Havant, Hants. The moorland bird is found in the area.

Curriers Arms Leighton Buzzard, Beds. Curriers dress and colour leather after it has been tanned. The curriers separated from the cordwainers in 1415, and were awarded their own coat of arms in 1583.

Cushy Butterfield Newcastle-on-Tyne. One of the characters mentioned in *The Blaydon Races* (*see* that entry). She appears also in Irving's painting of the subject.

Custom House London E16. The pub was built in 1789 as accommodation for Customs officers.

Cutler North Anston, near Sheffield. Sheffield and Rotherham have a Cutlers Arms and Worsbrough Dale near Barnsley a Cutting Edge. A cutler is a maker of knives and other cutting instruments. This region is well-known for the manufacture of such implements.

Cutter Weymouth and elsewhere. The small, single-masted sailing vessel, once used especially by excisemen in their pursuit of smugglers.

Cuttle Long Itchington, near Rugby. The sign shows a cuttlefish, also known as the inkfish because it ejects a dark fluid into the water to conceal itself from predators. The name is said to refer, however, to the 'cut' or canal which runs close by and the 'well' which was formerly behind the pub. 'Cut' and 'well' suggested 'cuttle', though one can never be sure, with this type of name, whether the name came first and was then 'explained' cleverly afterwards, or whether the name was suggested by the phrase.

Cutty Sark Falmouth and elsewhere. The inn signs usually portray the famous ocean clipper of this name, which stands in dry dock opposite the Royal Naval College at Greenwich. A pub there which was the Union rapidly changed to *Cutty Sark* when the ship arrived there in 1957. Built in 1869 the ship was in her time the fastest afloat, sailing from Sydney to London on one trip in seventy-five days, covering a record 363 miles on one of them. The pub in Barrow of this name prefers to illustrate on the sign the cutty (short, curtailed) sark (shift, rough shirt) which was worn in the Border country in the time of Robert Burns. *See also* Tam o'Shanter.

Cyder Apple *See* Apples.

Cyprus South Shields. A name which marked the placing of the island under British administration in 1878, by virtue of the Anglo-Turkish treaty.

D

Dagmar Arms London N15. In honour of the wedding of the Danish Princess Marie Dagmar to the future Tsar of Russia, Alexander III, in 1866.

Dairy Maid Aylesbury. The name of a stagecoach which ran from London to Buckingham, via Aylesbury. It carried news of the victory at Waterloo two days after it occurred in June, 1815.

Daisy Also Daisy Field. *See* Flowers.

Dalesgate Harrogate. Harrogate is the gateway to both Wharfedale and Nidderdale.

Dalesman Leeds. The sign shows a typical dalesman – one who inhabits the dales, or valleys – carrying a shotgun and accompanied by a spaniel.

Daley's Dandelion *See* Flowers.

Dame Agnes Mellers Nottingham. The widow of a prominent medieval burgess. She founded a free school in 1513 which later became the Nottingham High School for Boys.

Damory Oak Blandford Forum, Dors. The tree was a famous local landmark, but was cut down in 1755. The timber was sold for £14.

Dancing Cairns Aberdeen. The cairns referred to are the small Scottish terriers, suitable for driving foxes from their earths among the cairns (piles of stones raised as landmarks, memorials, etc). It seems they can also be taught to dance.

Dancing Weasel *See* Waltzing Weasel.

Dandie Dinmont Westlinton, Cumb. A breed of dog named after the character in Scott's *Guy Mannering*. The dogs have short legs and rough coats, and are of pepper or mustard colour.

Dandy Cart Newton Aycliffe, Dur. The light spring cart used by milkmen, especially. The origin of the expression is obscure.

Dandy Cock Disley, near Stockport. The bantam fowl, known as a spirited fighter. Dandy cock is its dialectal name.

Dandy Roll London EC4. A technical term in printing, the dandy roll (or roller) being a perforated roller which solidifies paper and impresses a watermark. The London pub is near the factory of Wiggins and Teape, paper manufacturers, whose employees are happy to refer to it as the Randy Doll.

Dangling Prussian Fictional. In Conan Doyle's story *His Last Bow*, Sherlock Holmes is talking to a German spy, who threatens to call for help. 'My dear sir,' says Holmes, 'if you did anything so foolish you would probably enlarge the too limited titles of our village inns by giving us *The Dangling Prussian* as a signpost'. Holmes may have been an expert on many subjects, but inn signs was not one of them, or he would never have referred to the 'too limited titles of our village inns'.

Daniel Lambert Leicester. Daniel Lambert (1770–1809) was keeper of the town jail in Leicester for many years, but was better known for his corpulence. He made money out of it by touring the country and exhibiting himself. At the time of his death he weighed almost fifty-three stones. His waist measurement, as evidenced by his waistcoat (now in a museum at Stamford) was 102 inches.

Daniel O'Connell Wolverhampton. There is also an O'Connell Arms in Manchester. Daniel O'Connell (1775–1847) was an Irish orator and political agitator who was a supreme advocate of Catholic emancipation. He became a member of parliament and was at one time found guilty of sedition or conspiracy when he argued for the repeal of the Act of Union, passed in 1801 when the Irish Parliament was dissolved. The sentence of a year's imprisonment was reversed by the House of Lords.

Danish Invader Empingham, near Stamford. This area was frequently invaded by the Danes before the time of the Norman Conquest.

Darby and Joan Crowle, near Scunthorpe. Another at Abington Pigotts, Herts. Henry Woodfall mentioned Darby and Joan in a ballad published in 1735. He is said to have had a certain John Darby and his wife in mind. The phrase subsequently came to mean a long-married, contented couple.

Darby's Corner Broadstone. Dors Darby was a local man who committed suicide and was therefore denied a burial in the churchyard. As was the custom of the time, he was buried near a crossroads which afterwards came to be known by his name.

Darnley Arms *See* Lord Darnley.

Dart Norwich. The pub sign is an outsize dartboard.

Dart Bridge *See* Bridge.

Dartmoor Halfway Bickington, Devon. Formerly an inn where coaching horses were changed, halfway to Ashburton from Newton Abbot.

David Copperfield Rochester. The novel (with hero of the same name) by Charles Dickens, was first published 1849–50. It was the book which Dickens himself liked best and in many of its details is a thinly veiled autobiography. At Birkenhead there is also a Copperfield.

David Garrick Hereford. There is also a **Garrick** at Stratford-on-Avon and elsewhere, and Garrick's Head, Bath and elsewhere. David Garrick (1717–79) was a famous English actor and theatrical manager. He had a simple manner of speaking and behaving which made the declamatory actors of his time seem foolish. He was one of Dr Johnson's circle of friends.

Davy Lamp Kelloe, Dur, and elsewhere. The safety lamp used by miners invented by the eminent English chemist Sir Humphry Davy (1778–1829). Davy surrounded the flame with wire gauze to prevent contact with dangerous gases. Although chiefly remembered now for the lamp, Davy was considered in his own lifetime to rank with Sir Isaac Newton in importance. For seven years he was President of the Royal Society. At Wallsend, T and W, there is a Davy.

Davy's Locker Millendreath, near Looe. The origin of the expression 'Davy Jones's locker', referring to the sea in its role as a grave for drowned seamen, is unknown. The first reference in print to Davy Jones as the spirit of the sea was in 1750. Partridge follows Professor Weekley in assuming that 'Jones' was originally 'Jones', itself a form of 'Jonah', and that the 'Davy' was added later.

Daylight Petts Wood, Kent. A tribute to William Willett (1856–1915), who was a tireless advocate of the Daylight Saving Scheme, which causes our clocks to be adjusted for

British Summer Time. This was adopted as a wartime measure in 1916 and made permanent in 1925.

Deacon Brodie's Tavern Edinburgh. Deacon Brodie was a town councillor and 'pillar o' th' kirk' who turned out to be a notorious scoundrel and bank-robber. The secrets of his double life were revealed at his trial in 1778. He and his accomplice, a grocer named Smith, were later hanged. Edinburgh seems to have a soft spot for William Brodie, however He is commemorated in another of the city's pubs, Deacon's Den.

Dean and Chapter Dunkirk, Kent. A compliment to the clerical dignitaries of neighbouring Canterbury. A 'dean' was originally in charge of ten clerics. Similar names are Dean's Walk in Gloucester and Old Deanery at Ripon, where the pub actually joins the cathedral.

Dean Swift London E1. Jonathan Swift (1667–1745) is known to most people as the author of *Gulliver's Travels*, though students of literature are aware of his other satirical works and his fine poetry. He became dean of St Patrick's. Dublin, his native city, in 1713.

Decoy Newborough, near Peterborough. Another at Fritton, near Lowestoft. Both pubs are near decoy lakes, used to attract waterfowl to a place where they can easily be watched.

Dee Miller Newton, near Chester. The River Dee, which for much of its length forms the boundary between England and Wales, is nearby. A once popular folk-song began: 'There was a jolly miller/Lived by the River Dee.' There is a Dee in the city of Chester, and nearby Heswall has a Dee View.

Deer Heraldic references to this animal normally refer to the hart, as in White Hart. Its presence, or former presence, in nearby forests causes it to be mentioned in many other pub names, either as something like Red Deer Croydon and London E1, or as Buck's Head, Little Wymondley, Herts, Roebuck Warwick, Fawn, Windsor, Hind, Stag, Royal Stag, Datchet, near Eton, etc. The barmen of pubs called the *Stag*, as at Watford, must get very tired of jokes about stag parties.

Deer's Leap Kingstanding, Birmingham and elsewhere. This is the trademark of the Mitchells & Butlers brewery, nearby at Cape Hill.

Deerstalker Nottingham. A Mitchells and Butlers pub, whose former house magazine was the *Deerstalker*, linking with their trademark *Deer's Leap*. The Nottingham pub is near Bestwood Park, used as a hunting ground by Charles II.

Defiance Ipswich. The name of a famous mail-coach which in the 1820s and 1830s ran nightly from the Swan with Two Nicks in London to Manchester, or for a ship of the Royal Navy. The first ship of this name was built in 1590 and there have since been at least nine others.

De Hems London W1. For a former landlord, a Dutchman who made the place famous for its beer and oysters.

Delver Arms Heaton, near Bradford. Dedicated to those who dig, for whatever reason, with a spade.

De Montfort Leicester. Simon de Montfort (1206–65), Earl of Leicester, was a powerful baron with liberal views. He was brother-in-law to Henry III but quarrelled with him. After the Battle of

Lewes in 1264, where he defeated Henry, he virtually founded the English House of Commons. He was killed at the battle of Evesham when fighting Prince Edward. Ten years later, with the approval of Edward I, the Statute of Westminster realised his vision of a Great Council or *Parlement* in which the business of the nation could be discussed and voted upon.

Denaby Main Tavern Conisbrough, near Doncaster. Denaby Main is the name of the local colliery.

Denbigh Yeoman *See* Yeoman.

Denham Express Denham, near Uxbridge. A name suggested by the *wagon-lit* (sleeping carriage) which was acquired by the pub owners in 1973. It was converted into a restaurant which became part of the pub. The coach itself was built in 1926 and has been carefully restored.

Denman's Head Sutton-in-Ashfield, Notts. Sir Thomas, later Lord Denman (1779–1854) was an eminent English judge and member of parliament for Nottingham. He became Lord Chief Justice in 1832. There is a Denman Arms in London SE15, while Mistley, Esx, has a Lord Denman.

Denmark Taunton. Christian IX, King of Denmark, stayed briefly in Taunton on one occasion when he was on his way to hunt at Dunster. The King's daughter Alexandra married the Prince of Wales, later Edward VII.

Denmark Arms London E6, Also at Ashford, Kent and Rochester. A reference to the visit to London of Christian IV of Denmark in the seventeenth century. His sister Anne became the wife of James I.

De Quincey's Glasgow. Thomas De Quincey (1785–1859) was an essayist and writer on miscellaneous subjects, but he is best known for his *Confessions of an English Opium Eater* (1822). He was driven to opium by physical suffering and became an addict, but managed to conquer the habit after eight years.

Derbyshire Yeoman *See* Yeoman.

Derby Turn Burton-on-Trent. The pub is situated at a junction on the Derby Road, which presumably suggested the name. The inn sign shows jockeys negotiating what is no doubt meant to be Tattenham Corner during a Derby race.

Derwent Blackhill, Dur. For the local river, which runs into the Tyne.

Deryk Carver Brighton. Deryk Carver was a local man who became England's first Protestant martyr. In company with sixteen others, all described as 'heretics', he was burned at the stake in Lewes in 1555, during the reign of Queen Mary.

Desert Rat Reigate. Another at Scunthorpe. The Desert Rats was a nickname given to the British 7th Armoured Division, a unit of the Eighth Army who fought in Europe and North Africa during World War Two. The name derived from the divisional sign, a jerboa, a jumping mouse found in African deserts.

Devereux Tavern *See* Earl of Essex.

Devil in the Boot *See* Boot.

Devil's Elbow Princetown, Devon. The local name of a tricky bend on the approach road across Dartmoor. The sign showed the devil sitting on a rock and surveying the S–bend.

Devil's Stone Shebbear, Devon. The pub is situated opposite an enormous stone, which is in front of the church. Tradition says that the devil left the stone there. The stone is turned over on 5 November each year, to the accompaniment of a peal of bells, just to make sure that the devil is not underneath.

Devil's Tavern *See* Prospect of Whitby.

Devon Dumpling Shiphay, near Torquay. 'Dumpling' can be used to describe a dumpy person, short and stout. Accordingly, the sign shows a buxom dairymaid, carrying the steaming delicacy on a platter. Lakenham near Norwich has a Norfolk Dumpling.

Devonshire Bath. The stagecoach of this name operated between Taunton and Salisbury.

Devonshire Arms London and elsewhere. This name is found in London, Devon, Derbyshire and Yorkshire especially, and reflects the ownership of large estates by the dukes of Devonshire.

Devon Tors *See* Tors.

Devon Yeoman *See* Yeoman.

Dew Drop Oxford and elsewhere. A popular pun: Dew Drop Inn for 'do drop in'. As it happens, the motto of the Distillers' Company, taken from the Song of Moses in Deuteronomy 32, is 'My speech shall distil as the dew'. The Oxford pub sign shows a large dew drop about to fall on a tiny elf. At Hathern, near Loughborough, it is falling from a tree leaf onto a garden flower. Swindon has a Do Drop Inn.

Dial Tavern Portsmouth and elsewhere. A name which normally indicates that there is a large public clock nearby, though it can also refer to a miner's or mariner's compass.

Diamond Jubilee Gaywood, near King's Lynn. A reference to the racehorse of this name, which won the Derby in 1900. The horse itself was named to commemorate Queen Victoria's diamond jubilee, the sixtieth year of her reign, which was celebrated in 1897.

Diamond XX Eccles, near Manchester. The special brew which was once made at Walker's Brewery in Warrington, now made at Allied Breweries in Burton-on-Trent.

Dickens *See* Charles Dickens.

Dick Hudson's High Eldwick, W Yorks. The unofficial name of the **Fleece**, referring to a previous owner, whose father came here in 1809 and ran the pub until 1850. Dick Hudson took over until 1880 and was succeeded by John Hudson, who remained as licensee until 1893.

Dick Turpin York and elsewhere. Dick Turpin (1705–39) was born in a pub at Hempstead, Esx (the Bell) and became a butcher. In his spare time he was a footpad, a kind of mugger. After a life which became more and more criminal he finally became a highwayman in 1735. The stories of his audacious robberies captured the public's imagination, but the authorities soon caught up with him. He was hanged outside the walls of York. He is remembered amongst other things for his famous overnight ride from London to York on his horse *Black Bess*, though Turpin did not actually make that journey (the legend was based on the escapade of an earlier highwayman). He had made his way to York via Lincolnshire, where he committed many robberies. There is a Dick Turpin's Cave at High Beech Hill, near Epping Forest and a Dick Turpin's Tavern in Bristol.

Dick Whittington South Oxhey, near Watford. Sir Richard Whittington, three times lord mayor of London, was a real person, born at Pauntley, Glos in the fourteenth century. His journey to London, subsequently attended by commercial and social success, somehow became corrupted into the Dick Whittington story of pantomime. Brewer solemnly repeats the absurd story that the 'cat' accompanying Dick in his travels was derived from the real-life Whittington's use of 'cats' or 'catts', a kind of sailing ship, though the first mention of such 'cats' occurs two hundred years after Whittington's death. Nevertheless, the cat is an essential component in the pantomime story, and occurs in pub names such as Whittington Cat at Whitehaven, Cumb, Whittington and Cat at London N19 and Hull. There is also a Whittington at Pinner and Kinver, W Mids, a Whittington Arms at Tonna, W Glam, a Whittington Stone in London N19.

Dieu et Mon Droit Great Stoughton, Herts. The royal motto of England, literally 'God and my right'. One of the rare pub names which is in another language – French in this case. The quotation is credited to Richard I at the battle of Gisors in 1198. He meant that he was king because God wished him to be so.

Diggers Rest Woodbury Salterton, Devon. Formerly the Salterton Arms, but an Australian became the owner and renamed it. The sign shows an Aussie asleep under a tree. 'Digger' was first used as a term of address on the goldfields of Australia and New Zealand in the mid-nineteenth century. Much later it became the nickname for an Australian soldier. *See also* Kangaroo.

Dighton Arms London SW18. For Robert Dighton, a painter. He painted the 'court of equity' which met in the Bell Savage inn on Ludgate Hill in 1776. The court was discussing the news of the American Declaration of Independence.

Dimsdale Arms Hertford. Thomas Dimsdale (1712–1800) was an eminent English physician, born in Essex but with a practice in Hertford. He became well-known for his use of vaccination as a defence against smallpox and was invited to Russia about 1768 by the Empress Catherine. She rewarded him for his professional services by creating him a baron and granting him a pension. As the sign of this pub shows, he was also granted the right to add the Russian eagle to his own coat of arms.

Dingman Leyland, near Preston. This is a local term for a production-line repair man, probably from the noise he makes with his tools. Centuries ago a 'ding boy' was a rogue.

Dinton Hermit Ford, near Haddenham, Bucks. John Bigg was born in the nearby village of Dinton, Bucks, in 1596. It is said that he was a good scholar and a confidant of Cromwell. He was one of the judges who passed sentence on Charles I. This is said to have affected his mental health. He became a recluse and lived entirely on bread and ale supplied by charitable friends. *See also* Hermit and Hermit of Redcoats.

Director-General London SE18. The name of a huge gun which was constructed at the Woolwich Arsenal.

Dirty Dick's London EC2, It is generally agreed that the original *Dirty Dick* was Richard Bentley, who kept a hardware store in Leadenhall Street. One story has it that he was once a fashionable man about town until his bride–to–be died on the eve of their wedding. He then became a recluse and lived in the filth that gradually accumulated around him. Another version of the story is that he was a businessman who discovered that his own slovenliness, coupled with the filth of his establishment, had made him very well known. Thereafter he remained dirty because it was decidedly profitable to do so. Modern by-laws do not allow this pub to be squalid, but the name still attracts many customers.

Dirty Duck Stratford-on-Avon and elsewhere. Several pubs have officially adopted this name, which usually began as a nickname for the Black Swan. The nickname was sometimes inspired by a badly painted sign. The naval tradition of calling HMS *Black Swan* the Mucky Duck is also reflected in pubs of this name at Gloucester, Lydford, Devon and Tismans Common, W Ssx.

Discovery Cardiff. The ship in which Robert Falcon Scott (1868–1912), British naval officer and Antarctic explorer, made his ill-fated voyage to the South Pole. He reached the Pole with four companions, but all died on the return journey.

Disraeli Arms *See* Beaconsfield Tavern.

Distillers Arms London W6. Another at London E3. The Distillers Company charter was granted in 1638. Their arms show the sun distilling drops of rain from a cloud, with a distilling apparatus below.

Dive Bar London SE1. In the US this name would suggest a drinking den of low repute. Here the name was used because of the nearby dungeons of a former debtors' prison.

Divers Great Yarmouth. The signboard shows a diving duck on one side, a helmeted human diver on the other.

Divers Arms Herne Bay. William Hooper Wood was a local man who indulged in smuggling. In the early 1830s he was caught and sentenced to five years' penal naval service. When that had expired he returned home and joined a diving company. From the proceeds of various salvage jobs he was able to build this pub.

Dixie Arms Market Bosworth, Leics. Named after the family of local squires, one of whom (Sir Wolstan Dixie) was elected Lord Mayor of London in 1585. The village grammar school endowed by the family welcomed the then unknown Samuel Johnson to its academic staff in 1741, when he took up his first teaching post.

Dixielanders Felling, near Gateshead. The pub holds a music-hall licence and offers 'oldetyme' entertainment. 'Dixieland' technically refers to jazz music in duple time characterised by ensemble and solo improvisation. Dixie itself, as a name for the southern states of the US, was first used by Daniel D Emmett in 1859, in a song called *Dixie*. This 'happy land of American negroes' is said to have been an estate on Manhattan Island which belonged to a Mr Dixie.

Dock Green Ashley Green, Leeds. This pub, which stands on the site of a former police-station, was opened in 1965 by Jack Warner who died in 1981 at the age of eighty-five. It was this actor who played the part of Sergeant Dixon in the long-running television series *Dock Green*.

Doctor Fosters Chorlton-on-Medlock, near Manchester. A 'fun pub' opened in 1982 and named after the nursery-rhyme character, the Dr Foster who 'went to Glo'ster, in a shower of rain./He stepped in a puddle, right up to his middle/And never went there again'. A nearby hospital provided obsolete equipment for decorative purposes, including bed-pans and a skeleton. *See also* Good Doctor.

Doctor Johnson Lichfield. Another at Clayhall, near Ilford. At Langley Green, near Crawley there is a **Dr Samuel Johnson**. Samuel Johnson (1707–84) is remembered mainly as a lexicographer, the compiler of *A Dictionary of the English Language* (1755). He was also a poet, essayist, critic and brilliant conversationalist, whose sallies in later life were assiduously noted by his biographer, James Boswell. His manner of speech, like his prose style, was ponderous but always incisive. He had a remarkable memory, and was able to recall apt quotations from the works he had read whenever he needed them. His critical judgements were heavily influenced by his strong moral views, but his intelligence and integrity made him the dominating literary figure of his age.

Doctor Syntax Preston and else-where. Originally the name of a ludicrous clergyman-schoolmaster who toured on his horse Grizzle in a series of parody picaresque travels. These were shown in drawings by Rowlandson, accompanied by verses written by William Combe. These works appeared between 1809–21, but the pubs usually took their name from a secondary source, the racehorse *Dr Syntax* which won the Derby in 1820.

Doctor W G Grace London SE20. William Gilbert Grace (1848–1915) dominated the game of cricket for some forty years. He was by profession a physician, but the cricket field was his natural environment. During his first-class career he scored nearly 55,000 runs, including 126 centuries, and took nearly 3,000 wickets. Three times he scored over 300 runs in an innings. He was for English cricket what Donald Bradman was later to become for the Australians.

Doffcocker Bolton. An invitation to doff (originally 'do off, ie 'take off') one's 'cocker', or pair of cockers, to be more accurate. Cockers are either high laced boots, or a kind of legging which was formerly worn during bad weather, especially when snow had fallen.

DOG *Dog* is found as a pub name at Ludham, Nflk and elsewhere and as an element in combination names such as Dog and Crook, Briashfield, near Romsey; Dog and Dart, Grappenhall, near Warrington; Dog in the Lane, Astley, near Shrewsbury; Dog i' th' Thatch, Wigan; Dog and Jacket, Bodymoor Heath, near Sutton Coldfield; Dog and Muffler, Coleford, Glos; Dog and Parrot, Newcastle-on-Tyne; Dog and Punchbowl, Lymm, near Warrington; Dog and Truck, London El. Coloured dogs are common: *See* Black Dog, to which may be added Blue Dog, Grantham and elsewhere in Lincs; Red Dog, High Halstow, near Rochester; White Dog, Ewhurst, E Ssx and elsewhere; Golden Dog, Shipham, near Thetford. Most of these colours are repeated with Greyhound replacing *Dog*. There is also a New Greyhound, Billesdon, Leics; Old Greyhound, Windsor; Racing Greyhound, Dumpton, near Ramsgate. There is a Lame Dog at Norwich, a Mad Dog at Odell, near Bedford. Entries will be found for many different breeds of dog, but one can add Setter Dog, Macclesfield; Beagle, Shute, near Axminster and elsewhere; Border Terrier, Cullercoats, Northld and elsewhere; Bull Terrier, Croscombe, Som and elsewhere; Norfolk Terrier, Thetford. Dog Tray, at Brighton, will recall for Shakespeare–lovers Tray, Blanch and Sweetheart in *King Lear*, just as Twa Dogs will be meaningful to lovers of Burns. Doggy pub names with rather a special sense include Bulldog, Gay Dog, Great Dane, Dog House and Dog Watch.

Dog and Bacon Horsham. A humorous corruption of 'Dorking Beacon', which can be seen on a clear day from outside the pub.

Dog and Bear Nottingham. A reminder that bear-baiting was formerly a popular 'sport'. A bear was chained to a stake and dogs encouraged to attack it. The pleasure was gained by seeing the dogs being cuffed or ripped apart and the bear bitten. Such baiting was made illegal in 1835.

Dog and Dart Warrington. The sign shows a bulldog wearing a Union Jack waistcoat. He is poised on his hind legs ready to throw a dart.

Dog and Doublet Sandon, near Stafford and elsewhere. A doublet was a close-fitting garment which was worn by men between the fourteenth and eighteenth centuries. It seems likely that a travelling showman, or showmen, dressed a dog in some kind of coat and caused it to perform tricks, such as jumping through a hoop. Such itinerant entertainers would have given their performances at or near the village inns. At Thorney, in Peterborough, where

there is a pub of this name, it has been suggested that wild-fowlers dressed their retrievers in brightly-coloured doublets so that they could more easily be seen. The Sandon story is that a former innkeeper was murdered and lay in his blood-stained doublet. His faithful dog tugged off the doublet and led neighbours by means of it to where his master lay. Another possibility is suggested by the sign at Thorney, where a poacher is shown to have hidden his dog inside his doublet. Brewer explains the phrase 'a dog in a doublet' by saying that it means a strong or resolute fellow. He explains that dogs used to hunt wild boar in Germany and Flanders and wear a kind of buff doublet. The sign Dog-in-Doublet is, in fact, found at Leabrooks, Derbs.

Dog and Duck Shardlow, near Derby and elsewhere. Such pubs are often near a village pond and refer to the 'royal diversion of duck hunting', favoured by Charles II. Ducks with pinioned wings were thrown into a pond and spaniels sent in to hunt them. The duck's only means of escape was by diving. Such 'sport' remained popular until the early nineteenth century. In many cases this pub name is simply a reference to duck hunters of the more usual kind and their retrievers.

Dog and Hedgehog Dadlington, near Hinckley. A former licensee is said to have admired an engraving showing a dog and hedgehog, entitled *A Rough Customer*. It was this engraving which served as a model for the inn sign.

Dog and Pot Stoke Poges. From the former ironmonger's sign of an andiron, commonly called a fire-dog, and a cooking pot. Bar-room imagination has produced an alternative story about a sluttish housewife who allowed her dog to lick plates clean, then wiped them with the dog's tail.

Dog and Trumpet London W1. Formerly the Marlborough Arms but renamed in 1973 when His Master's Voice celebrated its seventy-fifth anniversary. The company was known as The Gramophone Company until 1909, when it first made use of the famous picture showing Nipper, a fox-terrier, listening to the voice of his master issuing from a gramophone horn. The original painting, by Francis Barraud, hangs in the boardroom of EMI Records. There is another pub of this name in Coventry, next door to a music shop.

Dogger Bank Grimsby. The North Sea fishing grounds, once frequented by 'doggers', two-masted fishing vessels.

Doggett Coat and Badge London, SE1. Another at Margate. Also Coat and Badge, London SW15. Thomas Doggett, who died in 1721, was an actor and theatre manager. He instituted in 1716 a sculling race on the Thames, the oldest annual race in the British sporting calendar. The race takes place on or about August 1st each year under the auspices of the Fishmongers' Company. Six Thames watermen row between London Bridge and Chelsea, the winner obtaining the right to wear an orange coloured livery and a silver arm-badge, which is embossed with the White Horse of Hanover, the emblem of George I.

Dog Tray *See* Dog.

Dog Watch Glasgow. A nautical term for one of two shortened watches, of two hours instead of the usual four, which occur between 4 to 6 pm and 6 to 8 pm every day. Humorously explained as a watch which has been 'curtailed', but more likely to be connected with the earlier expression 'dog-sleep', a reference to fitful sleep. A derivation from 'docked (ie shortened) watch' has also been suggested.

Dolphin Norwich and elsewhere. The dolphin was looked upon by ancient seamen as a friendly creature who would help them in a storm by twining itself around the anchor cable. This would prevent the anchor from dragging and secure the safety of the ship. With such a reputation it was not surprising that Dolphin became a much used ship name, being used in the Royal Navy from 1648 to the present day. A dolphin also figures in many coats of arms, especially those of the Fishmongers Company and the Company of Watermen and Lightermen. In France the eldest son of the king was known as *Le Dauphin* from the mid-fourteenth century (*dauphin* being the French word for 'dolphin'). The name came from a family name – a common one in both France and England by the twelfth century. The *Dolphin* in Norwich was named in the early nineteenth century because local swimmers used it as their headquarters.

Dominoes Hartshorne, Burton-on-Trent. Also Domino, Corby and elsewhere. A reference to the popular pub game, played with twenty-eight rectangular pieces of wood or other material. A 'domino' is also a kind of cloak, originally worn by priests, and it is not clear how the word came to be transferred to the game. Double Six is a similar name.

Don Cossack Rochester. 'Cossack' literally means a nomad or vagabond, but to the English innkeepers who gave this name to their pubs in the early nineteenth century the term meant a Russian cavalryman of the kind who had caused Napoleon to retreat from Moscow. When the Crimean War began, British soldiers found themselves fighting the Cossacks, and many pubs which had been named in their honour were hastily renamed.

Don John Maltby, W Yorks. Named after the winner of the St Leger in 1838. In Bristol, there is a Don John's Cross, which relates to a monument of that name once in a nearby churchyard. The church has since been demolished and the site redeveloped. The pub has a pair of coats-of-arms as its sign.

Don Juan Cawood, near Selby. This pub was not named after the famous womanizer of Seville but a racehorse which won the St Leger in 1938.

Donkey and Buskins Layer-de-la-Haye, near Colchester. Buskins were leather leggings or gaiters worn by farm-workers. A local farmer who patronised the inn one evening had the considerate idea of transferring his buskins to the forelegs of his donkey, in order to protect the animal from thorns as it took his master home across the common. The incident became a local legend and has been perpetuated in the inn name and sign, the latter duly showing both farmer and donkey equipped with the leggings.

Donkey House Windsor. The pub is next to the Thames. It served as a watering place for the donkeys which pulled the river-barges, and as a place of refreshment for the bargees themselves.

Dook Falmouth. A local version of 'duke', namely the Duke of

Wellington, who is shown on the inn sign.

Dooley Walton, near Felixstowe. Officially this pub is the **Ferryboat**, but *Dooley* has been used by the locals for a century. It is a form of the word 'dool' or 'dole', which means a boundary mark – a post, stone or stretch of land left unploughed to form a path. In this case the dooley is the boundary path which leads down to the Walton-Harwich ferry.

Doon Dalmellington, Strath. The river which flows from Loch Doon into the Firth of Clyde.

Doris Pardoe's *See* Ma Pardoe's.

Dormers Wimborne. The kind of windows which project vertically from a sloping roof. They were originally known as dormitory windows.

Dormy House Willersey, Glos. Probably a house with dormer windows rather than a reference to the golfing term. There was, however, a pub called Dormy at Sheringham, Nfolk (now renamed Highwayman) which did refer to the golfing expression. 'Playing dormy six', for example, would mean that a player was six holes ahead with six holes still to play. Professor Weekley ingeniously suggests that the term derives from French *endormi*, 'asleep', because further exertion is unnecessary.

Dorset Knob Parkstone, Dors. For a locally-made bread roll.

Dorset Soldier Corfe Mullen, Dors. One of the directors of the brewery which owned this pub had commanded the local regiment.

Dotterel Reighton, near Bridlington. A species of plover, a reputedly stupid bird that allows itself to be caught. Its name is ultimately connected with 'dote', to act foolishly.

Double Barrel Stopsley, near Luton. The sign interprets the name in a double-barrelled way, showing two brewer's barrels and a double-barrelled shotgun.

Double Century George Green, near Slough. Harman & Co of Uxbridge, since absorbed by the Courage group, used this name to mark the opening of their 200th pub.

Double Decker East Looe, Corn. A reference to the pub's two bars, one above the other.

Double Dragon *See* Dragon.

Double Five Also Double Four. *See* Double Six.

Double Gloucester Gloucester. The county cheese which contains a substantial cream content and boasts of its richness of flavour.

Double Locks Exeter. The pub is beside the canal which has the locks.

Double O Two Yate, near Bristol. The Concorde aircraft known as Double O Two was built at nearby Filton. The pub was opened in 1971 by John Cochrane, deputy chief test pilot of the British Aircraft Corporation. The sign shows the plane in flight, together with two hands extended in a toast. One hand is French and holds a wine glass, the other is British and holds a beer tankard.

Double Six Basildon and elsewhere. The top-scoring piece in a set of dominoes. *See also* Dominoes. Similar names are Double Five at Whitburn, Loth, and Double Four, Northampton.

Dove and Olive Branch Hale, Ches. A familiar symbol in medieval times because of its common representation in church windows and the like. The Tallow Chandlers used three doves, each bearing an olive branch, in their coat of arms. The sign may have indicated their patronage, especially in the seventeenth century when tallow was much in demand for candlemaking and other purposes. The story of the dove and the olive branch, or leaf as it is in modern versions of the bible, is found in Genesis 8:8.

Dove and Rainbow *See* Rainbow and Dove.

Dovecot Billericay. The pub itself is shaped like a traditional dovecot. **Dovecote**, an alternative spelling of the same word, is found as a pub name at Laxton. Notts.

Dover Patrol London SE3. A tribute to the seamen who kept the Dover Straits open during the two world wars.

Dovey Aberdovey (now Aberdyfi). The river is mentioned also in the place-name. The latter means 'mouth of the Dovey'. The river flows into Cardigan Bay here.

Downs Woodingdean, near Brighton. Another at Clapton, E5. These pubs are close to the Sussex Downs and Hackney Downs respectively. Crawley has a most unusual Downsman, presumably on the analogy of dalesman. There is also a Downview at Worthing.

Dragon Welshpool and elsewhere. Not a common sign on its own, usually found as the George and Dragon, Green Dragon, Red Dragon. Occasionally these signs are 'reduced' to *Dragon*. In Nottingham, for example, there is a pub which was a *George and Dragon* for over two hundred years. In 1982 Shipstone's brewery removed George from the board, rewriting the legendary story to leave the dragon as the victor. The dragon appears on many coats of arms, notably that of the Tudor kings, accounting for the Royal Dragon at Portsmouth. The first ship of the Royal

Navy to bear the name was built in 1512, as part of the navy of Henry VIII. Dragons, represented as huge serpents with wings, often breathing fire, occur in the mythologies of many countries and are used as national symbols – as in the case of imperial China. It is perhaps rather surprising that it occurs so rarely as a pub sign. Dragon's Head is found at Whittington, Cumbria and Llangenny, Pwys. Llanelli has a Double Dragon and there is a Golden Dragon in London, SE4.

Dragoon Brampton, near Huntingdon and Colchester. This word is a corruption of 'dragon' and was first given to 'fire-breathing' carbines (firearms like muskets, only shorter). Later the word was applied to the soldiers who carried such weapons. Bold Dragoon is also found in Manchester; Canterbury has a Royal Dragoon. There was formerly a Light Dragoon at Bourne, Lincs and a Dragoons at High Garrett, near Braintree.

Drake Also Drake Manor, Drake's Arms. *See* Sir Francis Drake.

Drake's Drum Worcester and elsewhere. The reference is to a famous poem by Sir Henry Newbolt (1862–1938), written in honour of Sir Francis Drake. It contains the words: 'Take my drum to England, hang et by the shore,/Strike et when your powder's running low:/If the Dons sight Devon, I'll quit the port o' Heaven,/An' drum them up the Channel as we drummed them long ago.'

Drapers Arms London N1. Three imperial crowns appear on the arms of the medieval Company of Drapers, which may well also account in some cases for pubs called the Three Crowns.

Dreadnought London SE8. This has been the name of ships of the Royal Navy since 1573. In the present century it was the name of a battleship built in 1906 at Deptford, sold off in 1920, and was later transferred to Britain's first nuclear submarine, commissioned in 1963.

Dreghorn Irvine, Strath. The word means 'dry house' and relates to the local castle. London NW5 has a Dreghorn Castle.

Drewe Arms Drewsteignton, near Exeter. Another at Broadhembury, near Honiton. Said to be the family name of a 'rich grocer' of the early twentieth century. The 'Drew' in Drewsteignton refers to a Drew or Drogo who owned a farm here in the thirteenth century. 'Drew' occurs in several Devonshire place names but each is of a different origin eg Drewston was earlier Threwston and ultimately refers to a man named Thurweard or Thorward.

Drifter Lowestoft. A reference to a fishing boat using drift nets. Such boats once operated from this port.

Driftwood Spars St Agnes, near Truro. The spars used as beams for the ceiling were salvaged from shipwrecks in the nearby cove.

Drill Gidea Park, Esx. The sign shows a sergeant-major in full cry on the parade ground. The *Drill* at North Cheam interprets 'drill' in its agricultural sense, namely the furrow in which seed is sown. The sign shows a drill-harrow, a harrow used between the drills to get rid of the weeds. Other military signs include Drill Hall Vaults in Derby and Drill House. Stanford Rivers, Esx.

Drinker Moth Harlow. One of the many pubs in this town named after moths or butterflies. This particular moth has a long proboscis which it uses to suck liquids.

Drive *See* Cricket.

Drop Anchor Wraysbury, Bucks. An invitation couched in mariner's terms to stay for a while, and presumably an indication that the licensee is an ex-seaman who has dropped anchor permanently.

Drop Kick Low Moor, near Bradford. The pub is near the ground of the Bradford Northern Rugby League Club whose patrons would recognise this footballing term.

Drover Southend Common, near High Wycombe. Also Drovers, Bishop Thornton, near Harrogate, Drovers Arms, Steppingley, Beds, Drovers Call, Gainsborough, Drovers Rest. Carlisle. For those who conducted droves of cattle or sheep to market, often over large distances, such pubs were welcome ports of call.

Dr Samuel Johnson *See* Doctor Johnson.

Druid Corwen, Clwyd. Also Druid's Arms, Stanton Drew, Avon, Druid's Head, Brighton. Druids' Home, Manchester, Druids' House, Redruth, Druids' Rest. Manchester, Druids Tavern, Arnold, near Nottingham. There is also an Ancient Druid at Cowbridge, S. Glam and an Ancient Druids at Cambridge. Some of these signs refer to the Celtic priesthood of Gaul and Britain and a religion which venerated the oak and mistletoe, believed in immortality and reincarnation and probably practised human sacrifice. Elsewhere such pubs were the meeting places of the United Ancient Order of Druids, a friendly society founded in 1781. The sign of the Stanton Drew pub, in a place well known for its stone circles, shows a Druid priest about to make a ritual sacrifice.

Drum and Monkey Stamford and elsewhere. A reference to the travelling showmen who toured the country in former times with a monkey that performed tricks on a drum.

Drum Major Bodmin. The building here is part of the old barracks belonging to the Cornish Light Infantry. A drum major is the marching leader (often a senior NCO) of a military band, though he was formerly only responsible for the drummers.

Drummer London SW5. Also Drummer Boy, Market Lavington, Wilts, Drummers Arms, Newbury, Berks. Such signs usually refer to military drummers. The Market Lavington sign shows the boy accompanying the troops as they march.

Drunken Duck Hawkshead, Lancs. One of the best-known 'incident' type pub names. The traditional

story is that the innkeeper's wife found several of her ducks lying as if dead in the backyard. It turned out that they were in a drunken stupor, having eaten grain that had been soaked in ale from a leaking barrel.

Dryden Arms Liverpool. The same city has a Dryden Tavern. John Dryden (1631–1700) was an English poet, dramatist and critic. He was made poet laureate in 1668 but lost, the laureateship later when he converted to Catholicism. His best-known plays are probably *All For Love*, his version of the Antony and Cleopatra story, and his comedy *Marriage-à-la-Mode*.

Duchess of Sutherland London N19. This lady was the wife of the 2nd Duke of Sutherland and a friend of Queen Victoria. She died in 1868.

Duchy Arms London SE11. The pub is on land belonging to the Duchy of Cornwall.

Duck and Drake Yaxley, near Peterborough. Also Ducks and Drakes, London W2. The Yaxley pub is close to the Holme Fens Nature Reserve. 'Ducks and drakes' is also the name of the game whereby a flattish stone is made to skip across the surface of a pond as many times as possible before sinking. Sunderland has a Duck and Kangaroo.

Duke of Abercorn Enfield. The family seat of the dukes of Abercorn is near Queensferry, overlooking the Firth of Forth. It is now a National Trust property. The dukes owned vast estates in Greater London, reflected in such names as Abercorn at Stanmore, Abercorn Arms at Teddington.

Duke of Albany London SE14. This was the title granted to Prince Leopold, Queen Victoria's fourth and youngest son, when he

married in 1881. *See also* Prince Leopold and Albany.

Duke of Albemarle London W1. George Monk (1608–69) was a distinguished military leader who had much to do with the Restoration of Charles II. It was this monarch who gratefully raised him to the peerage. At Larkfield, near Maidstone there is a Monk's Head which refers to the same man.

Duke of Argyll London W1. John George Edward Henry Douglas Sutherland Campbell was Marquis of Lorne when he married the Princess Louise, fourth daughter of Queen Victoria, in 1871. He succeeded his father as 9th Duke of Argyll in 1900. For five years (1878–83) he was governor-general of Canada. Radford, Nottingham has a Marquis of Lorne.

Duke of Bedford London NW1 and elsewhere. The various signs show either the heads or coats–of–arms of the Russell family. The Russells first appeared prominently in the reign of Henry VIII and became wealthy landowners. The extent of their estates in London is indicated by many street names, such as Bedford Square, Russell Square.

Duke of Beaufort *See* Beaufort Hunt.

Duke of Bridgewater *See* Bridgewater.

Duke of Brunswick *See* Brunswick.

Duke of Buckingham Kingston-on-Thames. George Villiers (1592–1628), 1st Duke of Buckingham, was an English courtier and politician. He found favour first with James I, later with Charles I, but became very unpopular in the country. He was assassinated by a discontented naval officer.

Duke of Connaught Brighton and elsewhere. For Prince Arthur (1850–1942), the third son of Queen Victoria. He married a Prussian princess in 1879 and was

later governor–general of Canada
1911–16.

Duke of Edinburgh Oxhey near
Watford and elsewhere. After
Prince Alfred (1844–1900), second
son of Queen Victoria. He became
Duke of Edinburgh on his
marriage to Grand Duchess Marie
of Russia in 1874. In 1867 he
embarked on a voyage around the
world as commanding officer of
HMS *Galatea*. He became the first
English prince to visit Australia
and had the misfortune to be shot
at in Sydney, but the would-be
assassin only managed to wound
him. In 1862 Prince Alfred
declined the throne of Greece.

Duke of Marlborough St Albans and
elsewhere. John Churchill
(1650–1722) was a brilliant soldier
and statesman. Under James II he
crushed the rebellion of the Duke
of Monmouth. Later he won
many victories in the War of the
Spanish Succession. His wife,
Sarah Jennings (1660–1744) was
an influential friend of Queen
Anne, and it was during her reign
that Churchill's influence was
greatest. She created him Duke of
Marlborough and a nation grateful
for his victory at Blenheim
presented him with Blenheim
Palace. It was there that Sir
Winston Churchill (1874–1965)
was born. Related names
include Marlborough at Bath,
Marlborough Arms at
Woodstock, Marlborough Head
at Farnham and elsewhere,
Marlborough House at Oxford,
though the latter takes its name
more directly from a three-masted
warship of the Royal Navy. *See also*
Blenheim.

Duke of Monmouth Bridgwater.
Another at Oxford. James Fitzroy
(1649–85) was reputedly an
illegitimate son of Charles II and
Lucy Walters. He was created
Duke of Monmouth in 1663 and
treated as a prince. He later led an
unsuccessful insurrection against
James II, claiming the throne for
himself. He was defeated at
Sedgemoor in 1685 by General
John Churchill, later Duke of
Marlborough. Soon after his
capture he was executed in
London. There is a Monmouth
Arms in Shoreditch, and Lyme
Regis has Ye Olde Monmouth.

Duke of Wellington Hounslow and
elsewhere. Arthur Wellesley, 1st
Duke of Wellington (1769–1852)
was a British national hero after
his defeat of Napoleon I at
Waterloo 1815. He had earlier
had a distinguished military career
in India and Spain. Between
1828–30 he was prime minister;
later he was foreign secretary
1834–35. His popularity may be
judged by the fact that he is
mentioned on more English pub
signs than anyone except Nelson.
He was known as the Iron Duke,
and is honoured in that form at
Ramsgate and elsewhere. In
Limehouse he is the Waterloo
Hero. Chelsea sees him as the
Wellesley Arms, and there is a
Wellesley Tavern in Woolwich.
In Falmouth he is the Dook. His
portrait appears on several signs
where the pub name refers to the
battle of Waterloo.

Duke of Windsor Preston. This was
the title bestowed on Edward VIII
following his abdication in 1936.
He renounced the throne in order
to marry the twice–divorced Bessie
Wallis Warfield (Mrs Wallis
Simpson).

Duke of York Wellingborough,
Northants and elsewhere. There
have been many dukes of York
since the title was created by
Edmund in 1385. The claim to

the throne of Richard, Duke of York (d. 1460) led to the Wars of the Roses. The well-known song about the Grand Old Duke of York refers to Frederick Augustus (1763–1827). He was the second son of George III and commanded the English army in Flanders 1794–95. The song misrepresents the facts since the duke was only thirty-one, had 30,000 men, and there were no hills in the area where he was fighting.

Dukeries Edwinstowe, Notts. A reference to the ducal estates in Sherwood Forest.

Duke's Head Great Yarmouth and elsewhere. The Great Yarmouth pub has kept its name but changed the duke represented on the sign three times, from Cumberland to Clarence then Wellington. Other pubs of this name have no doubt also followed the fashion of the day, honouring whichever hero was currently in the news.

Duke without a Head Wateringbury, near Maidstone. A pub called the Duke's Head was due to be demolished and replaced by a new building. The magistrate's order, giving permission to transfer the licence, stated: 'Permission is given to remove the Duke's Head'. This duly affected the name of the new pub, though its sign shows a peer in morning dress, his head in place with a coronet perched on it.

Dumb Bell Taplow, Bucks. Another at Chalfont St Peter. The Taplow sign shows a young lady clinging to the clapper of a large bell. She is trying to prevent its ringing, for the sound of the bell would be the signal for her lover's execution.

Duncombe Arms Hertford. Thomas Slingsby Duncombe (1796–1861) was an English member of parliament, a witty and fluent speaker who was popular with the voters.

Dundas Arms Kintbury, Berks. It is not clear whether the name refers to Sir James Dundas (1785–1862) or to Sir Richard Dundas (1802–61). The former was actually Sir James Whiteley Deans but changed his name to Dundas in 1808. The latter had the slightly more distinguished naval career.

Dunkery Wootton Courtenay, near Minehead. The Dunkery Beacon, at 1350 feet, is the highest point on Exmoor. The hill itself is now referred to as the 'beacon', though originally that term referred to the signal fire which was lit on it in times of emergency.

Durham Heifer *See* Craven Heifer.

Durham Ox Beeston, Nottingham and elsewhere. This ox was bred by Charles Collings of Ketton, near Darlington. By the time it was six years old it weighed nearly two tons. The owner, who had paid the hefty sum of £250, made a substantial profit by touring the country with his prize ox in the early years of the nineteenth century, conveying the beast in a specially-built vehicle. The great impression made by this animal is reflected in the many pubs named after it, usually in towns which it visited on tour. The Ketton Ox at Yarm, Clev refers to the same creature.

Dust Shovel *See* Mother's Arms.

Dyers Arms Leek, Staffs. The pub is in an area known for its dyeing industry, originally based here because of the streams which ran in from the North Staffs moors. The arms of the Dyers' Company were granted in 1530.

Dying Gladiator Brigg, Lincs. The name of a famous statue in the Vatican Museum in Rome. It was seen by a former innkeeper while on holiday and he decided to make a copy of it. He placed his version of the statue above the front entrance and renamed the pub accordingly. There is a Gladiator in Gloucester.

Dyke Brighton. Also Devils Dyke, Poynings. For the local landmark known as the Devil's Dyke – a V–shaped cleft in the Downs. The legendary tale is that the Devil began to dig a trench which would cause the English Channel to flood the Weald, thus killing off the growing number of Christians in the area.

E

Eager Poet Milton Keynes. The 'poet' is Milton, while 'eager' is an approximation of Keynes ('keen'). A place–name pun.

Eagle Ross–on–Wye and elsewhere. A Christian and heraldic symbol, the eagle has been used as an inn sign since the fifteenth century. It was used to decorate church lecterns because it was the symbol of St John the Evangelist. For the Romans it was the emblem on their military standards. As a national symbol it suggests such countries as the USA, Germany and Russia. On pub signs it can be related to other things or events. The Ross-on-Wye pub, for instance, was the New Inn until 1969. It became the *Eagle* to commemorate the landing on the moon; Neil Armstrong descending from the lunar module *Eagle* to become the first man to step on the moon's surface. At Dereham in Norfolk the sign shows HMS *Eagle*, the aircraft carrier built in 1946, replacing one of the same name which was torpedoed in 1942. The sign at Plymouth also shows the aircraft carrier on one side, with a real eagle on the other side. At Mountain, near Bradford there is a Mountain Eagle. Kidderminster has an Eagle's Nest. *See also* Flying Eagle and Spread Eagle. Other related signs include Eagle Arms, London W6; Eagle Brewery Tap, Ryde; Eagle Tap, Kingston-on-Thames; Eagle Vaults, Witney; Eagles, Llanwrst, Pwys; Eagle's Head, Over Kellet, near Lancaster; Eaglet, London N7, Eagle and Chicks. Eagle bitter is brewed by Charles Wells of Bedford, who use the eagle as a trademark.

Eagle and Child Bury, Lancs and elsewhere. A reference to the arms of the earls of Derby, the Stanleys. Sir Thomas Latham, one of the family's ancestors in the four-teenth century, had an illegitimate son. He had the baby placed under a tree in which an eagle had built its nest. He then took his wife for a walk round the estate, and they 'discovered' the infant. Sir Thomas persuaded his wife that they should adopt it. In spite of this successful ruse he left most of his riches to his daughter Isobel, who married Sir John Stanley. In this way the Stanleys inherited both the estates and the heraldic eagle and child.

Eagle and Serpent Kinlet, Salop. The local squires here were formerly the Childes, whose arms showed an eagle and serpent. They were meant to symbolise courage and wisdom.

Earl Beatty *See* Admiral Beatty.

Earl Grey Edinburgh, and elsewhere. Charles Grey, 2nd Earl Grey (1764–1845) was British prime-minister 1830–34. He put through Wilberforce's act to abolish the African slave trade. His grandson, 4th Earl Grey (1851–1917) was governor-general of Canada, 1904–11. He is still remembered there on Grey Cup Day, when the football final between east and west Canada gives all Canadians an excuse for a party. There is a Lord Grey at Wotton-under-Edge, Glos.

Earl Haig Hounslow. Another at Gussage All Saints, Dors. Also

Lord Haig, Hertford; Sir Douglas Haig, Effingham; Haig, Sutton, Sry. Douglas Haig, 1st Earl Haig (1861–1928) was commander-in-chief of the British armies in France and Flanders in World War One, 1915–19. His name is associated with the British Legion's fund for disabled ex-servicemen, for which poppies are sold on Remembrance Sunday.

Earl Howe Holmer Green, Bucks. Another at Nottingham. Richard Howe (1726–99) was the British admiral who commanded the British fleet during the American Revolution. He is best remembered for his later victory (1794) against the French on the 'Glorious First of June'. This was the first sea-battle of the Napoleonic Wars.

Earl Kitchener *See* Lord Kitchener.

Earl Manvers Nottingham. This earldom dates from 1806. The family seat of the Pierreponts is at Thoresby Hall, near Ollerton, Notts.

Earl Marshal Liverpool. The earl marshal stage-manages state ceremonies and makes all arrangements for them. He is also governor of the College of Arms. Since 1672 the office has been held by the dukes of Norfolk.

Earl of Aberdeen's Arms New Deer, near Peterhead, Gramp. Also Aberdeen, Scarborough; Aberdeen Arms, Tarland, Gramp. George Hamilton Gordon, 4th Earl of Aberdeen (1784–1860) was foreign secretary under Wellington 1828–30. secretary for war under Peel 1841–46 and prime minister 1852–55.

Earl of Beaconsfield *See* Beaconsfield Tavern.

Earl of Cardigan Norwich. Also Lord Cardigan, London E3. James Thomas Brudenell, Earl of Cardigan (1797–1868) was the British general who commanded the light cavalry in the Crimean War. He was responsible for the Charge of the Light Brigade, which was seen by many at the time (1854) as a demonstration of reckless courage mainly thanks to a poem on the subject by Lord Tennyson. It contains such famous lines as 'Into the valley of Death/Rode the six hundred', also the telling comment: 'Someone had blunder'd'.

Earl of Chatham London SE18. William Pitt, 1st Earl of Chatham (1708–78) was a distinguished English statesman. He became head of a coalition government in 1757 and eventually retired because of mental disorder in 1768. His second son, William Pitt (1759–1806), also became prime minister. In spite of his title the Earl was known throughout the country at the height of his popularity as the Great Commoner. There is another pub of this name at Bridgend, near Lostwithiel, where the Earl was a local landowner.

Earl of Essex Basildon. Esx and elsewhere. Also Devereux Tavern, London WC2. Robert Devereux. 2nd Earl of Essex (1567–1601) was a soldier and favourite of Elizabeth I. He quarrelled with her when he married in secret the widow of Sir Philip Sidney (1590). In a later attempt to regain his standing at court he failed and was arrested. Tried for treason, Elizabeth signed his death-warrant and he was beheaded.

Earl of Sandwich London WC2. Edward Montagu, 1st Earl of Sandwich (1625–72) was an English admiral. He was actively engaged in restoring Charles II to the throne and was created Earl of

Sandwich soon after the king arrived at Dover. The 4th Earl of Sandwich, John Montagu (1718–92) was First Lord of the Admiralty in 1748 but was dismissed from the post. He held it again during the American war of independence, 'when the lowest depths of corruption were reached by the British navy' according to one commentator.

Earl of Warwick West Auckland, Dur and elsewhere. These signs are usually for Richard Nevil, Earl of Warwick (1420–71), known as 'Warwick the king-maker'. He gained his title by marrying Anne, daughter of the Earl of Warwick, and taking over the family's estates. He was also a nephew of Richard, Duke of York and a first cousin of Edward IV, besides being connected to many other noble families. Warwick was well-rewarded by Edward IV for defeating the Lancastrians in 1461 and securing for him the throne. He nevertheless quarrelled with Edward and proclaimed Henry VI to be king. Edward was temporarily driven out of the kingdom, but he returned in 1471 with an army which gained a decisive victory. Warwick was killed in the battle.

Earl Russell Bristol. Another in London NW1. Also Lord Russell, Leek, Staffs and Dresden, near Stoke-on-Trent. John Russell, 1st Earl Russell (1792–1878) was an English statesman who named the newly-formed Liberal Party and was twice prime minister, 1846–52 and 1865–66. His grandson was Bertrand Russell, 3rd Earl Russell.

Earl St Vincent Egloshayle, Corn. Another at Bristol and Ramsgate. Admiral Sir John Jervis (1735–1823) won a famous victory over a much larger Spanish fleet off Cape St Vincent in 1797. He went on to become 1st lord of the admiralty 1801–06, during which time he built up Britain's naval strength. He also recognised the outstanding qualities of the young Nelson and saw to it that he was promoted.

Early Bird Aspley, Nottingham. The communications satellite of this name was launched in 1965 and is shown on one side of the pub sign. Also a reference to the proverbial early bird which catches the worm, shown on the other side of the sign.

East Dart Postbridge, Devon. One of the headstreams of the River Dart, which rises on Dartmoor and runs into the English Channel at Dartmouth.

Eastern Union Railway Ipswich. This railway later became part of the Great Eastern Railway which was absorbed in turn by the London and North Eastern Railway. The initials E U R led to the nickname of the pub, the *Ere You Are*.

East India College Arms Hertford Heath. This pub was rebuilt in 1806 by the East India Company, a chartered company formed in 1600 to trade with India and the East.

East Kent Arms Whitstable and elsewhere. In Kent, as at Ramsgate and Folkestone a pub of this name commemorates the East Kent Railway, which once had a terminus nearby. Elsewhere the pub sign shows the griffin from the badge of the East Kent Regiment.

East Suffolk Tavern Aldeburgh. For the county regiment.

Ebor Harrogate. A short form of Eboracum, a later version of Latin Eburacum, name of the Roman legionary fortress and *colonia* at York. The original meaning was probably to do with yew trees, though it later came to be interpreted as 'boar town'. Harrogate is within the diocese of York, whose archbishop uses Ebor as the 'surname' of his official signature, according to ancient custom.

Echo Gravesend. In classical literature Echo was a nymph in love with Narcissus, who did not return her affection. She pined away until only her voice remained. *Echo* has been the name of many Royal Navy ships since the eighteenth century. During World War Two it was the name of a destroyer.

Eclipse Tunbridge Wells. The name of a stagecoach which was famous in its day. Pubs of this name at Egham, Sry and elsewhere (as also for the Old Eclipse at Mansfield) are for a horse which was born during the sun's eclipse in 1763 and named accordingly. He became a great champion, and sired countless others.

Eddystone Plymouth. The famous lighthouse erected by Sir James Douglas between 1879–82. It stands on a group of rocks about fourteen miles away. *See also* John Smeaton.

Edgar Wallace London WC2. Edgar Wallace (1875–1932) is best remembered for his detective thrillers, which remain bestsellers. This pub was renamed in his honour in 1975 and contains a fine collection of pictures, prints, etc, relating to the writer.

Edinburgh Castle Hastings and elsewhere. The castle is famous well beyond Scotland because of its tattoo, which is featured on the Hastings sign.

Edith Cavell Norwich. This famous English nurse and patriot was executed by a German firing squad in 1915, when she was fifty years old, causing a national outcry in Britain. She had been helping wounded British soldiers escape over the Dutch frontier from Belgium during World War One. Her grave lies in *Life's Green* at the south-east end of Norwich Cathedral.

Edward The Confessor Stevenage. This Anglo-Saxon king died in 1066, having ruled since 1042. His religious piety was the reason for his nickname, the Confessor. He is considered to have governed well, freeing his people from crippling taxes. He is remembered as the founder of Westminster Abbey.

Edward II Merriott, near Taunton. Edward (1284–1327) was king 1307–27. During his reign there was much dissension in the country and at court. He suffered defeat to the Scots at Bannockburn and after a generally unsuccessful reign was forced to abdicate. He was then brutally mistreated and killed. It is not clear why this pub chose to commemorate him: he was born in Wales and died at Berkeley Castle, near Gloucester.

Edward VII Chatham and elsewhere. Edward (1841–1910) was king 1901–10. He was the eldest son of Queen Victoria and was Prince of Wales for sixty years. The pub name is sometimes King Edward VII, as at London E15 and elsewhere. The signs at Barking and Eccles of Albert Edward also refer to him.

Eel Pie Twickenham. On Eel Pie Island, in the River Thames, which may have been named (if 'eel pie' is not a corruption of something quite different) because eel pies were eaten there by picnickers, or because of the island's shape.

Eels Foot Eastbridge, Sflk and elsewhere. In Eastbridge they explain this name as a corruption of 'Devil's Foot or Boot'. The legend is that the village priest managed to tie the devil in his boot, which he then flung far out to sea. There is a clear link here with Devil in the Boot (*see* Boot), a story which was widely known in earlier times.

Egmont Arms Midhurst, W Ssx. After John Perceval, 2nd Earl of Egmont (1711–70), who was First Lord of the Admiralty 1763–76. Mount Egmont in New Zealand was named in his honour (1770) by Captain Cook.

Egypt Cottage Newcastle-on-Tyne. In the early nineteenth century a row of houses were temporarily used as granaries, storing imported corn. The area became known as Egypt, biblical allusions being more common, and more widely understood, at that time than they are now. Joseph erected granaries in Egypt and stocked them during the years of good harvests. The story is told in Genesis 41.

Egyptian Queen Blaby, near Leicester. A 'theme palace' opened in the 1960s by Holes, the Newark brewers. The interior decor is suitably Egyptian, even the lavatory doors being carved sarcophagus-style. The sign compliments Queen Nefertifi (or Nefertari), whose mummy-case is one of the largest and most magnificent ever discovered. She was renowned for her beauty.

Eight Bells Beaminster, Dors and elsewhere. Since this is the normal number of bells in a peal, the sign is fairly common near rural churches. At Hingham and Wells, both in Norfolk there is a similar Eight Ringers. In seaside areas there may be a reference to the eight bells which signify the ending of a watch.

Eight Kings Portland, Dors. The sign shows eight playing–card kings, two from each suit, but the name may refer to eight 'kings' who paid homage to Edgar the Peaceful (or Peaceable) in the tenth century.

Eight Locks West Bromwich, W Mids. The locks are on the local canal system.

Eight Ringers *See* Bell.

Eilean Dubh Black Isle, Hghld. The Gaelic name for 'Black Isle', on which snow seldom lies even when neighbouring areas are 'white'.

Elastic Coventry. Elastic materials are manufactured in a nearby factory.

Elbow Room Paisley. A name that promises the customer that he will be able to move about freely inside, while hinting that he will be able to 'bend his elbow' satisfactorily as he drinks.

Elder Bush *See* Bush.

Eleanor Arms London E3. It is not clear whether this name refers to Eleanor of Aquitaine, queen of Henry II, or Eleanor of Castile, queen consort of Edward I. It was to commemorate the latter that the Eleanor crosses were erected to mark stages of her funeral journey to London, one of the best-known being at Charing Cross.

Electric Inn Birmingham. Also Electric Arms, Portsmouth. These were no doubt pubs which wished to advertise in the mid-nineteenth century that they were lit by the then newfangled electric light.

Elephant Andover. Another at Sheffield. Also Elephants at Smethwick. This animal provides a useful visual symbol, one which has a particular connection with drinking because of Cockney rhyming slang – 'elephant's trunk' = drunk. The phrase is often reduced to 'elephants.' A more recent association is with Carlsberg's Danish export lager. This is named *Elephant* with reference to the stone elephants at the gate of the Copenhagen brewery. Whitbread Fremlins of Kent is another brewery which uses the elephant as a symbol.

Elephant and Castle Trowbridge and elsewhere. A glance at the crest of the Cutlers' Company (used by them since 1622), which shows an elephant with a howdah on its back, the latter looking like a miniature castle, clearly reveals the origin of this name. The elephant was probably there on the coat of arms in the first place because ivory was used for knife handles. This simple explanation of the name will not please, or convince, those who insist on ingenuity. The legend that the name derives from *Infanta de Castile* will no doubt continue. By way of ingenious variation, Luton has a pub called the Elephant and Tassel.

Elephant's Head London NW1. This was the trademark of the Camden Brewery, which once stood opposite the pub. Other pubs of this name are at London E5 and Sevenoaks.

Elephant's Nest Horndon, near Tavistock. This was at first the nickname of the New Inn, a reference to its being the nest, or home, of a very large publican. He was obviously jolly as well as fat, and publicly accepted the joke against himself.

Eleven Cricketers Dartford. Another at Storrington, W Ssx. The Dartford village team of that time claims to have played its first fixture on the local pitch in 1723.

Eleven Ways Oldham, Lancs. It is said that there are eleven ways leading away from the pub.

Eliza Doolittle London NW1. The pub is near the Shaw Theatre and the pub is named after one of that playwright's best-known creations. In *Pygmalion* Eliza is the flower-girl who is taught to speak correctly by Professor Higgins. The musical based on the play was *My Fair Lady*.

Elizabeth of England Elmley Castle, near Evesham. The inn sign says that Elizabeth I visited the village on 20 August 1575. Her portrait is on one side of the sign, her retinue on the other.

Elm Norwich. Also Elms, London E11; Elm Tree, Radstock, Som, Elm House, Liverpool; Elm Park, Elm Park, Esx; Elm Shades, Earlswood, Sry. All such names appear to be inspired by the simple presence nearby of one or more elm trees. The number is often specified in the pub name, as with One Elm, Stratford-on-Avon;

Three Elms, Clewer, near Windsor; Four Elms, Cardiff; Five Elms, Dagenham; Nine Elms, Gravesend. Other names include Church Elm, Dagenham; White Elm, Woolpit, Silk; Bush Elms, Romford, Old Elm, Reading. *See also* Copcut Elm, Queens Elm.

Embassy Overcombe, Dors. Another in Aberdeen. Technically this is the residence of an ambassador, but the word was transferred easily to any building which was felt to be, or which its owners hoped would be, imposing. Thus it became a cinema name in the 1920s and 1930s and has since had other uses as a trade name.

Emigration Stockport. The name of a racehorse.

Emma Hamilton London SW20. Emma, Lady Hamilton (1765–1815) was a celebrated English beauty. She was at first the mistress, later the wife, of Sir William Hamilton, British ambassador to Naples. After 1798 she was the mistress of Lord Nelson. She bore him a daughter in 1801. Romney painted her portrait on many occasions. At Neston in Cheshire there is a Lady Hamilton.

Emperor Hadrian *See* **Adrian's Head.**

Emperor of India Portsmouth. The name of a Royal Navy battleship, suggested by Winston Churchill when he was at the Admiralty. The battleship served throughout World War One. The name was carried by a minesweeper during World War Two. There had been an earlier HMS *Empress of India*, a battleship named in 1891, which presumably accounts for that pub name in Islington. The more general Emperor and Empress have also been ship names, as well as naming pubs in Ipswich and Cambridge respectively.

Empire Bath. A patriotic Victorian sign, when the British Empire was one 'on which the sun never sets'. .

Empress Eugene Cardiff. Presumably a reference to Eugénie–Marie de Montijo de Guzman (1826–1920), wife of Napoleon III and Empress of the French 1853–70.

Empress of Russia London EC1. Catherine I (1684–1727) of Russia, second wife of Peter the Great, having been his mistress. When he died she ruled in his place for two years. The Russian empress known as Catherine the Great of Russia was a different person, Catherine II (1729–96), born a German princess. She married Peter III, but a group of conspirators headed by her lover, Grigori Orlov deposed him in 1762 in her favour. She was a cruel but effective ruler.

Encore Stratford-on-Avon. A suitably theatrical name for Shakespeare's town, and perhaps the call used by regulars instead of the usual 'Same again, please'. The sign shows an actor and actress taking their bow.

Endeavour Teignmouth. The name of a yacht which was a challenger for the Americas Cup in the 1930s. Also a pub of the same name in Whitby, the birthplace of Captain Cook, and named after one of his ships.

Engine Ashwell, Herts and else-where. This was earlier the Engine and Drum, the 'drum' being a cylindrical threshing machine which was driven by the steam-engine mounted on a horse-drawn wagon. The whole outfit must have been a great novelty when first seen in the English country-side. The pub sign at Kenilworth shows a prototype of the famous *Rocket* locomotive.

Engineer Harpenden and elsewhere. A reference to the driver of a railway engine, such an object being a great curiosity in this area in the 1860s, when the railway arrived. The sign at Dover shows a jolly toper enjoying his pint, with a railway viaduct in the background. At Newhaven in Sussex the sign portrays Brunel standing against the Avon Gorge at Bristol, his Clifton Suspension Bridge nearby and his ship the Great Britain underneath.

Engineer's Arms Salisbury. The sign shows a worker at a bench in a locomotive repair shop.

England's Gate Bodenham, H and W. The pub is near the Welsh border.

England's Hero *See* Lord Nelson.

English Rose *See* Rose.

Ensign Stewart Edinburgh. Stewart was a sergeant of the Scots Greys at Waterloo. He single-handedly captured one of Napoleon's cherished eagle standards and was promoted to ensign on the field of battle.

Enterprise London SE5 Another at SW3. The name of a steam-driven omnibus built in 1833 for the London and Paddington Steam Carriage Company.

Erewash Tavern Ilkeston. Erewash is the name of the local canal.

Escape London WC1. The pub name referred to the escape of many British servicemen during World War Two from prisoner–of–war camps. It was well supported by a sign which showed broken barbed wire in close up and a fortified camp in the background. The pub was opened by two distinguished escapees, Air Vice-Marshal Burton, the first British prisoner to make a home-run to England from a German camp, and Oliver Philpot, one of those who escaped from Stalag-Luft III by means of the wooden horse. The pub has now been renamed Mabels.

Esplanade Mill Bay, IOW. This word has certain specialised meanings, but mainly refers to a place for walking along a sea-front, as here. It is similar to a promenade, though the basic idea of an esplanade is that it is on a plane, ie level ground.

Essex Skipper Harlow. The first pub to be opened in Harlow New Town (in 1952), and the first of the moth and butterfly pub names in the area. One side of the sign shows the butterfly, the other shows the skipper of a boat on the Essex waterways.

Essex Yeoman *See* Yeoman.

Ethelbert Cliftonville. Also King Ethelbert, Reculver, near Herne Bay. The name of two Anglo-Saxon kings, though this pub name probably refers to the Ethelbert who died in 616, having been King of Kent.

Etruria Etruria, near Stoke-on-Trent. The pub is in Etruria Road. Pub, street and district derive their name from Etruria Hall, a house built by Josiah Wedgwood in the eighteenth century. Etruria is an ancient district in the north of Italy, famous for its Etruscan pottery.

Evening Star Colchester. Others at Dorking and Lisburn, Ant. This was the name of the last steam locomotive constructed for British Rail in 1960. It left the Swindon works in March, 1960. The name was most appropriate, recalling such famous early locomotives as Stephenson's *Morning Star* (also commemorated as a pub name), and fitting in with the names of Britannia Class Pacific loco-motives, such as *Polar Star*, *Royal*

Star, Rising Star, Shooting Star, though locomotive 92220 was a Standard Class 9 2–10–0.

Everest Sheffield. One of the pub names which marked the conquest of Everest in 1953 by the expedition led by Lord Hunt. The mountain itself is known to the Tibetans as 'Mother-goddess of the earth', or Chomolungma. The name in English derives from Sir George Everest (1790–1866), who was surveyor-general of India. Other pub names marking the conquest of the mountain include Summit at Shirebrook, Notts, Top of the World at Warner's End, Herts, and Sherpa, in Everest Road, Scunthorpe. The latter name is a tribute to Sherpa Tensing, who reached the peak with Sir Edmund Hillary.

Exchange Puriton, Som. The name of a stagecoach which ran between Bath and Exeter. The pub of this name at Holbeach, Lincs, has a sign which shows a trio of peasants exchanging a small pig for a bag of money.

Exeter Arms Also Exeter's Arms. *See* Hurdler.

Exeter Hall Cowley, near Oxford. The pub has close associations with Exeter College, Oxford, which was earlier known as Exeter Hall.

Exmoor Forest Simondsbath, Som. The pub is in an area which was part of the Exmoor Forest until the eighteenth century.

Eype Mouth Eype, near Bridport. The name of the local stream, which runs into the bay here, or possibly the name of a nearby hill. Ekwall, in his *Oxford Dictionary of English Place-Names*, tends to favour the latter.

Exile of Erin Manchester. An indication that the landlord who gave the name was an Irishman in exile. *Erin* is an ancient name for Ireland, now usually restricted to poetical use.

Exit 43 Leeds. The pub is close to Exit 43 of the M1 motorway.

Exmouth Exmouth. Sir Edward Pellew (1757–1833) became Lord Exmouth after leading an expedition against the notorious Barbary Coast pirates in 1816. During that battle his coat was torn by a cannonball. The Exmouth Arms is found at London E1 and London EC1, and there is a Lord Exmouth at Gillingham, Kent.

Eyrie Leeds. A variant of Eagle's Nest, which is found eg at Kidderminster, but the reason for the name is not clear. Hitler's Berghof at Berchtesgaden, the village near Salzburg, was known as the Eagle's Nest, but that is hardly likely to have suggested the pub name.

F

Fagan's Sheffield. The pub was the Barrel until 1985. It was renamed to commemorate Joe Fagan, who retired as publican after long service to his customers and the brewery.

Fagins Broadstairs and elsewhere. For the rogue character created by Charles Dickens in *Oliver Twist*. He teaches a gang of boys to pick pockets and is ultimately brought to justice.

Fair Maid of Kent Lower Walmer, Kent. Joan (1328–85), only daughter of Edmond Plantaganet, Earl of Kent, wife of Edward, the Black Prince, was known as 'the fair maid of Kent'. She was the mother of Richard II. She was also the very first Princess of Wales.

Fairmile Fairmile, Devon. A reference to a good stretch of the Exeter road at a time when most of it was of poor quality. The local legend about Cromwell chasing a cavalier as far as the inn, with a comment being exchanged about 'leading thee a fair mile' as the Royalist surrendered himself, is less imaginative than many bar-room speculations about pub name origins.

Fair Rosamund Botley, near Oxford. A lady who is said to have been the mistress of Henry II. In some accounts she was poisoned by Queen Eleanor. In others, after having two children by the king, she retired to Godstow Nunnery and died there of a broken heart. The sign shows her in a pastoral setting, holding a bunch of primroses.

Fair Seat Totnes. The pub is pleasantly situated beside the River Dart.

Fair View Colwyn Bay and elsewhere. Probably a name meant to appeal to hotel guests rather than frequenters of the bars.

Fairway Keyworth, near Nottingham. Also Fairways, Troon. Both pubs are near golf courses, where the fairway is cut grass, as opposed to the 'rough'.

Fair Winds Aberaeron, Dyfed. The pub is near the beach.

Falchion Darlington. A falchion is a curved broad sword. A replica of one hangs outside this pub, while differing stories account for its being of importance. One local legend concerns the slaying of a mythical beast which had devoured a few residents. Another says the weapon was used to slay Wat Tyler, leader of the Peasants' Revolt, in 1381.

Falcon Bude, Corn and elsewhere. The Bude name refers to a stagecoach which once operated a daily service across the Devon border. Elsewhere the name is a reminder that falconry was a royal sport for centuries. Falcons appear in the arms of Elizabeth I and William Shakespeare, amongst others. Port Erin, Isle of Man has a Falcon's Nest and Edinburgh a Falcon Arms.

Falcon Bearer Knutsford, Ches. A title which is given to the leader of the annual Knutsford Carnival.

Falkland Arms London WC1. Renamed in 1982 to celebrate the successful Falklands Campaign. The pub was formerly the Bull and Mouth. Before 1982 there were already *Falkland Arms* pubs at Dorking and elsewhere, perhaps associated with Lucius Cary,

Viscount Falkland (1610–43). He was secretary of state in 1641.

Fallen Knight Ashby-de-la-Zouch, Leics and Loughborough. An allusion to the jousting tournaments which were once held in the area.

Fallow Buck *See* Buck.

Falmouth Packet Germoe, near Helston. The packet boat which took the mail to various European ports once a week, as from 1703.

Falstaff Lincoln. Another in Plymouth. Also Falstaff Hotel, Falstaff Tap, both in Canterbury, Jolly Falstaff at Padgate near Warrington, Sir John Falstaff, Dover and elsewhere. This character appears in three of the Shakespeare plays. He is mountainously fat, a boastful liar, but fond of practical jokes and often acted as if he were a loveable old rogue. Some have seen in the character's name a play on 'Shakespeare', namely 'false-staff'.

Famous People For royalty see the various names beginning King, Queen, Prince, Princess, etc, though by convention living members of the royal family are not mentioned in pub names. One London pub was hastily named Lady Diana a month before that lady became Princess of Wales, but the Prince of Wales invariably refers to previous holders of that title. *See also* names beginning Duke, Lord, Earl, Sir, etc, plus a few beginning Lady for others of social note. Admirals and generals are very well represented on signs, led by Nelson and the Duke of Wellington. Most of the prime ministers since Sir Robert Walpole assumed that description occur on inn signs, even though the name may now have given way to an allusion such as Pipe and Gannex for Harold Wilson.

Other politicians occur fairly frequently, though they tend to be commemorated in this way after they have died rather than when they are still living. Writers do well, though Shakespeare is not honoured as frequently as one might think, or as he deserves. Dickens, Scott and Burns are naturally mentioned, while Pepys and Dr Johnson occur more often than one would expect. The name of Isaac Walton, being almost synonymous with Fisherman's Arms or Rest, is found on riverside inn signs. Other groups include men of the church, saints, artists, engineers, inventors, scientists and entertainers. There is a Bogarts, Charlie Chaplin, Cheekie Chappie, David Garrick, Jean Harlow, Kean's Head, Kemble's Head, Lancashire Lass, Lauder, Laurel and Hardy, Lillie Langtry, Marie Lloyd, Portman and Pickles, Sarah Siddons, Sir George Robey, and a Talma, but living actors and actresses, as can be seen from that list, are not mentioned. Television seems to have had relatively little impact on pub-naming, though one finds Captain Mannering, for the late Arthur Lowe, and Steptoe's. Finally there is a small group of men to whom pub enthusiasts are likely to refer as 'men of the beerage'. The great brewers such as Samuel Whitbread, Ben Truman, Joseph Benskin, Sir John Devenish and others are occasionally honoured by having pubs named for them. Local personalities are dealt with in individual entries where we have the facts, and there is a separate note about Women in Pub Names.

Fanny Grey Barnoldswick, Lancs. Commemorates a well-known trotting horse of the 1920s.

Fantail Kirkby, Liverpool. The type of domestic pigeon which has a fan-shaped tail.

Farmers Arms St Bride's Major, near Bridgend and elsewhere, especially in S Wales. The St Bride's sign shows the farmer sitting down to enjoy his pint, a cockerel on his shoulder, and a piglet and lamb at his knee. Associated names include the following:

Farmer, Catherington, Portsmouth; Farmers, Kempsey, H and W; Farmer's Boy, Kidderminster: Farmer's Glory, Haslingden, Lancs; Farmer's Home, Durley, Hants; Farmer's Man, Benson, Oxon; Farmer's Rest, Newcastle-on-Tyne. In addition, there are Farm House, Norwich; Farm Tavern, Hove; Farmyard, Youlgrave, Derbs.

Farne Seahouses, Northld. The Farne Islands lie off the coast of Northumberland and are well-known as bird sanctuaries.

Far Post Worthing. A football reference, not surprisingly, since the landlord is former England and Arsenal centre-forward, Malcolm MacDonald.

Farriers Arms Framlingham, Sflk. Also Farrier, West Bromwich, Farriers, Todenham, Glos. Farriers were obviously of some importance when horse travel was normal. The arms consist of three horseshoes, while the crest shows a hand holding a hammer.

Farthings Castle Bromwich, Warks. Another at Blackburn. The Castle Bromwich example picks up a local place name which derives ultimately from a field name. 'Farthing' was applied to a field of small size.

Fat Cat *See* Cat.

Father Red Cap London SE5. Mother Red Cap is the usual inn sign. This variation was no doubt inspired by it.

Fauconberg Arms Coxwold, N Yorks. Lord Fauconberg was married to Oliver Cromwell's daughter, Mary. The village tradition is that Mary brought her father's body to the Fauconberg home, at nearby Newburgh Priory.

Fawn Windsor. The young deer which can be seen in Windsor Great Park. The pub of this name in Plymouth is a reminder that *Fawn* is also the name of a ship, first used by the Royal Navy when a French ship called the *Faune* was captured in 1805 and added to the fleet.

Fazakerley Chorley, Lancs. Nicholas Fazakerley was a local lawyer and politician. He represented Preston, where there is also a Fazakerley Arms. He died in 1767.

Feathers Rickmansworth and elsewhere. Normally a reference to the plume of three ostrich feathers, first adopted as a crest by the Black Prince. At Ludlow the sign is for Arthur, Prince of Wales, who was the first husband of Catherine of Aragon. He died in 1502 and his younger brother, Henry VIII, married her a few years later. Variations of this sign include Feathers Royal, Aberaeron, Dyfed; Plume, Hungerford, Berks; Plumes, London NW10; Plume of Feathers, Rickford, Avon; and elsewhere; Prince's Feathers,

Winsford, Ches; Prince's Plumes, Cheltenham; Prince of Wales's Feathers, Kendal and Southampton. Perhaps the ultimate meaning of all these references to feathers is contained in the everyday expression 'a feather in your cap', meaning something you can be proud of. This in turn refers to an almost universal custom amongst primitive people of adding a feather to their hat or head-dress when they had killed an enemy.

Fellmongers Arms London SE1. Fellmongers were dealers in animal skins or hides, especially sheep-skins. 'Fell' in the sense of 'skin' is connected in origin with the word 'film'.

Fellows Nottingham. For the nineteenth-century company, Fellows, Morton and Clayton Brewhouse, which had premises here. The pub was opened in 1981 but is a recreation of a Victorian alehouse.

Fellowship Horfield, Bristol. The sign shows two employees of the British Aircraft Company greeting each other, against the background of a Brabazon airliner and a Bulldog bi–plane.

Fenman Stanground, Peterborough. Someone who lives or works on the Fens, low lands around The Wash which are covered completely or partly by shallow water.

Feoffees Rotherham. These are the members of a board of trustees who hold land for public purposes, usually charitable. The pub was originally built in 1776 as a School for the Poor and has been carefully preserved.

Ferret and Firkin London SW10. The 'ferret' is the half–tamed variety of the polecat which is used for destroying rats, driving rabbits from their holes, etc. The 'firkin' is a small cask holding a quarter of a barrel, or half a kilderkin. The *Ferret and Firkin* is one of a small chain of pubs which brews its own beer, and 'firkin' is used in the various names to forge the link. Other pubs are the Fox and Firkin, London SE13; Goose and Firkin, London SE1 and Frog and Firkin, London W11.

Ferrie Symond's Yat, near Ross-on-Wye. The sign shows two stalwart ferrymen, one holding his horse, punting their passengers across the River Wye. The licensees of this pub have owned and operated the ferry for over 300 years.

Ferry House London E14. A ferry used to connect Greenwich and the Isle of Dogs before the Foot Tunnel under the Thames was built in 1902. Also **Ferry**, Cookham, Berks.

Festival Inn Trowell, near Ilkeston. The village received 'a special award from the Festival of Britain organisers in 1951.

Festival House Norwich. The Norfolk and Norwich Music Festival has been held every three years at the nearby St Andrew's Hall since 1824. The original landlord was formerly a band-master of the Norfolk Regiment and a keen musician. The pub was a meeting place for the orchestra and chorus.

Festive Briton London E14. A reference to the 1951 Festival of Britain.

Fewsters Arms Bradford. The Oxford English Dictionary prefers to call these men *fusters*. They were makers of saddle trees, the wooden framework of saddles.

Fiddichside Craigellachie, Gramp. The pub is on the bank of the River Fiddich.

Fiddleford Inn Fiddleford, Dors. The name conjures up all kinds of visions to do with fiddlers of one kind or another, but the Fiddle–in the place name refers to an ancient personal name *Fitela*.

Fiddle i' th' Bag Burtonwood, near Warrington. The two pictures on the signboard show firstly an itinerant fiddler who was formerly well-known in the area. He always put his instrument away in a velvet bag after each performance. The second picture shows a kind of seed-sprayer used by local farmers.

Fiery Fred Darnal, Sheffield. Fred Trueman, the Yorkshire fast bowler, took 307 Test wickets for England. The pub was officially opened by him in 1982, and he is shown on the signboard bowling at top speed.

Fieryholes Bilston, W Mids. A reference to the furnaces in the nearby iron and steel works.

Fiesta Coventry. A fiesta, strictly, means the celebrations accompanying a religious holiday. Here it hints at the wide variety of entertainment available inside the pub, including 'music and dancing to suit all tastes'.

Fifteen Balls Penryn, near Falmouth. The fifteen balls in question are the roundels which appear on the coat of arms of Cornwall. They are arranged in triangular form. The **Cornish Arms** at Bodmin has fifteen half-roundels in bas relief on the sign.

53 Manchester The number of one of the city's oldest tram routes, now a well-used bus route. The pub was opened in 1979 by 'Inspector Blakey', a character in the television series *On the Buses* played by Stephen Lewis. Inside the pub the tram theme still dominates.

Fighter Pilot Canford Heath, Dors. A tribute to one of the best-known fighter pilots, Sir Douglas Bader,

who opened this pub in March, 1970.

Fighting Cocks St Albans and elsewhere. The St Albans pub is thought to date from the seventeenth century and takes the form of the original cockpit where the fighting cocks were let loose on one another. Cock-fighting was introduced to Britain by the Romans and was prohibited by Cromwell in 1653. It remained popular, however, until sterner measures against it were taken in the mid-nineteenth century. The birds were specially bred and equipped with steel spurs, while large sums of money were wagered on the outcome of the fights. Henry VIII and James I are said to have been royal admirers of cock-fights. At Ecclesfield, near Sheffield, there is a Fighting Cock, and signs of the Gamecock, as at Hereford, sometimes refer to the former presence of cockpits.

Fighting Harry Holt, Nflk. The inn sign shows Henry V in his armour, mounted and spurred and ready to do battle.

Filibuster Birmingham. Originally a term for a piratical adventurer; now best known in its sense of obstructing formal proceedings as much as possible by introducing points of order, etc.

Filly Setley, near Lymington, Hants. The pub is in the New Forest, an area well-known for its wild ponies. A filly is a young female horse, less than three or four years old (or five in the case of thoroughbreds).

Finger-post Offerton, near Stockport. Finger-posts are still to be seen in rural districts, set up at crossroads and indicating the direction to take for this or that place. Such signboards usually had the end shaped like a pointed finger.

Finishers Arms Bolton. Finishers perform the last operations in various manufacturing industries. Here the connection is with the local cotton and textile industry.

Finnygook Crafthole, Corn. The gook, or ghost, of a smuggler called Finny is said to haunt the area. He was killed whilst struggling to escape capture by the coastguards, or preventive men as they were formerly known.

Firebeacon Fulstow, near Louth, Lincs. A fire which is used as a signal, forerunner of such warning lights as those provided by lighthouses. Beacon is also found. There may be a heraldic reference to Edward IV or to the Admiralty.

Firebird Birmingham. A name which is applied to several small birds which have brilliant orange or red plumage, such as the Baltimore oriole or the scarlet tanager. This pub is any case known to its regulars as the Plastic Paris, because the lounge has been made to look like a French village square. The official name of the pub may have been suggested by Stravinsky's Russian fairytale ballet, which was first produced in 1910.

Firebox Yatton, near Bristol. The sign shows the footplate of a GWR locomotive. In the days of steam trains it was the fireman's job to keep the firebox topped up with coal.

Fire Brigade Bradford. At one time the local Fire Station was situated behind the pub. The sign shows a fire engine.

Fire Engine Marazion, Corn. In modern use this name usually refers to a machine (or vehicle mounted with such a machine) for putting out fires. It was also the local term for a steam engine, as in the Cornish pub name example. The engine was used in mines to pump out water. Other pubs called the *Fire Engine* are in Bristol and Oldham.

Firefly Hayes, GL. Another at Northampton. The firefly is a little insect which emits a phosphorescent light. Also the name of a twelve-foot dinghy, designed in 1946 by Uffa Fox. It has a moulded plywood hull and metal mast and is built at Hamble, Hants. This class of dinghy is raced in most parts of the country.

Firestone Brentford. The Firestone Tyre and Rubber Company was formerly nearby. The company was founded by Harvey Samuel Firestone (1868–1938).

First and Last Sennen, near Land's End and elsewhere. The Cornish pub once had a sign which said 'The last inn in England' on one side, 'The first inn in England' on the other. At Burham, near Rochester the sign of the pub is a woman's head, alluding to a saying that: 'without women the first part of our life would be deprived of assistance; the middle portion of pleasure; and the last of consolation'. At Great Yarmouth the pub of this name had a nickname *Cradle and Coffin* at one time. The licensee's wife was also a midwife, while the landlord also served as local undertaker.

First Edition London EC4. A pub in Fleet Street, formerly centre of the British newspaper world, and therefore using very appropriately a journalistic term. Another pub of this name is in the Isle of Dogs, almost opposite the new publishing works of the *Daily Telegraph*.

First in and Last out Larkhall, Bath. This sign was formerly common at the edge of a village or town, being the last licensed premises before the boundaries were extended. This was also the case until recently in the Larkhall area. The pub has now adopted the abbreviation **Filo's** as official; it has always been known as such to its regulars. The original name would probably have suggested the game of cricket to casual passers-by.

Fish Broadway, H and W. Another at Sutton Courtenay, near Abingdon. Also Fishes, North Hinksey, near Oxford, where the sign shows two perch and three pike swimming in a stream. Many publicans are keen fishermen, or have such amongst their customers, or have customers who drink like fish.

Fish and Duck Little Thetford, Nflk. The pub is near the junction of the rivers Cam and Great Ouse.

Fish and Quart Leicester. The pub was formerly patronised by porters at the city's fish market, who would quaff their ale by the quart. The inn sign shows a smartly dressed cod in waiter's uniform, carrying a drinks tray.

Fish and Ring London E1. The fish and ring are displayed on the heraldic arms of the city of Glasgow. They refer to a legend about St Kentigern, or Mungo, in which he miraculously saved the life of an unfaithful wife. She had given the ring to her lover, but the saint caused it to be found in the mouth of a fish caught in the river Clyde. The sign shows the saint with his cross in one hand, and a fish with a ring in its mouth in the other.

FISH AND SEA CREATURES A surprising number of different fish are mentioned in pub names. There is a Fish at Broadway, H and W, a Fish and Duck at Little Thetford, Cambs a Fish and Eels at Broxbourne, Herts, a Fishes at Highworth, near Swindon, a Three Fishes in Kingston-on-Thames and elsewhere, but from then on the references become far more specific. More sea fish are mentioned than freshwater fish, though amongst the latter the Trout is especially popular, together with Pike.

Fishermans Arms Pode Hole, Spalding and elsewhere. This area is well-known for the quality of the coarse fishing. There are many other pubs named for fishermen, both amateurs and professionals. They include: Fisherman, Fisher's Green, near Stevenage, Herts; Fisherman's, Bingley; Fisherman's Boy, West Pinchbeck, Lincs; Fisherman's Cottage, Reading; Fisherman's House, Rochdale; Fisherman's Haunt, Winkton, Dors; Fisherman's Joy, Selsey, W Ssx; Fisherman's Rest, Long Eaton, Derbs; Fisherman's Retreat, Marlow; Fisherman's Return, Kings Lynn; Fisherman's Hut, Leeds; Fisherman's Tavern, Whitby; Fishing Boat, East Runton, Nflk; Fishing Smack, Barking, Esx. For the last named *see also* Smack.

Fishmongers Arms London N22, and elsewhere. The Worshipful Company of Fishmongers were granted arms in 1512.

Fishpond Matlock Bath. The fishpond is opposite the pub. It is fed by the thermal waters which made this town well–known as a spa, and contains many goldfish.

Fist and Clippers *See* Hand and Shears.

Fitters Arms Peterborough. A compliment to the many patrons employed in the local engineering works.

Fitzhead Fitzhead, Som. The place name (and pub name) should correctly be *Fifehead*, a reference to the 'five hides' of land which formed the normal holding of a thegn, or feudal lord. The change to Fitzhead was obviously influenced by (aristocratic) family names such as Fitzpatrick, where Fitz– represents an Old French form of 'son', usually referring to an illegitimate son.

Fitzsimmons Arms Helston, Corn. Robert Fitzsimmons (1862–1917) was a Cornishman by birth, though he grew up in New Zealand. He became world heavyweight boxing champion in 1897 when he beat Jim Corbett. He had previously been middle-weight champion. His career spanned twenty-four years and involved him in some 300 fights.

Five Alls Cheltenham and else-where. This sign dates from the seventeenth century. It varies slightly from place to place (being found mainly in the West Country), but usually it shows a king with the caption 'I rule (for) all', a parson with 'I pray for all', a lawyer with 'I plead for all', a soldier with 'I fight for all' and a labourer with 'I work for all'. At Chepstow the labourer has become John Bull on the sign, and says cynically: 'I pay for all'. Another variant is to have a ploughboy saying 'I grow for all', as at Taunton where the sign has been reduced to the Four Alls. There was a popular jingle in the late seventeenth century which ran: 'King William thinks all,/Queen Mary talks all,/ Prince George drinks all./ Princess Anne eats all.'

Five Arrows Waddesdon, near Aylesbury. From the arms of Ferdinand Rothschild, who had this inn built in the nineteenth century in order to accommodate the servants of his guests.

Five Bells Bridport, Dors and elsewhere. In nautical terms 'five bells' could indicate 2.30 pm, or closing time, since the afternoon watch begins at midday. *See also* Two Bells.

Five Bells and Bladebone London E14. The first part of the name is as Five Bells above. The *Bladebone* recalls that on this site previously there was a slaughterhouse.

Five Elms *See* Elm.

Five Lions York. They appear on the city's coat of arms.

Five Miles from Anywhere, No Hurry Upware, Cambs. The message in the name seems to have been successful. The former tavern which bore it was frequently the scene of wild parties held by Cambridge students. The new pub that has taken over the name is noted more for the riverside views.

Five Pilchards Porthallow, Corn. A pilchard canning factory was next door at one time. They were packed in layers of five. There is a Three Pilchards at Polperro, Cornwall.

Five Ringers *See* Bell.

Five Wand Mill Gateshead. A local windmill with five sails, locally referred to as 'wands'.

Flag and Whistle Birchington, Kent. Another in York. An allusion to the equipment carried by railway guards.

Flamenco Fownhope, near Hereford. Previously the Highland Home, and decidedly Scottish, it became Spanish in its ambience and decor in 1964. The vigorous Spanish dance called the flamenco may have some connection with the flamingo bird (also *flamenco* in Spanish) because of the brightly coloured dresses worn by the dancers. The word actually means 'Flemish' which would apparently suggest 'gypsy' to a Spaniard.

Flarepath Hatfield, near Doncaster. There was formerly an RAF airfield nearby. 'Flarepath', with the sense 'a line of lights used to guide aircraft along a runway as they land or take-off', was first used at the beginning of World War Two.

Flash Harry West Bromwich. Originally intended to refer to the man who 'flashed' the furnaces every morning in local factories. It was accidentally taken to refer to the late Sir Malcolm Sargent, the distinguished conductor, who was affectionately known by this nickname. He is featured on the inn sign.

Flask London N6 and Fylingdales, near Whitby. When this pub was built in 1663, flasks could be obtained which could be filled with water from the nearby Hampstead Wells. The sign of the **Flask Tavern** in Hampstead, however, shows a soldier drinking from his flask on the field of battle. No doubt it contained something stronger than water.

Flat Cap Mottram, near Stockport. It is curious that a flat cap would now suggest to a Londoner a working man from the North. When John Marston used the phrase in the seventeenth century – 'wealthy flat caps that pay for their pleasure' – he meant a citizen of London. The reference was to the kind of flat cap sometimes worn by Henry VIII. It remained fashionable in London for a long time afterwards outside court circles, and 'flat-cap' still meant a Londoner in colloquial speech until the beginning of the eighteenth century.

Flat Iron Liverpool. The shape of the building on the plans suggested this name. At Salford the pub of the same name is located in the Flat Iron Market.

Flat Top Dewsbury, W Yorks. This pub was the Albion until 1976. The change of name conformed to popular usage in the area, the pub having a flat roof.

Flax Dressers Ashby-de-la-Zouch, Leics. The workers who prepared flax for the spinners, taking it through various refining processes. The linen industry was of importance in the area. Scutchers Arms, at Long Melford, Sflk, also refers to flax dressers. Scutchers beat the flax. At Newcastle-on-Tyne there is a Flax Mill.

Fleas House Huddersfield. Originally a nickname, the real name of the pub being the Fleece. Since 1978 it has officially been the

Palm Springs, borrowing the name of the exclusive winter resort in southern California.

Fleece East Dereham, Nflk and elsewhere. Not a pub where the customer will be 'fleeced', but a reference to the important wool trade. The prosperity of the nation depended upon it for several centuries.

Flemish Weaver Salford. Many weavers from Flanders settled here in the fourteenth century. They were brought over by Sir John Radclyffe in order to improve the local weaving trade. *See also* Bay and Say.

Fleshers Arms Dumfries. In Scotland 'fleshers' are butchers. Butchers Arms is found in England.

Fletcher Arms Angmering-on-Sea. John Fletcher (1579–1625) was a prolific English dramatist who frequently collaborated with other writers, especially Philip

Massinger. The plots of his plays tended to be rather complex.

Fletchers Arms Denton, near Manchester. The Company of Fletchers received a grant of arms in 1467. They were makers of and dealers in arrows. To fletch actually means to fit the feathers to an arrow.

Fleur-De-Lys St Albans and elsewhere. Also Fleur-De-Lis, Bedford: Fleur-De-Liz, Burham, near Rochester. Literally, 'lily-flower', but a heraldic lily rather than a real one. Its origin may have been an iris, or the top of a sceptre or battle-axe. It occurs in the royal arms of France and is thus symbolic of France in a general way. When Edward III assumed the title of 'King of France' the device was incorporated into English coats of arms, where it has since remained. It has also been adopted this century as the emblem of the Boy Scouts Association, but as a pub name it makes a fairly vague reference to royalty.

Flicks Rochdale. The pub was the Robin Hood until 1983. It is now a 'sound and light' pub which offers extracts from silent movies as one of its attractions. 'Flicks' is of course from the slang expression meaning 'cinema'.

Flint Knappers Brandon, Sflk. Knap means to break or snap with a short sharp blow. The flint knappers were the labourers whose job was to split flintstones.

Flintlock Hinckley, Leics. Another at Marsh, Devon. Technically a gun-lock fitted with a flint which produces a spark when struck by the hammer. This then ignites the gunpowder. Flintlock is commonly applied to the complete weapon, traditionally associated with old-time pirates, rather than to the lock.

Flitch of Bacon Little Dunmow, Esx. For a custom observed yearly on Whit Monday of giving a flitch or side of bacon to any married couple who can swear that they have not quarrelled or wished themselves unmarried during the previous year. The inn sign has a legend which reads; 'Painted in gold ye Flitch behold,/ Of famed Dunmow ye boaste;/ Then here should call fond couples all/ And pledge it in a toast.'

Floating Bridge *See* Bridge.

Floating Light Dob Cross, near Oldham. This pub stands at more than a thousand feet above sea-level. The lights of the inn appear to float in the air on a misty night.

Florence Nightingale Southsea. Also at Leeds and London SE1. Named of course for this famous nurse, a national heroine during the Crimean War, who was born in Florence, Italy, in 1820. By the time she died in 1910 she had reformed the British nursing service, and had caused thousands of little girls to be christened Florence in her honour. There is a Florence pub in Florence Street, London N1; a Florence Arms in Portsmouth.

Florin Birmingham. This coin, first minted in 1849, disappeared from British currency in 1971. It had been worth two shillings. It was originally made of silver, later of cupro-nickel, and was called a florin in the first place because it was floral – having a lily stamped on it.

Flouch Near Hazlehead, W Yorks. The local story about this name concerns the first landlord, who had a speech defect, a 'slouch lip'. The pub dates from the early nineteenth century, and it is interesting that Partridge records 'flouch' as meaning 'collapse, sag' at that time.

Flower Pot Hounslow. Also Flower Pots, Cheriton, Hants; New Flower Pot, Derby; Pot of Flowers, Stowmarket. Such signs came into being in the seventeenth century, having earlier placed the emphasis on the flowers, rather than the pot. These were always lilies, the emblem of the Virgin Mary. The Puritan dislike of saints and their symbols meant that adaptations had to be made to signs. The *Flower Pot* signs thus have a more respectable origin than might at first be thought, but it is well concealed. Names of this type given in recent times may simply refer to pots of flowers used as decorations.

Flowers The 'flower' group of pub names is dominated by the rose, which is treated separately under Rose. Flowers is found, as at Bacup, Lancs, but in that form reminds us of Flowers Brewery at Stratford-upon-Avon, which was closed in 1968. The name has been revived by Whitbreads for certain beers. A name like Bluebells of Scotland clearly has more to do with music than flowers, just as Black Tulip is more concerned with literature. Pot of Flowers, Hand and Flower and similar names have a religious origin which is explained in the entries. Primrose had a political meaning at one time, being strongly associated with Disraeli. Some of the genuine flower references in pub names are: Blooming Fuchsia, Ipswich; Bunch of Bluebells, Dudley Wood, W Mids; Camellia, Crossbush, near Arundel; Cornflower, Freshbrook, near Swindon; Daisy, Leeds; Daisy Field, Bardsley, near Oldham; Daley's Dandelion, Manchester; Flower of Kent, London SE13; Flower of the Valley, Rochdale; Hand and Marigold, Bermondsey; Lilacs, Isham, near Kettering; Lily, Bridport; Water Lily, Ipswich; Honeysuckle, Ramsgate; Pinks, Shenley, Herts; Poppy, London W2; Snowdrop, Lewes and elsewhere; White Heather, Ferndown, Dors.

Flushing Rye, E Ssx. For the Dutch seaport of this name (*Vlissingen* to the Dutch) to which boats from Rye regularly sailed.

Fly Boat Aspley, near Huddersfield. This term is applied to various kinds of boat. It was originally a boat used on the Dutch river *Vlie*. This was misheard in English and thought to be the word 'fly', meaning 'fast'. Its main modern use is for a boat used on canals. *See also* Shroppie Fly.

Flyer Chelmsford. This was formerly the name of a stagecoach. Church Fenton, near Tadcaster has a Fenton Flyer, but this has a railway association.

Fly House Barking, Esx. Some years ago huge swarms of bluebottles invaded the refuse dump in a nearby field. The pub name recalls the invasion.

Flying Bedstead Hucknall, Notts. The first vertical take-off and landing craft, which was immediately called 'the flying bedstead' because the experimental rig did indeed resemble such a thing, was tested at Hucknall aerodrome. The rig itself is now in the Science Museum at South Kensington. This pub was one of several named in the 1960s by the Kimberley Brewery, all based on a 'space-age' theme.

Flying Boat Calshot, near Southampton. The popular name of a seaplane which had a fuselage shaped something like a boat. Seaplanes were very much in the news in the 1920s and 30s, especially in 1931 when Britain won the Schneider Trophy (an international race for seaplanes) for the third time, and thus kept it permanently.

Flying Bull Rake, Hants. Two stagecoaches, the *Fly* and the *Bull*, used to call at this inn on the London to Portsmouth run and were responsible for its present name. So, at least, says one writer, though the *Bull* is a most unlikely name for a stagecoach. The same authority admits that the licensee of the pub prefers to tell the story of a mad bull which once came crashing into the bar.

Flying Childers Stanton-in-Peak, near Matlock and elsewhere. A racehorse which was trained by Sir Hugh Childers in the 1740s. It was the winner of many races.

Flying Dutchman Summerbridge, near Harrogate. The inn signs usually show the winner of the Derby in 1849. The racehorse had obviously been named after the ghostly ship which is supposed to haunt the seas near the Cape of Good Hope, luring other ships to destruction. The sign at Queenborough, Kent depicts this ship rather than the horse.

Flying Eagle Edgware. Commemorating Amy Johnson (1903–41), who flew solo from England to Australia in 1933, taking twelve days for the flight. She became a national heroine as a result of this exploit. She was later killed in a flying accident caused by bad weather. This pub is in Mollison Way, of significance because Amy married her fellow pilot Jim Mollison.

Flying Fox Colchester. Another famous racehorse, winner of the Derby in 1899, but the sign-painter has depicted a cheerful looking fox parachuting from the sky.

Flying Horse Banbury and elsewhere. Ultimately a reference to Pegasus, the winged horse ridden by Bellerophon in Greek mythology. Used as a heraldic device by the Knights Templar, to whom early examples of this sign may refer. More recently, in World War Two, Pegasus and his rider became the insignia of all British airborne troops. It should be remembered that stagecoaches were referred to at one time as 'flying machines', and their horses were 'flying horses' by association. As a general term for a fast–moving horse, the messengers of still earlier times may have inspired the name. Some writers have tried to link it with the quintain, used in tilting, but this seems unlikely.

Flying Horseshoe Clapham, near Lancaster. Flying Horseshoes, Sharpenhoe, near Bedford. 'Horseshoes' is a synonym for 'quoits' in some areas. The horseshoes are thrown at a peg stuck in the ground. The object of the game is to encircle the peg. This name can also be a variant of Flying Horse.

Flying Lady Crewe. A reference to the Rolls-Royce works which has been in Crewe since 1938. The flying lady is the unofficial name of the figurine that graced the radiators of Rolls-Royce cars. The company preferred to call it *The Spirit of Ecstasy*. A collection of Rolls-Royce pictures adorns the pub walls.

Flying Lancaster *See* Olde Lancaster.

Flying Machine Biggin Hill, Kent. The RAF airfield which became famous because of the Battle of Britain nearby. There is another pub of this name in Yeovil.

Flying Monk Malmesbury. Named for a monk, Elmer, who tried to fly from the Abbey Tower. The story is that he flew a good furlong before falling and breaking a leg. The pub has now made way for a supermarket.

Flying Saucer Gillingham. Another at Lutterworth, Rugby. Flying saucers have been with us by report since 1947. At least the patrons of these two pubs can truly claim to have seen one, and been inside for a visit.

Flying Scotsman Retford, Notts and elsewhere. Named for one of the most famous steam locomotives of all time, the first of Sir Nigel Gresley's Pacific class to appear after the 1923 formation of the London and North Eastern Railway. Its original number was 4472.

Flying Scud London E2. Another at Plaistow. These are both in the area of the London docks. Another pub of this name is at Earlswood, Sry. 'Scud' is ocean spray driven by the wind. Sailing ships were therefore commonly said to be 'scudding' along. The sign of the Bethnal Green pub shows a topsail schooner running before the wind.

Flying Shuttle Farnworth, near Bolton. A reference to the cotton-spinning machinery once used in the local mills.

Flyover Queensway, W Yorks. There is one nearby.

Foaming Tankard Birmingham. A sign which promised clients that they would get good measure, the copper tankard used by the innkeeper being filled to the brim. The same idea was sometimes conveyed by a Foaming Quart sign, as at Burslem and Norton Green. Oaken, near Wolverhampton has a Foaming Jug. Even more to the point were signs such as Full Measure, Hull, and Full Quart, Hewish, Som. There is also a Good Measure at Caldicot, near Chepstow.

Fob Watch Coventry. This pub has a living sign, an oversize version of a fob watch, which reminds passers-by of the city's former watchmaking industry. The 'fob' was a small pocket designed to hold a watch or money. The origin of the word is unclear, though Professor Weekley thought it might be a loan word from German dialect.

Fo'c'sle Maryport, Cumb. A suitably seafaring term for a pub in a port. The name represents the pronunciation of forecastle, which was originally a short raised deck, commanding a view over the enemy as from a castle. In the royal and merchant navies the forecastle is the living quarters of the crew, under the forward deck.

Fog in the Tyne North Shields. This was the Colonel Linskill until 1985. The new owner can see the Tyne from the pub windows, except on days when the fog rolls up the river.

Fold Stevenage. Fold Gate, Stradsett, Nflk, is a similar name. Both refer to sheep folds, or folds for other animals. 'Fold' in the sense of 'pen for animals' is unrelated to the word 'fold' meaning 'to turn something back on itself'.

Folly Padbury. Bucks and elsewhere. The Padbury pub shows a jester wearing his cap and bells. Follies at Bradford probably refers more to the antics of the patrons inside.

Fools Nook Sutton, near Macclesfield. The sign shows a clown leaning against an oak tree with what seems to be an ostrich egg at his feet, but the reason for his presence here is unknown.

Football There are football references of various kinds in pub names, as the following examples will indicate: Football, Swinton, W Yorks; Football Arms, Kirkcaldy; Football Tavern, Derby; Footballers, Ramsbottom; Footballers Arms, Burnley and Oldham; Footballers and Cricketers Public Arms, Linlithgow. Far Post, Worthing and Goalpost, Wolverhampton are also found. Names referring to specific teams are dealt with separately, but include Anfield Tavern, Airdrieonians, Canary and Linnet, Gunners, Hammers, Happy Wanderers and Trotters, Hawthorns, Magpies, Ninian Park Tavern, Pompey Tavern, Port Vale Tavern, Robins, Saints, Sky Blues, Spurs, Two Blues United. Some personalities of the game who have been commemorated are Jock Stein, Denis Law (King's Head), Bill Shankly (Shanks), Tom Finney, Stanley Matthews (Winger). There are other general references in such names as Ball, Intake, near Sheffield; Centre Spot, Sheffield and Greenock; Final, London WC2; Terrace, North Shields. *See also* Right Wing.

Footlights Newcastle-on-Tyne. Inspired by the local theatre.

Ford Holmfirth, near Huddersfield. The ford on the old packhorse road between Meltham and Holme Bridge is nearby.

Foresters Arms Farnham Common, near Slough, and elsewhere. The reference is to the Ancient Order of Foresters, a large friendly society with lodges, called 'courts', in the US and Britain. One such group used to meet at this pub. Southsea has a Bold Forester.

Forest Folk Blidworth, Notts. A book of this name was written in 1926 by James Prior Kirk, about the people who lived in the Sherwood Forest area in the early twentieth century.

Forest of Bere Denmead, Hants. A one-time forest area north of Portsmouth. Also Forest Rock, Charnwood, Leics, where the sign shows monks from nearby St Bernard's monastery in Charnwood Forest.

Forge and Hammer Machen, Gwent. Also Forge Hammer, Pleck, near Walsall and elsewhere; Forgemans Arms, Bristol. Such signs usually indicate the former presence of a smithy or foundry.

Forth Prestonpans, Loth. Also Forth Bank, East Wemyss, Fife; Forth Bridge, Queensferry. All inspired by the River Forth.

Fort St George in England Cambridge. On a former island in the river Cam, and said to be like Fort St George in Madras, South India. It was therefore called Fort St George at first, but *in England* was added later 'to avoid confusion'. It is difficult to see how anyone could actually confuse one with the other, but there it is. The sign shows an old fort, with ships approaching.

Fortune of War Babbacombe, near Torquay and elsewhere. One instance of this name in London in the early eighteenth century is known to have been a whimsical comment by a sailor–turned–landlord on the arm and leg he had lost in a sea-battle. At Woolwich the sign shows a sailing ship of this name. It was a merchant vessel which in times of war was armed and manned so that it could attack enemy shipping. Anything gained by such raids was considered the 'fortunes of war'.

Forty Foot Sheffield. The name of a 'drain' in Lincolnshire where employees of William Stones, an independent brewery, now part of Bass, held their annual fishing gala.

Fosse Way Leicester. The famous Roman road which ran from Exeter to Lincoln. The pub of this name at Aubourn near Lincoln has been renamed.

Foul Anchor Tydd St Giles, Cambs. This describes the badge of the British Admiralty. In general terms, a foul anchor is one which is hooked onto a wreck or another anchor.

Founders Arms London SE1. The Founders' Company was granted arms in the sixteenth century. They have as a motto: 'God the only founder'. This pub is built on the site of the foundry where the bells of St Paul's were cast. The cathedral itself is just across the river. Similar names include Foundry, Bristol; Foundry Bridge, Norwich; Foundry Vaults, Llangefni; Foundrymans Arm, Northampton; Foundry Arms, Bletchley, Bucks.

Fountain Stanmore, GL and elsewhere. This sign can be heraldic, referring to the crest of the Plumbers' Company and also the badge of the Master Mariners, or it can refer to a nearby spring or well. Before piped water was a normal part of everyday life such natural sources of water were of some importance.

Fountaine Linton-in-Craven, N Yorks. Richard Fountaine was the carpenter in this village in the seventeenth century. He travelled to London to seek his fortune and was there during the Great Plague of 1664–65, which kept him busy as a coffinmaker and undertaker. He contracted the plague himself but made a good recovery and returned to his village. Charles II made him a knight for his services to the needy folk of London, and for this and other blessings, Fountaine endowed a row of almshouses which are still in use.

Fountains London W2. The pub occupies part of the site known as the Water Gardens, in an area redeveloped in the 1960s.

Four Alls Taunton and elsewhere. Also Four Alls Vaults, Caernarvon. There was for a time in London a pub which converted this sign into Four Awls. In its true form it represents a slightly watered-down Five Alls (see Five Alls) and is perhaps even more widespread than that name.

Four Bells See Bell.

Fourburrow Truro. This is the name of the local hunt, which was founded in the 1750s.

Four Counties No Man's Heath, near Tamworth. The pub is at a meeting place of four counties, namely Derbyshire, Leicestershire, Staffordshire and Warwickshire. The sign shows them in map form, with their arms in the corners.

Four Crosses Hatherton, near Cannock and elsewhere in Staffs. For a former bishop of Lichfield. The arms of his see included four crosses.

Four Elms See Elm.

Four in Hand West Croydon and elsewhere. Sign-painters interpret this name either as a stagecoach driver in charge of four horses, or as a card-player holding four cards of the same denomination, eg aces.

Four-leafed Clover Clover Hill, near Norwich. Clover is generally associated with good luck: to be in clover is to be in a fortunate situation, like cattle in a field of clover. Clover normally has three leaves, the occasional four-leafed variety being traditionally associated with a special good fortune.

Four Lords St Blazey, Corn. The sign shows the quartet of local gentlemen who were jointly lords of the manor in this area in the sixteenth century. Their names were Rashleigh, Roberts, Pearce and Palkenhorn.

Four Seasons Harrogate and elsewhere. The Harrogate pub was opened in 1982 and is possibly unique in having four separate inn signs depicting each season. A similarly-named pub at Yate, near Bristol has a quartered sign.

Four Sisters London N1. The reference is to a former coffee-house run by four sisters.

Four Winds Falmouth and elsewhere. A sign found in ports, especially, and referring to the winds that were essential to the clippers and other sailing ships of former times.

Fox Twickenham and elsewhere. This sign has been used since the late fifteenth century. It has been disappearing from urban areas in recent years but is still common in the country, especially where fox-hunting occurs. The fox is often coupled with other animals or objects, but when alone he is likely to be seen in comic form, enjoying his pint of beer in a corner of the pub, for instance, while the hounds race by outside. Such a sign may also have a verse such as: 'I am a crafty fox, you see,/But there is no harm in me;/My master he has placed me here/To let you know he sells good beer.' At Felpham the sign shows a fox on one side and a cutter used by the Excisemen called the *Fox*, which at one time patrolled regularly between Shoreham and Southampton, on the other. Variant *Fox* signs include Barking Fox, at Barking, Esx, with a similar Catworth Fox at Catworth near Huntingdon; Hungry Fox, Gillingham; Crafty Fox, Chatteris, Cambs;

Running Fox, Leicester; Lazy Fox, Birmingham; Wheatland Fox, Much Wenlock, Salop; Wily Fox, Crumlin, Gwent; Blue Fox, Gunby, near Grantham; Black Fox, Liphook, Hants; Red Fox, Tiverton, Ches; Fox on the Hill, Dulwich; Fox under the Hill, Woolwich; Fox Revived, Norwood Hill, Sry; Fox's Brush, Ropsley, near Grantham; Fox and Cubs, Lilley, Oxon; Fox and Elm, Tuffley, Glos; Fox and Rabbit, Pickering, N Yorks; Fox Burrow, Lowestoft; Fox Hall, East Layton, N Yorks; Fox Hill, near Winchcomb, Glos; Fox House, Holmfirth, near Huddersfield; Fox Hunt, Halesowen, W Mids; Snooty Fox, Tetbury and elsewhere; Fox Covert, High Leven, N Yorks; Fox Hollies, Birmingham; Fox Vaults, Eccles.

Fox and Firkin *See* Ferret and Firkin.

Fox and Flower Pot Woking. The winning entry in a competition to find a name. It was felt it linked with the wildlife and gardens of the nearby Goldsworth Park.

Fox and Goose Ham Common, near Richmond, Sry and elsewhere. Early instances of this sign were a reference to *Reynard the Fox*, a medieval satirical tale which was highly popular. At Brent Knoll, Som, the sign refers to the carving on the bench-ends in the local church, which is in turn an allusion to the church (fox) carrying off the land (goose) of the laity. In many cases the inn sign must be an indication that the game called *Fox and Geese* (often *Fox and Goose*) was played there. This is a form of Nine Men's Morris. For an illustrated description of the game see Brewer's *Dictionary of Phrase and Fable* under 'Morris'. Another pub name reference to this game occurs in Marlipins.

Fox and Grapes Nottingham and elsewhere. Probably an allusion to Aesop's well-known fable. The fox tries to reach a bunch of grapes which he would dearly love to eat, but they are beyond him. He therefore declares that it is of no importance, since the grapes were sour anyway. It was this fable which gave rise to the expression 'sour grapes'.

Fox and Hounds Barley, Herts and elsewhere. A popular sign, not just in hunting country. The Barley sign is the best-known. It stretches right across the road, as many tavern signs used to do. Warminster has a Fox and Hound, which may be compared with the Fox and Dog, formerly at Rochdale. West Bromwich has a Fox and Dogs.

Fox and Knot London EC1. In the 1740s the tavern on this site had a landlord named Fox. His wife made head–dresses which incorporated the fashionable 'topknot' of the time.

Fox and Vivian Leamington Spa. The *Vivian* was added to the existing name of this pub, the more conventional Fox, by a former landlord. He had won a substantial amount of money by betting on a steeplechaser called *Vivian*, a horse often ridden by the Captain Becher of Becher's Brook fame.

Foxhunter Yelverton, Devon. The name of a famous show–jumper ridden by Colonel Harry Llewellyn at the Helsinki Olympics of 1952, where they were the winners of Britain's only gold medal. The pub of this name at Narborough, Leics is in the middle of fox-hunting country.

Foy Boat Ramsgate. 'The foyers of this town form a numerous and hardy class' said the writer of a book about Thanet in the early nineteenth century. 'To foy' was to go to ships with provisions and assist them when they were in distress. The boats used for this purpose duly became known as 'foy boats'. They operated from such places as Margate, Broadstairs and Deal as well as Ramsgate.

Foyle View Eglinton, near Londonderry. The Foyle is the name of the local river and lough.

Framesmiths Arms Bulwell, Nottingham. The frames made by these craftsmen were used in the hosiery and lace industry, still of importance in Nottingham.

Free Butt Brighton. The pub has a pleasantly punning sign which may commemorate an actual incident. A bowler-hatted drayman is lifting a butt of ale. He is about to be butted in the rear by the landlord's pet billy-goat.

Free House Longparish, Hants. Another at Stedham, W Ssx. Normally a term for a pub which is free of any brewery ties, and therefore able to offer a wide range of beers from different breweries. Brian Glover, in his *Camra Dictionary of Beer*, hints darkly that the term is 'often abused' nowadays.

Free Library Birkenhead. The pub itself is not a library, but is close to the site of the public library that was opened in 1864. The present-day public library is about a mile away.

Freemasons Arms London SE13. Also Freemason, Brighton; Freemasons Tavern, London, E16. The original freemasons were stone masons in medieval times who operated a closed shop union. They used secret signs in an effort to exclude what would now be called 'cowboy' builders. In modern times the freemasons are members of a fraternal society which does a certain amount of charitable work.

Free Press Cambridge. Named after a well-known radical journal of the 1830s, though there are still local newspapers of this name in East Anglia.

Free Trade Wigan. The free trade doctrine is that international trade should be free of all restrictions, such as import duties or quotas. In the 1840s its main advocates were John Bright, MP for Manchester, and Richard Cobden, MP for Stockport. The Liberal Party adopted it as official policy, and it became national policy between 1860 and 1932. There is a **Free Trader** at London, SE15. The difficulty of illustrating an abstract concept on an inn sign has been tackled in different ways. At Sileby, Leics, a fully-loaded and sorry-looking donkey is shown, being led along by his master.

French House London W1. This was the London centre for the Free French during World War Two. General de Gaulle is said to have drunk here, as is Dylan Thomas, though one cannot imagine them drinking together. This pub was formerly known by the name of York Minster.

French Revolution London SW15. The political upheaval that began in France in 1789, mainly a rebellion of the underprivileged classes against feudal oppression. Its effects were felt in many other countries, and some would say that it caused Europe to emerge from the Middle Ages into nineteenth century liberalism.

Friar Bacon Oxford. Also Bacon Arms, Newbury. The Friar at New Marston, near Oxford, also refers to him. Roger Bacon (1214–94) was born in Somerset but was educated at Oxford. He became a Franciscan monk but was often in trouble with his superiors. He was interested in natural science, and is respected for his experimental methods and direct observation. He wrote a general treatise on science, the *Opus Majus*, together with other works, but in 1278 his writings were declared heretical. He is sometimes wrongly said to have invented gunpowder and to have used both a telescope and microscope.

Friars Tavern Carlisle. The pub stands on the site of a Franciscan friary. It was established in the mid-thirteenth century and survived for nearly three hundred years. Plymouth has a Friary and South Bersted, Bognor Regis a Friary Arms. Ipswich has a Friar's Head and Hassocks, W Ssx a Friar's Oak.

Friar Tuck Arnold, near Nottingham, and elsewhere. The popular fat and jovial chaplain who accompanied Robin Hood and his band. He occurs as Fryer Tuck in Cheltenham, as if he were a fish-fryer. He is also the Jolly Friar at Blidworth, in Sherwood Forest country, while the Tuck's Habit refers to him at Bramcote, near Nottingham. Wakefield has a Friar Tuck's Tavern.

Friend at Hand Aylesbury. Also Friend in Hand, formerly at Hounslow; Friend in Need, Dover; Friendly Inn, Frankton, near Rugby; Friends, Llanelli; Friends Arms, Johnston, near Haverfordwest; Friendship,

Devonport and elsewhere. The sign at Aylesbury shows a shepherd holding a lamb in his arms. It is typical of the highly sentimental pictures which were popular in the nineteenth century.

Frigate London WC2. The type of naval vessel just as important in the modern Navy as in Nelson's era. The entrance to this pub has a ten foot high ship's figurehead which welcomes landlubbers aboard.

Frighted Horse Handsworth, Birmingham. It is commonly said that this sign was meant to be the *Freighted Horse*, ie a packhorse laden with goods. The change to *Frighted Horse* is always put down to carelessness on the part of an early sign-painter who could not read very well. The word 'freight', however, invariably meant a cargo carried by ship in Britain, though it took on a more general sense in the USA. Whatever the truth of the matter, the story of the illiterate sign-painter would be difficult to kill off.

Frog and Firkin *See* Ferret and Firkin.

Froghall York. The name of a successful racehorse.

Froize Chillesford, near Woodbridge, Sflk. The pub was built in 1980 on the site of an ancient alehouse, associated with the monks of the nearby priory. A 'froize', 'froise', or 'fraise' as it is also spelt, is a kind of pancake or omelette, usually served with slices of bacon.

Frozen Mop Mobberley, near Knutsford. This was the Warford Arms until 1950. The present name recalls a trivial incident in which a maidservant left a mop in a bucket of water overnight and found it frozen solid next morning.

Fruiterers Arms *See* Fruits and Vegetables.

Fruits and Vegetables It is the fruit of the Grape Vine, as at Peterborough and elsewhere, the Grapes, Ebberston, near Scarborough or Bunch of Grapes, London SW1 and elsewhere which most often represents this group. Winchester has an Old Vine, a reminder that the plant itself can survive for centuries, as well as the pub that bears the name. The apple is next in popularity and is treated separately under Apples. The cherry then seems to be dear to the Englishman's heart. There is a Cherry Arbour at Sparkbrook, near Birmingham; Cherry Gardens, Wigan; Cherry Grove, Rowbarton, near Taunton; Cherry Orchard, Chester; Cherry Tree, West Drayton, Bunch of Cherries, St Albans; May Duke (a variety of sour cherry), Reading. The Cherry Orchard, Chester is probably an accidental reminder of Chekhov's famous play, first produced in 1904, about a landowning family who are forced to sell their estate. Cherry Pickers is a far from accidental reference to a famous regiment. Pub name references also occur in the Greengage, Bury St Edmunds, Orange and Orange Tree, Pershore Plum, Pineapple, Strawberry. The Oranges and Lemons, at St Clements, Oxford, one of the best of the many nursery-rhyme references in pub names, has unfortunately been changed. Overseeing the above-mentioned names is the Fruiterers Arms, at Lewes, E Ssx. Vegetable references in pub names are relatively few, and are not always what they seem. Cabbage is a tailoring reference, Cabbage Patch an allusion to a rugby ground. The Oxnoble variety of potato is honoured by having at least two pubs named for it, and there is a Sack of Potatoes at Gosta Green, near Birmingham. Other such names include Bean, Hull; Beanstalk, Stirling; Cauliflower, Seven Kings, Esx; Rhubarb, Bristol. *See also* Artichoke, Bunch of Carrots, Purple Onion, Round of Gras.

Frying Pan London E1. Another at Wednesbury, W Mids. When street signs were commonly used by a variety of tradesmen in former times, the frying pan was popular with ironmongers. Some connection with that trade, or the visual simplicity of the sign, caused it to be taken over as a pub name.

Fullers Bath. The wine-shippers Fuller and Hicks used to occupy the premises.

Fullers Arms Berwick. Another nearby in Brightling, E Ssx. An eccentric squire who lived in this area at one time (died 1834). He was known as 'Mad Jack' Fuller, and built concrete follies in various places. Typical is the sixty foot pyramid which stands over his grave in Brightling churchyard.

Full House Monk Bretton, near Barnsley. In the game of poker this expression indicates a hand which consists of three cards of one value, two of another. It also manages to suggest the successful result of putting on a good show of some kind, and being rewarded with large audiences.

Full Measure Also Full Quart. *See* Foaming Tankard.

Full Moon Taunton and elsewhere. A convenient visual symbol, sometimes illustrated more elaborately on the sign than the name would suggest. The Taunton pub shows a group of Martian figures standing on a spaceship and watching other satellites in orbit. At Stokes Croft, near Bristol, a wolf is shown baying to the moon beside a snow-covered pine forest. At Morton, near Southwell a genial man-in-the-moon extends the invitation: 'Step in, my friends, and take a cup;/It is not dark, for the moon is up./Sit down refresh, and pay your way,/Then you will call another day.'

Full Pitcher Ledbury, H and W. One of the many signs which interprets the name in two ways. One side shows a graceful serving-maid carrying a pitcher on her shoulder. The other side shows a batsman receiving a full toss in his midriff.

Fur and Feathers Herriard, near Basingstoke. Eric Partridge in his *Dictionary of Historical Slang* notes that this expression was used by 1830, originally as 'fur and feather', later in the plural form, to mean either the game shot by sportsmen or the sportsmen themselves.

Furnham Furnham, near Chard, Som. A pub where the sign-painting illustrates the name only for those with some knowledge of the locality and its history. It shows a canal horse towing a barge down the Chard canal, which was built between 1834 and 1842. The village was at that time the centre of a busy area, but the canal did not pay its way and was closed in 1867.

Furze Bush *See* Bush.

Fwrrwm Ishta Machen, near Newport, Gwent. A Welsh expression which means 'resting place', or 'seat to sit on'. Formerly a spot where local women bought their wool for weaving, as recalled by the inn sign. It shows two salesmen, each carrying a large skein of wool on a pole over his shoulder, conversing with two women who are seated on a bench. They are wearing the traditional conical Welsh hats.

Fye Bridge *See* Bridge.

G

Gade and Goose Gadebridge, Herts. The local river is called the Gade. The 'goose' was no doubt felt to be pleasantly alliterative.

Gaff Falkirk. To a fisherman this term suggests the large hook used for landing fish. As a nautical term it refers to the spar to which the fore-and-aft sail is bent. The word also has more slangy meanings, such as a fair or cheap music-hall. To blow the gaff is to divulge a secret.

Gainsborough Tavern Sudbury, Sflk. Another at Rochester. Thomas Gainsborough (1727–88) was an English landscape and portrait painter, almost as popular at the peak of his career as Reynolds. He is known for his many elegant portraits of women, and above all for his *Blue Boy*. Greens and blues predominate in his work.

Galatea London SE15. Two ladies of this name are found in classical literature, one a sea nymph, the other a statue who came to life. The statue was made by Pygmalion, whose love for his own creation, Galatea ('milk white'), caused her to become a living woman, thanks to the intercession of the goddess Aphrodite.

Gallant Hussar Derby. The sign shows one of the lightly armed cavalrymen who rode into the 'Valley of Death' at Balaclava in the Charge of the Light Brigade. *See* Earl of Cardigan.

Galleon Fowey, Corn. At Great Baddow, in Essex, is a Galleons. The Spanish war ships often became valuable prizes for West Country seamen such as Sir Francis Drake because of the treasure they also transported.

Galliot Hoy *See* Hoy Tavern.

Gallipot Hartfield, W Ssx. The gallipots, small jars for ointment, which give this pub its name, are on display behind the bar. The pub was originally part of three cottages which incorporated a pottery, saddlery and small brewery, run as separate businesses by three brothers. Gallipots were brought in galleys from the Mediterranean as part of their cargo, so that 'galleypot' is sometimes found as an alternative spelling. The word was also applied jokingly to the sellers of the ointments, the apothecaries.

Gallon Pot Great Yarmouth. The sign is a large brass pot. The original building was destroyed in 1943 but was restored in 1959.

Galloping Major Edinburgh. Later known simply as the Pub, but originally named with reference to a favourite music-hall song which everyone could whistle or sing.

Gallows Dinnington, near Sheffield. Another at Ilkeston, Derbs. The Sheffield pub is located in Hangman's Lane, the other is near the site of a one-time gallows.

Gamecock Hereford and elsewhere. Also Game Cock, Cheltenham; Game Bird at Horley, Sry. The breed of cock which was formerly used in cock-fights. Game bird can also have the more general sense of bird which is suitable for hunting.

Gamekeeper Compton Dando, near Bristol. Another at Stevenage. For the man who helps raise and protect the wild animals and birds on an estate which may be used for game, hunting and shooting. The Compton Dando sign shows

George Hinton with his gun and retriever. He was gamekeeper for many years on a local estate.

Gandolfi Hanley Swan, near Worcester. Count Gandolfi was a wealthy Italian property owner who lived in this area for more than forty years. He died in 1970.

Gaping Goose Garforth, near Leeds. Another at Bradford. The Garforth sign originally showed a large grey gander with its neck fully extended and its beak gaping. There is another bird, allied to the stork, which is called a gaper.

Gardeners Arms Charlton, near Pershore and elsewhere. Also Gardeners at Awsworth, near Nottingham. The sign at Charlton was originally a horn of plenty with the text: 'By the sweat of thy brow shalt thou eat bread'. The Awsworth sign shows the gardener ruefully supporting his aching back. Luton has a Gardeners Call, Sheffield a Gardeners Rest, Boothen, near Stoke–on–Trent a Gardeners Retreat. There is a Garden in Belfast, a Garden Gate at Aldershot and a Garden House at Edgbaston.

Garden Tiger Harlow, Esx. One of the butterfly signs in this town. The reverse of the sign shows a ferocious tom cat rampaging among the flowers.

Garibaldi Iver, Bucks and elsewhere. Giuseppe Garibaldi (1807–82) was a great Italian soldier and patriot, remembered especially for his spectacular conquest of Sicily and Naples in 1860 with his 1,000 volunteer 'Red Shirts'. He visited London in 1864 to be presented with the Freedom of the City, and was received with much enthusiasm.

Garland Ipswich. A garland of flowers or feathers was used by brew-houses as a sign in the fifteenth century, possibly as a substitute for a crown. Some breweries still garland a new pub which is being opened.

Garland Ox Bodmin. It was formerly the custom at the local ox fair to decorate the champion ox with garlands of lilies. The owner of the champion also received a silver snuff box. Both garlanding and snuff box customs lapsed in 1879.

Garratt Gorton, Manchester. The works of Beyer, Peacock and Company are nearby. They were builders of the articulated steam locomotives known as the Garratt type.

Garrick Also Garrick's Head. *See* David Garrick.

Garter *See* Shakespeare.

Gate Northwood, GL and elsewhere. Proximity to a church gate, toll gate or town gate was usually enough to bring about this pub name. The sign in rural areas is still sometimes a miniature five-barred gate. It is traditionally accompanied by a verse such as: 'This gate hangs well, and hinders non,/Refresh and pay, and travel on.' At Carlton, near Market Bosworth, the reverse side of the sign has another couplet: 'Call at the Gate, and taste of the tap:/Drink and be merry, but lay off the strap.' The last phrase refers to the giving of credit, and means 'Don't ask for it'. There is a Gate Hangs High near Hook Norton, Oxon and another at Wrexham. The Gate-Hangs-Well is at Tipton, W Mids; similar names include Gateside, Coalhall near Ayr; Gateway, Manchester. London EC2 once had a Gates of Jerusalem.

Gatsby's Nottingham. Also at Cupar, Fife. The fictitious playboy created by the American novelist Scott Fitzgerald in *The Great Gatsby*.

The name is presumably meant to hint at the high-living style in the 1920s of the American upper-classes.

Gatwick Horley, Sry. Gatwick Airport is nearby.

Gauger Dundee. For the Customs and Excise official who measured capacities.

Gauntlet Kenilworth. The gauntlet was a glove worn as part of medieval armour. It was usually made of leather, covered with steel. When a knight threw down his gauntlet before an opponent he was issuing a challenge to combat. Jousting tournaments were held at Kenilworth Castle in Tudor times. The inn sign shows a knight astride his charger.

Gay Cavalier Devizes. This Wiltshire town was one of the Royalist strongholds during the Civil War, when the Cavaliers who supported Charles I fought against the Roundheads of the Parliamentarians. Dr Johnson defined 'cavalier' as a 'gay sprightly military man', though the term originally meant a soldier on horseback.

Gay Dog Lower Quinton, near Stratford-on-Avon and elsewhere. The former owner Joe Braddon was a noted breeder of boxer dogs. He subsequently became a judge at the annual Crufts Dog Show. The original sign showed a dog's head, but the present one is much more sophisticated. The dog is shown upright, using a walking-stick; he is attired in various colours, wears a cravat, and sports a flower in his buttonhole.

Gay Gordon Edinburgh. The nickname of a Gordon High-lander, a member of the regiment raised in the late eighteenth century by the Duke of Gordon. Gay Highlander at Peacehaven, E.

Ssx is a slightly unorthodox form of the same name.

Gay Trouper Newcastle-on-Tyne. After the performers at the nearby theatre. A 'trouper' is literally a member of a 'troop' of dancers or actors.

Gazebo Kingston-on-Thames. The architectural feature on a building, on the roof or high on a wall, which allows a person to 'gaze' over a long distance. This pub, opened in 1982, has in fact two gazebos as part of its architectural attractions.

Gazelle Glyngarth, near Menai Bridge, Anglesey. The gazelle is a small, delicate antelope found in North Africa, noted for its grace and the softness of its eyes.

General Abercrombie Arundel. Another at London SE1. James Abercrombie (1706–81) was a British general, one of the leaders of an expedition against the French in Canada in 1758, where he was defeated by Montcalm.

General Allenby Winterborne Zelstone, Dors. Also Allenby Arms, Plymouth; Lord Allenby, Southall, GL. Edmund Henry Hynman Allenby, 1st Viscount Allenby (1861–1936) was a British field-marshal who invaded Palestine and ended Turkish resistance in 1918. He was British high commissioner for Egypt 1919–25.

General at Sea Chatham. This name does not refer to a bewildered general, but to an admiral. 'General at sea' or 'General of the sea' was a title bestowed from the late sixteenth to the early eighteenth century on such men as Admiral Blake, who had indeed commanded an army before distinguishing themselves as naval officers.

General Burgoyne Great Urswick, Cumb. John Burgoyne (1722–92) led a poorly equipped army, untrained for frontier fighting, against the Americans in the War of Independence. He was forced to surrender at Saratoga in 1777, giving the Americans their first real victory of any note.

General Campbell *See* Sir Colin Campbell.

General Canrobert London E2. François Certain Canrobert (1809–95) was a marshal of France. He commanded the French forces in the Crimea 1854–55. He seems to be chiefly remembered in France for having had very long hair.

General Codrington Preston. Sir William John Codrington (1804–84) was the second son of Admiral Sir Edward Codrington. He commanded a brigade at the Battle of Alma during the Crimean War and eventually became commander-in-chief in the Crimea in 1855. He was governor of Gibraltar 1859–1865.

General Elliott Hinksey, near Oxford and elsewhere. General Elliott (1717–90) is chiefly remembered for defending Gibraltar against the Spaniards 1779–83. He was later created Baron Heathfield. A regular customer at the Oxford pub in the 1920s was Robert Graves, who found that none of the regulars knew anything about the general. He therefore wrote a poem which begins: 'He fell in victory's fierce pursuit/Holed through and through with shot,/A sabre sweep had hacked him deep/'Twixt neck and shoulder-knot./The potman cannot well recall,/The ostler never knew,/Whether that day was Malplaquet,/The Boyne or Waterloo.' Another regular at the Oxford pub of this name was a horse called Tom who did a local bread round. He was fond of a pint of beer and was

frequently given one in the 1940s and 1950s.

General Gordon Ipswich and elsewhere. Charles George Gordon (1833–85), known as 'Chinese Gordon', was a British soldier and administrator. He earned his nickname by commanding the Chinese army that suppressed the Taiping Rebellion. He was governor of Egyptian Sudan 1877–80. When he was killed in the siege of Khartoum the indignation felt in Britain helped to bring down Gladstone's government. The pub of this name in Gravesend, known simply as Gordons for a time after restyling, marked the centenary of the general's death by installing a portrait of him, in a Victorian frame, in the bar.

General Grant London E16. Ulysses Simpson Grant (1822–85) was commander-in-chief of the Union Army in the Civil War and later served as President on two occasions. An authoritative American commentator has said of him that he 'was possibly the most ill-fitted man for that office the nation has ever had'. He himself was honest, but his close associates were not.

General Havelock London N7 and elsewhere. Also Havelock, Blackburn; Havelock Arms, Dalston and Torquay; Sir Henry Havelock, Hastings. Sir Henry Havelock (1795–1857) was an English general who was a hero during the Indian Mutiny of 1857. He was responsible for the relief of Lucknow in that year, but died two months later.

General Jackson London SE20. Thomas Jonathan Jackson (1824–63), the Confederate general known as 'Stonewall Jackson' after he and his men had stood like a stonewall before the enemy at Bull Run. He was killed at the Battle of Chancellorsville. Next to General Robert E Lee he was the Confederacy's greatest general.

General Moore Plymouth. Named in 1982 in honour of Major-General Sir Jeremy Moore, leader of the land forces in the Falklands campaign.

General Napier Salford and elsewhere. General Sir Charles Napier (1782–1853) had a distinguished military career but is chiefly remembered for a joke. In 1843 he announced the capture of Sind (Pakistan) by sending a one–word telegram to the War Office: '*Peccavi*'. This translates from Latin as 'I have sinned', and was enough to tell those at home that Sind had been annexed. The general is remembered in Nottingham by the Sir Charles Napier. He was in charge of the troops who suppressed the local Chartist riots in 1839.

General Peel Leeds. Jonathan Peel (1799–1879) was an English general and politician, brother of the more famous Sir Robert Peel. The general was secretary of war 1858–59 and again 1866–67.

General Picton London N1. Also Picton, Haverfordwest; Picton Arms, Newport, Gwent. Sir Thomas Picton (1758–1815) served in the Peninsular Wars under Wellington and was with him again at Waterloo. He was killed there while leading a cavalry charge, impeccably dressed at the time in a top hat.

General Rawdon Luddenfoot, near Halifax. Sir George Rawdon (1604–84) played an active part in restoring Charles II to the throne in 1660.

General Smuts London W12. Jan Christian Smuts (1870–1950) was a South African statesman and soldier. He helped to create the Union of South Africa in 1910, and became prime minister of the country in 1919. He advocated the League of Nations and was later active in organising the United Nations. During World War Two he was again the South African prime minister and was a valued member of British war councils.

General Tarleton Newcastle-on-Tyne. Another at Ferrensby, N Yorks. Sir Banastre Tarleton (1754–1833) served in the War of American Independence, where he earned a reputation amongst the Americans for his extreme cruelty. He eventually surrendered with Cornwallis at Yorktown. He later represented Liverpool, where he was born, as a member of parliament.

General Wolfe Westerham, Kent (his birthplace) and elsewhere. James Wolfe (1727–59) commanded the expedition against Quebec. He forced an open battle with the French under Montcalm on the Heights of Abraham, winning a victory that was decisive in giving New France to England. Both he and Montcalm were killed in the battle.

Genevieve London SW16. The name of a car in the film *Genevieve* (1953), one of the veteran cars taking part in the London to Brighton run. The film was a minor classic, starring Kenneth More, Kay Kendall, Dinah Sheridan and John Gregson, and was also noteworthy for its harmonica theme music, composed and played by Larry Adler.

Gentil Knyght Canterbury. 'He was a verray parfit gentil knyght', says Chaucer in his *Canterbury Tales*, the knight being one of the pilgrims making their way to Canterbury.

Geoffrey Chaucer London SE1. Also Chaucer, Bootle, near Liverpool. Geoffrey Chaucer (*c.*1340–1400) is often referred to as the 'father of English poetry'. He is mainly known for his *Troilus and Criseyde* (1386) and the rich collection of stories known as *The Canterbury Tales* (begun 1387). He is the most important figure in English literature before William Shakespeare.

Geordie Ridley Blaydon-on-Tyne. George Ridley (1834–64) was a poet and folk-singer, born nearby at Gateshead. He wrote the Blaydon Races.

George Ruislip and elsewhere. London alone still has at least forty pubs of this name, which is universally popular. Originally it referred to St George, patron saint of England, though he is often coupled with a dragon. Since 1714 George has been kingly name in England, six different kings having borne it, and each of them (except George I) is referred to on signboards in different places. The George Tavern, London WC2 is unusual in referring to George Villiers, Duke of Buckingham in that way. Inn sign 'spotters' will occasionally notice that a pub called the *George* shows 'George and the dragon' on the sign, the name having been abbreviated. Records also show that some pubs which began as simple *George* later became George and Dragon when a new sign was painted.

George and Dragon Codicote, near Welwyn, and elsewhere. This sign is found as frequently as George. It refers to England's patron saint, who lived in the third or fourth century, of whom little is known in reality. The legend concerning his fight with a dragon, thus rescuing a maiden and causing thousands of people to be baptised, first appeared in the *Golden Legend* centuries after his death. The story, being so obviously untrue, has done George a disservice, causing many commentators to say that he did not exist. He almost certainly did exist, and was a good man, but his real deeds 'are known only to God'. As for the dragon, he has had the last word in Nottingham. A pub that had been the *George and Dragon* for centuries was suddenly reduced to the Dragon in 1982 by a local brewery.

George and Pilgrims Glastonbury. The inn was founded by the Benedictine community as a guest house for pilgrims to the local shrine. Their abbey was destroyed by Henry VIII at the time of the Dissolution and the guest house became an inn, originally named after St George. His cross is on one of three shields displayed above the entrance. A second shield bears the arms of Edward IV, while a third is dedicated to the founder of the abbey, Abbot John de Selwood. The 'Pilgrims' was added to the inn name at a later date.

George Borrow Oulton Broad, near Lowestoft. Another at Ponterwyd, near Aberystwyth. George Borrow (1805–81) was an English writer and linguist who travelled widely before settling near Oulton Broad. His novels are often autobiographical and present a succession of gypsies and adventures of all kinds. The best known are perhaps *The Romany Rye* (1857) and *Lavengro* (1851). He stayed at the Ponterwyd inn while writing *Wild Wales* (1862). There is a Romany Rye pub in Norwich.

George Canning *See* Canning.

George Eliot Nuneaton. The pen-name of Mary Ann Evans (1819–80), briefly Mrs Mary Ann Cross at the end of her life. She was born at Arbury, which is not far from Nuneaton. Her novel *Middlemarch* (1872) is considered by many to be one of the best novels in English. Other fine works include *Adam Bede*, *The Mill on the Floss* and *Silas Marner*.

George IV Queensbury, near Bradford and elsewhere. Also King George IV, London, SW7. This king, who reigned 1820–30, is seen more often on inn signs as the Prince Regent.

George Hudson York. George Hudson (1800–71) was a draper who became mayor of York and MP for Sunderland. He founded a prosperous banking company and made a fortune when he invested in the development of the railways. He subsequently lost his fortune and reputation by investing in more dubious enterprises.

George in the Tree Balsall Common, near Coventry. The pub was once the Royal Oak, with a signboard showing Charles II hiding in the tree. A licensee with little feeling for history is said to have had the head of Charles replaced by that of George III (then the reigning monarch) when the signboard needed repainting. A different local story is that the pub (and sign) had become the George, but after a gale one night the signboard was found to have disappeared. Only when a large elm tree across the road shed its leaves later in the year was the board discovered in its branches. The truth will probably never be known, but with pub names commonly changing because of a reinterpretation of the sign, it seems possible that the face in the original *Royal Oak* sign resembled either a royal George or a local man of that name.

George II Luton and elsewhere. George Augustus (1683–1760) was the son of George I. As George II he reigned from 1727. The pub which commemorates him at Chideock, Dors, shows him in command of his troops at Dettingen in 1743, during the war of Austrian Succession. He was in fact the last English monarch to lead an army on the field of battle.

George Stephenson Killingworth, near Newcastle-on-Tyne. George Stephenson (1781–1848) was an English engineer noted especially for the design and construction of locomotives. In 1814 he constructed a travelling engine which hauled coal from the mines, and in 1815 built the first engine to operate by steam blast. His most famous locomotive was the Rocket, winner of a contest in 1829 and later used on the Manchester-Liverpool railway. There is a Rocket pub in Birmingham and elsewhere, while Stafford has a Stephenson's Rocket and Preston a Stephenson Arms.

George III Penmaenpool, near Barmouth. George William Frederick (1738–1820) was the grandson of George II. He was king from 1760, but ultimately became insane. The sign at this pub shows the king on horseback on one side, while the other side has a fully-rigged schooner. It recalls the fact that the building was originally two separate buildings, one an inn, the other a ship-chandlery.

Ghillie Bar Edinburgh. A ghillie or gillie is a man who acts as guide and attendant to hunting and fishing sportsmen in the

Highlands. The word derives from a Gaelic word meaning 'lad', though the ghillies are often experienced older men.

Ghost Train Purton, near Swindon. Near an old railway bridge, and a reminder that the local station was closed as a result of the 'Beeching Axe' in the 1960s. Dr Beeching, later Lord Beeching, was chairman of the British Railways Board and recommended the closure of a great many non-profitable services. A Silent Whistle pub at Oakle Street, near Gloucester, owes its name to the same event.

Ghuznee Fort Gillingham, Kent. Ghuznee, otherwise Ghazni, Ghuzni, Ghizni, Gazna, is a city in Afghanistan. It was stormed by the British in 1839, retaken by the Afghans in 1842, and retaken by the British in the same year.

GI Hastings. Named in honour of the American servicemen who were based in Britain in the 1940s. The initials are normally explained as 'government issue' or 'general issue', from the letters stamped on articles provided by the US military supply department, but *Webster's Dictionary* says that certain articles such as garbage cans were listed with 'gi' against them because they were made of galvanized *i*ron. The pub was opened by a GI called Sergeant Hastings who came from Hastings in the USA and had married a girl from Hastings, E Ssx. In spite of all this the pub name has subsequently been changed (unnecessarily) several times. It is now the Town Crier.

Gibraltar Gardens Norwich. This riverside pub was once the house of a Flemish weaver in the sixteenth century. It became a tavern in 1704, the year that Gibraltar became a British

possession. Other pub names, such as Gibraltar at Blackburn, Gibraltar Castle at Batford, near Harpenden and Gibraltar Rock at Tynemouth, were probably inspired by the capture of the Rock by Admiral Rooke. *See also* Rock of Gibraltar.

Gigmill Stourbridge, The name of a machine used to raise the nap on cloth.

Gigolos Boston. A gigolo was originally a professional male dancing partner. The word literally means 'tall thin man', being a masculine form of *gigole*, 'tall thin woman'. Gigolo now suggests a man who is paid by a woman to be her companion and lover.

Gilbert and Sullivan London WC2. The original pub of this name was damaged by fire in 1979. The memorabilia of the famous pair was moved to a pub then known as the Old Bell now renamed as above. William Schwenk Gilbert (1836–1911), knighted in 1907, wrote the words of the comic operas. He drowned while attempting to rescue a companion. Arthur Seymour Sullivan (1842–1900), knighted in 1883, composed the music. The Gilbert and Sullivan operas were: *Thespis* (1971), *Trial by Jury* (1875), *The Sorcerer* (1877), *HMS Pinafore* (1878), *The Pirates of Penzance* (1880), *Patience* (1881), *Iolanthe* (1882), *Princess Ida* (1884), *The Mikado* (1885), *Ruddigore* (1887), *The Yeomen of the Guard* (1888), *The Gondoliers* (1889), *Utopia Limited* (1893), *The Grand Duke* (1896).

Gilded Cage Birmingham. A phrase that for older readers will recall a plaintive music hall song, written by Arthur Lamb in 1900, about a woman who 'was only a bird in a gilded cage'.

Giles London N1. The distinguished English cartoonist, Carl Ronald Giles was born in the Angel opposite this pub. He is especially associated with the creation of the dreadful 'Grandma Buggins' and her family, a famous feature of the *Daily Express*. Many of Giles's original drawings line the walls of the pub, which the cartoonist himself opened in 1973.

Gimcrack York. The pub is near the racecourse at York. The committee which manages the racing there is called the Gimcrack Club. The club holds an annual dinner at which the guest of honour is the winner of the Gimcrack Stakes, a six-furlong flat-race for two-year-olds which is run in August. The origin of the name Gimcrack is obscure, but appears to be taken from a horse which once ran at York some time before 1767. All that is known about the horse is that it lost.

Gimlet Maryhill, Glasgow. A small tool with a grooved shank used by carpenters to bore holes so that screws will enter easily, but also the name of a well-known drink. The latter consists of sweetened lime juice, gin or vodka and plain or carbonated water.

Ginger Tom *See* Cat.

Gin Trap Ringstead, Nflk. The pub has a collection of gins, or animal traps. 'Gin' in this sense derives from 'engine', whereas the drink is from 'Geneva'.

Gipsy Moth IV Plymouth. One side of the inn sign shows the biplane in which Sir Francis Chichester made a solo flight to Australia in 1929. He later used the name for several yachts, including the one in which he circumnavigated the globe between August 1966 and May 1967. *Gipsy Moth IV* is shown on the other side of the board. At Selby in West Yorkshire there is a Gipsy Moth which shows the plane, yacht and an actual gipsy moth. There is a Sir Francis Chichester at Plymouth. *See also* Lone Yachtsman.

Gladstone London N19. Another at Nottingham. Also Gladstone Arms, Peterborough and elsewhere. William Ewart Gladstone (1809–98) was the dominant personality of the Liberal Party 1868–94. He was prime minister on four occasions and was noted for his oratory and grasp of financial matters.

Glan Conway Llanrwst, Clwyd. 'Bank of the river Conway'. Similar names are Glan Severn, near Llangurig, Pwys, and Glantaff, Quaker's Yard, M Glam. Glamorgan itself contains the Welsh *glan*, 'bank' or 'shore'.

Glass Barrel *See* Barrels.

Glassblower St Helen's, Mers. The pub was opened in 1980, the name having been chosen by local people in a competition. It refers to the glass works of Pilkington Bros.

Glass House Bristol. In military usage the glass house is the guard room or the detention cells where prisoners are kept. Here the reference is to the local glass industry and the Flemish glass-workers who settled in the area at the end of the sixteenth century. Samples of the characteristic blue glass which they developed after their arrival are displayed behind the bar. At Nailsea nearby there is a Glasshouse, while in another part of Bristol there is a Glasscutter.

Glaziers Arms Ely. Another at Corby Glen, near Grantham. The Worshipful Company of Glaziers (1637) was originally a guild of those who glazed and leaded windows and painted glass. It still encourages the art of glass painting.

Gleaners Calverton, near Nottingham. Also Gleaners Arms at Talke, near Stoke-on-Trent. Gleaners were farm labourers who gathered up the ears of corn left by the reapers. Their work was made famous by Millet's painting *The Gleaners*, which shows three sturdy peasant women in sunlit fields. It hangs in the Louvre, in Paris.

Glengarry Avonbridge, near Falkirk. The name of a place in Grampian, but also a kind of woollen cap worn in the Highlands of Scotland. It rises to a point in front and usually has ribbons hanging behind it.

Glen Tavern Dumfermline. The Scottish glens are narrow valleys, often wooded, with streams running through them. There is a Glen Head in Duntochter, near Clydebank, and a Glen Kyle at Airdrie. Many pubs with the prefix Glen are found in Wales and Ireland as well as in Scotland.

Glevum Longlevens, Glos. This is the Roman name for Gloucester. It probably meant 'bright' in the sense of 'famous'.

Glider Dunstable. International gliding competitions are staged nearby. *See also* Windsock.

Globe Stratford-on-Avon and elsewhere. A name now associated with Shakespeare because of the Globe Theatre, where his plays were performed during his lifetime. The Stratford pub sign shows a wizard gazing into a crystal ball, but the name was clearly suggested by its Shakespearian associations. At Sampford Peverell, near Tiverton, the pub of this name has a globe on its sign together with Drake and his *Golden Hind*. At Lostwithiel, Corn, the reference is to an American ship which attacked a local frigate during the War of 1812. The skipper of the frigate was killed and is remembered here because he was a member of the innkeeper's family. The *Globe* has always been a popular pub sign, and there are still at least twenty pubs of this name in London. It was at one time associated with Portugal, and indicated that a tavern sold Portuguese wines. A new pub in Aldershot is called the Globetrotter.

Globe and Engine Sittingbourne. The sign shows a large station light suspended over a train which is alongside the platform.

Globe and Laurel Gillingham, Kent. After the Royal Marines, whose cap-badge shows a globe encircled by laurel leaves.

Glocester Flying Machine Brockworth, near Gloucester. The name of a stagecoach service in the mid-eighteenth century. It ran three times weekly from Gloucester to London and was drawn by six horses. It prided itself on being an express service, taking only two days to cover the 105 mile journey.

Gloster London SW3. The sign shows a member of the Gloucestershire Regiment (28th and 61st) in action at the Imjin River in 1951, during the Korean War. The regiment prefers the spelling 'Glosters'. Bristol has a Gloster House.

Gloucester Arms Penrith and Kingston-on-Thames. Richard, Duke of Gloucester stayed in Penrith in 1471 while the nearby castle was being repaired. The Duke was later Richard III.

Gloucester Old Spot Uckington, near Cheltenham. The name of a breed of pig.

Glovers Arms Reckleford, near Yeovil. The Glovers' Company was granted arms in 1464. In the early sixteenth century they were joined with the Leathersellers.

Glover's Needle Worcester. A glover's needle and thread appears on the sign together with the needle-like spire of St Andrew's church. Glove-making was a local industry here, accounting for the nickname of the church spire.

Glue Pot Swindon and elsewhere. Another at Harrogate, also one in London EC1. The Swindon pub refers to the carriage-making industry, part of the local involvement with the railways. Elsewhere the name refers to cabinet-makers.

Glynne Arms *See* Crooked House.

Gnu Inn *See* New Inn.

Goalpost Wolverhampton. The pub is opposite the ground of Wolverhampton Wanderers Football Club.

Goat and Barge Basingstoke. Opened in 1970, and preserving the names of two local pubs that were demolished when the town centre was redeveloped, the Goat and the Barge.

Goat and Compasses London NW1. Anthony Trollope comments on this name in his novel *Framley Parsonage* (1861): 'He came to a public house. It was called the *Goat and Compasses* – a very meaningless name, one would say; but the house boasted of being a place of public entertainment very long established on that site, having been a tavern in the days of Cromwell. At that time the pious landlord, putting up a pious legend for the benefit of his pious customers, had declared that – "God encompasseth us".' Trollope may not have been the first to offer the explanation that this phrase became 'Goat and Compasses', but

it has long been generally accepted and will no doubt go on being so, whatever arguments one brings against it. Those arguments are as follows: the Puritans are not on record as having used slogan names for inns, though a few fanatical groups imposed such names on their children – 'Fight-the-good-fight-of-faith', 'The-Lord-is-near', and so on. The amused reaction of non-Puritans to such names quickly killed them off. There are also satisfactory alternative explanations for *Goat and Compasses*. In his *Inns and Inn Signs* (1936) Charles R Swift drew attention to the scapegoat idea, the primitive belief that a goat could take on itself the ills and misfortunes that might afflict people, or other animals. Swift said that it was country practice in some areas to keep a goat with stock in the belief that this would keep the cattle healthy – all the sickness being borne by the poor goat. He also claimed that another practice was to parade a goat round a house where anyone was ill, so that the disease might be carried away in the goat's body. While this was happening the following would be recited: 'The goat that compass thee around/Is needful for compassing this end:/ That through whose compassment ye may be changed/From pain to happiness, disease to health.' This association of 'goat and compassing' is very suggestive, but there is another possible explanation. The arms of the Worshipful Company of Cordwainers shows a 'chevron' between three goats heads. To any normal eye the 'chevron' looks like a pair of open compasses. The Cordwainers were so called because they used goats' leather from Cordova, in Spain, to make highly fashionable shoes in the Middle Ages.

Goat in Boots London SW3. This pub was the Goat in the mid–seventeenth century. A former owner decided that he wanted a really striking inn sign and commissioned George Morland to paint it for him. The result was a sign with a goat which had huge horns and was armed with a cutlass. It was also booted and spurred. There is another pub with the same name in London NW1.

Goblin *See* Hob.

Gog and Magog *See* Magog.

Gold Cup Ascot and elsewhere. The Ascot sign refers to the flat race run on the famous racecourse each June. The race is run over two and a half miles and is open to colts and fillies three years and over. It was established in 1807.

Golden Anchor London SE15. A heraldic reference to the arms of the Lord High Admiral.

Golden Arrow Folkestone, Dover and elsewhere. For the famous express train running from London, Victoria, to Paris. The title was first used in 1929, when the service consisted entirely of first-class Pullman cars and a single journey cost £5. The increase in air travel soon made it impossible for the Southern Railway to be exclusive, and by 1931 second-class carriages had been added. Before World War Two the train always left Victoria at 11 am, after the war it left at 2 pm. The fortunes of the service are lovingly described in *Titled Trains of Great Britain*, by Cecil J Allen.

Golden Ball Bulwell, near Nottingham and elsewhere. This sign was used by many tradesmen in the past, probably because it was such a simple visual symbol. It seems to have no heraldic or religious significance. The royal orb is linked with Constantine the Great, who adopted a golden globe as a symbol and added a cross to it later when he was converted to Christianity.

Golden Bannock Lauder, Bdrs. For the flattish oatmeal cake eaten in Scotland and the North of England. Bannock Day is another name for Shrove Tuesday in parts of Scotland.

Golden Bowler Stubbington, near Fareham. The name symbolised for its first owner his retirement into civilian life from the Royal Navy, accompanied by a (golden) gratuity which enabled him to buy the pub.

Golden Cock Darlington. Formerly a sign used by many tradesmen. It is now seen on many pubs, though it does not name them, because it is the trade mark of Courage, owners of more than 5,000 pubs.

Golden Cross Coventry and elsewhere. The Coventry pub is said to have been built on the site of an ancient mint which made gold coins. The *Golden Cross* in Oxford, though the oldest pub in that city, has had several other names in its long history. It was the Cross Inn for at least two centuries, probably with reference to an earlier owner of the property, the bishop of Winchester. It is not clear why the cross became golden.

Golden Cup Bilston, W Mids and elsewhere. A heraldic reference to the arms of the Worshipful Company of Goldsmiths.

Golden Dragon *See* Dragon.

Golden Fleece Thirsk and elsewhere. In Greek legend the golden fleece was sought by the Argonauts. It was the fleece of a ram hung on a tree. The story may refer ultimately to a method of collecting particles of gold being washed down by rivers and streams by stretching sheepskins across the water. The Knights of the Golden Fleece is a chivalric Order founded in 1429 for the protection of the church. The Order's badge is a ram with a red band around its middle, which often in turn is used to illustrate the *Golden Fleece* inn sign.

Golden Hind Plymouth and elsewhere. A frequent pub name in Devon, the native county of Sir Francis Drake, who made the name of this ship famous. It had previously been the Pelican. The change was made by Drake to compliment his business partner, Sir Christopher Hatton, whose arms included a heraldic hind. Drake sailed the ship around the world 1577–80 and was knighted on board by Elizabeth I on his return. Pelican also occurs as a pub name and, is sometimes a reference to the ship. *See also* Sir Francis Drake.

Golden Inn Highampton, Devon. The pub was formerly a farm which at harvest time was surrounded by ripening corn. There is a similar Golden Acres at Solihull, a Golden Harvest at Greenmeadow, Cwmbran in Gwent and a Golden Sheaf at Riccarton, Strath.

Golden Key Snape, Sflk. Normally this is a religious emblem, a reference to St Peter or to St Petronilla. Christ said to St Peter: 'I will give unto thee the keys of the kingdom of Heaven.' (Matthew 16:18).

Golden Knight Huntingdon. A nickname earned by a local knight, Sir Henry Cromwell, in the sixteenth century. He spared no expense on his family home Hinchingbrooke House, which

had formerly been a monastery. It is now a school.

Golden Lion New Hillingdon, GL and elsewhere. A popular sign, referring heraldically to Henry I, or to the dukes of Northumberland, the Percys.

Golden Martlet *See* Martlet.

Golden Measure Lowgate, Hull. This sign, now gone, was a variant on Full Measure. The sign was a gilt gallon measuring can.

Golden Miller Cheltenham. A famous steeplechaser owned by the Hon Dorothy Paget. It won the Cheltenham Gold Cup for five successive years (1932–36) and the Grand National in 1934.

Golden Quaich *See* Quaich.

Golden Rose *See* Rose.

Golden Sovereign *See* Sovereign.

Golden Swift Harlow. The name of a moth, linking with other pub names on this theme in Harlow.

Goldfinger Highworth, near Swindon. The villainous character created by Ian Fleming in a novel of the same name. It was later made into one of the James Bond films, with a theme song called *Goldfinger* sung by Shirley Bassey. This pub was opened in 1972 by Ian Fleming's widow. The sign shows the villain himself, flanked by gold bars.

Golding Hop Plaxtol, Kent. A well-known variety of hop first grown by William Golding. The King and Barnes barley wine, Golding Ale, is named for the same reason.

Gold Medal Low Fell, near Gateshead. The gold medal was brought home from the European Championships in 1974 by local athlete Brendan Foster. He won the 5,000 metres in Rome that year. Edinburgh has a Gold Medal Tavern.

Golf Inn Montrose. Also Golf Tavern, Prestwick and elsewhere;

Golfers Rest, North Berwick; Golf Links, Pontmarnock, Dub, Golfers Arms, Christchurch, Dors and Golden Tee, Aberdeen. All such names are inspired by the presence nearby of golf links (a 'link' being a stretch of land near the sea) or a golf course, as it is normally called in the South. *See also* Fairway, Links, Hole in One, Nineteenth Hole.

Gondola Wollaton, Nottingham. The reference is to the gondola attached to a hot-air balloon, not to the Venetian boat. The pub is in an area known locally as Balloon Woods. Experimental work on a ballooning project was carried out there many years ago. Balloon races are still held during the summer in nearby Wollaton Park.

Gondolier London W2. The pub is in the area known as Little Venice because of the canals there. The Venetian gondolier is in charge of a 'gondola', a word which puzzles the scholars. It may have to do with a word meaning to 'see-saw'.

Good Companion Milton, Portsmouth. The inn sign depicts a dog.

Good Companions Brighton and elsewhere. The novelist J B Priestley made this phrase well-known when he published his *Good Companions* in 1929. As a pub name it usefully suggests an atmosphere within of friendliness.

Good Doctor Sheffield. The pub stands close by the old Royal Infirmary. A doctor is shown on the sign armed with his stethoscope.

Good Intent Fareham, Hants and elsewhere. This name is interpreted in various ways on the inn signs. The Fareham pub shows an in-shore naval cutter used for coastal defences around 1800. At Mollington, near Chester, a stagecoach of this name is depicted. At Puttenham, near Guildford, the sign shows a Puritan soldier praying on his knees at the entrance to a battle-tent, a fairly subtle pun compared to some inn signs. Kentish pubs of this name sometimes refer to a schooner which was engaged in smuggling in the 1830s between Rye and Dover. David Fisher's sign of *Good Intent*, Bristol depicts a mouthwatering cornucopia of fresh fruit.

Good Man Hunslet, near Leeds. In this case the pub name was no doubt inspired by the address, namely Goodman Street. Charles Hindley, in his *Tavern Anecdotes*, tells of a landlord who was looking for a new and unusual sign, and the Good Woman having been turned down as not very original, decided to put up a blank sign and call his pub the *Good Man*. His customers would constantly ask him where the good man was, since he was not on the sign. The reply was invariably: 'I'm still looking for one, but haven't found him yet'.

Good Measure *See* Foaming Tankard.

Good Samaritan London E1. Another pub of this name is in Ramsbottom, Lancs. The London example was no doubt inspired by the pub's location on the London Hospital estate. The name dates from 1937. The story of the good Samaritan is told at Luke 10. The Samaritan came from Samaria, an ancient city in Palestine, now Sabastiya, West Jordan.

Good Woman *See* Silent Woman.

Goose and Cabbage Plymouth. A reference to tailors. A goose (the plural form is *gooses*) is a tailor's smoothing-iron, so-called because its handle resembled a goose's neck. *See also* Cabbage.

Goose and Cowslip *See* Lord of the Manor.

Goose and Cuckoo Llanover, Gwent. Originally a nickname for the pub, or rather for its landlord and landlady. The name became the official one in the 1880s.

Goose and Firkin *See* Ferret and Firkin.

Gooseberry Bush Nottingham. The pub was built on the site formerly occupied by the Women's Hospital. Other pubs with a maternity link are the Stork at Rest and Baby in the Hand.

Goose Fair Bulwell, Nottingham. The pub was opened in 1982 and refers to the city's famous three-day fair, held each October. It dates from the thirteenth century and has been held every year except for the ten years lost in the two world wars.

Gordon Arms Fareham, Hants. The sign shows a kilted Highlander, a piper in his dress uniform. *See also* Gay Gordon.

Goshawk Mouldsworth, Chester. For the bird of this name, literally a 'goose-hawk'. In falconry goshawk is used for the female bird, the male being the tiercel or tercel. In Ireland goshawk is also applied to the buzzard and the peregrine falcon. The bird is large, with short wings.

Gospel Oak *See* Old Oak.

Governor's House Warwick. From 1860 until 1913 this was the house of the governor of the local Cape prison, which was finally demolished in 1933.

Goyt Whaley Bridge, near Stockport. The river Goyt rises in Goyt's Moss near Buxton and runs into the Mersey at Stockport.

Gracie's Banking Annan, Dumfries. The pub dates from 1916. The site is the steep bank of a brook, the Dickswell Burn, and was formerly owned by a Miss Gracie.

Grain Barge Peterborough. A floating pub in a converted barge which used to transport grain. It is near the old Custom House on the river Nene.

Grains of Beck Near Middleton-in-Teesdale, Dur. Known locally as the *Grainsy Beck* and referring to the little feeder streams, the grains, which eventually trickle into the river Lune, which in its upper part is called Lune Head Beck. 'Beck' is a brook or stream, especially one with a stony bottom.

Grampus Ilfracombe. For the dolphin-like sea creature, which blows out air and water.

Grand Duchess Plymouth. Marie of Oldenburg, a member of an aristocratic German family, visited Devon several times in the nineteenth century. She went especially to Paignton, where she is commemorated by the Oldenburg.

Grand Junction Crewe and elsewhere. Also Grand Junction Arms, London NW10. The Crewe example is for the railway junction. Other pubs of this name usually refer to the Grand Canal. The London pub has gardens for the use of bargees and others.

Grandstand Wrexham. Also Grand Stand, Knavesmire, York. In both cases for a nearby grandstand at a racecourse.

Grand Trunk Birkenhead. For the Leeds and Liverpool Canal, which opened in 1816. Financial problems caused the canal to take forty-six years to complete, though it is only 127 miles long.

Grand View Falmouth. The pub overlooks the bay and Pendennis Castle.

Grange Langton Green, near Tunbridge Wells. In its earliest sense a grange was a 'granary'. The sign shows a granger, or farm bailiff, watching one of his labourers, who is emptying a grain sack into a huge wooden vat. Perth has a Granary.

Granta Cambridge. For the river, also known as the Cam. The original meaning of the name may be 'fen river', but other possibilities exist. According to Eilert Ekwall, in his *English River Names*, the name should really be Grant. *Granta* he considers to be an artificial, learned form.

Grasshopper Cambridge and elsewhere. In Cambridge the reference is to the university lawn-tennis club. Elsewhere the sign is often heraldic, referring to the arms of Sir Thomas Gresham (1519–79), the English merchant and financier.

Gravediggers Southsea. The pub is near the main gate of the local cemetery.

Grave Maurice London E1. 'Grave' in this name is a title of nobility, equal to 'Count'. The reference is to Maurice, Prince of Orange (1567–1625), who was also Count of Nassau. He was a brilliant military leader who expelled the Spaniards from the Netherlands.

Great Britain Burslem, Staffs. The name of a famous ship designed by Isambard Kingdom Brunel. It was launched at Bristol in 1843, but subsequently foundered in the Falklands, and was brought back to Bristol in 1970 with money raised by public subscription. Since 1984 Port Stanley has had a new pub called SS Great Britain.

Great Bull *See* Bull.

Great Central Leicester. The name of the railway station, which was closed in 1969.

Great Dane Seaford, E Ssx. The sign here shows a bearded Viking warrior wearing his horned helmet. A longship and chariot are in the background. The pub of the same name at Hollingbourne, near Canterbury, shows a pair of Great Dane hounds on its sign. There is a local story about them having been kept at Leeds Castle nearby.

Great Dane's Head Beechamwell, near Swaffham, Nflk. The owner in 1976 kept a pair of Great Danes. There is a Great Dane at Seaford and Hollingbourne, near Canterbury.

Great Eastern New Ferry, Mers. The ship of this name, built by Brunel in the mid-nineteenth century. It was the largest ship afloat until the *Mauretania* claimed that distinction in 1907. The ship did not prove to be a commercial success as a passenger-liner, and was later used to lay cables. There is another pub of this name at Lowestoft where the reference is to the Great Eastern Railway.

Great Engineer *See* Brunel.

Great Harry Hemel Hempstead. One of the names of a galleon built in 1514, officially called *Henry Grace à Dieu* (Henry, thanks to God). With a name like that, it was not surprising that ordinary sailors bestowed a number of easier-to-say names on the ship. It became the *Great Carrack* ('carrack' being another word for 'galleon'), *Imperial Carrack*, *Henry Imperial* and *Harry*, as well as *Great Harry*. Another pub of this name at St Albans bearing this name shows a portrait of Henry VIII on its sign, though the name was originally intended to honour Henry VII. The 'Henry' referred to in the name of the galleon was Henry VIII.

Great Mersey Liverpool. For the River Mersey, which is likely to have meant 'boundary river' originally, ie the boundary between Northumbria and Mercia.

Great Northern St Albans. Also Great Northern Railway Tavern, London N8. The St Albans pub commemorated the branch line of the Great Northern Railway which had been extended from Hatfield in 1865. The Hornsey pub was built that same year to serve the nearby railway station opened in 1850.

Great Stone Northfield, Birmingham. There is a huge boulder standing in the old village pound, next to the pub. There is a churchyard opposite, giving rise to the local joke that beer is sold by the pint, by the pound, by the yard and by the stone.

Great Western Yeovil. Also Great Western Arms, London W2 and Warwick. The Great Western Railway reached Yeovil in 1856. The Paddington sign shows three of the company's locomotives; the sign in Warwick formerly showed an early locomotive, the *North Star*.

Grebe Stalham, Nflk. For the diving bird found on the neighbouring Broads. The bird has a short body, feet set well back and almost no tail.

Greek Plough Long Furrow, East Goscote, Leics. A 'theme' pub, justifying its name with its statues, urns, mosaics and the like. The pub is in a farming area.

Greenbank Falmouth. The green bank referred to was formerly to be seen at the head of the harbour. It has now been covered with buildings.

Green Barrel *See* Barrels.

Green Beret Walmer, Kent. For the Royal Marine Commandos; the American Special Forces, trained to fight guerillas, are also known as the Green Berets.

Green Carnation Richmond, Sry. This pub was the Blue Anchor until 1973. The new name was said to be in honour of Oscar Wilde, who once lived locally. He habitually wore a green carnation.

Green Coat Boy London SW1. Commemorates the Green Coat Hospital in Tothill Fields, Westminster for 'the relief of poor fatherless children'. It was founded by Charles I in 1633. The scholars of such charitable institutions were usually dressed in distinctive uniforms, especially blue, black or green coats. *See also* Greycoat Boy.

Greendale Oak Cuckney, near Mansfield. This was an oak or the estate of the Duke of Portland. In 1724 the Duke won a wager by driving a carriage-and-pair through the tree, an archway of ten feet by six feet having been cut in it.

Green Dragon Bishop's Frome, near Worcester and elsewhere. From the coat of arms of the earls of Pembroke. Apparently not connected with the *George and Dragon* story, though the Bishop's Frome sign interprets it in that way, showing Saint George and the dragon having a rest form their contest and drinking a flagon of ale. It is also true that on George and Dragon signs the dragon is usually green.

Green Gables Exeter. The pub itself has a green-tiled roof.

Greengage Bury St Edmunds. The variety of plum made popular by Sir William Gage of Norfolk, in the early eighteenth century. He also tried to launch a bluegage and purplegage.

Green Gingerman Hull. A street in the city is known as 'Land of Green Ginger'. Warehouses there were once used to store ginger and other imported spices.

Greenhouse Wollaton, Nottingham. A greenhouse has been added to the premises. Across the road from the pub is Wollaton Park, which has a well-known camellia house.

Green Howard North Ormsby, near Middlesbrough. A former landlord fought with the Green Howards in World War Two. Green Howards was originally a nickname of Alexandra, Princess of Wales's Own Yorkshire Regiment. It was adopted officially in 1920. The reference was to the green facings worn by the men, and to their colonel, Sir Charles Howard.

Green Jacket Shoreham-by-Sea, W Ssx. Also Royal Greenjacket, Oxford. The Green Jackets are the King's Royal Rifle Corps; Royal Green Jackets. The name was originally that of a cricket club formed by the 60th Foot and the Rifle Brigade. The Oxford pub was renamed in 1972 because of the new landlord's close connection with the regiment. The sign shows a bugle-major and there are military memorabilia inside.

Green Man Tunstall, near Snape and elsewhere. A common sign, not only in rural areas (London has thirty such signs). In modern times associated with Robin Hood and his men, who were supposedly dressed in Lincoln green cloth. They may well have been, since a cloth called Kendal green, from its manufacture in that place, or the lighter coloured cloth made in Lincoln was used for the clothes of foresters, woodmen and the like from the sixteenth century onwards. The Green Man was also seen in the May Day celebrations of former times – *see* Jack in the Green. Painters of inn signs

interpret this subject in very different ways. Some show a kind of wild man of the woods, some a respectable forester, some show Robin Hood. One way or another, people have been seeing 'little green men' for a long time.

Green Man and Black's Head Royal Ashbourne, Derbys. A fusion of two inn signs which occurred in 1825. The 'royal' was added after a fleeting visit by Princess Victoria in 1830. The sign is of the gallows type, bridging the street.

Green Man and Still London EC1. A herbalist and the still in which he distilled potions from green herbs, says one commentator, but there is no record of 'green man' ever being applied to a herbalist, not did they usually distil herbs. Larwood and Hotten, in their classic work on signboards, said that this sign was common, and that it began with the arms of the Distillers Company. These are supported by two Indians, represented by sign-painters as green men, or wild men of the woods. Later the green men became one green man, often Robin Hood.

Greenmantle Edinburgh. *Greenmantle* is the title of a novel by John Buchan (1875–1940), written a year after his most famous book, *The Thirty-Nine Steps*, and published in 1916. Buchan was born in Perth and had a brilliant career, first as President of the Oxford Union. He was later member of parliament for the Scottish universities, and in 1935 became Governor-General of Canada. He was raised to the peerage as 1st Baron Tweedsmuir in the same year. In 1938 he was chancellor of Edinburgh University.

Green Parrot Perranporth. The owner of the pub had a green parrot as pet. Parrot is also found as a pub name (there are three in Surrey). Manchester has a **Grey Parrot**. Hurlford, near Kilmarnock a Parakeet.

Green Star *See* La Verda Stelo.

Gregson's Well Liverpool. A well which was sunk by an early nineteenth-century landowner.

Gremlin Brecon, Pwys. The sign shows a cheerful pixie sitting on a toadstool in the moonlight, but a gremlin is supposed to be a wicked little creature which causes mechanical and electrical apparatus to go wrong. It was originally used to describe faults that developed in aircraft engines, and seems to have been used first in the early 1940s as RAF slang.

Grenadier London SW1. The pub was once an officer's mess for the Duke of Wellington's guards' regiments. There is a sentry box outside, and the mounting block which the Duke used to get onto his horse is on view. Colchester has a British Grenadier, no doubt inspired by the song: 'Some talk of Alexander, and some of Hercules,/ Of Hector and Lysander, and such great names as these;/But of all the world's brave heroes there's none that can compare/With a tow, row, row, row for the British Grenadier.' A 'grenadier' was originally a soldier who threw grenades. Later the term was used to describe the tallest and finest men in a regiment, It is only used now for the Grenadier Guards.

Gretna Tavern Carlisle. Also Gretna Green, Burnley; Gretna Green Wedding formerly at Newton Aycliffe, near Darlington. Gretna Green is the Scottish village only eight miles from Carlisle where English couples could once get married legally, even though they had no licence, had not called the banns and had no priest to officiate. After 1856 they had to stay there for three weeks first, which was probably a shrewd move by the hotel and innkeepers who lived locally rather than an attempt to make impetuous young couples who had eloped from England think again about what they were doing. Couples who are legally 'minors' can still marry at Gretna without parental consent.

Grey Bull *See* Bull.

Greycoat Boy London SE10. The Greycoat Hospital, a charity school, was founded in 1698 for 110 poor children of St Margaret's parish, Westminster. Since 1873 the school has been a day-school for 300 girls. *See also* Green Coat Boy.

Greyfisher Salisbury. A name one might expect to find in Scotland, where 'greyfish' is a name for young coalfish. The greyfish is known by different names in different parts of the country. One such name is dogfish, of interest because the otter has been referred to as a dogfisher, ie eater of dogfish. 'Greyfisher', unknown to the standard dictionaries, may have the same meaning, ie 'otter'.

Greyfriars Bobby Edinburgh. The Skye terrier who watched over the grave of his master in Greyfriars Kirkyard for many years in the mid-nineteenth century has become very famous. Bobby might have been forgotten, but Baroness Burdett-Coutts erected a drinking fountain in Candlemaker Row with a bronze statue of the dog surmounting it. The dog is seen as the perfect example of canine fidelity.

Grey Horse Kingston-on-Thames. A common name and sign in Yorkshire and Durham rather than elsewhere. There is also a Grey

Horses at Carlton-in-Lindrick, near Worksop. Grey horses are not really grey, they have a mixture of black and white hairs. They are always foaled black, then gradually become iron-grey, then turn white in old age.

Greyhound Beaconsfield and elsewhere. Inn signs interpret this name in different ways. They sometimes show a famous mail-coach which travelled between London and Birmingham, or another, as at Fenny Bridges near Honiton, which went from London to Exeter. The heraldic reference of this name is to the dukes of Newcastle, owners of land and property in many parts of the country. Usually the greyhound itself is shown. It has also been known as a gazehound, because it relies more on sight than smell. The greyhound was formerly used in the chase, but is now mainly associated with greyhound racing, or 'greycing'. The 'grey' of greyhound has nothing to do with the colour, but is a different word of uncertain origin. Hereford has a Greyhound Dog and Killinghall, near Harrogate a Greyhounds.

Gribble Little Torrington, Devon. Another at Oving, near Chichester. A small, yellowskinned apple which was first noted by this name in 1831.

Griffin Brentford, GL and elsewhere. A fabulous monster, supposedly the offspring of the lion and the eagle. Since it represented the attributes of the noblest animal and the king of birds, it was much used on coats of arms. Families called Griffin or Griffith have been especially fond of it when armigerous. There is a Gryphon at London N21 which shows the beast encountered by Alice as she wandered through Wonderland on its sign. The spelling variation is long established.

Griff Inn Drakeholes, Notts. The licensee here is J D Griffiths. There was therefore a reason to call the pub Griffin. This form of the name makes it even more apt.

Grosvenor London W7. Also Grosvenor Arms, London W1 and elsewhere. Grosvenor is the family name of the dukes of Westminster. The family has long held huge estates in London. Cheltenham has a Grosvenor Brewery and Bristol a Grosvenor House Tavern.

Grouse and Claret Rowsley, Derbys. Another at Henley–on–Thames. A name which manages to suggest an upper-class life style very effectively. Claret, a term used in England but not in France, originally referred to wines of a clear red colour. It is now used for the dark red wines of Bordeaux. Grouse has meanwhile taken on the secondary meaning of 'grumble'. It is tempting to see a connection between this and the bird, on the basis that a grouse has much to complain about, with hordes of people pursuing it with malicious intent, but the 'grumble' meaning began as soldier's slang in the nineteenth century and no link has yet been found with the bird meaning. There is a Grouse at Cabrach, Grampian and elsewhere.

Grove King's Nympton, Devon. The village takes its name from the River Nymet (now the River Mole). 'Nymet' probably means 'holy grove', which suggested the pub name. The sign has a crown above the grove to indicate the royal association, the area once having been used by the Wessex kings.

Growler Great Yarmouth. This was a slang term for a four-wheeled cab in the nineteenth century, shown on the sign. Partridge wondered in his *Dictionary of Historical Slang* whether the term derived from the driver's tendency to grumble or the creaking noises made by the cab itself. There was also a colloquial expression at the time 'to work the growler'. Its modern equivalent would be 'to go on a pub crawl', since it meant taking a cab and going from pub to pub.

Grub Pub St Ives, Corn. Not just a pub that offers food, but one that was converted from a food shop.

Gryphon *See* Griffin.

Guards Leamington Spa. The sign shows the badges of the five regiments of Guards: Grenadiers, Coldstream, Scots, Welsh and Irish. Portsmouth has a Guardsman.

Guinea London W1. The name of an English gold coin, first struck in 1663 when it had the nominal value of one pound. From 1717 a guinea was legal tender at the rate of twenty-one shillings. The original coins bore the figure of a little elephant and were made from gold which came from Guinea, in West Africa. The fluctuating value of the coins indicated the respect for gold – almost from their introduction they were worth more than their face value. The London pub was originally the Pound, referring to a cattle pound nearby. It then became the *Guinea*, and when that coin increased its value, took on the alternative name Ye Old One Pound One. There is another *Guinea* at Whitstable which refers to the finding of a treasure trove by a local man, John Gann. Birmingham has a Guineas.

Guinea Pig East Grinstead, W Ssx. The hospital nearby specialised in plastic surgery during World War Two. Some 600 patients who were treated there, mainly pilots and aircrews, became members of the Guinea Pig Club, referring to the innovative surgical work of Sir Archibald McIndoe and his colleagues. The sign shows a winged guinea pig descending in flames against the background of a shattered Spitfire.

Gun *See* Cannon.

Gun and Spitroast Horsmonden, near Tonbridge. This pub was the Gun (an ancient cannon being shown on the sign) until the late 1930s. The restaurant that is now attached to the inn has a spit on which to roast joints as one of its attractions.

Gun Barrels Birmingham. The inn sign here shows the type of battery guns used to fire official salutes.

Gunga Din's Colonial Inn Norwich. This was the Griffin until mid-1984. The new name must puzzle the younger patrons, not reared on Kipling's *Barrack-Room Ballads* and the poem about the Indian soldier, Gunga Din. The poem contains suitably pubby lines, such as: 'You may talk o' gin and beer When you're quartered safe out 'ere . . . ' but by far the most famous lines in the poem come at the end: 'Though I've belted you and flayed you, By the livin' Gawd that made you, You're a better man than I am, Gunga Din.'

Gunners *See* Arsenal Tavern.

Gupshill Manor Near Tewkesbury. The former manor, now an inn, has a sign which depicts a knight in armour on his charger, a reference to the battle of Tewkesbury in 1471. Edward IV's Yorkist army crushed the Lancastrians.

Gurkha Shreding Green, near Iver, Bucks. The pub was renamed in 1971 in honour of soldiers of the Brigade of Gurkhas, who were billeted nearby at the time. The Gurkhas are the ruling race of Nepal, an independent kingdom in the Himalayas. At one time the Gurkhas fought against the British, but since 1815 they have provided the British Army with men renowned for their loyalty and courage.

Guss and Crook Timsbury, near Bath. The sign shows a young miner on his knees hauling a laden truck of coal underground. The 'guss' in mining parlance is the rope–noose around his waist. It is attached by a 'crook' to the tub behind him.

Guy, Earl of Warwick Welling, Kent. A legendary hero whose story is told in Percy's *Reliques* (1765). The first account of Guy was written by an Anglo–Norman poet in the twelfth century. Later the stories of his deeds, including the slaying of the Dun Cow, Warwick, were accepted as fact.

Guy Fawkes Arms Scotton, near Harrogate. Guy Fawkes (1570–1606) was born in Yorkshire. He was one of the conspirators in the Gunpowder Plot, which was meant to kill James I and all the members of parliament on 5th November 1605. His arrest as he was entering the cellar of the House of Commons on the night of 4th November led to the execution of Fawkes and his friends, and eventually to the annual celebrations which occur each November on Bonfire Night.

Guy's Arms London SE1. Thomas Guy (c.1645–1724), bookseller and governor of St Thomas's Hospital, founded Guy's Hospital, 1721. Guy made his fortune not by selling books, but by speculating in South Sea stocks and shares. The hospital, near London Bridge station, is a famous medical teaching centre.

Gyngleboy Barnsley. A form of 'jingleboy', a slang term applied at first to a coin, later (nineteenth century) to a gold coin, then to a man who seemed to have plenty of money jingling in his pockets.

Gipsy Queen London NW5. A title assumed by Margaret Finch, who died at Norwood in 1760 at the reputed age of 109. The name also occurs as Gypsy Queen.

H

Haberdashers Arms London SW11.
Another at Knighton, near
Stafford. Originally the haberdashers were dealers in articles
such as caps. Later they dealt in
threads, tapes and ribbons. They
were granted arms in the fifteenth
century, and became prosperous
landowners. No-one is sure
where the extraordinary word
'haberdasher' comes from, with
the result that scholars and others
have speculated about the subject,
much as they have been inclined to
do about pub names. The most
ingenious suggestion so far is that
haberdasher derives from a
German phrase such as *Habt ihr
das?* 'Do you have that?'

Hackney Cab London E8 (Hackney).
An early form of taxi, the hackney
cab was for public hire, just as
hackney horses (later called 'hacks')
were for hire. Originally a hackney
was a horse that ambled along at an
easy pace, suitable for a lady rider.
It is not clear why they were called
after this London district, though
it is likely that there were meadows
there in former times where large
numbers of horses could graze.

Hadrian *See* Adrian's Head.

Haig *See* Earl Haig.

Halberd Ipswich. The military
weapon, a combination of spear
and axe, with a blade ending in a
point and a spear head. All this was
mounted on a shaft about six feet
long. Halberdiers acted as
bodyguards to Tudor monarchs,
and the Yeoman of the Guard still
carry halberds on ceremonial
occasions.

Halcyon Winchester. Another at
Peterborough. 'Halcyon days' are
days of peace and quiet. The
reference ultimately is to a fabled
bird which was supposed to build
its nest floating on the sea. The
bird had the power to charm the
sea and wind so that they remained
calm during the hatching of its
eggs. The kingfisher became
identified with this bird, but the
inn sign at Winchester shows a
bluebird.

Hale Fellow Halewood, near
Liverpool. The pub name was no
doubt inspired by the place name.
A 'hale fellow' would be one who
is free from injury or ill-health, a
whole fellow. By its sound,
however, it suggests the greeting:
'Hail fellow, well met'. Jonathan
Swift used the phrase in *My Lady's
Lamentation:* 'Hail fellow, well
met, All dirty and wet; Find out, if
you can, Who's master, who's
man.'

Half Brick Worthing. The pub is in
an area once occupied by brick
fields.

Half Butt Great Horkesley, near
Colchester. A large cask, holding
half as much as a butt. A butt could
contain 108 gallons of beer or 126
gallons of wine.

Half Crown Long Eaton, near
Nottingham. The coin of this
name ceased to become legal
tender in December 1969. The
Long Eaton pub sign shows a royal
crown cut in half. Facing it is a
halved coin. Other pubs of this
name are at Hereford and South
Benfleet, Esx. The latter pub was
formerly the Crown, but the
premises were partly demolished
by a runaway lorry. The rebuilt
pub took on the new name.

Half Penny Middlesbrough. The coin which ceased to be minted in March 1984, after national protests about its uselessness.

Halfpenny House Hipswell Moor, Richmond, N Yorks. This former pub, now a farmhouse, was named for the custom whereby a halfpenny was placed in a box by every customer, commemorating a toll that was once payable at this spot. The money so collected was handed over to local hospitals.

Half Sovereign *See* Sovereign.

Halfway Bridge *See* Bridge.

Halfway House Harefield, GL and elsewhere. Halfway Inn is also common. These pubs were originally on country roads and indicated convenient stopping places for travellers.

Halsetown Halse Town, near St Ives, Corn. The pub, and village, take their name from James Halse, a local businessman and member of parliament who died in 1838.

Halzephron Gunwalloe, near Helston. A Cornish term for 'Hell's cliff', referring to a nearby headland. (Other sources say the name refers to a 'moor on a cliff'.)

Hame Makers Arms Walsall. 'Hames' are the curved pieces of wood or metal which are put round the neck of a draught horse. They are either attached to the horse's collar, or form it themselves. Hames were once made locally.

Hammer and Stithy Ossett, near Wakefield. 'My imaginations are as foul as Vulcan's stithy', says Hamlet (Act 3, scene 2). The word derives from Old Norse and means 'anvil'. *See also* Blacksmith.

Hammer and Tongs Basingstoke. Not quite a straightforward reference to a blacksmith because of the slang use of this phrase, to go at it hammer and tongs, to have a violent quarrel. The slang meaning first occurs, according to Eric Partridge, in the eighteenth century. *See also* Blacksmith.

Hammer in Hand Ganders Ash, Herts and elsewhere. The Ganders Ash pub was converted from a blacksmith's shop in 1851. Similar signs include Hammer at Madeley, Hammer and Anvil, March, Cambridge, Hammer and Pincers, Sheffield. *See also* Blacksmith.

Hammers London E6. The local football team, West Ham United, are known as the Hammers.

Hampshire Bowman Dunbridge, near Romsey. A reminder of the forerunners of the Hampshire Regiment, the bowmen who served at Agincourt. *See also* Archery.

Hampshire Hog London W6. Such hogs fed on the acorns which were to be found in the vicinity of the New Forest. The reference here, however, is to a member of the Royal Hampshire Regiment. The Hampshires do not like the name, preferring to be known as the Hampshire Tigers.

Hampshire Rose *See* Rose.

Hampshire Yeoman *See* Yeoman.

Hampton Court Palace London SE17. The palace on the Thames created for Cardinal Wolsey in the early sixteenth century.

Hand Nottingham. Other pubs of this name are at Denbigh and Llandegla, Clwyd. The Nottingham pub borrowed its name from an inn which stood nearby until it was demolished in 1865, though the latter was a Bird in Hand. In former times a sign showing a woman's hand indicated a bawdy house, or brothel.

Hand and Crown Sawbridgeworth, Herts. This is said to be a reference to falconry, and the royal patronage of the sport.

Hand and Flower West Kensington. Another at Ham Common, Surrey. Also Hand and Flowers, Marlow, with another at Maidenhead. Pubs of this name were often originally called the Lily, the usual emblem of the Virgin Mary since it is the flower of purity. When the Puritans objected to such saintly references, innkeepers rapidly adjusted their signs and referred to the inn in a different way.

Hand and Glove Windsor. A falconry reference, but hand and glove is also an early form of the expression 'hand in glove', meaning 'a close relationship between people'.

Hand and Heart Peterborough and elsewhere. Two right hands holding a heart was an ancient sign of friendliness and agreement. Pubs of this name, or the similar Heart and Hand, Millbrook, Corn and elsewhere, were sometimes the meeting places of friendly societies. Heart in Hand, Bourne End, Bucks and elsewhere, is another variant.

Hand and Marigold *See* Flowers.

Hand and Pen London EC4. The pub is in Fleet Street, but the sign did nor refer originally to journalists. The scriveners who formerly worked in this area copied legal and other documents. The Inns of Court are nearby.

Hand and Racquet London WC2. A reference to the former royal tennis court, which was well used by Charles II. The court, which was nearby, survived until the mid-nineteenth century.

Hand and Shears London EC1. Some of the pub's patrons refer to it as the Fist and Clippers. Originally a meeting place for tailors and cloth merchants, especially just before and during the Bartholomew Cloth Fair, held each August from 1153 until 1855. The lord mayor attended the fair in its later years. He cut with a pair of tailor's shears the first piece of cloth to be sold. From this practice arose the custom of cutting a piece of tape or cord when 'opening' a new road, bridge, etc. There is another pub of this name at Church Hanborough, near Oxford. Merthyr Tydfil has a Glove and Shears.

Handford Rose *See* Rose.

Hand in Hand Brighton and elsewhere. Probably a variant of Hand and Heart, indicating a friendly greeting. It may also have been a name that avoided Puritan wrath in the seventeenth century, where Salutation would certainly have earned it. At Tadworth in Surrey the sign shows children hand in hand, using a zebra crossing.

Hangman's Tree Rowley Regis, W Mids. The sign shows a tree with a noose suspended from its branches. The story told locally is that a former landlord also acted as hangman in the area. There came a time when he was asked to string up his best friend. Rather than do this he hanged himself.

Hanover Cheltenham. Also Hanover Arms, London SE15; Hanover House, Sheffield. The royal house of Hanover succeeded to the English throne in 1714. The Hanoverian monarchs were George I, George II, George III, George IV, William IV and Queen Victoria though when the latter came to the throne in 1837 the thrones of England and Hanover were separated.

Hansom Cab York and elsewhere. What was once called 'the gondola of London', a two-wheeled horse-drawn cab with the driver mounted on a dickey behind. The reins go across the roof. These early taxis took their name from the architect who invented them, Joseph Hansom (1802–82) who was born in York. The pub of this name in London W8 has a real hansom suspended from the ceiling.

Happy Landing Stanwell, GL. The pub is not far from Heathrow Airport. Bristol has a Happy Landings. This pub's original sign showed a Bristol helicopter, but in 1982 it was changed to show a safely landed parachutist.

Happy Man Stapleford, near Nottingham and elsewhere. The identity of the happy man varies with the pub. At Stapleford the sign shows a smiling young naval officer with his arm round his bride-to-be. The man is the future Sir John Borlase Warren, who served with distinction during the Napoleonic Wars and rose to the rank of admiral. He also became the village squire. Other pubs remembering him are the Warren Arms at Stapleford and the Sir John Warren at Ilkeston and nearby Loscoe. There is also a Sir John Borlase Warren at Canning Circus, Nottingham.

Happy Matelot St Albans. The sailor is presumably happy because he is now safely ashore, and a long way inland.

Happy Prospect Reading. The pub is in Coronation Square, and the prospect is presumably that of a long and happy reign.

Happy Return Lenton, near Nottingham. In 1966 this pub replaced three others belonging to the same brewery which had been demolished a few years earlier. The brewery's chairman also declared that *Happy Return* was his favourite volume of the Hornblower series, by C S

Forester. The inn sign shows a fisherman with his catch. The pub of this name at Chard, Somerset, has a happy sailor with his kitbag slung over his shoulder on the sign. Brierley Hill, W Mids has a Happy Returns.

Happy Wanderer Framwellgate Moor, near Durham. The sign shows a helmeted miner with refreshment close at hand. Inside the pub is a collection of miners' lamps. It is thought that the name referred to the Yorkshire miners who moved into Durham when their own pits closed in the 1930s, perhaps especially to one such miner who became a Durham publican.

Happy Wanderers Bolton. The local football team, Bolton Wanderers FC, won the FA Cup for the fourth time shortly before this pub was opened in 1958. *See also* Trotters.

Harborough Melton Mowbray, Leics. Market Harborough is a nearby town. Northampton has a Harborough Arms.

Hardinge Arms *See* Viscount Hardinge.

Hardwick Hardwick Hall, Derbys. 'Hardwick' here means 'herd farm'.

Hardwicke Arms Arrington, Cambs. The earls of Hardwicke have distinguished themselves in various ways. Philip Yorke Hardwicke, the 1st Earl (1690–1764) was lord chancellor for twenty years and was immensely respected in that role. His eldest son, of the same name, had a successful career as a politician and writer. The 3rd Earl, again a Philip Yorke Hardwicke, governed Ireland as lord lieutenant 1801–05 and was Fellow of the Royal Society. The 4th Earl, Charles Philip Yorke Hardwicke became a rear-admiral.

Hare Harrow Weald and elsewhere. The animal which behaves in an unruly fashion each March, during the breeding season. This has led to expressions like 'mad as a March hare' and 'hare-brained'. The Hare and Tortoise, Plymouth is a reference to Aesop's fable.

Hare and Hounds Birkenhead and elsewhere. The Birkenhead sign shows two hounds dressed as huntsmen enjoying a pint of ale, watched by a hare. Elsewhere the sign depicts a hare-hunting scene of the more traditional kind, with a pack of beagles. At Kingskerswell, Devon, the name relates to the greyhound racing which takes place opposite the pub. Newport, Gwent has a Hare and Greyhound.

Harkaway *See* Hark to Bounty.

Hark to Bounty Slaidburn, near Clitheroe. Similar names include Hark to Dandler, Bury; Hark to Lasher, Edale, near Castleton; Hark to Melody, Haverthwaite, near Ulverston; Hark to Mopsey, Normanton, W Yorks; Hark to Nudger Dobcross, near Oldham, Hark to Rover, Leeds; Hark to Towler, Bury. These names all occur in hunting country, mainly in Lancashire, and refer to famous hounds, leaders of the pack. Rochdale once had a pub called Hark up to Glory, for the same reason. It was changed in 1921 to Harkaway. The explanation given at the time was that 'citizens of a serious turn of mind felt its former name to savour of irreligious interpretation.'

Harlequin London EC1. The pub is next to Sadler's Wells theatre and has a suitably theatrical atmosphere. A harlequin is the pantomime character in spangled dress.

Harnser Stalham, near Norwich. Another at Catfield, near Great Yarmouth. An East Anglian name, along with harn and harnsey, of the common heron. In the North the bird is also known as the hern, hernshaw, hernseugh or hernsew.

Harp Abergele, Clwyd and elsewhere. Welsh pubs of this name naturally show a Welsh harp. Normally the instrument is symbolic of Ireland. It was first adopted by Henry VIII as the Irish badge, while James I was the first king to include it in the royal arms. The pub name sometimes becomes Harp of Erin, as at London SE8 or Irish Harp, at Aldridge, W Mids.

Harp and Crown Gastard, Wilts. A name inspired by the union of Britain and Ireland in 1801, after the dissolution of the Irish parliament. The union remained in force until the setting-up of the Irish Free State in 1922. The sign here shows a lady harpist wearing a crown. Manchester has a Harp and Shamrock and Dundee a Harp and Thistle.

Harp of Erin *See* Harp.

Harrier Tipton, W Mids and elsewhere. Pub signs interpret this name in various ways. The Tipton pub shows a cross-country runner on one side, wearing the colours of Tipton Harriers Athletic Club. On the other side is a bird, the marsh harrier. At Hamble, Herts, the sign shows the aircraft developed by the local aircraft company. At Hucknall near Nottingham the jump-jet harrier is shown. This vertical take-off and landing aircraft was developed at the nearby Rolls-Royce Experimental Establishment. Marsh Harrier is also found at Stamford and Cowley, Oxford. There is a Merrie Harriers at Cowbeech, E Ssx.

Harrow Langley, near Slough and elsewhere. A common sign, referring to the contrivance which is used to break up clods of earth, stir the earth, root up weeds, cover seeds, etc, on farmland. At North Hykeham, near Lincoln, there is a Harrows.

Hart Sandsend, Whitby. A hart is a fully grown male deer, a stag. Since early times it has been the object of (royal) attention in the chase. The animal is well known for its branched horns, and there is a Hart's Horns in Hertford (where the place-name means 'ford used by stags'). Ashton-under-Lyne, Lanc, has a Hart's Head. At Gobowen, Salop, there is a hunting reference in Hart and Trumpet.

Harvest Weston-super-Mare. A slightly curious name to find in a seaside town, though there is such a thing as a harvest fish, found in North America. Perhaps the reference here is to the reward which comes at the end of a period of effort, a metaphorical harvest. At Frithville, near Boston there is a Harvest Man, which normally refers to a reaper but can also apply to certain insects, such as the longlegged spider, which are commonly found at harvest time. Harvest Home at Greet, near Cheltenham and elsewhere, is a reminder of the festivals which

were commonly held at the successful close of the harvesting.

Harvester Bingley, W Yorks. The name of a prize-winning show-jumper, ridden in the 1960s by Harvey Smith. He opened this pub in 1972. The inn sign shows him riding the horse.

Harvesters Stockwood, near Bristol and Nottingham. The sign of the Bristol pub says it all. One side shows a combine harvester, the other a group of men harvesting in the traditional way, with scythes.

Harvest Moon North Newton, near Bridgwater and elsewhere. This is the full moon in autumn, which gives longer spells of moonlight than usual. The phrase is also associated with a once-popular song which began 'Shine on, shine on harvest moon up in the sky . . . '

Hat and Beaver Atherstone, Warks. Another at Leicester. Both places are involved in hat-making. The sign is a reminder that hats made of beaver fur were formerly common.

Hat and Bonnet Luton. One of several signs in the town which refer to the local hatmaking industry.

Hat and Feathers Bath and elsewhere. The distinctive broad-brimmed hats, decorated with ostrich feathers, worn by Prince Rupert and the cavaliers, in the seventeenth century.

Hat and Tun London EC1. A well-known rebus sign, referring to the Hatton family whose mansion formerly stood nearby. The sign here was originally a beaver hat suspended from a pole with a small barrel, the tun, beneath it. There is a Sir Christopher Hatton in London EC1.

Hatch Hatch Beauchamp, near Taunton. 'Hatch' here means a gate leading into a forest.

Hatchet London EC4. Another at Lower Chute, Wilts. The London pub was named for a timber harbour which used to be nearby. The Lower Chute example refers to the hatchet which appears in the arms of the Foresters Company.

Hatchet and Bill Yaxley, near Peterborough. The reference is to two hedging tools, the second one being the bill-hook, often called a 'bill'. It has a long blade with a concave edge.

Hatchetts Bath. The name of the former owner. There is a Hatchett at Sherfield English, near Romsey, Hants.

Hatch Gate Bramshill, near Reading. A hatch gate is properly a wicket, a half door or gate with an open space above.

Hatters Arms Warton, near Tamworth. Another at Marple, near Stockport. For makers of, or dealers in hats. Hatters have acquired their reputation for madness only in modern times, and mainly thanks to Lewis Carroll. The expression 'as mad as a hatter' was originally American, and 'mad' meant 'angry'. 'Hatter' may therefore be a corruption of 'adder'.

Haunch of Venison Cheshunt, Herts and elsewhere. A sign normally found near a royal hunting forest. Venison is now thought of exclusively as deer-meat, but the word derives from latin *venari*, 'to hunt', and was formerly applied to the flesh of any animal, boar, hare, etc, which had been killed in the chase.

Hautboy Ockham, Sry. An early form of 'oboe', the wooden double-reed wind instrument of high pitch, the latter fact accounting for its name, from French *haut bois* 'high wood'. There was until about 1940 an Hautboy and Fiddle at Warmington, near Peterborough, both instruments being used to accompany Christmas carol singers.

Havelock Also Havelock Arms. See General Havelock.

Haw Bridge Tirley, Glos. The pub is by the bridge which crosses the River Severn.

Haw Bush *See* Bush.

Hawes Inn Queensferry, Loth. Originally this pub was Newhalls, a reference to Newhalls pier, just across the road. Ferry boats used to use the pier until the Forth Bridge was opened in 1964. In Scottish vernacular, the pub name became *Ha's Inn*, which led to the present name.

Hawk and Buckle Etwall, near Derby. Others at Llanefydd, Clwyd and Denbigh. A reference to falconry, and the French expression *en boucle*, which means that the hawk is tethered by a leash attached to a ring.

Hawkins Arms Probus, near Truro. Sir John Hawkins (1532–95) was an English naval hero, knighted for his prominent part in the defeat of the Spanish Armada (1588). He had earlier carried slaves from Africa to the West Indies. He died at sea while second in command to Drake.

Hawthorn Bush West Bromwich. Also Hawthorn Tree, Allesley, near Coventry. The heraldic reference here is to the arms of Henry VII. The Romans considered that a hawthorn bush would act as a protection against sorcery. They placed hawthorn leaves in the cradles of their newly-born babies.

Hawthornden Lasswade, Loth. The name of a glen eight miles south of Edinburgh. The estate there was once owned by the poet William Drummond. The Hawthornden Prize is now awarded annually for the best imaginative work in prose or verse by a British author who is under the age of forty-one.

Hawthorns West Bromwich. The local football team, West Bromwich Albion, have 'The Hawthorns' as their home ground.

Haychatter Bradfield Dale, Derbs. For the whinchat, a bird which makes its nest principally from dried grass.

Haycock Wansford, near Peterborough. A reference to a folkstory about 'Drunken Barnaby's Four Journeys to the North of England'. One of these occurred when Barnaby fell asleep on a haycock (which must have been difficult because a haycock is normally a bundle of hay in conical shape), which was carried along by the River Nene. When he woke it was to find the local people asking him 'Where away?' quoth they – 'from Greenland?' 'No,' says I, 'from Wansford Bridge in England.' There was some point to the last remark because Wansford is only a few miles from the former Holland division of Lincolnshire.

Hay Cutter Broadham Green, Sry. One of many names which refers to haymaking and its results. There is a Haymaker at Wadeford, Som; Haymakers at Cambridge; Bale of Hay, Birmingham; Load of Hay, Fordingbridge, Hants, with

another in London NW3; Hay Wain at Chelston, near Torquay – recalling the most famous painting of Constable, which he executed in 1821. It is now in the National Gallery. Churchover, near Rugby has a Hay Waggon; Hayloft is at Giltbrook, near Nottingham; Hay Nook is at Rotherham; Hay Rick at Nuneaton; Hay Stack at Canvey Island.

Hayling Billy Hayling Island, Hants. A locomotive which ran from Havant to Hayling Island until the railway line was closed in 1963. Since 1966 the locomotive itself has stood in the pub's forecourt.

Hayloft Giltbrook, near Nottingham. The pub displays a collection of old farming implements in its rafters.

Hay Tor *See* Tors.

Haywards Minehead. George Hayward ran a wine and spirit business here in the 1960s.

Headless Woman *See* Silent Woman.

Head of the River Folly Bridge, Oxford. College rowing crews compete for this title every June after their examinations. One crew tries to 'bump' another. The pub was opened in 1977 and a competition to find a name for it was organised by the *Oxford Mail*. This name was chosen from the 2700 entries.

Headstocks Cinderhill, Nottingham. The name applied to the bearings of revolving parts in eg lathes and planing machines. Here the reference is to winding machinery used at Babbington Colliery opposite.

Heart and Club Harlow. The name of a moth. It continues the common pub-name theme in this town.

Heart and Hand Also Heart in Hand. *See* Hand and Heart.

Heart of all England Hexham, Northld. The pub name makes rather a dramatic claim. Hexham is certainly a very ancient town, with a thirteenth century priory which contains the remains of a seventh century monastery.

Heart of Oak Hereford. Another at Pinhoe, near Exeter. Also Hearts of Oak, Drybrook, Glos and Barnstaple. The heart of an oak is the central part of the tree which has no sap, particularly prized in former times in shipbuilding. In Nelson's time some two thousand oaks would have been used to build a seventy-four-gun warship. The phrase 'heart of oak' has long been used figuratively to refer to a courageous man. As an eighteenth-century song put it: 'Heart of oak are our ships, hearts of oak are our men.' The sign at Barnstaple shows both sailor – an immaculately-clad bluejacket wearing his straw hat – and his ship.

Hearty Good Fellow Nottingham and elsewhere. The name was suggested by a ballad sung in the 1860s: 'I am a hearty good fellow, I live at my ease;/I work when I'm ready, I play when I please./With my bottle and glass many hours I do pass;/Sometimes with a friend, sometimes with a lass.'

Heath Robinson Bath. W Heath Robinson (1872–1944) was a cartoonist who specialised in showing whimsically intricate gadgets which performed simple tasks. The owner of this pub also happened to be a Robinson.

Heifer *See* Craven Heifer.

Heights of Alma *See* Alma.

Heilk Moon Scaleby, near Kirklinton, Cumb. The present landlord of the pub has no idea as to the name's meaning, but it appears to be a dialectal development of Old English *halh*, Middle English *halke*. The meaning has to do with a 'curve' or 'corner'. The pub sign appears to portray a gibbous moon, ie a moon which is more than half illuminated but is less than a full moon. It is, in a sense, the opposite of a crescent moon. The derivation from *halh* was suggested by Dr Wakelin, of Royal Holloway and Bedford College.

Helmsman Poole. Poole Harbour nearby is very popular amongst yachtsmen. The helm of a yacht is used to manage the rudder.

Helping Hand London WC1. The sign shows a man in the water being helped into a boat by someone who is lending a helping hand.

Help me through this World Bury, Lancs. Formerly a common sign, 'expressed on tavern signs, tradesmen's handbills and circus clowns' programmes by a man struggling through a globe – head and arms protruding on one side, his legs on the other – implying, thus far I have managed to get through the world by my own exertion; now afford me a little of your aid to enable me to accomplish the rest.' So Charles Hindley explains the name in his *Tavern Anecdotes and Sayings*. Others relate it to the drunkard's cloak, as it was known, a tub or barrel with holes for the head and hands, fitted on a drunkard like a jacket as a punishment. Puritan magistrates were fond of sentencing men or women to wear these. The same image of the person in a globe or barrel was often interpreted as Help the Poor Struggler, as at Hollinwood, near Oldham, Lancs; Struggler, Dearham, Cumb; Strugglers, Eagle, near Lincoln; Struggling Man, Dudley.

Helvetia London W1. In an area which was formerly the centre of

London's Swiss community. *Helvetia* is the Latin name for Switzerland.

Hemlock Stone Wollaton, Nottingham. The reference is to a local landmark at nearby Bramcote. The 'stone' is a mass of red sandstone rock of a peculiar shape. The hemlock plant has small white flowers and is poisonous.

Hemp Sheaf Stradbroke, Sflk. Crops of hemp are grown locally and stacked in sheaves.

Hen and Chickens Bristol and elsewhere. Also Hen and Chicken, Southwater, near Horsham. In the seventeenth century this expression was used to describe the Pleiads, the group of stars in the constellation Taurus. In the eighteenth century it was used to name a compound daisy, such as London Pride. By the late nineteenth century the expression was applied to a children's game. In slang, 'chickens' were small pewter pots mixed with larger pots (known as 'hens') and this looks a tempting source for the pub names. Before the seventeenth century however, a hen and chickens were symbolic in Christian art of God's providence, and that is probably the original reason for their use on street signs of various kinds, including taverns.

Hendras Carbis Bay, St Ives. The family name of the licensee, Hendra, originally meant 'someone who lived in a fixed abode'. Other Cornish pubs which take their names from a former or present licensee include Tyacks, Camborne; Webbs, Liskeard; Wheelers, Torpoint.

Hen–dy–dafarn–y–polin Porthy-rhydd, near Carmarthen. This Welsh name means 'the old inn with the pole' and refers to a toll pole barrier which was once stretched across the road here.

Hengler's Circus Liverpool. The pub takes the name of Britain's first indoor circus, which was on a site nearby until it closed in Edwardian times. The interior of the pub exploits the 'circus' theme.

Henry Cooper London SE1. This was the Lord Wellington until 1980, when it was renamed in honour of the popular former British and European heavyweight boxing champion. Henry Cooper performed the reopening ceremony.

Henry Fielding Dunball, Bridgwater. Henry Fielding (1707–54), not a man to stomach hypocrisy or vanity, was provoked by the publication of Samuel Richardson's novel *Pamela* (1740) to write a parody of it, *Joseph Andrews* (1742). He was probably also the author of *Shamela*, which appeared anonymously in 1741. Having discovered that he could himself write a novel, Fielding went on to publish *Tom Jones* (1749) and *Amelia* (1751). He wrote at a time when the English novel was only just taking on its accepted form and contributed to it greatly. He was born at Shapham Park, not far from this pub.

Henry V Monmouth. Henry V (1387–1422) was the son of Henry IV. He reigned from 1412. He was born in Monmouth Castle, and the town's marketplace is called Agincourt Square in honour of his victory there over the French. He was reckless in his youth but ruled wisely, restoring civil order and inspiring national pride. He was an excellent military tactician and became a popular hero, as Shakespeare's play makes clear.

Henry Ford Dagenham, Esx. Henry Ford (1863–1947) was the pioneer car manufacturer who introduced mass production methods into his factories. The pub is opposite Ford's Dagenham plant, and shows Ford holding a model of his 'Tin Lizzie'. The latter is also commemorated in the Model T at Waterton, near Bridgend and Mowden Park, Darlington.

Henry IV Fakenham, Nflk. Henry IV (1367–1413) was king from 1399. He was the son of John of Gaunt and the founder of the Lancastrian dynasty.

Henry Holland London SW1. Henry Holland (1746–1806) was the first architect employed by Whitbreads, the brewers. They named this house in his honour in 1960. Holland also designed Battersea Bridge and Brighton Pavilion.

Henry Jenkins Kirkby Malzeard, near Ripon. According to a memorial tablet in the church at Bolton–on–Swale, near Richmond, this man died in 1670 at the age of 169.

Henry Peacock Harrogate. A local worthy. He was appointed Master of the local workhouse in 1825 and also became a 'Town Improvement Commissioner'.

Henry VI London N1. Henry VI was the son of Henry V. Born in 1421, he became king when he was less than one year old. His uncles John of Lancaster and Humphrey, Duke of Gloucester ruled for him. After an unhappy life he died in the Tower of London in 1471.

Henry the Eighth Hever, Kent. Henry VIII (1491–1547) ruled 1509–47. The reign was comparatively peaceful for English people as a whole, though not for some of those who were close to him, notably two of his six wives, who were beheaded at his orders. Thomas Wolsey and Thomas Cromwell also suffered. The public loved him and seemed to forgive, or were unaware of, his ruthless pursuance of personal desires under the guise of public policy. Local tradition at Hever says that Henry courted Anne Boleyn in the castle there. There is a Hever Castle at London SE5, and a King Henry VIII in London N16.

Herbert Devonport. Herbert is the family name of the earls of Caernarvon, who owned land in the West Country. There is a Herbert Arms at Chirbury, Clwyd. It should also be noted that the trade sign of the Devenish Brewery, Weymouth, is 'Herbert the Tiger'.

Hercules Pillars *See* Pillars of Hercules.

Hereford Bull *See* Bull.

Heritage Cardiff. The pub was opened in 1984 and features old brewery bric-à-brac inside.

Hermit Burley–in–Wharfdale, near Ilkley. The hermit was a man named Joe Job. After his wife's death he built himself a hovel on the edge of Rumbald Moor. He eventually died in 1857 at the age of seventy-seven when some local lads offered him a doctored drink as a prank.

Hermit of Redcoats Titmore Green, near Hitchin. James Lucas barricaded himself inside his house after his mother's death in 1848. He lived in squalor until his own death in 1874. He is said to have worn at all times a red coat.

Herne's Oak Winkfield, near Windsor. This refers to a tree which was in Windsor Great Park until it was blown down in 1863. It was reputedly haunted by Herne, who was a forester centuries earlier.

Hero Overy Staithe, Nflk. The signboard here depicted Lord

Nelson, who was born in the vicarage of a nearby village, until 1963. The brewers then decided to put up a portrait of Wing Commander Guy Gibson, who gained his VC by leading the famous 'Dam buster' raid of 1943. Local objections caused Lord Nelson to be reinstated.

Heroes *See* Heroes of Waterloo.

Heroes of Alma *See* Alma.

Heroes of Lucknow *See* Sir Colin Campbell.

Heroes of Waterloo Waterlooville, near Portsmouth. This was the original name of the pub which led to the place name, though the pub itself is now simply the Heroes. It is said that the victorious troops on their way home after landing at Portsmouth rested in the area, or actually stopped at the inn.

Herongate Herongate, near Brentwood. The inn sign shows a heron perched on a five–barred gate, a humorous but incorrect interpretation of the place name. The Heron pub at Herne Bay may also have been inspired by the place name, especially since the heron is often hern in dialect, but as with Herongate the origin lies in Old English *hyrne*, 'corner' or 'angle'.

Hero of Aliwal Whittlesey, near Peterborough. Aliwal is in South Africa, and the hero who led a charge there in the deciding battle of the Sikh Campaign (1846) was Sir Harry Smith (1787–1860). The general was born locally, but later lived in South Africa.

Hero of Inkerman Bagshot, Sry. Inkerman is a town in the Crimea, near Sebastopol. On 5 November 1854, the English and French defeated the Russians there, after the latter had made an unexpected attack. Both sides lost great numbers of men. The battle is recalled also by the Inkerman, Ipswich, and Inkerman Arms at Rye Harbour and Luton.

Hero of Maida London W2. Close to Maida Vale, and honouring Sir John Stuart and his men who crushingly defeated the French in 1806. Maida is in southern Italy.

Hero of Switzerland London SW9. William Tell probably never existed but was supposed to be a native of Bürglen. He refused to obey Gessler, the Austrian bailiff, and was forced as a punishment to shoot an apple off his son's head. The story no doubt arose out of the revolt against the bailiffs which actually occurred on 1 January 1308.

Hero of Waterloo London SE1. The Duke of Wellington, or any of the soldiers who fought at Waterloo. The pub of this name which was formerly at Wollaton, Nottingham, was for the son of a local farmer. Lifeguardsman John Shaw died a hero on the field of battle.

Herschel Arms Slough. Sir William Herschel (1738–1822) was a pioneer astronomer who used systematic observations to discover the planet Uranus (1781). His sister Caroline worked with him, as did his son Sir John Frederick William Herschel (1792–1871).

Hever Castle *See* Henry the Eighth.

Hewitts Tavern Grimsby. This was the Duke of Wellington until 1984. It was renamed after the Hewitt Brothers, brewers here for many years.

Hibernia Angle, Pembroke. *Hibernia* was the Latin form of the Celtic name for Ireland. The Irish coast can be seen from this pub across St George's Channel.

Hide Away Stretton, near Chesterfield and elsewhere. Used of a pub which is hidden away, or was at the time of naming. In earlier times the phrase was also used of fugitives, stowaways and the like. Belfast has a similar Hide Out, though the suggestion here is that the pub's customers can escape from those who are bothering them.

High and Dry Waldershare, near Dover. A phrase that normally means 'deserted', left 'without help'. Here it is said to relate to the coal seam in the local pit, which is unusually free from seeping sea water.

Higher Mead Camelford, Corn. A reference to the high meadow which overlooks the town.

High Farm Holt Park, Leeds. The pub is on a new housing estate and incorporates a former farmhouse and barn.

Highflyer Ely. Another at Bradford. There was a highly successful racehorse of this name.

High Force High Force, Dur. The pub and place are named for England's highest waterfall. 'Force' is in general use in the North for 'waterfall'.

Highland Laddie *See* Bluebells of Scotland.

High Noon Sheffield. The licence for this pub was transferred from the Twelve O' Clock, which used to be in Savile Street.

High Roost Cleeve Hill, near Cheltenham. The pub is sited more than 1,000 feet above sea-level.

High Sheriff Rochdale. The pub is on land which originally belonged to the Entwisle family. Three members of the family have served as high sheriff of Lancaster.

High Span Rochester. The name refers to the nearby bridge over the river Medway, built in the 1960s.

Highwayman Dobwalls, near Liskeard and elsewhere. A reference to a local man, James Elliott, convicted of robbery on the highway in 1787 and hanged at Bodmin. The pub of this name at Skelmersdale, Lancs, refers to George Lyon, hanged at Lancaster in 1815. He was reputedly the last highwayman to suffer this fate. There is a Highwayman's Haunt at Chudleigh, Devon, and several highwaymen – Dick Turpin and the like – have pubs named after them. *See also* Wicked Lady.

Hill Chapel-le-Dale, near Carnforth, Lancs. The annual race which takes fell-climbers to the summit of Whernside, Pen-y-Ghent and Ingleborough (each over 2,000 feet) starts and finishes at this pub.

Hind Lutterworth, near Rugby. The hind is the female of the red deer, the male being the stag or hart. Early examples of this sign relate to St Giles, who is said to have withdrawn into a remote forest where a hind lived with him and supplied him with milk. When the king's huntsmen pursued the hind, St Giles caused thick bushes to spring up to protect it. There is a White Hind at Newark, and a Hind and Hart at London NW9. The latter name, however, is for two types of aircraft which used the former Hendon aerodrome. Wrightington, near Wigan has a Hind's Head.

Hit or Miss Stamford and elsewhere. A comment by the licensee on the random nature of a particular event, or life in general. The Stamford sign shows a blacksmith at his anvil.

Hob Bamber Bridge, Lancs. A reference to hobnobbing with someone, taking a drink with a good friend. The original sense was 'to clink glasses', and the expression is probably a form of hab-nab, meaning 'hit or miss', though one imaginative writer has tried to link it with hob in the sense of the side of a fireplace. 'Nob', according to this interpretation, referred to a small round table, but there is absolutely no evidence to support such an explanation. 'Hob' certainly can mean a sprite, a hobgoblin ('hob' in this instance being a pet form of Robert), and Hob in the Well, formerly at King's Lynn, was used in that sense. There is still a Hobgoblins in Edinburgh, while Liverpool has a Goblin.

Hobbit Monyash, near Bakewell, Derbs. Another at Sowerby Bridge, W Yorks. A reference to the benevolent, furry–footed creature, living in a burrow, created by Tolkien in his *Lord of the Rings*. Hobbits have a passion for food and tobacco. *See* Bilbo Baggins.

Hobbs Boat Lympsham, near Weston-super-Mare. The local legend is that a lady named Hobbs outwitted the Vikings when they landed here. She slipped the moorings of their ships, allowing them to drift down to the Bristol Channel.

Hobby Horse Minehead, Som. Another at Brynmawr, Pwys. This is the figure of a horse, made of wickerwork or some similar material, which is fastened round the waist of a morris dancer. The dancer then prances about like a horse. A simpler form of the device is a stick with a horse's head which children 'ride' as if it were a horse. An extended meaning of the phrase is any interest or topic which a person pursues with special devotion, as if he were riding a toy horse. A local tradition in Minehead relates hobby-horses to devices used to scare Viking invaders.

Hob Nails Little Washbourne, near Tewkesbury. The nails with large heads which were used to protect the boots of farm-labourers and the like. At one time it was possible to refer to a man as a 'hobnail', meaning that he was a clod-hopper, a clumsy awkward sort of man.

Hobson's Choice Cambridge. Another at London N15. Thomas Hobson hired out horses in the seventeenth century, but gave his clients no choice as to the horse which they would have. Each horse was hired out in strict rotation. His eccentricity might have lost him his trade, but instead seems to have endeared him to his clients, especially the poet Milton. Professor Weekley tried to throw doubt on this traditional explanation, quoting Richard Cocks, writing some years before Hobson's death: 'We are put to Hobson's choice to take such privileges as they will give us, or else go without.'

Hoedown Nottingham. This pub was the Gardeners until 1982. The change of name converted it into a kind of *Gardeners' Rest*. The sign shows two people raising their glasses in a toast rather than taking part in the square-dance called the Hoedown.

Hogarth Isle of Grain, near Rochester. William Hogarth (1697–1764) was an English painter and engraver of mostly satirical works. His portraits border on being caricatures. Some of his prints were designed to show the need for social reforms. His best known works are a series of engravings called *The Harlot's Progress, The Rake's Progress* and *Marriage à la Mode*.

Hog in the Pound London W1. The premises were formerly used by a butcher, whose sign showed a fat pig in a sty. The sty became a pound, an animal enclosure, when the house became an inn. Norwich has a Hog in Armour, Chislet, near Herne Bay a Hog and Donkey, and Cricklewood a Hog's Grunt.

Hog's Back Scale, near Farnham. The nearby natural ridge, with a road running along its top, is known by this name.

Hog's Grunt London NW2. A reconstructed barn which forms part of Production Village, a block of film studios.

Hogshead Sheffield. Also Hog's Head, Bournemouth, Leeds and Salisbury. The large cask of various capacities used for wines and beers is known as a hogshead.

Hogsmill Worcester Park, Sry. The name of a local river, derived in its turn from Hog's Mill, once owned by the Hog family.

Hole in One Cliftonville, near Margate and elsewhere. Normally pubs of this name are found near a golf course. They perhaps serve to remind the golfer who has been fortunate enough to achieve a hole in one that it is now his duty to buy the drinks.

Hole in the Wall Colchester and elsewhere. Various explanations have been offered for pubs of this name. They include references to holes in the wall of condemned cells, through which the prisoners could speak, or in the walls of debtors' prisons, through which supplies could be passed, or in the walls of a lepers' den, through which priests could put their hands in order to bless those inside. Sometimes the hole in the wall is a kind of spy-hole. It can refer to the position of a pub, as at Waterloo Station where the premises are beneath one of the arches of the

viaduct-type bridge, or the chief entrance to the pub can be through a narrow passage which breaks up the buildings facing onto the street as at Ashby-de-la-Zouch, Leics. In Richmond the hole is said to have been a hatch through which drinks were passed to coachmen, who waited outside for their passengers. In Chiswick the pub of this name attempted to call itself the Queen's Head, but returned to its former name when its regulars continued to use that version. The amusing sign shows a pig escaping through a hole in the wall. At Dumfries there is a Hole in the Wa'. The sign shows a schoolboy peering through it to look at a football match. Colne, Lancs has a Hole i' th' Wall.

Holeford Arms *See* Arboretum.

Holiday Ilfracombe. A sign presumably meant to attract the many holiday-makers who visit this town.

Holland Hatt, near Saltash, Corn. A local politician, Lord Holland, was active in the mid-nineteenth century. There is a pub of this name in Yeovil where the reference is to Holland linen, originally imported by Flemish immigrants, later made locally.

Hollies Winton, Bournemouth. There is an avenue of holly trees near the pub.

Hollins Bush Sheffield. 'Hollin' is an archaic or dialectal form of 'holly'. Walsden near Rochdale has a Hollins.

Holly Rodmell, near Lewes. Holly Bush, Hinckley and elsewhere; Holly Tree, Englefield Green, Sry, are associated names, as is Holly and Laurel, Holmwood, near Dorking. The latter, like the Holmbush at Holmbush, near St Austell, was clearly inspired by the place name, since holm is another form of 'holly'. This evergreen shrub, with its bright red berries, is now associated with Christmas decorations. Previously it was used by the Romans during the Saturnalia, the period of riotous celebrations extending over seven days, often ending in debauchery. The Saturnalia was also celebrated in December.

Hollywood Greats London W3. The pub opened in 1980 and has a name which indicates its theme. Chelsea has a Hollywood Arms, due to its location in Hollywood Road.

Holman Clavell Culmhead, near Taunton. The name refers to a clavel, or lintel, made of holm oak, which can be seen inside the pub.

Home Sweet Home Roke, near Oxford. The name of the home-brewed ale which was formerly sold here.

Honest Boy Washington, T and W. A reference to the supposed reply of the young George Washington (1732–99) when asked by his father who had chopped down the cherry tree: 'Father, I cannot tell a lie. I did it with my little hatchet.'

Honest Lawyer King's Lynn. Others at Folkestone, Southampton. The King's Lynn sign shows the lawyer with his briefcase in one hand, his head in the other. This joke, implying that the only honest lawyer is either dead or otherwise unable to open his mouth, is normally applied to signs like the Good Woman, Silent Woman, Quiet Woman.

Honest Miller Brook, near Ashford, Kent. Millers were notorious for their dishonesty in former times, especially the Middle Ages. There was a proverbial saying that 'Every honest miller has a thumb of gold', meaning that even if the miller wanted to be honest he would still grow rich because flour that should go into a loaf would stick to his thumb. The implication was that it was almost inconceivable that a miller should be completely honest.

Honeysuckle *See* Flowers.

Honiley Boot *See* Boot.

Honiton Awliscombe, Devon. The sign shows a square of lace, referring to the traditional industry of nearby. Honiton.

Hood Arms *See* Admiral Hood.

Hooden Horse Wickambreaux, near Canterbury. The hooden horse is similar to the hobby horse, worn about the waist of morris dancers. They come to this district each September when the hops are 'hooded' – placed in the oast house for drying.

Hook and Glove Farley, near Salisbury. Local woodsmen and foresters would hang up their hooks and gloves on special pegs when they came to this inn at the end of the working day.

Hook and Hatchet Chatham. Another at Hucking, near Sittingbourne. The reference is to the badge of a Chief Petty Officer Shipwright. At one time the Royal Navy had tree-felling rights so that they could obtain timber for ship-building in Chatham Dockyard and elsewhere.

Hoop and Grapes London EC3 and elsewhere in London. Formerly a popular sign, which may have originally been Hops and Grapes, the sign showing a bunch of grapes in a garland of hop leaves. The hoop from a beer barrel, together with the grapes, now serves the same purpose, to indicate that beer and wine is available.

Hoop and Toy London SW7. The sign shows a child's hoop and rocking horse but the reason for such a sign is not known.

Hoops Horns Cross, near Bideford and elsewhere. 'Hoop' is the name in the western counties for the bullfinch, deriving probably from the bird's cry. The birds were formerly so destructive in the Bideford area that fourpence a corpse was offered to local marksmen. Elsewhere this pub name refers to hoops of the more usual kind.

Hope Bridgwater and elsewhere. Another at Carshalton. The Bridgwater pub recalls a stagecoach which operated between Bristol and Taunton. The sign at Carshalton interprets the name differently. A Victorian young gentleman is on his knee proposing to his crinolined lady-love. Yet another interpretation is seen at Bristol, where the sign shows a small boy, ready at the wicket and holding a bat many sizes too big for him. The sign is based on a photograph of the landlord's son as a small boy. Ilford has a Hope Revived and Dalgety Bay, near Dunfermline a Hope Tryst.

Hope and Anchor Hope Cove, near Kingsbridge. The pub name was no doubt suggested by the place name, which uses 'hope' in its sense of 'small bay'. In Christian symbolism the anchor is the symbol of hope. At Hebrews 6:19 we find: 'Hope we have as an anchor of the soul.' The spare anchor on a ship was often called the 'hope anchor'. There is a Hope Anchor at Rye, E Ssx.

Hop Inn Winchester, Chichester and elsewhere. A name similar to Dew Drop Inn in that it issues a covert invitation to come inside. Associated names include the following: Hop Bag, Farnham, Sry; Hop Bine, North Wembley; Hop Blossom, Farnham, Sry; Hop Fields, Hatfield, Herts; Hop Flower, Inkersall, near Chesterfield; Hop Garland, Hemel Hempstead; Hop Kiln, Farnham, Sry; Hop Leaf, Basingstoke and Cooksbridge, near Lewes; Hop Market, Worcester; Hop Picker, Horsham and London E2; Hop Vine, Soham, near Ely. Coseley, W Mids has a Hop and Barleycorn, Aldridge near Walsall and Redcar both have a Hop and Grape and Rainham, Esx has a Hop and Vine. The pick of this bunch is probably the Hop n' Scotch, Harrogate, a fine pun.

Hop Pocket Paddock Wood, Kent. A 'hop pocket' is a very large sack containing one and a half hundredweights of fresh hops. They are kept in these pockets after being dried in the kilns, then about a year later they are ready for use.

Hop Poles Limpley Stoke, near Bath. Another at London W6. Also Hop Pole, Aylesbury and elsewhere. The hop vines used to be trained up hop poles, whereas they are now trained onto wires. At Alton, Hants, a pub called *Hop Poles* formerly had hop fields at the rear of the premises, the poles being repaired in the innyard.

Horn Reading. A name which can refer to the post-horn used by stagecoach guards, as here, or to the hunting horn.

Horn and Trumpet Worcester. Another at Kidderminster. Previously the sign of a musical instrument maker and repairer.

Hornblower Newport, Gwent and elsewhere. After Horatio Hornblower, the character created by C S Forester for a series of books from 1937 onwards. He begins as a midshipman but becomes an admiral, a knight and finally Lord Hornblower of Smallbridge.

Horn of Plenty Chatham and elsewhere. The colloquial way of referring to the Cornucopia, the goat's horn which Zeus presented to Amalthea, promising her that whoever had it would always have in abundance everything that was desired.

Horns Nursling, near Southampton. The driver of the brewery dray would sound a horn to announce his arrival here.

Horse The horse is one of the most popular animals to occur in pub names, though we have been unable to trace a single pub called *Horse*. Apart from named race horses (treated separately under Racehorses), there are signs for the Arabian Horse, Bay Horse, Brown Horse, Halifax and elsewhere, Chestnut Horse, Great Finborough, Sflk; Dray Horse, Hatfield; Dun Horse, Kendal; Galloping Horse, High Harrington, Cumb; Grey Horse, Pack Horse, Pied Horse, Shire Horse, Trotting Horse (*see* Trotter), White Horse, and so on. In Lincolnshire, near Grantham, there is of course a Blue Horse (*see* Series Naming). Other horsey names which do not actually mention 'horse' itself include Yorkshire Grey, Palomino and the like, or Black Mare, Old Grey Mare, Northchurch, Herts; Mare and Colt, Summerfield, Worcs; Filly, Nag's Head, Old Roan, Aintree. At least sixty different names refer to the horse as a working animal or sporting associate. The Iron Horse, needless to say, leads on to another topic.

Horse and Chains Bushey, near Watford. Extra horses were stationed at the foot of nearby Clay Hill in former times to assist with heavily-laden waggons. They were fitted with spiked shoes which enabled them to get a good grip.

Horse and Dorsers London EC4. 'Dorsers' or 'dossers' were wooden panniers *dos* in French). They were fitted to hang down the sides of packhorses, and can still be seen on some signs of the Pack Horse. The London pub is no longer there, but at North Luffenham, near Oakham there is still a Horse and Panniers.

Horse and Gears Newark. 'Gears' was used until the nineteenth century to refer to the harness of a draught horse.

Horse and Jockey Bentley, near Atherstone, Warks and elsewhere. The Bentley sign shows the local squire, Sir William Dugdale, riding *Cloncarrig* in the 1952 Grand National.

Horse and Panniers *See* Horse and Dorsers.

Horsebreakers Arms Hutton Sessaye, near Thirsk. A former licensee had previously added to his living by breaking-in horses. Birmingham has a Horsetrader.

Horse Guards Tillington, W Ssx. The name of this pub is used for both the Household Cavalry, which consists of the Life Guards and the Royal Horse Guards, or for the latter regiment only. The Royal Horse Guards (the Blues) have

their headquarters in Whitehall. Behind the eighteenth century building is Horse Guards Parade, where the Trooping of the Colour ceremony takes place each year.

Horse Shoe Bulwell, Nottingham and elsewhere. Often the name is given as Horseshoe. Also Horseshoes, Eye, Sflk and elsewhere. A simple visual sign, made more significant by the long-standing belief that a horseshoe brings luck. Originally it was said to be a protection against witches. Horse shoes are still nailed up by the superstitious (Lord Nelson was one). They must have their two ends pointing upwards, or the luck will 'run out'. *See also* Three Horseshoes.

Hotpot Manchester. Now associated with the dish of mutton or beef with potatoes and onions cooked in an earthenware pot with a tight cover. Formerly, in many areas, an expression used to describe a pot of warmed ale.

Hotspur Newcastle-on-Tyne. The famous nickname of Harry Percy (1364–1403), who was a gallant but decidedly hot-tempered fellow. He was the eldest son of the 1st Earl of Northumberland, and appears in Shakespeare's *Henry IV, Parts I and II*. Hotspur means 'fiery-spirited' as well as 'rash', and was presumably adopted by the Tottenham Hotspur Football Club in the former meaning rather than the latter.

Hour Glass Nelson, Lancs and elsewhere. The Lancashire pub has an hourglass in every bar. The distinctive shape of the hourglass makes it a convenient visual symbol, one which was formerly familiar from its presence in church. Preachers often had one on the pulpit in order to time their sermons. John Donne, the famous

seventeenth-century poet and preacher, was fond of turning the hourglass over with a dramatic gesture while remarking to his congregation: 'Let's have another glass together.'

House of Smiths Weston-super-Mare. The sign shows a tinsmith at his workbench, repairing a pewter pot. The name may have been suggested by the surname Smith.

House that Jack Built Bristol. Others at Salford and Wolverhampton. The title of a well-known nursery-rhyme, concerned with 'a man all tattered and torn, That kissed the maiden all forlorn, That milked the cow with the crumpled horn, That tossed the dog, That worried the cat, That lay in the house that Jack built.' The name would have an obvious appeal to licensees called Jack.

House without a Name Bolton. Another at Colchester. A logical misnomer, since the *House without a Name* is a name; therefore the house without a name is no longer without a name.

Howff Tavern Dundee. 'Howff' in Scottish vernacular means 'a favourite haunt'. Cottar's Howff is a similar name.

Hoy and Helmet South Benfleet, Esx. For 'hoy' *see* Hoy Tavern. The 'helmet' is said to have been a local term for the jetty where the hoys tied up, but the word is also a variant of 'helm', and could therefore have referred to the tiller.

Hoy Tavern London SE8. Another at SE10. A 'hoy' was a small vessel, usually rigged as a sloop, used to carry passengers and goods short distances near the coast. Ipswich formerly had a Galliot Hoy, which probably serviced the galliots (Dutch cargo boats) which visited that port. Poole has a Portsmouth Hoy, and Gosport an Isle of Wight Hoy.

Hub Coventry. A pub which is the centre of things, no doubt – its name suggested by its address in Wheelwright Lane.

Hufflers Arms Dartford, Kent. 'Hufflers' ferried goods from the chandlers to ships anchored offshore. They had no licence to do so, and were in some respects like the unlicensed cab-drivers who sometimes offer their services at airports and elsewhere. They seem to have also been called 'hobblers' and 'hovellers', which suggests that they were so called from living in hovels, rough cabins which they had built on the shore.

Hulstone Crackley Bank, Salop. In 1959, when this pub was opened, Jack Hulstone was foreman builder for the Ind Coope Brewery. His father had occupied the same position before him.

Humber Coventry. For the Humber motor company, which began in 1868 when Thomas Humber made his first bicycles. The company switched to cars from 1905 and was later absorbed by the Rootes group.

Humber Keel Beverley, Humb. A reference to the coal barges on the River Humber.

Humming Bird Harlow, Esx. For the humming bird hawk moth, so-called because its flight resembles that of a humming bird. The sign continues the moths and butterflies theme which is common to the town's pubs.

Hundred House Great Witley, near Worcester and elsewhere. The 'hundred' is a subdivision of a shire which has its own court. The sign at Great Witley shows the court in session. At Norton, in Salop, the pub of this name now has a grill

bar which used to be the court room. These hundred courts survived until the late nineteenth century.

Hungry Fox *See* Fox.

Hunter's Moon Crawley, W Ssx. Others at Llangattock, Pwys and Castle Bromwich. This is the full moon in October which follows the Harvest Moon.

Hunting This activity is well represented in pub names. Specific hunts, such as the Beaufort, Bedale, at Howe, N Yorks, Berkeley, Gloucester, Bramshill, Arborfield, Berks, Sparkford, Sparkford, Som, etc, are mentioned, as are especially famous hounds – *See* Hark to Bounty. There are general references to Huntsman and Hounds, Stag Hunt, Fox and Hounds, Hunters, and so on. The most famous huntsman of all, John Peel, is remembered at Bowness, Cumb.

Huntsman Holsworthy, Devon. Another at Falfield, Glos. The Holsworthy pub takes its name from Huntsman Ale, the popular name for beer produced by the Eldridge Pope Brewery in Dorset. A huntsman figure is used as the brewery's trade sign. The pub in Falfield, Glos called Huntsman's

House is near the headquarters of the Berkeley Hunt. Broomfield in Kent has a Huntsman and Horn, Spexhall in Suffolk a Huntsmen and Hounds.

Huntsman Hall Worcester Park, Sry. Henry VIII once hunted in this area, and a pack of beagles used to meet in the inn's backyard in the late nineteenth century.

Hurdler Stamford. Also Marquis of Exeter, Lyddington, near Uppingham; Exeter Arms, Uppingham; Exeter's Arms, Burrowden. The hurdler was Donald Finlay, later Marquis of Exeter, who won a gold medal for Britain at the 1928 Olympics in Amsterdam.

Hurdlers Arms Binley, near Andover. Also Hurdlemakers Arms, Woodham Mortimer, Esx; Hurdle, Morningcroft, Nflk; Hurdles, Droxford, near Southhampton. All refer to the hurdles used by farmers to erect temporary fences for sheep pens and the like. They were originally frames filled with wickerwork but are now usually open, like field gates.

Hurlers Near Haworth, W Yorks. A reference to participants in the game of hurling. In Cornwall this was a kind of handball; in Ireland it is a form of hockey. Here it is said to have been something similar to curling, with the stone being hurled along a road. The winner was the competitor who could complete the distance of five miles or so with the least number of hurls.

Huskisson Liverpool. Also Huskisson Vaults in the same city. William Huskisson (1770–1830) was an English statesman and financier who was killed in an accident at the opening of the Liverpool and Manchester Railway.

Hussar Hounslow. Another at Smethwick. Also Hussar Arms, Ayr; Royal Hussar, Brighton; Gallant Hussar, Derby. Hussars were originally a body of light horsemen organised in Hungary in the fifteenth century. The term was later applied to light cavalry regiments formed in other countries. Pub names mentioning hussars probably all refer to the 11th Hussars (Prince Albert's Own) who were involved in the Charge of the Light Brigade at Balaclava. *See* Earl of Cardigan.

Hustage Hyde, near Stockport. The name of a small lake nearby. It was used by local swimmers who formed themselves into a club known as the Hyde Seals. They later became world water-polo champions.

Hustler London E8. The word 'hustler' has become associated with an expert player of pool thanks to the 1961 film *The Hustler*. Paul Newman played the part of a professional player who met his match in Minnesota Fats, played by Jackie Gleason. In former times a hustler was one of a gang of pickpockets, who hustled their victims.

Hyde Park Dronfield, near Sheffield. The original owner of this pub is said to have been staying in London, near Hyde Park, when he first heard that a licence had been granted. The London park is thought to have consisted originally of one 'hide' of land. Plymouth and Salford both have a Hyde Park Corner.

I am the Only Running Footman
London W1, The longest pub
name in London, it is said, though
usually known more simply as the
Running Footman. A 'running
footman' was a servant who ran
ahead of his master's coach in
order to clear people out of the
way, pay tolls and so on. At night
he went ahead with torches. By the
beginning of the nineteenth
century only one such servant
remained in London, in the service
of the 4th Duke of Queensberry.
The inn sign shows him in action.

Ibex Chaddleworth, Berks. This is a
rather specialised version of the
Goat, referring to a species of wild
goat that lives in the Alps and
Apennines.

Igo Inn Lurgan, Arm. A pleasant little
Irish joke.

Ilkley Moor Ilkley. A reference which
even Southerners recognise as
alluding to a Yorkshire folk-song,
though the words of the song tend
to baffle them. They sometimes
come close to being English,
and begin: 'Wheer wer' ta bahn
w'en Aw saw thee On Ilkla
Moor baht 'at?'

Images Spinney Hill, Warwick.
A modern renaming (1984)
apparently meant to emphasise
that the customer has complete
freedom of choice in the pub. Its
former name, Hobson's Choice,
was not felt to be customer-
friendly. Yeadon, Leeds has an
Image.

Imp Southville, Bristol. This pub was
the **Southville** until 1980. The new
name was suggested by the
proximity of the Wills factory, part
of the Imperial Tobacco empire.
Imperial Tobacco shares are
referred to as 'Imps' in Stock
Exchange reports. The sign shows
the imp of Lincoln Cathedral – *see*
Lincoln Imp.

Imperial Arms Chislehurst, Kent.
Napoleon III (1808–73) came to
live in this area with his family
after his defeat in the Franco–
Prussian War (1870).

Independent London N1, also
Kossuth, Leeds. Louis Kossuth
(1802–94) was a Hungarian
revolutionary hero, a leading
figure in the Hungarian Revolution of 1848. In 1849 he was
briefly president of the Hungarian
republic, but when the Russians
came to the aid of the Austrians he
resigned. He spent most of his life
in exile. In 1850 he escaped to
England and addressed popular
demonstrations in Copenhagen
Fields, which then adjoined the
site where the London pub now
stands.

India Arms Winchester. The arms of
Earl Mountbatten are depicted.
He was the last British viceroy of
India in 1947.

Indian Stoke, near Devonport. The
inn sign is one that was previously
popular amongst tobacconists,
showing an Indian holding a pipe
or tobacco leaf.

Indian Queen Boston. An American Indian princess Pocohontas (1595–1617) married a Norfolk man variously described as John Rothe, Rolfe or Wrolfe. He had gone to Virginia when that territory was being colonised. The couple came to England in 1615 with their son Thomas and were received at court by Queen Anne, wife of James I. Pocohontas, who had become a Christian, died on board the ship at Gravesend which was due to take the family back to Virginia.

Inkerman Also Inkerman Arms. *See* Hero of Inkerman.

In–Laws Paisley. A variation on the 'inn' puns.

Inn at Whitewell Whitewell, Lancs. An interesting example of a natural phrase being promoted to name status, something that happens surprisingly rarely.

Innings Worksop, Notts. Commemorating the innings of Ted Alletson, locally born, at the Sussex ground in 1911. Alletson scored 189 runs in ninety minutes, the last eighty-nine taking only fifteen minutes. The pub was opened in 1975 by Geoffrey Boycott.

Inn of the Sixth Happiness Gant's Hill, Ilford. The film of this name was released in 1958, starring Ingrid Bergman as Gladys Aylward, a British missionary to China in the 1930s. The film also featured Robert Donat's last appearance, as a mandarin converted to Christianity. The film was based on *The Small Woman*, a novel by Alan Burgess.

Intrepid Fox London W1. Charles James Fox (1749–1806) was an English statesman who attacked British policy during the American War, urged the abolition of the slave trade and political freedom for dissenters. The landlord of this pub was one of his fervent supporters and is said to have given free beer during the election of 1784 to those who voted for Fox. 'Intrepid' means 'fearless'.

Invincible Portsea, Portsmouth. For the aircraft-carrier which acted as the flagship for the British fleet during the Falklands Campaign of 1982. Many other ships of the Royal Navy have borne this name since the eighteenth century. The pub of this name at Eyres Monsell, near Leicester, shows the aircraft carrier on its sign, but is said to have been named for the former battle cruiser which was Admiral Sturdee's flagship in 1914.

Irish Harp *See* Harp.

Iron Bridge *See* Bridge.

Iron Duke *See* Duke of Wellington.

Iron Grey Sandbach, Ches. One of the distinctive terms used for horses, greys being either dappled, iron (a dead lead colour), flea-bitten (or nutmeg). The sign shows a shire horse.

Iron Horse Wroughton, near Swindon, and elsewhere. It is said that Chief Sitting Bull of the Sioux tribe used this phrase when he first saw a locomotive. The sign at Wroughton shows a confrontation between a locomotive and a horse of coaching days, symbolising the end of one era of travel and the beginning of another.

Iron Maiden Bellshill, Glasgow. The Iron Maiden of Nuremberg was a box into which a victim was placed. As the doors of the box were closed the iron spikes which were fixed on their insides pierced the victim's body.

Iron Man *See* Man of Iron.

Ironmaster *See* Thomas Telford.

Ironmongers Arms Norwich. The Ironmongers Company were granted arms in 1455.

Iron Pear Tree Appleshaw, near Andover. A pear tree formerly stood nearby. Its hollow trunk was secured with iron bands.

Irwell Bacup, Lancs. For the river which rises north of Bacup and becomes the most important tributary of the Mersey.

Isaac Walton *See* Compleat Angler.

Isambard Brunel Bristol. Near the station which constituted the western terminus of the GWR, constructed by this great engineer to connect Bristol with London. *See* Brunel.

Isca Tavern Newport, Gwent. In this instance the name is for the Roman legionary fortress at Caerleon, Gwent. The word represents a Latin form of a British word meaning 'water', in the sense of 'river', and is more familiar as river names such as Esk, Usk, Axe, Exe.

Isis Tavern Iffley Lock, Oxford. The name used in the Oxford area for the upper part of the Thames. It probably came about because of the Latin name for the Thames, *Tamesis*, and the influence of Isis, familiar as an Egyptian goddess.

Island Tresco, Isles of Scilly. There is another pub of this name at Leysdown, Isle of Sheppey.

Island Queen London N1. A reference to Queen Victoria, who was fond of her house on the Isle of Wight, Osborne House, near Cowes. It was there that the queen died.

Isle of Wight Hoy *See* Hoy Tavern.

Isonomy Manchester. The word 'isonomy' refers to equal rights, in a legal and political sense, of the citizens of a state. It is not known why the name was chosen, but it may serve its purpose in luring customers in to ask what it means.

It's a man's world As far as pub names go, at least. Consider the following, most of which are dealt with as separate entries: Blue Man (in Grantham, where they once had a Blue everything); Brass Man, Newcastle-on-Tyne; Cannie Man, Hanworth, near Reading; Cottage Man, Kings Langley, Herts; Cunning Man; Farmer's Man (*see* Farmer's Arms); Good Man; Green Man; Grey Man, Bolton; Happy Man; Harvest Man (*see* Harvest); Hungry Man, Redditch; Iron Man (*see* Man of Iron); Labouring Man; Little Man, Wettenhall, Ches; Mortal Man; Machine Man; Morris Man, (*see* Morris Dancer); Muddled Man, West Chinnock, near Yeovil; Piltdown Man; Red Man, Kidderminster; Running Man, Halifax; Smiling Man, Dudley; Struggling Man (*see* Help Me Through this World); Travelling Man; Twelfth Man; Tything Man; Wakeman; Wild Man; Wise Man; Woad Man; Man at Arms; Man i' the Rock, Dysart, Fife; Man in Space; Man in the Moon; Man O' Clay; Man of Iron; Man of Steel; Man of Court Ashford, Kent; Man of Gwent; Man Of Kent; Man of Ross; Man of Trent; Man on the Moon; Man on Wheels; Man within the Compass, Whitwick, Leics; Old Man and Scythe. By contrast, 'woman' is rarely mentioned in pub names, though the word does occur in Good Woman or Silent Woman or Quiet Woman, (*see* Silent Woman), where she is usually the victim of a joke, and shown in a beheaded state.

Ivanhoe London SE5. The novel by Sir Walter Scott was published in 1819. It tells the story of Wilfred of Ivanhoe's love for Rowena and the more interesting love of Rebecca for him.

Ivy Tod London SW18. 'Tod' in this instance refers to a bushy mass. An ivy bush was often considered to be the favourite haunt of an owl, so the name could be the equivalent of 'Owl's Nest'. The plant was also dedicated to Bacchus, in the belief that it could cure drunkenness. Similar names include Ivy Tavern, Lincoln; Ivy Bower, Manchester; Ivy Bush, Lampeter; Ivy Bush Royal, Carmarthen; Ivy Cottage, Cattshill, H and W; Ivy Green, Moldgreen, Huddersfield; Ivy House, Tonbridge; Ivy Inn, Heddington, Wilts; Ivy Leaf, Manchester; Ivy Leigh, Liverpool; Ivy Plant, Leicester.

Izaac Walton *See* Compleat Angler.

Jaceys Bar Nottingham. Formerly the Old Plough; and earlier still the Plow. The new name is for the owners, J and C, or Jim and Charlie.

Jack and Jenny Witham, Esx. The inn sign depicts a jack-ass and jenny-ass.

Jack and Jill Coulsdon, Sry and elsewhere. The familiar nursery-rhyme characters who went up a hill to fetch a pail of water, with fairly disastrous results. The Coulsdon pub stands on a hill known locally as 'the Mount', and a well was discovered in the back garden when the pub was being built in the 1950s. At Clayton Ssx, the name is after a pair of working windmills on a nearby hill. At Allerton, near Bradford, there is a Jack and Gill, where 'gill' has the same pronunciation as the girl's name but refers to a measure of wine.

Jack Cade Old Heathfield, Esx. John Cade, referred to in Shakespeare's *Henry VI* as Jack Cade, was an Irishman who led a large body of Kentish insurgents towards London in 1450. He defeated an army which had been sent to stop him and entered the city. After a few days the mob was dispersed by the promise of a pardon. Cade fled to Lewes, E Ssx, where he was soon afterwards captured and killed.

Jackdaw Denton, near Canterbury. Richard Harris Barham (1788–1845), author of the *Ingoldsby Legends*, was at one time the vicar here. The best-known of the 'legends' was his poem about the 'Jackdaw of Rheims', which stole the ring of the cardinal-archbishop. Another pub of this name is at Tadcaster.

Jack Hobbs London W2. Sir John Berry Hobbs (1882–1963) was known throughout his outstanding cricketing career as Jack Hobbs. The Surrey and England batsman retired from first-class cricket in 1935, having scored over 60,000 runs, including 197 centuries. He was knighted in 1953.

Jack Horner Darlington. Also Jack Horners, Salford; Little Jack Horner, Stockport. The nursery-rhyme character, 'Little Jack Horner', who 'sat in a corner,/ Eating a Christmas pie;/ He put in his thumb,/ and pulled out a plum,/ And said, What a good boy am I.' It has been claimed that this refers to a real incident, when a certain John Horner, who was steward to the Abbot of Glastonbury, gained possession of the deeds of the Manor of Mells, a village near Frome. They were being sent in his care to Henry VIII, concealed for safety's sake in a pasty.

Jack in the Green Rockbeare, near Exeter. The sign shows a boy garlanded with ivy leaves. It was a custom on May Day for a boy, normally a chimney-sweep, to be concealed in a wooden framework which was covered with leaves and branches. He moved about through the crowds.

Jack of Both Sides Reading, and elsewhere. A pub of triangular shape, with views onto two roads. The sign shows a playing-card, a jack, which has heads facing in opposite directions. There are also two hands, one holding playing-cards and the other a glass of ale. At Maidenhead the pub of this name has a sign which shows the jack in a game of bowls surrounded by woods. At Bideford the sign relates the name to the card-game Euchre, in which the highest card is the jack of trumps, while the next highest is the other jack of the same colour. In another version of the game the jack acts as 'joker'.

Jack of Trumps March, Cambs. This pub is said to have been named as part of a chain reaction. A King's Head, using a playing–card sign, was established nearby at West Walton, causing another inn-keeper to name his house Queen of Trumps, at West Waltham Cambs., which in turn inspired *Jack of Trumps. See also* Jack of Both Sides.

Jack o' Lantern Loughborough. Another at South Ockenden, near Romford. A name that was originally applied to a night-watchman in the seventeenth century. It was then applied to an ignis fatuus, or will–o'–the–wisp, the phosphorescent light which hovers or flits over marshy ground. In some areas a jack o' lantern is the name for the lantern made from a turnip or pumpkin and used at Hallowe'en.

Jack o' Lent Midsomer Norton, Avon. A reference to a local tradition, in which the effigy of a knight (who is buried in the local church) was paraded during Lent.

Jack o' Newbury Binfield, near Wokingham. John Winchcombe of Newbury (d 1520) was a wealthy merchant engaged in the woollen trade. He equipped a small army of his own retainers to aid Henry VIII in his battle against the Scots at Flodden Field, 1513.

Jack Russell Swimbridge, near Barnstaple. Another at Old Marston, near Oxford. The name of a breed of dog, bred in the nineteenth century by the parson of Swimbridge, whose name they bear.

Jack's Booth Theale, near Reading. A popular prize fighter of the eighteenth century who had a boxing-booth behind the inn.

Jackson Stops Stretton, near Oakham, Leics. The name of local estate agents, who displayed their name prominently when this pub was put up for sale. The sale did not take place, and when the premises were licensed again local people had got used to seeing this name on the site.

Jack Straw's Castle London NW3. Jack Straw was one of the leaders, with John Ball and Wat Tyler, of the Peasants' Revolt in 1381. This rising began in Kent and Essex and came to London, forcing Richard II to make promises that serfdom and market monopolies would be abolished. At a second meeting with the king, Wat Tyler was killed by the lord mayor of London. The revolt was crushed and the promises forgotten.

Jack the Ripper London E1. The man who killed at least four, and possibly seven, prostitutes in the Whitechapel area of London in 1888. The fact that he was never caught or identified has allowed imaginative theorists full scope for their wild ideas ever since. Sadly now destroyed, we are informed.

Jacob's Ladder Falmouth. According to Genesis 28:12 Jacob saw a ladder which led up to heaven. The name is often attached to any long flight of steps, such as those which lead to this pub from the town centre. There is another pub of this name at Stratton St Margaret near Swindon.

Jacob's Post Wivelsfield, W Ssx. The unofficial name of the Royal Oak, and the former name of a pub at nearby Ditchling Common. It was there that Jacob Harris committed three murders in 1734. He was convicted at Horsham Assizes and hanged in chains, reputedly the last man to suffer this fate in England. A post stands on the site of the original gibbet.

Jacob's Well Honley, Huddersfield. The name alludes to the story told in the New Testament, John 4, concerning a woman of Samaria and Jesus. Jesus asked the woman to give him some water from Jacob's well and soon convinced her that he was the Messiah. As a pub name the allusion is rather irreverent, since it almost certainly refers to the comment by Jesus that 'Every one who drinks of this water will thirst again'. It is that idea of recurring thirst which appealed to publicans, rather than the words which Jesus added: 'whoever drinks of the water that I shall give him will never thirst.'

Jaguar Coventry. A reference to the motor car company, which took the name of Jaguar in 1936. The cars were originally known as SS Jaguars, referring to the Standard Swallow company which made them but the prefix was later dropped when the brutalities of Hitler's SS storm-troopers became apparent. There is another pub of this name at Stapleford, Nottingham.

Jamaica Bolventor, Corn. A reference to Jamaica rum, which was distributed from this inn in the days when smugglers operated a thriving industry. The inn was made famous by Daphne du Maurier's novel *Jamaica Inn* (1936), later filmed. Stonehouse, Plymouth has a Jamaica House and Leeds a Jamaican.

James I Norwich. This seems to be the only pub named for James I (1566–1625) of England, who was also James VI of Scotland. He was the son of Lord Darnley and Mary Queen of Scots, but accepted her execution in 1587 without protest. He relied on incompetent favourites such as Robert Carr, Earl of Somerset and George Villiers, 1st Duke of Buckingham and was unpopular because of his extravagance.

Jane Shore London E1. A London woman who died in 1527 in poverty, though she had lived in great luxury as the mistress of Edward IV and others. She had married, while still a girl, a goldsmith named William Shore but soon attracted the king's attention. After his death she became the mistress of Lord Hastings, who was beheaded by Richard III in 1483. Richard accused her of witchcraft and imprisoned her, but she later became the mistress of the Marquis of Dorset. Her life appealed to the imagination of ballad–writers and playwrights. One of the ballads tells in graphic detail, though without the authority of historical evidence, of her death by starvation in a ditch.

Jarnac Dalkeith, Loth. The name of a town in western France, which has an important trade in brandy and wine.

Jays Hoyland, Barnsley. The initials of the proprietors, Jim and John.

Jean Harlow Harlow, Esx. This pub was formerly the Painted Lady, a reference to the butterfly and conforming to the pub-name theme found throughout the town. The name apparently gave strangers a wrong impression of the clientele. The new name was suggested by the name of the town, which refers to a place where hundred-meetings were held. Jean Harlow was actually Harlean Carpentier (1911–37), who was a sensationally successful film star of the early 1930s. She was known as the 'blonde bombshell' or the 'platinum blonde', and had a personal lifestyle which matched anything she portrayed on screen.

Jeannie Deans Glasgow. Also Jeannie Deans' Tryst, Edinburgh. A reference to the heroine of Sir Walter Scott's novel *The Heart of Midlothian* (1818), though in the book she is always Jeanie Deans. The story has some basis in fact and concerns Jeanie's journey to London to see Queen Caroline and obtain a pardon for her sister, falsely accused of the murder of her child.

Jekyll and Hyde Turgis Green, Basingstoke. A reference to the novel by Robert Louis Stevenson, *The Strange Case of Dr Jekyll and Mr Hyde* (1886), in which the central character is alternately good and evil. The pub of this name in Norwich was renamed from the University Arms because of its split personality. The Jekyll room conforms to the older idea of what a pub should be, the Hyde room has a disco, a built-in video show and similar horrors.

Jenny Jones Llangollen, Clwyd. The heroine of a nineteenth century Welsh ballad, which is sung to the tune of *Cader Idris*. There is no evidence to suggest that she was a real person.

Jenny Lind Wimbledon and elsewhere. Jenny Lind (1820–87) was a singer who was known as 'the Swedish nightingale'. She sang in Europe and America, where she married the conductor Otto Goldschmidt in 1852. From 1883 she was professor of singing at the Royal College of Music. She also endowed many musical scholarships in England and Sweden.

Jeremy Bentham Tavern London WC1, The pub is in University Street, which is appropriate for a man who was one of the founders of University College London. Jeremy Bentham (1748–1832) was a philosopher who believed in utilitarianism, which holds that the goal of social ethics is to achieve the greatest good for the greatest number.

Jericho Tavern Oxford. The name of the biblical city was given in the seventeenth century to an area near Oxford. The sign shows a shield which bears the quotation: 'And the king said, "Tarry at Jericho until your beards be grown".' (2 Samuel 10:5) Out of context this looks like an invitation to have a leisurely drink, though the reason for King David's instruction was that Hanun had humiliated David's men by cutting off half their beards.

Jersey Lily Bristol. This was the nickname of the British actress Lillie Langtry (1852–1929), a noted beauty who was painted by Millais and Burne-Jones. Oscar Wilde wrote *Lady Windermere's Fan* for her. She was born in St Helier's, Jersey, as Emilie Charlotte Le Breton.

Jersey Tavern Weymouth. The largest of the Channel Islands, famous for its cattle. Swansea has a Jersey Marine Tavern.

Jet and Whittle Lower Tuffley, Gloucester. Another at Leamington Spa. The reference is to the Gloster aeroplane with a turbojet engine designed by Sir Frank Whittle (b 1907). This plane first flew from the Gloster Aircraft Works after tests at Cranwell. The sign shows a jet plane sky-writing the name Whittle. At Lutterworth, near Rugby, there is a **Sir Frank Whittle**.

Jimmy Shand Dundee. A well-known Scottish band–leader and television personality.

Jingling Geordie's Edinburgh. Said to be a reference to George Heriot (1563–1623), goldsmith to James I and philanthropist. He founded Heriot's Hospital at Edinburgh. He and his sister Judith are featured in Sir Walter Scott's novel *The Fortunes of Nigel* (1822).

J J's London E1. The licensee is Mrs J J Day.

John Baird London N10. John Logie Baird (1888–1946) was a Scottish inventor who was the first to demonstrate true television in 1926. He followed this in 1928 with the first transatlantic and first colour transmissions. His system was used by the BBC until 1937.

John Barleycorn Nottingham. Also Sir John Barleycorn, Hitchin. A jocular name for beer or ale or any malt liquor. He is referred to by writers such as Robert Burns, Sir Walter Scott and Nathaniel Hawthorne, and there is an old ballad about him in which he is described as of 'noble blood, well beloved in England, a great supporter of the Crown, and a maintainer of both rich and poor'.

John Brunt, VC Paddock Wood, Kent. John Brunt, a local man, was a captain in the Sherwood Foresters. He won the Victoria Cross in Italy in December 1944, but was killed in action the following day.

John Bull Exeter and elsewhere. This collective name for a sturdy Englishman was first used by John Arbuthnot in 1712. The same writer designated the French as Lewis Baboon, the Dutch as Nicholas Frog, and so on, but only *John Bull* was taken up by other writers. He is generally represented as a rather corpulent man, with a three–cornered hat, red waistcoat, leather breeches and carrying an oaken cudgel.

John Bunyan Coleman Green, Herts. John Bunyan (1628–88) was a Baptist minister and author of *The Pilgrim's Progress* as well as several other moral works. He spent nearly twelve years in Bedford jail because of his religious activities. The chimney stack of his former cottage is shown on the sign. He is remembered also in the Black Hat.

John Clare Gunthorpe, near Peterborough. John Clare (1793–1864) published several volumes of poetry, all of a rural nature, before he became insane in 1837. He had pursued a varied career as herd-boy, militiaman, vagrant and unsuccessful farmer. In a letter to a friend he once remarked: 'If life had a second edition, how I would correct the proofs.'

John Company London SW2, A name for the English East India Company, imitating the similar Jan Kompanie for the Dutch East India Company.

John Evelyn London SE8. John Evelyn (1620–1706) is best remembered for his *Diary*, which described his extensive travels in Europe and gave brilliant portraits of the people he met. He also wrote and translated books on gardening, architecture and the like. He has been described as a 'cultured dilettante'.

John Gilpin West Denton, near Newcastle-on-Tyne. John Gilpin is the central character of a humorous poem by William Cowper, *The Diverting History of John Gilpin,*

showing how he went further than he intended, and came safe home again.
He is said to be a linen-draper and 'train-band captain' (ie captain of a band of citizen soldiers). He sets off on a horse to follow his wife and children, who are in a carriage, but the horse bolts. Gilpin flies across London, losing his cloak, hat and wig as he goes. The turnpike men throw open their gates for him, assuming he is racing for a wager. After further adventures, he eventually comes home safely. Cowper is said to have based the poem on an incident that befell a Mr Beyer, who was still alive when the poem was published in 1782. Gilpin ends his poetic journey at Ware, in Hertfordshire, where he is commemorated by the Jolly Gilpin.

John Gregory Weymouth. The pub is named for its first owner and shows his coat of arms on the inn sign.

John Hampden Aylesbury. John Hampden (1594–1643) was an English statesman, one of the five members of parliament impeached by Charles I in 1642. He commanded a regiment for the parliamentarians and was killed in battle. He is mainly remembered as the defendant in the case of the *King* v *John Hampden* (1637–38), when he resisted the collection of ship-money as a tax. This had become obsolete, but Charles I tried to revive it without the authority of parliament. Hampden lost his case at the time, then the House of Lords ordered the judgement to be cancelled a few years later.

John Jorrocks Frittenden, Kent. The name of a character invented by the novelist Robert Surtees (1803–64) and featured especially in *Jorrocks's Jaunts and Jollities* (1838).

Mr Jorrocks is a sporting Cockney grocer, engagingly absurd and vulgar. A similarly named pub, Mister Jorrocks, is in Derby. *See also* Surtees and Cat and Custard Pot.

John Lyon Harrow. The man who founded the famous public school here in 1571. Its pupils have included Byron, Palmerston, Peel, Sheridan, Galsworthy, Cardinal Manning, Sir Winston Churchill.

Johnny Todd Kirkby, Liverpool. Name of a folk–song which was used as the signature tune of the long–running British television series *Z Cars* in the 1960s.

John of Gaunt Leicester and elsewhere. Also John o' Gaunt, Sutton, near Sandy, Beds; John o'Gaunt's Castle, Newcastle-under-Lyme, Staffs. John of Gaunt (1340–99) was Duke of Lancaster and fourth son of Edward III. 'Gaunt' is a corruption of Ghent, where he was born. He married first his cousin Blanche, daughter of Henry, Duke of Lancaster, whom he succeeded by right of his wife. When Blanche died he married Constance, daughter of the deposed King of Castile, Pedro the Cruel. He was viceroy for the senile Edward III and was, during that time, the ruler of England. His eldest son by Blanche became Henry IV. John of Gaunt seems to have had most success in choosing the right wife (by his third wife he was ancestor of the House of Tudor). He was not a competent general, and he became increasingly unpopular amongst the ordinary people. When Wat Tyler led an insurrection in 1381 it was John of Gaunt's palace which was destroyed. Nevertheless, he was for many years the most influential person in England. He is mainly referred to in pub names by a reference to his badge, the Red Lion.

John o' Groats near Thurso, Caithness. Another in London SE1. This name is well-known as that of the northernmost point of mainland Britain. It is thought to commemorate a bailee of the earls of Caithness who lived in the area at the end of the fifteenth century, the name originally referring to his house. John o' Groat is commonly said to have been a Dutchman, Jan de Groot, but he is also said to have had brothers called Malcolm and Gavin, also Dutch. For the moment the true explanation of his name remains in doubt.

John Peel Bowness, near Windermere. John Peel (1776–1854) was a famous huntsman of great style and pace. He is now remembered because of the song written by John Woodcock Graves (1795–1886): 'D'ye ken John Peel with his coat so gray?'

John Selden Durrington, near Worthing. John Selden (1584–1654), who was born locally, was a lawyer and antiquary, but is chiefly remembered as a writer and scholar. He was active in parliament's struggle with the crown and in the trial of George Villiers. In 1646 he became master of Trinity Hall, Cambridge. His writings dealt with the history of the English legal system, which led to the formation in 1887 of the Selden Society, which publishes ancient legal records. His wide range of intellectual interests also included oriental manuscripts, of which he amassed an important collection. His secretary Richard Milward noted down his sayings during the last twenty years of his life. These were published as *Table Talk* in 1689. Also Selden Arms in Worthing.

John Smeaton Austhorpe, Leeds. John Smeaton (1724–92) was born in Austhorpe. He was a civil engineer who constructed Ramsgate Harbour, the canal which extends from the Clyde to the Forth and other projects. He is remembered most of all for his work on the Eddystone Lighthouse. Winstanley's lighthouse on the Eddystone Rocks had been swept away by a storm, while a second was destroyed by fire. Smeaton's construction in 1759 lasted until 1882. The pub sign was copied from a portrait of the engineer by Gainsborough.

John Snow London W1. John Snow (1813–58) was a doctor in this area when a severe outbreak of cholera occurred in 1854. Snow came to the conclusion that the disease was water-borne, and was able to show that the local well had been polluted by leakage from a nearby drain. Dr Snow introduced ether into English surgical practice and administered chloroform to Queen Victoria at the birth of Prince Leopold in 1853. The pub stands on the site of the former Soho well and pump.

John Thompson Ingleby, near Melbourne, Derbs. Named after himself by the owner of the village pub. He is perhaps the only publican in England whose portrait adorns his own inn sign.

John Willie Lees Manchester. The pub was opened in 1978, taking its name from a local cotton manufacturer who was mayor of Middleton in 1828. Lees was also the owner of several taverns which he willed to his descendants. The present pub is jointly owned by two of them.

Joiners Arms London SE13. The Company of Joiners were granted a coat of arms in 1571. Joiners differ from carpenters in doing lighter and more ornamental work, but they take their name from the pieces of wood they join together.

Jollies Manchester. In nautical slang the 'jollies' are the Royal Marines. *See also* Royal Marine.

Jolliffe Arms Merstham, near Redhill, Sry. The name of a local family, one of whom was member of parliament for Petersfield, 1766–1802. His son was killed at the Battle of the Nile in 1798 at the age of twenty. Tablets in the local church commemorate both men.

Jolly This has long been a popular word with pub-namers, suggesting as it does someone who is of lively and happy disposition, jovial, laughing loudly as some-one does who is slightly, but pleasantly, intoxicated. In earlier, times the word also meant healthy and well-developed, splendid. It was also used, as now, as an admiring intensifier. Something could be described as good, or more forcefully as jolly good. A wide range of pub names therefore contain this element. It is especially popular linked to a trade or profession, as the following examples will show: Jolly Abbot, Newton Abbot, Devon; Jolly Angler, Leicester; Jolly Anglers, Yiewsley, GL; Jolly Bargeman, Ware; Jolly Beggars, Paisley; Jolly Blacksmith, Twickenham; Jolly Brewer, Kingston-on-Thames; Jolly Brewers, Fulham; Jolly Bricklayers, Cheshunt; Jolly Brickmakers, Redhill, Sry; Jolly Butcher, Farnham Royal; Jolly Butchers, Enfield; Jolly Carter, Hyde; Jolly Cobbler, Kingswood, Bristol; Jolly Collier, Radstock, Som; Jolly Colliers, Cotmanhay near Ilkeston; Jolly Coopers,

Flitton, near Bedford; Jolly Cricketers, Seer Green near Beaconsfield; Jolly Crofter, Stockport; Jolly Crofters, Horwich, Lancs; Jolly Dealers, Rockland All Saints, Nflk; Jolly Drayman, Gravesend; Jolly Drover, Sheet, Hants; Jolly Drovers, Consett, Dur; Jolly Farmer, Bagshot; Jolly Farmers, Buckland, near Reigate; Jolly Fenman, Sidcup; Jolly Fisherman, Barking; Jolly Fishermen, Stanstead Abbots near Ware; Jolly Friar, Blidworth; Jolly Friars, Lewes; Jolly Gardener, Canterbury; Jolly Gardeners, Watford; Jolly Guardsman, Windsor (until 1947); Jolly Hatters, Denton, Manchester; Jolly Londoner, Slough; Jolly Maltsters, Norwich; Jolly Masons, Rhosymedre, Clwyd; Jolly Milkman, London S14; Jolly Miller, North Warnborough, Hants; Jolly Millers, Cambridge; Jolly Ploughman, Bolton; Jolly Porter, Culham, near Abingdon; Jolly Postboys, Cowley; Jolly Potters, Cobridge, Stoke-on-Trent; Jolly Sailors, Buntingford; Jolly Shepherds, Barr; Jolly Sportsman, Chesham; Jolly Steward, South Shields; Jolly Tanner, Orford; Jolly Tanners, London SE1; Jolly Thresher, Lymm; Jolly Topers, Luton; Jolly Trooper, Bradenstoke, near Chippenham; Jolly Waggoner, Hounslow West; Jolly Waggoners, Rotherhithe; Jolly Waterman, Henley-on-Thames; Jolly Weavers, Banbury; Jolly Woodman, Burnham Beeches, Bucks. A few *Jolly* signs are dealt with separately below.

Jolly Bodger High Wycombe. Not an unflattering reference – though bodger is a clumsy worker, one who patches something together roughly. The skilled workers in the local furniture industry who fashion chair legs are 'bodgers'.

Jolly Brewmaster Cheltenham. Inspired by Whitbread's bottled Brewmaster Export Ale, launched in 1983.

Jolly Buffer Sheffield. The 'buffer ladies' used to work in the grinding shops of the cutlery trade, buffing or polishing the products.

Jolly Caulkers Chatham. The caulkers worked in the dockyards, making the ships watertight. They used oakum or a similar material to stop up the seams between the planking of the wooden ships. Afterwards, melted pitch was poured on.

Jolly Cockney London SE11. The sign shows a Pearly King cheerfully downing a pint of beer.

Jolly Cricketers *See* Cricket.

Jolly Fitter Longbridge, Birmingham. The Austin Rover Motor Works is nearby, and no doubt the fitters use this pub.

Jolly Gilpin *See* John Gilpin.

Jolly Falstaff *See* Falstaff.

Jolly Friar *See* Friar Tuck.

Jolly Higglers Radford, Nottingham. Higglers were wandering pedlars who bought up poultry and dairy produce and exchanged them in town for other commodities which they then sold in the country. The word 'higgle' is more familiar in modern times as 'haggle', which is what the pedlars undoubtedly did very well. The inn sign shows three such higglers.

Jolly Judge Edinburgh. They seem to be determined to have a happy legal profession in this city. The Tilted Wig is not far away.

Jolly Minister Northallerton, N Yorks. A reference to Heathcote Amory, who was chancellor of the Exchequer in 1959. He earned the gratitude of regulars throughout the land by reducing the price of beer by twopence a pint.

Jolly Roger Gosport. A term in use since the late eighteenth century for the pirate's flag. The 'jolly' is presumably ironic, given that the flag has a skull and crossbones. The 'Roger' is unexplained. At Airdrie, Strath, is a Jolly Rodger.

Jolly Sailor West Bromwich and elsewhere. The inn sign of the West Bromwich pub shows 'Smiler Joe', a worker at the local brewery named Joseph Weston. He joined the Merchant Navy during World War Two and was sunk with his ship. The pub was opened twenty years after his death, in 1962, and stands on the corner of the street where he was born. Apart from this particularly fitting individual tribute, the *Jolly Sailor* is a popular sign in coastal towns for obvious reasons.

Jolly Tar Hannington, near Swindon. Another at Wardle, near Nantwich. Normally the sign of a retired sailor who has become a publican. The Wardle sign shows a sailor of Lord Nelson's era dancing a hornpipe. Sailors were probably called 'tars' because they worked with tarpaulins, or tarred canvas.

Jolly Taxpayer Copnor, Portsmouth. The pub is near the local Inland Revenue office.

Jolly Toper Barlestone, near Market Bosworth. Also Jolly Topers, Round Green, Luton. 'Topers' are hard drinkers, though the term seems to have been used in gambling first of all. 'To tope' was to accept a wager by drinking to it.

Joseph Arch Barford, near Warwick. Joseph Arch (1826–1919) was a hedge-cutter who founded the National Union for Agricultural Workers in 1872. By 1884 he had succeeded in getting the vote for farm-workers, and in 1885 he himself became a member of parliament, representing the Liberal party. He retired to his native village in 1900.

Joseph Benskin Watford. The founder of the Watford brewery which was taken over by Ind Coope in 1966. In 1981 this pub was taken over by property developers who described it as 'much too valuable to continue as a public house'. Benskins Brewery was closed in 1972, but the name has at least been revived as a draught beer since 1980.

Joseph Pearce Edinburgh. The original owner of the premises, a wine-merchant.

Journey's End Ringmore, S Devon. Another at Yardley, Birmingham. R C Sherriff wrote his play about World War One in the Devon pub. The play *Journey's End* has been described as 'realistic in detail, romantic in spirit'. The Yardley pub, with a sign which shows a patch of grass which is pushing up a couple of daisies, is opposite the local cemetery.

Joyful Whippet Sompting, near Worthing. A name which now suggests a dog, but the earliest meaning of 'whippet' was 'a lively young woman'. The publican

here, when asked, had no idea as to why the pub bore this name. A great many licensees, unfortunately, are in a similar position.

Jubilee Folkestone and elsewhere. The inn sign usually makes it clear which jubilee is meant. The Folkestone sign shows silhouettes of Queen Victoria in 1837 and 1887, as does a similar sign at Pelynt, near Looe. Other pubs were named in 1935 for the Silver Jubilee of George V. In 1977 still more pubs were named for the Silver Jubilee of Queen Elizabeth II. Jubilee City in Derby was one such.

Judge Jeffreys Crockernwell, S Devon. George Jeffreys, 1st Baron Jeffreys of Wem (1648–89) was created lord chancellor. In the Bloody Assizes (1685) after the Duke of Monmouth's rebellion he sentenced about 300 prisoners to be hanged, had another 800 transported, and sentenced many others to imprisonment or whipping. All this was done in order to ingratiate himself with James II rather than administer justice. When James was overthrown Jeffreys was himself imprisoned. He died in the Tower of London.

Judge's Keep Glenluce, D and G. Local traditions say that this pub was run by a couple named Judge. They added to the premises in order to be able to put up travellers. One meaning of 'keep' is to provide board and lodging.

Judge Walmsley Billington, near Blackburn. Sir Thomas Walmsley (1537–1612) was a celebrated Lancashire lawyer. He is remembered also in the Walmsley Arms, Wigan, and the Walmsley Tavern, Great Harwood.

Juggs Arms Kingston, near Lewes. 'Juggs' is explained locally as a term for the men who brought fish from Brighton to Lewes, using carrier baskets. It is tempting to compare juggs with the Scottish jougs, from French *joug*, Latin *jugum*, 'yoke', but the Sussex carriers are said to have had baskets strapped to their backs rather than suspended from a yoke.

Jules Verne Coventry. Jules Verne (1828–1905) was a French novelist who introduced science fiction to a fascinated public. In 1865 he was already describing a journey to the moon, while a few years later he was *Twenty Thousand Leagues Under the Sea*. In modern times he is perhaps best known for the film versions of books such as *Around the World in Eighty Days*, first shown in 1956.

Jumbo Jet London SW5. This was the nickname immediately bestowed on the Boeing 747 when it was first seen in the late 1960s. It carries nearly 500 passengers. Those landing at Heathrow Airport, London, descend on a flight path which takes them over this pub.

Jumples Halifax. Jumples Ho is a Yorkshire place name, found also (several times) as Jumple Hole, Jumble Hole. The latter form indicates the meaning, which describes a topographical feature of a muddled or disorderly nature, or a stream which flows in a disorderly way. The extending of the name to a pub perhaps implies that disorderly conduct takes place there on occasion.

Junction Moldgreen, Huddersfield. Near a former tram junction. One of the vehicles is shown on the sign. Most of the *Junction* signs have railway associations. The one at Gosport shows a loco pulling a freight of oil tanks over a level-crossing.

Junction 23 Loughborough. Junction 23 on the M1 motorway is not far away.

Juryman London EC4. The pub is close to the Old Bailey, the Central Criminal Court.

Just Inn Lochgelly, Fife. Apparently a joke, like the Just Another which used to be in Stockport and the Just In Time which was in Hanley, Staffs.

Just Peters Holme-on-Spalding, near York. This was the Railway Inn until the closure of the local railway station in the 1960s. It was then renamed after the landlord of the time.

Jutland Preston. The pub was in Jutland Street until 1981. Jutland is a peninsula comprising most of Denmark and part of Germany. The Battle of Jutland, fought in 1916, was the biggest naval engagement of World War One. It was fought off the north-west coast of Jutland.

K

Kaffir Whetstone, near Leicester. The pub was opened in the 1880s, not long after the British victory over the Zulus, in South Africa. 'Kaffir' was a European name for Zulus and other Bantu–speaking natives.

Kangaroo Teignmouth. The pub is said to have been named by a former Australian owner. Australian connections of some kind probably account for the similarly named pubs at Aston-on-Clun, Salop and in Manchester.

Karozzin Preston, near Uppingham. The owners of this pub spent a holiday in Malta and were much impressed by the horse-drawn cabs of this name. Subsequent owners seem to have been less impressed, and the pub is now the Kingfisher.

Katherine Wheel *See* Catherine Wheel.

Keats Shanklin, IOW. John Keats (1795–1821) was an English lyric poet of outstanding quality, though little appreciated during his lifetime. Among his many well-known poems are *The Eve of St Agnes, Ode To a Nightingale, To Autumn, Ode To A Grecian Urn*, and so on. His letters are much appreciated. He developed tuberculosis in 1818, and died in Rome at a tragically early age.

Keel Barnsley. Also Keelboat, Washington, T and W. The reference is to a flat-bottomed vessel used on the Tyne and Wear to load colliers.

Keel Row Seaton Delaval, T and W. The Tyneside song of the 1860s, which includes the words: 'Weel may the keel row, that my laddie's in'. 'Keel' here has the same meaning as in Keelboat (*see* Keel).

Keepers Arms Quenington, Glos. The pub was converted from a pair of gamekeepers' cottages. There is another pub of this name at Trotton, W Ssx. At Kentisbeare, Devon, there is a Keepers Cottage.

Kemble's Head London WC2, John Philip Kemble (1757–1823) was a celebrated actor, especially of tragic roles. He became manager of the Drury Lane theatre in 1788, having been rather overshadowed on stage by his sister, Mrs Siddons.

Kendal Bowman *See* Archery.

Kenilworth Tavern Edinburgh. After the novel *Kenilworth* (1821) by Sir Walter Scott. He is said to have written the first draft of his novel whilst staying in Kenilworth. It concerns the tragic fate of Amy Robsart in the time of Queen Elizabeth I. Amy is falsely accused of infidelity, and despite desperate attempts to save her, falls through a trapdoor to her death. There is a Kenilworth Arms at London E17 and a Kenilworth Castle in both London N1 and W11.

Kennet Reading. Also Kennet Arms, Reading. The River Kennet runs into the Thames at Reading.

Kentish Cricketers *See* Cricket.

Kentish Drovers London SE15. A name commemorating the Kentish cattle-drovers who used to gather here when in London. They were 'drovers' rather than 'drivers' because of the 'droves' of cattle in their charge.

Kentish Rifleman Dunks Green, near Tonbridge. The sign shows a member of the local Home Guard.

Kentish Yeoman *See* Yeoman.

Keppel Also Keppel's Head. *See* Admiral Keppel.

Kersal Tavern Kersal, Salford. The place name here refers to an angle of land where cress grew.

Kettledrum Mereclough, near Burnley. The pub took its name from a racehorse, the Derby winner of 1861, rather than the musical instrument itself.

Ketton Ox *See* Durham Ox.

Kett's Tavern Norwich. Formerly Kett's Castle. Also Robert Kett, Wymondham. Robert Kett led an army of 20,000 farmers and labourers in an unsuccessful rebellion against the landowners in 1549. The owners were converting arable land into sheep pasture. The Earl of Warwick crushed the rebels and displayed the heads of their ringleaders on the castle walls.

Kew Gardens Tavern Kew, Sry. The Royal Botanic Gardens occupy an area of 288 acres and contain hothouses, conservatories, museums, etc, as well as the open garden beds. They were first established in 1759 and were presented to the nation in 1840.

Keystone Penn Place, Rickmans-worth. The reference is to the Keystone State, the nickname of Pennsylvania. The town has many connections with the Quaker William Penn, founder of that state, and his ancestors, and it was originally intended to name the pub William Penn. That scheme was abandoned when it was realised that he had been a lifelong teetotaller. As it happens, he was also opposed to the idea of naming places, streets and the like after people, which is why the streets in Philadelphia, and subsequently in many other American cities, became First Avenue, Second Avenue, etc, or were named after trees and flowers. It was as an act of deliberate malice that Charles II changed the suggested *Sylvania* into *Pennsylvania*.

Kicking Cuddy Coxhoe, near Durham. A 'cuddy' is a donkey in Scotland and the northern counties. It may derive from the name Cuthbert. In East Anglia 'dickey' is used for a male donkey, and there is a Kicking Dickey at Great Dunmow, Esx. (Norwich formerly had a Barking Dickey.) Kicking Donkey itself is found in Harwell, Oxon and elsewhere, for reasons which vary slightly in each locality. At Scarisbrick, near Ormskirk, for example, the name commemorates the donkey and cart which used to deliver small casks of ale from the premises to local farmhouses.

King Alfred Chippenham, Wilts and elsewhere. Also King Alfred's Head, Wantage, Oxon; King of Wessex, Basingstoke; Alfred The Great, formerly at Nottingham until 1973. Alfred, or Aelfred, was born at Wantage, Berks, in 849. He died in 901 or thereabouts (some sources say 899), having been king of the West Saxons since 871. He fought many battles with the Danes, eventually gaining victories because of his reforms of the national militia. He also brought about educational and judicial reforms of great importance, being himself a man of learning. His genuinely great services to his people led later to various legendary accounts of his life. There is a well-known story about the king taking refuge in a cowherd's hut, anonymously, and allowing the housewife's cakes, or bread, to burn because he was attending to other things. The housewife is said to have given him a good scolding.

King and Castle Brimscombe, near Stroud. This pub was renamed in 1985 in connection with the 150th anniversary of the Great Western Railway. One side of the sign shows a locomotive of the 'King' class, the other one of the 'Castle' class. Inside the pub is a wall plaque with historical details of the particular locomotives, together with pictures of others. The railway line from Swindon to Gloucester runs alongside the other side of the road.

King and Miller *See* Sir John Cockle.

King and Tinker Enfield. Like the King and Miller, this concerns another story of royalty coming into contact with an ordinary man who was not aware of his identity. The king in this case was James I, who became separated from his courtiers during the chase. At an alehouse he got into conversation with a tinker, who remarked that he would like to see what sort of man the king was. James answered that this would only be possible when everyone else was hatless, the meaning of which cryptic remark became clear when the courtiers arrived and immediately doffed their hats. The tinker then realised to whom he had been speaking. All this was the subject of a ballad which no doubt heavily embroidered whatever kernel of truth was originally present in the story.

King and Queen London SE9 and elsewhere. The inn signs interpret this name in different ways and for different reasons. The name was sometimes given because William and Mary were on the throne when the pub opened, in which case they, or one of them, is shown. In Portsmouth the pub of this name refers to the chess pieces. Highworth, near Swindon,

features the king and queen of hearts on a playing-card sign. At Wendover, near Aylesbury, Henry VIII is shown with the ghost of Anne Boleyn in the background.

King Arthur Belfast and elsewhere. Arthur was probably a British leader during the Anglo-Saxon invasion. A vast body of legendary tales were associated with him before the eleventh century and transmitted throughout Europe. The main facts of the legend are that Arthur showed his royal blood by drawing a sword from a stone. His own sword, Excalibur, was given to him by the Lady of the Lake. Arthur's court centred on the Round Table at Camelot, where gathered such knights as Sir Lancelot, who loved Arthur's queen, Guinevere, (Elaine of Astolat was in love with Lancelot), Sir Galahad, leader of the quest for the Holy Grail, Sir Gawain, the ideal knight, Sir Kay, Arthur's churlish foster brother. Also there was Merlin, the court magician, Morgan le Fay, Arthur's sister, and Sir Parsifal. Some of these individual figures are commemorated in pub names. At Tintagel, Corn, there is both a King Arthur's Arms and a King Arthur's Castle.

King Canute Canvey Island, Esx. Formerly the **Red Cow**. After floods here in 1953 the pub was ironically renamed as a hopeful deterrent against a similar occurrence. Southampton has a **Canute**, also honouring this Danish king who demonstrated to his foolish courtiers that he had no control over the tides. He reigned over England from 1017–35.

King Charles Bristol and elsewhere. The sign at Bristol is for Charles II. At Poole it is for Charles X of

215

France, who landed there in 1830 to begin his exile.

King Charles I Ventnor, IOW. Another at Kings Worthy, Hants. At Goring Heath, near Reading is a King Charles' Head, a rather grisly name when one remembers that Charles was beheaded in 1649. The Three Kings at Sandwich, Kent, shows three portraits of him, based on the Van Dyck painting which is now in Windsor Castle.

King Charles II London W1, also King Charles in the Oak, Short Heath, W Mids; Charles II, Worcester and elsewhere; Royal Oak, Woodchester, Glos and elsewhere. *See* Charles II.

King Charlie Wakefield. Enquiries locally have so far failed to reveal which king is meant, and why the familiar form of his name was used. The pub dates from at least 1851.

King Coel Colchester. The Old King Cole of the nursery rhyme, and remembered as such in the same town, which by popular tradition was named in his honour. The place name in fact has rather more to do with the River Colne than with the pipe-smoking monarch who was fond of his three fiddlers and a glass of something potent. The sign of the King's Head at Prestwood, Bucks shows him as such.

King David Brynmawr, Pwys. There was formerly another of this name at Abergavenny, Gwent. The shepherd boy who became King of the Hebrews, a great warrior who was also a musician and poet. Under his leadership the Hebrew tribes became a strong national state. He is popularly known for his victory over Goliath.

King Dick Bristol. The pub was opened in 1975 and the name is said to refer to Richard III. In Cockney rhyming slang a King Dick is a brick.

King Edgar Nottingham. Edgar was King of England from 959–75, earning the title of the Peaceful because civil order and prosperity marked his reign. At his death there was an immediate end to political unity. He was rightly honoured in Nottingham until 1971, but is now absent from English inn signs.

King Edward Birmingham. It is not clear which King Edward is referred to by this sign, though Edward VI has been suggested.

King Edward II Merriott, Som. Edward II (1284–1327) was king from 1307. There was much internal dissension during his reign, partly caused by his insistence on favouring Piers Gaveston, who was later murdered. Edward himself was finally forced to abdicate, and after brutal treatment he too was murdered.

King Edward VI Birmingham. Edward VI (1537–53) became king when he was in his tenth year. The country was actually ruled by his uncle, Edward Seymour, Duke of Somerset, though he was overthrown by John Dudley, Duke of Northumberland, who gained ascendancy over the boy-king. Edward was probably too ill to take much active interest in what was happening. He was only fifteen when he died.

King Edward VII Norwich and elsewhere. Edward VII (1841–1910) was the eldest son of Queen Victoria and remained Prince of Wales for sixty years while she reigned. He eventually became king in 1901. He is sometimes shown on inn signs in uniform, as at Longlevens, Glos, or in his coronation robes, as at South

Littleton, Worcs. The pub names Albert Edward, as at Barking and Eccles, Prince of Wales (seventy-five signs in London), and Edward VII at Chatham and elsewhere also refer to the same man.

King Edward VII *See* Edward VII.

King Ethelbert Reculver, Kent. Also **Ethelbert**, Cliftonville. Ethelbert, or Aethelbert, was King of Kent from about 560 until 616. He was the strongest ruler of the time in the south of England. St Augustine converted him to Christianity and helped him make Canterbury a great Christian centre. His queen was Bertha, who is shown on the sign of the Queen's Head, Canterbury. There was a later king of this name, brother of King Alfred, who became King of Wessex in the ninth century.

King George Portsea. Another at Barnet. An unsatisfactory name, giving no indication as to which of the six kings is meant.

King George IV *See* Prince Regent.

King Hal Liverpool. A reference to Henry VIII, often known as Bluff Hal because of his hearty manner.

King Harry St Albans. According to borough records, a reference to Henry VII. The pub of this name in Luton is for King Henry VIII.

King Henry II Newcastle-under-Lyme, Staffs. The town's charter was granted by this king, but the pub which commemorated him is no longer there.

King Henry VIII *See* Henry the Eighth.

King John Tollard Royal, near Salisbury. Another in Nottingham. Also Old King John, Ore, near Hastings; Old King John's Head, London E2. John (1167–1216) was King of England from 1199. He was the youngest son of Henry II. His barons united and forced him to sign the Magna Charta. The story of his treachery, tyranny and cruelty is told in Shakespeare's *King John*.

King Lear Aycliffe, near Dover. In Shakespeare's *King Lear* the King is conveyed to Dover by the faithful Earl of Kent to meet his daughter Cordelia. Lear recognises too late that she was the daughter who truly loved him, rather than her treacherous sisters Goneril and Regan. Much of the last act of the play is supposed to take place in the British camp, near Dover.

King Lud London EC4. The pub is at Ludgate Hill, which was explained in former times as a gate built by King Lud. The story is as mythical as the king himself, though a statue of 'King Lud' adorned Ludgate until it was demolished in 1760. He was supposed to have been a king of the Ancient Britons. There is another King Lud at Wishaw, Strath. London has also a New King Lud, which came into being when a redevelopment plan for Ludgate Circus proposed demolishing the *King Lud*. The new pub was built to replace the old, but the plan not put into effect.

King Mark of Cornwall Newquay. Sir Mark, King of Cornwall, held his court at Tintagel according to the Arthurian legends. He was a treacherous coward, despised by all true knights. They sent Dagonet, King Arthur's jester, to offer battle to King Mark, having convinced Mark that the fool was Sir Lancelot. Mark fled in terror, pursued both by the fool and by the laughter of the knights.

King of Belgium London SE1. Also King of the Belgians, Gravesend and Hartford, near Huntingdon. Leopold I of Belgium (1790–1865) married Princess Charlotte, daughter of George IV of England, but she died in 1817, the year after their marriage. At that time he was not king, only coming to the throne in 1831, so these signs are more likely to refer to Albert I (1875–1934) who led the Belgian resistance to the German invasion in World War One and was popular for his democratic ways.

King of Denmark London N1, Another at Ramsgate. Christian IV of Denmark came to England in 1606 to visit his brother-in-law, James I. It is said that the two of them 'caroused royally'.

King of Diamonds London EC1. Another at Langwith Junction, near Mansfield. The London pub is behind Hatton Garden, the centre of London's diamond trade. Elsewhere the name is similar to King of Hearts, as at West Walton, near Wisbech, making use of a convenient playing-card image.

King of Prussia Fowey, Corn and elsewhere. In London and elsewhere this sign refers to Frederick the Great. In 1756 he allied himself with England against the French and others and became a popular hero in England. The sign became an embarrassment in World War One, and at London N3 the sign was changed to King George V in 1915. Later the original name was restored as Old King of Prussia. In Cornwall the 'king' referred to is John Carter, a smuggler who operated out of Prussia Cove during his short but merry life (1770–1807).

King of Russia Penpercwm, near Abergavenny. The pub was the King of Prussia originally. The outbreak of World War One, with its attendant ill-feeling towards the Prussians, caused the first letter to be removed from the name. It has never been replaced.

King of the Belgians See King of Belgium.

King of Wessex See King Alfred.

King Oswy Hartlepool. King Oswy was King of Northumbria from 642–70. He is mainly remembered for his work in converting his subjects to Christianity.

Kings and Keys London EC4. The name represents an amalgamation of two licences which belonged to pubs called Three Kings and Cross Keys.

King's Arms Ockley, Sry and elsewhere. There are more than fifty pubs of this name in London alone. The arms shown on the signs obviously vary according to the king the artist had in mind. The sign would not have been used during the Commonwealth, but it has been a proud declaration of loyalty since the Restoration. It can also be a sly dig, as shown by the sign at Ockley, where Charles II is seen with his arms around Nell Gwynne. The allusion is to a story told by Charles Hindley in his *Tavern Anecdotes:* 'one of the courtiers (of Charles II), wishing to retire to some tavern for refreshment, inquired of another what house he would recommend, who wittily replied that he had better not go to the King's Arms, as they were full, but that the King's Head was empty'. Manchester has a King's Arms and Coronation.

King's Head London and elsewhere. A sign as popular as the King's Arms, and again with some fifty examples in London alone. The usual head shown on the signs is that of Henry VIII, but at least eight other monarchs are shown. Sometimes two kings share the signboard; at Chichester Henry VIII is on one side, Edward VI on the other. At Shotley Bridge, Dur, Henry shares the honours with Charles I. In *Tavern Anecdotes* Hindley describes an inn of this name near Ipswich which was distinguished by the publican's poem being added to it: 'Good people stop, and pray walk in,/ Here's foreign brandy, rum, and gin;/And, what is more, good purl and ale/Are both sold here by old Nat Dale.' The 'purl' referred to was an interesting drink, at first made by infusing wormwood or other bitter herbs into ale or beer. Later the name was applied to a mixture of hot beer and gin, also known as a dog's nose. This, together with a little ginger and sugar, was much favoured in the eighteenth century as a morning pick-me-up.

King's Head and Eight Bells London SW3. The sign here shows Charles II (looking more like Charles I) surrounded by eight handbells. The name arose either as an amalgamation of two separate pubs or because bells were rung when royalty passed by on the nearby river Thames. The former explanation seems to be far more likely.

King's House Glencoe, Hghld. A claimant for the title of Scotland's oldest inn. It was once used as a barracks for the troops of George II. They were stationed there in order to keep the Highlanders in subjection and to hunt for Bonnie Prince Charlie.

King's Manor Weybridge, Sry. Stands on the site of a hunting lodge used by Henry VIII.

King's Porter and Dwarf London EC3. A reference to two servants of Charles I. The porter, William Evans of Monmouth, was over seven feet tall. The dwarf was 'Sir' Jeffrey Hudson of Oakham, who was under four feet tall. Hudson originally worked for the Duchess of Buckingham and was first presented at court inside a monster pie dish.

King William IV Shenley, Herts and elsewhere. Also Sailor Prince, London SW7; Royal Sailor, Bath; Royal Tar, Brentford; Royal William, Birdlip, Glos; Nautical William, Leicester and elsewhere; King William, Shepton Mallet, Som. William IV (1765–1837) was the third son of George III. He joined the Royal Navy as a midshipman in 1779 and was soon a captain. He frequently disobeyed the orders of his superiors and violated the rules of discipline, so he was not allowed to command a ship. He was on the other hand promoted by 1801 to the rank of admiral of the fleet. As king he was given to ill-considered public utterances and was only moderately popular. His two children had died in infancy, and he was succeeded by his niece, Victoria.

Kirk Romaldkirk, N Yorks. A variant of Church. 'Kirk' is from an Old Norse word, 'church' is its Old English equivalent. It occurs also in Kirkcowan Arms, Newton Stewart, Wigtown; Kirkford Tavern, Cowdenbeath, Fife; Kirkgate, Kirkgate, Huddersfield; Kirk House, Strathblane, Stirling; Kirkless Hall, New Springs, Wigan; Kirkley Tavern, Lowestoft; Kirk Sandall, Kirk Sandall, near Doncaster; Kirkstall Arms, Liverpool; Kirkstile, Loweswater, Cumb; Kirkstone Pass, Kirkstone Pass, near Ambleside; Kirkstone Tavern, Liverpool; Kirkton, Dalrymple, near Ayr; Kirkton Arms, Kirkoswald, Ayr.

Kiss o' Life Wath-on-Dearne, near Rotherham. A reminder that on occasion a stiff drink revives one as the kiss of life might revive one in other circumstances. The original kiss of life was given by the prince to the Sleeping Beauty. The phrase is now used for the method of artificial respiration which involves breathing into another person's mouth.

Kitchener Arms Also Kitchener's Arms *See* Lord Kitchener.

Kite Osney, near Oxford. The bird of prey allied to the hawk and eagle. It is noted for its graceful flight, which is presumably why it gave its name to the kind of kites that are flown by children. The bird was formerly common in England and was known for its tendency to steal rags and other materials for its nest, hence the remark by Autolycus in *The Winter's Tale*, Act 4, scene 3: 'when the kite builds, look to lesser linen'. At Stretton Sugwas, Hereford, there is a Kite's Nest.

Kittiwake Hayling Island, Hants. For the kittiwake gull, so-named for its cry.

Kittiwitches Great Yarmouth. A local name for the narrow passages in the town.

Kiwi Hinckley, Leics. Others at Walton-on-Thames and Toomebridge, Antrim. The Apteryx, the flightless bird peculiar to New Zealand, hunts worms, insects and grubs largely by scent and usually at night. It is the rather unflattering though affectionate nickname of any New Zealander and occurs as a pub name when the owner has New Zealand connections. Auchtertool, near Kirkcaldy has a Kiwi Arms. Associated names are New Zealand, Aylesbury; New Zealand Arms, Derby and New Zealand Chief, Bolton.

Knapp Beaminster, Dors. A 'knapp' is a small hill, or more specifically, its summit. 'Knap' is the usual spelling.

Knavesmire York. The name of the city's racecourse, a place of execution in the fourteenth century, hence the 'knaves'.

Knight of Aveley South Ockenden, near Romford. The inn sign reflects the monumental brass which covers the tomb of Ralph de Knevvynton in the nearby church. He was a crusader.

Knights of St John London NW8. The pub is in the St John's Wood area, which originally belonged to the Templars. It was transferred to the Knights Hospitallers of St John when the Knights Templars were suppressed.

Kossuth *See* Independent.

L

Labourers' Rest Pleshey, near Chelmsford. This was formerly a cottage-cum-pub run by a farm labourer called Jack Staines. There was at one time a Labourers' Union in Burton-on-Trent.

Labouring Man Coldwaltham, W Ssx. On one side of the inn sign is a man using a scythe; on the other a blacksmith is working at his anvil. There was formerly a Labouring Boys in Isleworth.

Labour in Vain Yarnfield, Staffs, and Westergate, W Ssx. The sign was originally meant to imply that any attempts to brew ale as excellent as that available here would be 'labour in vain'. Sign-painters have had fun with the name, however, and the Yarnfield sign (imitated elsewhere) shows a housewife scrubbing a little black boy in a wooden tub. Underneath is the verse: 'Washing here can now be seen,/She scrubs both left and right;/Although she'll get him middling clean,/She'll never get him white.' This joke has led in turn to tales of a woman trying to hide the results of her extramarital adventures. Horsehay, near Telford has an All Labour in Vain for a similar reason.

Ladas Epsom. The winner of the 1894 Derby. This is one of the pubs where the names of the loos conform to the pub's theme, so Ladies and Gents have become Fillies and Colts.

Ladies' Mile Patcham, near Brighton. The inn sign shows a lady of high fashion riding her horse side-saddle along a stretch of road nearby. This was formerly used as a kind of parade ground for Regency belles to display themselves.

Lad in the Lane Erdington, near Birmingham. This was formerly the Old Green Man. It was used for a quiet drink by foresters working for the Earl of Warwick. Stone, near Greenhithe, Kent has a Lads of the Village.

Ladybower Ashopton, Derbs. Near the Ladybower Reservoir. The sign shows a Lancaster bomber in flight, and has the inscription: 'A tribute to 617 Squadron'. These were the famous 'Dam Busters', who used the stretch of water for practice runs before raiding the dams of the Ruhr valley in May 1943.

Lady Charlotte Dowlais, M Glam. Lady Charlotte Guest was the wife of a prominent local businessman in the mid-nineteenth century. She was a well-known benefactress, endowing several local schools.

Lady Diana London E8. Formerly the Prince Arthur, this pub was renamed in favour of Lady Diana Spencer two months before she became Princess Diana.

Lady Franklin London E3. Lady Jane Franklin (1792–1875) was the second wife of the celebrated Arctic explorer Sir John Franklin. He sailed on an expedition to find the Northwest Passage in 1845 and disappeared. Lady Jane fitted out five ships in the next ten years to search for her husband and his party. Finally, in 1859, one of the ships brought back evidence which proved that he had died twelve years earlier. Lady Jane was awarded the Gold Medal of the

Royal Geographical Society in 1860, in recognition of her efforts to find the missing explorers.

Lady Godiva Coventry. Lady Godiva was the wife of Leofric, Lord of Coventry, in the eleventh century. Leofric was being very severe on his tenants, which distressed his wife. She asked him to remove his impositions, and he agreed to do so – on condition that she ride naked through the streets of the city. She duly did so, and Leofric kept his word. Later embellishments to the story included the chivalrous behaviour of all but one of Coventry's inhabitants – the tailor who peeped at Godiva as she rode past. He was reputedly struck blind, and certainly gave rise to the expression 'Peeping Tom'. There is a Lady Godiva procession each year in Coventry, commemorating the good lady, while the villain of the piece is himself commemorated in the Peeping Tom at Burton Green, near the University of Warwick, and in Coventry. Coventry also has a **Leofric Hotel**.

Lady Hamilton *See* Emma Hamilton.

Lady Jane Whitwick. Leics. The unfortunate Lady Jane Grey (1537–54), whose home in early childhood was in the nearby Bradgate Park. Lady Jane was proclaimed queen in 1553, much against her will, Edward VI having named her as his successor (she was a great niece of Henry VIII). Nine days later Mary I took her place and imprisoned her. A few months later she was beheaded. The pub of this name at Shoreham-by-Sea, near Brighton, was renamed to honour the wife of a brewery executive in the early 1960s. It had formerly been the Tudor House.

Lady of Shalott Louth, Lincs. The title of a poem by Lord Tennyson. It concerns a lady who lives on the island called Shalott in great seclusion. One day she sees Sir Lancelot riding to Camelot. She falls in love with him but dies of a broken heart when her love is not returned. Tennyson was born at Somersby, a few miles from Louth.

Lady of the Lake Bridge of Allan, near Stirling. Another at Oulton Broad, near Lowestoft. In Arthurian legend the lady of the lake was Nimue. When Merlin was an old man he fell in love with her. She took advantage of that fact to wheedle his secrets from him, then enclosed him in a rock where he died. Sir Walter Scott's poem of this name concerns Ellen Douglas, who lives with her outlawed father on Loch Katrine. The king, under another name, asks for her hand, but she tells him she loves another. He generously offers her his protection in any case, and all ends well.

Lady Owen's Arms London EC1. Lady Alice Owen left several properties in trust to the Brewers Company in the seventeenth century. They were to be used for a free grammar school and as almshouses.

Lady's Finger Cleobury Mortimer, near Kidderminster. This is a popular name for the kidney vetch herb, which has pods resembling lady's fingers. There is also a variety of apple called Lady's Finger.

Ladysmith Arms Ballymena, Ant. The town of Ladysmith, in South Africa, was named in honour of the Spanish wife of Sir Harry Smith, who was British Governor of the Cape Colony from 1847–52. In the 1890s during the Boer War,

General White was besieged there for several months with 10,000 of his troops. He was finally rescued by General Buller.

La Marelle Glasgow. *La marelle* is the French name of the children's game we call hopscotch, where the 'scotch' refers to a line scotched, or scratched, on the ground.

Lamb London WC1. Another at Upton Noble, Som and elsewhere. The London pub is in Lamb's Conduit Street, commemorating a conduit (pipe or channel) built by William Lamb in the sixteenth century. It brought fresh water from the fields north of the city. The conduit was demolished in 1746. Lamb was a choral musician who served as a Gentleman of the Chapel to Henry VIII, but was known for his many works of charity and public benefaction. He died in 1577. The Somerset pub takes its name from the Lamb Brewery, which was formerly established in Frome.

Lamb and Flag Oxford and elsewhere. A heraldic sign, referring variously to the Knights Templar, the Merchant Tailors Company, St John's College, Oxford, etc. The lamb is of great Christian significance thanks to the passage in John 1:29 which reads: 'Behold the Lamb of God, which taketh away the sins of the world', thus equating the lamb with Jesus Christ. As a saintly emblem a lamb accompanies John the Baptist, St Agnes, St Catherine, St Genevieve and St Regina. The lamb and flag sign shows the Holy Lamb with a banner.

Lamb and Lark Oldham. Another at Keynsham, near Bristol. Apparently a reference to the sixteenth century proverb: 'Go to bed with the lamb and rise with the lark'.

Lamb and Lion Hambridge, Som. This was formerly the New Inn. The local story is that the parson, having remarked that too many of his 'flock' went into the pub like lambs and came out roaring like lions, offered to repaint the sign accordingly. The offer was accepted and carried out with skill.

Lambert's Leap Newcastle-on-Tyne. The former pub of this name recalled an incident which occurred in 1759. Cuthbert Lambert was riding nearby when his horse bolted. It jumped over the parapet of a bridge and made a leap of almost fifty feet. Lambert lived to tell the tale; the horse it was that died.

Lambeth Walk London SE1. The name of a dance which was featured in the musical *Me and My Gal* (1937) by Lupino Lane. This pub is in Lambeth Road, but there is an actual Lambeth Walk in London SE11. The Lambeth Walk is a kind of line dance.

Lambton Arms Houghton-le-Spring. Also Lambton Castle, Stockton-on-Tees; Lambton Hounds, Pity Me, Durham. John George Lambton, 1st Earl of Durham (1792–1840) was an English politician and diplomat. He was ambassador extraordinary to St Petersburg, Vienna and Berlin at various times, and was finally governor-general of the British provinces in North America.

Lambton Worm Chester-le-Street. A North Country dialect song tells the story of a monster worm caught by young Lord Lambton. He threw it down a well and went off to fight in the Crusades. The worm grew still larger and terrorised the district, eating cattle and children. Lord Lambton heard what was happening and came home to kill the worm. It should be noted that the earliest meaning of 'worm' was 'serpent' or 'dragon'.

Lame Dog *See* Dog.

Lammastide Hinton, near Berkeley, Glos. Lammastide refers to the period around Lammas, the first of August, which was originally celebrated as a 'loaf-mass'. Loaves of bread made from the first ripe corn were consecrated. 'Loaf', which in its Old English form was *hlaf*, was later misinterpreted as 'lamb'.

Lamorna Wink Lamorna Cove, near Penzance. In the West Country a 'wink' is a kind of winch used in the bow of a boat by fishermen to raise the anchor.

Lamp and Mantle Southampton. The pub was opened in 1984 but has a Victorian theme. A mantle, fixed around a gas-jet, becomes luminous as it gets hot and gives a brilliant light.

Lamp and Whistle Penzance. The reference is to the equipment of an old-time railway guard.

Lamplighters Shirehampton, Bristol. Joseph Swetman, a local business-man, built these premises in 1768 from the profits on his civil contract to light the town's oil lamps. There is a Lamplighter in Birmingham, another in Edinburgh. Perth has a rather poetic Lamplight.

Lamprey Gloucester. The lamprey resembles an eel and attaches itself to stones by means of its sucker mouth. The inn sign here shows a lamprey encircled by a crown, a reminder that lamprey pie was a royal delicacy in medieval times. Henry I died of a fever which developed from acute indigestion after eating a surfeit of lampreys. He loved eating them, but they invariably disagreed with him.

Lancashire Lass Rochdale. After the immensely popular singing star Gracie Fields (1898–1980), whose Lancashire humour and high spirits cheered the nation during the depressing years of the 1930s. She was born Grace Stansfield, but her mother shortened her name so that it could fit more easily on theatre signs. Gracie was certainly a 'Lancashire lass', but the singing comedienne was even more widely known as 'Our Gracie'.

Lancashire Union Hindley, near Wigan. The name of the local canal.

Lancaster Arms *See* Olde Lancaster.

Lancelot Liverpool. Another at London SW10. Sir Lancelot is one of the best-known knights in the Arthurian legends, the model of chivalry, bravery and fidelity. Shakespeare was therefore using the name ironically when he gave it to Lancelot Gobbo, Shylock's servant in *The Merchant of Venice*.

Land o' Cakes Manchester. A reference to Scotland by means of a quotation from Robert Burns. In his *Late. Captain Grose's Peregrinations through Scotland* he begins: 'Hear, Land o' cakes, and brither Scots . . . ' The cakes would be made of oatmeal.

Land of Liberty Rickmansworth, Herts. Originally named Land of Liberty, Peace and Plenty, referring to the nearby O'Connorville Estate. This was established in 1846 by Fergus O'Connor (1795–1855), the Chartist member of parliament, as part of a plan to form a National Co-operative. The enterprise was declared illegal and the estate was sold in 1857, the National Land Company having been wound up in 1851. In the meantime O'Connor himself had unhappily become insane and had been confined to an asylum.

Langtrys *See* Lillie Langtry.

Lanivet Lanivet, near Bodmin. Of interest for its sign, which shows Chi-Chi, the panda at the London Zoo eating bamboo shoots. They were sent to the zoo by local boy scouts when the animal first arrived in England. There are a wide variety of animals to be seen on British inn signs, but this is probably the only panda.

Lardicake Andover, Hants. The pub was formerly the Adelaide Tavern. It was renamed in honour of the local delicacy, which is made by a bakery behind the pub.

Larkman Norwich. The lark is the local river.

La Rouen Norwich. This pub was formerly the Plough. It was renamed in the early 1970s in honour of Norwich's twin city in France.

Larwood and Voce Tavern West Bridgford, Nottingham. This pub was opened in 1985 and stands within the confines of Notts County Cricket ground. Its name honours Harold Larwood (b 1904) and Bill Voce (1909–84), two of the finest fast bowlers England has produced. They were the spearhead of England's attack in the so-called 'Bodyline Tour' of 1932–33, when England defeated Australia to win the Ashes. The inn sign shows a set of stumps with a cricket ball at the centre.

Lass o' Gowrie Manchester. There were formerly pubs of the same name at Sunderland and Durham. There seems to have been a Scottish ballad of this name, of great appeal to expatriate land-lords.

Lass of Richmond Hill Richmond, Sry. The well-known song of this name, in which the lover proclaims: 'I'd crowns resign to call thee mine, Sweet lass of Richmond Hill', has been attributed to several writers. It is said to have been written for Frances L'Anson, who lived at Hill House, Richmond, N Yorks. There was formerly a pub of the name in its proper Yorkshire home, but it has closed, leaving the field clear for the usurper in Surrey.

Last Church Aston, Salop. Another at Barmouth. A shoemaker's last is a wooden model of a foot, on which he shapes a shoe. The Church Aston sign shows a man's hand holding such a last. Around it is the declaration 'All this day I have sought for a good ale, and now at The Last I have found it.' An old saying was: 'Cobblers and tinkers are the best ale-drinkers', which may have encouraged the early use of this sign. Liscard near Wallasey has a Wooden Last.

Last Drop Grassmarket, Edinburgh. Also at Sutton-in-Ashfield, Notts; Bromley Cross, Bolton; Cheltenham. A name which is capable of various interpretations. In Edinburgh said to be a reference to the last drink taken by Covenanters before they were hanged, but likely to be a rather more grim reference to their own last drop through the scaffold trapdoor. More innocently, a reference to ales and spirits that are of such quality that they will be drunk to the last drop.

Last House in England Saltney, near Chester. Close to the Welsh border.

Last Shift Braehead, Hamilton. A reference to miners at the local colliery.

Lathcleavers Arms Brighton. Lathcleavers were men who split timber into the thin strips of wood called laths, which are used in the building trade to support an outer coating of plaster, tiles, etc. Until 1982 there was an allied Lathrenders Arms at Wisbech, Cambs. These were the men who rendered walls with the first coat of rough plaster.

Lathkill Dale Over Haddon, Derbs. The Lathkill runs from Monyash into the Wye south of Bakewell. The 'kill' in the name has nothing to do with killing either men or beasts. It refers to a 'narrow valley'.

Lauder's Bar Glasgow. Sir Harry MacLennan Lauder (1870–1950) was a famous Scottish singer and entertainer. He received his knighthood in 1919, having raised a great deal of money for the war effort.

Laughing Fish Isfield, Esx. Formerly the **Station Hotel**, but the local railway line closed in the 1960s. The brewers therefore consulted the members of the local angling club, who used this pub as their headquarters, about a new name. Perhaps someone suggested Kingfisher, which in turn would have reminded some that the giant kingfisher of Australia is known as the Laughing Jackass, because of its cry. *Laughing Fish* appears to be a blend of the two. There is a Laughing Halibut in London SW1 and a Laughing Duck in Edinburgh.

Laughing Pirate Falmouth. A romanticised reference to the old-time sea pirates, who committed robbery at sea. As with highwaymen they now tend to be treated as heroes rather than criminals.

Laurel and Hardy London E11. The pub was named in 1979 to honour one of the cinema's best-loved pair of comedians. Laurel was Stan

Laurel (1890–1965), born at Ulverston in Cumbria as Stanley Arthur Jefferson (though rightly honoured there since 1977 by the Stanley Laurel). He was the brains of the partnership, devising the gags and virtually directing many of the films. He received a special Academy Award in 1960. Oliver Hardy (1892–1957) was the American member of the team, the fat man whose tie-twiddling and resigned look at the camera became world-famous. It was he who was continually being 'gotten into another fine mess' by Stan, to the delight of audiences since their first films together in the 1920s.

Lautrec's Walton-le-Dale, Preston. A reference to Henri de Toulouse-Lautrec (1864–1901). the French painter, known especially for his studies of music-halls, circuses and the like. This name is sometimes a pun on Toulouse when the house has 'two loos'.

La Verda Stelo Smallthorne, near Stoke-on-Trent. The pub was originally named Green Star, a name of significance to Esperantists, speakers of the artificial international language devised in the 1880s by Dr L L Zamenhof. The pub name was translated into Esperanto in 1975, and visitors can try speaking the language in the pub, where useful phrases such as 'Mi havos pajnton de Bass' can be employed if a pint of Bass is what is required.

Lawns Port Isaac, Corn. Another at Yate, Bristol. Inspired by nearby stretches of lawns.

Lawrence Sherriffe Arms Rugby. After the founder of the famous public school here, which dates from 1567. The school was most celebrated, however, during the headmastership of Dr Thomas Arnold (1827–42).

Lazy Fox *See* Fox.

Lazy Landlord Honiton, Devon. The owner, who is usually rushed off his feet, felt that he could safely afford to allude to himself jokingly in this way, since the regulars would see the point.

Leather Bottle Edgware and elsewhere. Associated signs include Old Leather Bottle, Belvedere, Kent; Leather Bottel, Northleigh, near Witney; Old Leather Bottel, London SW19; Leathern Bottel, Cranfield, near Bedford; Old Leathern Bottel, Lewknor, near Thame; Leathern Bottle, Godalming; Old Leathern Bottle, Wednesbury; Leatherne Bottel, Goring-on-Thames. All these names are a reminder that bottles were originally made of leather rather than glass. The variant spellings seem to have been influenced by Spanish *botella*, though the immediate source of the English word was French *bouteille*. Three leather bottles are shown on the arms of the Horners' Company, which united with the Bottlemakers Company in 1475.

Leather Craftsman Kettering. There is a local footwear industry. Bermondsey has a Leather Exchange, and at Hauxton, near Cambridge there is a Leather Gaiter. Gaiters were used to cover the ankles and lower legs.

Leathersellers Arms Watford. The Leathersellers Company was granted a coat of arms in 1479. They merged with the Glovers in 1502.

Lebeq's Tavern Bristol. There were several signs of Lebecks Head in London in the eighteenth century, all referring to a renowned chef and pastry cook. Outside his own house he hung a large portrait of himself. He eventually retired to Bristol.

Leckhampton Leckhampton, near Cheltenham. The name bears little relation to the sign, which depicts the Devil's Chimney, a rock pinnacle left by local quarrymen as a memorial to their work.

Leeds and Liverpool Brierfield, near Nelson, Lancs. A reference to the local canal.

Leefe Robinson Harrow Weald. Lieutenant William Leefe Robinson, VC, 'attacked an enemy airship under circumstances of great difficulty and danger, and sent it crashing to the ground as a flaming wreck'. This was the first Zeppelin to be shot down. It fell in flames at Cuffley, Herts, in the early hours of 3 September 1916. Leefe Robinson was serving at the time in the Royal Flying Corps.

Leg and Cramp Coventry. This name was selected by means of a public competition. It makes a humorous reference to the nearby Walsgrave Hospital.

Leg of Mutton Kirkby-in-Ashfield, Notts. This pub, closed in 1958, appears to have been the last surviving house to use a name which was formerly common. The leg of mutton was central to many a celebration in the local, such as that which marked the completion of an apprenticeship.

Legs of Man Douglas. The sign shows the arms of the Isle of Man. They traditionally show a willingness to kneel to England, kick at Scotland and spurn Ireland. A pub of this name at Redmire, near Leyburn, became known locally as the Three Kettle Spouts. There was formerly a Legs o' Man at Blackburn.

Leicester Arms Penshurst, near Tonbridge. The sign shows the arms of Robert Dudley, Earl of Leicester, the favourite courtier of Elizabeth I. She is said to have had secret meetings with him in this village.

Leicestershire Yeoman *See* Yeoman.

Leicester Tiger Leicester. After the local rugby football club.

Lemon Tree London W1. The name was probably inspired by the first appearance of lemons in the nearby fruit and vegetable market, Covent Garden.

Leodis Leeds. The pub name is no doubt meant to be an early form of the place name. Early spellings did in fact include *Loidis* and *Leodes*.

Leopard West Bromwich and elsewhere. Probably a heraldic reference to the Weavers' Company, whose arms show three leopards' heads.

Leopold *See* Prince Leopold.

Leprechaun Liverpool. The former Irish landlord chose this name to evoke his homeland. Leprechauns are supposed to be a kind of fairy in the form of little men. The word actually means 'small body'.

Letter B Whittlesey, near Peterborough. When applications for four new licences were being considered they were referred to as Letters A, B, C and D, since the houses concerned had no names at the time. The licence granted to 'Letter B' became the pub name. The inn sign shows a boy with his arm round a girl, though she clearly does not approve of the action. This is to be interpreted as 'Let her be.'

Letters Tattenhall, near Chester and elsewhere. Hindley thought that pubs of this name, which were once found more commonly than today, alluded to the phrase 'Alpha and Omega', as in the Revelation to John 1:8 – ' "I am the Alpha and the Omega," says the Lord God.' Alpha is the first letter of the Greek alphabet, Omega the last, so the phrase means 'I am the beginning and the end.' ABC was also used as a tavern name in former times.

Leviathan Watford. The leviathan is the name of a sea monster, real or imaginary, frequently mentioned in Hebrew poetry. It is also referred to in the *Book of Job*, and in Isaiah is equated with Satan. When the railways were spreading their tentacles in the 1830s, the railway system itself or the steam locomotives were referred to by many commentators as leviathan, using the word in its sense of 'something of (frighteningly) large size'. This pub was opened a year after the railway came to the town, in 1838, and by 1870 had changed its name to Leviathan Steamer. It subsequently reverted to *Leviathan*.

Leyland Tiger Leyland, near Preston. The heavy-goods vehicle which was manufactured locally.

Liberty Belle Southend-on-Sea. A pleasure steamer, but referring ultimately to the Liberty Bell in Independence Hall, Philadelphia, which was rung when the Declaration of Independence was rung adopted in 1776.

Lido Southport. The original Lido was the name of a bathing-place near Venice. In Venetian Italian the word means 'shore'. Since the 1930s the word has been used in English for any open-air swimming area.

Light Dragoon *See* Dragoon.

Lighter Topsham, Devon. Also **Lighterman**, Barking, Esx. The flat-bottomed barge used to unload ships which cannot be wharved. It takes its name from the fact that it 'lightens' the ship concerned.

Light Horseman Sheffield. Like the nearby Royal Lancers, the pub was named for the men who used the

Hillsborough Barracks. These were built in 1855 and relinquished by the War Office in 1926. By a curious twist, in the London slang of the early nineteenth century 'light horse-man' came to mean a thief who operated on the Thames. The name is also applied to a variety of fancy pigeons. At Dereham, Nflk, and Hounslow there is a Light Horse, referring to a body of light cavalry, though once again, in archaic slang, the term took on a different meaning. In the seventeenth century a 'light horse' was a prostitute.

Lighthouse Hoylake, Ches. A modern pub which has the history of Wallasey and its connection with shipping as a theme. The name refers to the New Brighton Lighthouse (Porch Rock) which was erected in 1827 for ships which were approaching Liverpool. The pub of this name at Burnham–on–Sea, Som refers to a lighthouse which used to guide ships into the River Parrett, thence to Highbridge and Bridgwater.

Light Railway Hulme End, near Buxton. The railway concerned ran from Leek to Hulme End from 1903 until its closure in 1934.

Lilacs *See* Flowers.

Lillie Langtry London NW6. Another in Norwich, Nflk. Lillie Langtry (1853–1929) was a famous actress and noted beauty, known as the Jersey Lily (and commemorated by a pub of that name at Bristol). She was born in St Helier's, Jersey as Emilie Charlotte Le Breton. Edward VII was one of her admirers, as was Oscar Wilde, who wrote *Lady Windermere's Fan* as a vehicle for her. She made one film in 1913, *His Neighbour's Wife*. In Nottingham, next to the Theatre Royal, there is now a Langtrys, formerly the Peach Tree.

Lilliput Hall London SE16. A former tavern on this site had many diminutive bars. The sign shows Gulliver striding into the walled city of Lilliput, to the consternation of its tiny inhabi-tants, though this hardly conforms to what happens in Jonathan Swift's story, *Gulliver's Travels*, published in 1726.

Lily Bridport, Dors. The lily is the flower of purity and is the usual emblem of the Virgin Mary. Formerly a popular sign, but one to which the Puritans had strong objections (as they did to all saintly references). During the Common-wealth period many *Lily* signs were therefore adjusted, becoming Hand and Flower, Flower Pot, etc.

Lima Arms Manchester. The pub is in Peru Street, so this name must have seemed a capital idea.

Limeburners Arms Newbridge, W Ssx. The pub was originally a row of three cottages occupied by men who burned limestone in kilns to produce lime. There is another pub of the same name at Kirkby-in-Ashfield, Notts. At Long Sutton, near Basingstoke, the Limekiln shows on its sign men unloading sacks of limestone from a waggon. (Arley, near Coventry, once had a pub called Waggon–Load of Lime.)

Lincoln Imp Lincoln. Another at Scunthorpe. The original imp is to be seen in the Angel Choir at Lincoln Cathedral. It shows a grotesque demon with long ears, with its right leg crossed over its left. The story is that he was turned to stone by angels for misbehaving in the Angel Choir, though misbehaving has long been the prerogative of choirboys. The Imp is now the emblem of Lincolnshire.

Linden Tree Lindfield, W Ssx. The pub name was suggested by the place name, both of which now refer to a 'lime' tree. The word 'linden' was shortened to 'lind', then changed into 'line'. A mis-hearing of combinations such as 'line-bark' seems to have given rise to 'lime-bark', etc, then 'lime'. This pub was formerly the Old Stand Up (due to its lack of space).

Lindum Lincoln. The modern place name is derived from the Roman form *Lindum Colonia*, 'the Roman colony at Lindum'. Ultimately Lindum refers to a pool or lake, probably Brayford Mere.

Ling Bob Wilsden, near Bradford. A place name which means either a 'cluster of heather' or 'place where a beacon was situated'.

Links St Anne's, Lancs and else-where. Also Links Tavern, Edinburgh; Links Bar, Carnoustie. Usually for nearby golf links, which took their name from the sandy ground near the shore on which golf was originally played.

Linny Coffinswell, Devon. Linny in the West Country is a form of 'linhay', a shed consisting of a roof resting on a wall at the back and supported at the front by pillars. Elsewhere it might be called a 'lean-to', or simply an open shed.

Lion There is a *Lion* at Nottingham, a Lion's Den at Great Holland, near Clacton, Lion's Head at Hertford and elsewhere, a Lion Revived at Bulwell, near Nottingham, a Lion Royal at Rhayader, and so it goes on. The king of beasts is very well represented in English pub names, mainly by the Red Lion of course, but in a variety of other colours, including the

Blue Lion at Rearsby, near Grantham and elsewhere. Most of these references stem from heraldry, families having wished to associate themselves with the lion's courage and strength.

Lion and Castle Norwich. A reference to the civic arms, adopted when Henry IV granted a charter to the city in 1403.

Lion and Column Ham Green, near St Budeaux, Plymouth. A heraldic reference to the arms of the Column family, members of which are associated with the local brewery.

Lion and Dragon Sawley, Long Eaton. Derived from the supporters of the arms of Henry VIII, Elizabeth I and Edward VI.

Lion and Fiddle Hilperton, near Trowbridge. Perhaps inspired by the more common Cat and Fiddle. The sign shows Leo playing his fiddle, with a couplet beneath: 'Here is music without sorrow;/ Pay today and trust tomorrow.'

Lion and Key London E10. A sign which first appeared during the Peninsular Wars, when Wellington captured Ciudad Rodrigo in 1812. This was considered to be the 'key' to Spain, and landlords showed a British lion holding the key in its paws.

Lion and Lamb Hounslow and elsewhere. In Christian heraldry, the lion is a symbol of the Resurrection, the lamb of the Redeemer.

Lion and Unicorn Liverpool. Another at Brighton. The heraldic reference was first to James I, later to Charles I and William and Mary. Unicorns have been written about since 400 BC and are mentioned several times in the Bible, where it is likely they refer to the wild ox. The mythical beast is white, with the body of a horse, tail of a lion, etc, but its most distinguishing feature is its single horn.

Lion Revived Bulwell, Nottingham. A pub called the

White Lion stood on the site previously.

Lion's Head Bishopsbourne, near Canterbury. The reference is to the coat of arms of Sir John Prestige, of Bourne Park.

Listen Inn Cann, near Shaftesbury, Dors. A punning name of the Dew Drop Inn type.

Lister Kirkcaldy, Fife. Joseph Lister, 1st Baron Lister (1827–1912) was an English surgeon who introduced antiseptic surgery. He also pioneered other important operative techniques. This pub is in Simpson Street, a happy reminder of Lister's contemporary, Sir James Young Simpson (1811–70), the Scottish doctor who was the first to use a general anaesthetic in childbirth. There is a Lister Tavern in Liverpool and a Listers Arms in Bradford.

Literary References Literary references in pub names cover a reasonably wide range. Dickens is well represented by the titles of his novels and the characters in them, so that we find Artful Dodger, Chelmsley Wood, Birmingham, Barnaby Rudge, Betsy Trotwood, Bleak House, David Copperfield, Fagin's, Mister Micawber, Pickwick, Nickleby's, Oliver Twist, our Mutual Friend, Sam Weller's, Sir Walter Scott is also popular, commemorated in names like Hawthornden, Ivanhoe, Jeannie Dean, Kenilworth Tavern, Lady of the Lake, Marmion, Peveril of the Peak, Rob Roy, St Ronan's Well, and Abbotsford. Shakespeare's Falstaff is naturally popular on inn signs, but other references to his characters are rare. Nursery rhymes are far more frequently quoted, as are the works of Lewis Carroll about young Alice. Children's stories and tales feature fairly prominently, in fact, and Dick Whittington, Robin Hood and the like are easily found. Individual books that have achieved great popularity are sometimes mentioned, so we find Beau Geste, Black Beauty, Blue Lagoon, Cruel Sea, Goldfinger, Good Companions, Hornblower, Lorna Doone, Moby Dick, Moonstone, Robinson Crusoe, Scarlet Pimpernel, Trumpet Major, Uncle Tom's Cabin, Westward Ho and Wuthering Heights, amongst others. Sherlock Holmes is represented, but he is without his trusty companion Dr Watson. Instead his arch enemy is found in Moriarty's. Of the poets, Burns is by far the most popular. References include Land O' Cakes, Tam o' Shanter, Twa Dogs and others. Film titles based on books can also occur – or almost. The 1958 British film *Inn of the Sixth Happiness* emerges in Essex as Inn of the Six Happinesses.

Little B Sale, Ches. The pub is in an area known as Brooklands. There was formerly a Brooklands Hotel, known locally as the Big B, and the Brooklands Tavern, which has survived and has now officially become *Little B*.

Little Barrow Lichfield. The reference is to a grave mound on the slopes above the city.

Little Brown Jug Birkenhead and elsewhere. Also Brown Jug, Dumpton, near Ramsgate. The Dumpton pub has a clock which plays the traditional (anonymous) song on the hour. Most people are familiar with the words: 'Ha, ha, ha, you and me,/ Little brown jug, don't I love thee.'

Little Bull *See* Bull.

little elephant Knaresborough. The name of the pub is given in lower-case lettering, while the inn sign shows Disney's elephant, Dumbo, flying above the house tops.

Little Gem Aylesford, Kent. This is a fairly modern descriptive name of an ancient pub. 'Little' is a factual description. The 'gem' is used figuratively, but few would argue with its use here.

Little Jack Horner *See* Jack Horner.

Little John Ravenshead, near Mansfield and elsewhere. After John Nailor, or in some versions of the Robin Hood story, John Little, Robin's faithful henchman. His nickname referred to his great height and girth. There is a pub of this name at Hathersage, Derbs, where Little John's body is said to have been buried. A grave in the churchyard, excavated in 1784, revealed the thighbone of a man who would have been about eight feet tall.

Little Mesters Sheffield. A reference to 'mister men' who stamped out blanks for the cutlery trade.

Little Owl Charlton Kings, near Cheltenham. The name of a steeplechaser which won the Cheltenham Gold Cup, run over three and a quarter miles, in 1981.

Little Rose *See* Rose.

Little Western Paddington. Near the terminus of the former Great Western Railway.

Little Wonder Harrogate. Another at Northfleet, near Gravesend. The racehorse which won the Derby in 1840 at odds of fifty to one. Little Wonder was also the nickname of Tom Sayers, an English boxer. In 1860 he fought an American heavyweight known as the Benicia Boy. The police stopped the fight after thirty-seven rounds.

Live and Let Live Downham Market, Nflk and elsewhere. This sign appeared in the mid-nineteenth century and was a comment by the owner-landlord on circumstances which he considered to be unfair. The opening of a rival pub, the loss of trade due to the opening of the railway, or the imposing of restrictions or taxes by a local authority would have been typical reasons for making this public protest. The Downham Market inn sign is one of many which interprets the name with humour. It shows a cat resting peacefully with a brood of newly-hatched chicks on its back.

Lively Lady Bracklesham Bay, W Ssx. The pub was opened in 1968, soon after Sir Alec Rose had completed his solo voyage around the world in a yacht of this name.

Liver Liverpool. Another at Chester. A mythical bird, invented in the seventeenth century by some humorist as an explanation of the place-name Liverpool. It was later adopted as the city's emblem. *Liver Birds* (pronounced *lyver*) was interpreted in the 1970s as the name of a successful television series, in which the birds were two girls who lived in Liverpool.

Liverymans Arms Peterborough. After the man who worked in the livery stables, which hired out horses. 'Livery' refers to the food and drink which a horse is given in order that it may live.

Livingstone Bath and elsewhere. David Livingstone (1813–73) was a Scottish missionary and explorer in Africa. He discovered the

Victoria Falls in 1855. When there had been no news from him for a considerable time, a newspaperman, H M Stanley, went out to search for him. He found him in 1871, greeting him with words that were to become famous in all English-speaking countries: 'Dr Livingstone, I presume?'

Lizard Lizard, Corn. The pub name refers to Lizard Point, which sounds as if it is the favourite haunt of small reptiles. The place name actually derives from two words in Old Cornish, *lis art*, and means 'high court'.

Llandoger Trow Bristol. The 'trow' in this name is a boat of *trough*-like shape. Such a boat had been used by a Captain Hawkins, who had used it to trade between the village of Llandogo, on the River Wye, and other places. The inn dates from 1664, and is said to have seen the meeting between the Scottish seaman Alexander Selkirk, who had been marooned on an island for four years, and Daniel Defoe, who subsequently wrote *Robinson Crusoe*.

Llawnroc Gurran Haven. This name is what is technically known as an ananym, and more commonly known as a back–spelling. It may have been suggested by the more famous Llareggub in Dylan Thomas's *Under Milk Wood*.

Llew Coch Dinas Mawddwy, Gynd and elsewhere. The name is Welsh for Red Lion.

Llewellyn *See* Prince Llewellyn.

Load of Hay *See* Hay Cutter.

Load of Mischief Rhyl and elsewhere. The original sign of this name was painted by William Hogarth (1697–1764), known especially for his satirical engravings. Hogarth was settling his score at a London tavern. His engraving of the same subject was accompanied by a couplet: 'A monkey, a magpie and a wife/Is the true emblem of strife.' Mischief Tavern, Norwich, was until 1850 the Man with a Load of Mischief. At Churchill, near Axbridge, Som, the *Load of Mischief* sign shows an attractive girl pushing a barrow–load of monkeys.

Loaves and Fishes Beccles, Sflk. A reference to the story told at Matthew 14:15 about the feeding of the 5,000 with only five loaves and two fishes, but interpreted locally as a reference to the ploughman's lunch which is made available here, together with fish caught in the River Waveney.

Lobster Sheringham, Nflk. Modern instances of this name are for the crustacean and its flesh, a popular delicacy. In the seventeenth century 'lobster' was a contemptuous name for a Roundhead soldier, referring to the armour plate worn by cuirassiers (horse soldiers who wore armour originally made of *cuir*, leather). The term was used later to refer to the soldiers' red coats. At Sale, Ches, there is a Lively Lobster. Aylesbury has a Lobster Pot, and Canvey Island, Esx a Lobster Smack.

Local Mansfield, Notts, and elsewhere. The Mansfield pub was probably the first to use the name in 1960. 'The local', meaning the local pub, seems only to have been in use since the 1930s.

Local Legends and Customs These are hinted at by only some thirty or so pub names, which is a great pity because the tales associated with them are usually interesting. To list them all here would spoil the browser's enjoyment, but see names like Ashen Faggot, Cuckoo Bush, Hooden Horse, Lambton Worm, Moonrakers, Rattlebone, Wakeman.

Lock and Key Pencarreg, Dyfed and elsewhere. 'Key' is an earlier form of 'quay' (which occurs in Lock and Quay, Bulbourne, near Tring). The reference is therefore usually to a local canal system, though some instances may refer to the locksmith's art.

Locks Near Geldeston, Nflk. The pub is on the banks of the River Waveney. In his *Waterside Pubs* Ronald Russell describes it: 'No approach road, access is by water or along a grassy track from the village over a mile away. There is no electricity, no gas, no running water . . .'

Lode's Head Magdalen, near King's Lynn. A 'lode' is a watercourse or channel.

Logan Rock Treen, near Penzance. The name of a local landmark, a 'rocking stone' which weighs about eighty tons.

Loggerheads Loggerheads, near Market Drayton. This was a common sign in the seventeenth century, alluded to by Shakespeare in *Twelfth Night*, Act 2, scene 3. Originally the sign would have shown two wooden heads with the inscription 'We three loggerheads'. The visitor was supposed to fall into the trap of asking where the third one was, whereupon he immediately became the third one himself. A variation was to say that the third man was inside the inn having a drink. Pictures of two asses were sometimes used instead of the thick log–like heads. There are other *Loggerheads* signs at Shrewsbury and Gwernymynydd, near Mold, Clwyd. At Tonbridge, Kent, there is a Three Logger-heads. Another sense of 'loggerhead' altogether has been used to interpret the *Loggerheads* sign at Narrow Marsh,

Nottingham: the term was also applied to the stout wooden post built into the stern of a whaling boat, to which the line was attached. Whaling relics were brought from Hull to Nottingham by bargees who used the River Trent.

London Weston-super-Mare and elsewhere. A frequent sign in south-western counties. Variants include New London, Poole; Royal London, Sidmouth. In the stagecoach era it was common practice for an inn to indicate where the coach which called there would go. London was obviously a common destination. In some seaside towns it was a steam-packet rather than a coach which would be making the journey. The signs are often illustrated by London landmarks or scenes. The Lyme Regis sign is perhaps typical, with a resplendent Beefeater seen against a background of the Thames and the Tower of London.

London and Paris Folkestone. A reference to the Golden Arrow service between the two cities which passed through Folkestone.

London Apprentice London EC1. Others at Isleworth and Smethwick. The Isleworth pub is certainly the best known of this name. It dates from the fifteenth century and was probably patronised by London apprentices who rowed here on their very infrequent days off. The pub contains prints of Hogarth's 'Apprentices'.

London, Chatham and Dover Railway Tavern London SW11. The name explains itself, and is one of the longest 'real' pub names in England, if one discounts recently-given names designed purely to gain an entry in the *Guinness Book of Records*.

London General London EC2. The pub contains many reminders of the London General Omnibus Company, which preceded London Transport.

London Hospital Tavern London E1. The pub is close to the London Hospital and is well used by its staff.

London Stone London EC4. After a milestone which is still to be seen set into a nearby wall. It is considered to be London's oldest relic, possibly the point used by the Romans to measure all distances from the city.

Lone Yachtsman Portsea, Portsmouth. The reference is to Sir Alec Rose, who completed a solo voyage round the world in his yacht 'Lively Lady' in 1968. The inn sign shows the yacht.

Long and Short Arm Lemsford, Herts. A reference to the two roads to which the pub has access. One of them is a long road, the other short.

Long Boat Birmingham. Another at Northampton. A reference to boats used on the nearby canal system.

Long Bow Tunbridge Wells. Named in 1938 in honour of a local resident, Mrs Nettleton, who was then joint world champion in archery.

Long John Silver Kewstoke, near Weston-super-Mare. The one-legged smooth-talking villain created by Robert Louis Stevenson in *Treasure Island*.

Long Man of Wilmington Patcham, near Brighton. The Long Man is cut into the turf of the downs at Windover Hill above Wilmington. It is 230 feet tall and since 1969 has had its chalk outline protected by concrete blocks. The man is thought to be the Saxon King Harold, and to have been created by those who lived in the now-ruined twelfth century abbey.

Long Reach Thanet Way, Whitstable. This pub, opened in 1965, renews the name of one which was demolished in 1958. The former pub was in an isolated place by the long reach of the river Dart, but was constantly flooded by the Spring tides.

Long Ship Hebburn, T and W. Another at Grimsby. A reminder of the Viking ships which raided the English coast centuries ago.

Long Stop Leicester. Another at Worcester. Both cities have county cricket grounds, and the name refers to one of the field placings in that game. By implication it invites customers to have a long and leisurely drink.

Looking Glass Brierley Hill, W Mids. The area is known for its glass-making industry.

Loosebox London SW7. The pub is in Cheval Place, from French *cheval* 'horse', (for the double reason that there were many stables here in the nineteenth century, and because the area was noted for the number of French people living there). The pub name continues the horse theme, a loosebox, otherwise known as a box stall or more simply as a box, being a large square stall in which a horse may move freely about without being tied up.

Lord Alcester Nottingham. Frederick Beauchamp Paget Seymour, 1st Baron Alcester (1821–95) was an English admiral who commanded the fleet in the bombardment of Alexandria, 1882. This resolved the Mediterranean crisis of that time.

Lord Allenby *See* General Allenby.

Lord Bexley Bexley Heath, Kent. Nicholas Vansittart, Baron Bexley (1766–1851) was chancellor of the Exchequer from 1812–23.

Lord Burleigh London SW1. William Cecil (1520–98) was an English statesman who occupied a position of great power, especially under Elizabeth I, whom he served for forty years. He was created Baron of Burghley (as it is often spelt, though his father came from Burleigh, Northants) in 1571.

Lord Byron Worksop, Notts, and elsewhere. Also Byron, Greenford, GL; Byron Arms, Portsmouth; Byron House, Bristol; Byron's, Nottingham. George Noel Gordon, Lord Byron (1788–1824) was a celebrated English poet whose romantic lifestyle matched the romanticism of his poetry. He was lame from birth, but grew to be a handsome man who was loved by women, though he seems to have been contemptuous of them. He married in 1815 Anne Isabella Milbanke and had by her a daughter, Augusta Ada. His wife left him, and a liaison with Miss Clairmont produced another daughter, Allegra, who died while still a child. Byron had abandoned England in 1816, spending much time in Italy. In 1823 he joined Greek insurgents at Cephalonia and soon became their commander–in–chief. He died of a fever at Missolonghi.

Lord Camden *See* Camden Arms.

Lord Campbell *See* Sir Colin Campbell.

Lord Cardigan *See* Earl of Cardigan.

Lord Cecil London E5. Edgar Algernon Robert Cecil, 1st Viscount Cecil of Chelwood (1864–1958) was a British statesman who helped draft the League of Nations Covenant. He was awarded the Nobel Peace Prize in 1937.

Lord Chancellor London NW8. This title, sometimes as lord high chancellor, is applied to the highest judicial functionary in England (senior judge and head of the legal profession). He is speaker of the House of Lords and the government's chief legal adviser in the Cabinet. He is keeper of the Great Seal, and amongst his various other responsibilities, is the general guardian of infants and lunatics. *See also* Woolsack.

Lord Clive Portsmouth. Another at Whitefield, Manchester. Also Clive Arms, Caerphilly, M Glam and Bromfield, near Ludlow. Robert Clive, Baron Clive of Plassey (1725–74), known as Clive of India, was a British soldier and statesman. In the service of the East India Company he won a series of victories, culminating in Plassey, 1757. He fought corruption and promoted reform, but on his return to England he was charged with having accepted large gifts in India. He was acquitted, but committed suicide.

Lord Clyde *See* Sir Colin Campbell.

Lord Collingwood *See* Collingwood.

Lord Combermere *See* Combermere.

Lord Cornwallis Tunbridge Wells. Lord Cornwallis is lord lieutenant of Kent. A previous holder of the title is honoured in pubs named Cornwallis.

Lord Crewe Arms Blanchland, Northld Another at Bamburgh, Northld. Nathaniel Crewe (1633–1721) was bishop of Durham and an abettor of James II. His wife is said to have been forty years younger than himself.

Lord Darnley Canongate, Edinburgh. Another in Glasgow. Also Darnley Arms, Gravesend. Henry Stuart Darnley (1541–67) was the second husband of Mary Queen of Scots. She became slightly disillusioned by him, discovering that he was stupid, insolent and wasteful with money as well as immoral. She was especially irritated when he participated in the plot against her favourite, the Italian secretary Rizzio, which led to Rizzio's murder in 1566. When Lord Darnley was recovering from an attack of smallpox, the queen had him taken to a solitary house called Kirk of Field, near Edinburgh. The house was blown up by gunpowder by the Earl of Bothwell in 1567, but the Earl was acquitted of Darnley's murder. He himself married Mary a few months later.

Lord Denman *See* Denman's Head.

Lord Duncan *See* Admiral Duncan.

Lord Elgin London W9. Thomas Bruce, 7th Earl of Elgin (1766–1841) is best remembered for the Elgin Marbles, which he removed from Athens to London in 1803. These were purchased by the nation in 1816 and are to be seen in the British Museum. They include parts of the frieze from the Parthenon and are of outstanding artistic merit.

Lord Eliot Liskeard. Sir John Eliot (1592–1632) was born locally. He was an English parliamentarian who vehemently opposed the actions of Charles I. The king committed him to prison in 1626, but parliament refused to function until he was released. The king again sent him to the Tower in 1629, saying that he should remain there until he admitted conspiracy against the throne. Eliot refused to do so and died in prison.

Lord Grey *See* Earl Grey.

Lord Haig *See* Earl Haig.

Lord Herbert *See* Herbert.

Lord High Admiral Plymouth and elsewhere. The title held by the supreme head of the Royal Navy, the present title-holder being HM Queen Elizabeth.

Lord Hood *See* Admiral Hood.

Lord Howard Blackburn. Another at Rochdale. Also Lord Howard of Effingham, Effingham Junction, Sry. Charles Howard, 1st Earl of Nottingham (1561–1626) was lord high admiral of England and commanded, nominally, the English forces against the Spanish Armada in 1588. Sir Francis Drake had more battle experience and made the decisions.

Lord Kelvin King's Lynn, Nflk. William Thompson, 1st Baron Kelvin (1824–1907) was a British mathematician and scientist, inventor of many improvements in the fields of telegraphic messages and thermodynamics. He introduced the Kelvin scale of temperature, in which water freezes at 273 degrees and boils at 373 degrees.

Lord Kitchener New Barnet. Another at Curbridge, Oxon. Also Earl Kitchener, Ipswich; Kitchener Arms, Trowbridge; Kitchener's Arms, Norwich. Horatio Herbert Kitchener, 1st Earl Kitchener (1850–1916) was a British field marshal and statesman. As commander-in-chief of the Egyptian army he reconquered the Sudan in 1896–8 and became its governor-general. Between 1900–1902 he conquered the Boers in South Africa. As secretary for war in World War One he expanded the army from twenty to seventy divisions, using a famous poster which showed him pointing directly ahead and saying: 'Your country needs you'. He was on his way to Russia for talks with the Tsar when the ship that was carrying him was sunk.

Lord Lyndhurst London SE15. John Singleton Copley (1772–1863) was born in Boston, USA. He made his career in England as a lawyer and entered parliament in 1818. By 1819 he was solicitor-general, by 1824 attorney-general, and by 1827 lord chancellor, a post he held on three separate occasions. He was created Baron Lyndhurst in 1827.

Lord Morrison of Lambeth London SW8. Herbert Morrison (1888–1965) was a popular minister of the Labour government. He was made a life peer in 1959. He was easily recognisable by his quiff of hair, which was much appreciated by political cartoonists, and to which justice has been done by the painter of the inn sign.

Lord Nelson Burnham Thorpe, near King's Lynn and elsewhere. This is the most common way of referring to Horatio Nelson, 1st Viscount Nelson (1758–1805) on inn signs, but as probably England's greatest hero he is mentioned in a variety of ways, indicated below. All in all one can safely say that there are more pubs named for him, directly or indirectly, than any other person. He was born at Burnham Thorpe, Nflk, and died on board the *Victory* at Trafalgar. His naval career began in 1770, and by the age of twenty-one he was a postcaptain. He came to real notice in the 1790s, in the war with France. His destruction of the French fleet at Aboukir (1798) ended Napoleon I's plan of conquest in the East. In 1801 he defeated the Danes at Copenhagen, but his greatest victory was at Trafalgar, where he destroyed the combined French and Spanish fleets. Before the battle he had hoisted the famous signal: 'England expects that every man will do his duty'. In private life Nelson had become involved with Emma, Lady Hamilton, wife of the British envoy to Naples. He left his wife for her, and they had a daughter, Horatia. Nelson had lost an arm in battle, and the sight of one eye, which gave rise to the famous instance when he put his spyglass to his blind eye so that he could not see a signal from his admiral to retreat. He went on to win the day against the Danes. The inn signs for him include: Admiral Lord Nelson, Bury and elsewhere; Admiral Nelson, Southwell and elsewhere; Lord Nelson's Arms, a slightly ambiguous sign at Winterslow, near Salisbury; Nelson Arms, Middleton-by-Wirksworth, Derbs; Nelson's Arms, Bristol; Nelson's Head, London E2; Nelson and Railway, Kimberley, Notts; Nelson Butt, Spilsby, Lincs; Old Nelson, Manchester; Brave Nelson, Brentwood; Pitt and Nelson, Ashton-under-Lyne; Norfolk Hero, Swaffham; Hero, Overy Staithe, Nflk. There was formerly an England's Hero at Gorleston. There are also pubs named Emma Hamilton and Lady Hamilton.

Lord of the Manor Crofton, near Wakefield. The pub stands on land once occupied by Manor Farm, belonging to the local lord of the manor. The brewery attempted to call the pub the Goose and Cowslip when it opened, but local people objected. At Upper Slaughter, in the Cotswolds, there is a Lords of the Manor.

Lord Palmerston Kilburn and elsewhere. Henry John Temple, 3rd Viscount Palmerston (1784–1865) was an English statesman, prime minister on two occasions. He was renowned for his reckless, 'gun-boat' diplomacy when foreign secretary, which on the whole increased British prestige abroad.

Lord Protector *See* Oliver Cromwell.

Lord Raglan Windsor and elsewhere. Also Raglan Arms, Southsea; Old Raglan, Chatham. Fitzroy James Henry Somerset, 1st Baron Raglan (1788–1855) was a British general who served in the Peninusla War and was military secretary to the Duke of Wellington. He was commander–in–chief of the British troops in the Crimea in 1854, but was thought by many to be rather ineffective in that role.

Lord Roberts Sandy, Beds and elsewhere. After Field-Marshal Earl Roberts VC (1832–1914), who was a distinguished British general. He served first in the Indian mutiny, but by 1885 he was commander-in-chief of the army in India. After service in. Ireland and South Africa he became commander–in–chief of the British army from 1900 until 1904, when this office was finally abolished. There is a Sir Frederick Roberts at Derby.

Lord Rodney Also Lord Rodney's Head. *See* Admiral Rodney.

Lord Rosebery Norwich. Also Rosebery Arms, Cheddington, Bucks. Archibald Philip Primrose, 5th Earl of Rosebery (1847–1929) was a Liberal member of parliament, prime minister briefly in 1894–95 when Mr Gladstone retired.

Lord Russell *See* Earl Russell.

Lord's Tavern London NW8. The original tavern was built by Thomas Lord (1757–1832), the man who began as a groundsman, then established his own cricket ground in 1797. In 1814 he transferred to the present Lord's, headquarters of the Marylebone Cricket Club and of cricket in general. Lord's Tavern was demolished in the interests of a new South Stand, but a replace-ment was opened in 1967. The Lord's Taverners, a cricket team of stage personalities which plays for charitable purposes, was so-named in 1950 because the idea was conceived in the pub. At West Meon, near Petersfield, Hants, there is a Thomas Lord, in honour of the man who began it all. He was well known as an ornithologist as well as cricketing enthusiast. He retired to West Meon in 1830 to take up farming.

Lord Stokes Leyland, near Preston. Lord Stokes was chairman of the British Motor Corporation when he opened this pub near the BMC plant.

Lord Warden Deal. Others at Hastings and Sandwich. A reference to the honorary position of Lord Warden of the Cinque Ports. The Duke of Wellington and Sir Winston Churchill are amongst those who have held it. Since 1978 it has been held by HM Queen Elizabeth, the Queen Mother.

Lord Wellington *See* Duke of Wellington.

Lorelei Porthcawl, M Glam. A name that recalls a rock on the River Rhine, near Bingen, which is a danger to river traffic, or the legendary siren who is supposed to have lured boatmen to their doom there. For some the name will recall another legendary siren, Marilyn Monroe, who played the part of Lorelei in the 1953 remake of *Gentlemen Prefer Blondes*.

Lorna Doone Galleywood, near Chelmsford. Another in Edinburgh. The novel *Lorna Doone* by R D Blackmore, published in 1869, was the most popular of this author's works but by no means his own favourite. The name also became that of a stagecoach which ran from Minehead to Lynton.

Louis Armstrong Dover. The pub was the Grapes until a new landlord came along who led a jazz-band in his spare moments. A portrait of Louis Armstrong (1900–71), the famous American jazz trumpet player, adorns the sign.

Louis Marchesi Tombland, Norwich. Louis Marchesi practised as a pastry–cook in Norwich. In 1926 he founded a society of business-men who met regularly at a round table to discuss ways of helping the less fortunate members of society. The Number 1 branch of the Norwich Round Table still hold their meetings in this pub, which displays many mementoes associated with what is now an international movement.

Love Pool Sellack, H and W. The pond opposite this pub is called the Lough Pool, 'lough' itself meaning a pool, though it has a special meaning in Ireland where it can refer to a lake or an arm of the sea. In the latter sense it corresponds to Scottish 'loch'; in the former sense it is normally pronounced *luff*, and it is that which caused the change to 'love'.

Lover's Leap Stoney Middleton, Derbs. The pub is at the foot of cliffs from which a young lady is said to have jumped in a suicide bid. She was saved by her crinoline gown which acted as a parachute. Similar tales are told in other parts of the country to gullible visitors. The residents of Kirkby Over-blow, for instance, tell of a love-lorn maiden who threw herself from Almes Cliff, only to be saved by her voluminous petticoats. The incident is said to have caused the place-name to come into being.

Lower Bell Between Maidstone and Rochester. The reference may be to a 'low-bell', used in night-time fowling. The birds are first stupefied by the noise of the bell, then blinded by the glare of lights, so that a net can easily be thrown over them. The sign-painter has chosen to illustrate the name by showing an elegantly-dressed suitor about to call at a house. Two belles await him, one at an upstairs window, the other downstairs. *See also* Upper Bell.

Loyal Toast Southend. A name which provides an excuse, if any be needed, for a drink at almost any time, especially to a member of the armed services. The loyal toast to the King or Queen is drunk sitting down by the Royal Navy, allegedly because one English king who stood up to acknowledge the toast cracked his head on a beam.

Lucknow *See* Sir Colin Campbell.

Luck Penny Stafford. By local tradition, a farmer selling livestock always returned something to the buyer for luck. Miss Mitford (1787–1855), in one of her books, writes: 'All the savings of a month, the hoarded halfpence, the new farthings, the very luck penny, go off *in fumo* (in smoke) on that night.' 'Luck penny' did not necessarily mean one penny. *The Times* reported in 1890 that a man had bought a horse for £100 and received back £5 'luck penny'.

Lugger Chickerell, Dors and elsewhere. The vessel once used to patrol the south coast, looking out for smugglers. It carried a lugsail – four-cornered and hung obliquely. The saying: 'once aboard the lugger and the maid is mine' is a version of: 'I want you to assist me in forcing her on board the lugger; once there, I'll frighten her into marriage'. This occurs in John Benn Johnstone's *The Gipsy Farmer*.

Lumbertubs Moulton, near North-ampton. A nearby lane became known as Lumbertubs Lane because it was used by shopkeepers for the disposal of their rubbish. 'Lumber' refers to any objects which are no longer felt to be useful, while the 'tubs' would probably have been used for butter. The pub was built on a site adjoining the lane and was originally called Boothville. The present name dates officially from 1960.

Lumley Arms Maltby, near Middlesbrough. The sign is based on a drawing of Lumley Castle in County Durham, once owned by the earls of Scarborough. The pub is on land that also once belonged to that family. There was a Lumley Castle in Nottingham until 1961.

Lumphinnans Cowdenbeath, Fife. The name of a nearby village, referring to a church dedicated to St Finnan.

Luttrell Arms Dunster, Som. This pub began as the Ship but changed its name in 1779 in favour of the Luttrells, the family who had occupied the nearby castle since 1404.

Lygon Arms Broadway, H and W. General Edward Lygon was one of Wellington's commanders at Waterloo. After his death his butler was allowed to become licensee of this pub, on condition that it bore the family name. It had previously been the Whyte Harte. There is another *Lygon Arms* at Feckenham, near Droitwich.

Macaulay Arms London W8. Thomas Babington Macaulay, Baron Macaulay of Rothley (1800–59) was a historian and author who had a distinguished career in parliament. His best-known work was his *History of England from the Accession of James II*, in five volumes (1849–61). His poetry, *Lays of Ancient Rome* (1842), was very popular.

Macbeth London N1. The eleventh century Scottish king, murderer of Duncan. The pub has a tiled wall which shows scenes from Shakespeare's play *Macbeth*. At Deeside, near Aboyne in Grampian there is a Macbeth Arms.

Mace Bearer Bury St Edmunds. The pub is modern, but honours the official who performs this ancient function, carrying a mace, as a symbol of authority, before a high functionary such as a mayor.

Machine Man Long Wittenham, near Abingdon. The sign shows the threatening figure of a monster robot against a stormy skyline. The landlord would seem to be trying to tell us something.

Mad Cat Pidley, near St Ives, Cambs. The name of this pub reminds us that painters of inn signs expose their work to a highly critical audience. An attempt to paint a sign for the White Lion, which was the name of the pub at the time, was not too successful as far as the regulars were concerned. They promptly referred to the *Mad Cat*, which has now become the official name.

Mad Dog Odell, near Bedford. The original owner of the pub had a King Charles spaniel. It is shown on the inn sign in a state of frenzy, chasing a cat, presumably one of its regular occupations.

Madeira Falmouth. Another at Torquay. Also Madeira House, Stonehouse, near Plymouth. The wine which comes from the Madeira Islands, owned by Portugal, was formerly delivered direct to the taverns from the ships which brought it to England.

Mad Hatter Manchester. Another at Warrington. Also a Madhatters in Edinburgh. The reputation of hatters was ruined for ever by Lewis Carroll, who drew attention to the American expression 'as mad as a hatter' when he created the character in *Alice in Wonderland*. Brewer takes the expression at face value and says that the use of mercurous nitrate in the making of felt hats may have caused hatters to behave oddly. He also cites a seventeenth-century hatter who gave away all his possessions and lived on dock leaves and grass. This all sounds very plausible until one remembers that 'mad' in the original expression meant 'angry', and it has long been suggested that the original phrase was 'mad as an adder'. The hatters themselves will no doubt prefer this version.

Maenllwyd Rudry, M Glam. The name is Welsh for 'grey stone slab', the pub being built of knobby stone.

Mafeking Hero Bishop's Waltham, Hants. Formerly the Wheatsheaf, but renamed after the 217-day siege of Mafeking, in South Africa, had been relieved in 1900. The pub name honours men from the village who survived the siege, together with their leader, Lord Baden-Powell. Journalists of the time invented the verb 'to maffick' to describe the exuberant behaviour of the London crowds when the relief of Mafeking was made known.

Magazine Leicester. The original meaning of 'magazine' is storehouse. It came to mean more specifically a storehouse for military provisions, including arms and ammunition. Later still it was applied to the chamber of a repeating rifle, which contains a store of cartridges. It had also taken on the separate meaning of a publication which was a 'storehouse' of general information. This pub is located near the Magazine Gateway, a remaining part of the old city walls and now constituting the museum of the Royal Leicester Regiment.

Magdalen Arms Gorleston-on-Sea, Nflk. The pub was built in 1955 and is on an estate which Sir John Fastolfe bequeathed to Magdalen College, Oxford, in 1480. There is another pub of this name in Oxford itself. Magdalen (pronounced *mawdlin*) College was founded in 1458.

Maggie Murphy's Tywyn, Conwy. The name of a popular hostess of the late nineteenth century.

Magic Hour London NW2. The pub forms part of Production Village, a converted film studio which provides family entertainment of different kinds.

Magician's Nephew Macclesfield. This was formerly the Hole in the Wall. In C S Lewis's book for children, *The Magician's Nephew*, Diggory has to go through a hole to get to Narnia, the magical country.

Magna Charta Lowdham, near Nottingham. The document, also known as the Magna Carta, which King John was obliged by his barons to issue in 1215. It guaranteed them certain privileges and in more general terms asserted the supremacy of the constitution over the king. John later repudiated the charta on the grounds that he had been forced to sign it, and civil war resulted. The inn sign here shows him using a quill pen to put his signature to the document.

Magnet and Dewdrop London E14. The magnet is said to pull in the customers who might otherwise have missed the invitation 'do drop in'.

Magog London EC3. One of a pair of giants in British legend. The Gog and Magog, which was formerly in Manchester, commemorated them both. There is also a New Gog in London E16. The effigies of the two giants stood at the Guildhall in London, but were destroyed in the Great Fire of London. Their replacements were destroyed in an air raid in 1940, but further replacements were put up in 1953. There are references to Gog and Magog in the bible. In Revelations they are symbols of the world's hostility to the Church. In Ezekiel Gog personifies the powers hostile to the people of God. This makes the presence of the two figures at the Guildhall seem a little strange, but in the British legend they were taken to the palace which was formerly on the site and forced to be porters (gatekeepers) there.

Magpie Epsom. Another at Stapleford, near Nottingham. The bird that began as a simple *pie* or *pye*. The *Mag* is from the name Margaret. There are many allusions to this bird in folklore. If one taps at the window it is supposed to be a death-warning. In some parts of the country it is unlucky to meet one, and especially to kill one. In the following rhyme, the reference is to the number of magpies seen: 'One is sorrow, two mirth,/Three a wedding, four a birth,/Five heaven,/six hell,/Seven the devil's ain sell.' Other tales concerning the bird include its refusal to enter Noah's Ark, its inability to complete its nest, and its warning of stormy weather to come if seen flying alone. In former times it was best not to be behind a Devonshire peasant if he saw one, since he would spit over his shoulder three times to avoid ill-luck.

Magpie and Stump London EC4. The sign shows the bird perched on the stump of an old tree. It may refer to the badly painted arms of Anne Boleyn, which should show a white falcon on the root of a tree. It has been suggested that 'magpie' has its slang sense of 'halfpenny,' and that 'stump' refers to 'stumping up', ie paying the bill, but the pub is older than the first recorded instance of magpie used in that sense. Site redeveloped – pub no longer exists, says our scout.

Magpies Nottingham. Another at Coleshill, Bucks. The Nottingham pub reflects the nickname of Notts County Football Club, who wear black and white shirts. Their ground is nearby.

Maiden Over Earley, near Reading. Another at Pelaw, near Gateshead. 'Maiden' has long been used in the secondary sense of 'yielding no results', a thought which led to the cricketing expression 'maiden over', an over which produces no runs. The sign-painter at Earley was forced into a punning interpretation of his subject, and showed a maiden jumping over a set of cricket stumps.

Maiden's Head Maidenhead. Others at Evesham, Whitwell, near Hitchin and Canterbury. King's Lynn has a Mayden's Heade. In this case it seems to be fitting that the pub name at Maidenhead reflects the place-name, which is explained as 'landing-place of the maidens', (Maidenhead is on the Thames). There are many other thirteenth century references to such landing-places. As John Field says in his *Place Names of Great Britain and Ireland*, 'the exact significance is obscure'. Place names of this type perhaps gave rise to the inn signs which were noted in London in the fifteenth century. For the inn signs a heraldic justification was sought, and a link with the Mercers' Company or the Duke of Buckingham has been suggested. As for the original place names, Stokes suggested that a maiden's hythe, or 'head' used in that sense, meant that the landing-place was a very safe one, easy to use, so that even a young girl could cope with it.

Maid Marian Arnold, near Nottingham. Another in Norwich. Robin Hood's lady-love, who wandered with him in Sherwood Forest, not too far distant from this pub. Marian, according to one version of the story, was really Matilda, daughter of Robert Lord Fitzwalter. King John loved her, but she rejected him in favour of Robin. Drayton described her: 'Her clothes tucked to the knee, and dainty braided hair,/With bow and quiver armed, she wandered here and there/Amongst the forest wild. Diana never knew/Such pleasures, nor such harts as Mariana slew.'

Maid's Head Mildenhall, Sflk, and elsewhere. Normally a reference to a fish, the young of the skate, thornback or shad.

Mail Cart Spalding, Lincs. The sign shows an old-time horse-drawn conveyance with a top-hatted driver holding the reins.

Mail Coach Tuxford, Notts and elsewhere. The mail coach was introduced in 1784 with a trial run from Bristol and Bath to London. The coaches soon replaced the mail carts and carriers of mail on horseback. The coaches continued in use until 1846, by which time the railways had proved their superiority. At Lyndhurst, Hants, there is a Mailmans Arms. Hounslow has an Old Mail Coach.

Main Band Bullgill, near Maryport. A mining term in Cumbria, describing a seam of coal.

Majestic Bondgate, Darlington. The pub was named after a paddle-steamer of former times. Time has in turn overtaken the pub itself, now gone.

Malakhoff Tower Great Yarmouth. Also Malakhov, Tewkesbury. This tower was one of the principal defences of Sebastopol, in the Crimea. In 1855 it was stormed by French forces, with some British help, during the Crimean War. The French thought enough of the victory to name a suburb of Paris *Malakoff*.

Maldon Grey Chilton, near Sudbury, Sflk. The sign shows a grey horse.

Malin Derby. Known by this name, but properly the Cox and Malin Wine Vaults, reflecting the use of the premises before the pub was licensed.

Mallard Stevenage and elsewhere. The name of a famous steam locomotive which set a world speed record of 126 mph in 1938 on a measured stretch of line between Grantham and Peterborough. The Stevenage pub and at least two others show the locomotive on their sign. Elsewhere the reference is to the male of the wild duck. At All Souls College, Oxford 'The Mallard' refers to a festival celebrated on January 14th each year in former times. It commemorated the finding of a very large mallard in a drain when digging for the foundation of the college.

Mall Tavern London W8. Also Mall, Woodhall Spa, Lincs. The London sign shows the game of pall-mall in progress, Charles II being the player. Pall-mall, sometimes called pell-mell, was played with a boxwood ball. This was struck with a mallet in order to drive it through an iron ring suspended at a height in a long alley. Pall Mall, London SW1 and The Mall, leading to Buckingham Palace, are on the sites of former alleys where the game was played.

Mallyan Spout Goathland, near Whitby. The spout is a forty foot waterfall in the locality.

Malta Harpenden. Another at Allington Lock, near Maidstone. This former British crown colony was annexed to Britain in 1814, which caused pubs to be named after it at the time. During World War Two the island was merci-lessly bombed for three years. In 1942 it was awarded the George Cross for gallantry in the face of this bombardment.

Maltese Cat London SW15. Polo was played for many years in the Roehampton area where this pub is situated. The *Maltese Cat* is a polo pony – 'past, pluperfect, prestissimo player of the game' – featured in a short story by Rudyard Kipling. It can be found in *The Day's Work*, 1898. The sign of this pub is a model of the pony.

Manage Horse Bath. 'Manage' is an earlier form of 'Manège', a riding school or academy; also the exercises carried out in horsemanship.

Man and Barrel *See* Barrels.

Man at Arms Bitteswell, near Rugby. In the late Middle Ages this term referred to any soldier, but especially one who was heavily armed and on horseback. Here the sign shows a knight in armour.

Mandeville Arms Hardington Mandeville, near Yeovil. Mandeville is the family name of the earls of Essex, once landowners here.

Manger Bradfield Combust, near Bury St Edmunds. The sign shows an example of a trough from which animals on a farm take their food. No other pub seems to be named after this common agricultural object, which has such strong Christian associations.

Manhattan London E9. Another at Arbroath. The name of a well-known cocktail, consisting of sweet vermouth, rye or bourbon whiskey, and sometimes a dash of bitters. The cocktail in its turn was named for the borough of New York City, which took its name from the Indian tribe who formerly lived there.

Man in Space Eastwood, Notts. Opened in 1966 by the Kimberley Brewery as the second of a series of names related to the space age. The sign shows an astronaut dangling in space at the end of his cord. Other pubs of this name are at Trentham, near Stoke-on–Trent and Stockwood, Bristol.

Man in the Moon London SW3. Another at Stevenage. The figure of a man in the moon has long been discerned, and various suggestions have been made through the centuries as to his identity. A popular belief has been that he is the man who picked up a bundle of sticks on the sabbath day. He is referred to in Numbers 15:32–36. He was stoned to death for disobeying the Lord's commandment. The reasoning was that he had disobeyed the law regarding Sunday, and was therefore sentenced to a perpetual moon-day, but the sabbath which the man disregarded was a Saturday. Nevertheless, *Man in the Moon* signs have long shown a man with a bundle of sticks. Sometimes he has a lantern and is accompanied by a dog. This seems to have become common by the seventeenth century, since Shakespeare, in *A Midsummer Night's Dream*, says: 'The man with lantern, dog, and bush of thorn/Presenteth moonshine.' At West Heath, Birmingham, the pub of this name was changed to Man on the Moon immediately after Neil Armstrong's landing in 1969.

Man o' Clay Bentilee, near Stoke-on-Trent. The pub is in the Potteries, and uses the local name for a potter.

Man of Gwent Newport. The pub was named when the county was still called Monmouthshire. It is now Gwent, after an ancient province.

Man of Iron Stapleford, near Nottingham. A reference to the nearby Stanton Ironworks, the largest of its kind in Europe. The sign shows a furnace-man at work. A similar Iron Man at Coventry refers to workers in the iron foundries there. Spennymoor, Dur has an Ironworks.

Man of Kent Ashford, Kent and elsewhere in the county.

Traditionally the description of a man born to the east of the River Medway, while those born to the west of it claim the title Kentish man. Curiously, there appears to be no pub called Kentish Man. Rainham, near Chatham has a Men of Kent.

Man of Ross Ross-on-Wye. John Kyrle (1637–1724) lived here. His house was converted into an inn after his death. The name of the pub refers to his many local benefactions.

Man of Steel Pontfaen, Gwent. A reference to the workers in the nearby modern steel plant. Sheffield has a Steel Inn.

Man of Trent Clifton, Nottingham. The pub is not far from the River Trent. The sign shows an angler on its banks completing a catch.

Man on the Moon Cambridge and elsewhere. This has been a popular sign since the celebrated touch-down on the lunar surface on 20 July 1969. Neil Armstrong stepped onto the moon at 3.56 am BST the following day, making the remark that was destined to be recorded in every dictionary of quotations for evermore: 'That's one small step for Man, one giant leap for mankind.' The pub of this name at Ipswich has a model of the Eagle lunar-module craft in the foyer. It is perhaps upstaged by the Spotted Cow at Brockham, Sry, opened in 1962. The sign there shows the nursery-rhyme animal which jumped over the moon, flanked by a frustrated-looking American eagle and Russian bear. Round the cow's neck is a medallion which says: 'First over the moon'. There is another nursery rhyme reference in the sign at Norwich of Man in the Moon. The sign depicts an astronaut on the moon, but recalls: 'The man in the moon came down too soon/And asked his way to Norwich/He went to the south, and burnt his mouth/With supping cold pease porridge.'

Man on Wheels Luton. The name was suggested by Peter Smith, director of the Luton Museum. Apart from hats, the town's main industries are all connected with wheels of one kind or another. Brightly coloured cartwheels hang from the ceiling. The pub was opened in 1970.

Manor House West Bromwich. The pub is an old manor house, a fine example of medieval timber-framed building.

Manor of God Begot Winchester. Originally a sanctuary, the property of St Swithin's monastery. Until the end of the seventeenth century anyone was safe from punishment while he remained within these walls, unless he had committed a treasonable offence.

Man o' War Birmingham. In this instance, transferred from the name of a famous American racehorse.

Mansion House Bridgwater. The pub is next door to the (real) Mansion House, where meetings of the town council take place. The pubs of this name at Camberwell and Kennington are no doubt for the Mansion House in London, the official residence of the lord mayor of London, at the Bank.

Man with a Load of Mischief *See* Load of Mischief.

Manxman Lewes. Another at Blackburn. Licensees proudly advertising their birth in the Isle of Man.

Ma Pardoe's Netherton, W Mids. Also Doris Pardoe's. These are the usual nicknames of the Old Swan, recalling the landlady of former times.

Maple Leaf Newark. Others at Worcester and West Durrington, W Ssx. The Newark pub has a Canadian theme. The Canadian national anthem, since 1867, has been 'The Maple Leaf Forever'.

March Hare Stevenage. Others at Nottingham and Broughton Hackett, H and W. The character in Lewis Carroll's *Alice in Wonderland*. Hares really do behave strangely in March, their rutting season.

Margaret Catchpole Ipswich. The inn sign here shows a fight between Revenue men and smugglers on one side, and Margaret Catchpole at full gallop on a horse on the other. The reference is to a Suffolk folk-heroine who stole a horse on which to ride to London, dressed as a sailor. She wanted to visit her lover, William Laud, a smuggler. Margaret was sentenced to death for horse-stealing, but was instead transported to Australia in 1801. There she married well and became respectable. Perhaps this was inevitable with a name like Catchpole, which means a 'sheriff's officer', especially one who arrests people for debt. In Old French a *cachepol* went around seizing poultry in default of money.

Marie Lloyd London N1. Marie Lloyd was the stage-name of the immensely popular music-hall artiste, born Matilda Alice Victoria Wood (1870–1922). She took the name Bella Delamare at first, but became Marie Lloyd when she appeared at the Star Palace of Varieties, Bermondsey, in 1885. She borrowed her name from *Lloyd's Weekly Newspaper*.

Marine Great Yarmouth. The sign shows a Royal Marine in red coat and white trousers on guard duty.

Marine Grotto Marsden, Dr Peter Allan took up residence in the local caves at the beginning of the nineteenth century. He was not exactly a hermit, since he brought up a family of eight children, though he is sometimes referred to as such by the locals. This pub has its own lift to convey customers up and down the cliff face.

Marisco Lundy Island. Named after the first ruler of Lundy, William de Marisco (or Marsh). He supported Richard I and rebelled against Richard's brother, John. There is another pub of this name at Aveley, Esx, which may be for Richard de Marisco, who was chancellor in the early thirteenth century. Lundy Island is at the mouth of the Bristol Channel.

Maritime and Nautical Names A wide range of names is found referring to those who go to sea and the ships in which they sail. *See* Ship Names, and Admirals. Sea-battles of the past, such as Trafalgar, Portobello and Jutland are often mentioned, as are the Valiant Sailors who fought in them. Many ex-sailors seem to become publicans. They Drop Anchor in a Safe Harbour, and so on. Ports may well have a Harbour Inn, as at Axmouth, Devon. Those with a special interest in maritime matters might care to make their own collection of such pub names. We were well past the 150 mark when we stopped counting.

Markers' Retreat Denon, near Gravesend. There is a firing range nearby. The markers examine the targets and record the scores, but retreat to this pub for safety.

Market House Glastonbury. Others at Langport, Som, and Dewsbury, W Yorks. At Glastonbury the auctioneers collected their monies in the inn and no doubt took something to soothe their vocal chords.

Market Side Nottingham. The Sneinton Market is held nearby each week. Until 1981 this pub was the Sir Robert Clifton, a former member of parliament for the city and local landowner.

Market Tavern Brecon. The name is of the Market House, Market Side type, but this pub is distinguished by its sign, which manages to include a bull's head, a ram, a sheepdog, a shepherd's crook, a jar of ale, fronds of wheat and a sprig of hops.

Mark Lemon Broadfield Barton W Ssx. Mark Lemon (1809–70) was an English journalist, dramatist and novelist, but is perhaps most noteworthy for having been one of the joint founders of the magazine *Punch*. He was also its first editor, 1843–70. He published a 'jest book' in 1867.

Mark Twain Rochdale. Mark Twain was the famous pen–name, derived from the leadsman's call on a Mississippi boat indicating the depth of water, of Samuel Langhorne Clemens (1835–1910). He was first noticed as a writer in 1865 when his *Jim Smiley and his Jumping Frog* appeared. In 1869 he published *The Innocents Abroad*, but his masterpieces were *The Adventures of Tom Sawyer* (1876) and *The Adventures of Huckleberry Finn* (1884).

Marlborough Also Marlborough Arms, Marlborough Head, Marlborough House. *See* Duke of Marlborough.

Marlborough House Oxford. The sign shows a three-masted warship, one of the ships of the Royal Navy named in honour of John Churchill, Duke of Marlborough (1650–1722), victor of Blenheim, Ramillies, Oudenarde and Malplaquet.

Marlipins Shoreham-by-Sea, W Ssx. This name refers to a board game which was played from the end of the fourteenth century, correctly known as merels. The game was played between two players, each of whom had the same number of pins (which sometimes became pegs, discs or pebbles). Merels derives from a word in Old French which meant a token coin, or counter, and it took on various corrupt forms in English, including miracle, moral, marl and morris. Nine men's morris is in fact another name for this game, as is Fox and Geese. There can be no doubt about this explanation of the name, though local tradition tries to insist that 'marl' was a Saxon word for 'tax', and that the pins were pins of ale. 'Marl' has never had such a meaning.

Marlow Donkey Marlow, Bucks. This was the local name for a small tank engine that worked the Marlow branch railway line to Reading from 1897. It was superseded by a diesel unit in 1962. About this time the Railway Hotel was renamed to commemorate the engine.

Marlpit Norwich. Marl is a kind of soil consisting of clay mixed with carbonate of lime. It is much used as a fertiliser.

Marmion Tamworth. Also Marmion Arms, Haltham, near Horncastle; Marmion Tavern, Portsmouth. *Marmion* is the title of a narrative poem by Sir Walter Scott, published in 1808. It concerns the doings of Lord Marmion. These include forgery to achieve his own ends, and other misdeeds, and hardly seem to justify the naming of a Royal Navy destroyer, HMS *Marmion*, in 1915. After this was sunk *Marmion* became the name of a minesweeper.

Marne Bishop's Stortford, Herts. This pub was opened in 1984. It takes its name from the river that runs through the French town of Villiers sur Marne, with which Bishop's Stortford is twinned.

Marquess London N1. Marquis is now the commoner form of this word in English, which specifies a degree of the peerage between duke and earl. A particular marquis is usually specified on an inn sign, but apart from the *Marquess* example there is a Marquis at Rusthall, near Tunbridge Wells and a Marquis Arms at Fforestfach, near Swansea.

Marquis Cornwallis Also Marquis of Cornwallis. *See* Cornwallis.

Marquis of Anglesea London NW1. Another at Bow Street, WC2. Henry William Paget (1768–1854) was an English general who commanded the British cavalry at Waterloo. He lost a leg during the battle. It was kept and buried with him when he died forty years later. The sign of the Marquis at Rhosybol is also for this popular soldier, whose statue stands on a 250–foot column near the Menai Bridge.

Marquis of Camden *See* Camden Arms.

Marquis of Carabas Northampton. A fictitious title for an aristocrat who supposes that the whole world has been created for his own benefit. He was made fun of by Perrault in his *Puss in Boots* and is also mentioned in Disraeli's novel *Vivian Grey*.

Marquis of Exeter *See* Hurdler.

Marquis of Granby Esher and elsewhere. John Manners (1721–70), Marquis of Granby, is honoured in a great many pub names because he set up so many of his own men as tavern keepers when they left the army. He himself was Colonel of the Royal Regiment of Horse Guards by 1758, and commander-in-chief of the British army in 1766. After his death the following lines were published: 'What conquest now will Britain boast/Or where display her banners?/Alas, in Granby she has lost/True courage and good Manners.' His courage was often displayed on the battlefield, not least when he led a cavalry attack against the French in the Battle of Warburg. He lost his hat and wig as he rode at the head of his men, and there is a popular but erroneous belief that the phrase 'to go at it bald-headed' arose at that moment (1760). (The phrase began as American slang.) In spite of Granby's popularity, it was Frederick Duke of York who was known as the Soldier's Friend, though the phrase certainly described the Marquis as well. At least twenty pubs in London are named after him, including a Marquess of Granby at London WC2.

Marquis of Lorne Radford, Nottingham and elsewhere. Also **Lorne**, Dollar, near Falkirk; Lorne Arms, Aberdeen. Many of these signs are for John George Edward Henry Douglas Sutherland Campbell, Marquis of Lorne (1845–1920). He was a member of parliament for Argyllshire (now Strathclyde) and governor-general of Canada 1878–83. He married the Princess Louise, fourth daughter of Queen Victoria, in 1871. The signs in Scotland may refer to one of the marquis's ancestors, a general who fought with Marlborough.

Marquis of Queensberry Wigston, near Leicester. John Sholto Douglas, 8th Marquis of Queensberry (1844–1900) is known for the Queensberry Rules, which governed boxing from 1872, though they were formulated a few years earlier by the marquis and John G Chambers. The marquis was also involved with Oscar Wilde in the famous libel case which caused Wilde to be sent to prison. Lord Alfred Douglas, Wilde's friend, was the son of the marquis.

Marquis of Salisbury London N1. Robert Arthur Talbot Gascoyne–Cecil, 3rd Marquis of Salisbury (1830–1903), was a Conservative statesman and diplomat, three times prime minister. He served as his own foreign minister. At Purewell, Dor, the pub of this name is for his grandson, leader of the House of Lords 1942–45 and again 1951–57.

Marquis of Wellington London SE1. The Duke of Wellington is meant.

Marquis of Westminster Westminster. Robert Grosvenor, 1st Marquis of Westminster (1767–1845) was a member of the family which owned immense estates in London, marked by such names as Grosvenor Square, Eaton Square, etc.

Marrowbone and Cleaver Kirmington, Hum. 'Rough music' was formerly provided by butcher boys who each held a marrowbone and a cleaver, striking them to sound different notes as if they were bells. Newly–married couples were often serenaded with such music in the seventeenth century.

Marsh Harrier Stamford. Another at Cowley, Oxford. The bird is sometimes known as the marsh hawk, and was earlier called the moor buzzard.

Martello Folkestone. Others at Eastbourne; Holywood, Down. Martello towers are circular forts with massively thick walls, usually built at the coast with a view to preventing enemy landings. Over seventy of them were built at the beginning of the nineteenth century when it was feared that Napoleon would invade England. The towers take their name from Cape Mortella in Corsica where there was a tower of this kind. The English fleet captured it in 1794, but could not quite master the original form of the name.

Marten Leicester. The pub is in Martin Street, which presumably suggested the name. The marten is of the same family as the weasel, though slightly larger. Its fur has long been valued.

Martha Gunn's Brighton. Martha Gunn was a well-known local personality, officially the Beach Superintendent. She died in 1815, aged 89. The pub was renamed from New Inn in 1972 as a result of a competition organised by the brewers.

Martingale Reedham, Nflk. A device intended to keep a horse's head down. There are various kinds of martingale, known as the Cheshire, Irish, Indian, Running, Standing, etc. The origin of the word is something of a mystery.

Martlet Langford Budville, Som. Also Martlets, Bognor Regis; Golden Martlet, Hellingly, near Hailsham. In heraldry the martlet is an imaginary bird without feet. It is used for the fourth son of a nobleman, signifying that no property will come to him. The Langford Budville example was a reference to Lord Langford. Martlet is also a name for the swift, though often used in former times for the house-martin or swallow.

Martyrs Tolpuddle, near Dorchester. The Tolpuddle Martyrs were six farm labourers who tried to form a trade union in 1834. A local bench of landowners sentenced them to seven years transportation to Australia, apparently looked upon as a martyrdom at the time. There was in any case a public outcry and the men were brought back after two years. The pub was renamed from the Crown in 1971.

Mary Rose Cheslyn Hay, near Walsall. Another at Portsmouth. The Portsmouth pub was formerly the Gloucester. It was renamed by Whitbreads to remind everyone of the support the brewery had given to the Mary Rose Trust. The Trust managed to raise the *Mary Rose* from the bed of the English Channel off Spithead in 1982–83. It had been Henry VIII's flagship, but sank in 1545. The Cheslyn Hay pub was a new one and took a name which was being much publicised at the time.

Mash Tub Melton Mowbray. This seems to be an error for Mash Tun, which is found at Winchester and North Bradley near Trowbridge. In brewing the mash tun is filled to a depth of several feet with grist (milled malt) and then hot liquor is run in to form a porridge-like mass. After several hours the liquid is run off, now in the form of sweet wort. (These brewing technicalities are dealt with in the *Camra Dictionary of Beer* by Brian Glover.)

Masons Arms Basford. Nottingham, and elsewhere. A popular name,

occurring at least seven times in London alone. The Company of Masons, who cut stone into shape for building purposes, was granted a coat of arms in 1473.

Master Brewer Hillingdon, GL. Another at Wickersley, near Rotherham. 'Master' here means 'extremely skilled'. A few other masters are honoured in pub names. They include: Master Builder's, Bucklers Hard, Hants; Master Cooper, Middlesbrough; Master Gunner, London EC4; Master Mariner, Cambridge and Barry (normally the captain of a merchant vessel); Master Potter, Cheadle, Ches.

Master Builder's House Bucklers Hard near Beaulieu, Hants. A pub since 1926, and formerly the house of Henry Adam, a master shipbuilder in the eighteenth century. Such ships as Nelson's *Agamemnon* were built here. Adam himself died in 1805 – the year of Trafalgar – aged 100.

Master Robert Hounslow, GL. The racehorse of this name won the Grand National in 1824. The pub has now become a motel.

Matapan Dagenham. Cape Matapan is the southernmost point of the Peloponnese, Greece. During World War Two a British naval force defeated the Italians near this cape.

Matelot Calderwood, Strath. Also Matelots, Queensbury, Bradford, The French word for 'sailor'. A naval officer of World War Two reports that the term was frequently used by sailors to describe themselves and their messmates.

Mauretania Wallsend-on-Tyne. Another at Bristol. In ancient geography this name referred to northern Morocco and part of Algeria, but it is best known as the name of a Cunard liner, built at Wallsend in 1906.

May Duke Reading. A variety of sour cherry. The tempting derivation from *Médoc* in France is dismissed by the Oxford English Dictionary.

Mayfield Newquay. The pub is beside a field where May Day dancing used to take place. Rochdale once had a pub of this name.

Mayflower London SE16 and elsewhere. As few people will need reminding, this was the name of the ship in which the Pilgrim Fathers sailed to America in 1620. The Rotherhithe pub was once the Shippe. It has been restored but recreates the atmosphere of the seventeenth century. It holds the unique privilege of being able to sell both English and American postage stamps.

Maypole Burnham, Bucks and elsewhere. Most of the pubs of this name stand near the site of an ancient maypole, the decorated pole bedecked with streamers, around which dancers move gracefully on May Day. Such May Day celebrations are very ancient in origin and were considered to be pagan by the Puritans, who suppressed them. They survive nevertheless in many areas, where a May Queen is still elected annually.

Mazeppa Wednesbury, W Mids. Another at Aston, Birmingham. The title of a poem by Lord Byron, published in 1819. It tells the story of Ivan Stepanovitch Mazeppa, a Polish nobleman, or rather an incident that befell him as a young man. He was discovered in embarrassing circumstances with the wife of a local magnate. As punishment he was bound naked to the back of a horse which was then lashed into madness. The horse galloped off and only stopped when it fell dead.

Mazeppa was rescued by peasants and lived to tell the tale.

Meadery Gulval, near Penzance. Also Mead House, Newlyn; Waterside Meadery Penzance. The references are to places where mead was made – mead being a fermentation of honey and water.

Meadow Covert Edwalton, near Nottingham. The sign shows two men in Norfolk jackets trying to wing a high–flying pheasant. The name was chosen by referring to an early map of the area and seeing what it was called before development.

Medway Wouldham, near Rochester. The river which flows into the Thames estuary at Sheerness. Chatham has a Medway Queen a boat name.

Melancthon's Head Derby. This name disappeared in 1910, having attracted a lot of attention until then from writers on pubs. It was a slightly erroneous form of Melanchthon, the name adopted by Philip Schwarzerd (1497–1560), a German scholar and humanist. He worked with Martin Luther, but was more conciliatory than he. He helped establish a German school system and supported a capitalist economic system. Polyglot readers will have noted instantly that Melanchthon was merely a Greek translation of his German name, which could be Anglicized as 'black earth'.

Melbourne Arms Melbourne, near Derby and elsewhere. Also Melbourne Bar, Derby; Melbourne Vaults, Otley, W Yorks. William Lamb, 2nd Viscount Melbourne (1779–1848) was the prime minister who taught statecraft to the young Queen Victoria. Melbourne, in Australia, was named for him; it had earlier been known as Dootigala. Melbourne was separated from his wife, Caroline Lamb, who wrote minor novels which had little interest for the public and had an affair with Lord Byron which was of much greater interest to the public.

Mendip Gurney Slade, near Bath. Another at Frome.
At Bishopsworth, near Bristol there is a Mendip Gate. The Mendip Hills extend twenty-three miles from Axbridge in Somerset. They include the famous Cheddar Gorge and numerous caves, some of which have yielded human and animal prehistoric remains.

Mercers Arms London E1. Another at Coventry. The Company of Mercers (drapers) received their first charter in 1393. They dealt mostly in costly materials such as silk.

Merchants Arms Stapleton, Bristol. After the Worshipful Company of Merchant Taylors, founded in 1327. They originally made armour lining and men's clothing, then became general merchants.

Merchant Venturer Redcliffe Hall, Bristol. A form of merchant-adventurer. Associations of such merchants financed exploratory voyages with a view to establishing trading posts abroad, importing goods, and so on, in the sixteenth and seventeenth centuries. The Bristol-based merchants were especially active.

Mercia Cross Cheaping, Coventry. Another at Mynydd Isa, Clwyd. The kingdom of Mercia in Anglo–Saxon England consisted more or less of the Midlands as they are today. It was gradually taken over by Wessex after the death of Offa in 796.

Meridian Bollington, near Macclesfield. The name means 'midday', though if the licensee who named the pub was Scottish, he would have had a midday dram

in mind. The name also suggests that it is the highest point, of success, splendour, or whatever.

Merlin Pinkneys Green, near Maidenhead. The pub was opened in 1959 and local residents were asked to name it. The streets on the housing estate had been named for types of aircraft used in World War Two, and *Merlin* was the name of the Rolls-Royce engine that powered them all. Elsewhere, as at Pontypridd and Andover, Hants, the name is for the wizard of Arthurian legend. The Andover sign shows him clutching his crystal ball. Leeds has a Merlin's, as does Edinburgh. At Chalfont St Giles, Bucks there is a Merlin's Cave, recalling a subterranean construction in the royal gardens at Richmond in the eighteenth century. The interior of this 'cave' was decorated with astrological signs, and Merlin himself was the chief attraction. There is a New Merlin's Cave in London WC1.

Mermaid Blackshaw Moor, near Leek, and elsewhere. The Blackshaw Moor pub is about a mile from Mermaid Pool. Legend has it that a certain Joshua Linnet was responsible for a local witch-hunt in former times. It led to a girl being drowned in the pool. Three days later, as her persecutor walked by the pool, she reached out and grabbed him, pulling him under the water. At Poole and Hedenham in Norfolk the inn sign depicts the famous bronze figure at the entrance to Copenhagen harbour, a memorial to Danish seamen who lost their lives in World War One. Historically, the Mermaid Tavern was a famous London pub in Cheapside, London. It was frequented by Raleigh, Beaumont, Fletcher, Donne, Ben Jonson and Shakespeare, to name but a few, and was celebrated much later by John Keats: 'Souls of poets dead and gone/What Elysium have ye known,/Happy field or mossy cavern,/Choicer than the Mermaid Tavern?/Have ye tippled drink more fine/Than mine host's Canary wine?' The best-known *Mermaid* is the ivy-clad old inn at Rye, which claims to have been re-built in 1420.

Merrie Harriers *See* Harrier.

Merriemead Sampford Peverell, near Tiverton. The modern sign of this pub shows dancing festivities on the village green, or meadow.

Merrie Mouth Fifield, Oxon. The former lord of the manor here was called Murimuth, which may indeed have begun as a nickname for someone who had a merry mouth.

Merry Cricketers *See* Cricket.

Merry Fiddlers Becontree Heath, near Dagenham. The name is meant to hint at the musical entertainment provided every night and the merry atmosphere to be found within. Our informant says, 'Pub demolished years ago. Site is now a supermarket.'

Merry Maidens Maiden Erleigh, near Reading. The sign shows a trio of mini-skirted maidens performing the twist. This dance, popular in the 1960s, is well described for future generations in the *Longman Dictionary of Contemporary English:* 'the dancers twist arms, legs and bottom in time with fast noisy music, but remain in the same place.'

Merry Monarch London N1. Another at Leicester. Charles II was known as the Merry Monarch.

Merry Wives of Windsor Windsor. This play by Shakespeare, written in 1600 or 1601, is said by Dennis to have been written at the command of Elizabeth I to show Sir John Falstaff in love. She had been highly pleased at the portrayal of this character in *Henry IV*, Parts One and Two. In the *Merry Wives*, Falstaff sends identical love-letters to two women, both of whom are already married. His designs on them merely end in various discomforts for him, such as being covered with foul linen and tipped into a ditch, and later being given a good thrashing.

Mersey Birkenhead. Others at Liverpool and Tranmere. The river which runs into the Irish Sea. Liverpool also has a Mersey Beat, referring to the musical style that began with the Beatles.

Metal Bridge Metal Bridge, Cumb. As one might surmise, there was a metal bridge here at one time. It was in use from 1820 to 1915.

Metropolitan Uxbridge. The sign here shows a tube train. Uxbridge is the terminus of the Piccadilly line. The pub of this name at Wokingham has a composite picture on its sign, showing St Paul's, Eros, the Post Office Tower, Big Ben, Broadcasting House, an Underground sign and a guardsman, a kind of tourist's guide to London in a single picture.

Mexico Longrock, near Penzance. Also Silver Wheal, Metherell, near Callington; Mexico Fountain, Landore near Swansea. Experimental silver mines appeared in Cornwall in the early 1820s. They were referred to in local vernacular as 'wheals', and were often associated with Mexico because that country was then the world's foremost producer of silver. The silver mines did not last long, especially when a gale blew down the rigs of the Long Rock mine in 1823.

Midday Sun Coulsdon, near Croydon. Named after a racehorse which won the Derby in 1937.

Midland Railway St Albans. The sign shows a blue diesel engine of the Midland Railway. A former pub of this name at Warmley, Bristol, is now the Midland Spinner. This was the nickname of the local train which used to stop here, the pub having formerly been the station. On its conversion to a pub it became the *Midland Railway* but changed to its present form in 1976.

Mid–Wales Pantydwr, Pwys. One can compare this name to Centre of England, near Coventry.

Mighty Fine Portsmouth. If this pub were anywhere but Portsmouth, one would say that the licensee had been struck by a phrase used by an American visitor and had decided to indicate the excellence of his establishment by using it. The phrase was also Dickensian, however, occurring for instance in *Oliver Twist*. Dickens, born in this town, would probably have approved of the name.

Mighty Hood Rodwell, Weymouth. HMS *Hood* was the Royal Navy's biggest warship, a 42,000 ton battlecruiser that was sunk in a matter of seconds by a direct hit on her magazine. This occurred in 1941 during an engagement with the German battleship *Bismarck*. Of the 1500 crew-members, only three survived the explosion. *See also* Admiral Holland.

Milecastle Haltwhistle, Northld. The pub is near Hadrian's Wall and has a full-size replica of a Roman chariot standing outside. The wall when built had mile-castles, fortifications every (Roman) mile.

Milestone Exeter. The pub sells only soft drinks, non-alcoholic beers and wines. It was set up in 1985 by the Devon Council on Alcoholism and the Exeter Community Alcohol team to help people with a drink problem. It is in the basement of an office block, and those who named it clearly see it as a highly significant step.

Military Names There are even more references to soldiers and battles on land than there are to sailors and battles at sea. The battles begin with that of 1066 and continue through nearly 1,000 years of our history. The average person may not be too familiar with the Boer War, the Peninsular War, the Crimean War etc, but in many areas names still commemorate skirmishes with Danes or Vikings as battles of a more local nature. The Battle of Waterloo, Brighton, and the Duke of Wellington made a particularly strong impact on pub names, but in many areas military names still commemorate skirmishes of a more local nature with the Vikings. Individual regiments are often mentioned, either because they were stationed near a particular pub or because the owners served in them. Such names will quickly emerge as the pages of this book are turned. We noted over 250 of them.

Miller of Mansfield *See* Sir John Cockle.

Millhouse Moreton, Wirral. The pub is a former millhouse and still has a large waterwheel in its lounge bar.

Millstone Hathersage, Derbs. The circular stone, one of a pair, used in grinding corn.

Millwey Between Chard and Axminster. The sign shows activity at a local flour mill.

Milton's Head Nottingham. Also Milton Head, Chalfont St Giles, in his native county of Buckinghamshire. John Milton (1608–74) was a poet and prose writer who became Latin secretary in Cromwell's government. He defended the imprisonment and execution of Charles I, and at the Restoration he was fined and driven into retirement. By this time his arduous duties had left him blind. He dictated his two epic poems *Paradise Lost* and *Paradise Regained*.

Minden Rose Bury St Edmunds. The pub is opposite the barracks which were once the headquarters of the Suffolk Regiment. This was the senior of the six Minden regiments, responsible for a famous victory at the Battle of Minden, 1 August 1759, against the French. The advance to the battlefield lay through gardens which were full of roses. Many of the men picked them and put them in their hats, establishing a custom which some regiments still observe on 1 August every year, though the Royal Welch Fusiliers maintain that they had no time to pick roses that day. Portsmouth has two pubs named Battle of Minden, at Hilsea and Kingston.

Minders Arms Oldham, Lancs. Another at Middleton, near Manchester. After the machine-minders in the local factories.

Miners Mexborough, S Yorks. Another at Risehow, Cumb. Also Miners Arms, North Molton, Devon and elsewhere; Miner's Lamp, Pemberton, near Wigan; Miners Refuge, Hurst, near Ashton-under-Lyne; Miners Rest, Washington, T and W and elsewhere. There are references to tin, copper, lead or coal miners, according to the district and age of the pub. Dordon, near Tamworth has a Merry Miners. *See also* Mines and Mining.

Miners Standard Winster, near Matlock. Referring to a standard dish formerly used to measure lead ore. A sixteenth-century example of such a dish can be seen at nearby Wirksworth.

Minerva Plymouth. The pub was built by a retired sea–captain and named after his last ship. The ship itself was named for the Roman equivalent of Athena, the goddess of the household arts. There is a stained-glass window showing this goddess at the front of the pub, and a statuette of her behind the bar.

Mines and Mining In Durham pubs are often named for individual collieries, while Cornwall still has many references to its former tin mines. The Miners are frequently mentioned, as in Miners Rest or Miners Arms, Coalminers Arms, Boldon Lad, Sturdy Lads, etc. Allusions to mining also occur in names like Main Band, Last Shift, Black Diamond. Altogether we found about fifty such names.

Minster Tavern York. Another at Ely. In both cities the pub of this name is near the minster, or cathedral church.

Minstrel Boy Coventry and elsewhere. Either a reference to the Minstrel Boy in Thomas Moore's *Irish Melodies* or to a famous racehorse. The *Melodies* were very popular indeed, and rightly so since they included such songs as 'Believe Me if All Those Endearing Young Charms' and 'Oft in the Stilly Night'. The relevant poem begins: 'The Minstrel Boy to the war is gone,/ In the ranks of death you'll find him,/His father's sword he had girded on,/And his wild harp slung behind him.'

Mint Exeter. King Athelstan set up a mint in Exeter in the tenth century. Silver coins were minted here until the end of the seventeenth century. The pub of this name at Banstead refers to the plant – *see also* **Mitcham Mint**. There is no connection between the two kinds of mint, the first of which derives from Latin *moneta*, money, the second from Latin *menta*, the name of the plant.

Miranda Liverpool. This name was invented by Shakespeare for the heroine of *The Tempest*, his last play. It means that she was 'worthy to be admired'. In the play she is the daughter of Prospero, exiled duke of Milan. When Ferdinand is shipwrecked on the island where she lives they instantly fall in love.

Mischief Tavern *See* Load of Mischief.

Mister Jorrocks *See* John Jorrocks.

Mister Micawber Glasgow. Mr Wilkins Micawber is a character in *David Copperfield* by Charles Dickens. He is a great optimist, confident of success at all times though never successful. He is an amiable but erratic man, and is said to be based on Dickens's father. At the end of the novel we hear that he has become a magistrate in Australia. At London EC3 there is a Mr Micawbers.

Mitcham Mint Mitcham. Also Mint, Banstead, Sry. In an area which was formerly noted for the cultivation of aromatic herbs, such as mint, lavender, etc.

Mitre Oxford and elsewhere. A reference to the deeply cleft hat,

having the shape of a pointed arch at the front and back, worn by bishops and some abbots. A

symbol of the bishop's office. It makes a convenient visual symbol and has been used as an inn sign since the fifteenth century, especially in cathedral towns. At Tonbridge the sign is said to be a corruption of 'martyr', because the church of King Charles the Martyr is nearby, but that may well be mere coincidence. There is no real reason to suppose that these two words would be confused. There was a tavern of this name off Fleet Street, London, where Dr Johnson loved to sit up late with Boswell, Goldsmith and other cronies.

Mitre and Keys Leicester. A pious combination of two religious symbols, the mitre for the bishop, the keys for St Peter.

Moby Dick Chadwell Heath, near Ilford. Another at West Kirby, Mers. *Moby Dick*, by Herman Melville, was published in 1851 and has always been popular. It tells the story of a cunning and ferocious whale named Moby Dick. Captain Ahab lost his leg hunting it, and he has vowed his revenge. After a long chase Ahab and Moby Dick join in a battle which lasts for three days. Moby Dick was for whales what the more recent Jaws has been for sharks, but Melville saw no reason to allow man to be the victor in the struggle.

Model T *See* Henry Ford.

Mole Mullacott Cross, near Ilfracombe. Another at Monk Sherborne, near Basingstoke. Also Molescroft, Beverley, Humb; Mole Trap, Chipping Ongar, Esx; Three Moles, Selham, W Ssx. The mole is a small furry animal that eats insects and likes to dig holes. It has weak eyes and no external ears. Molescroft refers to an enclosed field which is frequented by the animals.

Molly Millar Wokingham. After a celebrated local beauty of the eighteenth century, an innkeeper's daughter. Reputedly the toast of all the local gallants, she resisted them to a man and died a spinster.

Mona Liverpool. Also Mona Castle, Seacombe, Mers. Mona is the Latin name for the Isle of Anglesey, according to most modern scholars, though the reference by Caesar was long thought to refer to the Isle of Man.

Monarch of the Glen Liverpool. The name of a famous painting by Sir Edwin Landseer (1802–73), showing a stag surveying his territory. It has been much reproduced.

Monkey House Buckland, near Portsmouth. This pub was officially the **Crown**, but was known as the *Monkey House* because of the pet monkeys kept by a former landlord. When the pub was modernised the nickname was made official.

Monkey Puzzle London W2. The sign shows a Chilean pine. Its twisted prickly branches caused the botanist Archibald Menzies, who introduced the tree to England in 1796, to remark that it would puzzle even a monkey to climb it.

Monk's Head *See* Duke of Albemarle.

Monmouth Lostwithiel, Corn. An indirect reference to the *Duke of Monmouth* in this case, being the name of a ship which sank offshore with many local people on board.

Monmouth Arms *See* Duke of Monmouth.

Monolulu London N8. Prince Monolulu was a racing tipster who frequented the racecourses dressed as an Indian chief until his death in 1965. He was an Ethiopian by birth, actually named Peter Charles MacKay.

Mons Liverpool. It was at Mons, in Belgium, that the British and German forces fought their first engagement in World War One.

Montgomery of Alamein Hampton Magna, near Warwick. Bernard Law Montgomery, 1st Viscount Montgomery of Alamein (1887–1976) was the British field marshal who became nationally famous after his victory at Alamein in 1942. The pub is on the site of the former headquarters of the Royal Warwickshire Regiment. The present name of the pub was bestowed in 1978, replacing 'Bout Time, a comment on the long delay before a pub was built.

Monument London EC3. Another at Newbury. The London pub is near the Monument which commemorates the Great Fire of London, 1666. It is 202 feet high and can be climbed for a view over London. The pub offers an alternative way of spending one's time. We are told that this pub has been demolished and the site is a Docklands Light Railway station.

Moodkee Great Malvern. Moodkee, or Mudki, is south of Lahore, in India. In 1845 the British, under Gough, defeated the Sikhs there. This pub was named by an English army officer who returned from there.

Moon Wotton-under-Edge, Glos. Another in London, WC1. This sign is less common than Half Moon, Full Moon, etc. The Wotton pub sign shows two lovers in silhouette against a smiling moon. The London pub was taken over by the proprietor of the Sun Inn nearby. He changed the name from George and Dragon. As it happens there was once a Moon and Sun in London EC1. There is still a Moon and Stars to be found in Norwich and New Eastwood,

Notts, and the following also await moon-struck drinkers: Blue Moon, Leicester; Garway Moon, Garway, near Hereford; Harbour Moon, Looe; Heilk Moon, New Moon, Biddesham, Som; Red Moon, Bexley Heath; Rising Moon, Matley, near Stalybridge. *See also* Full Moon and Harvest Moon.

Moon and Sixpence Tintern, near Chepstow. Another at Hanwell, near Banbury. The Tintern pub was formerly the Masons Arms. It changed its name in favour of the novel by Somerset Maugham, *The Moon and Sixpence* (1919), when the author visited the pub.

Moon and Sun London EC1. This was a rebus name (the pub is no longer there) meant to suggest the Monson family, who were landowners in Lincolnshire and Hertfordshire.

Mooneys Irish House London WC2. A name which may fairly be said to speak for itself.

Moonlighters Pegwell, near Rams-gate. Presumably a reference to smugglers, 'moonlight' being on a par with 'moonshine'. In modern times 'moonlighting' has taken on the meaning of working while declaring oneself to be unemployed.

Moonraker Bradford and elsewhere. A name which is increasingly being used in the 1980s, perhaps due to the influence of Ian Fleming's James Bond story, *Moonraker*. The older inn sign is Moonrakers, as at Swindon and elsewhere, where the reference is to men from Wiltshire. They earned this nickname when they were discovered trying to rake the reflection of the full moon from a pond, believing it to be a large cheese. Wiltshire people themselves have an explanation for this. They say that a gang of smugglers were in the act of

retrieving casks of brandy, which they had hidden in a pond, when the Revenue men appeared. The leader of the gang pretended to be an idiot and explained about the cheese. It was the Revenue men who were the real fools for believing their story. A vaguely similar tale lies behind the Cuckoo Bush.

Moonstone Liverpool. In *The Moonstone* (1868), by Wilkie Collins, the stone is a huge diamond which is taken from an Indian idol. Sergeant Cuff, who is often said to be the first fictional detective, solves the mystery of its disappearance.

Moor Cock Garsdale, near Sedbergh, Cumb. Moor cock is another name for the red grouse. Shooting parties intent on bagging the bird often call in at this remote inn which stands well over 100 feet above sea-level. Another pub at Oakenclough, near Preston, bears the name. The Moorcock at Langdale End, near Scarborough, is for a racehorse which won the Richmond Gold Cup three times in succession.

Moorings Sowerby Bridge, W Yorks. This pub was a former warehouse. It stands in a canal basin where the moorings referred to are to be found.

Moot House Bingham, Notts. Also Moot Meet, Netherton, near Dudley. A 'moot', to the Anglo-Saxons, was a meeting, especially a meeting which had to make a judgement of some kind, like a court of law. Later it came to mean a legal action, and at the inns of court the word referred to a hypothetical case which students would discuss for practice. The word survives in the phrase 'a moot point', meaning one that can be argued about.

Mops and Brooms Well End, near Borehamwood, Herts. The explanation for this name offered in the village is that it commemorates a fight between villagers and gipsy travellers, in which mops and besom brooms were used as weapons.

Morgan Link Top, Malvern. The sports car of this name, still manufactured locally. H F S Morgan made his first car in 1909, a three-wheeler (which gave it a tax dispensation) known as the Moggie to enthusiasts. A four-wheeled Morgan appeared in 1936, though the three–wheeler continued to be made until 1950. The pub is a mecca for car freaks.

Moriarty's London NW1. The pub is at Baker Street tube station, and has a Sherlock Holmes' theme. Professor Moriarty, the Napoleon of crime, was of course Holmes' great rival. He and Holmes fell to their death, locked in each other's arms, in 1891, though popular demand forced Conan Doyle to revive Holmes in 1905 and explain that he had survived the fall, then spent a few years in Tibet.

Morley Arms Plymstock, Devon. John Morley (1838–1923) was a statesman and man of letters. He was editor of the *Fortnightly Review* 1867–83, and wrote a number of good biographies. He was also secretary of state for India, 1905–10.

Morning Gun Macclesfield. At the turn of the century workers gathered here in the early morning, awaiting the signal to begin work. Such is the local explanation, although the workers are more likely to have been in their places of work, listening for such a signal. The inn sign formerly showed a cannon.

Morning Star Aberdare and elsewhere. The name of a famous locomotive built by Stephenson for the Great Western Railway.

Morris Dancers Castleton, Derbs and elsewhere. Also Morris Dancer, Harold Hill, near Romford and Kelsall, Ches; Morris Man, King's Heath, Northampton; Morris Clown, Bampton, near Oxford. Morris dancing was introduced to England in the reign of Edward III from Spain, where it was the dance of the Moriscos (Moors living in Spain as opposed to those living in North Africa, though no doubt the latter also had the dance). It is said to have been a military dance originally, but in England it became a comical representation of society in general, from king and queen (Maid Marian representing her), to clown. There seems to have been an attempt to link the dance with the Robin Hood legend, though the exact form of the dance, the costumes worn, etc, have come to vary slightly in different areas. The Bampton pub, named for Bavian, the fool, claims to be the home of the dance in England.

Mortal Man Troutbeck, near Windermere. The phrase is taken from the couplets which accompanied the original sign. On one side was an ill-looking wretch, on the other a man who was in the best of health, though he had a red pimply nose like that of Bardolph in Shakespeare's *Henry IV*. The sign was painted by one Ibbetson, a painter who was on holiday, in order to settle his bill. Mine host at the time was Tommy Burkett. The couplets ran: 'Thou mortal man, that liv'st by bread,/What is it makes thy nose so red?'/'Thou silly elf with nose so pale,/It is with drinking Burkett's ale'.

Mortimer's Cavern Nottingham. In 1330 soldiers of the young Edward III are said to have entered the castle here through a tunnel. They came to arrest Roger Mortimer, lover of Queen Isabella, who together had usurped the throne and murdered Edward II.

Mortimer's Cross Mortimer's Cross, near Leominster. The pub is close to the site of a battle which took place in 1460, part of the Wars of the Roses. The sign shows Edmund Beaufort, Duke of Somerset, and Richard, Duke of York, picking a red and white rose to represent the Lancastrians and the Yorkists respectively.

Moss Rose *See* Rose.

Moth and Lantern Cottam, near Retford. This was formerly the Grenville Arms, but the pub's new owner organised a competition in 1981 to find a more appealing name. The *Moth and Lantern* is symbolic of the pub's attraction, drawing customers as a moth is drawn to a bright light.

Mother Hubbard Loughton, Esx. Another at Doncaster. No doubt a comic reference to the poverty of the landlord. The Mother Hubbard story, relating how she 'went to the cupboard/To get her poor dog a bone/But when she got there/The cupboard was bare/ And so the poor dog had none,' was related by Sarah Catherine Martin in 1805. In the full story Mother Hubbard trots hither and thither looking for something with which to feed the dog, who performs extraordinary feats.

Mother Huff Cap Great Alne, near Alcester. 'Huff cap' is strong ale, the drinking of which huffs one's cap, or makes one's head swell with pride and arrogance. The term was common in the sixteenth century; today we would talk about strong drink which 'goes to one's head', but the thought is the same. The sign here shows a serving wench offering foaming liquor to a traveller, suggesting that the artist was associating 'huff cap' with the 'head' of the beer itself, the froth. This erroneous explanation of the term is given in many books about pubs.

Mother Red Cap Luton and elsewhere. Mother Redcap was probably a general term for an 'ale-wife', as Monson-Fitzjohn suggested in his *Quaint Signs of Olde Inns*, derived from the wearing of a red cap. He quotes a verse: 'Old Mother Redcap, according to her tale,/Lived twenty and a hundred years by drinking good ale,/It was her meat, it was her drink and medicine besides,/And if she still had drunk ale, she never would have died.'

Mother's Arms Fictional. There is a fine flight of fancy from Charles Dickens in *Martin Chuzzlewit*. 'What are we?' said Mr Pecksniff, 'but coaches? Some of us are slow coaches; some of us are fast coaches. We start from the *Mother's Arms*, and we run to the *Dust Shovel*.'

Mother Shipton Knaresborough, N Yorks, and elsewhere. According to Richard Head, in his *Life and Death of Mother Shipton* (1641), this was Ursula Southiel (1488–1561), who married Tony Shipton when she was twenty-four. She is supposed to have been born in a cave at Knaresborough. Her fame derives from the predictions she made, which included the foretelling of the Gunpowder Plot, the death of Cardinal Wolsey, the development of the steam-engine, telegraph, aircraft etc. One wonders if she predicted that pubs would still be named for her in the

1980s, in places as far from her native town as Portsmouth.

Moulders Arms Cheshunt, Herts and elsewhere. Also Moulders Rest, Masbrough, near Rotherham. Moulders made the moulds used in iron-casting.

Mount Newmarket, Sflk. Another at Stanton, near Broadway. The sign here shows a mounted jockey. At Stanton the reference is to the climb up to the pub, which stands at the summit of a sloping street.

Mountain Lutton, near Ivybridge, Devon. A reference to the pile of earth connected with china-clay mining.

Mountain Eagle *See* Eagle.

Mounted Rifleman Stone, near Faversham, Kent. A former licensee was a founder member of the East Kent Mounted Yeomanry, formed as a volunteer force against an expected invasion.

Mount Skip Midgley. Halifax. The pub is on a steep hillside, the Great Mount. 'Skip' is recorded first in the mid-eighteenth century as part of the inn name, and poses a problem. In Yorkshire place names it sometimes means 'sheep'.

Mouse Westbury-on-Trym, Bristol. The original sign here showed a field mouse on an ear of wheat. It now shows a mouse dressed in Sunday best, propping up the bar with a pint of beer in front of him. Mousetrap occurs at Bourton on the Water, Glos.

Mowers Arms Moston, near Manchester. The name is said to recall a mowing contest in which two men each mowed an acre with his scythe. The winner was the village inn keeper, who had drunk only cold tea as refreshment instead of the alcohol consumed by his rival. He renamed his inn after the event.

Mowlem Swanage, Dors. After a local businessman who was born in 1788 in humble circumstances but prospered.

Mr Micawbers *See* Mister Micawber.

M S & L Manchester. After the Manchester, Sheffield and Lincolnshire Railway which became the Great Central Railway in 1899 when it built a line from Sheffield to London.

Mucky Duck *See* Dirty Duck.

Mudlark London EC2. A reference to the film *The Mudlark* (1950) which featured Andrew Ray as the juvenile lead. In the film the expression was used for a boy who searched in the river mud at low tide for any items of value. The word originally applied to thieves who waited by a ship and received small stolen packets from the crew. Later it came to mean a seashore scavenger, and later still, a street Arab, a homeless vagrant living in the streets.

Mug House Claines, near Worcester. This was a seventeenth-century term for an alehouse, 'mug' being used in the sense of 'pot' or 'ewer'. This pub is distinguished by standing entirely within a graveyard.

Mulberry Bush Liverpool. Another at Kempston, near Bedford. Also Mulberry Tree, London N19, another in Ipswich. The *Mulberry Bush* refers to a children's game which involves dancing around in a circle while singing 'Here we go round the mulberry bush'. The leaves of the tree are used to feed silkworms.

Muscular Arms Glasgow. A Glaswegian joke name which has become well-known elsewhere

Museum Farnham. Dors. The local museum was established by the Pitt-Rivers family. The inn sign shows the family arms on one side, a statue from the museum on the other. The Museum Tavern in London WC1 stands opposite the rather better-known British Museum.

Musical Names Music is now an inescapable part of pub life, and music of one kind or another has long been mentioned in pub names. The Bugle and Horn signs nearly always refer to coaching signals, but many musical instruments are mentioned besides, ranging from the Banjo, Liverpool, through the Bass Drum, Stretford, near Manchester and the Organ, Ewell, Sry and elsewhere to the Pipers at Dagenham and beyond.

Fiddlers are often mentioned as at Aberdeen and Glasgow, but often as Merry Fiddlers or Fiddlers Three as at Runcorn and Clayton, near Bradford, where 'Old King Cole' seems to be the source. The Welsh Harp and Irish Harp are possibly used more as national symbols than instruments. There is a Musicians Arms at Waterhead, near Oldham and elsewhere, and a few individuals are honoured. These include Old Duke (Ellington) at Bristol and Louis Armstrong at Dover, and there is a Charlie Parker's in Edinburgh. There is a Paganni in Liverpool. Gilbert and Sullivan are com-memorated, as are Brahms and Liszt, though the latter has obviously more to do with being drunk than a liking for their music. *See* Songs.

Mussel Down Thomas, near Plymouth. Mussels are found nearby. The name of the shellfish means literally 'little mouse' (as does the 'muscle' of the human body) because of its shape.

Mustard Pot Norwich. Another at Whinburgh, nearby. No doubt for real mustard pots (manufacture or use). The pub is associated by name with the famous Mustard Shop in Norwich which contains memorabilia relating to the local manufacture of Colman's mustard.

Mystery Southsea. The mystery was how the pub managed to stay undisturbed when the whole harbour area was redeveloped.

Mytton and Mermaid Atcham, near Shrewsbury. The reference is said to be to Sir John Mytton (died 1834), a local squire, whose sporting interests included the 'mere maids' of the village. The sign shows Sir John on one side astride his horse. He holds a tankard of ale, and a miniature mermaid is seen emerging from the froth. The other side of the sign shows a mermaid combing her hair. In her mirror can be seen Sir John, wearing hunting rig and a lecherous grin.

Nab Gate Harwood, near Bolton. 'Nab' means either the summit of a hill or a projecting peak of some kind. 'Gate' can mean a 'path' as well as gate in the modern sense. There is also a Nab's Head in Nab Lane, Samlesbury, near Preston.

Nadder Dinton, near Salisbury. The river which rises near Shaftesbury and flows into the Avon at Salisbury. Ekwall dismisses any theory about the name having to do with water snakes and gives it as 'running water'.

Nag's Head London WC2 and elsewhere. A 'nag' is a small riding horse or pony, and early signs showing a nag's head probably indicated that one could be had for hire from the inn. The modern inn sign painter sometimes interprets his subject humorously. Thus, at Martock, Somerset, the sign put up in 1979 shows a shrewish old woman with her hair in curlers, while the sign at St Leonard's, E Ssx, shows a woman with her head in a muzzle. Some ladies might be justifiably upset at such signs, for although 'nag' has long meant to complain persistently in order to persuade someone to do something, the noun applied to a person who does this is not feminine. Less controversial is the sign of the pub behind the Royal Opera House in Covent Garden, which shows a fine circus pony.

Nailers Arms Bourneheath, H and W. Also Nailmakers Arms, Hemsworth near Pontefract; Jolly Nailor, West Bromwich, another at Atherton, Lancs. 'Nailor' was a frequent early spelling. Nail-making was an important trade in the Middle Ages, giving a family name to many a Nailer, Nayler, etc. The Nailbox at Folkestone is also said by some commentators to be connected, though this word in printers' slang referred to a favourite place for backbiting.

Nancy Burton Pidsea, Humb. A racehorse of this name won several Classic races in the 1850s.

Napoleon Boscastle, Corn. Another in Guildford. Bradford has a **Bonapartes**. The Cornish inn received its name in 1807. Local levies were being raised in many towns to prepare for an expected invasion by Napoleon's troops. It fell to the inn keeper to gather volunteers from amongst the local men, who promptly dubbed him 'Napoleon'. The joke might have been misunderstood by strangers, but the same village also had a Wellington, which still exists. Some English signs may be after Napoleon III, who came to England in 1871 to begin his exile.

Narrow Boat Nottingham and elsewhere. For the long, narrow boats used on canals.

Narrow Gauge Neath. Another at Merthyr Tydfil. A term applied to a railway, such as that used in a colliery, which uses a narrower gauge (distance between the lines) than the standard four feet eight and a half inches. Originally, when there was a 'broad gauge', the narrow gauge was itself four feet eight and a half inches.

Naseby West Humberstone, Leicester Naseby is a village in Northamptonshire. In 1645 the Parliamentarians, led by Cromwell and Fairfax, heavily defeated the

Royalists under Charles I and Prince Rupert in the Battle of Naseby.

National Hunt Cheltenham. Cheltenham is the centre of national hunt racing, ie steeplechases and hurdle races rather than flat races.

Natterjack Evercreech, Som. This pub was once the Railway Inn. When the local line was closed in the 1960s it became the Silent Whistle. Since 1976, Conservation Year, it has been named for the species of British toad which has a yellow stripe running down the middle of its back, though the name also manages to suggest a man who is always ready for a natter.

Naughty Pigeon Tretharres, near Newquay. Said to be a reference to the bombing habits of local pigeons, a disturbance to snoozing holiday-makers.

Nautical William *See* King William IV.

Nautilus North Shields, T and W. The pub is in Verne Road, from which it may be assumed that it was named for the submarine in Verne's *Twenty Thousand Leagues under the Sea* (1870). The ultimate derivation is Greek *nautilos*, 'sailor'. There was subsequently a Royal Navy submarine of this name, and the USS *Nautilus*, launched in 1955, was the world's first nuclear-powered submarine.

Naval and Military Taunton. Also Naval and Military Arms, Gosport. A reference to the Royal Marines.

Navarino London E8. The pub is in Navarino Road and refers to a naval battle of 1827. *See* Admiral Codrington.

Navigation Lapworth, near Henley-in-Arden and elsewhere. The word 'navigation' used to mean a 'canal, waterway' (as well as other things), and the men who built the canals were therefore known as 'navigators', shortened to 'navvies'. The latter still exist, though a 'navvy' is a labourer now who is engaged in heavy excavating work of any kind. This connection of 'navigation' with 'canal' has often been forgotten. The inn sign at Wootton Wawen, for instance, formerly showed ships' officers taking readings with sextants, though the pub itself stands almost beneath the aqueduct which carries the canal across the Birmingham-Stratford road. Since 1946 the sign more correctly shows a canal narrow-boat. At Erdington, near the Fazeley Canal, a sign shows a ship in full sail – not exactly appropriate for a canal, and clearly a misunderstanding by the sign-painter.

Needle Gun London E3. This was a nineteenth-century term for a gun in which the cartridge was exploded by the impact of a needle. By 1880 it was being described as 'not at all a satisfactory arm'.

Needlemakers Arms Ilkeston, Derbs. Another at Studley, Warks. Reflecting a local industry of former times.

Needles Alvaston, near Derby. The pub is in Bembridge Drive, one of many streets in the area which link with the Isle of Wight. The Needles are three isolated chalk rocks off the western extremity of the island, near the entrance to the Solent.

Nell Gwynn(e) Arnold, near Nottingham and elsewhere. Eleanor Gwynn(e) (1650–87) worked as an orange-seller at the Drury Lane theatre in London before appearing there as an actress at the age of fifteen. She was especially successful in comic roles, where her sprightly personality could be seen at its best. She was also an excellent dancer. When she laughed it is said that her eyes almost disappeared because she laughed with such abandonment. Happily, everyone laughed with her, and she was very popular. She had various adventures with different men, including Charles II, by whom she had two children. The king was still thinking of her as he died, and asked that she should be cared for. In Covent Garden she is also commemorated in the Nell of Old Drury.

Nellie Dean London W1. The pub is in Dean Street, named after a seventeenth century dean of the ecclesiastical kind. 'Nellie Dean' is the name of a well-known song, composed by Henry W Armstrong, an American. 'Nellie Dean', according to Mrs Armstrong in 1961, was a 'fictional' name. Her husband wrote other songs for ladies who were figments of his imagination.

Nelson Arms Also Nelson's Arms, Nelson Butt, Nelson's Head, Nelson and Railway. *See* Lord Nelson.

Nelson's Quarterdeck Warrington New Town. The pub is in Admirals Road, and was opened in 1980 by Commander Kinch and some of his men from HMS *Tartar*. The naval theme is continued inside the pub.

Nene Wisbech, Cambs. The river Nene runs past Wisbech to The Wash.

Neptune London SE16. Also Neptune Hall, Broadstairs. The name of the Roman god of the sea and of the eighth planet in the solar system, discovered in 1846.

Nest Norwich. The pub is built into the main stand of the city's football club. Norwich City. The team are known as the Canaries because of the colour of their shirts, and this no doubt suggested the pub name.

Neuk Hopeman, near Elgin, Grampian. 'Neuk' is a Scottish form of 'nook', a secluded corner (where one may drink peacefully).

Never Turn Back Caister-on-Sea, near Great Yarmouth. In 1901 the local lifeboat was launched in a severe gale, in an attempt to help a ship in distress. The lifeboat itself capsized, with the loss of many of its crew. At the inquest the coxswain, James Haylett, was asked why the lifeboat had continued towards the ship it was trying to help in such terrible conditions. He replied 'Caister men never turn back, sir!' There is a similar Never Say Die pub at Jaywick, near Clacton-on-Sea.

Nevill Crest and Gun Eridge Green, near Tunbridge Wells. Nevill Crest refers to the arms of the Nevill family, marquesses of Abergavenny, whose family seat is here. The **Gun** was another pub at one time, but the two names were put together when the licence was transferred. At Birling, near Maidstone, the Nevill Bull is also a heraldic reference to this family.

Neville Gateshead. Also Neville Arms, Wendons Ambo, Esx. Neville is the family name of the earls of Warwick, owners of large estates in various places.

Neville's Cross London NW6. The name of a former village now part of the city of Durham, significant because of the battle that took place there in 1346. Edward III's army routed that of King David II of Scotland.

Nevison's Leap Pontefract. Also Nevison, Leigh, Lancs. References to 'Swift Nick', a highwayman, and a leap he made when escaping from pursuers.

NEW Some two hundred different pub names begin with the word 'new', indicating that an old name is being restored to use, or rather, was being restored to use when the pub was named. We have not attempted to provide entries for all such names, since a great deal of duplication would have been involved. Try ignoring the 'New' in the name and look for an entry under what follows it.

New Black Bull *See* Bull.

New Black Cap London NW1. The pub is on the site of an old court house. Older readers will recall that before the abolition of capital punishment, judges in full formal dress donned a black cap when sentencing prisoners to death.

New Broom Rotherham. Another at Checkley, Staffs. The Rotherham pub is on the Broom Valley estate, where bushes of yellow broom used to grow in great profusion. The Checkley sign shows a housewife wielding a besom.

New Bull *See* Bull.

New Bull's Head *See* Bull.

New Flower Pot *See* Flower Pot.

New Forest Emery Down, near Lyndhurst, Hants. The sign shows two wild ponies sheltering under a tree in the New Forest, the national park managed by the Court of Verderers. Lyndhurst stands within it. The forest was new in 1079, when William I carried out an afforestation policy.

New Gog *See* Magog.

New Inn Worle, Som and elsewhere. The Gloucester pub, like several others which bear this name, is very ancient. They were once new, later examples sometimes replacing inns which had previously stood on the site, and the name, though simple, is perfectly honourable. Nevertheless, many *New Inns* become something more 'trendy' in modern times, and will no doubt change their names again in the future to something trendier still. Many *New Inns* came into being in the sixteenth century as a result of Elizabeth I's complaints about the lack of suitable places to stay. There is a joke sign at Waltham Abbey, Esx, where the sign shows a gnu, the African member of the antelope family which looks like a buffalo. At Stedham, W Ssx, the pub name has far less subtly been changed to **Gnu Inn**.

New King Lud *See* King Lud.

Newlands Eynsham, near Oxford. The sign shows two astronauts exploring the rocky terrain of a new planet. Their spaceship is in the background, and a crescent moon shines overhead.

New London *See* London.

New Merlin's Cave *See* Merlin.

New Penny Leeds. Others at Fenton, Staffs, and Cheltenham. The sign of the Cheltenham pub shows the penny introduced in February, 1971.

News House Nottingham. At one time the national news was read out to patrons from broadsheets, the primitive newspapers of the eighteenth century.

New Shovels Blackpool. The new pub replaced the Shovels, which referred to clay-mining operations at nearby Marston Moss in the nineteenth century.

Newstead Abbey Bulwell, Nottingham. A reference to the historic building which was founded as a priory by Henry II in 1170. It was later the home of the Byron family.

Newton Pippin *See* Apples.

New Vic Nottingham. The pub is in the Victoria Centre, a shopping and market centre opened in 1973. The name was obviously chosen in the knowledge that the *Old Vic* existed in London. The theatre was once the Royal Victoria Hall, and earlier still the Coburg. There is an Old Vic pub in Stamford.

New White Bull *See* Bull.

Nickleby's Manchester. *Nicholas Nickleby*, by Charles Dickens, was published in 1838–39. In the course of the story Nicholas manages to confound Wackford Squeers, who runs a so-called school ironically named Dotheboys Hall. Squeers 'does' the boys by starving and ill-treating them instead of educating them. Nicholas also gets the better of his evil uncle and saves his sister from a fate worse than death, marriage to a revolting old man, Gride. As a reward he woos and wins Madeline, and all ends happily, with Squeers sent to Australia, the uncle dead by his own hand and Gride murdered.

Nicky Tam's Tavern Edinburgh. In Scotland a nicky-tam is a piece of string or whatever worn below the knee by a workman. It keeps his trouser-leg lifted from the ground if he is doing dirty work, stops dust rising up his leg, etc.

Nightingale London N8. Another at London N22. It was in North London that John Keats wrote his 'Ode to a Nightingale', the 'immortal bird'. As proof that absolutely nothing is sacred, it must be reported that a 'nightingale' was once a prostitute in slang usage, being most active at night.

Night Jar Worle, near Weston-super-Mare. A clever use of the name of a bird to suggest an evening drink. The bird was long known in some rural areas as the 'goatsucker', from its supposed habit of sucking milk from goats. Its other names include 'puck-bird' and 'puckeridge'.

Night 'n Day Birmingham. The pub is at the ATV Centre. It borrows the name of a famous Cole Porter song to suggest the nonstop activity at the centre.

Nile Burslem, near Stoke-on-Trent. The pub is in Nile Street. The reference is to the battle of the Nile, or the Battle of Aboukir Bay as it should be called. In 1798 Lord Nelson defeated the French here and restored British prestige in the Mediterranean. Mrs Hemans later wrote a poem, *Casabianca*, in which she celebrated the heroism of Louis Casabianca, captain of the French flagship in this battle. He and his thirteen year-old son, Giacomo, who refused to leave his side, perished. The poem has taken on countless ribald versions since, but originally began: 'The boy stood on the burning deck/ Whence all but he had fled;/The flame that lit the battle's wreck/ Shone round him o'er the dead.'

Nine Elms Gravesend. After the district of Greater London, SW6, or named, as the district was, after a clump of nine elm trees (which in turn became the name of a farm).

Nine Pins Low Fell, Gateshead. Another name for skittles, the game in which nine pins, bottle-shaped wooden objects, have to be knocked down by bowls.

Nine Saxons Basingstoke, Hants. The skeletons of nine Saxons were recovered years ago from a burial ground discovered in the vicinity. The sign shows a Viking warrior, presumably thought to be responsible for their death, surrounded by nine skulls.

Nineteenth Hole Aberdeen and elsewhere. The light–hearted golfing reference to the clubhouse, the normal destination after a round is completed at the eighteenth hole. At Buxton the name is 19th Hole.

Nineteenth Hundred York. The city celebrated 1900 years of existence in 1971.

Ninian Park Tavern Cardiff. The home of Cardiff City Football Club.

Noah's Ark Plymouth and elsewhere. The story of Noah's Ark has always appealed to the popular imagination, and the sign of an ark would have been instantly recognisable in the Middle Ages, when *The Deluge* was always presented as a mystery play. The ark also features in the arms of the Shipwright's Company, who have as a motto: 'Within the Ark safe for ever'. One can see that such a slogan would appeal to innkeepers. In rhyming slang 'Noah's ark' could be used for a 'nark', an informer to the police, park or lark, in the sense of 'a bit of fun'. The latter meaning also does no harm to the innkeeper's cause.

Noble Art London NW3. This phrase seems to have been used first by Henry Fielding in his novel *Tom Jones*. Before then there had been references to the 'noble science of defence'. The phrase is now firmly established as boxing's own, and is used here in a pub which has a boxing gymnasium attached to it.

Nobody Doddiscombsleigh, S Devon. The origin of this name is unknown, which allows free range for all sorts of local tales. One concerns some travellers who knocked at the door one night, but the landlord refused to open the door or admit that he was there. The travellers told people in the next town that nobody was in the pub they had called at, though the locals knew better. Another story tells of a solitary drinking landlord who often called to would-be customers that there was nobody in, and refused to let them enter. There may, on the other hand, have been a joke about a sign that showed someone's head and no body, as many signs do. The present landlord can at least inform enquirers that 'Nobody knows' when asked about the name. The sign shows a traveller in Elizabethan dress with his horse nearby. There is also a Nobody Inn at London N1.

Nodding Donkey Gainsborough, Lincs. The colloquial name for the kind of pump which is used on oil-rigs. Several of them can be seen near this pub, which opened in 1980.

Noel Arms Whitwell, Leics and Chipping Campden. Noel is the family name of the earls of Gainsborough.

Nog Inn Wincanton, Som. A pleasant pun on Noggin, which is found at Risley, near Warrington. A 'noggin' is a small quantity of spirits, or the vessel which holds it. The *Nog Inn* joke would be especially effective in East Anglia, where 'nog', in the eighteenth century, described a strong beer brewed locally.

Non Plus Morton-on-Swale, near Northallerton. This was the name of a racehorse which had some success, in spite of its name. One meaning of 'to nonplus' is to bring to a standstill.

Nont Sarah's near Scammonden, Huddersfield. The popular licensee here in the nineteenth century was known to one and all as 'Aunt Sarah', or Nont Sarah in local speech.

No. 1 Also No 10; No 20 Vaults. *See* Number Names.

Noon Sun *See* Sun.

No Place Plymouth. Another at Gosport. The Plymouth pub is said to be on the site of a brutal murder in the eighteenth century. The name probably reflects a superstitious feeling that reference to the place should be avoided.

Nore Sheerness. Nore is the name of a sandbank in the Thames estuary, off Sheerness, marked by a lightship and buoys. The anchorage around it was much used by the Royal Navy in the eighteenth and nineteenth centuries.

Norfolk Hero *See* Lord Nelson.

Norfolk Terrier *See* Dog.

Norfolk Wherry Norwich. A 'wherry' is a large, barge–like boat. This pub is named after one called the *Albion* which saw service on the local Wensum and Yare rivers, carrying anything from coal, sand, manure, marl to manufactured goods. Wherry is also found at Langley, Nflk, and in Norwich. There used to be a Wherrymans Arms in the area, but it has become the Sutton Staithe.

Norland Hessle, Humb. This was the Eight Bells, but was renamed as a tribute to the Hull passenger ferry which played a vital part in the 1982 Falklands Campaign.

Norman Hastings. Another at Norman Cross, near Peterborough. Also Norman Arms, Derby and Fulham; Norman King, Dunstable; Norman Knight, Wallingford; Norman Warrior, Lowestoft. References to the Norman Conquest, when William the Conqueror defeated Harold in 1066 at the Battle of Senlac, or Hastings. William was Duke of Normandy, the region in the north-west of France lying between Brittany and Picardy. At Norman Cross (a place name which has been in existence since the tenth century) they tell a tale about French prisoners in the Napoleonic Wars being hanged when they tried to escape. The 'Norman' in the place name and pub name actually refers to 'Northmen', ie men from Norway, who were in these parts centuries earlier.

Normandy Arms Blackawton, near Dartmouth. In 1944, before the Normandy invasion by allied troops, whole villages in this area were evacuated and used as a battle–training ground.

Norseman Hemsby, near Great Yarmouth. Others at Greenock and Weisdale, near Lerwick. The last-named is Britain's most northerly public house. After the Norwegian Viking, also referred to in the Norsk, Glasgow.

North Briton London N1. The name of a periodical established by John Wilkes (1727–97). He was an English politician and self-publicist of note. In issue forty-five of his magazine he attacked George III, for which he was at first imprisoned, though he was soon released. By that time he had become a popular hero. He wrote a scandalous *Essay on Woman* (Pope's more famous *Essay on Man* appearing in 1734) and was expelled from parliament. After many battles, in which he became a symbol of opposition to tyranny, he became lord mayor of London. Eastergate, W Ssx, has a Wilkes Head.

Northern Lights Fintray, Aberdeen. Also Northern Light, Liverpool. The popular name for the Aurora borealis ('northern dawn'). These are bands of coloured light seen in the night sky in the most northern parts of the world. The similar lights seen in the most southerly regions are the Aurora australis.

Northern Star London N11. Another at Ballymoney, Ant. After the north, or pole, star.

Northgate Caerwent, Gwent. The inn sign shows a fully–armed centurion on guard by the fortified north gateway of this former Roman settlement. At Launceston, Corn there is both a *Northgate* and Westgate for a similar reason. Oxford has a Northgate Tavern; Chester has Northgate Arms.

North Pole Ramsgate and elsewhere. This inn sign appeared in London in the 1860s, long before the pole was reached by the American explorer Robert Edwin Peary, in 1909. It may have arisen from a simple pole used as a sign and jokingly referred to as the 'north pole'.

North Star Chessington, Sry and elsewhere. The name of the famous locomotive built by George Stephenson for the Great Western Railway. It was at one point shipped to New Orleans (Minnesota, the North Star state would have been more appropriate), intended for the New Orleans Railway. The money could not be found to pay for it and it was duly returned. It had a 'sister', the Morning Star. *See also* Evening Star. Some *North Star* pub signs probably show the pole star rather than the locomotive.

Northumberland Arms London SW15 and elsewhere. After the dukes of Northumberland, owners of land and property in various parts of the country.

North Western St Albans. A railway

reference, to the London and North Western branch line from Watford, opened in 1858. There is another pub of this name at New Mills, near Stockport.

Norton Erdington, Birmingham. The reference is to a famous British motor cycle, shown on the sign. The Norton was made locally. At Cold Norton, near Colchester, the pub name echoes the place name.

Norway Perranarworthal, near Truro. The pub is close to the wharf where timber from Norway was unloaded, mostly in the form of pit-props for the Cornish tin-mines. The river has now silted up the creek, and ships such as the one on the sign, a Viking longboat, could no longer enter it.

Nosey Parker's Thornton, near Bradford. Another at Exeter. This slangy reference to someone who is over–inquisitive about other people's affairs is only recorded in the present century. Brewer's suggestion that it refers to a sixteenth century archbishop of Canterbury is therefore hardly to be taken seriously. Nosey had previously been used as a nick-name for someone with a large nose, such as the Duke of Wellington, or Oliver Cromwell. 'Parker' was also a London slang term by the mid-nineteenth century, referring to the kind of well-dressed man who could be seen strolling in a park. It is just possible that 'nosey parker' therefore meant an inquisitive man in a general sense, and that no particular member of the Parker family was responsible for the phrase.

Nottingham Mutley Plain, Plymouth. The sign shows the castle and the coat of arms of the city of Nottingham. The original inn stood in Nottingham Place, the town having several streets called after other English towns. There may be a reference to one of the ships of the Royal Navy which has been called *Nottingham*.

Nottingham Arms Westgate-on-Sea, Kent. Named by the first landlord for his birthplace. There are other pubs of this name in Nottingham, Derby, Tewkesbury, Birmingham and London E16, as well as a **Nottingham House** in Sheffield. Some of these no doubt refer to one or other of the earls of Nottingham.

Nottingham Castle Nottingham. Others at Kirk Hallam, near Ilkeston and London N1. The Nottingham inn sign depicts the original castle, begun by William the Conqueror in 1068. Inside the pub prints show the castle in various stages of construction. Elsewhere the castle is shown on signs as it is now.

Noughts and Crosses Polperro. The local story is that a bakehouse previously stood on this site. The lady who ran it somehow managed to keep her accounts by using an o for a loaf that was sold, crossing it with an X when it was paid for. Her shop became known as Noughts and Crosses.

Nova Scotia Bristol. Another at Airdrie. It was the Bishop of Bristol who arranged the Treaty of Utrecht, which ceded Nova Scotia to Britain. This Canadian province had formerly been part of Acadia. The sign shows a full-masted schooner ploughing through the icy waters of the North Atlantic.

Nowhere Plymouth. Plymouth Breweries itself explained this name in a letter as follows: 'When a husband was asked by his wife where he had been, and he did not wish her to know he had been to the pub, he could truthfully reply –

"Nowhere".' One would have thought that this joke would have worn thin very quickly.

Nuffield Arms Cowley, Oxford. William Morris, 1st Viscount Nuffield (1877–1967) was an industrialist and philanthropist. He was until 1952 chairman of Morris Motors. He gave large sums of money to Oxford University and endowed the college which bears his name. There is another pub named for him at Perivale, GL.

Number Names There was a period in the nineteenth century when it was easy to obtain a licence from the magistrates (rather than the Excise) to brew beer. In 1869 there were 134,000 licensed brewers in England and Wales. Today there are fewer than 200 brewers (who can offer their product for sale, that is). Licenses for beer-houses, during the peak period, were issued to numbered houses, some of which did not bother to name their premises in the traditional way. A few of these numbered houses, which have subsequently become legitimate pubs in every sense, survive. For all practical purposes, the number has become the name, one which can take various verbal forms as seen in the examples below: No 1, Southampton and Kelty, near Edinburgh; Number One, London EC1, Number One Vaults, Kirkgate, Wakefield; Number Three, Layton-with-Warbreck, near Blackpool; Ye Olde Number Three, Bollington, Ches; Number IV, Salford; Number Five, Hereford and York; Number Seven, Ledbury; Old Number Seven, Barnsley; No 10, Swansea (10 Union Street, not a reference to Downing Street); Number Ten, Liverpool,

(Elliott Street); Old Number Eleven, Scarborough and Hereford;
One and Three, Oldham (13 Manchester Street, but avoiding a direct reference to 'thirteen'); No 20 Vaults, Wakefield; One Five One, Great Yarmouth; One Hundred, North Shields. There was formerly a Big Eighteen at Newark and a Twenty-five at Northampton.

Nurseryman Beeston, near Nottingham. The pub is opposite the former site of Lowe's Nurseries. On one side of the sign the panama-hatted expert is holding aloft a pot of begonias; on the other he is tending his tomato plants. There is a Nursery at Heaton Norris, near Stockport and a Nursery Arms at Chichester.

Nut and Bolt Yattendon, Berks. The licensees here are John and Val Bolton, and their name no doubt suggested the pub name.

Nutshell Bury St Edmunds. The smallest pub in Britain. In March 1984 101 men and a dog managed to squeeze into it, while the local radio station gave a live running commentary on the event. The breed of dog is said to have been slightly uncertain beforehand and a total mystery afterwards. Bar-room conversation in this pub must be very much to the point, since everything that is said is 'in a nutshell'.

Nut Tree Murcott, near Bicester, Oxon. The locals say that a prolific hazelnut tree once grew in front of the pub. Passing children no doubt recite: 'I had a little nut tree, nothing would it bear/But a silver nutmeg and a golden pear;/ The king of Spain's daughter came to visit me,/And all for the sake of my little nut tree.'

O

Oak Leamington Spa and elsewhere. In some instances a simple reference to the tree, as in Oak and Ivy Burton-on-Trent and elsewhere, Oak and Saw Taplow Bucks (formerly frequented by wood cutters). There may be a link with a place name, as in Oakdale, Dors, less obviously in the Oak Tree, which is in the London suburb of Acton. 'Ac' is the Old English word for 'oak', so that the place name means 'oak settlement'. *See* British Oak, Heart of Oak for naval connections with the tree. *See* Royal Oak for names connected with Charles II and his adventure in the Boscobel Oak. The Oaks at Stenton, Loth refers to the race for three-year-old fillies first run in 1779. Other variations on the theme include Oak Beck, Harrogate; Oakfield, West Croydon; Oakhill, Beckenham; Oak Leaf, Barnsley; Oakleigh, Sale, Ches; Oak Tree Root, Howe Bridge; Oak Vaults, Hull; Oakwood, Eastwood, Glos; Oakwood Mill, Bream, Glos.

Oak and Acorn Taunton. This town was a Royalist stronghold during the Civil War. There is therefore a tradition that the pub name alludes to Charles II (*see* Royal Oak), the 'acorn' referring to his chances of regaining the throne and 'sprouting' again.

Oak and Black Dog Stretton-on-Dunsmore, Coventry. Probably an amalgamated sign, created by a landlord who moved from a Black Dog inn to one called the Oak or vice-versa, and hoped to retain his previous customers. Some commentators insist on seeing an anti-royalist allusion to Charles II, claiming that he was known to his detractors as 'The Black Dog' because of his swarthy appearance, but evidence for this is not forthcoming.

Oast House Icklesham, E Ssx. The kiln used for drying hops or malt, both of which are used to make beer. Names of this type are very rare in the county where they might be expected – Kent. *See* Hop Pocket.

Occupations We have found references in British pub names to over 400 different occupations, either in a form such as Florist, as at Portsmouth, Hop Picker at London E2, etc, or as

275

Brushmaker's Arms, Upham, near Southampton, Fewsters Arms, Bradford, etc. Apart from those guilds and liveried companies such as the Distillers and Goldsmiths, who do have armorial bearings, the word 'Arms' is often added to an occupational description almost as if it meant 'pub frequented by'. Thus one finds names like Coalheavers Arms, Peterborough, Dyers Arms, Leek; Ropemakers Arms, Exeter, and so on. Amongst this solid representation of the nation's industrial life, past and present, there is the occasional exotic reference, eg to a Toreador at Birmingham, where the pub is in the Bull Ring Centre, and to a Snake Catcher at Brockenhurst in the New Forest, or a Welsh Bard at Neath. Women are very rarely mentioned specifically, though there is a Witch at Lindfield, W Ssx. There was a Three Washerwomen at Norwich, but even that has now disappeared.

Octavian Crakehall, N Yorks. The name of a famous racehorse, winner of the St Leger in 1810.

O'Connell Arms *See* Daniel O'Connell.

Oddbottle Hull. Probably inspired by an oddly-shaped bottle which could be displayed to customers. At Wembury there is a similar Odd Wheel. Oakham has an Odd House, Edinburgh an Odd Spot, though the latter probably has more to do with the slang phrase in which 'spot' means a 'drop of liquor, especially Irish whiskey', than with the pub's location. In Ashton-under-Lyne the Odd Whim was no doubt that of the original landlord in taking on the pub.

Oddfellows Arms Stratford-on-Avon and elsewhere. Several pubs bear this name, which originally referred to the Independent Order of Oddfellows (Manchester Union), a social and benevolent society with branches throughout the UK and in many other countries. Active since the early nineteenth century, and said to derive its name from a remark made about the founding members. The Odd Fellows at Stratford-upon-Avon has two signs which interpret the name in a Shakespearian context, depicting four 'odd' characters from the plays. Falstaff is paired with Bottom the weaver; Shylock with Touchstone the jester.

Odessa Coombe Hill, Tewkesbury. Named in 1854 when this Black Sea port was being bombarded by the British and French fleets in the Crimean War. Also Odessa Arms, London, E9.

Offa's Dyke Broughton, Deeside. The defensive earthwork which runs along the England-Wales border, probably built by order of Offa, King of Mercia in the eighth century, in an attempt to protect his kingdom from the Welsh.

Oily Johnnie's Winscales, Cumb. Commemorating a former licensee who sold paraffin oil as a sideline.

Old We have in our records over 500 different pub names which begin with *Old* or Olde (also Ye Old, Ye Olde – *see* Ye). Many of these names are treated individually below, but in the majority of cases we would simply have been duplicating names had we dealt with both a name and that same name prefixed by *Old*. If the name you are looking for is not below, try looking for it in alphabetical order without the *Old* or *Olde*. The word is used in pub names for various reasons. It can describe a genuinely very old pub, or refer to an old person whose name has been given to the pub. It is frequently used in the sense of 'former'. The Old Albion was a ship called the *Albion* that formerly existed. The Old Mint is a place which was formerly connected, rather loosely, with a mint. Sometimes a pub is built on the site of one which was demolished and takes the name of the former pub in an act of commemoration. The Old Bull or whatever in such cases simply refers to a Bull which was once here. Old is also frequently used in an affectionate way, as in terms of address. 'Old boy' and 'old girl' are friendly expressions, if outdated, which are meant to indicate familiarity, not make a comment on someone else's age. In the well-known song, the line 'down at the old Bull and Bush' was probably meant in that way, ie the pub name was Bull and Bush, not Old Bull and Bush. Finally, the word old is often used in a pub name for purely advertising purposes. As our late friend John Leaver once put it, the idea is 'to instil an atmosphere of bygone days into the minds of the patrons'. In such cases *Olde* is likely to be used. The superfluous final 'e' is simply a reflection of times when spelling had not yet become standardised, so that the same word could appear in a variety of forms. *Olde* is not an older variant of *Old*, simply a variant that was found in former times but would be considered an illiterate mistake today.

Old Airport Tremorfa, Cardiff. The sign shows an old biplane flying over the civic airport.

Old Albion Crantock, Corn. The name was originally for a locally-built schooner, but the sign shows HMS *Albion*, a ninety-gun warship built at Plymouth in 1842. The Royal Navy has since had other ships of this name, including an aircraft-carrier.

Old Barrel *See* Barrels.

Old Beams Ibsley, Hants. The pub is based on a pair of fourteenth-century cottages and incorporates the old beams mentioned in the name.

Old Bell and Steelyard Woodbridge, Sflk. The steelyard referred to in the name is attached to the front of the pub, and recalls the days when the publican offered the services of a public weighbridge as well as serving drinks. The weight from the steelyard has been removed for reasons of public safety, but the contraption still works.

Old Berkeley Hunt Watford. The name of a fox-hunt established in the eighteenth century. The kennels are near Aylesbury and the hunt extends over country in Buckinghamshire and Hertfordshire.

Old Bill London W7. A famous cartoon character created by Captain Bruce Bairnsfather in World War One. He was a walrus-moustached veteran of the Flanders mud. Typical was the cartoon which showed Old Bill with another soldier under fire in a waterlogged shell hole, with Bill saying: 'Well, if you knows of a better 'ole, go to it!'

Old Boots London WC1. There was a famous 'boots', a man who cleaned customers' shoes and boots, at Ripon in former times, who was known as *Old Boots*. His fame rested on the fact that, thanks to a longer than usual nose and chin, he could hold a coin between them. Nowadays the expression indicates durability, someone who is as 'tough as old boots.'

Old Bull *See* Bull.

Old Bull and Bush London NW3. The pub has a bar named for the music-hall singer Florrie Ford, who made Harry Tilzer's song about this pub so famous. Florrie invited her audiences to 'Come and make eyes at me' and 'have a drink with me, down at the Old Bull and Bush.' The word 'old' in the song was used in its affectionate sense, just as a man might address a friend as 'old man', without having his age in mind. There has been a natural tendency to include it in the pub name, which commemorates the fact that the inn was once a farmhouse by means of the 'bull'. William Hogarth, the painter, was a later owner who planted a garden there, from which the 'bush' may derive, but a bush in any case been a tavern sign since Roman times. The tribe of ingenious etymologists have nevertheless been at work with this name, pronouncing it a corruption of Boulogne Bouche. This translates as Boulogne Mouth, said to be the origin of the Bull and Mouth, formerly at Holborn, which might have been the Bowl and Mouth, indicating that food was available. The Boulogne Bouche explanation of Bull and Bush is as absurd as the derivation of Shakespeare from Jacques-Pierre, another explanation foisted on us by those who seem to believe that English is merely French badly spoken.

Old Cat *See* Cat.

Old Cellars Tenterden, Kent. The premises were formerly those of a wine merchant. The old cellars and barrels are still there.

Old Circus London N17. The interior of the pub has a circus theme.

Old Clink Callington, Corn. The one-time local lock-up, built to accommodate two persons, is opposite the pub. 'Clink' was originally the slang name for a particular prison in London SE1. By the eighteenth century it had become the general term for a small place of detention. The name recalls the sound of chains which were attached to the ankles of prisoners in former times.

Old Coastguard Mousehole, Corn. The Coastguard Service began as an anti-smuggler force. It now performs general police functions in coastal waters.

Old Cock Droitwich. Others at Harpenden and London EC4. The Droitwich sign shows a Silver Grey Dorking cockerel. The caption says: 'The oldest English breed, dating from Roman times'. *Old Cock* has the advantage of sounding a friendly name, mates having addressed each other in this way since the eighteenth century.

Old Comrades Wellington Heath, near Ledbury. The sign shows an old soldier in civilian dress, complete with medals, moustache and bowler hat.

Old Contemptibles Birmingham. A nickname of the British Expeditionary Force which fought at Mons in 1914. The soldiers themselves adopted the name when they were told that the Kaiser had referred to 'General French's contemptible little army', which may or may not be true. The surviving veterans of the BEF held their last parade in 1974 in the presence of HM Queen Elizabeth.

Old County Cricket Ground Tavern Leicester. Also Old Cricket Ground, Sheffield. Pubs where the respective county players can get a few extras.

Old Court House Kingswinford, W Mids. The earls of Dudley formerly held their court leet here. This was a court held before the lord of the manor and attended by residents of the district. It appointed constables, aleconners and other local officials, but by the nineteenth century had virtually disappeared. The pub sign, which shows a Bill Sykes-type burglar in the dock, with top-hatted Peelers on either side, is therefore rather anachronistic.

Old Cricket Ground Also Old Cricket Players. *See* Cricket.

Old Crome Norwich. John Crome (1769–1821), the landscape painter who founded the Norwich School, was often called by this name. He had a son John Bernay Crome (1794–1842) who painted in a very similar style. The name was chosen by means of a competition run in the *Evening News*, and was especially appropriate. Crome was born in a pub and painted several local inn signs in his day.

Old Crown Hayes, GL. The sign shows one of the old crown coins, so-called because they were stamped with crowns. The last coin of this name was worth five-shillings, or twenty–five modern pence.

Old Crutched Friars London EC3. A corrupt form of 'Crossed Friars', Friars of the Holy Cross, who had a small monastery nearby. They wore a red cross on their habit and carried a silver cross before them. The word 'crutch', meaning the support used by someone who is crippled, also derives from Latin *crux* 'cross', being shaped with a crosspiece, but there is no truth in the ridiculous story that the Crutched Friars were themselves all crippled.

Old Deanery *See* Dean and Chapter.

Old Duke Bristol. Originally named for the Duke of Wellington, now for 'Duke' Ellington, Edward Kennedy Ellington (1899–1974), the famous black American jazz musician. The pub has become a jazz mecca because of the interest of the licensee.

Old Dungeon Ghyll Langdale, Cumb. The sister of the poet William Wordsworth, Dorothy, kept a journal when she lived in this part of the world. She noted that a 'ghyll' was a 'short and, for the most part, narrow valley, with a stream running through it.' The Journal also refers to 'those fissures or caverns, which in the language of the country are called dungeons.'

Old Ebor York. *Ebor* is the Latin name for city of York; *Old Ebor* was the name of a racehorse.

Olde Lancaster Desford, Leicester. This name looks back to two previous names, Flying Lancaster and Lancaster Arms. The latter name was the first, and was a reference to the land belonging to the duchy of Lancaster. A later landlord had flown a Lancaster bomber during World War Two. He changed the name and sign, which then showed aircraft VN-N of 50 Squadron, the plane he had piloted.

Oldenburg *See* Grand Duchess.

Olde Tippling Philosopher Caldicot, near Chepstow. 'To tipple' originally seems to have meant to sell drink, especially strong drink, to the public. It quickly took on its sense of drinking strong drink. Today the word 'tippler' suggests someone who drinks constantly but never quite gets drunk. This pub name could refer to a philosophical inn keeper, though a reference to the famous philosophers Plato and Socrates has been suggested. They were hardly 'tipplers', but are said to have been fond of wine in moderation.

Olde Watling London EC4. A reference to Watling Street, a famous Roman road which began at Dover and ran through Canterbury, London, St Albans, Dunstable to Wroxeter.

Old Father Thames London SE11. Alexander Pope refers to Father Thames in 1704. He seems to have been the first to use the phrase. The Americans in their literature sometimes refer to the Mississippi as 'father of rivers'. 'Old Father Thames' became the subject of a popular song, telling us that 'Kingdoms might come, and kingdoms might go, but old Father Thames keeps rolling along, down to the mighty sea.' This pub looks on to the river.

Old Folks at Home Tonbridge. The pub name borrows the title of a song by Stephen Collins Foster (1826–64), the writer of many highly successful songs amongst his total output of 175 numbers. He was also responsible for the *Camptown Races, My Old Kentucky Home, Poor Old Joe, Beautiful Dreamer* and *Jeanie With the Light-Brown Hair*. According to him, the old folks lived on a plantation, 'way down upon the Swanee Ribber'. The inn sign here shows a pig sty and its occupants. It seems to be a joke that some would consider offensive in the extreme.

Old Ford Llanhamlach, near Brecon. A simple name, imaginatively illustrated on the inn sign. On one side a vintage Ford car is crossing a ford; on the other a smart young fellow in morning coat and topper is wading across the ford with a young lady in his arms.

Old Fourpenny Shop Warwick. Originally the Warwick Tavern, but the name now reflects a time when the navvies working on local canal and railway cuttings could buy a number of refreshing items here, all at a cost of fourpence. The sign shows four Victorian 'bun pennies', and is based on brass-rubbings from actual pennies which were photographed, then enlarged.

Old Friar Bridgnorth. The sign shows a cheerful monk tapping a cask in the cellar. Beneath him are the lines: 'I am a friar of Orders Grey/ Who lived in the Friary over the way./Though my Friary's gone I still have cheer:/Come in and taste our excellent beer./Yet still be temperate with the same – /Nor bring this house to evil fame.'

Old Gatehouse Oxford. On the site of a gatehouse where tolls were collected until 1868. The sign shows a highwayman jumping over the toll-gate, with an enraged toll-collector shaking his fist with rage.

Old General Hyson Green, Nottingham. After a local eccentric, Benjamin Mayo (1779–1843), an inmate of the workhouse. Twice a year he took it upon himself to review a parade of raggle-taggle schoolboy troops in the Old Market Square. The townsfolk tolerantly recognised him as 'Commander of some forces there/And intimate with Mr Mayor'. A statue of the general, who was less than five feet in height, stands above the pub entrance, showing him in scarlet coat and epaulettes.

Old Gresham London EC2. The pub is in Gresham Street. Both are named after a sixteenth century merchant, Sir Thomas Gresham (d 1579). He founded the Royal Exchange in London, which led to the City becoming the financial centre of Europe. He also founded Gresham College.

Old Grindstone Sheffield. The pub stands at the corner of a lane which leads to several former quarries, source of grindstones.

Old Hainault Oak Ilford, Esx. A reference to an ancient oak which once stood in Hainault Forest nearby. Part of this area was deforested in 1851.

Old Ham Tree Holt, near Trowbridge. A local landmark that was blown down in 1888; an elm tree which stood nearby at Ham Green.

Old Harry Poole, Dors. A local reference to two rocks which stood in the sea near Poole harbour entrance, known as Old Harry and his wife. The wife was washed away in the 1940s and Old Harry has himself almost disappeared. Perhaps, therefore, it is time to change the name of this pub, since Old Harry not only means 'the devil', but a composition used by vintners to bedevil their wine.

Old Hat London W13. The reference is to the Old Hats' Club, the world's first pigeon-shooting club, founded in 1777. In colloquial speech the phrase 'old hat' has come to mean something that is old-fashioned, or stale news, or something taken for granted. Huddersfield has an Old Hatte.

Old Hob Bamber Bridge, near Preston. When open coal fires were usual, the hob was a kind of metal shelf used to cook food or heat water. The inn sign here shows a roaring fire and a kettle on the hob.

Old House at Home Burton, near Chippenham and elsewhere. A once-popular ballad gave rise to this name. It was a kind of 'Home thoughts from abroad' of soldiers. The Burton sign shows on one side a soldier dreaming of home; on the other side he is on his way home. At Chichester an English and Scottish soldier are enjoying a pint outside an old thatched inn. At Edenbridge, Kent, the jokey sign shows a pig with pipe in mouth leaning over his sty.

Old Jack Calverhall, Salop. At one time a 'jack' was a general term for a leather beer jug, coated on the outside with tar, and more specifically called a 'black-jack'. In this instance the reference is to a specific jug which was lined with horn and silver mounted. It was produced at village celebrations in Calverhall, when it became everyone's ambition to drain it with a single quaff. It was kept at this inn, but disappeared about 1860.

Old Justice London SE16. There was an eighteenth-century inn here called Justice in the Mint, perhaps an ironic reference to the debtors, thieves and others who traditionally found some kind of sanctuary in the area known as the Mint.

Old King Stockport. This was formerly the King George IV but its regulars constantly referred to it as the *Old King*. The nickname became official in 1975.

Old King Cole *See* King Coel.

Old King John Also Old King John's Head. *See* King John.

Old King of Prussia London N3. This pub was the King of Prussia until 1915, but references to Germany were not acceptable during World War One. The pub became the King George V. Some time after the end of the war it took on its present name.

Old Leather Bottle Also Old Leather Bottel, Old Leathern Bottel, Old Leathern Bottle. *See* Leather Bottle.

Old Man and Scythe Bolton. Also Man and Scythe, Kearsley; Cross

Scythes, Bolton. The *Old Man and Scythe* sign was originally Old Father Time, but the sign was later altered to show a jester with a scythe. The allusion was to Sir William Trafford, a wealthy landowning royalist in the seventeenth century. When he was told that Cromwell's troops were about to visit him, he hid the family treasures under some straw, disguised himself as a rustic, and was found by the troops making sweeping movements in the air with a scythe. They believed they had come upon the village idiot and left him alone.

Old Mill Baginton, near Coventry. A converted mill, where the massive mill wheel can be seen through a glass screen which fills an interior wall.

Old Miller of Mansfield *See* Sir John Cockle.

Old Mint Southam, near Leamington Spa. Charles I stayed in this fourteenth-century building after the battle of Edgehill in 1642. He ordered the local nobility to bring their silver so that it could be melted down and made into tokens, for the payment of his troops.

Old Mitre Tavern London EC4. The pub was built in the sixteenth century by the bishop of Ely for the use of his palace servants. *See also* Mitre.

Old Monken Holt Barnet. This whole area has long associations with monks of one kind or another. High Barnet once belonged to the Abbey of St Albans; Friern Barnet to the Knights of St John of Jerusalem. A 'holt' is a small wood, and no doubt it belonged to and was used by monks. Local tradition says that it was a hiding place for monks, but 'holt' in that sense is used of animals, as in Otters' holt.

Old Nelson *See* Lord Nelson.

Old New Bourton-on-the-Water, Glos. Another at Laxey, Isle of Man. The Bourton pub was entirely rebuilt in 1935. The name was chosen to recall the old pub while acknowledging the new one.

Old Number Eleven Also Old Number Seven, Ye Olde Number Three. *See* Number Names.

Old Nun's Head London SE15. The pub is at Nunhead Green, itself named after the original Nun's Head, or Nun as it seems to have been. There are records of several such signs in London, and there is no reason to believe the stories of a beheaded nun which supposedly gave rise to the name.

Old Oak London NW7. This was formerly the Gospel Oak, referring to a nearby tree which marked the boundary between Highgate and Hampstead. During the annual 'beating of the bounds' procession a reading from the Bible would take place when the oak was reached.

Old Packet House Broadheath, near Altrincham. 'Packet' here is short for 'packet-boat', one of which is shown on the sign. Packet-boats ran regular services, carrying mail, goods and passengers.

Olde Parish Oven Thorpe Salvin, near Worksop. The pub itself dates from 1972, but it was built on the site of an oven which served the whole parish. The oven door has been built into a small fireplace inside the pub.

Old Parr's Head London W14. Another at London N1. Also Parr's Head, London NW1. There was formerly an Old Parr at Gravesend and another at Rochester. 'Old Parr' was the name by which Thomas Parr was known in the later stages of his long life. He was reputedly born in 1483, but this cannot be proved. It is certain that he died in 1635. If his birthdate was correct that would have made him 153 years old. He was old enough to attract the attention of the Earl of Arundel, who took him to the court of Charles I. He was a Shropshire farm-hand who married for the first time at eighty, it is said, and for the second time at 120. Almost inevitably, he is said to have fathered a child by his second wife, but all that can safely be said is that he was genuinely a very old man when he died, and had become something of a celebrity.

Olde Pipemakers Rye, E Ssx. The pub displays a fine collection of pipes. The very first tobacco-pipes appeared at the end of the sixteenth century. (Bramber, W Ssx, has a pipe museum.)

Old Pomona Newcastle-under-Lyme, Staffs. Pomona was the Roman goddess of fruit and its cultivation. Latin *pomum* means 'fruit' or 'apple'. Sheffield has a Pomona.

Old Pond Hove Edge, Brighouse. The pond was opposite the pub. It is said to have been used for the usual seventeenth century sport of ducking unfair tradesmen, scolds and the like.

Old Raglan *See* Lord Raglan.

Old Rangoon Clifton, near Bristol. This was the Dog and Duck until 1984. Rangoon is the capital and chief seaport of Burma. 'Old' Rangoon presumably refers to the time in the nineteenth century when it was taken by the British (1834 and again in 1852).

Old Rectifying House Worcester. In the nineteenth century this term was used of a place where water was rectified, or purified, for public consumption.

Old Roof Tree Middleton, near Morecambe. This pub was converted from an old farmhouse, one wing of which was known as Roof Tree Cottage. A tree had grown up through the roof. Part of its trunk may still be seen embedded in the wall.

Old Rose *See* Rose.

Old Rosins Darwen, Lancs. In his *Inns and Inn Signs*, Charles Robert Swift quotes a 'once popular ballad *Old Rosin the Beau*'. The opening words of this song were: 'I have travelled the wide world over,/And now to another I'll go,/I know that good quarters are waiting,/To welcome old Rosin the Beau.'

Old Sal Longton, near Stoke-on-Trent. A nickname for the Mossley Colliery at nearby Adderley Green.

Old Scarlett Dogsthorpe, near Peterborough. Sir James Yorke Scarlett (1799–1871) was an English major-general who served with distinction with the Heavy Brigade at the Battle of Balaklava (1854).

Old School House Ockley, Sry. The original school house dated from the seventeenth century. It was converted into a pub in 1965. The sign shows a cap-and-gowned schoolmaster armed with a cane. The name of the pub is chalked on his blackboard.

Old See-ho Shorne, near Gravesend. 'See-ho!' was the cry which indicated that a hare had been seen during coursing, the sport of chasing hares with greyhounds. London's Soho derives its name from a similar huntsman's cry.

Old Sergeant Enfield. The inn sign is based on a portrait of Sergeant Arthur Stevens, a Chelsea Pensioner. Sergeant Stevens served in the Seaforth High-landers. There is another pub of this name at London SW18.

Old Seven Sisters London N15. Seven elm trees were responsible for the pub name and name of the district. They are mentioned on a map of 1754 and stood at the corner of Seven Sisters Road, near Page Green.

Old Sheer Hulk London SE18. A reference to the hulk or body of a disused ship which is fitted with shears – hoisting tack. The spelling used in the pub name is usual, but 'Shearhulk' would be more correct. The hulks near Woolwich were used to house French prisoners–of–war in the Napoleonic wars.

Old Slipper Shrewsbury. The reference is to the man who 'slipped' or released the grey-hounds at coursing matches.

Old Smiddy Pencaitland, East Lothian. The English equivalent of this name is found at Welcombe, near Bideford, in the **Old Smithy**. Both refer to a blacksmith's workshop.

Old Smuggler Whitby. Also Old Smugglers, St Brelade, Jersey. Another at Alfriston, E Ssx, where the pub was once the home of Stanton Collins, leader of a local gang of smugglers. He seems to have been successful in that role, but was hanged for sheep-stealing.

Old Spot Daybrook, near Nottingham. Another at London E7. The name of a racehorse owned by the Duke of Newcastle, who owned land in the Nottingham area.

Old Stingo Liverpool. Also Old Stingo Vaults, Liverpool. Stingo was originally a slang term for strong ale or beer. It was used as a trade name by several breweries for a potent barley wine. In the past it would have been served when stale and flat after long maturation.

Old Stocks Loudwater, near High Wycombe. The stocks were the well-known instrument of punishment used to humiliate delinquents in former times. The victim's ankles, and sometimes his wrists as well, were confined between planks, keeping him in a very awkward sitting position. They would originally have been made of stocks, ie tree trunks stripped of their branches.

Old Success Sennen Cove, Corn. The name has been variously explained as referring to prosperity brought to the village by the Pilchard Seine Net Company, which set up here and recruited crews in the inn, and as a reference to the joining of Atlantic sea cables to land lines.

Old Tanyard Merthyr Tydfil. 'Tanyard' is another word for 'tannery', a place where skins are converted into leather.

Old Thatch Hoden's Cross, near Wimborne. Another at Broughton, Humb. Also Old Thatched Inn, Ilfracombe; Old Thatched House, Shirley, near Southampton. Simple descriptions which have been given name status.

Old Tom Oxford. The famous bell of this name, which commemorates Cardinal Thomas Wolsey, founder of Christ Church College, is in the college clock tower, almost opposite the pub.

Old Trafford Manchester. For the cricket ground of this name, home of the Lancashire County Cricket Club and scene of many a memorable test match.

Old Tramway Stratford-on-Avon. The horses used for the horse-drawn tram service to Moreton-in-Marsh were once stabled here. The pub was earlier known as the Old Railway.

Old Transporter Halton Brow, near Runcorn. There was formerly a transporter bridge here which carried road traffic over the upper reaches of the river Mersey.

Old Tup Gamesley, near Glossop, Derbs. A 'tup' is a male sheep, a ram. The expression is mainly used in the North and in Scotland.

Old Vic *See* New Vic.

Old Vine *See* Fruits and Vegetables.

Old Volunteer Carlton, near Nottingham. The reference used to be to an Old Contemptible (*see* **Old Contemptibles**), with the sign showing such a World War One soldier. The brewery decided on a new sign, put up while the landlord was on holiday. It shows a soldier peeling a huge pile of potatoes as part of his fatigue duty. The landlord was not amused.

Old White Bull *See* Bull.

Old Wine Shades *See* Wine Barrel.

Ole Frank Oulton Broad, Sflk. The common heron is known in local dialect as the 'frank' because of its cry.

Olive Branch Canterbury. The olive was an ancient symbol of peace, hence the expression 'to hold out the olive branch'. Ultimately it is a reference to the story in Genesis, when the dove returned to Noah's Ark bearing an olive leaf, proving to Noah that the flood was subsiding. The scene is portrayed on the arms of the Shipwrights' Company, which seems to have inspired the Canterbury pub sign. In Ipswich there is a similar Olive Leaf. *See also* Dove and Olive Branch.

Oliver Bath. Dr W Oliver was a physician in Bath in the late eighteenth century. He invented a delicately flavoured hard dry biscuit, the Bath Oliver, which found favour with the Prince of Wales (later George IV). Dr Oliver left the recipe for his biscuit to his coachman, who set up in business to make and sell it.

Oliver Cromwell St Ives, Cambs and elsewhere. Also Cromwell, Hull and elsewhere, Cromwell's Head, Gloucester and elsewhere, Lord Protector, Huntingdon. Oliver Cromwell (1599–1658) was a military leader and parliamentarian who became lord protector of England in 1653. This followed the defeat and execution of Charles I. Opinions of him vary widely, though his military genius was not in doubt any more than his personal strength of character. His son Richard Cromwell was unable to follow in his footsteps. Some of the *Cromwell's Head* signs were reputedly celebrations of his death and the rapid restoration of the monarchy.

Oliver Twist Portsmouth and elsewhere. Usually because Charles Dickens had some kind of local connection, justifying the use of this well-known character. The pub of the name in London E10 puns on the fact that it is on a twist or bend in Oliver Road.

Omnibus Attercliffe, Sheffield and elsewhere. Also Omnibus and Horse(s). Horse-drawn omnibuses first appeared in the late 1820s and were novel enough to inspire pub names and signs. The name was further used when motor omnibuses replaced trams. 'Omnibus' actually makes a very suitable pub name because it means 'for all' in Latin.

On Broadway London. Situated on Broadway, NW7.

One and All Penzance. The motto on the Cornish county badge. *See also* Fifteen Balls.

One and Only Maidstone. This proud boast of uniqueness appears to be justified as far as its name is concerned.

One and Three Also One Five One; One Hundred. *See* Number Names.

One Bell *See* Bell.

One Bull Bury St Edmunds. The reference is to a papal 'bull', a document sealed with a bulla, or metal seal. In pre-Reformation times these bulls were solemn, official letters in which the pope issued his instructions to the Roman Catholic clergy.

One Elm *See* Elm.

One Five One Great Yarmouth. A simple number name, based on the address of the pub, 151 King Street.

199 London EC2. The pub at 119 Bishopsgate. Now the called White Hart.

One Tun London EC1 and W1. The 'tun' is a cask capable of holding 216 gallons. Three Tuns is more common, but there may be a pun intended on 'one ton', used in the popular pub game darts to indicate a score of 100.

Open Arms Coventry. A pleasant pun making use of a common pub-name element in order to suggest that a welcome is in store.

Open Hearth Corby, and the other steel town of Scunthorpe. A name which those in the steel industry would interpret in the technical sense of the open-hearth steel-making process. To others it would merely suggest domestic comfort around an open fire. *See also* Man of Steel.

Opera Tavern London. Situated near the Royal Opera House, Covent Garden.

Oporto Tavern London E14. Oporto is an important city and sea-port in northern Portugal. The wine which was shipped from there to England was at first called Oporto, later 'port'.

Ops Room Portreath, Corn. Premises which housed the Operations Room of the Royal Air Force's South-Western Command during World War Two.

Orange Brewery London SW1. This may merely have been something which was easy to illustrate on the inn sign, though it could have been prompted by Prince William of Orange, later William III, or by the famous orange-seller Nell Gwynne. The 'Orange' in Prince William's case refers to a French town which was earlier Arausio, meaning 'high place'. *See also* Nell Gwynn(e).

Orange Tree Hitchin and elsewhere. A fairly common name. The orange tree is said to have been introduced to England by Sir Thomas Gresham is the late sixteenth century. It would have had some novelty value as a pub sign.

Orchard West Huntspill, Som. A cider orchard is alongside the pub.

Ordinary Fellow Chatham. Named in 1935, when George V was celebrating his Silver Jubilee. The king was much moved by the cheering of the London crowds as he drove to St Paul's Cathedral and remarked to the Archbishop of Canterbury: 'I can't really understand all this; after all, I am only an ordinary fellow.'

Ordnance Arms Stibbard, Nflk and elsewhere. Once housed the troops who produced the first Ordnance Survey map of Norfolk. The London pubs which bear this name recall the purely military senses of 'ordnance', namely 'artillery', or 'the supply of military stores and materials'.

Organ Ewell, Sry and elsewhere. An early licensee made barrel-organs. This may also account for the similarly-named pub at Hollingworth, Ches.

Original Alfred Moodie's Wakefield. The pub occupies premises which previously housed a wine and spirits business. It was that business which represented Mr Moodie's first, or original, venture. The name was also clearly meant to convey the idea that he was an interesting individual.

Original Dog and Partridge Nottingham (until 1969). A reminder that there is no copyright law relating to pub names. This pub began as the Dog and Partridge. A pub immediately opposite then announced that it was the Old Dog and Partridge. The name battle then continued with the use of 'Original'. Many common pub names are found throughout the country with 'Original' added to them, suggesting that arguments have taken place about seniority. Some examples are Original Ball, Maesbury, Salop, Original Bay Horse, Horwich, Lancs, Original Oak, Leeds, Original Seven Stars, Leyland, Lancs, Original Swan, Cowley, Oxford. Original White Hart, Ringwood, Hants, Original Woodman, London SW11. In Fulwood, Lancs, it was even necessary for a pub to call itself Original Withy Trees (a type of willow). A Manchester pub appears to have forestalled any such arguments by calling itself simply the Original.

Orlando Bognor Regis. The name of one of Charlemagne's knights, of great stature and strength, much celebrated in medieval literature. He owned an ivory horn, Olifant, which could be heard for twenty miles. The horn features on the inn sign.

Ormonde's Head Tetbury, Glos. Named after James Butler, 1st Duke of Ormonde (1610–88). He accompanied Charles II into exile and was made lord high steward of England at the Restoration.

Osprey Nutbourne, Chichester. A bird which was once known in this area but now fights for its survival in Scotland. Another pub of the same name at West Howe refers to HMS *Osprey*, a Royal Navy Air Station which is at nearby Portland.

Ostler Uffculme, Devon. The ostler was the odd-job man of the coaching era, whose main job was to take care of the horses. The word is a corruption of 'hosteler'. There is another pub of this name in London E8, and an Ostler's Arms in Leeds.

Ostrich Colnbrook, near Slough and elsewhere. The original building was a 'hospice', a guest-house run by monks. The word is thought to have been corrupted into 'ostrich'. Another pub of the same name near Ipswich is based on the coat of arms of Sir Edward Coke (1552–1633), an eminent lawyer who became speaker of the House of Commons. He was the local lord of the manor.

Other Side of the Moon Toton, near Nottingham. Opened shortly after the launching of the Russian sputnik in 1959. *See also* Man in Space.

Otter Otterbourne, Hants and Ottershaw, Sry. There are obvious place-name links in both Otterbourne and Ottershaw. Otter's Head at Glenrothes, Fife makes use of the animal's distinctive shape to provide an easily recognisable sign name. Otter and Fish also occurs at Hurworth-on-Tees. Otter's Pool looks slightly out of place in modern Manchester.

Our Mutual Friend Stevenage. The Dickensian novel of this name appeared in weekly parts 1864–65. Perhaps the pub namers wanted to suggest that the pub was also full of interesting characters.

Outpost Barnsley. This name was used by the Kimberley Brewery because the pub concerned represented at the time the furthest point of their marketing activities.

Outrigger Kingston, Sry. Referring to the boats frequently seen passing this riverside pub. An outrigger was originally the iron bracket fixed to the side of the boat with a rowlock at its outer edge, so that the leverage of the oar would be increased. The name was then extended to a boat fitted with outriggers.

Overdraught Largs, Strath. A deliberate pun which manages to imply that too much drinking will lead to shortage of money. 'Draught' beer is 'drawn' from its barrel, but a 'draught' also refers to the quantity of liquid drunk in one breath.

Owain Glyndwr Corwen, Clwyd and elsewhere. In Salop, at Ford found in the English form Owen Glendower. Cardiff has a Glendower. The man concerned is a Welsh hero who led the last major revolt against the English. He was highly successful in the period 1401–06 but disappeared after a defeat in 1415.

Owd Betts Norden, Rochdale. A reference to a former landlady, 'old Betty'.

Owd Boots Nottingham. A modern renaming, referring to a collection of bric–à–brac, including various kinds of old boots, which is there to divert the customers. There was some objection to the name from Boots, the chemists, who have a superstore just around the corner.

Owl and Crescent Calshot, Southampton. From the arms of the Flying-Boat Squadron, later the Sunderland Squadron, stationed in the area in the 1930s.

Owl and the Pussy Cat Laindon, Esx. The conveniently easy-to-illustrate pair created by Edward Lear (1812–88). As is well known, 'they went to sea in a beautiful pea-green boat; They took some honey, and plenty of money, Wrapped up in a five-pound note.' A solitary Owl occurs in North London, while St Helen's has an Owl's Nest.

Ox Abingdon. In this instance there is a street-name link, since the pub is in Oxford Road. Pubs are often named after a particular prize-winning animal, or a special breed. Examples include Blackwell Ox, Sutton-on-Forest, near York; Castle Howard Ox, York; Fat Ox, Whitley Bay and Tenterden; Black Ox, Llandovery; Grey Ox, Hartshead, W Yorks; Ketton Ox, Yarn, Clev; Spotted Ox, Tockwith, near York; Swiss Ox, near Berwick, Ssx. Another street-name link occurs in London NW2, where the Ox and Gate is found in Oxgate Lane. Ox and Plough occurs more than once, while Ox Cart, Bretton, near Peterborough, Ox Lea, Shepshed, near Loughborough, and Old Ox, Shillingstone, Dors are further variants found mainly, for obvious reasons, in rural districts. *See also* Durham Ox, Garland Ox.

Oxford and Cambridge London W6. The annual boat race between the two universities passes under the nearby bridge. There was another pub of this name which changed to the Oarsman, perhaps to avoid a clash with the street name in which it stands, New Oxford Street.

Oxfordshire Yeoman *See* Yeoman.

Oxnoble Manchester. The name of a variety of potato which was popular in Lancashire, especially, in the early nineteenth century. A pub in Bolton also bears this name.

P

Pacific Liverpool. Another at Birkenhead. The Pacific Ocean was named by Magellan in 1520. He chose a word meaning 'peaceful' because his journey was one of calm seas and mild weather. *Pacific* has been used to name Royal Navy and other ships from time to time.

Packet Boat Bolton-le-Sands, near Lancaster and elsewhere. Also Packet, Dogdyke, near Coningsby; Packet House, Eccles; Paddington Packet Boat, Cowley Peachey, near Yiewsley. These are all references to the boats which were named for the packets of goods they carried on regular services, though they also carried the mails and passengers.

Pack Horse Egham, Sry and elsewhere. A reminder of the horses which carried packs of goods, such as corn and wool, in the days before canals, railways and the like, catered for bulk transport. Pack horses often travelled in trains of up to forty at a time. They would have been a familiar sight on the roads, and the men in charge of them would have been very regular customers at inns, seeking refreshment for themselves and the horses. There is a Pack Horses at St Blazey, Corn. Mapledurham, near Reading, has a Pack Saddle.

Pack Horse and Talbot London W4. Probably an amalgamation of two licences. It has been suggested that the talbot would have acted as guard dog to a traveller with a pack horse, but a talbot was used for hunting, not as a guard dog.

Pack of Cards Combe Martin, near Ilfracombe. The original premises here were built by a local squire named Lee in the late seventeenth century. The squire had won a fortune by gambling at cards. He arranged for the building to have four floors, thirteen doors and fifty-two windows. Originally his house, the *Pack of Cards* became an inn when he died in 1716.

Paddington Stop London W9. A halting place on the Grand Union Canal is meant. The pub has a canal-boat theme.

Paddle Steamer Cardiff. A boat propelled by a paddle-wheel.

Paddock West Molesey, Sry. The pub is close to a former racecourse, where horses still regularly graze. A 'paddock' at a racecourse is the small enclosure where the horses are assembled before a race.

Paddy's Goose Trealaw, near Tonypandy. Originally a nickname for a pub which was properly a Swan, White Swan, etc. The Trealaw pub sign shows a man (presumably Paddy) making off with a goose tucked under his arm.

Padwell Sevenoaks, Kent. The pub has a well in the cellar, fed with clear spring water, but the 'pad' in the name is no doubt the dialectal word for 'toad'.

Paganini Liverpool. After Niccolo Paganini (1782–1840), an exceptional virtuoso on the violin and composer of some violin concertos, caprices, etc. He toured Europe, coming to Britain in 1831–32 for a highly successful visit.

Pageant York. An early meaning of this word was 'the movable structure on which a miracle play was performed'. York is one of the

four towns where these medieval
religious dramas were presented.

Painted Lady Coventry. There was
formerly a pub of this name at
Harlow, where the town's pubs
have a moths and butterflies
theme. (The 'painted lady' is a
butterfly.) That pub has since
become the Jean Harlow. In
Walsall a proposal to use *Painted
Lady* as a pub name in 1959
brought immediate protests from
local prigs. The pub became the
Leather Bottle.

Palace *See* Silver Jubilee.

Palatine Manchester. Another at
Accrington. Lancashire is one of
the counties referred to as a county
palatine (others are Cheshire and
Durham) because it comes under
an Earl Palatine. Such an earl has
jurisdiction within a territory
which would normally belong to
the *palace*, ie the sovereign. Latin
palatinus means 'of or belonging to
the palace'. The Palatine Hill in
Rome had the palaces of the early
Roman emperors built on it.

Palm Beach Falmouth. There are
palms in the garden alongside and
the beach is nearby, but the name
obviously conjures up an image of
luxury because of the Palm Beach
winter resort in California.

Palmerston *See* Lord Palmerston.

Palm Tree Basford, near
Nottingham. The pub is in an
area where the street names
commemorate the Egyptian
Campaign of the 1880s. The pub
of the same name at North
Elham, near Canterbury had as its
first licensee a member of Captain
Cook's South Seas expedition,
who had no doubt seen many a
palm tree on his voyage and
perhaps hoped for palmy days in
his retirement. A third pub of this
name is at Woodnesborough,
near Sandwich.

Palomino Newmarket. Strictly
speaking this is neither a type nor a
breed of horse but a description of
a colour. A palomino is of a pure
gold colour with a flax or silver
mane and tail, and was perfected in
the USA by crossing thoroughbreds and Arabs of the required
colour on native stock. The word
means 'like a dove' in Mexican
Spanish. The sign here shows a
horse with a lady rider on one side
and a horse in a circus ring on the
other.

Panama Luton. One of the pub
names referring to Luton's hat-
making industry. Related names
are Blockers Arms and Boater.
The Panama hat was first made in
Ecuador but distributed to the rest
of the world from Panama.

Pandora Flushing, near Falmouth.
Also Pandora's Box, Bonby,
Humb. The Flushing pub was a
Ship until 1791. It was renamed by
Captain Edwards of HMS *Pandora*
who later ran his ship on to a reef
and sank it, for which carelessness
he was dismissed the service. His
ship, and the pub at Bonby, were
named for the Pandora of Greek
legend, the first mortal woman.
She had a box or casket filled with
all the evils which afflict mankind.
She opened the box and released
them upon the world, retaining
only Hope. (In another version of
the story the box contained all the
blessings of the gods, which were
lost when the box was opened,
only Hope remaining.)

Pandy Tonypandy. Another at
Dorston, near Hay-on-Wye. A
name to strike terror into a
schoolboy of the nineteenth
century, when a 'pandy' meant a
caning, but here a reference to
fulling, the process by which cloth
is cleansed and thickened by
washing and pounding it. The inn

sign at Tonypandy shows the process in operation.

Panniers Yelvertoft, near Rugby. Panniers were large baskets used for carrying foods of various kinds, such as bread, fish and fruit (Latin *panarium* 'bread basket'). Later they were specifically the baskets on either side of a saddle of a pack horse.

Panther London E2. Another at Reigate Heath, Sry. The panther is a leopard, especially a large, black one. In America the name is applied to the puma or cougar, occasionally to the jaguar. In Word War Two the name was associated with the German cruiser tank which weighed forty-four tons and had a speed of thirty mph.

Pantiles London NW10. A kind of curved roofing tile, such as are found at this pub. Schoolboys used to apply the term to jammy cakes. For a short time in the nineteenth century London itself was known jocularly as Pantile Park, because of its roofs covered with these tiles.

Papermakers Arms Tonbridge and elsewhere, especially in Kent. Also Paper Mills, Stamford and Wansford, near Peterborough. The papermakers could reputedly be recognised by their trembling hands in past times, a result of constantly agitating paper moulds. Torvill, near Maidstone has a Royal Paper Mill.

Parachute *See* Red Beret.

Paradise House Tunstall, near Stoke-on-Trent. Until 1982 there was also a pub of this name in Oxford, in Paradise Street. The name referred to the medieval fruit garden kept within the walled grounds of the Penitentiary Friars at St Ebbes.

Paraffin Lamp Livingston, Loth. 'Paraffin' was discovered by Baron

Karl von Reichenbach in 1833. He gave it this name because it had 'little affinity' with other bodies.

Paris Coverack, near Helston. The steamship *City of Paris* ran aground here in thick fog in 1890. It was salvaged and refurbished, then sold to the king of Spain for use as a royal yacht.

Parish Pump Weston-super-Mare. A reminder of the time when water had to be fetched from the pump that served the whole parish. The phrase was also used figuratively, as in 'parish pump politics', to refer to matters of local interest only. Here it clearly has a 'local' interest.

Park Exmouth. Another at Tottenham. These two pubs interpret the name in widely differing ways. At Exmouth the sign shows a couple of young lovers strolling through a park in Victorian times. They each have on riding costume, complete with top hats. The London sign shows a parking meter.

Parker's Vaults Shepton Mallet, Som. Thought to refer to Admiral Sir Hyde Parker, remembered especially for an order he gave that was ignored. When he signalled the retreat, Nelson clapped his eyeglass to his blind eye so that he could not see it and went on to win the battle against the Danes, 1801.

Parliament Oak Mansfield Woodhouse, Notts. The local tradition is that Edward I held a meeting of his nobles under the branches of an oak tree in Sherwood Forest. This happened in 1290, and gave the tree its name.

Parrot Shalford, near Guildford and elsewhere. Also Parrot and Punchbowl, Aldringham, Sflk. The parrot has long been recognised as a useful pub bird. It provides a sign-painter with a brightly coloured model, and amuses customers inside the pub with its mimicry. The modern phrase 'as sick as a parrot' is presumably a reference to psittacosis.

Parr's Head *See* Old Parr's Head.

Parson and Clerk Streetly, near Sutton Coldfield. The local parson and squire quarrelled violently at the end of the eighteenth century, eventually taking the cause of their dispute to court. The squire won the case, celebrating by setting up on the roof of the Royal Oak a caricature figure of the parson, head bowed as if in prayer. Behind him was his clerk, holding aloft an axe. The pub name commemorates the event.

Parson's Nose Melksham, Wilts. The reference is to the rump of a chicken or goose. The earlier term for a fowl's rump was 'pope's nose'.

Passage Dawlish. Passage House, Saltash and elsewhere. Most of these signs refer to places where it was possible to obtain a passage on a ferry.

Patch Box Bradley, near Bilston. This was a box in which a fashionable lady of the seventeenth or eighteenth century would keep the patches she wore on her face. The patches were made of black silk or court-plaster (ie sticking-plaster) and were cut into fanciful shapes, such as stars or half moons. They were probably worn originally by a royal personage to hide ugly facial blemishes, and continued to be useful for that purpose, but they also drew attention to the fairness of the wearer's complexion. Patches were usually worn by women, occasionally by men.

Patent Hammer Low Moor, Bradford. From a piece of machinery that was used in the nearby ironworks, established in 1791.

Pathfinder Maltby, near Rotherham. Also Pathfinder Hotel, Leeds. The Maltby sign shows the badge and motto ('We guide to strike') of the Royal Air Force's Pathfinder force. These were specially selected and trained pilots and navigators of bombers who dropped flares over a target area in World War Two.

Patna Plymouth. The name of an Indian town on the Ganges. In 1763 there was a revolt against the British. The local nawab ordered the massacre of many English residents. In 1857 several of the Sepoy regiments here took part in a mutiny. On the whole, not a place of pleasant associations from the British point of view.

Patriots Arms Chiseldon, near Swindon. The sign shows a Victoria Cross medal imposed on the silhouette of a tin-hatted soldier.

Patten Arms Warrington. Also Pattenmakers Arms, Duffield, Derbs. Pattens were a kind of overshoe. They consisted of a wooden sole mounted on an iron oval ring. By wearing them pedestrians were raised an inch or two above the mud and filth that would have covered the roads in former times. They were also useful in wet weather. John Gay referred in the eighteenth century to 'good housewives' who 'safe through the wet on clinking pattens tread'. The clattering noise that the pattens made gave rise to the phrase 'to run on pattens' where the meaning was to talk a lot and make a great noise.

Paul Jones Tavern Whitehaven, Cumb. John Paul Jones (1747–92) was born in Scotland but fought for the Americans in the War of Independence. He raided the Cumbrian coast and is said to have led a party ashore at Whitehaven. Naval historians have much praise for his capture of the *Serapis* in 1779. Jones later joined the French, then the Russian navy, where he achieved the rank of vice-admiral. The type of dance known as the Paul Jones, imported to Britain from the USA in the 1920s, was named in his honour.

Paul Pry Peterborough and else-where. The name of a play by John Poole, produced in 1825, with the title–character being a man who constantly meddles in other people's affairs because he has nothing to do himself. The play was popular, and signs often appeared in a town after its performance at the local theatre. Inn signs show Paul Pry listening at doors marked 'Private', etc.

Paviers Arms Oxford. Also Paviours Arms, London SW1. Both names are forms of 'pavers', the men who laid down paving stones. 'Pavier' was an early spelling, no longer used.

Pavilion London SW11. 'Pavilion' is used here in its original sense of 'tent', especially one used by royalty as a temporary head-quarters. The pub is said to be on the site of such a royal pavilion. The sign shows a uniformed Indian orderly standing outside it.

Pavilion End London EC4. A term used to describe one of the two 'ends' at certain cricket grounds. The pub has an old–time cricketing theme, with bar staff dressed in whites.

Pax Thorp Arch, near Wetherby, W Yorks. *Pax* is the Latin word for peace. In some parts of the country it is the word used by children when they want to drop out of a chasing game temporarily, the equivalent of 'Truce'. In public school slang the phrase 'be good pax' meant 'be good friends' from the late eighteenth century.

Paxton Arms London SE19 and elsewhere. Sir Joseph Paxton (1801–65) was an architect and gardener, mainly remembered for the Crystal Palace building at the World's Fair in London, 1851. He was knighted for designing it and superintending its building.

Peabody Arms London SE1. George Peabody (1795–1869) was an American financier and philan-thropist who made his fortune in London. He gave away large sums to various charities, doing much to help raise the standard of education in the American south. He also built blocks of flats for the poor in London.

Peace and Plenty Great Yarmouth. Others at Sittingbourne and Playden, E Ssx. Said to refer to a return to normality (or an idealised normality) with the ending of the Napoleonic wars in 1815. The phrase occurs in Shakespeare's *Cymbeline*, Act 5, scene 5, where there are references to Britain flourishing in peace and plenty.

Peacock Rowsley, Derbys and elsewhere. Also Peacocks, Torquay. This bird obviously offered great scope to sign-painters. It sometimes has a heraldic significance, as at Rowsley, where it links with the Manners family, earls and dukes of

Rutland. In some instances the reference may be to a family named Peacock. The surname would originally have indicated someone who was especially proud of himself. There is one example of a Peahen, the object of the peacock's magnificent display, at St Albans.

Peakstones Alton, near Cheadle. This term was sometimes used for millstones which had come from the Peak District.

Pearly King London E3. After the Cockney costermonger in his ceremonial dress, a suit covered entirely with mother-of-pearl buttons. There was fittingly a Pearly Queen at London E1, but it has now become the Hayfield Tavern.

Pear Tree Charfield, Glos. Suggested by the presence of such a tree, or an indication that perry, a drink like cider, only made from pears instead of apples, was for sale.

Peat Peat Inn Cross, Fife. Also Peat Pitts, Ogen, near Halifax; Peat Spade, Longstock, Hants. Peat is partly decayed vegetable matter, decomposed by water. It is dug out of peat bogs and used for fuel, or as manure.

Pebble Ridge Westward Ho, near Bideford. A reference to the protective barrier around the low-lying farmlands, often flooded at the season of high spring tides.

Peckett's Flyer Fishponds, Bristol. This pub was the Railway until the 1960s. When Peckett's locomotive works were closed – the works being named for Samuel Peckett, an engineer who invented a type of saddle-tank locomotive – the pub changed its name. The inn sign shows one of his engines which is in the Bristol Industrial Museum.

Pedestrian Northampton. Also Pedestrian Arms, Carlisle;

Pedestrians Arms, Brighton. Such pubs should sell obviously Walker's Mild or Bitter, but the Walker pubs are mostly on Merseyside.

Pedigree Oswestry, Salop. A reference to the pedigree animals sold in the local cattle market.

Peel Blackburn and elsewhere. Also Peel Arms, Bolton; Peels Arms, Padfield, near Glossop and Macclesfield; Peeler, Clifton Down, Bristol; Robert Peel, Watford; Sir Robert Peel, Chatham and elsewhere. Sir Robert Peel (1788–1850) was twice prime-minister, but is perhaps best remembered today for his act as home secretary in 1829 when he established the London police force. Early members of that force were known as Peelers or Bobbies in his honour. He himself was nicknamed Orange Peel early in his career, because of his hostility to Catholics. Sir Robert was thrown from his horse while riding in the park and died from his injuries a few days later. The various signs which commemorate him often show the peelers in their formal uniforms.

Peel Castle Peel, Isle of Man. The castle at Peel was originally called a 'peel', which means 'castle'. The place then borrowed the name from the castle. All this means that *Peel Castle* means 'castle–castle'. (With this one may compare the place name Penhill, where the Welsh *penn* has been added to Old English 'hill' to give a name meaning 'hill-hill'. A Penhill in Lancashire became Pendle, and had another 'hill' added to it, so that it is now 'hill-hill-hill'. The record is held by Torpenhow Hill, which means 'hill-hill-hill-hill'.)

Peeping Tom *See* Lady Godiva.

Peep o' Day Worcester. Eric Delderfield, in his *British Inn Signs*, singled out this name to describe it as 'attractive'. He was thinking of it in its sense of 'early dawn'. The name once had a far more sinister association, which Mr Delderfield did not mention. In the eighteenth century the Peep of Day boys were members of a Protestant organisation who visited the homes of Roman Catholics at dawn in search of arms. In some areas Peep of Day is a name for the Star of Bethlehem plant. It was also used in 1836 by Mrs T Mortimer as the title of a book, subtitled: 'A series of the earliest religious instructions the infant mind is capable of receiving'.

Peewit Astwick, Beds. Another name for the lapwing (where 'wing' was originally a word meaning to totter or waver, not the wing of a bird). 'Lap' derives from another word meaning to 'leap'. All this 'leaping' and 'tottering' refers to the bird's flight. 'Peewit' is an allusion to its cry, which sounds something like peewit.

Pegasus Southmead, Bristol, and elsewhere. The name of Bellerophon's winged steed in Greek mythology, it was adopted in World War Two as the insignia of all British airborne troops. At Southmead the name also refers to a type of aircraft engine built locally. Flying Horse is sometimes a variant of this sign, which Charles Dickens discovered as Pegasus's Arms. He remarks, in *Hard Times*, that 'the Pegasus's Legs might have been more to the purpose.' At Vange, near Basildon, Esx there is a Winged Horse.

Peg and Whistle *See* Pig and Whistle.

Peggotty's Great Yarmouth. Another in Leicester. After the faithful old nurse of the hero in *David Copperfield*, by Charles Dickens. In later life she becomes rather plump, so that 'whenever she made any little exertion after she was dressed, some of the buttons on the back of her gown flew off. She marries Barkis the carrier, who leaves her well provided for when he dies.

Peggy Bedford Longford, near Heathrow Airport. After a Victorian licensee who ran what was then the King's Head. She is said to have been a very popular lady.

Peldon Roşe *See* Rose.

Pelham Buckle Crawley, W Ssx. A reference to the silver buckles included in the arms of the Pelhams (dukes of Newcastle). They commemorate the capture of the French King John, at the Battle of Poitiers (1356) by John de Pelham. Immingham, Humb has a Pelham.

Pelican Bilborough, near Nottingham and elsewhere. After the distinctive-looking bird, which prompted one wit to write: 'The *Pelican* at Speenhamland/It stands upon a hill./You know it is the *Pelican*/By its enormous bill.' Some signs, however, show the ship in which Drake made his global voyage in 1577. He later changed its name to *Golden Hind*, an allusion to the coat of arms of his partner, Sir Christopher Hatton. This sign can also refer to the arms of Bishop Fox, founder of Corpus Christi College, Oxford.

Pembroke Yeoman *See* Yeoman.

Pen and Wig Nuneaton, Warks. The pub is adjacent to a firm of solicitors. Similar names include Pen and Parchment, Basingstoke and Stratford-on-Avon.

Penbeagle Croft St Ives, Corn. The pub is built on the site of a crofter's property on Penbeagle Hill.

Pendre Cilgerran, near Cardigan. The name is Welsh for 'top of the town'.

Pen Inn Newton Abbot, Devon. The sign shows a quill pen resting in an inkstand.

Penny Black London EC1 and elsewhere. The name of the first adhesive postage stamp, issued in 1840. It bears the head of Queen Victoria. The pub is close to the GPO's biggest sorting office at Mount Pleasant close by Sheffield's pub of this name is situated in the basement of the city's Head Post Office.

Pennycomequick Plymouth. Pennycomequick is a well–known Devonshire place name, originally the name of a farm. The name refers to the farm's profitability, brought about by good soil. It was recorded first in the seventeenth century and has nothing to do with Cornish words such as *pen y cwm wic*, as some would have us believe.

Pennyfarthing Oxford and elsewhere. A pub name that is 'catching on' in the 1980s. The Oxford sign is a pennyfarthing bicycle, named for its having one large wheel and one small wheel, like the old penny and farthing coins. The pub is in a street which has been called Pennyfarthing in one form or another since the Middle Ages, apparently because a town bailiff bore that name. In Nottingham the Colonel Burnaby was renamed in favour of the bicycle in 1982. Raleigh Industries, who now make 2,000,000 cycles each year began in nearby Raleigh Street in 1888.

Penny Pot Waltham, near Canterbury. From the middle of the nineteenth century, 'penny pots' in slang usage were the pimples that appeared on the face of a man who drank too much. The phrase seems to have had no other usage. The earthenware pots in which pennies were collected seem to have been restricted to Scotland, where they were known as 'penny-pigs', not because they were shaped like pigs, but because 'pig' or 'piggin' meant a very rough earthenware pot. Our modern piggy-banks have no doubt come about because the word was misunderstood. Fragments of these poor quality pigs or piggins, which became known as 'pigs and whistles', may have led, ultimately, to another well-known pub sign.

Pensioners Arms Southampton. One might have expected to find this pub in Chelsea, where the local football team has this nickname. The first licensee was presumably pensioned from the armed services.

Pepper Hill Manchester. After the peppermint plants which grew in this district in former times.

Perch Binsey, near Oxford. The common freshwater fish, shown on the sign. Inside the pub is a photo of the American submarine of this name, presented by the American Embassy to the landlord, himself an ex-submariner. South Stoke, near Wallingford, has a Perch and Pike.

Percy Hobbs Morn Hill, Winchester. The pub was formerly the New Inn. In 1982 it was renamed after a man who had been a regular at the pub for 62 years. Whitbreads think this to be the first pub named for one of its customers. The sign shows the gentleman concerned wearing his well-known cap.

Periscope Walney Island, Cumb. The pub has a periscope in working order, one that was used for training purposes. The Vickers shipyard at Barrow-in-Furness is not far away, breeding ground of many a nuclear submarine.

Periwinkle Wombwell, near Barnsley. The name refers to the creeping evergreen plant, or to the small sea animal now usually called the 'winkle' and eaten as a delicacy.

Perseverance Bedford and elsewhere. The Bedford example is in Bunyan Road and no doubt alludes to the author of the *Pilgrim's Progress*. John Bunyan certainly provided a good example of steadfast application to a particular aim, which the pub name suggests. Elsewhere there are inns which are named for the well-known stagecoach of this name. Others may be for HMS *Perseverance*, the name of a troopship in the 1850s.

Persevere Edinburgh. The name was suggested by the town motto of nearby Leith.

Pershore Plum *See* Plum Tree.

Pestle and Mortar Wantage, Oxon. Another at Grimsby. The 'pestle' is a club-shaped instrument used to pound substances in the 'mortar',
a vessel made of marble or something equally hard with a cup-shaped cavity in it. Together the pestle and mortar symbolise the pharmacist's trade, and were frequently used as the sign of a druggist. There is usually a reason for borrowing it as an inn sign, such as the take-over of a druggist's premises.

Peter Boat Leigh-on-Sea, Esx. A dredgerman's double-ended boat, which can be steered either way.

Peter de Wint Lincoln. Peter de Wint (1784–1849) was a fine painter of watercolours. He was born in Stone, Staffs, to Dutch parents and was associated with Lincoln through his marriage in 1810 to a local girl.

Peter Pan Dogsthorpe, near Peter-borough. The character created by James Matthew Barrie (1860–1937). The play was first produced in 1904. It caused floods of Peters to be named, and introduced the name Wendy, which Barrie invented when a young friend addressed him as 'friendy-wendy'.

Peter Tavy Peter Tavy, Devon. A reference to the church of St Peter by the river Tavy.

Petrol Station Pub Padbury, near Buckingham. The authors believe this to be the most boring pub name in Britain. *See also* Pumps.

Peveril Nottingham. A reference to William de Peverel, natural son of William the Conqueror, who commanded Nottingham Castle in 1068 after his father's conquest of Britain.

Peveril of the Peak Manchester. The name of a coach which ran between Manchester and London, though the coach in turn had clearly borrowed the name of the novel by Sir Walter Scott, published in 1823. The story is set in the time of Charles II. The title character is Sir Geoffrey Peveril, descendant of the natural son of William the Conqueror (*see* Peveril).

Pewter Pot Lewes, E Ssx. Another at Kimberworth, near Rotherham. Pewter is an alloy of tin and lead (usually). Pewter pots were formerly in common use, especially as beer tankards. They now tend to be collected for display.

Phantom Coach Canley, near Coventry. The pub is on an old coaching route between Coventry and Cheltenham. One night a coach left this inn and disappeared, never to be seen again, other than on the present inn sign.

Phene Arms London SW3. The pub is in Phene Street, named for Dr John Samuel Phené who leased a large house there in the nineteenth century. By the time he died in 1912 the house was full of architectural curios. Dr Phené was also an enthusiastic planter of trees in urban streets.

Philharmonic Liverpool. The best-known pub in this city, opposite the Philharmonic Hall. The pub was built at the turn of the century and is of great architectural interest.

Phoenix London N18 and elsewhere. The fabulous bird which every few 100 years or so sets fire to itself and emerges from the ashes to begin a new life. In some instances the pub name refers heraldically to the Seymours, dukes of Somerset. Others may recall the *Phoenix Theatre*, now called *Drury Lane Theatre*. In Harlow, Esx, the name is for the phoenix moth. At one time there were phoenix-men in London, in the employ of the Phoenix Insurance company. They seem to have been an early kind of fireman.

Piccadilly Caerwys, Gwent, and elsewhere. The famous London name is derived from 'piccadils', borders of cut work inserted on the edge of an article of dress. They were made nearby. The Caerwys pub takes its name from a racehorse which had borrowed it from London. In Caerphilly, M Glam, the choice of the name was no doubt inspired by the wish to have a *Piccadilly* in *Caerphilly*.

Pickerel Cambridge. Another at Stowmarket, Sflk. Also Three Pickerels, Mepal, near Ely. A pickerel is a young pike.

Picketty Witch Yeovil. A corruption of the Old English words for a 'piked wyoh-elm', piked meaning pointed. 'Witch' has long been an alternative spelling of 'wych'.

Pickwick Manchester and elsewhere. Samuel Pickwick is the chief character in *The Pickwick Papers*, by Charles Dickens, and one of that author's most popular creations. He is a benevolent old gentleman, chairman of the Pickwick Club. He wanders off with three of the club members and becomes involved in a series of loosely connected adventures. One or two of the pub signs show Sir Harry Secombe depicting this character.

Picton Also Picton Arms. *See* General Picton.

Pied Bull Enfield and elsewhere. For a bull of more than one colour. At Streatham the sign is a ceramic picture on the outside wall instead of the usual hung sign. Bulls used to graze on the common opposite. There is a Pied Calf at Spalding. Slough has a Pied Horse, a description usually applied to a horse which is basically white but has patches of other colour. The term has also been applied to a zebra.

Pied Piper Scunthorpe and elsewhere. The Pied Piper of Hamelin is a well-known story of events that are supposed to have taken place in the thirteenth century. He was a 'pied' piper because of his dress, which was chequered or of various colours, but perhaps the attraction of this name for pub owners (the name is becoming more common) is the joke on him being 'pied' in another sense – 'pie-eyed' or intoxicated.

Pied Wagtail London SE2. This looks like a name chosen by an ornithologist licensee, but it is highly suspicious. 'Pied' probably has its joke sense mentioned under

Pied Piper. A 'wag-tail', according to Eric Partridge's *Dictionary of Historical Slang*, was a term for a harlot. The actual bird does wag its tail, and there is an old superstition that when it alights it should wag it nine times before beginning to run about or feed. Should the number of wags be less or more, it is very unlucky for the person who is counting. It sounds like a story a 'wag' would invent, but it is recorded solemnly in *A Dictionary of English and Folk-Names of British Birds*. Like the dictionary mentioned above, this also had an avian author, H. Swann.

Pier Tavern Burnham-on-Sea, Som. The sign shows an old-time pleasure steamer tied up at the pier. The Royal Pier at Clevedon (another at Weston) refers to a royal visit in the past. Beaumaris, Anglesey, has a Pier Head; Cowes, IOW has a Pier View.

Pig and Whistle Littlehempston, near Totnes. This name is neither as common as is normally supposed, nor is it very old. When Lilley-white examined 17,000 London signs up to the nineteenth century he was unable to find a single example of *Pig and Whistle*. We estimate that in the 1980s about ten British pubs are so identified. The *Oxford English Dictionary* gives several examples of the phrase 'pigs and whistles', dating from 1681. 'To go to pigs and whistles' at one time meant 'to be ruined'. If going to pigs and whistles was going to ruin, and constantly going to inns was also going to ruin, then 'pigs and whistles' would be associated sooner or later with the inns. From there it would be a short step to naming an inn *Pig and Whistle*, first as a nickname, then as an 'official' name. Those not satisfied with such an explanation might like to play around with an association of 'pig', as in Sussex pig, a drinking vessel shaped like the animal, and expressions like 'wet one's whistle', meaning to 'have a drink', current since the seventeenth century. The bar-room etymologists tend to favour a derivation from 'peg o' wassail', an unrecorded phrase which would, if it had ever existed, mean something like 'a measure of good health'. Derivations from pyx and housel, pightle and wassail, piggens and whatever are not to be taken seriously. The visual image conjured up by this sign is pleasantly exploited in the Littlehempston sign. It shows a porker playing a penny whistle and dancing around, reminding us all not to take matters like this too seriously. At Helions Bumpstead, Esx, the licensee has made his own decision about this name and called his pub Peg and Whistle. Edinburgh has the delightful variant Pig and Thistle. *See also* Penny Pot.

Pigeon Pair Kingswood, near Reigate. A reference to boy and girl twins, from a belief that pigeons always produce two eggs, which in turn produce a male and female bird.

Pigeon Pie Sherburn-in-Elmet, N Yorks. A former delicacy.

Pig in Pound Romford. There is a local cattle market where pigs would be impounded. Pub no longer exists, we are told.

Pig of Lead Bonsall, near Matlock. An oblong mass of metal obtained by smelting is called a 'pig'. Compare pig-iron.

Pig on the Wall Droylesden, Manchester. The pub was built on the site of a farm. Some of its beams, and bricks from the piggeries, were used in the building.

Pig's Nose East Prawle, Devon. The name of a rock off the nearby headland, though the sign shows a real pig with a ring in its nose.

Pike Stoke-on-Trent. Also Pike and Eel, Cambridge and Overcote Ferry, near St Ives; Pike and Heron, Tinsley, near Sheffield; Pike and Musket, Walton, Som, and Tuffley, near Gloucester; Pike House, Berry Hill, near Coleford; Pike View, Bolton. The word 'pike' has at least three senses in pub names. One refers to the voracious fish found in rivers and lakes. A second meaning is 'pikestaff', a weapon consisting of a long wooden shaft with a pike, or spike, at the end of it. Pike also means a hill with a pointed summit, or a peak.

Pilchards Burgh Island, near Bigbury, Devon. Also Three Pilchards, Polperro; Pilchard, Newquay. The small sea fish allied to the herring, found in large numbers off the coast of Devon and Cornwall. The Burgh Island pub can only be reached on foot by walking over from Bigbury at low tide. *See also* Five Pilchards.

Pilgrim Much Birch, near Hereford and elsewhere. Also Pilgrim's Rest, Battle, E Ssx and elsewhere; Pilgrim's Bottle, Great Linford, near Milton Keynes. Pilgrims journeyed to various sacred places, such as Canterbury, where the tomb of Thomas à Becket was much visited. The hospices where they stayed overnight would originally have been religious houses.

Pilgrim Fathers Scrooby, Notts. It was a Puritan congregation from Scrooby which decided to migrate to America and eventually left Plymouth on the *Mayflower*. The term *Pilgrim Fathers* arose only at the very end of the eighteenth century but now applies specifically to those who founded the colony of Plymouth, New England, in 1620.

Pillar Box London EC1. The pub is very close to the headquarters of the Post Office. The sign shows a corner of an envelope with its stamp. Inside the pub is a framed display showing the history of the pillar box. Nearby there is a Royal Mail.

Pillar of Fire London NW4. This phrase occurs at Exodus 14:24 in the famous passage that tells of Moses leading the people of Israel through the Red Sea, the waters of which had parted before them. The Egyptians were in pursuit, but 'in the morning watch the Lord in the pillar of fire and of cloud looked down upon the host of the Egyptians'.

Pillar of Salt Droitwich. Another at Leftwich, near Northwich. Both names refer to a local salt industry, while recalling Lot's wife, turned into a pillar of salt when she looked back at Sodom. Pillars of rock salt in curious shapes are found near the Dead Sea.

Pillars of Hercules London W1. The two rocks which mark the entrance to the Mediterranean; one is the Rock of Gibraltar, the other is Mount Hacho. The ancients explained that they were originally one rock, but Hercules tore them apart so that he could get to Gades (Cadiz). There are several pubs, eg three in London, which honour **Hercules** himself. As Hercules or Heracles he is the most popular hero in the Greek and Roman legends, renowned for his extraordinary strength and courage. There is a Hercules Pillars at London WC2.

Pilot Exmouth and elsewhere. Also Pilot Boat, New Brighton, near Wallasey and Bembridge, IOW; Pilot Cutter, Blyth, Northld. All references appear to be for those who pilot some kind of boat or ship. The Exmouth sign shows the coxswain of the local lifeboat, Dido Bradford, who retired in 1971 after thirty-six years of service. The Pilot Cutter refers to a small boat used to guide a much larger one in difficult waters.

Piltdown Man Piltdown, near Uckfield, E Ssx. A reminder of a famous scientific fraud, which began in 1912 when Charles Dawson and Sir Arthur Smith Woodward announced that they had discovered the skull of a new genus of man at Pilt Down. It was not until 1953 that closer examination showed the jaw to be that of an ape, while the rest of the skull was that of a man. It is thought now that the hoax was deliberately planned to make Smith Woodward look foolish.

Pimlico Tram London SW1. The pub contains nostalgic memorabilia, including photographs of trams, maps, etc. 'Pimlico' is an interesting name because it is thought to have been the name of an inn keeper, Ben Pimlico, who lived in the area that now bears his name in the sixteenth century. His family name was first transferred to his inn, then to the district.

Pin and Bowl Wokingham. A reference to ninepins, or skittles.

Pindar of Wakefield London WC1. A 'pindar', or 'pinder', as it should be, was a keeper of a pound for stray animals. According to the Robin Hood legend, one of these minor officials, called George-a-green, who performed his duties in Wakefield, W Yorks, resisted Robin Hood and his friends Will Scarlett and Little John single-handed, when they attempted to trespass. The Elizabethan playwright Robert Greene wrote a comedy about the incident, which seems to have caught the popular imagination.

Pineapple Dorney, near Slough and elsewhere. There are several pubs of this name in the Manchester area, but it occurs elsewhere. The fruit was introduced to England in the seventeenth century and was no doubt a considerable novelty. Some pubs which bear the name were no doubt near fruit markets where they were sold.

Pink and Lily Parslow's Hillock, Bucks. The two flowers are shown on the sign. There is a similar Pinks at Shenley, near Radlett; Herts.

Pink Domino West Hartlepool. One meaning of 'domino' is the kind of half-mask worn at a masquerade, though the word really applies to the complete outfit.

Pink Elephant Stoney Stretton, Salop. One of the mythical animals one is supposed to see when under the influence of drink. There may be a connection with the Cockney expression 'elephants', short for 'elephant's trunk' and rhyming on drunk, though Julian Franklyn in his *Dictionary of Rhyming Slang* suggests that the pink elephants came first.

Pint Pot Sutton Coldfield. Also Pinters, Renton, near Glasgow; Pint 'n' Pie, Hanley, near Stoke-on-Trent. That authority on drinking matters, Sir John Falstaff, addresses the hostess of the inn as 'Pint-pot' in *Henry IV* Part One, perhaps reflecting general Elizabethan usage.

Pipe and Gannex Knowsley, near Liverpool. A reference to the pipe and Gannexcloth coat favoured by

Sir Harold Wilson. He was prime minister when this pub opened in 1968.

Pipers Dagenham, Esx and Ashcott, near Glastonbury. After the Dagenham Girl Pipers. The pub at Ashcott shows a Highland piper on its sign. It is said that James II sent Highland troops to the area to crush the Monmouth Rebellion. Kettering has a Piper.

Pippin Hereford. An apple of various varieties, often made more specific, as in Wyken Pippin, for an apple first grown at Wyken, near Coventry. The word is useful for pub namers, partly because of its pleasant associations, eg applied to a person who is thought to be rosy-cheeked and healthy as a term of address. Lord Byron addressed his wife in this way. There is also an in-built joke (as it were), made more obvious by the Pip Inn, Glasgow, and the Pipp Inn, Clayton-le-Dale, near Blackburn.

Pirate Penzance. *See* Gilbert and Sullivan.

Pit Laddie *See* Boldon Lad.

Pit Pony Easton, near Bristol. Another at Ashton–in–Makerfield, near Wigan. A reminder of the ponies that used to haul the coal-trucks underground.

Pitt's Head Coventry. Another at London E16. After William Pitt (1759–1806), known as William Pitt the Younger. His father had been the most popular statesman in England. Pitt followed him into parliament at the age of twenty-two, and was prime minister at the extraordinary age of twenty-four. He was renowned for his debating, and was a master of sarcasm, but it is said that those who listened to him were always more aware of the speaker than the message.

Place Names As a matter of policy we have ignored, with a few excep-

tions, pub names which are simply the names of the places where they happen to be. There is, for example, a Scole Inn at Scole, in Norfolk, and there are many hundreds of similar names. There are one or two instances where a place is named after an inn (Adrian Room's *Concise Dictionary of Modern Place Names, in Great Britain and Ireland*) but in the vast majority of cases the place name came first, and the pub simply borrowed that name. To have taken the matter a stage further and explained the origin of the place names in such instances would have made this a dictionary of place names instead of pub names. Those who are interested in that topic should consult the publications by county of the English Place-Names Society, which are held by most public reference libraries, or the *Concise Oxford Dictionary of English Place Names*, by Eilert Ekwall. For the names of major towns, readers would be well advised to consult the more up-to-date *Names of Towns and Cities in Britain*, by Nicolaisen, Gelling and Richards, published by Batsford, or *Place Names of Great Britain and Ireland*, by John Field, published by David and Charles.

Place Next Door Manchester. Seemingly a euphemism for 'pub', derived from: 'I'm just popping to the place next door'.

Plainsman Mapperley Plains, Nottingham. Another at Stanley, Dur. The Mapperley name was obviously inspired by the place name, but recalls the 1937 western film *The Plainsman*. It starred Gary Cooper as Wild Bill Hickok, James Ellison as Buffalo Bill and Jean Arthur as Calamity Jane.

Plaisterers Arms Winchcombe, Glos.

After the Worshipful Company of Plaisterers (1500), 'plaisterer' being an obsolete form of 'plasterer'. Plasterers Arms is actually more common as an inn sign, being found at Oxford, Warwick and in London. The Plaisterers have as a motto 'Let brotherly love continue'.

Plank, Hook and Shovel Holbeach Bank, Lincs, until 1960. The plank here was used to walk across the dyke, the hook was on the wall close to the front door, and from it was suspended a shovel. The latter was used to remove the horse dung that often collected in the lane when drivers of a pony-and-trap disappeared into the pub. The dung was transferred to a handy rhubarb patch.

Plant Doncaster. The pub is opposite the local locomotive works, referred to as 'the Plant'. This use of the word came from the idea of planting, ie establishing, a new industry in a place where there was none.

Plastic Paris *See* Firebird.

Plate of Elvers Longney, near Gloucester. 'Elvers' are young eels. The inn sign here shows a diner tucking into a plateful, his tankard of beer beside him.

Platform 1 Tavern Pannal, near Harrogate. Also Platform, Southampton. These are no doubt pubs that remain thankfully stationary when the world of someone who has drunk too much starts to spin around.

Playground Manchester. The word can be applied to any 'place of recreation'.

Playing Cards Playing cards often feature on pub signs. There is a Queen of Diamonds in Liverpool, a Queen of Clubs in Bristol, a Queen of Hearts in Edgware and a Queen of Spades in Boston. At Langwith Junction, Notts there is a King of Diamonds; Bloxwich, Walsall has a Knave of Hearts, while there is a Knave of Clubs at London E2 and elsewhere. There is an Ace of Spades at Oldham, and a punning Ace of Clubs at Ingoldmells. Skegness. Sometimes a name such as the King's Head or the Queens is illustrated on the sign by the appropriate quartet of cards. The Eight Kings at Portland shows two kings from each of the suits. A slight variation occurs in Jack of Trumps, March, Cambs. It is said that the Queen of Trumps at West Walton, near Wisbech was named in order to out-do the neighbouring King of Hearts.

Pleasure Boat Hickling, near North Walsham. The pub is in an area known for cabin-cruising on the Norfolk Broads.

Plimsoll Arms London N4. Also Plimsoll Ship, Hull. Samuel Plimsoll (1824–98) was a native of Bristol. It was while he was member of parliament for Derby that he managed to get through the Merchant Shipping Act of 1876. This caused a mark or line to be put on merchant ships to define the maximum load that could be taken on board. The ship, when fully loaded, must not sink below it. Before Plimsoll's time it is certain that the overloading of merchant ships had caused a great many accidents at sea, resulting in the loss of many lives.

Ploddy House Taynton, near Gloucester. Said to take its name from land which was swampy, making it necessary to plod through it.

Plough Oxford and elsewhere. This remains one of the commonest pub names in Britain, having been in regular use since at least the sixteenth century. Its alternative spelling Plow is still found. Apart from the farm implement itself, signs often show the group of seven stars in the Ursa Major constellation which have the shape of a primitive plough. In many places this name should offer a warning to university and other students not to spend too much time drinking, since a candidate who fails to pass an examination is said to be ploughed. That in turn presumably causes the candidate to have a furrowed brow. Associated names include a Plough and Furrow at Dereham, Nflk. Plough and Harrow, Epsom; Plough and Horses, Cove; Plough and Tractor, Great Knightley, Esx. At Great Burstead in Essex there is a Burstead Plough.

Plough and Sail Snape, Sflk. Another at Crossbush, near Arundel. The Alpha and Omega of farming are represented in this sign. The plough begins the whole process, preparing the ground for sowing; the windmill (represented by one of its sails) grinds the ripened corn. The Snape sign depicts the 'sail', however, as a sailing barge, one of those which formerly carried away the grain from the adjacent quay. The Crossbush sign has a pair of pictures, one showing a plough with a sailing ship, the other showing it with windmill sails. At Bristol there is a Plough and Windmill.

Plough and Shuttle Marsham, Nflk. In former times many people in this area combined agricultural work with weaving at home.

Ploughboy Burraton, near Saltash. Another at Lincoln. A reminder of the days when working on the farm filled what are now called schooldays. Culter, near Aberdeen, has a Ploughman.

Ploughshare Beeston, near Dereham, Nflk. The 'share' of the plough is the iron blade which does the cutting of the ground. It is allied to the word 'shear', as in to cut with shears.

Plume Also Plumes; Plume of Feathers. *See* Feathers.

Plummet Line Halifax. The ball of lead attached to a line which is used by builders, carpenters, and the like in order to ensure that the vertical line is true (from Latin *plumbum*, 'lead').

Plumpers Sheffield. 'Plumper' has various possible meanings, but is said to refer in this instance to the kind of outrageous lies or 'tall tales' that are sometimes told in bars.

Plum Tree Pershore, H and W. Pershore is famous for its plums, so much so that there is a Pershore Plum pub, at Winchester. London N1 has a Plums, on the site of a former fruit garden.

Pluto Corby, Northants. The name of the Roman god of the underworld. In World War Two it was the code name for the

pipelines which conveyed fuel across the English Channel for the Allied armies. This code name is an acronym from the initial letters of 'pipe line under the ocean'. Much of the pipeline was constructed in Corby's steelworks. There is a Pluto's Place in Leicester.

Plymouth Arms Stratford-on-Avon. The earls of Plymouth formerly had their country seat at Hewell Grange not far away at Bromsgrove. Another pub of this name is at Cardiff.

Poacher Scunthorpe. Also Poachers, Ide, near Exeter and Piddletrenthide, Dors; Poacher's Pocket, Walderslade, near Chatham, others at Chelynch, Somerset, and Carlton, near Saxmundham. The Walderslade sign shows a poacher being arrested. His extra-large jacket pocket has been torn on a barbed-wire fence to reveal a brace of pheasants. Acocks Green, Birmingham has a Lincoln Poacher and Wangford, near Beccles a Suffolk Poacher. There are pubs at Spalding, Stamford and Metheringham, near Lincoln called Lincolnshire Poacher, referring to the folksong of that name.

Podger Garforth, near Leeds. A podger is a foundry implement used for turning large bolts. The sign shows a gigantic spanner.

Podium London EC2. Used in the sense of a raised platform around an arena. This pub is on the second-storey shopping platform at the Barbican.

Poet's Corner Nottingham. 'For Henry Kirke White: he might have been great/Had an early death not sealed his fate./ Admired by Southey, Byron too,/ Remembered now by very few.' He died in 1806, aged 21.

Pointer Alresford, near Wivenhoe. Also Pointers, Whitwood Mere, near Castleford; Pointer Dog, Hethersgill, Cumb. The dog which stands rigidly when it scents game, usually with one foot raised.

Pointsman Stalybridge. The man whose job it is to check the points on the railway line.

Polecat Prestwood, Bucks. The landowners here in 1750 were the Policate, or Polecatt, family. It is just possible that they derived their name from the animal, which is small, fierce, dark-brown in colour and smells disgustingly. In the Middle Ages such words were sometimes imposed on people as insulting nicknames.

Politician Glasgow. After 'that insidious and crafty animal, vulgarly called a statesman or politician' (Adam Smith 1723–90).

Polzeath Perranporth. Dr T F G Dexter, in his *Cornish Names*, explains this as 'dry pool'.

Pompadour Corringham, Esx. Also Pompadours, Harold Hill, near Romford. The nickname of the 2nd Battalion of the Essex Regiment, derived from the purple facings, or cuffs and collars, of their uniforms. That colour happened to be the favourite of Madame de Pompadour, then the mistress of Louis XV of France.

Pompey Portsmouth. The naval nickname for Portsmouth, and the nickname of Portsmouth Football Club whose ground at Fratton Park is nearby. The exact origin of the nickname is not known. In the North of England the same name was applied to an undersized boy. Southsea's Pompey Tavern has now become the Pompey Beer Bar.

Pony and Trap Newton, near Chew Magna, Avon. Another at Cullompton, near Exeter. The trap was a two-wheeled carriage on springs, usually a gig, and with its pony before it was a regular sight in country areas within living memory. The carriage was probably called a trap because it was a rattletrap (also a slang term for 'mouth', now also abbreviated to 'trap'). There is a Trap at Oldham and Glossop, Derbs.

Pope's Grotto Twickenham. Alexander Pope (1688–1744) lived here at Twickenham for twenty-five years. When he was not writing or translating poetry he laid out and developed a highly original garden, almost every trace of which has disappeared. The grotto connected the lawn to the main garden. In 1740 Pope wrote some 'Verses on a Grotto by the River Thames at Twickenham, composed of Marbles, Spars and Minerals', comparing it to a 'mine without a wish for gold' and saying that only a special kind of person should be allowed there: 'Let such, such only, tread this sacred floor,/Who dare to love their country, and be poor.'

Pop Inn Rutherglen, near Glasgow. Another at Edinburgh. In Tatworth, Som, there is an Olde Poppe Inn. The name has taken on a new meaning with the advent of 'pop music', to which some customers do not wish to listen.

Poplar Kitten Harlow. The name of a small puss-moth, and one of a series of such names in this town.

Poppinjay London EC4. The pub was opened in 1976 on the site of a thirteenth century house which was identified by the sign of the Popyngaye. The name, which is probably more correctly spelt as Popinjay, as at Basingstoke, and Rosebank, Strath, refers to a dummy parrot which was suspended from a pole and used as a target for archery practice.

Poppy *See* Flowers.

Porcupine London SE9 and elsewhere. This rodent, with a body and tail covered in defensive quills, appears in some coats of arms. The word has also been applied to various machines which have a large number of projecting spikes or teeth, eg a kind of mashing machine used in brewing.

Porpoise Porthtowan, near Truro. The blunt-nosed sea mammal, allied to the whale, which is occasionally seen in the bay near the pub.

Portcullis Hillesley, Glos and elsewhere. The framed metal gate at the entrance to a castle which could be lowered quickly on chains as a defence. 'Portcullis' literally means 'sliding door or gate'. Its distinctive shape, and its symbolic representation of stout defence, made it a popular heraldic symbol. It refers heraldically to the dukes of Beaufort, Henry VII, Henry VIII, and City of Westminster, etc. It can also be seen on the 'tail' side of the modern penny. At Butleigh, near Glastonbury, there is a Rose and Portcullis, where the Tudor rose has been added to the sign.

Porter Bath. Also Porters Arms, Plymouth; Porter and Sorter, E Croydon. The last name refers to both railway porter and Post Office sorter, since the station and sorting office are both nearby. Market porters were formerly such good drinkers that an ale, the predecessor of stout, was named for them. By the beginning of the nineteenth century porter was an immensely popular drink. In 1814 a vat containing 130,000 gallons of this ale burst, drowning eight people. The accident happened at

Meux's London Brewery in Tottenham Court Road. A pub name referring to this drink is the Porter Butt, Walcot, Bath.

Portland Arms Nottingham and elsewhere. A reference to the dukes of Portland, descended from William III's favourite, Hans Bentinck. The dukes owned a great many estates in different parts of the country, and property in London. William Henry Cavendish Bentinck, 3rd Duke of Portland, was prime minister in 1783 and again 1807–09.

Portland Roads Portland, Dors. 'Road' here is used in the sense of 'sheltered water where vessels may safely lie at anchor'. The harbour is protected by a massive break-water, mentioned in another local pub called the Royal Breakwater.

Port Mahon Oxford. Port Mahon is in Minorca, and was captured by the British in 1708. This pub was named a few years later, perhaps by a licensee who took part in that action.

Portman and Pickles Halifax. The pub was formerly the William Dighton but was renamed in 1984 for two of the town's famous sons. Eric Portman (1903–69) was a distinguished stage actor who appeared in some films. Wilfred Pickles (1904–78) was mainly a radio personality, presenter of 'Have A Go' for twenty-one years. He also acted in one or two films, playing Yorkshire roles.

Portobello Also Portobello Arms, Portobello Star. *See* Admiral Vernon.

Port Out and Starboard Home Peterborough. The name is the supposed derivation of the word 'posh', though the expert on slang usage, Eric Partridge, thought the ultimate derivation of that word was from Romany. Posh is significant in Peterborough because the local football team, Peterborough United, are known in the League as 'the Posh'.

Port Royal Exeter. This ancient pub takes its name from the dockyard town of this same name near Kingston, the Jamaican capital. The present sign shows the map of Jamaica, with a galleon in the background.

Portsmouth Chawleigh, Devon. Also Portsmouth Arms, Umberleigh, Devon. After Lord Portsmouth, local landowner and Master of Foxhounds for thirty years during the nineteenth century.

Portsmouth Hoy *See* Hoy Tavern.

Port Vale Tavern Hanley, near Stoke-on-Trent. After the Port Vale Football Club, the local professional team.

Posada Wolverhampton and elsewhere. Spanish *posada* means 'tavern', as well as 'shelter'.

Post Whiddon Down, Devon. Also Post Boy, Biggleswade, Beds and Ferryhill, Dur; Post Boys, formerly at Camberley, Sry. References to those who carried the mail in former times, using inns like these to change mail bags.

Poste Haste Wakefield. The cry of 'Post haste' was formerly heard in many an inn yard as postal messengers galloped in. They were demanding to be given priority so that they could continue their journey quickly. To do something 'post haste' came to mean to do it as quickly as possible.

Postgate Egton Bridge, N Yorks. The pub is named for Father Nicholas Postgate, who caused offence in the seventeenth century when he baptised a child as a Roman Catholic. He was sub-sequently hung, drawn and quartered at York.

Postillion Paston Ridings, near Peterborough. In its earliest use, this referred to a post boy, or swift messenger. It then came to have its usual meaning of a man who rode the near horse of the leaders when four or more horses were used in a carriage. Occasionally he rode the near horse of a pair, in which case he became the driver.

Post Office Stroud, Glos, and elsewhere. Also Post Office Arms, Boxmoor, Herts; Post Office Tavern, Bristol; Post Office Vaults, Wantage, Oxon; Poste House, Liverpool. These names are a reminder that inns sometimes provided certain post office facilities, collecting local mail for dispatch and acting as a kind of primitive sorting office for incoming letters.

Pot Black Glasgow. This new pub borrowed its name from the BBC television series about snooker which ran for many years.

Pot Kiln Frilsham, Berks. This term is used for a small lime kiln in which lime is derived from limestone.

Pot of Flowers *See* Flower Pot.

Pot o' Four Cow Green, Halifax. The name is said to allude to wool-combers, four of whom would use the same pot to heat their combs. An unsociable man was called a 'pot o' one'.

Pot Still Glasgow. A reference to a kind of still used to make whisky. Heat is applied directly to the pot instead of by means of a steam jacket. The pub specialises in malt whiskies.

Potter Fenton, near Stoke-on-Trent. Also Potters Arms, Middleport and elsewhere; Pottery Arms, Brentford. Such signs are mainly to be found in The Potteries.

Potter's Wheel Porthill, Staffs and elsewhere. Actually a revolving table on which the potter moulds

his clay, but always described as the 'wheel'.

Pound Leebotwood, Salop and elsewhere. The enclosure in which stray animals were impounded.

Powder Monkey Wallsend-on-Tyne. In naval slang a powder monkey was a boy who carried gunpowder from the magazine where it was stored to the guns. The term was used as a nickname for a mineshaft near the pub, where explosives were used.

Prancing Horse Thatcham, near Newbury. A prancing horse can be seen on the badge of the Ferrari racing-car. It was originally to be seen on the fighter aircraft of the Italian World War One flying ace, Francesco Baracca. Barraca's parents persuaded Enzo Ferrari to adopt it for his cars after their son's death. Many members of the Ferrari Car Club use this pub.

President Lincoln Walsall. Another at King's Lynn. After Abraham Lincoln (1809–65), sixteenth president of the USA, assassinated by John Wilkes Booth. He was the man who spoke of 'malice toward none; with charity for all'.

Pretoria Okehampton. The Devonshire Regiment gained battle honours during the Boer War at Pretoria, South Africa.

Pretty Pigs Amington, near Tamworth, Staffs. Formerly the Reppington Arms, in honour of a local landowner. The new name records a particularly fine litter of piglets born to the landlord's sow.

Pride of Pimlico London SW1. With this Pimlico pub one may compare **Pride of Stepney**, London E1; Pride of the Isle, London E14, where the reference is to the Isle of Dogs. Bristol has a slightly more puzzling Pride of the Forest in the centre of town, surrounded by roads and factories.

Pride of the Valley Churt, near Hindhead. After David Lloyd George (1863–1945), the Liberal politician, who was known by this nickname. He became prime minister in 1916 and held the post until 1922. He was later raised to the peerage as 1st Earl Lloyd-George of Dwyfor. Churt became his country seat.

Primrose London EC2. Another at Tonbridge. Also Primrose Hall, Combe Valley, Dover; Primrose View, Oldham. This flower became a 'rose' by mistake, the earlier form of its name being 'primerole'. Another mistake was made by Queen Victoria, who sent primroses to Disraeli's funeral believing that they were his favourite flowers. The Primrose League was founded in the same belief. The London pub, however, was named because of the nearby flower market.

Prince Liverpool. The pub is in Prince Edwin Street, and presumably refers to that seventh-century Prince, or King, of Northumbria.

Prince Albert London and elsewhere. A popular name – London has more than thirty pubs which bear it. It honours Francis Albert Augustus Charles Emmanuel (1819–61), second son of Ernest I, Duke of Saxe-Coburg-Gotha. He married his first cousin Queen Victoria in 1840 and became Prince Consort in 1857. Albert is found at Kingston-on-Thames and elsewhere; New Cross has a Royal Albert, London NW3 a Prince Consort, Preston a Royal Consort. Some of the Coburg pubs were also in honour of Prince Albert. Other variants include Albert Arms at Esher, Albert House at West Ham, Albert Park at Middlesborough, Albert Vaults in Manchester, Albert Dock and Albert Hall in Hull, and Albert Oak, Plymouth. Manchester's Albert Square even has a Square Albert.

Prince Alfred Burton-on-Trent and elsewhere. Prince Alfred (1844–1900) was the second son of Queen Victoria. He was known also as the Duke of Edinburgh. The Greeks elected him to be their king in 1862 but he declined the offer.

Prince and Princess of Wales London SE17. A name celebrating the marriage of Edward, Prince of Wales, to Alexandra, daughter of Christian IX of Denmark, in 1863.

Prince Arthur Brighton and elsewhere. After Arthur William Patrick Albert (1850–1942), third son of Queen Victoria. He was also known as Duke of Connaught and Earl of Sussex.

Prince Blucher Twickenham. Another at Tiverton, Devon. Also Prince of Waterloo, Bristol and elsewhere. Gebhard Leberecht von Blücher, Prince of Wahlstadt (1742–1819) was a famous Prussian field-marshal. He defeated Napoleon at Laon in 1814, and commanded the Prussian army at Waterloo in 1815, though then 73 years old. He was popular in Britain and received the freedom of the City of London.

Prince Charles Forest Town, near Mansfield, Notts. Names like this do not refer to present members of the royal family, who do not appear on inn signs while they are alive, (with the sole exception of the former Lady Diana). *See* Bonnie Prince Charlie. The Prince Charlie, Liverpool, also refers to the bonnie prince.

Prince Christian Windsor. Thought to be for Christian of Schleswig-Holstein, who married Princess

Helena, Queen Victoria's third daughter, in 1866.

Prince Consort *See* Prince Albert.

Prince Edward London E9. Another at London N7. After the Prince of Wales, later Edward VII. Royal Edward Blackburn, also refers to him.

Prince Ernest London E8. Apparently for Prince Alfred, whose second name was Ernest. *See* Prince Alfred.

Prince Frederick Sundridge Park, Bromley. After Frederick William, Crown Prince of Prussia (1831–88). He married Princess Victoria Adelaide, Queen Victoria's eldest daughter, in 1858.

Prince George London E8 and elsewhere. Another reference to the Prince Regent.

Prince Imperial London SE16. After Louis, son of Napoleon III (who lived in exile in England at the end of his life). The prince fought with the British forces in the Zulu war of 1879 and was killed. He is commemorated also by the Prince Louis at Dover and Farnborough, Hants.

Prince Leopold Upton Lovell, Wilts. Leopold (1853–84) was the fourth and youngest son of Queen Victoria. In 1881 he was created Duke of Albany and Earl of Clarence, titles which are also reflected in pub names. At Southsea, he is remembered by the Leopold Tavern.

Prince Llewellyn Dowlais, M Glam. Also Llewellyn, Cilmey, near Builth Wells, Pwys; Welsh Prince, Newport, Gwent. After Llewellyn, Prince of Wales from 1242–82. He revolted against Edward I of England and fell in battle.

Prince Louis *See* Prince Imperial.

Prince Madoc Colwyn Bay. Madoc or Madog was reputedly the discoverer of what is now called America, circa 1150. His name means 'fortunate'. He was the subject of a poem by Southey in 1805.

Prince of Wales Dilton Marsh, Wilts and elsewhere. This very common sign (nearly 100 in Greater London alone) mainly refers to Edward (1841–1910), eldest son of Queen Victoria. He eventually became Edward VII in 1901. The Dilton Marsh sign is one that refers instead to Edward II when he was still Prince of Wales in 1301. Some signs also show Edward the Black Prince, who was also Prince of Wales.

Prince of Wales's Feathers *See* Feathers.

Prince of Waterloo *See* Prince Blucher.

Prince Regent Tiverton, Devon and elsewhere. Also Regent, Clevedon, Som and elsewhere; Regency Tavern, Bath, Brighton and elsewhere. This title was given to George Augustus Frederick (1762–1830), son of George III, in 1811, when his father's insanity made it impossible for the king to govern the country. The prince was hardly a responsible person himself, and has been aptly described as a bad husband, bad father, bad subject, bad monarch and bad friend. He was, on the whole, roundly hated by one and all, both as Prince Regent and as George IV.

Prince's Castle Headington, Oxford. The sign shows a prince in his red cloak looking at his white mountain castle in the distant mist, but the name does not seem to have a specific reference.

Prince's Feathers Also Prince's Plumes. *See* Feathers.

Prince's Head London SW11. The particular prince whose portrait is displayed on the inn sign varies, though the 'Black Prince', son of Edward III, is popular. There are many opinions as to the reason for his nickname. He was probably 'black' because of his cruelty, but it is commonly said that he wore black armour. Dr Brewer remarks that in fact he wore gilt or 'gold' armour.

Prince's Motto Barrow Gurney, Avon. The motto of the Prince of Wales is *Ich dien*, German for 'I serve'. There are those who believe the motto to be a corruption of Welsh *Eich dyn*, 'your man', words which Edward I used when he presented his son to the assembly at Caernarvon.

Prince's Plumes *See* Feathers.

Princess Nottingham. When this pub had a sign it showed a medieval princess. Llanelli has a Princess Head.

Princess Beatrice London NW1. Beatrice (1857–1944) was the fifth and youngest daughter of Queen Victoria.

Prinny's Brighton. The nickname of the Prince Regent was Prinny. He was responsible for the building of Brighton's Royal Pavilion, which typifies his own extravagant personal style.

Printers Arms Bury and elsewhere. Torquay improves this sign, which seems to be more common in the North than the South, by making it Printer's Elbow.

Printer's Devil London EC4 and elsewhere. The traditional name of the errand boy in a printer's office, used since the seventeenth century. 'The black art' as a joking name for the printer's trade is a much more recent expression.

Printer's Pie London EC4 and elsewhere. A reference to a mass of type which has become mixed up, perhaps as the result of someone knocking over a forme of type.

The person who does this normally buys drinks all round to atone for his carelessness.

Privet Bush Privett, near Petersfield, Hants. A pub name inspired by the place name, the latter meaning 'privet copse'. The privet is an evergreen shrub, with smooth dark-green leaves and clusters of small white flowers, succeeded by small black berries.

Prizefighters Crawley Down, W Ssx. Formerly the Royal Oak. When a professional boxer, Don Cockell, became licensee here in 1970 the name was changed to mark a long association between the pub and the boxing fraternity.

Promenade Perranporth. This originally referred to walking in a leisurely way with a view to displaying to others how well-dressed and elegant one was. The name was then transferred to the place where such walking was done. Promenade concerts sometimes accompanied this activity. The 'real' promenaders, at the Albert Hall 'proms' each year, are those who stand, as if pausing in the course of a stroll.

Propeller Croydon. A link with the former airport.

Prospect Chapelhay, near Weymouth. The name of a square-rigged trading schooner that was formerly well known locally.

Prospect of Whitby London E1. A London dockland pub which takes its name from a coal-supply-ship which used to moor nearby. It called in at Whitby on its way south from the Tyne to the Thames. The present name dates from 1777. The pub is said to have earned the nickname Devil's Tavern at one time because of the number of thieves and smugglers who frequented it.

Proud Salopian Shrewsbury. 'Salopian' means 'of Shropshire'. Shown on the sign is Alderman Thomas Southam, wearing his mayoral robes. He was a member of a local family of brewers.

Pub Edinburgh. Formerly the Galloping Major. There is a Pub in the Park at Southampton and a Public House at Draperstown, Londy.

Puddlers Arms Briton Ferry, near Neath. Puddlers were the men who stirred molten iron in a furnace, so as to expel the carbon. The general sense of 'to puddle' is to dabble or poke about, especially in mud or shallow water.

Puffin Weston-super-Mare. This bird nests on Lundy Island in the Bristol Channel. Its name possibly derives from the puffy downy covering of the young bird or from the fact that it is puffed out in shape. One of its many alternative names is bottle-nose.

Puffing Billy Killingworth, near Newcastle-on-Tyne. A locomotive built by William Hedley in 1813, known by this name because of the alarming amount of smoke it belched forth. It was in service until 1862 and is now in the Science Museum at South Kensington. Apart from the pubs which bear this name, it is also splendidly illustrated on the sign of the Railway at Blandford Forum, Dors.

Pullet Sholver Green, Oldham. A young hen, or for those in the trade, a hen which has begun laying and has not reached the first moult. Also a slang term for a young girl, leading to the phrase 'pullet-squeezer', a womanizer who likes young girls.

Pullman Cressing, near Braintree, Esx, and elsewhere. The Cressing sign shows an example of the railway coach, built to luxurious standards by and named for the Pullman Carriage Works, Illinois. Such saloon and sleeping-car coaches were designed by George Pullman (1831–97) of Chicago.

Pump House Brighton and elsewhere. Named after the presence nearby of some kind of pump house. The one at Brighton was used to pump sea-water into baths.

Pumps Nottingham. Two illuminated Shell petrol pumps adorn the entrance to this newly updated pub, formerly the Exchange Hotel. They are purely for decorative purposes, but lead to this extraordinary name. There was once a term 'pump-sucker', which meant a teetotaller, and various other slang expressions, most of them now thankfully obsolete (since they were all decidedly obscene) which included 'pump'.

Punch and Judy London WC2. The brewers think that this pub, opened in 1980 as part of the Covent Garden complex, is on the site of the first Punch and Judy show to be given in England. It originated in Italy and was brought here in the seventeenth century.

Punchbowl Abingdon and elsewhere. Punch, as a drink, was established in England by the 1630s. It seems originally to have been a sailor's drink. There is doubt about the origin of the word, though it has been associated with the word for 'five' in several Indian languages. There is no evidence, however, that five ingredients were always used. Nowadays, anything (or almost anything) can become an ingredient, according to the taste of the person making the drink. The drink is normally made in a large bowl, hence the name of the pub. Such pubs at one time would have sold punch, especially to the

Whig political party meetings, it is said. At Hindhead, Sry, the name refers to the Devil's Punchbowl, a large depression in the hillside. Monmouth has a Punch House; Punchbowl and Ladle is at Penelewey, near Truro.

Puncheon Whitehaven, Cumb. The name of a seventy-two gallon cask, no longer used.

Punch Tavern London EC4. The magazine *Punch* was first thought of in this pub in 1841. 'Punch and Judy' shows were held nearby in Ludgate Circus and suggested the name. Cartoons from the magazine are on display.

Pure Drop Poole, Dors. 'Drop' usually refers to a tiny quantity of liquid. In a drinking context it means 'a large quantity of alcohol', as in a sentence like: 'I had a drop too much to drink last night'. In this pub the name promises that it will be of high quality.

Purple Emperor Harlow. The name of a butterfly, one of a series of such names in Harlow.

Purple Onion Edinburgh. An interesting name, apparently of no special significance (ie not listed in the *Oxford English Dictionary*, one of whose original co-editors was C T Onions).

Push Inn Beverley, Humb. A name which cunningly conveys the impression that the pub is always packed with customers.

Puss in Boots Hazlewood, Derbs, and elsewhere. Also Puss 'n Boots, Acomb, near York. The character in the sixteenth-century story, familiar in its pantomime form, which does extremely well for its master.

Puzzle Hall Sowerby Bridge, W Yorks. There is a maze here for the amusement of patrons.

Pyewipe Pyewipe, near Lincoln. The local name for the lapwing, also known as the peewit. The pub was once a meeting-place for wildfowlers.

Pyle Cock Wednesfield, near Wolverhampton. 'Pyle' is said to be the reddish-ginger colour of fighting cocks, three of which are engraved on the pub's windows.

Pyrotechnists Arms London SE15. After the makers of fireworks.

Q

Quadrant Chorlton-cum-Hardy, near Manchester. Another at Clifton, near Bristol. The instrument used to take angular measurements in astronomy and navigation. The basic meaning was a quarter of a circle, a shape that suggested The Quadrant as the name for the curved end of Regent Street, London. The name is also sometimes used to describe a square, or quadrangle.

Quaich Glasgow. A form of Gaelic *cuach*, 'cup', used to describe a shallow drinking cup formerly used in Scotland. It was usually made of small wooden staves hooped together, and had two ears or handles. Arbroath has a Golden Quaich.

Quakers' Yard Quakers Yard, Glam. Lydia Fell was a wealthy Quaker who left land in the seventeenth century as a 'suitable repository for the dead'. The Welsh name for the village translates as 'graveyard of the Quakers'.

Quantock Gateway Bridgwater. Also Quantock, Eastcombe, Som. The range of hills in Somerset, nine miles long and an area of great natural beauty. The Bridgwater sign shows two young hikers surveying the view.

Quarry Keinton Mandeville. Som. The local quarries produce blue lias stone for monumental masons. Quarry Arms is at Clayton, near Bradford; Quarryman's Arms is at Box Hill. Wilts, and Blackburn; Quarrymen's Arms is at Trefil, near Tredegar, Gwent. The Quarry Gate, Oxford, is named for a gate that used to shut off the former footpath to Headington Quarry.

Quarterdeck Parkstone. Dors. Originally a deck which covered roughly a quarter of a vessel's surface, above the half-deck. In later usage it referred to the deck used by senior officers and passengers. It is a naval custom to salute the quarterdeck when boarding a ship.

Quarter Gill North Berwick and elsewhere. All these signs are found in Scotland and refer to a quarter of a pint (of something strong).

Quart Pot Wickford, Esx. Another at Milton-under-Wychwood, Oxon. Margate has a warning about attempting the impossible, Quart in a Pint Pot. 'Quart' refers to a quarter of a gallon, two pints. In centuries past beer was commonly drunk by the quart.

Quavers Ryker, near Newcastle-on-Tyne. This pub was the Hope and Anchor until 1982. It is now a disco pub, so *Quavers* is probably meant to suggest both music and the shaking of the floor (and the people on it) as frenzied dancing takes place.

Quay Kingsbridge, Devon. Also Quayside, Brixham and Belfast; Quay House, Connah's Quay, Deeside; Quay Tavern, Felling, near Gateshead. The *Quay* pub has one of the largest signs anywhere, worth studying in detail. It shows an old–time quayside scene, but has been fixed so high on the wall that it cannot properly be observed.

Queen London SW18 and elsewhere. The signs show various

queens, eg Queen Anne at London SW8; Elizabeth I at Tadcaster, N Yorks; young Queen Victoria, Cwmbran, Gwent; Victoria as child and grandmother, Penzance.

Queen Bee *See* Busy Bee.

Queens Preston. The signboard shows those great ocean liners, the *Queen Mary*, *Queen Elizabeth* and the *QE2*. The similar sign at Morecambe shows four playing-card queens.

Queen's Windermere and elsewhere. The Windermere sign shows a queen surrounded by the heraldic arms of England, Scotland, Wales and Northern Ireland.

Queen's Arms Watford and else-where. A popular sign, at least twenty-six of them still in the London area. Different queens are referred to, as in Queen's Head, Queen. It used to be a common joke amongst commercial travellers, if asked where they stayed in a particular city, to say 'in the *Queen's Arms*' if they happened to live there, and thus stayed at home.

Queensberry Rules *See* Marquis of Queensberry.

Queen's College Arms Pamber End, Basingstoke. The land on which this pub is situated belongs to Queen's College, Oxford. The sign shows the college coat-of-arms.

Queen's Elm London SW3. As every pub should, this one has a plaque on a wall inside explaining the name. Elizabeth, I visiting Lord Burghley, sheltered from the rain under a nearby elm tree.

Queen's Head Box, Wilts, and elsewhere. Elizabeth I was the subject of many early signs, but this royal lady was not at all pleased at the way amateur sign–painters had represented her. Signs that offended her were knocked down and burnt, and by royal proclamation in 1563, future signs were forbidden unless they followed an approved example. The sign is still fairly common, with twenty-five examples in central London alone. It takes various visual forms, including Anne Boleyn, with block and axe in background, at Box; Jane Seymour at Colney Hatch, Herts; Catherine of Aragon at Dogmersfield, Hants, where that queen first met Prince Arthur, her first husband; a chessboard queen at Maidstone; a queen of clubs at Iron Cross, near Evesham; Queen Anne as a young woman at Neath, W Glam; Catherine Howard and Elizabeth of York at Stratford-on-Avon; Elizabeth I at Newark; the head of Queen Victoria on a penny black postage stamp at London N21, near the Post Office sorting centre; Queen Bertha, wife of King Ethelbert, at Canterbury.

Queen's Head and Artichoke London NW1. The sister of Henry VIII, widow of Louis XII of France, was passionately fond of artichokes (it is said). She persuaded her chief gardener to call his tavern by this name. That tavern has gone, but the name survives here.

Queen's Larder London WC1. The pub is in Queen Street, which was named for Catherine of Braganza, the unpopular wife of Charles II. The pub name is modern, with a sign showing the Queen of Hearts about to place a tray of tarts in her larder. Watching her do it is her Knave.

Quicksilver Mail West Coker, near Yeovil. A famous mail-coach of former times, the only one to be given a nickname. It ran between London and Devonport at the (then) astonishing average speed of just over ten miles per hour.

Quids Inn Chester. 'Quid' has been a slang term for one pound for at least a century, and was earlier applied to a guinea. 'Quids' meant money in general. The origin of the term is not clear, though it is usually linked to Latin *quid(dam)*, 'something', ie the wherewithal. 'Quids in' is a fairly modern phrase meaning that one has bought something at bargain price. The pun in *Quids Inn* could also extend to quids of tobacco being chewed, where 'quid' is related to 'cud'.

Quiet Woman *See* Silent Woman.

Quill Tavern Edinburgh. Another at London SW15. The Edinburgh pub is near the Law Courts, where quill pens were formerly much used by solicitors and others.

R

Rabbie Burns Also Rabbie's Bar. *See* Robert Burns.

Rabbit Luton. When the pub was built the area was known as Coney Fields, 'coney' or 'cony' being the older word for 'rabbit'. The name also occurs in Cambridge and Southport. London E12 has a Three Rabbits.

Rabbits Stapleford Tawney, near Romford. Said to be a corruption of rabbets, the grooves along the edge or face of a piece of wood or stone, into which the end or edge of another piece is fitted. The term would have been familiar to carpenters.

Raby Arms Hart, near Hartlepool. Also Raby Hunt, Summerhouse, near Darlington; Raby Moor, Cockfield, Barnard Castle; Raby Castle, formerly at Hull. Raby is a place name in Cheshire and Durham, meaning 'settlement near a boundary mark'.

Race Hill Brighton. The pub is at the foot of Elm Grove Hill. At the top is the local racecourse, and half way up the hill is another pub called the Race Horse. Other pubs of the latter name are at Taunton (where the jockey Dave Dick is shown on his horse *Dunkirk*), Cambridge, Hereford, Tiverton and Warwick. At Kettlewell, near Skipton, there is a Racehorses.

RACEHORSES It seems to have been fashionable in the nineteenth century to name pubs after racehorses, especially those that won the Derby. Examples are Amato, Blenheim, Blink Bonny, Cadland, Cossack, Cremorne, Flying Dutchman, Highflyer, Ladas, Little Wonder, Voltigeur. In some instances it must have been the money won by betting on these horses that enabled people to become owners of pubs. At least sixty horses have been honoured by having pubs named after them.

Racing Greyhound *See* Dog.

Rack and Manger Between Stockbridge and Winchester. An indication that horses could be fed, the rack and manger being receptacles for hay and fodder.

Raddle Hollington, near Stoke-on-Trent. A door or fence made with intertwined raddles – thin laths twisted between upright stakes.

Radjel Pendeen, near Penzance. Explained locally as a term for an excavated mine tunnel or a fox's lair. The sign shows a fox on a heap of boulder rubble.

Raffled Anchor North Shields. The reference is to an anchor which has become entangled, or to one with finely-notched edges.

Raffles Plymouth and elsewhere. Sir Thomas Stamford Bingley Raffles (1721–1826) was an English naturalist and administrator. He was lieutenant-governor in Java in 1811 and later held a similar post in Sumatra. He made a large collection of the animals, plants, etc of those places. He advised on the annexation of Singapore in 1819, and is still remembered there in the famous Raffles Hotel. E W Hornung used Raffles as the name of his gentleman burglar and cricketer in several books from 1899 on.

Rag Doll Edinburgh. Also Rag Doll's Head, Birmingham. Apart from its normal meaning of a doll made from rags, this term has also been applied in the past to a slatternish woman.

Raglan Arms *See* Lord Raglan.

Ragleth Little Stretton, Salop. Ragleth Hill is to the east of Little Stretton and has lent its name to several streets in the area. The licensee here is an American from Vermont, possibly the only American publican in Britain.

Railway and Bicycle Tubs Hill, Sevenoaks. The sign shows a heavily bewhiskered man riding a pennyfarthing bicycle over a railway bridge.

Railway and Naturalist Prestwich, near Manchester. The pub was used as headquarters of the local botanical society until the outbreak of World War One. It was also much used by the railway workers who built the line to Radcliffe, opened in 1879.

Railway Engineer London NW7. This pub was formerly the Railway. In 1973 it changed to Royal Engineer, in compliment to the soldiers at the nearby Royal Electrical and Mechanical Engineers Barracks. There were local objections, leading to the present compromise name in 1983.

Railway Medina Cowes and Newport. The Medina is the river that divides the Isle of Wight into two halves.

Railway Names The coming of the railways in the nineteenth century made a huge impact on life in Britain, and this was naturally reflected in the naming of our pubs. Thus we find the Railway, London EC2 and elsewhere; Railway Arch, Weymouth; Railway Bell, Folkstone and New Barnet; Railway Bridge, Burton-on-Trent; Railway Carriers, Southsea; Railway Engineer, London NW7; Railway Guard, Epsom; Railway Junction, Hitchin; Railway Posting, Newport Pagnell; Railway Signal, Llanelli; Railway Steamer, Shefford, Beds; Railway Telegraph, Thornton Heath, Sry; Railway Terminus, Bridport; Railway Train, Kidderminster. There is also a Railroad at Bristol and a Railway and Bicycle at Sevenoaks. All these are merely the tip of the iceberg. Many of the individual railway companies that existed in different parts of the country before they began to merge as larger groups, and finally as British Rail, are still commemorated in local pub names. Also taken over as pub names are locomotive names, especially those of George Stephenson's Morning Star and North Star. Such names create many difficulties for pub-name researchers unless they, know that a locomotive is shown on the sign: the name alone is not sufficient indication since locomotive names were themselves transferred from a number of other naming systems. A glance into *British Locomotive Names of the Twentieth Century*, by H C Casserley, published by Ian Allan, will make the problem apparent. The Great Western Railway, for example, named at least 150 locomotives for castles. The LNER also had some castle names. We find over a hundred pub names which mention a specific castle by name, but it is very difficult to know whether the pub name borrows from the railway or from the castle itself (or from an ocean liner such as the *Stirling Castle*). Apart from locomotives, named train services often feature as pub names. They are the subject of *Titled Trains of Great Britain*, by Cecil J Allen, published by Ian

Allan. Railway enthusiasts who take a close look at pub names and get out their notebooks will eventually find about 200 references to the subject ranging from Atmospheric Railway to Whistle Stop.

Railway Steamer Shefford, Beds. 'The reek of the labouring horses steamed into it', says Dickens, in *A Tale of Two Cities*. 'Steamer' here also applies to a labouring horse. It is seen on the sign pulling a railway wagon in a goods yard.

Rainbow Allesley, near Coventry and elsewhere. Also Rainbow's End, Steeple Langford, near Salisbury. The latter name refers to the pot of gold which awaits anyone who digs at the spot where a rainbow touches the earth. This legendary tale may have influenced other uses of *Rainbow*, in use as a sign since the seventeenth century. Clearly its distinctive shape and colouring made it useful as a visual sign. Other associations with *Rainbow* include the Rainbow Division of the American Army in World War One, so named because they were recruited from all sections of the community. Rainbow Corner, a Lyons Corner House at Shaftesbury Avenue, was named for them in World War Two and became a meeting place for Americans in London. The Rainbow Room is also a well-known restaurant in New York.

Rainbow and Dove Harlow, Esx. Another in Leicester. Also Dove and Rainbow, Hartshead, near Sheffield. A sign adopted by the Dyers Company. It was the dyers who performed each Whitsuntide the mystery play *The Deluge*, about Noah's Ark and the flood. The rainbow and dove feature in the story, as they do in the account in Genesis 9.

Rake Littleborough, near Oldham. The sign shows a rake of the human kind, a rake-hell as he was known more fully. This was the name for a man of immoral habits, idle and dissipated. The man on the sign has a flowing cape, tall hat and a lecherous leer. In the background can be seen the old coach road over the Pennines.

Rake and Pikel Saighton, near Chester. The pub was converted from a pair of labourers' cottages in 1939. The 'pikel' is a local word for a long-handled pitchfork.

Ralegh's Cross Brendon Hill, near Watchet, Som. Simon de Ralegh was one of Richard II's men who fell in battle. He was brought home for burial and crosses were erected in two places where his bier rested on its journey. This was one of them, the other was at Low Cross, near Upton.

Ram Derby and elsewhere. The male sheep, which appears in the arms of the Worshipful Company of Clothworkers and other livery companies connected with the wool trade. In use as a sign since the fourteenth century.

Ramada Hebburn, T and W. This appears to be Arabic *ramada* 'to be hot', more familiar as Ramadan, the Moslem Holy Month. It sometimes falls in midsummer. A place–name link (and joke) may be intended.

Ram and Hogget Bradfield, Esx. A 'hogget' is a yearling sheep, though the word can also be used of a young colt.

Ram and Teasel London N1. The teasel is a plant of the thistle family, used for centuries to tease cloth, which raises a nap on the cloth's surface. Since the early nineteenth century the work has been done by a machine, also called a teasel (or teazle, teazel, etc). The *Ram and Teasel* sign was therefore symbolic of the wool trade, and both objects were used heraldically with that in mind. There is a Teasel at Bromley, Kent; Panteg, Gwent, has a Teazel.

Rambling Miner Chacewater, near Truro. A freelance miner who moved around, obtaining casual work here and there instead of staying at one mine.

Ram Jam Stretton, near Oakham. The Ram Jam Inn formerly issued a little booklet about itself (undated, but double rooms were advertised for two pounds a night) in which it explained at great length how it came to get its name. It chose to repeat the story of a traveller who told the innkeeper's wife that he could tell her how to draw mild and bitter ale from the same barrel. He then made a hole in one side of a barrel and told her to ram her thumb against it. Then he made a hole in the other side and told her to jam her other thumb in that. At that point he remembered that he had no spile-pegs to put in these holes, and went away to get them. The landlord later found his wife still with her thumbs rammed and jammed in the barrel, while the traveller had disappeared without paying his bill. This story, said the booklet, 'provides us with an interesting sidelight on the credulity of human nature in general and of innkeepers' wives in particular'. Leaving aside the remark about innkeepers' wives, the story certainly does comment on people's credulity if they are willing to believe a story like this. In another version of the story it is the landlord who falls for the trick, while the trickster has in mind a little dalliance with the landlady. A different story concerns a publican who brought home from India the recipe for a rare liqueur, which he named for his 'ram-jam', his Indian servant. The liqueur became famous, but he died with its secret intact. After all this one is almost reluctant to report that ram-jam had two well-established meanings in the nineteenth century. 'To ram-jam' meant to stuff oneself with food, but 'ram-jam full' simply referred to any place that was filled with people, or any receptacle that was absolutely full. In a way, the inn's own explanation of the name is much better, symbolising as it does how ordinary people are willing to believe almost any story, however outrageous, when it comes to explaining a pub name.

Rampant Cat *See* Cat.

Rat Anick, near Hexham. Also Rat Catchers, Cawston, near Norwich; Rats Castle, St Albans; Rats Cellar, Aberdeen; Rat Trap, Stratton St Margaret, near Swindon. In former times a 'rat', in colloquial speech, was a drunken person

taken into custody. To be as drunk as a rat, to get the rats, or have the rats, or see the rats, or even to be in the rats, all referred to a state of extreme intoxication. In spite of these associations between rats and drinking, the pub names probably have other derivations. Rat catchers were important officials who did a legitimate job. *Rats Castle* was a nickname given to a pub which had become derelict and was overrun with rats. When the pub was rebuilt the nickname stuck. *Rat Trap*, apart from being a real trap, was also the name for a wire-framed bustle, used to improve a dress, though this is probably not what the ladies who wore such things called it.

Rattlebone Sherston, near Malmesbury, Wilts. A legendary local hero, John Rattlebone. He was attacked by marauding Danes centuries ago and mortally wounded in the stomach. He clutched a tile to his body to prevent the blood gushing forth and fought on to the bitter end. The sign captures the gruesome-ness of the story.

Raven New Basford, Nottingham. This bird was sacred to the Druids, and was known in Norse mythology as Woden's bird. Two ravens, one black, one white, sat on the god's shoulders and told him all that passed in the world. King Arthur was reputedly changed into a raven and still lives. There are many local beliefs about the bird, the most popular being that it is an omen of something unpleasant. Shakespeare refers to the bird in that way, also to another curious belief: 'Some say that ravens foster forlorn children,/The whilst their own birds famish in their nests.' (*Titus Andronicus* 2.2) The bird

nevertheless features in some coats of arms, and it is said that in the late seventeenth century the sign indicated Jacobite sympathies on the part of an innkeeper.

Ravensbourne London SE6. The name of a river which flows past Bromley into the Thames at Deptford. The sign is nevertheless said to commemorate a raven called Bob, mascot of Whitbread's Chiswell Street Brewery until 1941, when it disappeared after an air-raid.

Ravenser Hull. The name of a village on the Humber which was destroyed by floods in the fourteenth century.

Reading House Clevedon. The pub was once owned by the Simonds Brewery at Reading.

Real Mackay Glasgow. A variant of the expression 'real McCoy', as it tends to be in the South, used for any genuine article, especially good Scotch whisky. Mackay was the name originally used in this expression, which dates from before 1900. Speculation as to its origin remains just that, speculation.

Rechabites Rest Winsford, Ches. A jokey name for a pub, though the joke will be lost on those who do not realise that the Independent Order of Rechabites is a large friendly society, founded in 1835, for total abstainers. Its lodges are called 'tents'. They take their name from the Rechabites, mentioned in Jeremiah 35 as a good example of men who obeyed their father's command not to drink or build houses, but to live always in tents.

Recruiting Sergeant Great Yarmouth and elsewhere. The man who would tour the country, setting up an office at a tavern, and induce local men to join the ranks of the army. The men bound themselves by accepting the King's shilling. It is said that unscrupulous sergeants dropped a shilling into a pint of beer, which they offered to a victim. When the drinker emptied his glass and the coin became visible he would take it out, only to find that he had thus accepted the shilling. Pewter pots with glass bottoms were introduced so that this trick could not be practised. At Mollington, near Banbury, there is a Recruit.

Red Admiral Weston-super-Mare and elsewhere. The butterfly of this name. The pub at Weston (formerly the Prince of Wales) changed name when its new owner brought with him a fine collection of butterflies for exhibition in the bar.

Redan Norwich and elsewhere. A military term for a kind of trench. It is especially associated with the Crimean War and the siege of Sebastopol. The sign at Norwich shows a local hero, Major-General Charles Windham, leading a final successful charge there. A similar military term for a field fortification is found in the Redoubt, Wakefield.

Red Barrel Kenilworth. The name of one of Watney's bottled beers. *See also* Barrels.

Red Beret Chelmsford. *The Red Beret* was the name of a film which starred Alan Ladd as a member of the Parachute Regiment. It was released in 1953. Journalists sometimes referred to men of the Parachute Regiment as 'Red Devils', but 'Red Beret' was never a nickname, even though a true description of the headgear that was worn from 1942 onwards. There is a Parachute at Henlow, Beds.

Red Bull *See* Bull.

Red Cat Greasby, near Birkenhead. The local chapel has a sandstone figure projecting from the wall, thought to have been a lion's head originally but known as the 'red cat'.

Red Comyn Cumbernauld, Glasgow. Sir John Comyn, nephew of King John of Scotland, had red hair and a ruddy complexion. He was known as Red Comyn to distinguish him from a kinsman who was Black Comyn. Red Comyn was stabbed to death by Robert Bruce in the church of the Minorites, Dumfries, in 1306.

Red Cross Henley-on-Thames. Also Red Cross Knight, High Wycombe. A reference to St George of England, who is the Red Cross Knight in Spenser's *Faerie Queene*. His badge is a red cross on a white background. The modern use of Red Cross, to indicate the neutrality of ambulances and hospitals in war, was suggested by the Swiss national flag, though this has a white cross on a red background. The Red Cross movement began in Switzerland as a result of the Geneva Convention, 1862.

Red Dog *See* Dog.

Red Dragon Wrexham and elsewhere. This is now a reference to the Welsh flag, though in Cumbria it is said to relate heraldically to the earls of Cumberland. It was adopted in the seventh century as the standard of King Cadwallader, and later featured in the arms of the Tudors. In modern times it is also the name of a beer brewed by Brains Brewery, who have a red dragon as their symbol.

Red Duster South Shields. Naval slang for the Red Ensign, used only by British merchant ships since 1864.

Red Earl Northampton. The pub is on the Spencer Estate, and refers to John Poyntz Spencer, 5th Earl Spencer. He had a distinguished political career, becoming viceroy of Ireland and 1st lord of the admiralty. He had a red beard. Princess Diana is a descendant.

Red Fox *See* Fox.

Red Ginn Bradford. The original pub was built in the eighteenth century, when there was some coal-mining in this area. The inn sign was painted red and showed a 'gin', a machine used for hoisting. The spelling 'ginn' may have been used to distinguish it from gin, the spirit, but spelling was none too accurate in the eighteenth century.

Red Hackle Jarrow, T and W. The red feather, taken from the neck of a cock, worn in the bonnet or beret of the Tyneside Scottish Regiment.

Red Hart Hartcliffe, Bristol and elsewhere. Also Red Deer, London E1 and Croydon. The *Red Hart* refers to the male red deer.

Red Heart Ruddington, near Nottingham. The pub has a wrought-iron sign, with a heart over-painted in red. The heart is supposed to be that of Mary I. In the year she died Calais was lost to the English (1558). Mary was grieved at its loss and declared on her deathbed (it is said) that the word Calais would be found engraved on her heart.

Red Jackets Camborne, Corn. A general reference to the red-jacketed soldiers who came to this area from Bodmin in 1873. The miners had rioted and the troops came to restore order.

Red King Prestwich, near Manchester. The Red King is a character in *Alice Through the Looking Glass*, by Lewis Carroll, 1872. His queen was intended by Carroll to be 'the concentrated essence of all governesses'.

Red Lion Thames Ditton and elsewhere. In 1986 there were at least 600 pubs bearing this name, the most popular of all pub names. Its early use was due to John of Gaunt, the most powerful man in England for much of the fourteenth century (*see* John of Gaunt). A red lion is also a heraldic reference to Scotland. When James I (also James VI of Scotland) came to the throne he diplomatically ordered that a heraldic red lion should be displayed in public places. London has a Red Lion Court, Street and Square, all named for inns of this name. The Old Red Lion, London WC2 is on the site of a well-known sixteenth-century inn: It is said that prisoners on their way to execution were sometimes allowed to take a last drink there. Red Lion Lane does not seem to exist, but at one time that expression was used jokingly to refer to the throat.

Red Post Peasedown St John, Som. The red post marked the spot where the post-boys exchanged mail in former times.

Red Rose Rochdale. Another at Oldham. Formerly popular in Lancashire, referring to the badge of Edmund Plantagenet, 1st Earl of Lancaster.

Red Rover Northampton and elsewhere. The name of a well-known stagecoach.

Red Shoot Linwood, Hants. The pub is in the New Forest. The name refers to a wood which harboured red deer.

Redstart Barming, near Maidstone. For the bird of this name, where '-start' is from Old English *steort*, 'tail'.

Red, White and Blue Oxford and elsewhere. Another way of referring to the Union Jack and an expression of patriotism. The Oxford pub sign chooses to show a croquet lawn, complete with hoops and balls coloured red, white and blue.

Redwing Lympstone, near Exmouth. Not in this instance for the kind of thrush known by this name, but for a fourteen foot dinghy. It was designed by Uffa Fox for use in the West Country and always has red sails.

Refuge Stalybridge. A suitable drinking place for refugees. 'Refuge' simply means a place of security and comfort.

Regent Clevedon, Avon, and elsewhere. In Clevedon a reference to a stagecoach of this name. Often a direct reference to the Prince Regent.

Reindeer Northwood, GL and elsewhere. Sometimes called a 'Raindeer' on early signs in London, but its name derives from the reins used when it is drawing a sledge. The animal's magnificent antlers make it very distinctive, though it now has rather a sentimental Father Christmas image.

Rembrandt Manchester. Harmenszoon van Rijn Rembrandt (1606–69) was a famous Dutch painter and etcher who was at one time the most popular painter of his day. His reputation suffered badly when he painted in 1642 what was generally known as *The Night Watch*, focusing strong light on a few central figures and leaving the rest in shadow. This departed from the conventions of the time. By 1657 Rembrandt was bankrupt. He painted many fine self–portraits during his last period of poverty and retirement. In all he painted some 700 pictures and produced a great many superb etchings.

Rest and be Thankful Wheddon Cross, near Dunster, Som and elsewhere. This was obviously a standard phrase by the early nineteenth century. The *Westminster Gazette* referred to 'a few who adopt rather too much of the rest-and-be-thankful principle' in 1894, and the Oxford English Dictionary quotes from an 1843 publication a reference to people sitting on a rest-and-be-thankful stone. There is another pub of the name at Arrochar, Strath, while Portrush in Antrim has a Rest Awhile. The Rest and Welcome is at Melbury Osmond, Dors.

Restoration Cheltenham. This name disappeared in 1981 but referred to the restorative powers of the local spa water rather than the Restoration of Charles II.

Reveller Yafforth, near Northallerton. The name of a racehorse, winner of the St Leger in 1818.

Revenue Devonport. The sign shows Revenue men of the eighteenth century waiting on the cliffs, ready to pounce on some smugglers who are rowing their contraband ashore.

Rhadegund Cambridge. An alternative spelling of Radegunde, the name of a sixth century saint who founded the monastery of Holy Cross at Poitiers. Another saint of this name was a thirteenth-century German servant girl of great piety and charity who was torn to death by wolves.

Rhino Chaddesden, Derby. The former Offilers Brewery had a policy of using bird and animal names for their new pubs. This is obviously short for rhinoceros, an animal named for its 'nose-horn' in Greek. 'Rhino' therefore means 'nose'.

Rhubarb *See* Fruits and Vegetables.

Rhubarb Tavern Bristol. The pub is in an area where rhubarb once grew abundantly.

Richard Cobden Cocking, W Ssx and elsewhere. Also Cobden, Leicester, Cobden Arms, Cobridge, Staffs and elsewhere, Cobden's Head, London E2. Richard Cobden (1804–65) was an English politician who played a major part in getting the Corn Laws repealed. These restricted the import and export of grain and had caused prices to rise. In 1860 he negotiated an Anglo-French treaty which greatly increased trade between the two countries.

Richard I London SE10. Richard I, known as Richard Coeur de Lion or Richard Lionheart (1157–99) was King of England from 1189. He went on the third Crusade in 1190 and was absent from England for much of his reign, having been taken prisoner while on his way home by Leopold II. There is a Coeur de Lion at Bath.

Richard III Leicester. Richard III (1452–85) was king from 1483, when he murdered his young nephew Edward in the Tower of London. The Earl of Richmond confronted him at Bosworth Field, where Richard was killed. Richmond became Henry VII. Richard was the last Yorkist king, and his death finally brought to an end the Wars of the Roses. He is commemorated in other pubs at Luton and York, and shown on the sign of the King's Arms at Beaumaris, Anglesey.

Richmond Arms Richmond, Sry and elsewhere. A reference to the various dukes of Richmond.

Ridge and Furrow Gloucester. A reference to ploughing in a way that produces strips of raised soil with deep furrows alternating between them. The Ridger, at West Kirby, refers to the plough-man who does this. Bedlington, Northld, has a Ridge Farm, probably referring to one on a stretch of elevated ground.

Ridgewood Edenthorpe, near Doncaster. The name of a successful racehorse.

Ridgeway Newport, Gwent. A ridge of high land. The sign shows it in winter being used for sledging.

Rifleman's Arms Glastonbury, Som. 'Arms' suddenly reminds us of its other meaning here, the fact that it can refer to firearms as well as heraldic arms. The pub itself is not especially military in character.

Rifle Volunteer Watford. Another at St Anns Chapel, near Gunnislake, Corn. Also Rifle Volunteers, Maidstone; Rifle Volunteer Arms, Stafford. The volunteer soldiers of the past, who had to find their own instructors and rifles before the government would accept their services.

Riga House Chelmondiston, near Ipswich. Riga is the capital and chief seaport of the Latvian Soviet Socialist Republic. This pub name commemorates the shipments of timber that came from Riga to the nearby quay.

Rig Dyke Rawmarsh, near Rotherham. A ridge dyke, erected to protect low-lying land from flooding.

Rights of Man Thetford, Nflk. The title of a two–volume work by Thomas Paine (1737–1809), in which he defended the French Revolution. He was born near Thetford, but spent much time in America. Paine fled to France when the English authorities charged him with sedition. He upset the French and was imprisoned there. His *Letter to Washington* (1796) upset the Americans, and when he returned there in 1802 he was ostracised.

Right Wing Duddingston, near Edinburgh. This phrase now carries a political suggestion, that Conservative views are held. Forty years ago it would immediately have suggested football, and a player like Stanley Matthews.

Ring London SE1. The sign shows a boxing ring in use.

Ringmaster London W14. The pub is near Olympia, where a circus was the usual Christmas entertainment for many years.

Ringers Also Ringers' Rest. *See* Bell.

Ring of Bells Norton Fitzwarren, near Taunton and elsewhere. Often a name for a pub used by the local bell-ringers. Ring o' Bells, Bideford and elsewhere, is a popular variant. The sign at Ashcott shows the bells themselves in a belfry. At Keswick the ringers are seen holding the bell-ropes. Barnsley has a sign which shows a set of hand-bells.

Ring o' Roses Holcombe, near Bath. A reference to the nursery rhyme, 'Ring a ring of roses, A pocketful of posies, Atishoo, Atishoo, we all fall down.' Whether or not this rhyme refers to the Black Plague, as has been suggested, seems to depend on whether 'roses' was ever used to describe the facial rash of the sufferers. There is no evidence that it was. Bunches of sweet-smelling flowers may well have been used to hide the smell of corpses, however, and there is something rather sinister about 'we all fall down'.

Ringwood Castle London E17. The castle itself is in Hampshire. The people who developed this area in the nineteenth century came from that county.

Rising Buck Sheinton, near Shrewsbury. Also Rising Deer, Thurcroft, near Rotherham. 'Rising' is used here in the sense of an animal emerging from a covert or lair.

Rising Flame Great Yarmouth. Formerly the Station Stores. The sign now shows a North Sea drilling rig with a blazing gas flame.

Rising Sun Wimborne Minster, Dors, and elsewhere. Also Sun Rising, Claydon, near Banbury. A common heraldic symbol, referring to Edward III, Richard III and to many landed families. The Wimborne sign is said, however, to be a reference to William of Orange, who passed through the village on his way to London to become king.

Rising Trout *See* Trout.

Riverboat Kidderminster. Another at Shrewsbury. These names refer to the rivers Stour and Severn respectively. Other river-inspired names include Riverhead, Sevenoaks; Riverside (for the Exe) Exeter and elsewhere; River View, Earith, near Huntingdon, and Cork; Riverway (for the Trent) Nottingham.

River Don Eastoft, near Scunthorpe. The Yorkshire river of this name formed with its southern arm part of the boundary between Lincolnshire and Yorkshire. Other rivers of the name are in Durham and Lancashire.

River Parrett Bridgwater. This river rises in North Dorset and runs into Bridgwater Bay.

Rivers and Canals A great many pub names are simply transferred river or canal names. At least eighty different rivers are mentioned by name, and the various canal systems are well represented. Those with a special interest in river names should consult *English River Names*, by Eilert Ekwall, published by the Oxford University Press.

RMA Tavern Eastney, Hants. After the Royal Marines Artillery.

Roach Bolton. Also Roach Bank, Whitefield, near Manchester; Roaches Lock, Mossley, Manchester. The freshwater fish of the carp family, or from the surname Roach.

Road to Morocco Northampton. One of several films which starred Bob Hope, Bing Crosby and Dorothy Lamour. The series began with *Road to Singapore* in 1940. *Road to Morocco* appeared in 1942 and was probably the best. The sign shows a camel and rider.

Roaring Donkey *See* Blazing Donkey.

Roaring Meg Lincoln. This was the nickname of a huge cannon used here by Royalist forces during the Civil War.

Robert Burns Southampton. Another at Millwall. Also Burns' Arms, Catrine, Strath; Burns' Cottage, Manchester; Burns' Head, Patrington, Humb; Burns' Tavern, Bamford, near Rochdale; Burns' Howff, Glasgow (*See* Howff Tavern); Rabbie Burns, Edinburgh; Rabbie's Bar, Ayr; Robbie Burns, Houghton-le-Spring, T and W. Robert Burns (1759–96) is Scotland's best-loved poet, noted for his spontaneous simplicity, his deep emotional response to life and his humour. He was responsible for 'Auld Lang Syne' and 'Comin' thro' the Rye', as well as the longer 'Tam o' Shanter', 'The Cotter's Saturday Night' and hundreds of other poems. His lifestyle was unconventional, or as some would say, dissipated, and he died tragically young.

Robert Burre Clacton-on-Sea. The pub is a converted farmhouse, which was leased by the Bishop of London to Robert Burre in 1375.

Robert de Mortain St Helens, Hastings. The brother of William the Conqueror, reputedly the builder of Hastings Castle.

Robert E Lee London N15. Robert Edward Lee (1807–70) was the general in chief of the Confederate armies during the Civil War. He was a great commander and a man of exalted character; idolised by the South. He was eventually forced to surrender to General Grant in 1865 and subsequently became president of Washington College.

Robert Kett *See* Kett's Tavern.

Robert Peel *See* Peel.

Robert Tinker Manchester. Robert Tinker (1766–1836) was the proprietor of Tinker's Gardens (later called Vauxhall Gardens) in the area then called Collyhurst. Brass bands, balloon ascents and fireworks were amongst the entertainments offered to the public.

Robin Hull and elsewhere. Also Robin's Nest, Lisburn, Ant and elsewhere; Robins, Bristol. The last-named refers to Bristol City Football Club, elsewhere for the bird, originally the redbreast, Robin being added (= Robert).

Robin Adair Newcastle-on-Tyne. The present words of this song were written by Lady Caroline Keppel about 1750, and were addressed to a young Irish surgeon whom she loved. She eventually married him and he went on to become Surgeon–General to George III. The previous words of the song had referred to an Irish member of parliament of the same name.

Robin Hood Nottingham and elsewhere. At least 100 pubs are currently named for this legendary outlaw of medieval England. Hindley says that the name spread in the nineteenth century, as the Ancient Order of Foresters (founded in 1834) opened new courts, or lodges. Robin himself, of course, lived in Sherwood Forest with his merrie men and Maid Marian, and acted like an unofficial taxman, robbing the rich to help the poor. Associated names include Old Robin Hood, Gloucester; Robin Hood's Retreat, Bristol; Robin Hood and Little John, Stevenage and elsewhere. There are also pubs named for Little John, Maid Marian, Friar Tuck and Will Scarlet. The popularity of the *Robin Hood and Little John* sign no doubt stems from the old rhyme: 'You gentlemen and yeomen good/Come in and drink with Robin Hood/If Robin Hood be not at home/Come in and drink with Little John.'

Robinson Crusoe London N16 and elsewhere. Daniel Defoe wrote *Robinson Crusoe* in 1719, basing it on the experiences of Alexander Selkirk. Defoe was nearly sixty at this time, and when it was clear that the book was successful lost no time in writing a follow-up. The book has contributed to the English language in a curious way, giving us 'girl Friday', alluding to Crusoe's faithful servant, so named because Crusoe met him on that day. As a pub name *Robinson Crusoe* is becoming more popular in the 1980s. The signs vary, but that at Stoke Newington evocatively shows merely a large footprint.

Rob Roy Buchlyvie, near Stirling. Others at Dumfries and Edinburgh. The novel by Sir Walter Scott of this name was published in 1817. The title character is Rob Roy Macgregor, who was a real-life outlaw. He was capable of being just, however, and was generous on occasion, so he has been called the Scottish Robin Hood. He died in 1734.

Rock and Heifer *See* Craven Heifer.

Rocking Chair Londonderry. Wakefield has a Rocking Horse. The journey from the *Rocking Horse* to the *Rocking Chair* seems to symbolise man's existence. *See* Mother's Arms.

Rocket *See* George Stephenson.

Rockmans Arms Froncysyllte, near Llangollen. The rockman is a skilled worker in a slate quarry who gets out the slate rock.

Rock of Gibraltar Bletchington Station, near Oxford. The pub here is named after the former Gibraltar Bridge road. At Gibraltar itself there is a Rock pub, its sign showing the rock, the colony's coat-of-arms, the union jack and an aircraft carrier in the foreground.

Rod and Line Tideford, Corn. Rod and Reel at Crianlarich, Cent. Names that no doubt hook a certain type of customer.

Rodney Also Rodney Arms, Rodney's Head, Rodney and Hood. *See* Admiral Rodney.

Roebuck Ruardean, Glos, and elsewhere. The male of the roe deer, the small species of 'spotted' deer.

Roe View Terrydremond, Londy. The river Roe is nearby.

Rogues Retreat Flackwell Heath, near High Wycombe. Presumably a reference to the pub's past rather than its present customers.

Roll Call Butlocks Heath, near Netley, Hants. There was a barracks nearby during the Napoleonic Wars. The roll-call was also the name of the signal that called the men together as well as a reading of their names.

Rolling Mill Llanelli and elsewhere, especially in South Wales in steelmaking centres. Swindon has a Rolling Mills relating to the railway workshops here.

Roman Mexborough, S Yorks. Also Romans, Silchester, Hants, and Southwick, near Brighton; Roman Galley, Chislet, near Canterbury; Roman Quay, Stembrook, near Dover; Roman Ridge, Sheffield and Scawsby, near Doncaster; Roman Urn, Cheshunt, Herts; Roman Way, Luton and London NW6. All these names serve as a reminder that Britain was occupied by Roman legions for nearly 400 years. They finally left at the beginning of the fifth century.

Roman Bath York. A Roman bath was discovered beneath the pub when alterations were being made in 1930. It can now be seen through an observation window in the lounge bar.

Roman Camp Aylmerton, near Cromer. Some local archaeological discoveries prompted the name.

Romany Northampton. A gipsy, or the gipsy language. *Rom* in that language means 'man' or 'husband'.

Romany Rye *See* George Borrow.

Romper Marple, near Stockport. A former landlord won a lot of money on a horse called *Miss Romper*.

Romping Cat Bloxwich, near Walsall. This was the Sandbank Tavern until 1957, but showed on its sign a heraldic lion from the arms of Sir Gilbert Wakering, lord of the manor in Elizabethan times. The nickname of the pub locally was then made official.

Romping Kitling Styal, near Stockport. 'Kitling' is a dialectal word for 'kitten'.

Roost Belfast. Others at Coleraine and Portaferry. Usually associated with hens, but the word can also mean to pass the night somewhere.

Ropemakers Arms Chatham. Another in Exeter. Also Ropers Arms, Boston; Ropery, Gainsborough. Pubs where the customers know the ropes. This was an especially important trade near dockyards.

Rorty Crankle Plaxtol, near Sevenoaks. The place name Plaxtol means 'playground', and the pub name was chosen to blend with it. 'Rorty' was a curious slang word in the nineteenth century, with a number of related meanings summed up in 'do the rorty – have a good time. 'Crankle' means a bend or twist. The pub stands at the junction of School Lane and High Street.

Rosary Thorpe Hamlet, Norwich. Named after the Rosary Cemetery nearby. 'Rosary' can mean a rosegarden as well as the beads used by Roman Catholics as an aid to memory when reciting prayers.

Roscoe Arms, Liverpool Also Roscoe Head and Sir Henry Roscoe, also in Liverpool. Sir Henry Roscoe (1833–1915) was professor of Chemistry at Manchester University and member of parliament for South Manchester. The other examples could be for him, or for Thomas Roscoe (1791–1871) an eminent translator and scholar who was born in Liverpool, or William Roscoe (1753–1831), his father, a poet, historian and author who was also born in Liverpool.

Rose The rose is by far the most popular flower to be mentioned in pub names. *See* Red Rose, White Rose, Tudor Rose (under Tudor Arms), Yorkshire Rose and the like for the development of its use as a national heraldic symbol. Some of the combination rose names are listed in separate entries below, but the general range of names is illustrated by the following: Rose, Strelley, near Nottingham; Rose Valley, Norwich; Rose in Bloom, Whitstable; Rose in Hand, Cinderford; Rose in June, Margate and elsewhere; Rose in the Valley, Chatham; Rose of England, Portsea and elsewhere; Rose Garden, Holmer near Hereford; Rose Grower, Bramcote Hills, Nottingham; Rose and Laurel, Bath; Rose and Lily, Rotherhithe; Rose and Olive Branch, Virginia Water, Sry; Rose and Shamrock, London SW1; Rose and Thistle, Frimley Green, Sry; Rosebud, Accrington and elsewhere; Bloomin Rose, Hunslet Moor, near Leeds; Briar Rose, Cork; English Rose, Bristol and elsewhere; Golden Rose, Cambridge; Hampshire Rose, Purbrook, Hants; Handford Rose, Ipswich; Little Rose, Cambridge; Moss Rose, Kearsley, near Bolton; Old Rose, Radford near Nottingham; Peldon Rose, Peldon, near Colchester; Union Rose, Rochdale. Individual varieties of rose such as Super Star also occur, apart from those that share their names with pubs. (The Admiral Rodney, as a pub name, is normally a direct reference to the

admiral, but it could be for the rose of that name. There are many similar examples). *See also* Rose Revived, Minden Rose and Yellow Rose.

Rose and Castle Braunston, near Daventry and elsewhere. The Braunston pub is beside a canal and reflects the theme of the old narrow-boat decorations.

Rose and Crown Lenton, Nottingham and elsewhere. Over sixty London pubs bear this name, and it is found extensively throughout the country. The sign indicates loyalty to the monarch and to England, and has done so since the early seventeenth century. The 'Merrie Olde England Pavilion' at the Walt Disney Centre, Florida, features a pub of this name.

Rose and Portcullis *See* Portcullis.

Rose and Thistle London SE5. Another at Frimley Green, near Camberley. A reference to the uniting of the English rose with the Scottish thistle, eg when James VI of Scotland became James I of England in 1603.

Rose and Woodbine *See* Woodbine.

Rose Cottage Norton Fitzwarren, near Taunton, and elsewhere. Also Rose in Hand, Drybrook, Glos. These names are said to relate to the rose that was given by the tenants of cottages as peppercorn rent to the owners. 'Peppercorn' is used here to signify something of no value. The *Oxford English Dictionary* quotes an example of a 'bunch of may' being used for such a rent in the seventeenth century.

Rose Grower Bramcote Hills, Nottingham. A partner for the same brewery's Nurseryman nearby. Paintings of roses are found inside the pub.

Roseland Philleigh, Corn. The roses in the front courtyard justify the name. The well-known Trelissick Garden is also across the channel. Perhaps they should try to reintroduce the term 'rose-parley' here: in the sixteenth century it referred to 'pleasant conversation'.

Rosemary Branch London SE14. Another at London SE27. Branches of rosemary were used for decoration, especially at weddings and funerals. The plant symbolises both fidelity to one's partner and remembrance.

Rose of Denmark London SW13 and elsewhere. A reference to Alexandra, Princess of Wales, who was Danish by birth. The wild rose was her favourite flower, and as Queen Alexandra she inaugurated Alexandra Rose Day in 1912 to mark her fiftieth year of residence in England. Rose emblems were sold to the public to raise money for hospitals, a practice which still continues.

Rose of England Portsea, near Portsmouth. Another at London NW5. A thoroughly patriotic sign, given that the rose itself signifies England. More local references are found in Rose of Kent, Deptford; Rose of Mossley, Liverpool; Rose of Lee, Lee, London SE13. The latter pub manages to suggest the Cockney's cup of Rosie Lee, or tea. There is a Rose of Lancaster at Chadderton, near Oldham and a Rose of York at Richmond, Sry.

Rose Revived Hadlow, near Tunbridge Wells and elsewhere. Originally a reference to the Restoration of Charles II in 1660. A publican named Rose is said to have revived the pub of this name at Newbridge, Oxon.

Rose, Thistle and Shamrock Burslem, near Stoke-on-Trent. Another at Hanley, Staffs. The use of three national emblems to signify the union of England, Scotland and Ireland on 1 January 1801. Southampton has a similar Rose, Shamrock and Thistle.

Rosie O'Grady Brighton. A reference to 'Sweet Rosie O'Grady', subject of a music-hall song: 'And when we are married/How happy we'll be/I love sweet Rosie O'Grady/And Rosie O'Grady loves me!'

Rossetti London NW8. Dante Gabriel Rossetti (1828–82) was the son of an Italian exile who wrote patriotic verse. Dante himself was a poet and painter of considerable merit, aligning himself as a painter with the so-called Pre–Raphaelites, who painted as they believed the Italian painters had done before Raphael, in the sixteenth century. They concentrated on serious biblical and literary themes and used bright colours and great detail. Rossetti's poems appeared in a journal edited by his brother. His sister, Christina Georgina Rossetti was also a lyric poet, often dealing in a melancholy way with religious themes.

Rother Easebourne, near Midhurst. Also

Rother Arms, Bexill-on-Sea; Rother Valley, Northam. After the river Rother, which rises near Rotherfield and falls into the Channel at Rye. Other rivers of this name rise near Priors Dean, Hants, flowing into the Arun near Pulborough, and near Pilsley, south of Chesterfield, flowing into the Don at Rotherham.

Round Bush *See* Bush.

Roundhead Bretton, near Peter-borough. Others at Reading and Kidderminster. This was a nickname for a Parliamentarian soldier during the Civil War in the seventeenth century. Such soldiers objected to the degenerate long curly hair of the Royalists and cropped their own hair very short. The Bretton pub pursues the theme of Cromwell and his men inside.

Round House London E16. Others at London WC2 and Bath. Historically this was the name for a prison. The 'round' referred to the patrol of the guards and did not necessarily imply that the building was round in shape.

Round of Beef Cradley Heath, W Mids. A slice of beef cut from the upper part of the back leg, and giving a new meaning to that old pub phrase 'my round'.

Round of Gras Badsey, near Evesham. A round of 'gras', or asparagus, comprises thirty shoots in a bundle, as shown on the sign. The pub is in the fertile Vale of Evesham where market fruits and vegetables are grown.

Round Stone near East Preston, W Ssx. The pub is on the Roundstone by-pass and refers to a millstone which was placed over the grave of a suicide, buried by custom at a crossroads. A stake was also driven down through the hole in the centre of the stone to prevent a ghostly return of the dead man. The sign shows it all, including the skeleton's grimace at the weight of the millstone.

Rovers Return Manchester. Another at Blackburn, built in the early 1970s when Blackburn Rovers had just been relegated to the Second Division. Local people naturally hoped to see them return to the First Division. The name was given in the knowledge that the *Rovers Return* of the television soap-opera *Coronation Street* was probably the best-known pub in the country.

Rowan Tree Uddingston, Strath. Another at Dundee. Rowan is another name for the mountain ash, often planted outside Scottish houses to ward off evil.

Row Barge Guildford and elsewhere. A barge propelled by oars, especially one used to convey royalty on state occasions.

Rowing Machine Witney, Oxon. 'Rowing' here is used in a very special sense, referring to the raising of a pile on cloth. The rowing machine was a horse-driven contraption which did this job. Witney has long been famous for the manufacture of blankets.

Rowley Rag Rowley Regis, W Mids. The local name for the stone from the quarries here, used for road making.

Royal Albert London SE14 and elsewhere. A variant of Prince Albert, perhaps suggested by the launching of HMS *Royal Albert* in 1854 (by Queen Victoria, naturally). At St Budeaux, near Devonport there is a Royal Albert Bridge, commemorating the opening of the local railway bridge across the Tamar by Prince Albert in 1859.

Royal Anchor *See* Anchor.

Royal Archer Edinburgh and elsewhere. The Royal Company of Archers traditionally act as bodyguards when the sovereign is in residence at Holyrood Palace in Edinburgh. *See also* Archery.

Royal Arms Attleborough, Nflk and elsewhere. The coat of arms of the reigning monarch has been borrowed as an inn sign since the Restoration (1660) to indicate allegiance to the crown. Former signs which showed odd-looking lions and dragons, swans and falcons, boars and antelopes, etc, were often attempts to reproduce some aspect of the royal arms.

Royal Arthur Corsham, Wilts. For HMS *Royal Arthur*, the local naval training and leadership school.

Royal Artillery Arms Willenhall, W Mids. Also West Huntspill, Som. *See* Artillery.

Royal Ascot Cheltenham. The name of the four-day race meeting at Ascot in June. The royal party drive down the course and the whole occasion is a social event of importance.

Royal Blenheim Oxford. A famous stagecoach of this name which ran from Oxford.

Royal Breakwater *See* Portland Roads.

Royal Charlie London E14. There was an older pub here called the Royal Charles which referred to the ship the *Charles II*, taken by the Dutch in 1667.

Royal Children Castlegate, Nottingham. According to tradition the children of Princess Anne, daughter of James II, played with those of the local innkeeper. (After her marriage to Prince George of Denmark in 1683 Princess Anne had five children from seventeen confinements. Four of the children died before the age of two, the fifth died at the age of eleven).

Royal Consort *See* Prince Albert.

Royal Cricketers *See* Cricket.

Royal Dragoon *See* Dragoon.

Royal Duchess London E1. Opposite this pub is a Royal Duke. It is not clear which name inspired the other.

Royal Duchy Falmouth. A reference to the duchy of Cornwall, the huge estate established by Edward III in 1337 for the Black Prince. It has been inherited by the sovereign's eldest son ever since, and is currently administered on behalf of Prince Charles by a government trust.

Royal Escape Brighton. Charles II was obliged to escape to France in 1651. It was a Brighton skipper.

Captain Tattershall, who took him there, changing the name of his brig to *Royal Escape* after Charles had returned safely, in 1660. The grateful monarch provided the captain with a gratuity which he used to establish himself in the Old Ship at Brighton. Another Brighton pub, the Royal Stuart, refers to the same escape.

Royal Esk Musselburgh, Loth. The Scottish river Esk is formed by the union of the North Esk and South Esk and flows into the Firth of Forth at Musselburgh.

Royal Exchange Paddington and elsewhere. This would normally refer to the building at Cornhill, London, but the painters of inn signs prefer to have fun with it. The Paddington sign shows Richard III on his knees, offering his crown to a yokel who holds a feeble-looking nag. Below are the words: 'A horse, a horse, my kingdom for a horse.' At Basingstoke the sign recalls the execution of Charles I as England exchanged the monarch for Oliver Cromwell.

Royal Forest Coleford, Glos. Another at Ascot. Also Royal Forester, Callow End, near Worcester; Royal Foresters. Cinderford. A reminder of royal hunting activities in former times.

Royal French Arms Throckley, near Wylam, Northld. A group of royalist French clergy refugees who were housed in this area after the Revolution in 1789. They returned to France in 1802.

Royal George Birdlip, Glos and elsewhere. The Birdlip sign shows George III in uniform surveying the local mansion which he owned. The Bermondsey sign shows a ship of this name, built at Woolwich in 1756. It foundered at Spithead in 1782 with the loss of 800 lives.

The name was subsequently used for other Royal Navy ships.

Royal Gloucestershire Hussar Frocester, Glos. The sign shows on one side a hussar (*see* **Hussar**) in full uniform on his horse, on the other the regimental arms and a list of its battle honours. An example of what the sign-painter can achieve (in this case John Cook of Whitbreads was responsible).

Royal Greenjacket *See* Green Jacket.

Royal Head Llanidloes, Pwys. This name amalgamates two others, the Royal Oak and King's Head. The sign shows Edward III (1312–77).

Royal Hunt Ascot. Royal Huntsman, Williton, near Taunton. Signs which link with Royal Forest.

Royal Hussar *See* **Hussar**.

Royal Inn Atherton, near Manchester. A rare name in this form, though 'royal' occurs as an element in many pub names. As an appendage, eg Angel and Royal, Grantham, Golden Lion Royal, Dolgellau, Gynd, it often indicates a single visit by a member of the royal family.

Royalist Market Harborough, Leics. Another at Stow-on-the-Wold, Glos. The local people supported the Royalist cause during the Civil War of 1642–46.

Royal Lion Lyme Regis, Dors. 'Confused lion' might be an appropriate name for this pub. It began as the Golden Lion, became the Red Lion, switched to White Lion then took its present name in 1856. The Prince of Wales, later Edward VII, stayed incognito while on a walking tour with his tutor.

Royal London *See* London.

Royal Mail Taunton and elsewhere. Pubs of this name are often close to a Post Office sorting centre. Others have historical connections with mail coaches. The Taunton sign shows the driver of such a coach controlling his horses.

Royal Marine Plymouth and elsewhere. The Plymouth pub is for the Commandos, whose barracks is at Crownhill. At Combe Martin, near Ilfracombe the pub was adopted by the Royal Marine Depot at Lympstone. The sign at Walton-on-the-Naze, Esx, shows the landlord's stepson serving with the Corps, complete with his bugle and drum.

Royal Midshipman *See* Clarence.

Royal Mortar London SE18 and elsewhere. The name of a gun manufactured at the Woolwich Arsenal, around the middle of the nineteenth century. It was made of brass and had a five and a half inch bore, weighed 150 lbs and was able to project a twenty-four pounder shell up to 600 yards. Such guns were installed on ships. It is said that another pub in London, originally the King's Head and showing Charles I on its sign, became the Royal Martyr after his execution, which in turn was corrupted to *Royal Mortar*. Charles I was certainly described as the Royal Martyr, but by Macaulay in the nineteenth century, not in the seventeenth century.

Royal Nip Edinburgh. Wherein may be obtained a nip of whisky of outstanding quality, or so the name implies.

Royal Oak Mayfield, E Ssx and elsewhere. This sign is second in popularity to the Red Lion, well over 500 pubs bearing the name in the 1980s. Charles II, together with his aide Colonel Carless, hid from noon to dusk in the Boscobel Oak, near Shifnal, Salop, in order to escape from the Roundhead soldiers who were pursuing him. Charles had suffered defeat at the Battle of Worcester, 1651. After the Restoration of Charles II to the throne it was declared that 29 May, the king's birthday, should henceforth be celebrated as Royal Oak Day as an act of thanksgiving. The popularity of the pub sign may be attributed to genuine rejoicing that the monarchy had been restored, but it also comments on the appeal of particular human incidents, comprehensible even to a child, over the great events that shape our history. Signs usually show the king in the tree, but variants include the portrayal of the medal which was struck to commemorate the occasion, seen at Newingreen, near Hythe. Indirect references to the main event occur when a pub is named for one of the ships which has borne this name. The first was launched in 1664 and sunk by the Dutch in 1667. It is seen on the sign at Cartmel, Cumb. At Shoreham, near Sevenoaks, the name is for the battleship sunk in 1939 in Scapa Flow. At Nailsea, Avon, the pub was named for the Royal Oak Brewery. There is still a Royal Oak strong cask ale, made by Eldridge Pope. Portsmouth seems to be the only town to have an extended form of this name – Royal Oak Tree.

Royal Pavilion Tavern Brighton. The Prince Regent's fantasy palace is nearby. The Royal Pavilion was built in Mogul style with Chinese decor by Holland and Nash.

Royal Pier *See* Pier Tavern.

Royal Sailor *See* King William IV.

Royal Saxon London W2. An allusion to King Alfred.

Royal Scot Crewe and elsewhere. The name of a train service from Euston to Glasgow, hauled by the Royal Scot 4–6–0 engines. The first of these, built in 1927, numbered 6100, was the *Royal Scot*. Other locomotives in the series had names like *Royal Scots Grey, Black Watch, Royal Scots Fusilier, Scottish Borderer, Cameron Highlander*, etc. The old sign at Crewe showed the *Royal Scot* engine on one side, with Bonnie Prince Charlie on the reverse.

Royal Sovereign London E5. There were several ships of the Royal Navy which bore this name, the last being a battleship of 1915. The seventeenth-century ship was famous, and was known also as *Sovereign of the Seas*. The name is also that of a well-known variety of strawberry and a beer brewed by Kentish Ales.

Royal Squadron Ryde, IOW. The Royal Yacht Squadron is based here. 'Squadron' here has the sense of a small body of seamen assigned to a particular duty.

Royal Standard Derby and elsewhere. The royal flag or standard has changed through the centuries, reflecting the course of history. Edward III introduced the fleur-de-lys of France, James I the Scottish lion and the Irish harp, and so on. The present standard dates from the accession of Queen Victoria. At Hastings, King Harold's standard is shown, used at the Battle of Hastings in 1066.

Royal Standard of England Forty Green, near Beaconsfield. The name dates from the seventeenth century, when Charles II visited the Royalist innkeeper.

Royal Stuart Brighton. A reference to Charles II, one of the Stuart kings. There is a

Royal Stewart at Worthing, also referring to one of this dynasty.

Royal Table Bristol. As with Royal Nip at Edinburgh, 'royal' is used to suggest something of out-standing quality – in this instance the food provided. There was once a Royal Bed in this city.

Royal Tar *See* Clarence.

Royal Tiger Leyland, Lancs. The name of a bus built by the Leyland Company.

Royalty Christchurch, Dors. Another at Otley, W Yorks. Christchurch has the remains of a twelfth-century castle, which may have inspired this name.

Royal Victoria and Bull Rochester. Recalling a visit to the town by Queen Victoria, which caused the Bull to be renamed.

Royal William *See* King William IV.

Royal Yeoman Grimstone, near Dorchester. The Queen's Own Dorsetshire Yeomanry, founded in 1881.

Royal York Bath. George, Duke of York, later George V.

Rubaiyat Glasgow. *The Rubaiyat of Omar Khayyam* was a translation of the *rubais* or quatrains of a Persian poet, by Edward Fitzgerald, first published anonymously in 1859. Omar Khayyam ('tent-maker') was an eleventh-century poet. The poem contains his thoughts on the mysteries of existence, and concludes that one should drink and make merry while life lasts.

Rubbing House Epsom. Where horses were rubbed down.

Ruddy Duck Peakirk, near Peterborough. The name of a reddish duck which can be seen in the nearby Wildfowl Trust enclosure.

Rugby The game of rugby is not referred to all that frequently in pub names. At Twickenham, the home of Rugby Union Football in England, there are naturally references to the game itself, as in Rugby Tavern (another at Cubbington), also to the famous ground, as in Twickers and Cabbage Patch. Rugger Tavern, Attleborough, near Nuneaton is close to the local rugby ground.

Wigan has a Ball and Boot, and the group includes Drop Kick, Low Moor, Bradford; Fair Play, Bridgend; Leicester Tiger, Leicester, Touch Down, Hartlepool and Up and Under. Cwmbran, Gwent.

Rugglestone Widecombe-in-the-Moor. The local name for a nearby 'rocking stone' on Dartmoor.

Rule and Compass Bulkington, near Nuneaton. Also Rule and Square, Edlesborough, near Dunstable. Signs meant to attract carpenters and masons.

Rumbling Tum Glasgow. Only Glasgow could stomach a name like this.

Rumboe London EC4. (Old Bailey) At one time 'rumbo(e)' was a slang term for a prison. The pub stands on a corner of the site of the old Newgate Prison.

Rummer King's Lynn and elsewhere. The name of a large drinking glass. The word derives from Flemish or Dutch *roemer* and has nothing to do with rum. It is traditionally explained as meaning 'Roman' glass. Cardiff has a Rummer Tavern.

Rumples Rye, E Ssx. Another at Belfast. The Rye inn sign shows Rumpelstilzchen, as he is in the original German story, or Rumpelstiltskin as he becomes in English. It concerns a dwarf who aids the miller's daughter to spin straw into gold for the king, whom she marries. The dwarf gave his assistance on condition that the first daughter of that union should become his bride. He agrees to release the queen from this obligation if she can discover his name. It is a name that is probably almost as useful as the breathalyser – if you can say it you're still sober.

Rum Puncheon Boston. Another at Swansea. A cask (*see* Puncheon) containing rum.

Rum Runners Southampton. A reference to the men and ships engaged in rum smuggling.

Running Buck See Buck.

Running Footman See I am the only Running Footman.

Running Fox See Fox.

Running Horses Erith, Kent. Another at Mickleham, Sry. The Erith pub is for the wild horses which once roamed through the Erith marshes. For the Mickleham reference *see* Cadland.

Running Pump Catforth, near Preston. A pump is built into the front of the inn, which dates from 1834. It served the whole community at one time.

Runnymede Egham, Sry. The pub is close to Runnymede itself, famous as the spot where King John was compelled by his barons to set his seal on the Magna Carta in 1215. There is another pub of this name at Newcastle-on-Tyne. *See also* Magna Charta.

Runt-in-tun Maynards Green, E Ssx. A rebus name inspired by Runtington Farm nearby. The farm name goes back to an Old English personal name, Hrunta. In its pub name form we have a small pig in a large barrel.

Runway Bucksburn, near Aberdeen. A reference to Dyce civil airport.

Rupert Brooke Grantchester, near Cambridge. Rupert Brooke (1887–1915) was a highly promising young poet who was killed while on active service in World War One. He wrote a poem called *The Old Vicarage, Grantchester* in which he described that 'lovely hamlet' in glowing terms, but probably his best known poem is *The Soldier*, a sonnet which begins: 'If I should die, think only this of me:/That there's some corner of a foreign field/That is for ever England.'

Ruskin Arms London E12. John Ruskin (1819–1900) was an English author and critic, especially of art and architecture. Later he turned to the question of social reforms. Ruskin College Oxford was named in his honour.

Russells Nottingham. This was the Clinton Arms until 1983. The interior decor now relates to Jane Russell, who made many films in the 1950s and one or two afterwards. She was in *Gentlemen prefer Blondes* (1953) and the far less interesting *Gentlemen marry Brunettes* (1955).

Rusty Axe Kingsbury Episcopi, Som. Said to be for an axe that was left behind by a withy-cutter and never claimed.

Rutland Belton, near Uppingham. A reminder of what was England's smallest county until it disappeared, from an administrative point of view, in 1974.

Sack of Potatoes *See* Fruits and Vegetables.

Safe Harbour Fowey, Corn. Others at Ipswich and Birmingham. Literally true, or used metaphorically.

Saffron Saffron Walden, Esx. Saffron was extensively cultivated here from the time of Edward III until the late eighteenth century. Saffron was thought to be of medicinal value at one time. It is now used for colouring and flavouring purposes.

Sailor Prince *See* King William IV.

Sailors Safety Dinas, Dyfed. This pub is right next to the sea but is tucked securely into the dunes.

Sailor's Return East Chaldon, near Dorchester. The sign shows a sailor home on leave being greeted by his wife, whose lover is trapped in a cupboard. Presumably a reminder that sailors may have a wife in every port, but that a wife may also have her fling.

Saint Some 70 different saints are mentioned in British pub names. An indication is given below of the range of names that occur, and there are individual entries for a few names of particular interest. In most cases, however, a saintly pub name has simply been borrowed from a nearby church which is dedicated to a saint, or the reference to the saint is secondary. When a pub is called St Ives, for example, one can be fairly sure that it is a place of that name that is alluded to, rather than a direct reference to Saint Ia. Some saints are well known as patrons of a country or profession and may have had their names attached to

pubs for that reason, but most are obscure people about whom a great many legends and very few facts are known. It should be said that sign-painters generally do their homework, referring to Butler's four volumes on the lives of the saints, or the more accessible *Penguin Dictionary of Saints* or similar works, and correctly show individual saints in the right kind of dress and accompanied by the correct traditional symbols. The symbols composed a primitive Christian heraldry in the Middle Ages, allowing illiterate church-goers to identify a particular saint by the tongs with which he tweaked the devil's nose (St Dunstan), his keys (St Peter) or whatever. The exact identification of some of the saints listed below would be impossible, since many bear the same name or are known by different versions of the same name. Finally, there are other pub names which allude to saints without actually mentioning that word, as in Catherine Wheel. Brief notes are added below as appropriate: St Agnes, St Agnes, near Truro; St Albans, Cheltenham, Rochdale and Liverpool; St Andrew's Hall, Norwich; St Andrew's Head, London E14; St Andrew's Tavern, London W1 – patron saint of Scotland; St Ann's, Nottingham; St Anne's Castle, Great Leigh, near Chelmsford; St Anne's Cross, Faversham; St Anne's Vaults, Liverpool – probably for the mother of the Virgin Mary; St Aubyn's, Hove; St Aubyn's Arms, Crowan, near Helston; St Aubyn's

Vaults, Devonport; St Bernard's Grange, Birmingham; St Bride's Tavern, London EC4; St Buryan, St Buryan, near Penzance; St Clair Arms, Castletown, near Thurso; St Clair Tavern, Kirkcaldy; St Clements Bar, Aberdeen – a Saint Clements is also the name of a drink consisting of orange and lemon juice mixed, believed to have been invented by a barman in a BBC club. It alludes to 'The Bells of St Clements' in the children's playground song which begins 'Oranges and Lemons'; St Crispin, Worth, near Sandwich; St Cuthbert's, Scorton, near Richmond, N Yorks; St David's, formerly in Manchester – patron saint of Wales; St Day, St Day, near Redruth; St Denys, St Denys, near Southampton; St Domingo, Liverpool; St Dunstan, Langley, near Macclesfield; St Dunstan's, Sutton, near Prescot – patron of blacksmiths; St Edmund's Head, Bury St Edmunds; St Faith's, formerly at Norwich; St Fagan's Castle, Penarth; St Giles Gate Stores, Norwich until the 1960s; St Govan's, Bosherton, near Pembroke; St Helen's, Chesterfield and Derby; St Helier's Arms, Carshalton, Sry; St Hilda, Liverpool; St Ives, Neath, W Glam; St James Tavern, London W1 – there was a leper hospital here dedicated to St James; St James Wine Vaults, Bristol; St John's, St John's, near Torpoint, Corn; St John's Arms, Melchbourne, near Bedford; St John's House, Penzance; St John's Tavern, Southwark and elsewhere; St John's in the Vale, near Thirlmere, Keswick; St John's Head, Great Yarmouth – where the sign shows the head of St John the Baptist on a silver salver, demanded as a reward for Salome's dancing; St John of Jerusalem, London EC1 – recalling the religious nursing order, the Knights Hospitallers of St John of Jerusalem, founded in the eleventh century. Revived in the nineteenth century and now controls the St John Ambulance Brigade; St Johnstoun, Perth; St Julian's, Newport, Gwent; St Kew, St Kew, near Wadebridge, Corn; St Lawrence, St Lawrence, near Ventnor; St Lawrence Stone, Stone, near Dartford; St Leonards, St Leonard's, near Ringwood, Hants – *see also* Startled Saint – St Leonard's Arms, London E14; St Levan, Devonport; St Loyes, Exeter – patron of farriers; St Luke's, Birmingham; St Luke's Head, London EC1 – patron of brewers; St Machar Bar, Aberdeen; St Margaret's Tavern, St Margaret's, Twickenham; St Mary's Arms, Portsmouth; St Mary's Gate, Arundel; St Mary's Vaults, Stamford; St Matthew's Tavern, Manchester – patron of tax-collectors; St Matthias, Birmingham; St Mawes, St Mawes, near Truro; St Michael's, Leuchars, Fife; St Michael's Mount, Barripper, Corn; St Mungo's Arms, Lockerbie, Dumfries – *see also* Fish and Ring – St Nicholas, Stevenage, Herts; St Nicholas Arms, Carlisle; St Nicholas House, Bristol; St Olave, formerly at Folkestone; St Oswald's Arms, Featherstone, near Haltwhistle, Northld; St Owen's Cross, St Owen's Cross, near Hereford; St Patrick, Liverpool; St Patrick's Tavern, Standish, near Wigan; St Patrick's Well, Bampton, near Penrith – patron saint of Ireland; St Paul's Tavern, Birmingham and elsewhere; St Peter's Tavern, Manchester – *see also* Cross Keys – St Petrock, formerly at Bodmin; St Philip's Tavern, Manchester; St Quintin's Arms, Harpham, near Driffield, Humb; St Tecla, Chepstow; St Thomas's Cross, Newton, near Rugby – also remembered in Thomas à Becket; St Thomas Bar, Arbroath; St Vincent, Manchester and Birmingham; St Vincent Arms, Norton Disney, near Lincoln; St Vincent Rocks, Bristol; St Wilfrid's, Ripon; St Winifred's, Liverpool.

St George London SW1 and elsewhere. The patron saint of England appears most frequently on inn signs of the George and Dragon, but there are five *St George* signs in London, for instance. St George and Dragon is found at Norwich and Clyst St George, near Exeter. Cheltenham has a St George's Vaults.

St Helena London SE16. After the volcanic island in the South Atlantic where Napoleon was exiled in 1815 until his death in 1821. The island has an area of about forty-seven square miles and a permanent population of some 4,000 Europeans, Asians and Africans.

St Leger Tavern Doncaster. Another at Sheffield. Also St Leger Arms, Laughton-en-le-Northen, near Rotherham. The St Leger race for three-year-olds, run at Doncaster in September each year, was named for Colonel Anthony St Leger in 1778, though first run two years earlier. It is the last of the season's Classic flat races.

St Martin's Brewery Chichester. Also St Martin's Tavern, London NW1. St Martin is the patron saint of drunkards, only because his feast day happens to fall on the Vinalia or feast of Bacchus (11 November). He is also the patron saint of innkeepers. The saint himself is best known for having given his cloak to a naked beggar, 'in whom he was led to recognise Christ'. This incident prompted the Water Poet, John Taylor, to write in 1636: 'If it be true, some ancient writers spoke,/That Martin to a beggar gave his cloak:/Those that have cloaks, let them this tavern find,/And there they and their cloaks may well be lined.'

St Peter's Finger Lytchett Minster, Dors. A particularly well-known sign, showing the saint with his left forefinger pointing aloft to heaven. Many writers have moralised about this encouragement to think of spiritual rather than worldly matters. It is said, however, that 'finger' was a local interpretation of Latin *vincula* 'chains', used to describe the celebration of Peter's release by the angel from the chains in which Herod Agrippa I had confined him. This incident sometimes causes the saint to be shown with a chain as an emblem instead of his usual key or keys.

St Ronan's Well Innerleithen, Bdrs. The title of a novel by Sir Walter Scott, published in 1823. It concerns the idle life of fashionable society in the Scottish spa of St Ronan's Well.

Saints Millbrook, Southampton. The nickname of the Southampton Football Club, whose ground is nearby.

St Stephen's Tavern London SW1. The pub is fitted with a bell which summons the many members of parliament who use this pub back to the House of Commons if there is about to be a division. St Stephen's is used as a synonym for the House of Commons, though strictly speaking it refers to the entrance, which was originally a chapel dedicated to the saint.

Sair Inn Linthwaite, near Huddersfield. 'Sair' is a dialectal form of 'sour'. At one time the pub cellar was kept too warm, affecting the quality of the beer. A new landlord chose the present name to remind himself not to make the same mistake as his predecessor.

Salamanca Wrenbury, near Nantwich, Ches. The capital of Salamanca province, Spain. In 1812 Wellington decisively defeated the French army there.

Salamander Dudley and elsewhere. The winner of the Grand National in 1866 bore this name, and was honoured on some inn signs. The salamander itself was supposed in ancient times to be a lizard-like creature which was able to live in fire. It has been part of the Ironmongers' coat of arms since 1455.

Salisbury London SW1. The lease of the pub was acquired from the Marquis of Salisbury in 1892.

Sally Port Portsmouth. This word has a special meaning in Portsmouth, where it refers to a landing place set apart for the use of men-of-war's boats. The general meaning of the word is an opening in a fortified place through which troops may make a 'sally', a sudden sortie.

Salmon Apsley End, near Hemel Hempstead, and elsewhere. The fish which anglers enjoy catching and others enjoy eating. The sign was found in London in the seventeenth century when, it is claimed, salmon could be caught in the Thames.

Salmon and Ball London E2. The ball was possibly added because mercers used the inn, the reference being to a ball of silk.

Salmon Leap Totton, near Southampton. The sign shows a fish 'climbing' a waterfall, which may itself be known as a 'salmon leap', on its way to its breeding place.

Salt Box Liverpool. Another at Harrogate. A box of salt was kept nearby in winter months. Drivers of horse-drawn trams used the salt in snowy conditions.

Salters Arms Darlington. After the Worshipful Company of Salters (1558), originally a guild of producers and sellers of seasalt and those who preserved food with it. There is a Salter at Weaverham, near Northwich, and a Salters at Cradley Heath, W Mids.

Saltersgate near Whitby. A reference to the illegal traffic in salt in the eighteenth century, when that product was heavily taxed. It was carried by packhorse to this isolated inn, as were fish landed at Whitby. The fish was salted and distributed by other packhorse trains throughout the North.

Salt Horn Thornton, near Bradford. Probably a large salt cellar in the shape of a horn, of the kind which was placed in the centre of a dining table. Important dinner guests sat 'above the salt', less important guests were 'below the salt'.

Salt House Clevedon, Avon. The pub was formerly the home of a man who owned the local salt-manufacturing business.

Salty Dog Ilfracombe. The sign shows Popeye the Sailor.

Salutation Gibb, Wilts, and elsewhere. An early religious sign referring to the Annunciation, the greeting and proclamation of the Archangel Gabriel to the Virgin Mary. The Puritans objected strongly to such signs, and they were transformed in various ways, eg into the Soldier and Citizen. The Gibb sign is non-religious, showing a Victorian gallant kneeling before his lady-love.

Same Yet Prestwich, near Manchester. Local legend says that this pub, formerly the Seven Stars, was due to be repainted. Asked what colour scheme was to be adopted, the landlord replied 'Same yet', meaning 'Same as it is now'.

Samson Gilsland, near Brampton, Cumb. Also Samson's Castle, London SE1; Samson and Lion, West Bromwich and elsewhere. Samuel Pepys drank at a London *Samson* in 1661. The exploits of this popular biblical hero have always had a great appeal. He was to the Philistines what Sylvester Stallone, in his various roles, is to his opponents. A man of prodigious strength, not exactly a thinker, and as putty in the hands of an attractive woman, he personifies the macho image. He slew a lion while still a young man, and a few thousand Philistines along the way, but was ultimately betrayed by Delilah.

Samuel Pepys London EC4. Others at Slipston, near Kettering and Gillingham, Kent. Samuel Pepys (1633–1703) is best known as a diarist, though he was a diligent naval official, secretary to the Admiralty, and in 1684 was president of the Royal Society. His diary was written in cipher and was published only in 1825. It contains an intimate record of his domestic, social and political life and thus provides a vivid picture of life in the Restoration period.

Samuel's Lichfield. A name which the man referred to would no doubt have thought highly impertinent. Dr Samuel Johnson (*see* Doctor Johnson) was born here. There is another *Samuel's* at Old Hill, W Mids, not far away.

Samuel Whitbread London WC2. The founder of the famous brewery, which began business in 1742. There are now over 7,000 Whitbread pubs. The company also has an interest in several other breweries.

Sam Weller's Birmingham. Sam Weller was the 'Boots' at the *White Hart*, afterwards servant to Samuel Pickwick in *The Pickwick Papers*, by Charles Dickens. His loyalty to his master is such that he has himself arrested for debt in order to be able to join Pickwick in prison.

Sand Boy Bawsey, near Kings Lynn. In modern times it is perfectly normal to hear someone being described as 'happy as a sand boy', the phrase conjuring up an image of a boy playing with sand on a beach. In the nineteenth century the phrase was always 'as jolly as a sand boy', which gave point to Dickens's remark in *The Old Curiosity Shop*: 'The *Jolly Sandboys* was a small roadside inn of pretty ancient date, with a sign representing three Sandboys increasing their jollity with as many jugs of ale and bags of gold . . . ' (There was formerly a Jolly Sandboy at Englefield Green, Surrey, but the name disappeared in 1956). In 1823 a *Dictionary of the Turf* said: 'As jolly as a sandboy' designates a merry fellow who has tasted a drop. The same dictionary also made it clear that 'sand boys' were boys who drove carts laden with sand. They dug it from sand pits and went around selling it where they could.

Sandpiper Ainsdale, near Southport, and elsewhere. A member of the plover family, named for its clear piping note.

Sandringham King's Lynn. The village of Sandringham is seven miles away. The estate there was acquired by the Prince of Wales, later Edward VII, in 1863 and the Hall has been a royal residence ever since. George VI (1895–1952) was born and died there.

Sandsifter Gwithian, near Hayle, Corn. After the men who once panned the local streams, washing the sand in the hunt for various metals.

Sandy Bay Towyn, near Abergele. This North Wales resort has one.

Sans Pareil Frindsbury, near Chatham. A French phrase meaning 'without equal', in use for centuries to describe anything of high quality. The traditional translation was 'nonesuch' or 'nonsuch', the latter form (like *Sans Pareil* itself) being used to name varieties of apple and pear. A French ship named *Sans Pareil* was captured by the Royal Navy in 1794, and the name was afterwards used for other British ships, including a battleship. Compare *Nonpareil* 'no equal', which has had similar naval use.

Saracen's Head Southwell, Notts and elsewhere. To the Greeks and Romans, a Saracen was a nomad of the Arabian desert. The word came to mean 'Arab', then 'Moslem', especially with regard to the Crusades. Noble families whose members had taken part in the Crusades tended to include thereafter a Saracen's head as part of their arms. It was then transferred to inn signs in the normal way. The inn signs usually show a typical Arab or Turk. The Southwell inn is particularly well-known because Charles I surrendered to the Scots there in 1646.

Sarah Mansfield Willey, near Rugby. A former landlord of this Free house named the pub in honour of his mother, using her maiden name.

Sarah Siddons Brecon, Pwys. Also at Warwick and Cheltenham. Sarah Siddons (1755–1831) was a celebrated English tragic actress. She was born in Brecon at the Shoulder of Mutton. She was renowned for her beauty and deportment and is said to have lived a blameless life. Her most famous role was that of Lady Macbeth.

Satchmo's Bonnyrigg, Loth. Another at Kirkcaldy, Fife. The nickname of the famous black American jazz trumpeter, Louis Armstrong, derived from 'satchel mouth'. *See* Louis Armstrong.

Savernake Forest Savernake, near Marlborough. Formerly a royal forest, Savernake is now leased to the Forestry Commission. It occupies some 2,000 acres.

Saxon Escomb, near Bishop Auckland, and elsewhere. The Saxons were a Germanic people whose recorded history begins in the second century. By the sixth century they were fully established in England along with the Angles. This pub name normally occurs where there is a Saxon church or where evidence of Saxon residence has been found. Bournemouth has a Saxons, and similar names include Seven Saxons, Kingston-on-Thames; Nine Saxons, Basingstoke; Two Saxons, Chelmsford. The Saxon Tavern, London SE6, was formerly the King Alfred.

Saxon Chief Maidstone. Also Saxon King, Spalding, Lincs, and Harold Hill, Romford. Compare Royal Saxon, London W2. All references to a Saxon ruler, probably King Alfred.

Saxon Horn Rainham, Kent. The Saxons once occupied this county and left behind traces of their existence. Horns were used as drinking vessels.

Saxon Mill Guy's Cliffe, Warwick. The pub is a converted mill that was used in Saxon times, now scheduled as a historic monument.

Saxon Warrior Bulford Camp, near Devizes. There are traces in the area of a Saxon encampment.

Scales Lichfield. The sign shows a jockey being weighed in. Earlier signs usually showed the balance included in the arms of the Worshipful Company of Goldsmiths.

Scaramouche Glasgow. Scaramouch, as the name is usually spelt, is a stock character in traditional Italian farce. He is usually dressed in Spanish costume, as he was originally meant to ridicule the Spanish don. He is a boastful coward in the Falstaff mode.

Scarborough Arms London E1. After the Earl of Scarborough whose private army assisted Churchill at Sedgemoor, 1685. At Scarborough itself there is a Scarborough Castle. Dewsbury has a Scarborough Tavern.

Scarlet Pimpernel Haverhill, Sflk and elsewhere. The scarlet pimpernel is a small annual plant with scarlet flowers which close in rainy or cloudy weather. One is seen on the inn sign at West Huntspill, Som. The flower was adopted as the emblem of Sir Percy Blakeney, the hero of several novels by Baroness d'Orczy. He saved many people from the guillotine during the French Revolution and hid his true identity behind this pseudonym. 'Pimpernel' derives from words meaning 'two wings' according to the *Oxford English Dictionary*. Professor Weekley, in his *Etymological Dictionary of Modern English* has a rather more startling suggestion to make. He traces it to a kind of baby-Latin word *pipinna* and compares modern French baby-talk, *faire pipi*, to urinate.

Scarsdale Arms London W8. Kensington Market is on the site of the former Pontings store, which in turn had replaced Scarsdale House. This was a house belonging to the Curzons, Viscounts Scarsdale. The Curzons lived there until 1894.

Scholar Gipsy Kennington, near Oxford. *The Scholar-Gipsy* was a poem written by Matthew Arnold (1822–88) and published in 1853. It was based on the legend of an Oxford scholar who tired of seeking advancement and joined a band of gypsies. He still haunts the Oxford countryside, it is said.

School Inn Ackworth, near Pontefract. There is a boarding school here run by the Society of Friends, or Quakers.

Schooner Shoreham-by-Sea and elsewhere. Usually a reference to a sailing ship, originally with two masts, later with three or four. A schooner is also a glass, usually for sherry but in the USA and Australia especially, for beer.

Scotch Heifer *See* Craven Heifer.

Scotchman and his Pack Bristol. The sign shows a pedlar walking up hill behind his horse-drawn dray. He is carrying wheel chocks in case they should be needed. A similar name is the Scotsman's Pack at Old Dale, Hathersage. It commemorates the packmen who called at the inn on their way south, offering wares such as tweeds.

Scotch Pine Betws, near Ammanford, Dyfed. Of significance in this area because of its use for pit props.

Scotch Piper Lydiate, near Southport. The local legend here concerns one of Bonnie Prince Charlie's soldiers who deserted his regiment after the 1715 rebellion and married the innkeeper's daughter. The inn was a Royal Oak at the time but was renamed for the new member of the family.

Scots Grey Bulwell, Nottingham. The Royal Scots Greys were so-named because they were mounted on grey horses. Units of the regiment were stationed locally at the time of the 1840 riots. Nottingham formerly had another inn called Scots Greys.

Scots Wha Hae *See* Wallace Arms.

Scottish Queen Sheffield. Mary Queen of Scots was imprisoned for a time in Manor Castle, opposite this pub.

Scrogg Newcastle-on-Tyne. Scrog or scrogg is a stunted bush. In the plural it refers to a thicket, or brushwood.

Scutchers Arms *See* Flax Dressers.

Sea Birds Forty Foot, near Flamborough, Humb. Flamborough Head is particularly noted for the sea birds which breed there.

Seagull Crantock, Corn and elsewhere. Common in coastal towns, as indicated by its correct name, the common gull. 'To gull' someone is to make a fool of him, and a 'gull' is a simpleton. This may come from the bird's habit of eating anything that is thrown at it, or 'swallowing anything'. Children occasionally recite: 'Sea-gull, sea-gull, sit on the sand;/It's never good weather when you're on the land.' Edinburgh has a Seagull's Nest.

Sea Horse London EC4. and elsewhere. A name applied to the walrus, also to a fabulous creature that is supposed to have the fore parts of a horse and the tail of a fish. The London pub is built on the site of the famous Mermaid Tavern, destroyed by the Great Fire of London. (The Ladies lavatory inside has 'Mermaids' on the door; the Gentlemen are referred to as 'Divers'.)

Seal Netherseal, near Burton-on-Trent. The pub name was clearly influenced by the place name, in which the 'seal' means a shaw, or wood.

Sea Lion Penarth, S Glam. Another at Burslem. A name given to several types of seal which have large ears. The Burslem example may have been brought about by a travelling menagerie which passed through the Potteries. It caused several other *Sea Lion* pubs to be named, but they have since disappeared.

Sea Urchin Bournemouth. The original meaning of 'urchin' was hedgehog, and this spine-covered mollusc is also known as the 'sea-hedgehog'. The name now manages to suggest a mischievous brat playing in the sea.

Seaweed Woolston, near Southampton. An unlikely name for a pub, but no doubt the seaweed referred to makes its presence known by its unpleasant smell.

Sebastopol Windsor. Another at Minting, near Horncastle, Lincs. An important seaport in the Crimea and a popular resort for the Russians. In 1854–55 it was captured and destroyed by British, French and Turkish forces after an eleven-month siege. It took another terrible pounding from the Germans in 1942.

Second Best King Cross, Halifax. Originally the Allanfold, but taken over by the younger of two brothers who had formerly been in partnership but had quarrelled. The elder brother apparently told the younger that he'd always be 'second best'. Users of the pub say it is now 'second to none'.

Second West Lidget Green, Bradford. The pub has a cowboy theme.

Sedan Chair Bristol. This was an enclosed seat mounted on two poles, carried by two men, one in front and one behind, and used to carry a person through the streets. It was introduced to England by Prince Charles (later Charles II) and the Duke of Buckingham on their return from Spain in 1623. Beau Nash gave them his seal of approval and they became very fashionable until horse-drawn cabs eventually replaced them. A converted sedan chair, said to have belonged to the Duke of Cumberland, is used as a telephone booth in Shepherd's, London W1. The men who carried the chairs are remembered in the Two Chairmen.

Sedgemoor Weston Zoyland, near Bridgwater. Sedgemoor is three miles from Bridgwater, and is the place where the Royalist troops of the Catholic monarch James II defeated the Duke of Monmouth's Protestant forces in 1685.

Seine Boat North Shields. A boat which uses a seine net, one which hangs vertically in the water. Its ends are then drawn together to enclose the fish.

Selsey Bill Selsey, near Chichester. The name of the headland at the tip of the Selsey peninsula, so named because its shape resembles a bird's beak.

Selsey Tram Donnington, near Chichester. Recalling a horse-drawn tram that ran locally until 1932. The enterprise rejoiced in the title of The Hundred of Manhood and Selsey Light Railway. 'Manhood', the name of the ancient 'hundred' (sub-division of a county) is a corruption of Old English words meaning 'common wood'.

Series Naming Occasionally a series of pub names is found which reflects a deliberate policy. At Harlow in 1951 it was the suggestion of Dr Stephen Taylor (now Lord Taylor of Harlow) that the pubs in that New Town should be named after moths and butterflies. Seven different breweries joined in this unique enterprise, comprising at one time a series of seventeen. The signboards now remaining show contrasting interpretations of their names, one literal and the other humorous, eg the Small Copper butterfly being paired-off with a bright new farthing. During the 1960s, after the launching of the Russian *sputnik* in 1959, the Kimberley Brewery near Nottingham decided to launch its new pubs into the space age, beginning with the Other Side of the Moon. In the same decade the Wiltshire brewery of Wadsworths systematically named all its new pubs after birds. More recently a small chain of pubs in London has included 'Firkin' in each name to produce the Fox and Firkin, Ferret and Firkin, Frog and Firkin and so on. In Grantham and district there are a number of 'Blue' inns, dating from the time when Lord Dysart, a prominent Whig and owner of most of the inns in this area, decided to make his political allegiance clear.

Setter Dog *See* Dog.

Setting Sun *See* Sun.

Seven Saxons *See* Saxon.

Seven Seas Clydebank. Another at Grimsby. After those 'that go down to the sea in ships and do their business in great waters', as Ecclesiastes puts it. The seven seas are the North and South Atlantic, the Antarctic, the Arctic, the Indian, the North and South Pacific Oceans.

Seven Sisters Seaford, E Ssx. Others at London N17 and King's Lynn. Also Old Seven Sisters, London N17. At Seaford a reference to a series of chalk cliffs. At London N17 for seven elm trees, removed in the 1840s.

Seven Stones St Martins, Isles of Scilly. After a group of rocks between Land's End and the Scilly Isles.

17th/21st Lancer Lenton, Nottingham. A name chosen by Colonel Hanson, chairman of the Kimberley Brewery when this pub was opened in 1973, in honour of his old regiment. The sign shows the regimental motto 'Death or Glory' surmounted by a skull and cross-bones. Inside the pub is a display of military regalia.

Seven Ways St Judes, Bristol. The pub is at a point where seven roads meet.

Seven Wives Green End, St Ives, near Huntingdon. A reference to the nursery rhyme: 'As I was going to St Ives/I met a man with seven wives,/Each wife had seven sacks,/Each sack had seven cats,/Each cat had seven kits:/Kits, cats, sacks and wives,/How many were there going to St Ives?' All these are illustrated on the sign.

Severn Trow Stourport, H and W. The local boats which carried goods from Stafford and Worcester down to Bristol on the river Severn. 'Trow' is applied in different parts of the country to various types of boat or barge.

Sexey's Arms Blackford, Som. Hugh Sexey was a local ploughboy in the sixteenth century. He is said to have run away to sea, indulged n piracy, then achieved respectability as a public official under Queen Elizabeth. He founded a local school and hospital.

Seymour Arms Blagdon, Som. Seymour is the family name of the dukes of Somerset.

Shaftesbury South Harrow. Also Shaftesbury Arms, Richmond, Sry. Anthony Ashley Cooper, 7th Earl of Shaftesbury (1801–85) was a noted philanthropist who did much to free child workers from industrial bondage. He was president of the British and Foreign Bible Society, the Evangelical Alliance and many similar organisations.

Shafto Arms Langley Moor, near Durham. An allusion to Bobby Shafto of the nursery rhyme, first published in *Songs for the Nursery*, 1805. It begins: 'Bobby Shafto's gone to sea/Silver buckles at his knee/He'll come back and marry me,/Bonny Bobby Shafto!'

Shah Hemel Hempstead and elsewhere. Also Shah of Persia, Poole, Dors. The latter pub has a four-sided sign which commemorates the visit to England by the Shah of Persia in 1887. 'Shah' means 'king'.

Shakespeare Stratford-upon-Avon and elsewhere.
William Shakespeare (1564–1616) was born at Stratford and married Anne Hathaway there in 1582. It is thought that he worked for a while as a schoolmaster, but all that is certain is that he left Stratford for London and became connected with the theatres there. His earliest dramatic writing was the three parts of *Henry VI*, which date from 1590–91. We know relatively little about Shakespeare's life, but we have thirty-seven plays and some wonderful poetry which remain as his supreme gift to his fellow men. It is almost unbelievable that one man should have been able to write so much of such quality, a thought that has caused scholars

to suggest that he had many collaborators or that someone who was more formally educated was the real author, not Shakespeare. Such topics may be pursued elsewhere: in the context of pub names it must be said that Shakespeare does not make the impact that one would expect. There are far more references to Dickens and his novels than to Shakespeare's plays on British inn signs, though Falstaff is naturally popular. It is interesting also to see what Shakespeare had to say about inn signs. In *Titus Andronicus* Act 4, scene 2 he refers scornfully to some men as 'ye alehouse painted signs' He means that they are not real men, merely copies of them. In the second part of *Henry VI*, Act 3, scene 2, Queen Margaret says to the king: 'make my image but an alehouse sign.' She means: 'let me die and be remembered only as a tavern sign.' The same play ends with the dukes of York and Somerset fighting. Somerset is killed, and there is a comment from Richard, Duke of York, that 'underneath an alehouse' paltry sign, The Castle in St Albans', Somerset lies dead. Purists might wonder what a Roman general is doing in *Titus Andronicus*, making a reference to Elizabethan tavern signs, but the references in *Henry VI* are not anachronistic. Bryant Lilleywhite, in his *London Signs*, is able to show that the King's Head and Castle signs were both in use in Henry VI's reign. It is interesting that these three Shakespearean references to inn signs come in the early plays of the 1590s, when Shakespeare was no doubt spending much of his time in taverns or alehouses. Perhaps, too, someone somewhere has done a doctoral thesis about

Shakespeare and his inns. How many does he mention by name, one wonders? There is the Garter Inn in *The Merry Wives of Windsor* and the Centaur in *A Comedy of Errors*. There is, happily, a Centaur to be found in Portsmouth. Windsor, to its shame, seems to have lost its Garter.

Shambles Edinburgh. Others at Carlisle and Lutterworth. The original meaning of this word (in plural form) is a slaughterhouse. Manchester has a Wellington Shambles. The Lutterworth pub was formerly a butcher's shop.

Shanks Liverpool. The affectionate nickname used by Liverpool fans and players for Bill Shankly, manager of the Liverpool Football team. He retired in 1974 having taken the club to many Cup wins and Championship titles.

Shannon Bucklesham, near Ipswich. The Shannon is Ireland's chief river, 240 miles long. It rises on Cuilcagh Mountain in County Clare and flows past Limerick into the Atlantic Ocean.

Shannon *See* Chesapeake and Shannon.

Shant Holmfield, Halifax. Explained locally as deriving from 'shanty town', a collection of crudely-built huts and cabins used to house the workmen on the railway while it was being constructed. In Australia a 'shanty' is in any case a public-house.

Share and Coulter Herne Bay. The sign shows these two blades of a plough, the coulter being fixed in front of the share.

Shaven Crown Shipton-under-Wychwood, Oxon. The sign shows a tonsured friar holding up a wine goblet and looking decidedly cheerful. This inn was formerly a pilgrim's hostel associated with Cistercian monks.

Shark Harlow, Esx. The shark moth, continuing the moths and butterflies theme of the pub names in this town.

Shave Cross Inn Shave Cross, Dors. The pub name and place name are said to refer to monks who were making a pilgrimage to the shrine of St Wita at Whitchurch Canonicorum. They had their heads shaved, or their tonsures renewed, as an act of humility before they completed their journey.

Sheaf West Haddon, near Daventry. Also Sheaf of Wheat, St Ives, Corn; Sheaf and Sickle, Long Lawford, near Rugby. When corn was still harvested by hand, the sickle was used to cut it. It is a tool with a hook-shaped blade which is held in the hand. The corn was then gathered into sheaves, or bundles, which were stood in the field and left to dry. 'Sheaf' is also used of a quiverful of arrows, as instanced by the Sheaf of Arrows, Wimborne, Dors. The sign is a heraldic reference to the Cecil family who own nearby Cranborne Manor.

Shears Halifax and elsewhere. Also Shearer Arms, Portsmouth; Shearers Arms, Owslebury, near Winchester; Shearmans Arms, Wottonunder-Edge, Glos; Sheepshearers, Burgh Heath, Sry. Both a shearer and a shearman used shears in their jobs. The former sheared the wool from the sheep, the shearman used shears to cut cloth. The *Shears* sign can therefore refer to either. In Halifax, where there are three pubs of this name, it would have been the clothmakers who came to the pubs, but at Collingbourne Ducis, Wilts, the *Shears* indicated that sheep drovers stayed there overnight on their way to Weyhill market.

Sheep Heid Duddingston, Edinburgh. A Scottish form of 'sheep head'.

Sheepshank London W11. Apart from meaning the shank, or leg, of a sheep, a sheepshank is a kind of knot which is cast on a rope to shorten it temporarily.

Sheet Anchor Sunderland. Another at Whitmore, Staffs. This is technically a ship's largest anchor, used only in an emergency, though it has the metaphorical meaning of something that can be relied upon when all else has failed. Perhaps the idea is to make the regulars think of the pub in those terms.

Sheiling Glasgow. A Scottish word for the summer hut used by a shepherd.

Sheldrake Jaywick, near Clacton-on-Sea. Otherwise known as the sheldduck, 'sheld' referring to the 'different colours' of this species. It can be found on the marshes near the pub.

Shelley Arms Oxford. Percy Bysshe Shelley (1792–1822) was an English poet, expelled from Oxford University because of a pamphlet he wrote on *The Necessity of Atheism*. He then eloped with sixteen-year-old Harriet Westbrook, leaving her after three years. She drowned herself soon afterwards. Shelley went off to Italy with Mary Godwin, whom he later married. (She is remembered for her novel *Frankenstein*.) Shelley himself was drowned while sailing. He is remembered best for some fine lyrics, such as 'Ode to the West Wind', 'To a Skylark', 'The Cloud', and so on, though he wrote many longer works.

Sheltered Deck Sunderland. A pleasant variation on the 'refuge' theme.

Shenanigans Hull. This curious word, of disputed origin, now mainly refers to light-hearted conversation and 'goings-on'. It had the earlier sense of trickery.

Shepherd Doddingshurst, Esx. A figure much loved by the pastoral poets, who often implied that the shepherd's existence was ideal. 'Shepherd' also has Christian significance, of course, referring to Christ, or to the spiritual leader of a 'flock'. Shepherds are mentioned in many pub names, often in urban districts as well as rural. Some examples are: Shepherd and Crook, Burmarsh, near Dymchurch, the crook being a long staff with a crooked end that can be hooked round a sheep's hind leg; Shepherd and Dog, Fulking, W Ssx; Shepherd and Flock, Runfold, Sry and Luton; Shepherd and Shepherdess, Beamish, Dur, where they are said to refer to lead figurines which were patriotically melted down for ammunition during the Napoleonic Wars; Shepherdess, London N1; Shepherds, Rawtenstall, Lancs; Shepherds Arms, Tilbury; Shepherd's Boy, Oldham and Dewsbury; Shepherd's Bush, Stafford; Shepherd's Call, Hyde, Ches; Shepherd's Cottage, Tipton; Shepherd's Crook, Southsea, Hants; Shepherd's House, Woodley, near Reading; Shepherds' Hall, Long Handborough, near Woodstock; Shepherd's Hut, Eton Wick, near Windsor; Shepherds' Rest, Taunton; Shepherds' View, Barnston, Mers.

Shepherd's Tavern London W1. Edward Shepherd, who died in 1747, was an architect and property owner. The pub was built on ground belonging to him.

Shepley Spitfire Totley, near Sheffield. The Shepley family were local landowners. A son of the family flew a Spitfire during World War Two and was shot down. His parents instituted a Spitfire Memorial Fund which raised the money to pay for an aircraft which was named the Shepley Spitfire. This too was shot down, though the pilot survived. The pub opened in 1979. Thornaby-on-Tees has a Spitfire.

Sheridan Stafford. Richard Brinsley Sheridan (1751–1816) was a playwright and politician, also director and part-owner of the Drury Lane Theatre, London. His most successful plays were *A School for Scandal* and *The Rivals*. He represented Stafford in parliament after 1780 and was renowned for his oratory.

Sherlock Holmes London WC2. This was the Northumberland Arms until 1957, and was mentioned as such by Sir Arthur Conan Doyle in *The Hound of the Baskervilles*. The stuffed head of the hound is one of the pub's attractions, together with a replica of this famous fictional detective's study at 221b Baker Street.

Sherpa *See* Everest.

Sherwood Inn Sherwood, Nottingham. Also Sherwood Oak, Walderslade, near Chatham; Sherwood Ranger, Retford, Notts. All references to Robin Hood's forest, some portions of which still remain. The name means 'wood belonging to the shire'. The Sherwood pub has a Robin Hood as its neighbour.

Shinglers Arms Middlesbrough. 'Shingles' were pieces of wood, thin but with one end thicker than the other, with parallel sides. They were used as house-tiles instead of slates or other tiles, and shinglers were the men who laid them.

Shiny Sheff Lodge Moor, Sheffield. The pub was opened in 1970 and named for HMS *Sheffield*, the cruiser launched in 1936. It was nicknamed *Shiny Sheff* because it was finished in bright Sheffield stainless steel. Its successor, a missile destroyer, was sunk during the Falklands War. The inn sign shows that warship under a map of the Falklands. The battle honours of the original ship, together with various mementoes, are displayed inside the pub.

Ship Burcombe, Wilts, and elsewhere. A common sign, with a fully-rigged schooner often being shown, though the inn sign at Caerleon-on-Usk in Gwent shows a Roman galley. The Burcombe inn was originally a **Sheepe**, but some old ship's timbers were used during structural alterations and caused the change of name. At Styal, Ches, the name is said to derive from 'shippen', an old dialect word for 'cattle-shed' or 'cowhouse'. 'Shippen' looks as if it should be connected with 'sheep', but it has more to do with 'shop', as in 'workshop'.

Ship Afloat Bridgwater. The opposite of Ship Aground, which is found at London E5. and elsewhere.

Ship Ahoy Bridlington. The traditional cry from the look-out announcing that another ship has been seen.

Ship and Castle Bristol, and elsewhere. A ship and castle are both represented in Bristol's coat of arms. Other instances may represent amalgamated signs. *See* Combination Names.

Ship and Plough Hull. Another at Kingsbridge, Devon. An amalgamation of common signs, or a reference to the taking of a ship's position by reference to the Plough constellation.

Ship and Shovel Barking. The labourers who shovelled grain and ballast from ships and barges used this pub. There are two others in London with the same name, also referring to shovellers of coal and other products who left their shovels outside the pub when they came for a drink.

Ship and Whale London SE1. The pub dates from 1664 and was originally the Ship. The name was extended when a whale was seen in the Thames. A tract of 1658 entitled *London's Wonder* had earlier described 'the taking and killing of a great whale near to Greenwich upon the third day of June'. Evelyn refers to this event in his Diary.

Ship 'Anson' Portsmouth. Modern pubs named for a specific ship tend to use the ship's name on its own. In the past it was often preceded by the word 'ship', as in the following examples: Ship Albion, Spalding; Ship 'Centurion', Whitstable; Ship 'Defiance', Wisbech; Ship 'Leopard', Portsmouth; Ship 'Victory', Chester; Ship 'York'. London SE16.

Ship Ashore Niton, IOW. Ship-ashore establishments were set up by the Royal Navy until the middle of the nineteenth century in order to select oak trees suitable for ship building. An ensign was hoisted, and naval discipline and customs prevailed. The nearest innkeeper would often rename his inn in honour of this lucrative source of income.

Ship Centurion *See* Centurion.

Ship in Distress Stanpit, Dors. A reference to a tragic incident off Hengistbury Head nearby. It involved the Revenue cutter *Osprey* and cost the life of the captain.

Shipley Boat Shipley, near Heanor. Derbs. There are two canal locks in front of the inn, the Erewash canal having been built in the 1770s to serve the nearby coal-mines.

Shipmate Middlesbrough. One who serves on the same ship. The pub comes complete with fo'c'sle and chart room.

SHIP NAMES Ship names are often transferred to pubs, for reasons which vary in each individual case. Such names make an interesting study in themselves, and we can highly recommend two books about them which have served us well: *British Warship Names*, by Captain T D Manning and Commander C F Walker, published by Putnam, and *Ship Names*, by Don H Kennedy, published by the University Press of Virginia. Apart from such ship-name borrowings, a great many types of boats and ships are referred to in pub names, ranging from the barge and brigantine to the windjammer, yacht and lifeboat.

Ship on Shore Sheerness. A sailing ship called the *Lucky Escape* ran aground here in 1858. It had a cargo of cement which was loaded in barrels. The sea-water turned the cement into barrel-shaped blocks which can still be seen near the pub.

Shipwrights North Hylton, near Sunderland. Also Shipwrights Arms, Salcombe and elsewhere. After the Worshipful Company of Shipwrights, 1605, the largest of the livery companies.

Shire Horse Coventry and elsewhere. Also Shire Horses, York. The latter pub was formerly the Sea Horse. It was renamed when the brewers Samuel Smith of Tadcaster recommended deliveries of beer in York by horse-drawn drays. Shire horses are the heaviest of all English draught breeds. They evolved from the 'Great Horse' of Elizabethan times, when it carried a man in full armour. It is an immensely powerful horse but has a docile temperament.

Shirley Poppy Shirley, near Croydon. After the poppy first grown by the Reverend W Wilks in the vicarage at Shirley, 1880.

Shoe Exton. near Southampton. The sign here depicts the old woman of nursery-rhyme fame and the enormous shoe she lived in, together with her brood of children. At Horton, near Blyth, Northld, is a Shoes.

Shoemaker Norwich. Another in Leicester. Also Shoemakers

Arms, Montacute, near Yeovil. Connected signs are Shoehorn, Huddersfield, for an instrument now usually made of metal but originally made of horn, and Shoestrings, Dundee. 'Shoestring' is now nearly always used in the metaphorical sense of working on a shoestring, ie working on a very low budget. The allusion here is to the constant threat of a shoestring (or shoelace) suddenly snapping.

Shooting Star Borehamwood, Herts. A meteor, though also the name of the American cowslip, which has large rose-purple or white flowers. It is also the name of a British Rail 'Britannia' class Pacific locomotive.

Shorthorn Appleton Wiske, near Northallerton. The popular breed of beef cattle, from which Polled Shorthorns and Dairy Shorthorns have been developed.

Shoulder of Mutton Oswaldtwistle and elsewhere. A popular dish at inns in former times.
The Shoulder of Mutton and Cucumbers at Yapton, near Arundel, served it with a cucumber sauce to stagecoach travellers. In some village inns it probably indicated that the innkeeper was also the local butcher, while at Calverton, near Milton Keynes, the name is said to derive from the shape of the land on which the pub is situated.

Shovel Cowley, near Uxbridge. There was formerly a Shovellers Arms in Portsmouth, named for the gangs of stokers who worked on the ships. The shovel is used for lifting loose materials, such as earth, coal, malt, etc. A spade is used for digging, but the two words are sometimes inter-changed. There is also a shovel hat, so called from the supposed resemblance of its front and rear

brims to the curved blade of a shovel. It was worn mainly by ecclesiastics in the nineteenth century.

Showman Cullompton, Devon. Formerly the Railway, but renamed because the pub overlooks a field where a number of travelling showmen have their winter headquarters. The sign shows one of them trying to convince an audience that a two-headed dwarf is genuine.

Shrew Beshrewed Hersden, near Canterbury. The sign shows a shrewish woman being ducked in a pond. 'Shrew' was once applied to a malignant man, but it later became exclusively a reference to a scolding wife. The phrase 'Beschrew thee' meant 'Devil take thee'.

Shrimp Morecambe. Also Shrimper, Southport; Shrimp and Turtle, Sandwich. The crustacean similar to a prawn, eaten as a delicacy.

Shroppie Fly Audlem Wharf, near Crewe. The pub is on the Shropshire Union Canal. Its name refers to a horse-drawn boat that was worked on a 'flying' basis – around the clock – because it contained a perishable cargo.

Shropshire Lad Harlescott, near Shrewsbury. The title of a book of poems, *A Shropshire Lad* (1896) by Alfred Edward Housman (1859–1936). Many of the poems have been set to music by British composers, eg *On Wenlock Edge*, a song cycle by Vaughan Williams.

Shrubbery Ilminster, Som. Another at Tipton, W Mids. Also Shrubbery Cottage, Oldwinsford, W Mids. The Ilminster pub was previously a private house which had a particularly fine shrubbery.

Shuttle and Loom Darlington. Opened in 1980, this pub has a well-developed theme reflecting the town's former flax-weaving industry.

Sidewheeler Babbacombe, near Torquay. A paddlesteamer with its wheels at the side, as opposed to a sternwheeler.

Sidmouth Arms *See* Addington.

Sidney Arms London EC1 and elsewhere in London. Sidney is the family name of the earls of Leicester.

Sign i' the Cellar Golborne, near Wigan. There was formerly a pub at nearby Leigh called My Sign is in the Cellar. Such names are hardly above board.

Silent Whistle *See* Ghost Train.

Silent Woman Widford, near Chelmsford and elsewhere. A common European joke lies behind this sign, which is often **Quiet Woman**, as at Earl Sterndale, near Buxton and elsewhere, Good Woman, as at Doncaster, or **Headless Woman**, as at Duddon, near Tarporley, Ches. The last example makes the point, as does the couplet that was sometimes seen: 'Here is a woman who has lost her head./She's quiet now – you see she's dead.' At Leek, Staffs, the sign of the *Quiet Woman* shows a ghostly decapitated lady and Henry VIII lurking in the background. At Halstock, Dors, the same sign may refer to St Judwardine, executed by her brother for becoming a Christian. At Coldharbour, Dors, the *Silent Woman* is said to recall a threat made to the wife of an innkeeper, whose marketplace prattling threatened the safety of some smugglers. They threatened to remove her tongue unless she held it. Local references apart, one cannot escape from the basic thought behind these signs, that women – in the opinion of men – tend to talk too much. Compare the seventeenth century use of *Silence* by the Puritans as a girl's name, *Tacy* or *Tacey* in its Latin form. A contemporary writer said that such names properly reminded females of the admonition of St Paul: 'Let the women learn in silence, with all subjection'. All this makes it unnecessary to look for ingenious explanations of *Headless Woman*, as some writers have done, attempting to link the name with the 'heedless' virgins described at Matthew 25.

Silks Bristol. Formerly the Malt and Hops, but the pub is next door to the Law Courts. 'Silk' is used allusively for a Queen's Counsel, who has the right to wear a silk gown. This was one of the meanings exposed by the new inn sign, first shown on Leap Year Day, 1984. The other was the silken underwear of the female barrister shown on the sign. Lady members of the legal profession were quick to give their opinion of this 'degrading and embarrassing' sign, though the brewery claimed it merely followed the light-hearted pattern of many modern signs.

Silver Ball St Columb Major, near Newquay. A reference to a game played locally since the sixteenth century. The ball is made of apple wood covered with silver and it has to be carried to one of two troughs at each end of the town which serve as goals. The game is played each year on Shrove Tuesday, with teams coming in from surrounding villages.

Silver Bullet London N4. The sign illustrates the combined rail-air-rail London to Paris service of this name.

Silver Cod Hull. Hull is the major fishing port in Britain, so there is nothing fishy about this name.

Silver Fountain Betws-y-Coed, Gynd. A poetical reference to the famous Swallow Falls, a great tourist attraction in this picturesque area.

Silver Fox Taverham, near Norwich. An albino fox was once tracked down and shot in the woodlands which were formerly in this area.

Silver Ghost Alvaston, near Derby. The pub is near the Rolls-Royce works. From 1907 until 1925 the six-cylinder *Silver Ghost* was the only Rolls-Royce car on sale. Some 6,000 of them were produced. The inn sign here shows a 1907 model on one side, while the other shows a floating apparition.

Silver Herring Great Yarmouth. Another at Kilkeel, Down. For the sea fish and those engaged in catching it.

Silver Jubilee Cheltenham. The pub was the **Palace** until 1977, when it was renamed to mark the twenty-fifth year of Elizabeth II's reign. The pub sign formerly showed Buckingham Palace. The *Silver Jubilee* at Chatteris, Cambs, is for the Pacific class locomotive which first ran in 1935.

Silver Lion Lilley, near Hitchin. A heraldic reference to the local Sowerby family.

Silver Oyster Monkwick, near Colchester. The silvery oyster is shown on the sign together with a fishing boat. The oyster fisheries at the mouth of the river Colne have been famous for centuries.

Silver Tassie Hamilton, Straith and elsewhere. A tass, or tassie, is a cup or small goblet, especially one made of silver. The word can also refer to the contents of the tassie. All examples of the pub name occur in Scotland, where tass and tassie are used in local speech. Found also in Scottish literature, Sir Walter Scott using tass in *Rob Roy*, and Burns has: 'Ye'll bring me here a pint of wine, A server and a silver tassie.'

Silver Thread Paisley. The town is noted for the manufacture of cotton thread and was once famous for its shawls.

Silver Wheal *See* Mexico.

Simon the Tanner London SE1. This name has been solemnly explained as a tavern kept by a man named Simon who had been a tanner, or who catered for tanners, but it must surely be an allusion to an old Cockney joke. This concerned a banking transaction of St Peter, 'who lodged with one Simon a tanner', a reference to Acts 10:32. A 'tanner' is one who converts skins into leather, but it was until recently the slang word for sixpence. Until the end of the nineteenth century, 'simon' was also a slang word for sixpence, indeed it was probably that slang usage which gave rise to the later use of tanner in the same sense.

Simple Simon Emscote, Warwick. There is a large pie factory opposite the pub. It may be remembered that 'Simple Simon met a pieman/Going to the fair:/ Said Simple Simon to the pieman,/ "Let me taste your ware".'

Sippers Millbay Docks, Plymouth. The sign shows a sailor holding a keg of rum under one arm while he holds his daily tot aloft with the other. In Navy parlance, two sippers equalled one gulper, two gulpers equalled one tot. The tradition of issuing a daily rum allowance in the Royal Navy came to an end in July 1970.

Sir Alexander Fleming London W2. The Scottish Nobel Prize-winner (1881–1955) who discovered penicillin in 1928 while working at St Mary's Hospital, near this pub.

Sir Alf Ramsey Tunbridge Wells. Opened in 1973 by Sir Alf, a former England football player who was manager of the national side when it won the World Cup in 1966.

Sir Alfred Hitchcock London E11. The English film director (1899–1980), who was in Hollywood from 1940, was a specialist in the suspense thriller who loved to shock an audience. He was also a personality in his own right, with an instantly-recognisable face and voice. He made his first film in 1925 and was making films like *Psycho* and *The Birds* in the 1960s.

Sir Charles Napier *See* Admiral Napier.

Sir Christopher Wren London EC4. The outstanding English architect (1632–1723) whose works are notable for dignity and elegance. He is best known for his work on St Paul's Cathedral, which he recreated after the Great Fire of London (1666), but he built a great many other churches. He was also responsible for Chelsea Hospital, parts of Greenwich Hospital, the garden facade of Hampton Court Palace, the Temple, etc. He is buried in St Paul's, where there is a famous epitaph relating to him, attributed to his son: *Si monumentum requiris, circumspice* – If you would see his monument, look around.

Sir Colin Campbell Coventry and elsewhere. Also General Campbell, Burnley; Lord Clyde, Walmer, Kent and elsewhere. Colin Campbell (1792–1863) was a distinguished British field-marshal, mainly remembered for the relief of Lucknow, India, in 1857. He was made Baron Clyde of Clydesdale in 1858. The first landlord of the *Lord Clyde* was under the command of the general at Lucknow. There was formerly a pub called the Lucknow in Portsmouth, and there is still a Heroes of Lucknow in Aldershot.

Sir David Brewster London SE13. A Scottish physicist (1781–1868) who improved lighthouse illumination and is said to have invented the kaleidoscope.

Sir Douglas Bader Martlesham Heath, near Ipswich. Officially opened in 1979 by Sir Douglas himself, recalling that at one time during World War Two he had commanded a fighter squadron here. The Bader Arms at Tangmere, near Chichester likewise pays tribute to him, as does the Fighter Pilot which he opened in 1970. This legless airman, a legend in his own lifetime (1910–82) epitomised for many the spirit of 'The Immortal Few' who won the Battle of Britain in 1940. He was knighted in 1976 for his services to the disabled.

Sir Douglas Haig *See* Earl Haig.

Sir Ernest Shackleton London SE21. A British explorer (1874–1922) who was a member of Scott's expedition 1901–04 and commanded his own south polar expedition 1907–09. On that occasion he located the south magnetic pole and achieved important scientific results. He died while on another expedition to Enderby Land.

Sir Evelyn Wood Chelmsford. An eminent soldier (1838–1919) who was born at nearby Braintree. He served with the Naval Brigade in the Crimea, gained the Victoria Cross during the Indian Mutiny, fought in the Ashanti and Zulu Wars and was Commander-in-chief of the Egyptian army. He also wrote an autobiography: From *Midshipman to Field Marshal*.

Sir Francis Burdett King's Newton, near Melbourne, Derbs. A local landowner (1770–1844) who was member of parliament for Westminster 1807–37. After publishing a speech which denied the right of the House of Commons to imprison delinquents, his own arrest was ordered. He barricaded himself into his house and resisted for four days.

Sir Francis Chichester *See* Gipsy Moth IV.

Sir Francis Drake Plymouth and elsewhere. Sir Francis Drake (1540–96) is mainly remembered for the part he played in the destruction of the Spanish Armada in 1588, though he made many other adventurous voyages. His popularity is reflected in the many pubs named for him, such as the Admiral Drake in Portsmouth, the Drake in Hull and elsewhere, the Drake's Arms at Bishopswood, Som, the Drake Manor at Buckland Monachorum and Drake's Drum at Worcester and elsewhere. In his native county of Devon the name of his famous ship, the Golden Hind, is frequently found as a pub name.

Sir Frank Whittle *See* Jet and Whittle.

Sir Frederick Roberts *See* Lord Roberts.

Sir Garnet Wolseley Nottingham and elsewhere. Pontypool, Gwent, formerly had a Sir Garnet. A distinguished soldier (1833–1913) who rose to the rank of field-marshal. He served in Burma 1852–53, the Crimean War and the Indian Mutiny. He was commander of the Nile Expedition sent by Gladstone to the relief of Khartoum in 1884–85.

Sir George Robey London N4. George Robey was the stage name of George Edward Wade (1869–1954), a music-hall comedian who was known as 'the prime minister of mirth'. This pub (formerly the Clarence) was renamed in his honour in 1968. He once worked at the local Empire Theatre.

Sir Henry Havelock *See* General Havelock.

Sir Henry Roscoe *See* Roscoe Arms.

Sir Humphrey Chetham Manchester. A local merchant and philanthropist (1580–1653) who endowed the city's famous music school, a blue-coat hospital and a public library.

Sir Isaac Newton Woolsthorpe, near Grantham and elsewhere. The physicist, mathematician and philosopher (1642–1727) who is mainly remembered for deriving the law of gravity and formulating the laws of motion. He did a great deal of work on the nature of light and invented a reflecting telescope. He also managed to act as member of parliament for Cambridge University, was Master of the Mint and reformed the English currency system and became President of the Royal Society in 1703, a post he held until he died. In the popular imagination he is associated with an apple tree and a falling apple which led him to the law of gravity. That story was first told by Voltaire, who heard it from Newton's niece. The Grantham pub is not far from his birthplace in the village of Woolsthorpe.

Sir Jeffrey Amherst Seal Chart, near Sevenoaks. Sir Jeffrey (later Lord) Amherst (1717–97) was the English general responsible for the capture of Montreal from the French in 1759. He also captured a French fort on Lake Champlain called Crown Point and on his retirement gave that name to his house. It also became the name of the Crown Point pub at nearby

Ightham. The Amherst Arms at Riverhead is another pub which commemorates the general in his home county of Kent.

Sir John Barleycorn *See* John Barleycorn.

Sir John Borlase Warren *See* Happy Man.

Sir John Cass London E9. The lord mayor of London (1665–1718) and founder of two schools in Hackney. He is also remembered in Cassland Road, Homerton.

Sir John Cockle Mansfield, Notts. Also Miller of Mansfield, Goring-on-Thames; Old Miller of Mansfield, London SE1 King and Miller, Retford, Notts, and Stocksbridge, Sheffield. An old ballad, kept in the Pepys Collection at Mansfield Public Library, tells the story of Henry II losing his way in Sherwood Forest. He came across a miller who offered him hospitality, including a dish of venison. Since only the king had the right to hunt deer in the forest, this could have had dire consequences. Instead it appealed to the king's sense of humour and he knighted the miller for his services. The sign shows the miller receiving that honour.

Sir John Devenish Cheriton Bishop, near Exeter. Also Devenish Arms, Portland. The founder of the Devenish Brewery at Weymouth in 1742. There are now two breweries and the company runs more than 300 pubs in the southwest of England.

Sir John Falstaff *See* Falstaff.

Sir John Franklin London E14. Another at London N1. The navigator and arctic explorer (1786–1847) who served at Trafalgar and was later sent to trace the coastline of North America. This involved a walk of some 550 miles. His career advanced steadily, and in 1845 he was sent on an expedition to discover the North West Passage. It is thought that he did discover it, but he never returned. *See* Lady Franklin for the continuation of the story.

Sir John Lawrence London N11. An English statesman (1811–79) and administrator in India. He was governor-general there 1863–69. He was known as the 'Saviour of India' for his services during the Sepoy Mutiny.

Sir John Moore Bilston. Another at Bodmin. A British general (1761–1809) who is best remembered for his burial service, which took place in the citadel at Corunna, Spain, where he was killed by Napoleon's troops. The Reverend Charles Wolfe wrote a poem *The Burial of Sir John Moore at Corunna* which became extremely popular: 'Few and short were the prayers we said,/And we spoke not a word of sorrow;/But we steadfastly gazed on the face that was dead,/And we bitterly thought of the morrow.'

Sir John Morden London SE13. A London merchant (1623–1708) who founded a 'charitable college' at Blackheath.

Sir Joshua Reynolds Plympton, near Plymouth. The celebrated portrait painter (1723–92) who was born locally. Of great social gifts as well as artistic, he entertained the great literary figures of his day and was known for his eloquence. He was the first president of the Royal Academy. With the help of assistants he completed over 2.000 works.

Sir Laffalots Aberdeen. A cheerful variant of Sir Lancelot.

Sirloin Hoghton, near Preston. Another at London E4. Also Sirloin of Beef, Southsea. A sirloin, or surloin as it is also spelt, is the upper part of a loin of beef, the choicest section. The word comes from French, where the prefix indicates 'over' or 'above'. There is a pleasant but totally untrue story about James I knighting on the spot a loin of beef served to him and thus bringing 'sirloin' into existence.

Sir Paul Pindar London EC2. A wealthy London merchant (died 1650) and ambassador. He had a passion for architecture and spent vast sums on beautifying St Paul's Cathedral and his own mansion. The mansion was demolished when Liverpool Street Station expanded, but its original front is preserved in the Victoria and Albert Museum.

Sir Ralph Abercrombie Hanford, Staffs. Sir Ralph Abercrombie, or Abercromby, (1734–1801) was a distinguished British general. The *Dictionary of National Biography* says of him that he 'shares with Sir John Moore the credit of renewing the ancient discipline and military reputation of the British soldier'.

Sir Richard Grenville Bideford. A naval hero (1541–91), cousin of Sir Walter Raleigh. He is remembered for his bravery in trying to pass through a large Spanish fleet off the Azores in 1591. His own seven vessels were attacked by fifteen Spanish ships, whereupon he and his men fought hand-to-hand for fifteen hours. He eventually surrendered when only twenty of his men remained alive, and died himself a few days after the battle. According to Tennyson, who glorified the incident in his poem *The Revenge* (the name of Grenville's ship), his men 'blest him in their pain,/'And Sir Richard said again: "We be all good English men/Let us bang these dogs of Seville, the children

of the devil,/For I never turn'd my back upon Don or devil yet. " '

Sir Richard Steele London NW3. An essayist, poet and playwright (1672–1729) mainly remembered for his association with Joseph Addison and their combined work on *The Tatler* and *The Spectator*. In 1713 he was elected member of parliament for Stockbridge, but an injudicious pamphlet led to his expulsion from the House in 1714.

Sir Robert Peel *See* Peel.

Sir Roger Tichborne Alfold, near Horsham, W Ssx. Roger Tichborne, heir to a Hampshire baronetcy, disappeared in 1854 when his ship was wrecked. In 1865 a man in Wagga Wagga, Australia, announced that he was the missing baronet. He came to England in 1866 to pursue his claim. After the longest court case in British criminal history, the man was shown to be Arthur Orton, son of a London butcher. He was sentenced to fourteen years' penal servitude. There is a Tichborne Arms at Tichborne, near Alresford, Hants.

Sir Sidney Smith London E1. Another at London SE11. An admiral (1764–1840) who successfully opposed the French in the Mediterranean during the Napoleonic Wars.

Sir Solomon Belton, near Doncaster. The name of the horse which won the St Leger in 1850.

Sir Tatton Sykes Wolverhampton. The squire of Sledmere, Humb (1772–1863) who loved horse-racing. He is said to have witnessed the running of the St Leger seventy-four times, including the time in 1846 when his own horse, named after himself, was the winner. The Sledmere Tavern, Dudley, also remembers him.

Sir Thomas Paxton *See* Paxton.

Sir Thomas White Coventry. A wealthy citizen of London (1492–1566) who became lord mayor of London in 1553. He founded St John's College Oxford and was one of the founders of the Merchant Taylors' School.

Sir Thomas Wyatt Maidstone. Sir Thomas Wyatt the Elder (1503–42) was a favourite at the court of Henry VIII and used by the king as an ambassador. He wrote lyric poetry of high quality, mostly of an amatory nature. His son (1520–54) served with distinction as a soldier, but then attempted to prevent Queen Mary from marrying Philip II. He had some success fighting against royalist forces, but was captured in London and executed for treason.

Sir Walter Raleigh Dartmouth and elsewhere. An English statesman, adventurer and man of letters (1552–1618) who was a favourite of Elizabeth I but not of James I, who had him convicted of treason and executed. Raleigh was engaged in the colonisation of America and is said to have introduced potatoes and tobacco to England. He is also remembered for his gallantry in laying his cloak over a puddle so that Elizabeth I would not wet her feet. This scene is illustrated on the inn sign at East Budleigh, Devon, close to his birthplace. Raleigh's writings include some worthwhile poetry and philosophical works.

Sir Walter Scott London N4. Another at London E8. The Scottish novelist and poet (1771–1832) who wrote mainly historical romances. The titles of several of his novels have been used as pub names (eg Kenilworth, Peveril of the Peak, Ivanhoe) and there are also references to some of the fictional characters he created. Scott invested his money in a publishing house which collapsed, leaving him with debts of £114,000. For the rest of his life he worked incessantly in an effort to pay off the debt in full, to the detriment of his health. Creditors received payment in full from money earned by his books, though Scott himself was by this time dead.

Sir Walter Tyrrell Cadnam, Hants. The pub is in the New Forest area, near the Rufus Stone, where William Rufus, son of William the Conqueror, met his death. Sir Walter Tyrrell is the man who, according to tradition, fired an arrow which glanced off an oak tree accidentally with fatal results. Others say that the arrow was deliberately aimed. These events took place in 1128.

Sir William Grindleford, near Sheffield. After Sir William Bagshawe (1771–1832), a local landowner and high sheriff of Derbyshire in 1805.

Sir William Courtenay Dunkirk, near Canterbury. An archbishop of Canterbury (1342–96) who was also chancellor of Oxford University in 1367. He came to Canterbury in 1381.

Sir William Gomm London SE16. An English general (1784–1875) who served in the Peninsular Wars, then at Waterloo. He was Commander-in-chief in India 1850–55.

Sir William Walworth London SE17. The lord mayor of London (died 1385) who is mainly remembered for having killed Wat Tyler in 1381. This act effectively ended the Peasants' Revolt.

Sir Winston Churchill London W8 and elsewhere. Also Churchill, Bamford, Rochdale, and elsewhere; Sir Winston, Annesley Woodhouse, Notts; Winston, Churchill, Som; Winston Churchill, Dunstable. After Britain's leader during World War Two and prime minister on two other occasions. Winston Leonard Spencer Churchill (1874–1965) first entered parliament in 1900. In World War One he was 1st lord of the admiralty. He was later chancellor of the Exchequer, then replaced Chamberlain as prime minister in 1940. He became a symbol of the nation's resistance to its enemies. Apart from his political career, Churchill was active as an author of histories, biographies and memoirs. He was awarded the 1953 Nobel Prize in Literature. He found time for other hobbies, one of which is commemorated at Marston, near Oxford, in the Bricklayer's Arms. Inn signs often show the great man giving his famous V for Victory sign and smoking one of the cigars which he loved.

Sitwell Arms Renishaw, Derbs. Also at Horsley Woodhouse, Derbs. Sir George Sitwell had three children who became well-known poets, writers and critics. Dame Edith Sitwell (1887–1964) was of remarkable appearance, nearly six feet tall and usually dressed in medieval fashion. She was a distinguished poetess and critic, awarded several honorary doctorates. One brother was Sir Osbert Sitwell (1892–1969), poet and novelist, who worked with Dame Edith and their brother Sacheverell Sitwell on the anthology *Wheels*. Sacheverell Sitwell (b 1897) was sheriff of Northamptonshire 1948–49, and is also a well-known critic and poet.

Six Bells *See* Bell.

Six in Hand Croesyceiliog, near Pontypool. The normal way of speaking about a team of horses controlled by one person. West Croydon has a Four-in-Hand.

Six Lords Singleborough, near Buckingham. This pub closed in 1933, but commemorated six noblemen who passed through the village on their way to London, where they were due to be executed for their part in the 1715 Rebellion. One of them, Lord Nithsdale, managed to escape from the Tower dressed in his wife's clothes.

Six Packs Market Harborough, Leics. The six packs of hunting hounds which are well-known in this area. They are the Atherstone, Belvoir, Fernie, Pytchley, Quorn and Woodland packs.

Six Ringers Felmersham, near Bedford. The sign shows six bell-ringers at work in the local church.

Sixteen String Jack Theydon Bois, near Epping. Another at Stratford St Mary, near Colchester. This was the nickname of John Rann, an eighteenth-century highway-man. He wore eight coloured strings round each knee of his breeches, and was known for his love of fine clothes. He went to the gallows, it is said, in a new pea-green suit.

Skate Arbroath. The large flat fish, at the centre of a local fishing industry.

Skiddaw London W9. The name of a mountain in Cumberland, 3,054 feet high. There is a well-known reference to it in Lord Macaulay's poem *The Armada:* 'And the red glare on Skiddaw roused the burghers of Carlisle.'

Skiff Newcastle-on-Tyne. The name of different types of boat, originally a small seagoing boat adapted for rowing or sailing, attached to a ship. It now tends to refer to a long narrow racing boat, outrigged and fitted with a sliding seat.

Skinners Arms London EC4 and elsewhere. The Worshipful Company of Skinners (1327) was originally a guild of fur merchants. The pub in London EC4 is in the shadow of Beaver House, head-quarters of the Hudson's Bay Company. We are told that the pub has been demolished and the site redeveloped.

Skittlers Arms Broadstone, Dors. 'Western skittles' is played throughout the West Country. Teams of eight men each bowl seven hands, using a ball that usually weighs five pounds. Henry VIII was a keen player.

Sky Blue Coundon Green, Coventry. The colour of the Coventry City Football Club's playing kit. Their ground is nearby.

Skylark Clearbrook, near Yelverton, and elsewhere. The bird that soars into the air while singing. A favourite name for small seaside pleasure boats, it was also given to a British solid-fuel research rocket during the International Geophysical Year, 1957–58.

Skyrack Tavern Leeds. 'Rack' refers to clouds being driven along by the wind in the upper air.

Slab House East Horrington, near Wells, Som. For the stone slabs outside Wells on which food was left for the townsfolk during the plague of 1644.

Slap Up Waterbeach, near Cambridge. This clever pun alludes to the sound of water slapping against something solid (Waterbeach is on the river Cam) while using a phrase that has meant 'excellent' or 'first-rate' since the 1830s to comment on the quality of its own food and drink.

Slatters Canterbury. Slate-layers, or slaters. Slatters is a dialectal form.

Slaughter House Liverpool. The unofficial name of a pub that has no official name. It was converted from a slaughterhouse during the reign of George III.

Sledmere Tavern *See* Sir Tatton Sykes.

Sleeveboard Arms Honiton, Devon. A sleeveboard is a board on which sleeves are ironed.

Slinky Toppers Luton. For the 'gracefully slender' top hats made here, part of the town's hat-making industry.

Slip Much Marcle, near Ledbury, and elsewhere. The other examples are all in Lancashire and Yorkshire. The Much Marcle (H and W) pub commemorates a 'wondrous landslip' which occurred in 1575, demolishing the local church.

Slipper Northampton. The town is well-known for the manufacture of all kinds of footwear.

Slippery Sam's Petham, near Canterbury. For a local smuggler who was at work between 1730–60.

Slipway Sunderland. The slipway in the local ship-building yard is used for launching purposes.

Sloop St Ives, Corn and elsewhere. Either a small one-masted vessel much used by Excisemen in former times, or a small ship-of-war. The latter was highly manoeuvrable in shallower waters. It developed into the type of vessel which was later classified as a frigate.

Slow and Easy *See* Ca'canny.

Slubbers Arms Rochdale. Another at Huddersfield. To slub wool or cotton is to draw it out and twist it after carding, so as to prepare it for spinning. Since the 1830s it has been done by slubbing machines, operated by slubbers.

Slug and Lettuce Stratford-on-Avon. Renamed in 1983, having been the

Phoenix. It now has a large salad counter. The two signboards tell the story behind the name. One shows a lettuce leaf before the slug gets to work on it, and afterwards, whilst the other then shows a village cricket match in which a batsman slugs a ball for six through the pavilion window into a bowl of lettuce. There is another pub of this name at Winkfield, near Windsor.

Smack Leigh-on-Sea, Esx. Another at Whitstable. A smack is a single-masted fishing vessel. The word derives from Dutch *smak* with the same meaning. Burnley has a Smackwater Jack's.

Small Arms Birmingham. A reference to BSA (British Small Arms), a local company, originally engaged in making firearms but well known also for bicycles and motor cycles.

Small Copper Harlow, Esx. One of this town's butterfly signs, though the reverse side of the sign shows a bright farthing coin as a second interpretation of the name. This coin disappeared from official currency at the end of 1960.

Smelters Arms Castleside, near Consett, Dur. The smelters are the men who melt down iron ore and the like in order to extract from it the metal. The word is connected with 'melt'.

Smithfield Blythe Bridge, near Stoke-on-Trent. Another at Higherland, nearby. A reference to Smithfield Market in London, which specialises in meat and poultry. The Blythe Bridge sign shows a butcher hanging up a carcase; the Higherland sign shows a cattle market. In London EC4 there is a new pub called Smithfields (Past and Present).

Smithfield Porter London EC1. The pub is adjacent to the meat market and shows a porter on its sign, wearing his smock-like coat and flat-topped hat.

Smiths Arms Godmanstone, near Dorchester and elsewhere. The Godmanstone pub measures only twenty by ten feet. Under the sign it says: 'Originally a blacksmith's shop where Charles II once stopped to have his horse shod. When he asked for a drink, the blacksmith replied "I have no licence, Sire". So there and then the King granted him one.' *See also* Blacksmiths.

Smithys Nottingham. Formerly the **Crown**, but renamed in 1983 when the brewery discovered that it stood on the site of a former blacksmith's forge. At Tingley, near Wakefield there is a Smithy, while at Rhualt, Clywd there is a Smithy Arms. *See also* Blacksmiths.

Smoker Plumley, Ches. The name of a white racehorse owned by the Prince Regent. It won many races between 1790–93.

Smokers Arms Grimsby. For those who cure fish by a smoking process, preserving it and adding a special flavour at the same time.

Smokey House Marldon, near Paignton. Smoke signals were sent from here to the boats of smugglers, according to local tradition. Opening the door would cause smoke to belch out of the chimney.

Smugglers Anstruther, Fife. This pub was once associated with men who brought their contraband from France to supply the earl of Strathmore. A passage from the inn led to their hide-out. Smugglers' inns are normally found in the West Country, where pubs anywhere near the coast hardly feel respectable these days unless they can claim that gangs of criminals once used the premises.

Names include Smugglers Barn, Bembridge, IOW; Smugglers Den, Cubert, near Newquay and Morecambe; Smugglers Haunt, Trickett's Cross, near Wimborne; Smugglers Roost, Rustington, W Ssx.

Snaffle Bit Glasgow. The snaffle is the simplest kind of bit, or mouthpiece of a horse's bridle. It acts directly on the horse's mouth and is in general use for racing, jumping and hunting.

Snake Bamford, Derb. It is popularly supposed that this name alludes to the twists and turns of the road on which it stands, but there was once a carving of a snake over the front door. That was taken from the arms of the Cavendish family, who owned large estates in this area.

Snatchems Heaton, near Bolton. This is the unofficial name, generally used, of the Golden Ball. The nickname is said to derive from the press gangs of former times who snatched drunken customers as they left and pressed them into naval service.

Snipe Patcham, near Brighton and elsewhere. The snipe has a long straight bill and is usually found in marshy places. Its habit of wading in 'gutters', small channels of water, causes it to be known in some areas as the guttersnipe.

Snooty Fox Tetbury, Glos and elsewhere. This sign is becoming more popular in the 1980s. The first of these was at Tetbury, where the fox was shown as an elegant dandy. At Chester he is shown hiding high above the hounds.

Snowball Brierfield, near Nelson. This name has more associations than one might think. It is possible to eat, drink, read about and smell a snowball as well as throw it. It is the name of various dessert dishes or confections which are made to look like snowballs; as a drink it is a mixture of Advocaat and lemon; in George Orwell's *Animal Farm*, Snowball is the character who represents Trotsky, and in the garden a snowball is either a Guelder rose or one of its clusters of white flowers. Once a word starts to take on other meanings the whole process seems to snowball.

Snowcat Cambridge. The sign shows a profile of the special vehicle with caterpillar tracks used to convey the members of the trans-Antarctic expedition, led by Sir Vivian Fuchs, in 1957–58. This team became the first to traverse the continent, covering 2,200 miles in ninety days. Sir Vivian opened the pub in 1959.

Snowdrop Lewes, E Ssx. There was an avalanche of snow here in 1836 which buried a group of cottages and caused eight deaths. Another pub of this name near the village of Lindfield, not far away, shows a bunch of the flowers on the sign.

Snow Goose Cove, near Farnborough, Hants. The sign here is a reproduction of a well-known painting by Peter Scott. The name itself was suggested by Paul Gallico's romantic novel, *The Snow Goose* (1941).

Snuff Mill Frenchay, near Bristol. The pub was opened in 1967 and recalls a flour mill run by a miller known as Snuffy Jack. He had the habit of sniffing snuff which he had put on to his forearm. Bridgwater has a Snuff Box.

Snug Glasgow. Also Snug Bar, Dalmellington and Cumnock, both in Strathclyde. The snug or snuggery is the traditional name for the bar-parlour of an inn, derived from its earlier use as the name for a bachelor's den – a small, comfortable room where one may be quiet. The ultimate origin of this expression seems to lie in a nautical phrase, 'to snug down', meaning to make everything tidy.

Soho Studley, Wilts. A hunting call used to direct the attention of others to a hare, or to encourage the dogs. The London district of Soho was once used for hare-hunting.

Soldier Dick Furness Vale, near Stockport. Said to relate to a soldier who was given refuge here in the seventeenth century by the local innkeeper. He was wounded, and the innkeeper's wife nursed him back to health. He subsequently stayed on and became a popular local character who could be prevailed on to tell stirring tales of his adventures. He died in 1621.

Soldier's Return Ickenham, near Uxbridge. One side of the sign shows an eighteenth century soldier being welcomed home by his wife and daughter. The other side shows a mini-skirted young lady flying to the arms of a modern soldier.

Sole and Heel Rackheath, near Norwich. Local workers were taken to the Norwich shoe factories every day in convoys of buses.

Sole Bay Southwold, Sflk. Named after an indecisive battle which took place in 1672 during the third Dutch war. A Dutch fleet attacked an English and French one commanded by James, duke of York, later James II. The Dutch, commanded by de Ruyter, eventually retired.

Solent Cowes. Another at Ryde. The Solent is the channel between the Isle of Wight and the mainland of Hampshire. It is about fifteen miles long.

Solway Workington, Cumb. The Solway Firth is an inlet of the Irish Sea separating Cumbria from Dumfries and Galloway. The Esk and Eden rivers flow into it and it broadens to a width of twenty-two miles.

Somerset and Dorset Tavern Burnhamon-Sea, Som. Named after the branch line of the Great Western Railway which opened in 1858.

Songs Songs that have led to pub names are usually traditional, such as Ash Grove, Auld Lang Syne, Blaydon Races, Bluebells of Scotland, Bobby Shafto, Burlington Bertie, Champagne Charlie, Keel Row, Lambeth Walk; Lass of Richmond Hill, Lincolnshire Poacher, Linden Lea, Little Brown Jug, Minstrel Boy, Nellie Dean, Old Folks at Home, Robin Adair, Scots Wha Hae, Sospan Fach, Tipperary. *Tipperary* features on its sign the song's opening bars in musical notation.

Sorbonne Edinburgh. The university in Paris, which no doubt sends many students on courses to Edinburgh University. The Sorbonne was named after its founder. Robert de Sorbon (1201–74), chaplain and confessor to Saint Louis.

Sorrel Horse Ipswich. A horse of a light chestnut colour.

Sospan Fach Pwll, Llanelli. The title of a song much admired by Welsh rugby football fans. The title means 'Little Saucepan' and relates a tale of domestic disorder.

Sound and Vision London W1. The pub is surrounded by film company offices, recording studios, viewing theatres and the like. It was opened (in Dean Street) in 1982.

South Downs Felpham, near Bognor Regis. The chalk hills which extend through Sussex to Beachy Head. They provide good sheep pasture and have produced the Southdown breed, commemorated in a pub at Worthing.

South Stack Holyhead. Named after the nearby lighthouse.

Sovereign Whitstable and elsewhere. The name of Britain's standard gold coin from 1817–1917, with a value of twenty shillings. There was an earlier gold coin of this name minted from the time of Henry VII, when it had a value of 22*s*. 6*d*., to the time of Charles I, by which time its value had fallen to ten shillings. There is a Half Sovereign at Canley, near Coventry, a Sovereigns at Fareham, Hants, and a Golden Sovereign at Norwich.

Sow and Pigs Thundridge, near Ware and elsewhere. This name derives from a card-game called 'My Sow's Pigg'd', said to have been popular with farmers. There are references to it in the seventeenth century, but it seems to have disappeared by the early nineteenth century. There are other pubs of this name at Toddington, near Dunstable and West Bromwich.

Spa Stonehouse, Glos. The sign shows two country women drawing water from a well, supervised by the parson.

Spade and Shovel Eye, near Peterborough. A decidedly down-to-earth name.

Spade and Becket Cambridge and elsewhere. The 'becket' is a large hook on which the spade is hung, the latter being used to dig peat in the Fens. 'Becket' is properly a nautical term, used of a small loop of rope or a hook which keeps loose oars and the like tidy. It can also be a 'bracket', and may be a corruption of that word.

Spade Tree Newton Burgoland, near Leicester. This is a dialectal reference to the handle of a spade. The original landlord here made spade trees.

Spangled Bull *See* Bull.

Spaniard's Inn London NW3. Various reasons are advanced to account for the name of this pub: it was the residence of the Spanish Ambassador to the court of James I; it was run by two Spanish brothers; it was used as the Spanish embassy; its first landlord had been a servant of the Spanish Ambassador, and so on. Lilleywhite in *London Signs* says the building dates only from 1700, which would make several of the explanations impossible, but clearly there was a Spanish connection of some kind. There is a Spaniard at Hindhead, Surrey, also at Colchester and a Spaniards at Saltash, Corn.

Spanish Galleon London SE10. A name suggested by paintings in Greenwich Hospital, which became a Royal Naval College in 1873, showing engagements with the Spanish Armada.

Spanish Lady Saltdean, near Brighton. It was decided to make this a Spanish theme pub. It has a Barcelona Bar and a Castile Saloon.

Spanish Patriot London SE1. Also Spanish Patriots, London N1. References to the Peninsular War, when Britain assisted Spain in ousting Napoleon, who had declared his brother Joseph to be King of Spain in place of the Bourbon royal family.

Spanker Nether Heage, near Derby. Used of any fine person or animal, and the name of a racehorse – the immediate source of this pub name. Smollett, writing in the eighteenth century, had 'a buxom wench' in mind when he wrote: 'turn me adrift in the dark with such a spanker'.

Spanking Roger Miles Platting, Manchester. Major Roger Aytoun of the Royal Manchester Volunteers. He was a local hero at the time his regiment disbanded in 1783. 'Spanking' meant 'fine', 'excellent'.

Sparkford Sparkford, Som. The sign shows the Sparkford Hunt, led by its Master of Foxhounds, Colonel Dyer.

Sparrow Letcombe Regis, near Wantage. Also Sparrows, London E15. One of the commonest British birds, small and brownish-grey. Sparrow-pie or pudding was once eaten, and had the reputation of making the eater sharp-witted.

Sparrowhawk Edgware. This is now the general term for the kind of hawk which preys on sparrows and other small birds. In former times it denoted the female of the species, the male being called the musket (or musquet) hawk. This pub name commemorates Ella, countess of Salisbury. She granted the manor of Edgware to her son Nicholas and his wife in return for the annual gift of one sparrowhawk. There is an Old Sparrowhawk at Wheatley Lane, Lancs.

Spearsmans Arms Thornley, near Durham. A variant of spearman, one skilled at throwing a spear. The Normans were in this area in the eleventh century.

Speckled Skipper Ashton, near Oundle, Northants. The name of a butterfly which is shown on the sign, cleverly contrived in a mosaic of copper nails.

Speckled Trout *See* Trout.

Spectre Pluckley, Kent. The pub is reputed to be haunted.

Speech House Forest of Dean, Glos. An inn since the 1860s, earlier a court house where justice was dispensed by the Verderers of the Forest.

Speed the Plough Hitchin and elsewhere. There was an old saying 'God speed the plough!' where 'speed' means to make successful. The phrase was used to express a general wish that all would go well for arable farmers.

Spencer Arms Chapel Brampton, near Northampton. The home of Earl Spencer, Althorp House, is nearby. The sign shows his coat of arms.

Sphinx Cottingley, near Leeds. In Greek mythology the Sphinx was a monster with the head of a woman and the winged body of a lion. The Sphinx had the habit of proposing a riddle to the people of Thebes and murdering those who were unable to solve it. It was finally solved by Oedipus, whereupon the Sphinx slew itself. Perhaps because it was associated with a problem that was difficult to 'fathom', the Royal Navy used *Sphinx* many times to name a ship. The last was sunk by aircraft in 1940. The name was later used for the naval base in Egypt, 1941–46.

Spice of Life London W1. Apparently a reference to the comment by William Cowper (1731–1800) in his poem *The Task*: 'Variety's the very spice of life,/That gives it all its flavour'. The pub is in an area where there are many variety theatres.

Spider's Web Aberdeen and elsewhere. *See* Cobweb, 'cob' being another word for 'spider'. Armagh has an amusing Spider's Rest.

Spindlemakers Arms Preston. The makers of the spindles used in spinning, originally made of wood, later of metal.

Spink Nest Birkby, near Huddersfield. 'Spink' is a dialectal word for chaffinch, suggested by its note. In Yorkshire the name is also applied to the yellow bunting.

Spinnaker Swanwick, near Southampton. A large three–cornered sail carried by racing yachts and used to run before the wind. The name is said to derive ultimately from *Sphinx*, the name of the yacht which first used such a sail.

Spinner and Burgamott Comberbach, near Northwich, Ches. The second word in this name is a form of Bergamot, which apart from being the name of a tree is also a term used to describe a kind of tapestry, made of flock and hair mixed. The hair would have come from goats or oxen. This type of woven fabric was first produced at Bergamo, in Italy, but it seems to have been produced in Comberbach as well.

Spinners Arms Colne and elsewhere, especially in Lancashire. A general tribute to those engaged in the cotton industry.

Spinning Jenny Accrington. The name of an early form of spinning machine in which several spindles were set in motion by a band from one wheel. It was invented by James Hargreaves about 1764, though not patented until 1770. Hargreaves was probably born in Blackburn. He died in Nottingham 1778, where he had set up a mill. That city also has a pub of this name, opened in 1979.

Spion Kop Hemsworth, near Wakefield. The name of a hill near Ladysmith, Natal, for which a battle was fought in 1900 during the siege of Ladysmith. That Boer War battle seems to have led to the naming of the Kop, the hill-like terrace, at Liverpool's football ground. Spion Kop was also the name of the Derby winner in 1920.

Spirit Vaults Bath and elsewhere. Normally a reference to premises which previously belonged to a wine-merchant, especially one who sold gin. At Worksop a pub of this name opened in 1976 also has a pharmacy on the premises. Previously liquor was sold in a snug at the rear of the chemist's shop.

Spital Chester. In Spital Walk, and named for a hospital. Leicester, has a similar Spitalhouse Tavern. The Spital Beck at Flaxton, near York and Spital Bridge, Peterborough, also derive ultimately from 'hospital', especially one dealing with particularly contagious diseases leading to disfigurement and having beggars and other destitute persons as patients.

Spofforth Liverpool. Frederick Spofforth (1853–1926), the Australian cricketer earned the nickname of *The Demon Bowler*. There are photographs of him inside the pub and he is also shown on the sign.

Sport The Sportsman at Stratford-on-Avon has a sign which shows him wearing various sports gear and accessories. There are other pubs of this name where the reference is more specific, to stag hunting, for instance. Sandyway, Som, has a Sportsman Arms, Taunton a Sportsman's, Sheffield a Sportsmans Group, Uxbridge a Sportsmans Hall, Copnor near Southsea a Sportsmans Rest. Old Hill, W Mids, has a Sportsman and Railway. In general terms, racing, hunting, fishing, golf, rowing, archery and bowls are well catered for in pub-name terms. There are a few boxing names, two or three mention athletics, and sports such as hurling are lucky to be mentioned in a single instance, in this case Hurlers at Haworth, W Yorks. Wrestling names mainly recall the wrestlers of the past, especially those of Cumberland.

Sporting Life London E2. Another at Wheatley, near Halifax. The London pub contains items connected with jockeys.

Spotted Bull *See* Bull.

Spotted Cow Brockham, near Betchworth, Sry, and elsewhere. The Brockham sign shows the cow wearing a medallion around her neck inscribed 'First over the Moon'. She is flanked by an American eagle and a Russian bear. The allusion is to the nursery-rhyme; 'Hey diddle diddle,/The cat and the fiddle,/ The cow jumped over the moon;/ The little dog laughed/To see such sport,/And the dish ran away with the spoon.'

Spotted Dog Smart's Hill, near Tonbridge and elsewhere. The Kent sign was supposed to refer to the three leopards on the coat of arms of the Sydney family. The pub's name reflects public opinion of the original artist's work.

Sprat Didcot, Oxon. Also Sprat and Mackerel, Brixham, which is a fishing port. The sprat is a small fish and the word is sometimes applied to other small things. At one time it was the slang word for a sixpence.

Spread Eagle Midhurst, W Ssx and elsewhere. An eagle with its wings spread out was established as a national emblem by the Romans. It is associated heraldically with many countries, including Austria, Germany, Russia, Spain and France. The white-headed American eagle with outspread wings is the emblem, of the United States. The British noble families who make use of a spread eagle in their coats of arms usually

'imported' the device after trips to foreign parts, beginning with the Crusades. The Midhurst pub refers to the Viscounts Montagu, who were once the local lords of the manor. At Stourton, Wilts, the name of the pub belonging to the National Trust is derived from the arms of the Hoare family, the bankers.

Springbok London W12. The springbok is a kind of antelope which abounds in South Africa, and which is used as the national emblem of that country. It has a habit of springing almost directly upwards when excited, hence its name. The Springboks are the South African rugby football team. This pub is in South Africa Road.

Springer Bristol. The pub was formerly the Spring Gardens. A new landlord had a pet springer spaniel (one of the larger varieties of spaniel) and renamed the pub accordingly. The dog is seen on the sign.

Spurmakers Arms Walsall. After the local spurriers. Spurs are the metal pricking instruments worn on the heels of a horseman's boots, used to encourage the horse to greater efforts. They come in different types: box, dropped, hammerhead, OK, polo, racing and rowelled.

Spurs London N17. After the Tottenham Hotspur football team. *See* Hotspur.

Spyglass and Kettle Wigmore, near Gillingham. In 1946 the Phoenix Brewery wished to amalgamate two pubs called the Lord Nelson and the Steam Engine. The brewery's employers were invited to suggest a new name and sign. The present sign shows an admiral looking through his spyglass while standing on the footplate of a very early locomotive. 'Kettle' was once applied to iron-clad or iron vessels of any kind, and was presumably used as a locomotive name.

Spyway Askerwell, Dors. Said to have been used by smugglers as a look-out post.

Square Albert Manchester. The pub is in Albert Square.

Square and Compass Worth Matravers, Dors. Another at Gloucester. Also Square and Compasses, Great Shelford, Cambs, and elsewhere. A reference to basic tools used by carpenters, joiners and stonemasons.

Square Rigger London EC4. The pub was opened in 1963 and reproduces in its entirety an eighteenth century frigate. Fowey, Corn, has a Square Rig. Sails which are placed in the line of the vessels length are known as fore-and-aft. Pub now demolished.

Square Ring Hartlepool. An allusion to the boxing ring, which was originally formed by a ring of spectators but is now square.

Squinting Cat Clipstone, near Mansfield. Notts. The sign here won first prize in a paint-a-pub-sign competition organised by Shipstone's Brewery. It shows a cat who has sampled the contents of a leaking barrel (*see* Drunken Duck). There are other pubs of this name, including one at Pannal, near Harrogate, where a previous landlady is said to have squinted from behind her curtains at approaching customers. Locals say she was known as 't'owd cat'.

Squire Chipping Sodbury, Glos. Another at London SE6. Also Squires, Ballygowan, Down. The Chipping Sodbury sign shows Squire George Osbaldestone (1787–1866) who was only five feet high but excelled as an all-round sportsman. Two of his feats,

accomplished in order to win wagers, were to catch a fox, badger and otter, all within thirty-six hours, and to ride two hundred miles in less than ten hours. To achieve the second of these he changed horse every five miles. The squire also indulged in fencing, shooting, boxing and rowing.

Stable Door Buckfastleigh. Another at Middleham, N Yorks. Presumably a reference to the proverbial saying that it is too late to shut the stable door when the horse has bolted.

Staff Camberley, Sry. The Staff College is at Camberley, a college where selected army officers are trained for staff appointments.

Staff of Life Shottermill, Sry. Others at Ticknall, near Melbourne and Sutton-in-Ashfield, Notts. There is a seventeenth century proverb: 'Bread is the staff of life'. The Shottermill pub is on the site of a former water-mill where flour was ground. The Ticknall sign shows a cottage loaf.

Staffordshire Knot Lanesfield, near Bilston. Another at Hanford, near Stoke-on-Trent. Also Staffordshire Volunteer, Bushbury, near Wolverhampton; Staffordshire Yeoman, Stafford. The Staffordshire Knots was originally the nickname of the South Staffordshire Regiment, now amalgamated with the North Staffordshire Regiment to form The Staffordshire Regiment (The Prince of Wales's). In his book *How the Regiments got their Nicknames*, Tim Carew tells a heart-rending story of the 38th Foot being sent to Antigua in 1706 and being forgotten by the War Office for the next sixty years. No new uniforms were issued in that time, so old ones were patched up with brown holland. A piece of this material was worn behind the cap badge afterwards in memory of that period and became known as the Staffordshire Knot. Others explain the knot as derived from the coat of arms of the barons of Stafford. Decorative knots are certainly used in heraldry, and are also worn on uniforms – eg a black mourning knot, but getting at the truth of this matter appears to be a knotty problem.

Staffordshire Yeoman *See* **Yeoman**.

Stag Watford and elsewhere. Also Stag's Head, Golspie, Sutherland and elsewhere; Stag Hunt, Ponsanooth, near Truro; Stag Hunters, Brendon, Devon; Stag and Hound, Kilwinning, Strath; Stag and Hounds, Iver Heath, Bucks and elsewhere, Stag and Huntsman, Hambleden, near Marlow; Stag and Pheasant, Coventry. The stag is a male deer, especially a red deer, in its prime, ie its fifth year. Most of the signs mentioned above refer to hunts, stag hunting having been a favourite royal sport in times past. Occasionally there is a heraldic reference, or a particular incident is commemorated, as at Ponsanooth. The sign there dates from an incident in 1805 when an exhausted stag fell into a local mine-shaft, fatally pursued by a pack of hounds.

Stage Door Nottingham. The pub is near the stage door of the Theatre Royal.

Stagg *See* Swann.

Stamps North Bersted, near Bognor Regis. Formerly the Rising Sun, but reopened in 1983 with a name that looks back to The Stamp House, which once stood on this site. Its rooms and corridors were completely covered from floor to ceiling with over three million postage stamps.

Standard Northallerton, N Yorks. The English defeated the Scots at the Battle of the Standard three miles from here in 1138. The battle earned this name from the standard which was raised on a wagon and placed in the centre of the English army. On a single pole the flags of St Cuthbert of Durham, St Peter of York, St John of Beverley and St Wilfred of Ripon were displayed. St Cuthbert's flag was looked upon as a particularly lucky omen.

Standard Bearer Coventry. A local man bore Edward III's personal standard at the Battle of Crecy in 1346. English longbows were used for the first time and helped the English defeat a French army which was three times as large as their own.

Standard of England Basford, Nottingham. Another at Ash Vale, near Aldershot. Another version of Royal Standard.

Stang Foot near Barnard Castle, N Yorks. 'Stang' occurs in Yorkshire place names, especially names of hills, and means a pole of some kind that marked the summit. Here the name means 'foot of Stanghow'.

Stanley Laurel *See* Laurel and Hardy.

Staplecross *See* Cross.

Star Dorking and elsewhere. Originally a religious symbol, referring either to the star of Bethlehem or to the Virgin Mary, one of whose titles is 'the Star of the Sea' (*Stella Maris*). Since 1634 a sixteen-pointed star has also appeared in the arms of the Worshipful Company of Innholders, formerly a guild of innkeepers. The *Star* as a pub name dates from the fifteenth century. The inn of this name at Alfriston, E Ssx is said to date from 1450. **Ye** Olde Starre in York claims to date back to the reign of Henry VIII. More recent pubs sometimes show an insignia, such as the Star of India medal. The popularity of the sign, with its conveniently easy-to-recognise shape, is demonstrated by the city of Norwich. At one time it could boast of pubs called Star, Morning Star, New Star, Old Star, Golden Star, Star and Crown, Seven Stars and Moon and Stars.

Star and Garter Windsor and elsewhere. Also Star and Garter Royal, Wolverhampton. A reference to the Most Noble Order of the Garter, the highest order of knighthood in Britain. Instituted by Edward III about 1348 when, according to a pleasant tradition, he picked up a garter which had accidentally slipped from the leg of the Countess of Salisbury at a court ball. Edward noticed that some of those present were looking at him in a knowing way as he stood with the garter in his hand. He therefore slipped the blue band around his own knee, saying as he did so, *Honi soit qui mal y pense*, 'evil be to him who evil thinks'. The Order is limited to the sovereign, other members of the royal family, and twenty-five knights. The 'star' forms part of the insignia.

Star and Waggon Droitwich. A line from the works of Ralph Waldo Emerson (1802–82) was 'Hitch your wagon to a star'. This was taken up and used in a once-popular song. The pub sign here illustrates the idea literally.

Star Castle St Mary's, Isles of Scilly. The local castle was built in 1593 and has a star shape.

Stardust Thurso, Caithness. The name of a popular song, and used metaphorically to describe a dreamlike magic quality or feeling, as if one were as light and airy as stardust.

Stargazer Selsey, W Ssx. One who spends his time thinking and talking about impractical schemes instead of getting on with what needs to be done. The word had far more obscene meanings in the eighteenth century, but they are now obsolete.

Star in the East London SE10. Another at Kemptown, Brighton. Also Star of the East, London E14. Matthew 2:1 has: 'There came wise men from the east to Jerusalem, Saying, Where is he that is born King of the Jews? for we have seen his star in the east, and are come to worship him.'

Star of Brunswick *See* Brunswick.

Star of India Nunhead. The Most Exalted Order of the Star of India was instituted by Queen Victoria in 1861. It was used to recognise services to India and the loyalty of the Indian princes, but it has lapsed since 1947.

Star Royal Oxford. This was the Star until 1975. The sign shows the Magi on their camels looking up to the Star of Bethlehem.

Start Bay Torcross, near Kingsbridge. One of the most attractive signs in the country, with its own thatched roof. It portrays the beauty of the local landscape. The bay takes its

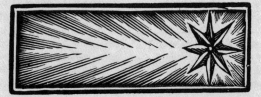

name from Stuart Point, named because it was thought to resemble a 'tail' (Old English *stoort*).

Starting Gate Redcar and elsewhere. The name is used in several places which have a racecourse.

Startled Saint West Malling, Kent. The sign shows St Leonard looking startled as fighter aircraft buzz round his halo. This saint is a local one, by tradition, and the name imagines his reaction to the Hurricanes and Spitfires from nearby Biggin Hill, the famous RAF fighter station of World War Two. The pub was patronised by many of the pilots.

Starving Rascal Amblecote, near Stourbridge. This pub was the Dudley Arms until 1977. The present name commemorates an incident which occurred earlier this century. A tramp appeared at the inn door one winter's night, asking for shelter. He was refused admittance but stayed on the doorstep. His frozen body was found there next morning. The sign shows the tramp on one side, and his ghost on the other, since naturally he has come back to haunt the place.

Steamboat Trent Lock, near Nottingham. Others at Burntisland, Fife, and Ipswich. The facade of the Trent Lock pub has been painted to represent a steam boat. A more popular sign is Steam Packet, as at Devonport and elsewhere. *See* Packet Boat.

Steam Wagon Shrewsbury. A name given to both road and rail vehicles which were propelled by steam. They were once made locally at the Sentinel Waggon Works – later taken over by Rolls-Royce.

Steering Wheel Bury St Edmunds. A pub where they take turns to buy you a drink?

Stephen Langton Friday Street, near Abinger, Sry. Stephen Langton (died 1228) became archbishop of Canterbury in 1207. He supported the barons against King John and was the first subscribing witness to the Magna Carta (*see* Magna Charta).

Stephenson's Rocket *See* George Stephenson.

Stepping Stones Westhumble, near Dorking. Others at Stourbridge and Broadstone, Dors. The Westhumble sign shows medieval travellers using stepping stones to cross the river Humble.

Steptoe's Sheffield. Another at London N16. Named for the father and son characters in the highly popular television series *Steptoe and Son*, about rag-and-bone men. The Sheffield pub picks up on the junk theme in its decor. The series ran from 1964–74 and starred Harry H Corbett as the younger man, Wilfrid Brambell as his father.

Stewards Arms Southampton. After the stewards on the ocean liners which use this port.

Stewponey Stourton, near Stour-bridge. Officially the Stewponey and Foley Arms, with the sign showing the arms of the Foley family, who made a fortune as iron masters. According to the locals, Stewponey, is a corruption of Estepona, in Spain. It was the birthplace of a girl who married an English soldier during the Penin-sular Wars. He returned to run the pub and named it, in honour of her native village, but the locals found the name too much of a mouthful. Now sadly demolished.

Sticky Wicket Redditch. Another at Wolverhampton. An allusion to the saying about 'batting on a sticky wicket', ie being on uncertain ground, making a statement which it may be difficult to justify or engaging in an enterprise which is risky. On a sticky wicket, in cricket, the ball is likely to bounce in an unexpected way.

Still Lincoln. Another at Boston. Also Still Vaults, Spalding. The apparatus which is at the heart of the distilling process, by which alcohol is produced. The still is a closed container in which a liquid is turned to vapour by heating, then recovered as it condenses. The sign was formerly common in London, presumably as a simple indication that alcoholic drinks were sold.

Still and West Country House Portsmouth. A blended name derived from two pubs originally, one being the Still, the other the East and West Country House. The latter pub was demolished in the late nineteenth century, leaving the other to absorb part of its trade and name.

Stilton Cheese Stilton, near Peterborough. In the middle of the eighteenth century the cheese made by a Mrs Paulet of Melton Mowbray was sold by her relative, Thornhill, at the Bell Inn, Stilton. The fame of the cheese spread from there. It is still made mainly in the Vale of Belvoir, Leics. There is another pub of this name at Somerby, near Melton Mowbray.

Stingray Harwich. The long tail of this fish has a flattened sharp-pointed bony spine near the middle. It is serrated on both sides and can inflict a very nasty wound.

Stiperstones Minsterley, near Shrewsbury. A dialectal reference to the 'steep' stones of the nearby rocky hills.

Stirrup Cup Scraptoft, near Leicester and elsewhere. This name refers to a drink taken by one who is already on horseback and is ready to depart, the hunting equivalent of one for the road. The Master of Foxhounds normally takes such a drink, offered by the landlord of the pub where the hunt has assembled. In the Highlands that courtesy was formerly extended to all the members of the hunt. Sir Walter Scott writes in *Marmion*: 'Lord Marmion's bugles blew to horse;/Then came the stirrup cup in course;/Between the baron and his host/No point of courtesy was lost.'

Stobsmill Gorebridge, near Dalkeith, Loth. A stobmill or stobsmill is a windmill pivoted upon a central post (the 'stob', which in Scotland and some other dialects is a stake or post).

Stocks Furzehill, near Wimborne, Dors and elsewhere. The well-known instrument of punishment by which an offender was made to sit in a public place with his ankles secured by two planks with small apertures. Sometimes the hands were also secured in a similar way. The use of stocks continued until the nineteenth century

Stockyards Gloucester. A reference to the cattle pens in the local market.

Stokers Arms Blackburn. After those who feed and maintain a furnace.

Stone and Faggot Little Yeldham, Esx. 'Faggot' here has the meaning of a bundle of sticks used to make a fire. In the village bakery, in the eighteenth century, faggots were used to heat stones on which bread was baked. This name was adopted when the bakery was converted into an inn.

Stonegallows Bishop's Hull, near Taunton. Thomas Gage was hanged nearby in 1910. He murdered Elizabeth Styling, wife of a local farmer. 'Stone' here is a place name; the gallows would have been made of wooden beams in the usual way.

Stonehenge Bulford Camp, near Salisbury. The most important prehistoric monument in Britain, on Salisbury Plain. The stones are thought to have been erected about 3,500 years ago. Stonehenge takes its name from the stones which 'hang' between upright stones. The use to which Stonehenge was put is still something of a mystery, though it is probable that it was for some kind of sun–worship.

Stork Wigan and elsewhere. The white stork is a visitor to Britain, apart from the birds which are in captivity. The bird is seen more regularly in Germany, Hungary, etc, where it often builds a nest on the roof of a house. It is considered to bring good luck when it does so, and no doubt this habit led to the tales about storks bringing babies. According to legend the bird also looks after its parents when they are old and unable to find food for themselves.

Stork at Rest Gravesend. The pub was built on the site of a maternity hospital, destroyed in World War Two. The sign shows Doctor Stork at ease in his surgery, a jar of ale at hand and contentedly puffing a cigar.

Stormy Petrel Tern Hill, Market Drayton. Storm petrels, or stormy petrels as they have also been called since the eighteenth century, are so named because their appearance is thought to indicate that stormy weather is approaching. At sea they are said to seek the wake of a vessel when a storm is due. 'Petrel' is thought to allude to St Peter, the Apostle who walked on the sea at Galilee. The terns referred to in the place name are also sea-birds.

Stour Blandford St Mary, Dors. Also Stour Vale, Christchurch; Stour Valley Tavern, Birmingham. There are various English rivers called Stour. The one in Kent rises near Lenham and flows into Pegwell Bay. Another rises near West Wickham, forms the boundary between Essex and Suffolk, and flows into the sea at Harwich. Another rises at Stourhead and flows into the Avon at Christchurch. A fourth rises near Tadmarton. Oxon, and flows into the Avon near Stratford-on-Avon, while the fifth rises near Halesowen and flows into the Severn at Stourport.

Stow Away Stow Hill, Newport. There is a similar place–name joke in the Stowaway, Stowe St Lichfield. Neath has another pub of this name.

Strad Sheffield. The name obviously suggests a violin made by Antonio Stradivari (1644–1737) and referred to as a Stradivarius. However, the pub is in Stradbroke Drive and Strad appears to be what is known as a back formation.

Strawberry Barrow-in-Furness and elsewhere. Also Strawberry Gardens, Stockport. The fruit, or a drink made from it. Its name probably derives from its habit of strewing itself over a patch of ground, though from an early time straw was used to protect it. At Entwhistle, near Manchester, there is a Strawberry Duck, presumably a reference to its colour.

Strawberry Special Draycott, Som. The original sign by David Fisher done in 1977 showed a GWR pannier-tank engine hauling a truck-load of enormous strawberries: a nostalgic allusion to the fruit vans used by the old Cheddar Valley line which closed in 1968.

Strawplaiters Luton. Luton was for a long time the centre of the straw-plaiting industry, introduced in the reign of James I. The manufacture of straw hats was later replaced by that of felt hats.

Street Names A great many pubs bear the same names as the streets they are in. Only local historians would be able to sort out which came first, the inn or the street.
For London pubs, especially, consulting a good street name dictionary can often provide the clue to the origin of a name There have been about ten different dictionaries of London street names published, but we have mainly consulted while preparing this book *London Street Names*, by Gillian Bebbington, published by Batsford, and *The Streets of London*, by S Fairfield, published by Macmillan.

Struggler Also Strugglers, Struggling Man. *See* Help me through this world.

Student Prince Luton. The sign shows a scene from the operetta of this name by Sigmond Romberg (1887–1951), the Hungarian composer who settled in New York, then Hollywood. *The Student Prince* was first performed in 1924.

Studio 4 Norwich. The nearby headquarters of Anglia Television is the converted Agricultural Hall. This pub opened in 1958, just as the conversion had taken place. Anglia House, as it had now become, had three studios, so the pub became *Studio 4*. Luton has a Studio 2.

Sturdy Lads Monk Bretton, near Barnsley. In a coal–mining area with a long tradition of providing tough jobs for its work force.

Sturdy's Castle Tackley, near Oxford. The sign shows two men engaged in a bitter struggle. According to local tradition they were named Sturdy and Castle, and one of them killed the other. He was hanged on gallows specially erected where the pub is today. This happened in the eighteenth century, and the original name of the pub, **Sturdy and Castle**, has since changed to its present form.

Styrrup Rossington, near Doncaster. A variant of stirrup, the rider's foot-rest which is attached to the horse's saddle by leather straps.

Submarine Plymouth. This word was first used to describe a boat that could operate under water in 1899. The crews that serve in the submarines of the Royal Navy form an élite within the Service. For American tourists the name no doubt suggests that they will be able to obtain a large sandwich in the pub, generously filled with meat, cheese, onion, lettuce and tomato, and known as a submarine or sub because of its shape. It is also known as a torpedo.

Success to the Plough Rochdale. An updated version of Speed the Plough.

Suffolk Punch Ipswich and elsewhere. Also Old Suffolk Punch, London N4. A strong and hardy horse, mostly bred in Suffolk.

Sugar Loaf London EC4 and elsewhere. Also Sugar Loaves, Little Chalfont, Bucks and Sible Hedingham, Esx. In 1707 Lady Moseley paid over £3 for a sugar loaf, according to her Household Book, in which she carefully kept her accounts. It would have been conically shaped, like a very large ice-cream cone, and made of refined sugar. This was the normal method of marketing sugar until the early 1800s, and a sugar loaf was once an instantly recognised shape. The name was applied to other objects, such as a hat which was worn during the Tudor and Stuart periods, or a hill, eg the famous *Sugar Loaf* at Rio de Janeiro, Brazil. A sugar loaf would originally have been the sign of a grocer, but its convenient visual form made it attractive to tavern-keepers, who have been using it since the seventeenth century.

Sultan Wimbledon and elsewhere. Sultan Azizi of Turkey visited England in 1869. A Royal Navy ship was named in his honour, as were some pubs, four of which are still found in London.

Summit *See* Everest.

Sumpter Horse Penwortham, near Preston. The word 'sumpter' originally meant the driver of a packhorse. Later it came to mean the horse itself, and later still it meant the pack carried by the horse. That seems to be the meaning here – a horse carrying a sumpter.

Sun Yeovil and elsewhere. Also Sun in Splendour, Leamington Spa; Midday Sun, Coulsden; Noon Sun, Rochdale; Setting Sun, Hull; Sun House, Whatley, near Frome; Sun Mill, Chadderton, near Oldham; Sunbeam, Kennoway, near Leven, Fife; Sunnyside, Nuneaton and Northampton; Sunray, Osmington, near Weymouth; Sunsea, St Ives, Corn; Sunshine, Farlington, Hants. Most of these names are modern and reflect a contemporary attitude towards the sun, expressed in 'a

place in the sun', which means to have a fortunate situation which gives favourable opportunities. The early uses of *Sun* as a tavern sign made use of its simple visual form. It was painted as a circle with a few rays around it, and often filled in with eyes, a nose and a mouth. One or two modern signs, by contrast, are very elaborate. At Long Marston, near York, the sun image is shown together with the head of Edward IV and white and red roses. The sign at Yeovil shows Apollo, the sun god, driving his chariot.

Sun and Slipper Clows Top, near Kidderminster. The sun here is a heraldic reference to the local Blount family. The slipper is said to refer to an occasion when one of that family fought a duel at the inn wearing his carpet slippers.

Sun and Thirteen Cantons London W1. The name was given by an innkeeper of Swiss origin in the mid–eighteenth century, at which time there were thirteen cantons (small political divisions) united together in a defensive league. Modern Switzerland has twenty-five cantons. The area of Soho where this pub is situated is still something of a Swiss centre in London.

Sundowner Dunoon, Strath. The name given in various countries to a drink taken at sunset, though the expression is also well-known in its Australian sense, of a tramp who arrives at a ranch in the evening, too late to do any work that day but in time for a meal and a night's lodging. These he is given in the expectation of the following day's work, but he moves on. The word could usefully be applied to those who arrive in a pub ten minutes before closing time and have time to be bought a drink, but not time to finish it and buy one in return.

Sun in the Sands London SE3. The sign shows a shepherd driving his flock along the road towards the setting sun. Kentish drovers used to pass this way on their journey to the London market. When they climbed Shooters Hill, having taken a week to get that far, and saw the setting sun through a cloud of dust and sand thrown up by the hooves of the sheep, they knew they were near the end of their journey.

Sun Rising *See* Rising Sun.

Super Star Newcastle-under-Lyme. The name of a prize-winning and very popular rose.

Surf Rider Newquay. This resort is known for its rolling waves, and riding them is a popular sport.

Surprise London SW3. Another at London EC1. This name has frequently been used by the Royal Navy to name ships of various kinds. The Chelsea pub was named for the frigate which carried Napoleon's body from St Helena to France.

Surrey London WC2. The pub is in Surrey Street, on land owned by the Howards. Various branches of that family held the dukedom of Norfolk and the earldoms of Arundel and Surrey.

Surrey Cricketers *See* Cricket.

Surrey Oaks Newdigate, near Dorking. There are two magnificent oak trees outside the pub.

Surrey Yeoman *See* Yeoman.

Surtees Tow Law, Dur. Also Surtees Arms at nearby Shildon. The novelist Robert Smith Surtees (1803–64) lived in this area. He was particularly successful with the creation of John Jorrocks, the sporting Cockney grocer, who has pubs named after him in Kent and Derby. *See also* Cat and Custard Pot.

Suspension Bridge *See* Bridge.

Sussex Brighton. The sign shows a steam locomotive.

Sussex Coaster Peacehaven. The sign shows a trading vessel.

Sussex Cricketers *See* Cricket.

Sussex Ox *See* Ox.

Sussex Pad Lancing. The reference is to a footpad, a thief who operated on foot rather than on horse, like the highwayman. Pads, or footpads, were simply the eighteenth-century equivalent of muggers.

Sussex Yeoman *See* Yeoman.

Sutton Arms London EC4. The pub is in Carthusian Street, named for the monks who came from Chartreuse in France and were founders of the Charterhouse monastery. (Charterhouse is a corruption of Chartreuse.) Thomas Sutton (1532–1611) was a merchant and philanthropist who turned the monastery into a hospital for the poor. It later became a public school, which moved out to Godalming, Sry, in 1872. Charterhouse is now a 'home of rest'.

Sutton Staithe Sutton, Nflk. 'Staithe' is another word for a landing-stage, or wharf. The word is used especially of a waterside depot for coal shipments.

Swallow Wellingborough. The pub is in Nest Lane. There is another pub of this name in the village of Swallow, near Lincoln, where the place name probably derives from a river name, not the bird. Warsop, Notts, has a Swallows; Blurton, near Newcastle-under-Lyme has a Swallows Nest.

Swan Thames Ditton and elsewhere. In use as a tavern sign since the fourteenth century, either as a direct allusion to the majestic bird itself or to a coat of arms which featured it. In the latter role it was much favoured by Henry VIII and Edward III. The sign remains fairly popular, with some thirty examples in Greater London. At Clare, Sflk, there is a particularly fine wrought-iron sign. The *Swan* at Pangbourne has special literary associations with both Kenneth Grahame and Jerome K Jerome. The White Swan is a frequent variant; *see also* Black Swan

Swan and Pyramids London N12. An amalgamation of two former signs, the 'pyramids' referring to sugar loaves. *See* Sugar Loaf.

Swan and Rushes Leicester. The sign shows the swan in its nesting environment. The rushes in the background also help to emphasise the whiteness of the bird's plumage. Also Swan in Rushes, Loughborough.

Swann Guist, near Dereham, and elsewhere. A variant of Swan, a leftover from the times when spelling was anything but standardised. Before the present century the majority of people were illiterate. Written records of all kinds show that those minor clerical officials and others who were entrusted with committing words and names to writing, frequently adopted their own idiosyncratic spelling system. The preservation of spellings like *Swann* in modern times is meant to show that the pub concerned is of great age. (Compare Stagg for Stag at Hatfield Heath, and Starr for Star in Manchester.)

Swan Revived Newport Pagnell, Bucks. The reference is to a licence being renewed after having been allowed to lapse, rather than to a bird being saved. The pub was formerly a Swan.

Swan's Nest Exminster, Devon. Swans nest on the nearby river Exe. Associated names include Swan and Cygnet, Swanland, Hull, Swan and Cygnets, South Laggan, Hghld; Swan and Three Cygnets, Durham.

Swan with Two Necks Armitage, Staffs and elsewhere. Also Swan with Two Nicks, Leeds and elsewhere; Two-necked Swan, Great Yarmouth. This sign first appeared in London in the sixteenth century, when 'neckes' was the spelling of the last word. There are many seventeenth-century references to another London inn as either *Swan with Two Necks* or *Two-necked Swan*. There appear to be no early examples anywhere of a *Swan with Two Nicks*, but at a meeting of the Antiquarian Society in 1810 Sir Joseph Banks propounded his belief that this was the origin of the name, referring to the nicks made on the beaks of swans to show who owned them. For centuries ownership had been restricted to royalty; Elizabeth I granted the privilege of owning swans to both the Dyers' Company and the Worshipful Company of Vintners. Swans belonging to the Vintners were identified with two nicks on the upper mandible. Since there was a justifiable reason for speaking about swans with two nicks, but none that one can imagine for speaking of swans with two necks, and since the Vintners clearly had connections with taverns all over the country, and since the *Oxford English Dictionary* tells us that 'neck' is an obsolete variant of 'nick', it seems safe to assume that Sir Joseph Banks was correct. It would be easier still to make that assumption if at least one early example of *Swan with Two Nicks* was found. One possible reason for the neck variant is that illustrating on a sign the two nicks on a swan's beak would have been a problem – showing a swan with two necks, if that is what the early sign-painters did, would have been easier and more eye-catching. As a footnote to all this, at Chorley, Lancs, there is a Swann with Two Knecks.

Swedish Flag London E1. The name was obviously suggested by the pub's address, in Swedenborg Gardens. Emanuel Swedenborg (1688–1772) was a Swedish scientist, philosopher and theologian. Several experiences of divine revelation convinced him that he was the direct instrument of God. His followers certainly believed this, and founded the Church of the New Jerusalem after his death. He was buried in the Swedish church which stood in Swedenborg Gardens until its demolition in 1921.

Sweeney and Todd Reading. The name of a highly popular melo-drama about a 'demon barber' of Fleet Street who murdered his customers was *Sweeney Todd*. It was concocted by Dibdin Pitt for a novelette in 1847. Various versions of the story have since appeared, and there was an early film on the subject.

Swinging Plaice Gloucester. Presumably customers perch at the bar to drink a bass or two, then flounder about.

Swinging Sporran Eccles and elsewhere. A sign that is becoming more popular in the 1980s, though in England rather than Scotland, reflecting the English obsession with the kilt and what is worn under or on top of it. The sporran is the ornamental pouch which is worn by Highlanders in front of the kilt. It is usually made of skin with the hair left on and is decorated with tassels. The word in Gaelic means 'purse'.

Swingletree Kelly Bray, near Callington, Corn. The sign shows the crossbar, pivoted at the middle, to which the traces of a horse are fastened. 'Tree' is used here in its sense of a piece of wood shaped for a particular purpose. 'Swingle' is from 'swing' and refers to the swingletree's movement.

Swinside Newlands Valley, near Keswick, Cumb. Swinside is found several times as a place name in this part of the world and refers to a place where swine, or pigs, were kept.

Swiss Cottage London NW3. Another at Lincoln. The district takes its name from a Swiss chalet-type cottage which once stood here, the property of a toll-collector. A pub was built on the site in the early nineteenth century and reconstructed in a vaguely Swiss way after World War Two. Newtonabbey, Ant has a Swiss Chalet, and in the same county, at Ballyvoy, there is a Swiss Lodge. Braintree, Esx, has a Swiss Bell, and London SE15 a Swiss Tavern.

Sword and Castle Chilcompton, Som. These appeared on the badge of the Bristol and North Somerset Railway, which was opened in 1873.

Swordfish Newlyn, near Penzance. The sign shows the fish with its upper jaw projecting like a sword and the *Swordfish* bi–plane. The latter was flown from a Fleet Air Arm station nearby during World War Two by a pilot who later became landlord of this pub.

Sword in Hand Westmill, Herts. This is either a religious symbol, referring to St Paul or one of the other saints whose emblem is a sword, or a heraldic allusion. In a figurative sense the phrase means 'militant'.

Swordsman Stamford Bridge, near

York. At a battle which took place nearby in 1066, a month before the Battle of Hastings, a Norse swordsman displayed outstanding courage in holding a bridge over the Derwent. He was eventually killed by a Saxon who floated downstream hidden in a tub, together with his spear.

Swyndlestock Carfax, Oxford. The site of this former tavern is marked by a plaque on the inside wall of Barclays Bank at the Carfax. It was here that a brawl between Town and Gown occurred in 1355 which led to the deaths of sixty students alone, though they are said to have emerged as the winners. The name is a variant of Swingletree, though perhaps used in its earlier meaning of a board used in dressing flax or hemp.

Tabard Hereford and elsewhere. Chaucer's Canterbury pilgrims set out from the *Tabard* in Southwark. It was demolished after a fire in 1676. The sign at Hereford shows the kind of tabard worn by heralds, a coat with no sleeves emblazoned with the arms of the sovereign. As worn by knights, the tabard was a short-sleeved surcoat, open at the sides, emblazoned with his personal coat of arms and worn over his armour. This was truly his 'coat of arms'.

Tabby Cat Chandler's Ford, Hants. A cat which is of a brownish, tawny or grey colour, marked with darker parallel streaks, but loosely used of a female cat.

Tafarn-y-Sospan Pwll, near Llanelli. This translates from Welsh as Saucepan Tavern. *See* Sospan Fach.

Taj Mahal St Albans. The Taj Mahal is the world's most celebrated mausoleum. It was built 1632–50 in pure white marble by Shah Jahan at Agra, India, as a memorial to his favourite wife. The name is variously translated as 'distinguished abode' or 'gem of buildings' (*Mumtaz Mahal* in its original form), which may be true of this pub.

Talbot Welshpool and elsewhere. Also Talbot Arms, Birmingham and elsewhere; Talbot Head, Rochdale; Talbot Bier Keller, Blackpool. A variety of hound formerly used for tracking and hunting, white with black spots, heavy–jawed and with long ears. It had remarkable powers of scent and was the ancestor of modern fox and stag hounds. Its name derives from the fifteenth-century Talbot family, who used the hound on their coat of arms.

Talisman Hitchin. Another at Wolverhampton. A charm endowed with supposed magical powers which will allow extraordinary things to be achieved. Some might say that alcohol is a kind of liquid talisman.

Talk of the Town Cleethorpes, Lincs. A place which is talked about by everybody (because of its excellence). At Nuneaton there is a **Town Talk**, where a place to gossip about doings in the town is implied.

Tall Cranes Govan, Glasgow. A comment on a distinctive shipyard sight.

Tallow Tub Manchester. A tub in which tallow is kept or melted. Tallow is hard animal fat which is used for making candles, dressing leather, etc.

Tally Ho Eastbourne and elsewhere. The hunting cry which announces that a fox has been viewed. Some weird and wonderful etymologies have been proposed, such as a corruption of French *il est haut* 'he is high' ie 'off, but the expression is probably as meaningless as 'Yoicks'. The *Tally Ho* was the name of a stagecoach in the nineteenth century and it is occasionally that which appears on the inn sign, as at Eastbourne.

Talma Tavern London SE26. François Joseph Talma (1763–1826) was a famous French tragic actor, educated in England. He was the first to introduce to the French stage the custom of wearing the costume of the period represented in the play. His wife was also a well-known actress.

Tamar Crownhill, Plymouth. Another at Calstock, Corn. The river which rises east of Morwenstow and eventually flows into Plymouth Sound.

Tam o' Shanter Dumfries and elsewhere. Originally the name of a drunken farmer in a poem of the same name by Robert Burns. The poem was published in 1791, and tells of how Tam interrupts a witches' sabbath. He is pursued by one of the witches, Cutty Sark, to the Doon river, only just escaping with his life. (The witch was named for the short shirt she was wearing). Tam o' Shanter was later applied to a kind of bonnet made of wool, with a flat circular crown which is about twice the circumference of the head. It was once worn by Scottish ploughmen but has been adapted for more fashionable wear in modern times. There was a horse called *Tam o' Shanter* in the nineteenth century which had considerable success, and some pubs were named for it. At Tamworth, Staffs, its use was obviously suggested by the place name. Kilmarnock has a Tam o' Shanter Arms; Perth a Twa Tams.

Tandem Kirkheaton, near Huddersfield. Another at Oxford. The Kirkheaton pub sign shows a pair of trotting horses in a tandem harness. The Oxford sign shows a two-horse gig, a reference (according to Paul J Marriott in his *Oxford Pubs Past and Present*) to the practice of students in times past of taking a one-horse gig as far as this pub, adding another horse there and continuing to Steventon station for the train to London. This was before 1840, when Oxford got a station of its own, and when only one-horse gigs were allowed within the city boundary.

Tan Hill Inn Arkengarthdale, near Reeth, N Yorks. *The Times* published a picture of this desolate pub, 1732 feet above sea-level and thus the highest in Britain, in February 1963. The photograph showed it completely surrounded by snow and totally cut off, and remarked that it had had no customers so far that year. The pub was first established to serve the King's Pit, and indeed bore that name itself until the mine closed in 1932. The nearest village is five miles away.

Tankard Edinburgh and elsewhere. This is now a one–handled jug, usually of pewter but occasionally silver, sometimes with a lid. It was originally a drinking vessel made of hooped staves, something like a miniature wooden tub. In that respect it resembled the Scottish quaich. Haslingden, Lancs, has a Tankards; Cheltenham a Tankard and Castle Foaming Tankard is also found at Birmingham.

Tanners Arms Rochdale and elsewhere. Also Tanner, Runcorn; Tanners, Skelmersdale; Tanners Hall, Stoke Newington; Tannery, Walsall. All refer to the trade of tanning, converting hides into leather by steeping them in suitable solutions, etc. Children are still occasionally told that their hides will be tanned if they do not mend their ways. 'Hides' in this instance usually means their backsides, though when the expression was first used it simply meant 'skins', while the 'tanning' referred to 'treating' them.

Tansy Green Bolton. 'Tansy' is applied to various plants and grasses, but it also meant in some areas a merrymaking or festival held on Shrove Tuesday. This pub name probably refers to a village green where such a tansy was traditionally held.

Tantivy Watford. This originally meant 'at full gallop', probably echoing the sound of the horses' feet as they did so in the sound of the word itself. Also used as a cry of encouragement in the hunt to go at full gallop. The word is often erroneously applied to the sound of the huntsman's horn used for this purpose.

Tap and Tumbler Nottingham. This was probably a reference originally to two kinds of entertainment offered at the neighbouring Theatre Royal, but on the sign 'tap' is interpreted in its beer cellar sense of tapping a barrel instead of tap-dancing. The other side of the sign shows a travelling showman. Bristol has a Tap and Barrel.

Tappit Hen Aberdeen. Literally a hen which is 'topped', ie with a crest, but applied to a drinking vessel with a knobbed lid and a capacity of anything from one to six quarts. The slim neck and broad body of the vessel give it a hen-like shape and the lid is the crest. The term is only used in Scotland.

Tarantella Frodsham, near Warrington. The name of an Italian peasant dance of rapid motion, the rhythm of which was skilfully caught by Hilaire Belloc in his poem *Tarantella:* 'Do you remember an Inn,/Miranda?/Do you remember an Inn?/And the tedding and the spreading/Of the straw for a bedding,/And the fleas that tease in the High Pyrenees/And the wine that tasted of the tar?'

Tartar Frigate Broadstairs, Kent. *Tartar* has been a popular name with the Royal Navy. The frigate which was given this name was the eighteenth to bear it. 'Tartar' means a native of Tartary, which at one time was looked upon as anywhere from the Crimea to the borders of China. The Tartars have long been considered a very violent people, and to call someone a Tartar, man or woman, is certainly no compliment. Nevertheless there is a Tartar pub at Cobham, Sry.

Tatie Garth Holmrock, near Ravensglass, Cumb. The reference is to a place where potatoes are grown or stored.

Tattersall's Tavern London SW7. Tattersall's was a London auction room for bloodstock near Hyde Park Corner 1766 and still functions at nearby Brompton. Tattersall's Committee is an unofficial body which supervises betting on horse-races, while Tattersall's ring refers to the principal betting enclosure on a racecourse. This pub is built on the former site of Tattersall's offices and has a racehorse theme. All of these derive their name from a Richard Tattersall who was a stud-groom to the Duke of Kingston in the eighteenth century.

Taverners Aveton Gifford, Devon. A group of touring actors who used to perform in the village. The sign shows a pattern of black masks.

Taylor Arms *See* Timothy Taylor.

Teasel Also Teazel. *See* Ram and Teasel.

Teddington Hands Teddington, near Tewksbury. Originally the Cross Hands. It stands at a crossroads.

Teddys London NW4. A reference to King Edward VII.

Teign Teignmouth. Also Teign House, Christow, near Chudleigh; Teignmouth, Exeter. The river which rises at Teign Head on Dartmoor and flows into the sea at Teignmouth.

Telegraph London W12. The name of a famous stagecoach which ran between London and Exeter, driven by Charles Ward. It was said to be the fastest coach of the age. In Taunton the pub of this name is said to allude to messages telegraphed by flags or beacons during the Civil War.

Telstar Drongan, near Ayr and elsewhere. The name of the first communications satellite to amplify the signals it relayed. It was launched from the US in 1962 and was superseded by Syncom.

Temple Temple Cloud, near Bristol. The hospice of the Knights Templar, later the property of the Knights of St John, which gave the village its name.

Tenbell Norwich. Formerly the Ten Bells. It was once possible to stand outside this pub and hear the bells in ten different belfries.

Tennis Court Warmley, Bristol. There was formerly a tennis court nearby.

1066 Battle, E Ssx. Also 1066 Tavern, Canvey Island, Esx. Commemorating one of history's most famous battles, which took place on 14 October 1066. The small but well-trained army of William the Conqueror were victors over the Saxon King Harold and his men. It was the first and most decisive battle of the Norman Conquest.

Terminus Bognor Regis and elsewhere. Usually a reminder of a local tramway system and its terminus. The Chesterfield sign shows an open-topped tram; the Cardiff pub of this name is on the former terminus site.

Tern Yate, near Bristol. Another at Chipping Sodbury. The long-winged sea-bird of the gull family; the sea–swallow.

Test Match West Bridgford, Nottingham. The pub is near the Trent Bridge cricket ground where Test matches are played.

Thack Hurlford, near Kilmarnock. The same town has a Wee Thack. A Scottish form of 'thatch'.

Thames Head near Cirencester. Also **Thames Tavern**, Windsor. The Thames rises near Ewen and Somerford Keynes, south of Cirencester. It forms the boundaries of several counties as it makes its way past London to the sea. With the Thames flood barrier now in operation, there is a Thames Barrier Arms at London SE7.

Thatcher Liverpool. Also Thatchers, Great Warley, Esx and Woodley, near Reading; Thatchers Arms, Theale, near Reading and elsewhere; Thatched Cottage, Wokingham; Thatched House, Barking; Thatched Inn, Abbotsham, near Bideford and Keymar, W Ssx. Thatched Barn at Cockfosters. Herts changed to *Thatchers* in 1983. Thack is also found in Scotland, and was the original form of 'thatch'. All refer to straw-based coverings for a roof, 'cover' being the original sense of the word, of the same family as the 'toga' worn by the Romans.

Theatre Tavern Great Yarmouth and elsewhere. Referring to a nearby theatre. Stockton-on-Tees has a Theatre.

Thirst and Last Hildenborough, near Tonbridge. A modern variant on **First and Last**.

Thirsty Kipper Port Erin, Isle of Man. Eric Partridge in his *Dictionary of Historical Slang* says that 'kipper' in naval slang meant, until the turn of the present century, a stoker. The allusion was to his being roasted by his work in the engine room on the coal-fired ships.

1314 Whins of Milton, Stirling. A reference to the Battle of

Bannockburn, which took place on 24 June 1314. Robert the Bruce defeated Edward II.

Thirteenth Volunteer Mounted Cheshire Rifleman Stalybridge, Ches. The name explains itself and was formerly accepted by the *Guinness Book of Records* as the longest pub name in Britain. The present holder of the Guinness title is a London challenger in South Kensington called Henry J Bean's but his Friends all call him Hank Bar and Grill.

This Ancient Boro' Tenterden, Kent. The sign shows the borough seal, the town's charter having been granted in the fifteenth century by Henry VI.

Thistle Camelon, near Falkirk. The heraldic emblem of Scotland, adopted by James III. Formerly found as a London sign, often as 'Thistle and Crown'. Stevenston, Strath, has a Thistle and Rose. *Compare* Rose and Thistle.

Thomas à Becket London SE1 and elsewhere. Thomas à Becket (1117–70) was Archbishop of Canterbury when he was murdered in his own cathedral by supporters of Henry II. The king and Becket had been opposed on a number of issues, but it is not clear whether Henry ordered the murder. In 1174 he did penance at what was now the tomb of Saint Thomas à Becket, the Church having recognised him as a martyr. His shrine attracted countless pilgrims thereafter, including those in Chaucer's *Canterbury Tales*.

Thomas Cook Leicester. Thomas Cook (1808–92) was a Baptist preacher and advocate of temperance who organised a train excursion in 1841 from Leicester to Loughborough that was the first of its kind. From that came the international travel agency which bears his name. Cook's most spectacular feat was to transport 18,000 men up the Nile in 1884 for the attempted relief of General Gordon.

Thomas Dutton Egerton, near Bolton. The founder of the Blackburn Brewery in 1799. Ownership of the brewery passed to his son and grandson.

Thomas Eldred Ipswich. Thomas Eldred (1586–1622) was a local man who became a master mariner, later a high official in the service of the East India Company.

Thomas Lord *See* Lord's Tavern.

Thomas Neale London E1. Sir Thomas Neale was an influential courtier who became a speculative builder at the end of the seventeenth century. He bought an area known as the Marshland and laid out seven streets radiating from a central point. In the middle was a Doric pillar which had seven sundials on it, facing each of the streets. The pillar, minus the dials, is now at Weybridge, Sry. Neale, who was also Master of the Royal Mint, is remembered in London by *Neal (sic) Street* and *Seven Dials*.

Thomas Telford Leegomery, near Telford. Another at Margate. Also Telford Arms, Edinburgh. Thomas Telford (1757–1834) was an eminent Scottish engineer. The son of a shepherd, he was apprenticed at an early age to a stone mason. He later removed to London and was soon engaged in civil engineering projects of an important nature. In 1796 he completed an iron bridge over the river Severn, then followed work on the Ellesmere Canal, a bridge over the Dee valley and the Caledonian Ship Canal. The latter, together with the Menai suspension bridge, are regarded as his finest works. The town of Telford itself has a pub called the Ironmaster.

Thorn Tavern Norwich. This was named after the church of St Michael–at–Thorn (destroyed in World War Two), which in turn was named for the thorn bushes which surrounded the graveyard. There is a Thorns at Horley, Sry; Inverness has a Thorn Bush; Matlock a Thorn Tree (another at Langley Mill, near Nottingham).

Thoroughbred Polegate, E Ssx. The sign shows a thoroughbred racehorse.

Thrasher Ipswich. This word is another form of 'thresher' and refers to those who formerly thrashed corn by hand, using a flail. This arduous task is now undertaken by combine-harvesters.

Three Arrows Boroughbridge, near York, and elsewhere. The Boroughbridge pub name refers to the Devil's Arrows, three monoliths which are thought to date from the Bronze Age and to be connected with pagan rituals. The largest of these stone pillars is about thirty feet high. Elsewhere this pub name is a heraldic reference to the guild of Fletchers, who made or dealt in arrows.

Three Bells See Bell.

Three Blackbirds Luton and else-where. This bird is very common but is mentioned surprisingly little in folklore. 'Blackbird' was used as a general term before 'raven', 'crow', etc, distinguished between such birds, and these may be meant in this sign, which appeared in London in the seventeenth century. It has not very con-vincingly been suggested that it alludes to the Jacobites, showing the landlord's sympathy with their cause. It is also the case that

'blackbird' was used in mainly nautical slang to describe a Negro slave, but such usage is unlikely to have spread to inn signs. On the whole it is likely that the bird itself is meant and that three was convenient for signboard arrangement.

Three Bridges The Meadows, Nottingham. After the bridges in the neighbourhood which span the river Trent.

Three Bucks London EC2. After the roebucks on the arms of the Worshipful Company of Leathersellers (1444). There is a Leathersellers' College at Bermondsey.

Three Bulls' Heads See Bull.

Three Castles London EC4. A reference to the arms of the Worshipful Company of Masons (1677).

Three Chimneys Biddenden, Kent. The sign shows a French officer of the Napoleonic era standing beneath a three-way signpost. There was at one time a prison camp for such officers in the area. Those who gave their word that they would not abuse the privilege were allowed to go for walks, but not beyond a point where three lanes met. To the officers that point was known as *les trois chemins*, 'the three ways'. The locals heard this as the 'three chimneys'. Such international misunderstandings can work both ways. French soldiers in a hospital where there was an English nurse thought that as she left the ward each night she called out 'Six hairs', to which they duly responded in French, '*Six poils*'. She was actually saying, in English, 'Sleep well!'

Three Choughs See Chough.

Three Cocks Three Cocks, near Glasbury, Pwys. The village is named for the inn, in English, at least. The Welsh name for it is Aberllynfi, 'mouth of the river Llynfi'. The pub of this name at Tetbury, Glos, shows two cockerels pecking grain. Behind them a third cock can be seen on top of a church steeple, acting as a weather-vane.

Three Colts Buckhurst Hill, near Epping. A colt is a young male horse. If a thoroughbred, it is described as a colt from the time it is taken from its dam until it is five years old. Other breeds are colts until they are three or four years old.

Three Compasses Kingston-on-Thames and elsewhere. Compasses were used on the arms of the guilds of carpenters, joiners and masons, three pairs being a specific reference to the carpenters.

Three Conies Thorpe Manderville, near Banbury. Also Three Rabbits, London E12. 'Cony' or 'coney' was an early term for rabbit and is still the term used in heraldry. *Three Conies* was in use in London in the sixteenth century, referring at that time to a dealer in poultry and game animals. In earlier times village innkeepers frequently ran other businesses along with their tavern activities.

Three Cranes York. The name was suggested by the commercial cranes nearby, but the sign shows three of the wading birds of this name, executed skilfully in coloured tiles.

Three Craws Tavern Montrose, Tays. 'Craws' are Scottish crows.

Three Crowns Lichfield and elsewhere. This sign is interpreted in various ways by the sign-painters. In some instances the reference is to the Magi, the three wise men, who may have been astrologers but are often called kings, who came to Bethlehem to visit the Christ child. Later signs add a portrait of James I and refer to his being the first monarch to rule over England, Scotland and Wales. In some instances the sign refers heraldically to the Worshipful Company of Drapers (1364). Elsewhere the sign has become three crown coins, a reminder that in London the nickname for a *Three Crowns* pub was commonly Fifteen Bob or Fifteen Shillings, a crown being worth five shillings.

Three Crutchers Strood, Kent. The original sign here showed three Crutched Friars, ie friars distinguished by a cross on their backs. *See* Old Crutched Friars.

Three Cups Harwich and elsewhere. This sign was found in the sixteenth century. It refers to the Worshipful Company of Salters (1558), producers and sellers of sea–salt. At Punnetts Town, E Ssx it is said that 'cup' is the dialectal word for the source of a stream, and that there are three such sources there.

Three Daws Town Pier, Gravesend. This bird is now usually referred to as the jackdaw, though 'daw' is the earlier term, and the only one used by Shakespeare, for instance. The thieving habits of the bird are well known, and the significance of three daws together is perhaps summed up in an old saying: 'When three daws are seen on St Peter's vane together then we're sure to have bad weather'.

Three Elms *See* Elm.

Three Fishes Kingston-on-Thames and elsewhere. In Kingston three fishes appear in the civic coat of arms. There is probably a heraldic reference elsewhere, or the fish market may have been nearby, as in Shrewsbury until 1857.

Three Frogs Wokingham. The original sign here is said to have been three barley sheaves, changed when a Belgian landlord began to serve frogs' legs to his customers on special occasions. The French themselves used to refer to Parisians as frogs, because toads appeared on the arms of the city. When it became known in the eighteenth century that the French ate the back legs of certain frogs, *Frog* or *Froggie* became the usual nickname for a Frenchman, though earlier it had applied to the Dutch.

Three Goats Heads London SW8. These appear on the arms of the Worshipful Company of Cordwainers (1439). They made boots from goatskins from Cordova, Spain.

Three Hammers St Stephens, near St Albans. From the arms of the Worshipful Company of Blacksmiths (1571). In 1838 the premises here consisted of a tavern attached to a blacksmith's shop.

Three Hats Milton Regis, Sittingbourne. The original sign showed three kinds of hat – a shako (a military cap shaped like a section from a cone, with a peak and a plume), a naval hat of the Napoleonic era, and a billycock (a kind of bowler hat made originally by William Coke). This sign was replaced by one showing three Mexican sombreros draped over a cactus bush.

Three Hills Bartlow, near Cambridge. The hills referred to are the ancient grave mounds, or tumuli, which dominate the church and village.

Three Horseshoes Ripley, Derbs and elsewhere. Horseshoes normally come in sets of four, but it has been suggested that those horses being brought to the blacksmith's near the village inn of this name would normally have been going there because they were minus one shoe. The real explanation of the name has more to do with heraldry, referring to the Worshipful Company of Farriers (1673) and to the Ferrers family, earls of Derby, whose family name does not indicate that they were farriers, as it happens. It derives from a French place name. The Ripley sign nevertheless concentrates quite rightly on the humorous explanation, showing a horse squatting on its haunches and ruefully holding up a faulty shoe for inspection. Single Horseshoe inn signs are found, possibly referring to their reputation for being lucky, and Four Horseshoes occurs at Thame, Oxon, and Kentisbeare, Devon. There are even Five Horseshoe signs at Remenham Hill, Oxon, Stanstead Abbots, Herts, and Barholm, Lincoln.

Three Jays Sunninghill, near Ascot. The jay is something like a magpie, though the name is also applied at times to the jackdaw, the Cornish chough and the missel thrush. A person described as a jay either talks too much, dresses flashily or is rather stupid, all of which reflect medieval ideas about the bird. As a modern house name, *Three Jays* almost always refers to three people living in the house whose names begin with J.

Three Johns London N1. Three eighteenth century Johns are referred to, John Wilkes (1727–97), John Horne Tooke (1736–1812) and John Glynn (1722–79). For Wilkes *see* North Briton. Horne Tooke is usually described as a politician and philologist. He was at first a vicar, then a Liberal politician who engaged in controversies with Wilkes. He was imprisoned for libel in 1767–68, and in 1794 was tried for high treason and acquitted. Glynn was a lawyer and politician who is chiefly remembered for defending Wilkes in the cases related to the publication of the *North Briton*.

Three Kings Twickenham and elsewhere. This sign has been in use since at least the sixteenth century and usually refers to the Magi, the three wise men from the East who visited the Christ child in Bethlehem. Imaginative writers have adorned them with the names Balthazar, Caspar and Melchior, but there is no evidence to support those names, or to confirm that they were kings. There is another tradition that their bodies were recovered in the East in the fourth century, removed to Constantinople, then to Milan, then to Cologne in 1162. The cathedral in Cologne certainly claims to possess the relics, and the Three Kings of Cologne could formerly be found as an inn sign. In Threekingham, near Sleaford, Lincs, a village which must have the clumsiest name in Britain, there is a *Three Kings* pub which refers to three Danish kings killed nearby in 869. The sign at Sandwich, Kent, shows three portraits of Charles I. At Theale, near Reading, there is a Three Kings Booth.

Three-legged Stool Worksop, Notts. The pub was opened in 1978 on the site of a Northern Dairies depot. The milking theme is continued inside the pub with the names of the lavatories – 'Cowmen' and 'Milkmaids'.

Three Lions Wimborne, Dors and elsewhere. A heraldic reference, to the county's coat of arms at Wimborne but elsewhere to

Richard I, or to other armigerous families such as the Fitzherberts.

Three Loggerheads Tonbridge, Kent. *See* Loggerheads, though *Three Loggerheads* is the more correct form of the name.

Three Lords London EC3. William Boyd, 4th Earl of Kilmarnock, Arthur Elphinstone, 6th Baron Balmerino and Simon Fraser, Baron Lovat are the lords referred to here. After the Jacobite Rebellion of 1745 these Scottish peers were found guilty of high treason and beheaded on Tower Hill. The inn sign shows them, together with the executioner's axe and block, while the bars are called 'The 45' and 'Culloden'.

Three Lums Aberdeen. 'Lum' is Scottish chimney, as in the saying 'Lang may your lums reek' – long may your chimneys keep smoking.

Three Mariners Hythe, Kent, and elsewhere. The original sign of the Hythe pub showed only one mariner, alluding to the 'elderly naval man' who occurs in W S Gilbert's *Bab Ballads*, 'The Yarn of the *Nancy Bell*'. 'Oh, I am a cook and a captain bold,/And the mate of the *Nancy* brig,/And a bo'sun tight, and a midshipmite,/And the crew of the captain's gig.' After being shipwrecked this jolly tar was obliged to eat both his shipmates.

Three Marines Eastney, near Southsea. There is a local training base for the Royal Marines.

Three Men in a Boat Walsall. Jerome Klapka Jerome (1859–1927) was born in Walsall. An exiled Hungarian named Klapka also lived there and was a frequent visitor to the Jerome household. Jerome became a reporter, then tried teaching, but by 1889 he had made his mark as a writer with *Idle Thoughts of an Idle Fellow*. His most famous book, remembered in this pub name, appeared in the same year. It sold a million copies in America alone.

Three Merry Boys Formerly in Lambeth. Farmer Richard Marsden converted his cowshed into a taproom and named it after his three sons. The youngest of them was landlord here 1903–21.

Three Merry Lads Sheffield. The original sign showed John Bull and three cheerful young men, representing the landlord and his sons.

Three Mile Inn Great North Road, Newcastle-on-Tyne. The pub is exactly three miles from the city centre.

Three Mill Bills Nassington, near Peterborough. A mill bill was a steel adze used for dressing millstones. It had a wooden handle known as a 'thrift'. There were formerly mills in the neighbourhood. West Bradford, near Clitheroe, has a Three Millstones.

Three Moorhens Hitchin. This bird is also known as the water hen. It had a reputation at one time for frequenting castle moats, and was occasionally referred to as a moat hen. It also likes fish ponds, and there was formerly one near this pub.

Three Nuns London EC3. This name is now associated with a tobacco, the trade name, according to Adrian Room in his *Dictionary of Trade Name Origins*, having been chosen for fairly arbitrary reasons. In London this pub name is for *Sorores Minores*, the Little Sisters of St Clare, whose nunnery is recalled in the *Minories*. At Mirfield, W Yorks the pub of this name adjoins the Kirklees Priory where Robin Hood is said to have been tended on his death bed by three nuns. Loughborough also has a pub of this name.

Three Old Castles Keinton Manderville, Som. For the three towers that appear in the Bristol civic arms.

Three Pickerels. *See* Pickerel.

Three Pigeons Banbury and elsewhere. This was formerly a common London sign, used by various tradesmen and not just tavern keepers. It does not seem to have any heraldic significance and is something of a puzzle. It might have been used in a secondary sense, a pigeon being amongst other things a simpleton, or dupe, in colloquial speech. Had the earlier signs shown only two pigeons, leaving the spectator to be the third (*see* Loggerheads), that might have made sense. The signs all seem to occur in the South rather than the North, where pigeon-fanciers are more plentiful.

Three Pigs Edgefield, Nflk. This was the Bacon Arms, but when the local landowner, Lord Bacon, refused his permission for the family arms to be shown on the sign in 1976, the name was changed. It now has a sign which shows three piglets with their trotters entwined.

Three Pilchards *See* Five Pilchards.

Three Rabbits *See* Three Conies.

Three Ravens Tilmanstone, near Deal. A heraldic reference to the Rice family, owners of the local manor for many generations.

Three Shires Little Langdale, near Grasmere. This was the Tourists Rest until 1952. It was renamed because Cumberland, Westmoreland and Lancashire could all be seen on a clear day. The first two have since merged as Cumbria.

Three Swans Frome, Som. They appear in the arms of Richard,

Provost of Wells in the fifteenth century. The sign of the Market Harborough, Leics, pub of this name is a superb example of wrought-iron workmanship, dating from about 1700.

Three Tuns Barnstaple and elsewhere. A 'tun' is a large cask containing wine and other liquids, with a capacity of two pipes, or four hogsheads, or 252 old wine gallons. Tuns were used for wholesale distribution, for retailing purposes the measures were gallons, pottles (half-gallons), quarts and pints. Three tuns appear in the arms of the Worshipful Company of Vintners (1437) as well as the Worshipful Company of Brewers (1437), hence the widespread use of this sign.

Three Wheatsheaves Lenton, Nottingham. Another at London N1. They are seen in the arms of the Worshipful Company of Bakers (1486). Thropton, Northld, has a most unusual Three Wheatheads.

Three Willows Birchanger, near Bishop's Stortford. The sign here is in cut-out style and shows three cricketers of different centuries. The changing shape of the bat since the eighteenth century can be seen. The nineteenth-century figure in the middle, with a bushy beard, is no doubt Doctor W G Grace.

Three Witches Stratford-on-Avon. A reference to the Weird Sisters of Shakespeare's *Macbeth*. The sign shows three conical witches' hats resting on a broomstick.

Throstle's Nest Wigton, Cumb and elsewhere. Also Thrush, Bury. 'Throstle' is a provincial and archaic word for song thrush. The Wigton pub is said to be named because a local resident in the

eighteenth century who had been on a journey referred to the area as the 'throstle's nest of England' on his return.

Thule Lerwick, Shetd. This was the name given by the ancients to the extreme northern limit of the world. There has been much debate as to where Thule was supposed to be. William Camden and some others considered it to be the Shetland Isles. Thule is also the name of the US air base in Greenland, named no doubt for Virgil's *Ultima Thule*, the end of the world.

Tibbie Shiel's St Mary's Loch, Selkirk. Tibbie is a diminutive of Isabella, the name of the landlady here for many years in the nineteenth century. She died in 1878 at the age of ninety-five. She had become something of a celebrity because writers such as De Quincey and Robert Louis Stevenson had stayed at the inn. The 'shiel' in the name is presumably 'shelter', as in Sheiling.

Tichborne Arms *See* Sir Roger Tichborne.

Tickell Arms Whittlesford, Cambs. Thomas Tickell (1686–1740) was a poet and translator, an intimate friend of Joseph Addison. His literary work was regarded as adequate, but not of the highest quality.

Tickled Trout *See* Cunning Man.

Tide End Cottage Teddington, GL. The pub is near Teddington Lock – the highest point to which the tide comes up the Thames.

Tiger London SE7 and elsewhere. In the early nineteenth century this was a slang term for a boy-groom dressed in a smart livery, especially one of striped black and yellow. Little Negro boys were especially fashionable in this role. Elsewhere there may be a heraldic reference. The Tiger's Head, for instance, at Bromley and London SE6 is said to relate to the arms of Sir Francis Walsingham.

Tiger Moth Bedford and elsewhere. The Moth was a light aircraft built by De Havilland in 1925. From it developed the *Gipsy Moth* and the *Tiger Moth*. These aeroplanes are especially remembered because of the record-breaking flights made in them to Australia by Sir Francis Chichester and Amy Johnson respectively. *See* Gipsy Moth IV and Flying Eagle.

Tigh–an–Truish Clachan Bridge, near Oban. A Gaelic name meaning 'house of trews (trousers)'. After the Jacobite Rebellion in 1745 Highland soldiers serving in the British army were not allowed to wear kilts. On their way home on leave they changed from trews to kilts at this inn – or enough of them did to suggest the name.

Tight Line Loch Awe, near Dalmally, Argyll. This area is famous for its angling. The name indicates that a fish has taken the bait and is running.

Tilbury Datchworth Heath, Herts. The name of a light open two-wheeled carriage, fashionable in the first half of the nineteenth century. This two-seater was designed by John Tilbury, a London horse-dealer.

Tilden Smith King's Lynn. The name of a schooner which often loaded here in the 1860s. The ship is said to have been named for its Kentish owner.

Tilly Whim Durlston, near Swanage, Dors. This is the name of a nearby cave. 'Tilly' may have to do with the kind of clay known as 'till', and 'whim' presumably is used in its early sense of a fantastic creation of any sort.

Tilt Boat London EC3. 'Tilt' here refers to a cover of coarse cloth, a kind of tent or awning. It was fixed to large rowing boats on the Thames to give protection to passengers. Such boats were used from the mid-fifteenth century, especially between London and Gravesend.

Tilted Wig Edinburgh. A pub where members of the legal profession can relax.

Tilt Hammer Birmingham. A heavy hammer used for forging, fixed on a pivot. As an eccentric wheel revolves the hammer is alternatively tilted up and allowed to drop.

Tim Bobbin Burnley and elsewhere. Tim Bobbin was the pseudonym of John Collier (1708–86), the son of a country parson who achieved some fame as an artist and dialect poet. He was sometimes known as the Lancashire Hogarth, though one critic said: 'No more inappropriate designation could have been selected. He lacked not only the artistic skill of Hogarth but that moral indignation which made the pencil more powerful than the preacher's voice.'

Timothy Taylor Braithwaite, near Keighley. Founder in 1858 of the brewery in Keighley which is looked upon by many as the best in the country. It has won more championship medals than any other brewery. The Taylor Arms at nearby Stanbury also refers to this man.

Tinker and Budget Oswaldtwistle, Lancs. 'Budget' here is used in the sense of a bundle, a collection or stock, the contents of a bag which was itself originally called a budget. Such a bag, usually made of leather, was used by the chancellor of the Exchequer to carry his papers giving financial estimates to the House of Commons. This led to the modern use of the word for the estimates themselves. The itinerant craftsmen who went around repairing metal pots and the like were called 'tinkers' from the noise they made when striking metal.

Tin Mine Tavern Trewellard, near Penzance. The pub has a display of mining equipment, underground maps, etc, relating to the Cornish tin mines.

Tinners Arms Zennor, near St Ives, Corn. Another at Blackburn. Also Tinmans Arms, Lower Lydbrook, Glos; Tinworks Arms, Llangennech, near Llanelli. After tin miners and workers. The Zennor pub sign shows a mermaid beckoning and refers to a local tale about a church chorister who was once lured into the sea by a mermaid. The former sign, showing a young 'tinner' (tinman), was stolen.

Tin Pot Gustard Wood, Herts. A reference to a rich recluse named James Gustard, who lived locally in the 1850s. He was the owner of a Cornish tin mine.

Tintern Abbey Liverpool. A famous ruined abbey in Gwent, north of Chepstow. It was founded in the twelfth century for Cistercian monks. It inspired Wordsworth's poem: *Lines Composed a few miles above Tintern Abbey*.

Tipperary Meer End, near Kenilworth. Another at London EC4. The name of a market town and county in the Irish Republic, but perhaps best known because of the song 'It's a Long Way to Tipperary' by Harry Williams and Jack Judge which was immensely popular with the troops in World War One. The Meer End pub shows the musical notation of the first few bars on its sign and claims that the song was composed there in 1912. The *Concise Oxford Dictionary of Quotations* dates it several years earlier. The London pub of this name dates from the late nineteenth century.

Tipples London E2. Also Tipplers, Edinburgh and Great Yarmouth. *See* Olde Tippling Philosopher.

Tithe Barn Cockermouth, Cumb. Another at Preston. 'Tithe' means 'tenth part', and the tithe barn is where the parson's share of the corn, the tenth part to which he was entitled, was kept. Hebden Bridge, W Yorks has a Tythe Barn.

Titton Titton, near Stourport. The rebus sign here shows a blue tit on the roof of the building.

Toastmaster Burham, near Rochester. Formerly the Royal Exchange. The pub was renamed when the new landlord took over. He had been a toastmaster – the person who announces the toasts and introduces the speakers at public dinners – in the City of London.

Toby Jug Bickington, N Devon and elsewhere. Also Toby Inn, Brighton and elsewhere; Toby's Head, Coventry; Toby Tavern, London E15; Toby House, Folkestone. After the jug in the form of a stout old man wearing a long coat and a three-cornered hat, an eighteenth century costume. Also known as a Toby fill-pot. Brewer traces the name Toby Philpot to a poem adapted from Latin by Francis Fawkes in 1761. He also attributes the design of the jug to Carrington Bowles and says that Ralph Wood was the potter who made them in great numbers. The name also occurs in O'Keefe's *Poor Soldier* (1782): 'Dear friend, this brown jug which now foams with mild ale . . . was once Toby Filpot, a thirsty old soul/As e'er cracked a bottle, or fathomed a bowl.' Some have tried to link the name with Harry Elwes, a Yorkshireman who lived in the eighteenth century and of whom it is said that he once drank two thousand gallons of beer without taking food. At Bickington the landlord has a fine collection of the jugs.

Toddle Inn Belfast. Another at Shotts, Strath. Another variant of the Dew Drop Inn type.

Toll Gate Chadwell Heath, near Romford and elsewhere. Also **Toll** Bar, Tollhouse Hill, Nottingham; Toll Down, Wilts; Toll Bridge, Nottingham; Tollhouse, Coggeshall, Esx; Toll Point, Denton, near Manchester. All references to places where it was necessary to pay a fee for the use of a stretch of road, bridge, etc.

Tom Cobley Spreyton, Devon. Another at Paignton. The man immortalised in the well-known folk song *Widdicombe Fair* was Uncle Tom Cobley, or Cobbleigh as it is in some versions of the lyric. The inn sign at Spreyton shows a portrait of the original man, said to have been born and to have died in this village. The singer of the song wants to borrow the grey mare of Tom Pearse (or Pearce) and go to Widdicombe Fair with Bill Brewer, Jan Stewer, Peter Gurney, Peter Davey, Dan'l Whiddon, Harry Hawk, Old Uncle Tom Cobley and all.

Tom Cribb London SW1. Tom Cribb (1781–1848) began life as a coal-porter but found fame as a prize-fighter. He was the champion of England, his fights drawing huge crowds, who knew him as the Black Diamond (referring to his coal-portering days). Later he became the innkeeper at this pub, then known as the Union Arms. Its name was changed in his honour in 1960.

Tom Crocker Bigbury-on-Sea, Devon. Named after a notorious local smuggler who operated from a cave on nearby Burgh Island which came to be known as Tom Crocker's Hole.

Tom Hoskins Leicester. Opened in 1984 next door to the old family brewery founded by Tom Hoskins. The brewery owns a few other pubs.

Tom Mogg Burtle, near Bridgwater. This was formerly the Railway, referring to the old Somerset and Dorset branch line. It was renamed in 1980 after a popular 'regular' who lived nearby. He acted as signalman at Edington Junction and is seen on the sign wearing his uniform and ringing a large brass bell.

Tommy Ducks Manchester. This was the Prince's Tavern when it opened in 1867, the name of the licensee being Tommy Duckworth. He asked for his name to be added to the sign as the resident proprietor, but the sign-painter miscalculated the amount of space he needed. Eventually he only had room for one more letter after Tommy Duck, so Tommy Ducks appeared on the sign. The name appealed to the locals and subsequently became official.

Tommy Wass Beeston, Leeds. The pub was converted from a farmhouse in the late 1920s. Tommy Wass was the farmer who owned the place at the time.

Tom o' Bedlam Chadwick End, near Solihull. 'Bedlam' here refers to the Hospital of St Mary of Bethlehem, in London, founded as a priory in 1247. By 1402 it was specifically a hospital for lunatics. It was originally sited in

Bishopsgate, but it was re-sited near London Wall in 1676 and transferred to Lambeth in 1815. Bedlam seems to have been the popular pronunciation of Bethlehem from at least the fourteenth century. By the seventeenth century, when a popular pastime was to go to the hospital to watch the antics of the inmates, Tom or Jack o' Bedlam had become a general term for a madman and 'bedlam' itself referred to a general uproar. Tom o' Bedlams were later those inmates of the hospital who had been released as harmless and given a licence to beg. There were others who found it advantageous to pretend to be mad for begging purposes.

Tom o' the Wood Rowington, near Warwick. This was the Old New Inn until 1975. The new name came from a local windmill, one of three with individual names – the others being *Grinning Jenny* and *Bouncing Bess*.

Tom Sawyer's Tavern Looe, Corn. After the boy hero created by Mark Twain (Samuel Langhorne Clemens) in his tales of life in Missouri, *Tom Sawyer* (1876) and *Huckleberry Finn* (1884).

Tom Thumb Blaby, near Leicester. Another at Stockport. This name for a tiny man has been in use since the sixteenth century and has its equivalent in French *Poucet*, German *Däumling*. Phineas T Barnum, the American showman, brought the name to life in the nineteenth century by exhibiting 'General Tom Thumb', an American dwarf whose real name was Charles Sherwood Stratton (1838–83). The 'general' was summoned to Buckingham Palace to meet Queen Victoria during his English tour. There had earlier

been a burlesque opera called *Tom Thumb*, based on a play by Henry Fielding. It had a successful run at the Haymarket Theatre in 1778. There is an anecdote about Liston, the actor who made a great success of the role, being invited out to dinner and asked afterwards to perform his dance 'before the children went to bed'. Liston took his hat 'and danced out of the house, never more to return'.

Tom Tiddler's Tavern London NW1. The immediate source of the pub name seems to have been a cartoon character called Tom Tiddler, but he was named in turn for an old children's game in which Tom Tiddler is a player who tries to stop others crossing into his base.

Tom Treddlehoyle Pogsmoor, Barnsley. This was the pen–name of Charles Rogers, who lived in this area in the 1820s and wrote pieces for the local *Almanack*. The pen–name was suggested by the treadles operated by local women in the 'hoyles', ie 'holes' (a reference to cellars). The pub sign here illustrates a scene from one of Tom's stories, in which he described his late arrival home, and how he had awakened the whole village by making so much noise. The villagers took their revenge by putting him on a donkey, facing backwards, and urging the donkey into the village pond.

Tontine Iron Bridge, Telford and elsewhere. Also **Cleveland Tontine**, Staddle Bridge, N Yorks. The original tontine was initiated by Lorenzo Tonti, an Italian banker who lived in France, in the middle of the seventeenth century. It was a method of raising money whereby subscribers had to gamble on how long they would live. The interest or profit was shared out each year between those who had subscribed. The last remaining survivor received the entire amount, his share having increased as others died. The term by the nineteenth century was being applied loosely to various friendly societies which shared out their funds at the end of each year, and it is probably these slate clubs, or 'dividing societies' which led to several pub names. The *Cleveland Tontine* refers to a specific fund-raising exercise for the building of the inn, which was to serve the new Thirsk-Yarm turnpike, completed in 1804. Profits were to be shared amongst all participants until only three survived, at which time the inn was to become theirs in proportion to the number of shares they held.

Toot and Whistle Toothill, near Swindon. A neat place-name link and reference to the nearby railway centre at Swindon.

Top House New Coundon, near Bishop Auckland and elsewhere. Also Top of the Hill, Rye, E Ssx and Ryde, IOW; Top o' the Trent, Biddulph, near Stoke-on-Trent; Top of the Toun, Kirkcaldy; Top of the Town, St Albans and Torquay; Top of the Walk, Edinburgh. Descriptions of the pub's location coupled with a suggestion of excellence. The latter idea is more emphatic in Tops, London W11.

Top of the World *See* Everest.

Top o' the Morning London E9. A cheerful greeting which hints that the pub has a decidedly Irish flavour.

Top Twenty With pub names being changed all the time, and with many of them now being listed in Yellow Pages only under the names of the licensees, it is almost impossible to make an accurate count of the most popular pub names. However, using the information that is available we would suggest that the top three names, in order, are Red Lion, Crown and Royal Oak. The other top names, as far as we can judge, are those following – but the order in which they are given is alphabetical only: Anchor, Angel, Bell, Bull, Coach and Horses, George, George and Dragon, King's Head, Nelson (Lord/Admiral), New Inn, Plough, Railway, Rose and Crown, Swan, Wellington (Duke of), White Hart, White Horse.

Torch Wembley Park, GL. The pub was opened in 1948, shortly after the Olympic Games of that year had been held in Wembley Stadium. The sign shows the traditional carrying-in of the Olympic torch to the stadium.

Toreador Birmingham. The pub is in the Bull Ring Centre. The toreador is the mounted bull-fighter in Spain (Latin *taurus* 'bull').

Tormohun Torquay. Torquay was earlier called Tormoham, though Tormohun would have been more accurate since the manor passed to the Mohun family in the thirteenth century. Torquay was originally the name of a small nearby village but replaced Tormoham as the resort developed in the nineteenth century.

Torridge Bideford. The name of the river which rises near Hartland and flows to the Taw at Barnstaple Bay.

Tors Belstone, near Okehampton. 'Tor' is a common place-name element in the south west, referring to rocky outcrops or hills (or their peaks). There is a Devon Tors at Yelverton, and a Hay Tor at Ilsington, near Newton Abbot. Other associated names for pubs include Brentor, Brentor; near Tavistock; Burrator, Dousland, near Yelverton; Kestor, Manaton, near Newton Abbot.

Toss o' Coin Holmfirth, Huddersfield. This pub was the Junction formerly, and was put up for auction. Two bidders maintained that they had made the last bid, so the matter was settled by the toss of a coin rather than starting the auction again.

Touch Down Hartlepool. The pub adjoins the ground of the local rugby club. The aim of the players in the game is to touch the ball down behind the goal line of the opponents in order to score points.

Tournament London SW5. The Royal Tournament is held each year in the nearby stadium at Earls Court. The inn sign shows an earlier kind of tournament in which knights showed their skill at jousting.

Town and Gown Dundee. A phrase originally used in Oxford and Cambridge to distinguish between the townsmen and women and those connected with the university. The relationship between the two factions has not always been a happy one – *see* Swyndlestock.

Town Crier Chelmsford and elsewhere. The official, usually dressed in a robe, who made public proclamations, attracting attention with a bell and his cries of 'Oyez, oyez'. The latter derived from French and meant 'Hear ye' but was frequently interpreted by local children as 'O yes' calling for an answering cry of 'O no!'

Tower Redhill, Sry. Another at Slapton, Devon. The Redhill inn sign shows the London Post Office Tower (now Telecom). It refers to the fact that Redhill is the post office centre for this area of the county. At Slapton the reference is to the nearby tower of the Chantry of St Mary, founded in 1372. The pub of this name at Otterburn, Northld, is itself a castellated stone building and is based on a Norman tower.

Town Hall Richmond, N Yorks and elsewhere. Named because of its proximity to the town hall, just as Town Wall Tavern, Coventry, and Town Pump, Boston, are close to where those items were. *Town Hall* sometimes becomes Town House, as in Dundee and Horsmonden, Kent, though this expression also applies to houses other than public buildings.

Town Mouse Burnley. A reference to the mouse in Aesop's fable, or in later versions of it. In 1621, for instance, Henryson produced his *Town and Country Mouse*, in which the town mouse invites the country mouse to come and see how grandly he lives. A cat nearly kills them both, and the country mouse remarks that he prefers his more modest life, coupled with his freedom from such dangers. Most versions of the tale refer to the different lifestyles of town and country dwellers, to their mutual lack of understanding and to the relative merits of the two types of existence.

Town of Ramsgate London E1. Years ago the fishermen of Ramsgate used to sell their catches from the Old Wapping steps alongside the pub.

Town Talk *See* Talk of the Town.

Trader Birmingham. Also Traders Arms, Mellor near Blackburn; Traders Inn, London NW8; Traders Tavern, Glasgow. After those who make their living by buying and selling. The word 'trade' particularly applied in earlier times to the import and export of goods. The sailing ships carrying such goods were referred to as 'traders' and often benefited from Trade Winds, Birmingham and Barrhead, near Glasgow. The latter, were named using 'trade' in its earliest sense of 'track' or 'path', and meant winds that blew steadily in the same direction, not winds that were good for traders. Plymouth has a pub called Trader Jack's (the Barley Sheaf until 1983), named after a mythical sea-trader.

Tradesman Bideford. Also Tradesmans Arms, Stokenham, Devon. This term was originally applied to craftsmen of various kinds. It is now used of retailers, those who deliver goods from shops, etc.

Trafalgar Brighton and elsewhere. Also Trafalgar Arms, London SW17; Trafalgar Bay. York; Trafalgar Tavern, London SE10. Cape Trafalgar is a headland on the Atlantic coast of Cadiz, near the Strait of Gibraltar. It was here on 21 October 1805, that Lord Nelson achieved a magnificent victory over the Franco-Spanish fleet, ending Napoleon's sea power and the threat of an invasion of England. Nelson himself was killed in the action.

Trafalgar Maid Chatham. This pub replaced the New Inn which was badly damaged in World War Two. It was named after Jane Townshend, who lived next door to the old pub for many years. She was on board HMS *Euryalus* during the Battle of Trafalgar.

Tram Allensmore, near Hereford. Also Tramcar, Southwick, near Sunderland; Tramway Tavern, Colchester; Tramcar Vaults, Glasgow; Tramway, Great Yarmouth and elsewhere.

Terminus and Old Tramway are also found. Tramways were originally blocks of wood or stone sunk into the ground in parallel lines so that wagons had a firm surface to run on. They were used in or near mines. The use of rails sunk into the ground came later, as did the public tram cars which used them to carry passengers. The tramway system has mostly been abandoned in Britain, though it is still found in Blackpool. Many European cities have modernised their trams and use them to great effect.

Trap *See* Pony and Trap.

Travellers Rest Grasmere, Cumb and elsewhere. An 'obvious' name which the sign painters often enliven. The Grasmere sign shows a bewhiskered cyclist sipping a pint while his dogs wait for him. His pennyfarthing leans against the wall. At Stow-in-the-Wold the sign shows two yokels seated back to back on a donkey, eating their lunch. The pub of this name at London E7 is in Cemetery Road. Travellers of the past, using horses and coaches, really did need and made use of inns. Other names which mention them are Travellers Call, Manchester and Marple Bridge, Ches; Travellers Friend, Reading and elsewhere; Travellers Home, Woolwich; Travellers Joy. Telford and Rayleigh, Esx; Travellers Tryst (place of meeting), Edinburgh; Travellers Welcome, East Hagbourne, near Didcot; Travellers Well, Skewen, near Swansea.

Travelling Hen Pontshill, near Ross-on-Wye. After a hen which was found to have ridden on the back axle of a lorry which travelled from Pontshill to Birmingham. It made the return journey in the driver's cab and laid an egg. The local tale is that this same hen hitched a ride on the same lorry to Cardiff, and laid another egg on the journey home. The New Inn was therefore renamed in honour of the travelling hen, which was present at the opening ceremony. It should be said that this is only one version of the story. In another the hen made a nest on top of the petrol tank, laid a clutch of eggs and hatched them out. In the meantime the lorry had made several long-distance journeys.

Travelling Man West Boldon, T and W. Another at Oadby, Leics. In modern usage, a man who makes no long-term emotional or other commitments but constantly 'moves on'.

Trawl Grimsby. Also Trawler, Liverpool and Brixham. The Grimsby sign shows a large fish caught in a net. In trawling the net is dragged along the bottom of the sea-bed.

Treaty of Commerce Lincoln. The Treaty of Commerce was made between England and France in 1860, and was arranged by Richard Cobden, the Victorian advocate of Free Trade.

Treble Chance Southmead, Bristol. Another at Basildon, Esx. A phrase introduced by the football pool companies, referring to the guessing as to which games will be drawn rather than be won away or at home. The Southmead sign shows three horses and their jockeys approaching the winning–post.

Tree References to oak trees dominate this group of pub names and are treated separately under Oak. Name collectors might care to see how many varieties of tree they can spot in other pub names. They will find many references to the elm, but alders, almonds, cedars, firs and the like have all been mentioned when those trees are close to the pub concerned. Our own collection of 'tree' names shows that some fifty different varieties are recorded, including the Monkey Puzzle, Lemon Tree and Bannut Tree.

Tree Inn Stratton, near Bude, Corn. Others at Rugeley, Staffs and London SW7. The Stratton pub was formerly the Ash Tree, and probably a simple reference to a tree that was nearby. Antony Payne was born at the inn in 1610. He grew to be seven feet four inches tall and weighed thirty-eight stone. Some commentators have therefore linked the inn name to the man because he was 'as tall as a tree'. Payne's portrait by Sir Godfrey Kneller is in the Royal Institute of Cornwall at Truro.

Trent Cockfosters, Herts. Also Trent Navigation, Nottingham; Trent Port, Gainsborough; Trent Tavern House, Bucknall, near Stoke-on-Trent; Trent Valley, Lichfield. References to the river which rises on Biddulph Moor in Staffordshire, and joins with the Ouse to form the Humber. There is another Trent in Dorset, a river also known as the Piddle. The Trent Bridge Inn, Nottingham, refers to the county cricket ground, where Test matches have been played since 1899.

Trevithick Arms Camborne. Richard Trevithick (1771–1833) is said to have invented a steam-carriage which could carry passengers on ordinary roads. It was demonstrated for the first time in Camborne on Christmas Eve, 1801.

Triangle Triangle, near Halifax. Others at Derby, Peterborough and Chasetown, W Mids. The Yorkshire village was named for the pub, which in turn was named because of its location on a triangular piece of land between the turnpike to Lancashire and Oak Hill.

Trinity Brewery Bath. An old brewery which was absorbed by West Country, which was in turn absorbed by Whitbreads.

Trinity Foot Swavesey, near St Ives, Cambs. The brewery chairman was Master of the Trinity College Foot Beagles while at Cambridge University. This pack of hounds used for hunting hares originated in the 1880s.

Triple Plea Halesworth, Sflk. The sign shows an old man on his death bed. He is surrounded by his parson, doctor and lawyer, while the devil is in the background with a trident. The three professionals are pleading for the man's soul, corpse and estate respectively and are arguing as to who has the greater claim. The devil seems to know the answer to the question.

Trip to Jerusalem Brewhouse Yard, Nottingham. This pub is probably the best known in Britain because of its unique features. It is hollowed out of the rock on which Nottingham Castle is built and is honeycombed with caves and passages. The date 1189 AD is painted on the outside wall and this, together with the name, has given rise to a tradition that Crusaders assembled here before setting off for the Holy Land. Against this one has to point out that the name cannot possibly date from the twelfth century, 'trip' being unrecorded in English in any sense that would be meaningful here until at least the fourteenth century. 'Trip', incidentally, always seems to have meant a journey that was either short and sharp, or for amusement rather than serious purpose, which is hardly fitting in a crusading context. Some commentators have attempted to explain 'trip' as meaning 'stay' or 'stop', but the word has never at any point had such a sense. Borough records refer to a brewhouse under Nottingham Castle in the early seventeenth century, but their first mention of this pub by name occurs only in the eighteenth century. It seems likely then that these premises were those of a brewhouse which served the castle, construction of which began in the eleventh century, and may themselves be of very great age. Conversion into an inn probably came in the eighteenth century.

Triton Sledmere, Humb. Another in Liverpool. The name of a sea-god in Greek mythology, part man, part fish. He blows a conch, or shell, to soothe the oceans. The US Navy used the name for their second nuclear-powered submarine. It also named a submarine of the Royal Navy, lost in 1940, and had previously been used to name many other warships.

Trocadero Birmingham. Originally the name of a fort captured by the French at Cadiz in 1823. It was then used to name a building at the Paris Exhibition in 1878. This was reconstructed for the 1937 Exhibition under the name of *Palais de Chaillot*. It is across the Seine from the Eiffel Tower. The name was taken up and used by various hotels and restaurants in Britain.

Troglodyte Fairford, Glos. This word translates from Greek as 'one who gets into a hole'. It is meant in a literal sense and refers to a cave-dweller. Also applied at times to someone who prefers to live alone. Jenny wrens, or kitty wrens, are

Troglodytes to ornithologists.

Trollope Arms Uffington, near Stamford. Anthony Trollope (1815–82) is remembered for his Barchester novels, such as *Barchester Towers* (1857), *Framley Parsonage* (1861), *The Last Chronicle of Barset* (1867), etc. Some of these works have recently enjoyed a revival in television adaptations. Trollope was remarkably productive, given that he wrote part–time, doing an arduous clerical job during the day. His mother also wrote a great deal, supporting her family with novel-writing after her husband had failed as a solicitor and later as a shopkeeper. Her eldest son, Thomas Trollope, also published many works, including fiction, all of which are now forgotten.

Trooper Windsor and elsewhere. Also Troopers, Newport, IOW; Loyal Trooper, South Anston, S Yorks; Valiant Trooper, Aldbury, near Tring. This term was first used about 1640 for a soldier who was part of a group of cavalry. Latin *troppus*, from which 'troop' derives, means a flock.

Trot Inn Edinburgh. Another variation of Do Drop Inn, or Drop Inn. *See* Dew Drop.

Trotter Crickham, Som. The sign here shows a trotting pony. Similar names are Trotting Horse, Ludlow and Clyffe Pypard, near Swindon; Trotting Mare, Knolton Bryn, near Wrexham; Trotters Arms, Ramshaw, Dur.

Trotters Bolton. The nickname of the local Football League team, also known as the Happy Wanderers. Their official title is Bolton Wanderers.

Troubadour South Ockendon, near Romford. Technically a medieval singer-poet of France, Spain and Italy who was mainly concerned with chivalry and gallantry, but applied to others who sing and compose ballads.

Trouble House Cherington, Glos. The troubled history of this pub is now safely in the past. There were problems in the Civil War when a skirmish took place here. Two landlords later committed suicide, and there was a Luddite uprising in the early nineteenth century. On a more positive note, there was once a 'Trouble House Halt' on the Kemble to Tetbury branch line because of the pub's isolated position, which must have made it the only pub in Britain to have what was almost a private railway station. The halt disappeared in the 1960s when British Rail ran into troubles of its own.

Trout Wolvercote, near Oxford. Another at Bickleigh, Devon. Also Rising Trout, Saxmundham; Speckled Trout, New Milton, Hants; Tickled Trout, Wye, Kent. After the freshwater fish which is valued for sporting and eating purposes. The Wolvercote pub dates from the sixteenth century and overlooks Godstow Bridge, the Thames weir and Trout Island and has been used by generations of Oxford students. The Bickleigh pub is near a former trout hatchery in the river Exe. The *Tickled Trout* refers to a fish caught in the hand by gently stroking it.

Trowel and Hammer Lowestoft and elsewhere (mainly in East Anglia). The tools used by masons, bricklayers and the like. Said to be associated with a former guild of craftsmen.

True Blue Wick, near Littlehampton. This phrase now means a loyal Conservative. In the seventeenth century it applied to the Scottish Presbyterian or Whig party, the Covenanters having adopted that colour to distinguish themselves from the royal red.

True Briton Sheerness and elsewhere. The name of an East Indiaman, a sailing ship of large tonnage engaged in the East India trade, which disappeared on her eighth voyage with all hands. Inland pubs of this name may express a general patriotism. This was a favourite way of signing anonymous letters to the press about political matters in former times. Reading has a True Patriot.

True Heart Bishopstone, near Swindon. The sign shows Cupid shooting an arrow into a large heart.

True Lover's Knot Tarrant Keyneston, Dors. Another at Northwood, GL. An ornamental knot, consisting of a double-looped bow or two loops intertwined, was often given by one lover to another in former times. Shakespeare refers to them in *Two Gentleman of Verona*, where they are made of 'silken strings', but they could be made in other materials. They were sometimes worn as hair ornaments, worked into rings, used as cake decorations, and so on.

Trumpet Pixley, near Ledbury. Also Trumpeter, Chesterfield. Formerly a London sign as well, and possibly a synonym, in a loose sense, of Bugle Horn, connected with the delivery of the mail. The instrument was used for military purposes before being included in the orchestra.

Trumpet Major Dorchester. Thomas Hardy (1840–1928) was born nearby and wrote his novel *The Trumpet Major* in 1880. It is a simple and pleasant tale set in the time of the Napoleonic Wars. The trumpet-major of the title is John Loveday. He has problems in his courtship of Anne Garland and eventually goes away with his regiment 'to blow his trumpet till silenced for ever upon one of the bloody battlefields of Spain'.

Trusty Servant Minstead, near Lyndhurst, Hants. Another at Chelmsley Wood, Birmingham. The Minstead sign is based on a sixteenth-century painting kept at Winchester College. The symbolic figure shown has the qualities thought to be necessary in a trustworthy servant – a padlocked pig's snout represents the ability to keep secrets, the ears of a donkey represent patience, the feet of a stag represent swiftness in the execution of a master's errands.

Try Again Bristol. A reference to the long efforts that were made to obtain a licence for the premises, though the sign shows a frustrated angler trying to land his catch.

Tucker's Grave Radstock, Som. A reference to a local man who hanged himself in 1747 in a barn near the present inn. As was the custom he was buried in unconsecrated ground, said to be where the car park of the inn is today.

Tuckingmill Tuckingmill, near Camborne. This is another term for a fulling mill, where cloth was cleaned by beating and washing.

Tuck's Habit Bramcote, near Nottingham. The sign shows Friar Tuck tucking into some food. There is a Tuck Inn at Cheadle, Ches.

Tudor Arms Reading. Also Tudor Close, Ferring, near Worthing; Tudor House, Bath; Tudor Tavern, St Albans; Tudor Rose, Coulsdon, Sry and elsewhere. 'Tudor' is from the Welsh family name Tewdwr, which in turn is usually associated with Theodore, though that may have become confused with a native Welsh name containing the element *tud*, 'tribe' or 'country'. Owain Tudor married Catherine, the widow of Henry V, and his grandson, Henry VII, became the first king of the Tudor dynasty. The other Tudors were Henry VIII, Edward VI, Mary I and Elizabeth I. The Tudor period was from 1485 to 1603. The Tudor rose was adopted as a badge by Henry VII. It combines a red and white rose.

Tufted Duck St Combs, near Fraserburgh, Gramp. After the bird also known as a tufted widgeon, which has a tuft of narrow feathers on its crest.

Tulip Tree Richmond, Sry. After the tree which has flowers like large tulips. Visitors to the nearby Kew Gardens are able to admire them. The Tulip itself is celebrated in Leeds. The name of this flower derives ultimately from a Persian word meaning 'turban', which the expanded flower was thought to resemble.

Tumbledown Dick Camberley, Sry. Another at Farnborough, Hants. One of the nicknames applied to Richard Cromwell (1626–1712). He succeeded his father Oliver Cromwell as Lord Protector of England in 1658 but was totally inadequately equipped for the job. He was a mild and unambitious man, virtuous but not very bright. He was probably greatly relieved when he was forced to resign in 1659. The rest of his life was spent in peaceful obscurity, much of it in France and Switzerland.

Tunnel House Coates, near Cirencester. The pub is near the Thames-Severn canal, constructed in 1783 and now derelict. The canal included a tunnel two and a half miles long between Coates and Sapperton, and this inn was built as a hostel for the men who constructed it. Barges had to be 'legged' through the tunnel, the bargees lying on their backs and pushing with their feet on the ceiling or walls. Cymmer, M Glam has a Tunnel, and there is a Tunnel Tavern at Rhymney, Gwent, and Jarrow.

Tup Cumnock, Strath. Also Old Tup, Gamesley, near Glossop, Derbys. A chiefly Northern and Scottish term for a male sheep, a ram.

Turbinia Fossway, near Walker-on-Tyne. Another at Newton Aycliffe, Dur. Charles Parsons (1854–1931) perfected the turbine for marine use but failed to interest the admiralty until he made a dramatic appearance at the Spithead Review in 1897. His steamship *Turbinia* cruised at an estimated thirty-seven knots and proved that his vessel had great manoeuvrability. The admiralty adopted his invention within two years and Parsons was knighted.

Turfcutters Arms East Boldre, Hants. 'Turf' here means a slab of peat, dug for use as fuel. Turfcutting was once a local occupation.

Turf Tavern Nottingham. The Turf has been used to describe everything to do with horse-racing since the mid–eighteenth century, hence the modern 'turf accountant', or bookie. The Turf and Feather, Padgate, near Warrington, refers both to horse-racing interests and cock-fighting.

Turkey Turkey Street, Enfield. The pub name was obviously suggested by the place name, though the latter has nothing to do with turkeys. It was earlier Tuckey Street. For that matter, the turkey has nothing to do with Turkey. The name was originally applied to the guinea-fowl, an African bird imported to Europe through Turkish territory. It was then transferred to the present bird, which has always been North American. There is another pub of this name at Bexhill-on-Sea. Norwich and Hunsdon, near Ware have a Turkey Cock, a term for the male bird which is also applied to anyone who struts around in a pompous way.

Turk's Head Wednesbury, W Mids and elsewhere. In most instances a variant of Saracen's Head. The expression was applied to various other objects, such as a kind of thistle, a round long handled broom or brush and a round cake tin which has a conical core in the centre. The Wednesbury sign shows the ornamental knot called a Turk's head, seen here as ropework adorning the tiller-post of a canal narrow-boat.

Turners Arms Blackburn and elsewhere. Also Turners, London EC2. After the Worshipful Company of Turners (1604) which was originally a guild for wood turners. They made domestic articles turned on lathes.

Turnpike High Wycombe and elsewhere. Originally this term was used of a spiked barrier which was put across a road for defensive purposes. The name was later transferred to the barrier which was erected to stop travellers until a toll was paid. Turnpike Trusts are said to have controlled some 20,000 miles of roads at one time.

'Turnpike' can refer to the barrier itself, the **Toll Gate** where the fees were collected or the road for which the fee was collected. In Scotland it can also be applied to a spiral or winding stair. At London N16 there is a Turnpike House.

Turnstone Hopton, near Lowestoft. The bird which has the habit of turning over stones as it seeks its food.

Turpin's Cave High Beech Hill, near Loughton, Esx. Also Turpin's Tavern, Sutton-on-Derwent, Esx. The 'cave' is reputed to be one of the hiding-places used by Dick Turpin, who frequented this area.

Turtle Bay Southend-on-Sea. The pub was opened in 1984 and is decorated in tropical style. The better-known *Turtle Bay* is the district around the UN head-quarters in East Manhattan.

Twa Corbies Cumbernauld, near Glasgow. A reference to an old ballad of this name about two ravens. 'As I was walking all alane,/I heard twa corbies making a mane:/The tane unto the tither did say,/"Where sall we gang and dine the day?" '

Twa Dogs Brigham, near Keswick. The poem by Robert Burns about a dialogue between Caesar, a gentleman's dog, and Luath, a ploughman's collie. They end up by agreeing that it is better to be poor, since the poor eat anything with good appetite, sleep soundly because they work hard, stay at home with their families because they have no money for travelling, and so on. The ploughman is presumably Burns himself: 'A rhyming, ranting, raving billie,/Wha for his friend an' comrade had him,/And in his freaks had 'Luath' ca'd him,/After some dog in Highland sang,/Was made lang syne – Lord knows how lang.'

Twa Tams *See* Tam o' Shanter.

Tweed Spittal, near Berwick-on-Tweed. Also Tweedside, Portbrae, Peebles. The river that rises in Tweed's Well, Bdrs and flows into the North Sea in Northumberland at Tweedmouth. The cloth called tweed got its name by accident, it was properly tweel, a Scottish form of twill.

Twelfth Man *See* Cricket.

Twelve Bells *See* Bell.

Twelve Knights Margam, near Port Talbot. A reference to twelve noblemen appointed by William the Conqueror to maintain order on the English/Welsh border. The Three Knights at Corntown, near Bridgend, also refers to these peace-keepers, who were occasionally called to quell local rebellions.

Twenty Churchwardens Cockley Cley, near Swaffham, Nflk. This village is one of ten parishes which constitute a church group, and each parish has two church wardens. At the opening of this pub in 1968 they were all presented with long-stemmed clay pipes, known as 'churchwardens' in the nineteenth century. They were also given tankards engraved with the name of their parish, to be kept at the pub for their use as required.

Twentyfive *See* Number Names.

Twickers Twickenham. The nickname of the nearby rugby union football ground, the home of English rugby.

Twin Foxes Stevenage. The inn sign shows the Foxes concerned, twin brothers who were Albert Ebenezer Fox and Ebenezer Albert Fox. They were notorious poachers in this area until the turn of the present century. They are seen on one side of the sign with guns under their arms, their dog in the background. The other side of the sign shows a pair of fox heads.

Twist and Cheese Lower Stondon, Beds. The 'twist' is a roll or loaf made from twisted dough. It is seen on the inn sign here as part of an attractive ploughman's lunch.

Two Bells Folkestone. At sea a bell is rung every half hour during a 'watch', which normally lasts for four hours (though 'dog-watches' last only two hours). Two bells therefore indicate that an hour has passed since a watch was begun. *See also* Five Bells.

Two Blues Bishop Auckland, Dur. After the colours of the local amateur football club, originally formed of players from a nearby theological college. Most of the students there had come from Oxford (dark blue) and Cambridge (light blue).

Two Brewers Chipperfield, Herts and elsewhere. A fairly common sign since the seventeenth century, with at least seventeen still remaining in London alone. The 'brewers' are usually draymen, who deliver the beer, seen carrying a cask between them, slung from a pole.

Two Bulls' Heads *See* Bull.

Two Chairmen London W1 and SW1. The men who carried the Sedan Chair. There was some criticism when the latter was introduced in the 1630s that Englishmen were being degraded 'into slaves and beasts of burden', but it flourished nevertheless. Defoe mentioned in 1702 that a sedan chair and its two chairmen could be hired for a shilling an hour, and compared the men to gondoliers. The Crown and Two Chairmen is also found.

Two Friends Blofield Heath, Norwich. The sign here used to show two crossed hands against a background of international flags. It now shows a little girl in Victorian dress feeding her pet duck.

Two Mile Oak Abbotskerswell, Devon. This oak tree stands two miles from the village and marks the point where a person could legitimately call himself a 'traveller' on a Sunday, and thus have a drink.

Two-necked Swan *See* Swan with Two Necks.

Two Palfreys Doncaster. The sign shows the two palfreys, light horses used by women, which were given by Robert de Turnham to King John at the end of the eleventh century. In exchange he was allowed to hold a Fair at Doncaster in the year 1200.

Two Poplars Wokingham. For the two trees which were planted in front of the pub when it opened in 1926.

Two Puddings London E15. A former licensee used to distribute plum puddings on Christmas Eve to the local poor. He would stand with one pudding on each side of him.

Two Sawyers Canterbury and elsewhere. The sawyers were considered to be unskilled workmen and were not incorporated into the guilds of carpenters, joiners and ship-wrights. This sign, which usually shows two men using a double-handed saw, therefore replaces what would otherwise have been the Sawyers Arms.

Two Saxons *See* Saxon.

Two Ships *See* Chesapeake and Shannon.

Two Woodcocks London SW2. This bird is allied to the snipe, and has a long bill, large eyes and plumage of mixed colours. It is also renowned for being gullible, and easy to catch, which is why Fabian says of Malvolio, in Shakespeare's *Twelfth Night:* 'Now is the woodcock near the gin (trap)'. There is also a variety of apple called a woodcock.

Tyacks Camborne, Corn. Tyack is a Cornish surname meaning 'farmer'.

Tyburn House Birmingham. Tyburn was the place of public execution for Middlesex until 1783. It was at the junction of the present Oxford Street, Bayswater Road and Edgware Road. The name came from a small brook which used to run past Marylebone to the Thames at Westminster. It gave rise to the village of Tyburn (later Marylebone) and a district known as Tyburnia. Because of its association with hanging, the name also entered into various phrases that reflected the grim humour of times past. A Tyburn blossom was a young thief or pickpocket who would eventually ripen into the fruit of the Tyburn tree, ie the gallows. A Tyburn face was a 'hangdog' look, a Tyburn collar the fringe of beard worn under the chin, and to preach at Tyburn cross was to be hanged, alluding to the speeches that those who were to be hanged were allowed to make to the crowds of spectators. The pub sign here shows a hanging.

Tyke Thornton, Bradford. Since 1700 this has been the nickname for a Yorkshireman. It may have been insulting to begin with (or it could have arisen simply because Yorkshiremen referred to 'tyke' when other people tended to say 'dog') but it has long been accepted by Yorkshiremen themselves, as this pub name illustrates.

Tylers Rest Tilehurst, near Reading. The pub name was no doubt suggested by the place name, and the two do in fact go well together. Tilehurst is a place where tiles were made (or found), so a tiler (tyler is a variant) was certainly at work here centuries ago.

Tyne Newcastle. Also Tynedale, Corbridge, near Hexham; Tyne Dock, Templetown, near South Shields; Tynemouth Castle, Jarrow; Tynemouth Lodge, North Shields. The river Tyne has two headstreams which join near Hexham and flow into the North Sea at Tynemouth. There is another river of this name in Scotland, for which the Tyneside Tavern at Poldrate, near Haddington, Loth is named.

Tynte Arms Enmore, Som. A Colonel Tynte bought this pub for his sergeant-major, Edward Calland, who named it in his honour.

Tythe Barn *See* Tithe Barn.

Tything Man Winterbourne Dauntsey, Dor. A form of tithing man, which by the seventeenth century had two meanings, the main one being a parish peace-officer, or petty-constable. The phrase could also be used of a man who collected the tithes – *see* Tithe Barn.

Tywarnhayle Perranporth. Cornish for 'house on the estuary', or interpreted very freely as 'house near water'. There is a stream behind the pub which was used by tin–miners in the past to wash ore.

U

Udder Place London EC2. A modern off–beat name, but hardly a happy choice. It suggests a milk–bar rather than a pub and the joke is at the expense of West Indian pronunciation.

UEA Pub Norwich. It is attached to the University of East Anglia.

Ugly Duckling Haywards Heath, W Ssx and elsewhere. The Haywards Heath sign shows a forlorn-looking Donald Duck at the side of a pond. The general reference is obviously to the story by Hans Christian Andersen (1805–75) about a duckling who is not like other ducklings, and despairs until he finds that he is in fact a cygnet.

Ulsterman Magherafelt, Londy. A native of Ulster, often mistakenly used as an alternative for Northern Ireland. Ulster in fact comprises the six counties of Antrim, Armagh, Down, Fermanagh, Londonderry and Tyrone with the addition of the three counties of Cavan, Donegal and Monaghan which belong to the Republic of Ireland. Associated names are Ulster Arms, Newtonards; Ulster Inn, Armagh; Ulster Tavern and Ulster Vaults, both in Belfast.

Umbrella Cheltenham. This is said to be a reference to Neville Chamberlain, who visited Hitler in 1938 armed with nothing more than an umbrella. William Plomer has in his *Father and Son* (1939) the following: 'A pleasant old buffer, nephew to a lord,/Who believed that the bank was mightier than the sword,/And that an umbrella might pacify barbarians abroad:/Just like an old liberal/Between the wars.'

Umpire *See* Cricket.

Uncle Tom's Cabin Wincanton, Som and elsewhere. One of the pub names which is becoming more popular in the 1980s. The novel of this name was published in 1852 by Mrs Harriet Beecher Stowe. It concerns a Negro slave of unaffected piety who faithfully serves his master, who is compelled to sell him to a slave-dealer because of his shortage of money. Uncle Tom suffers greatly at various hands and dies. The story is said to have contributed to the cause of those who were fighting against slavery and helped to bring about emancipation. At Wincanton it is said that there was a coach-driver of the 1830s who was known as Uncle Tom, and who called at the inn three times a week. The pub was named for him on his retirement, which was clearly after the publication of Mrs Stowe's book.

Underwriter London EC3. The pub is in the City area where the main insurance companies have their head offices. An underwriter is an insurance agent, especially one who deals in marine insurance, the name deriving from his 'under writing', or signing, of the insurance policies.

Unicorn Ripon and elsewhere. Also Unicorn's Head, Langar, Notts; Unicorn and Star, Thurmaston, near Leicester. The unicorn is a legendary animal which supposedly has a horse's body and a single long horn projecting from its forehead. The horn is thought to possess magical properties. The unicorn has sometimes been identified with the one-horned rhinoceros. The word was also used for a Scottish gold coin in the fifteenth and sixteenth centuries, and was applied to the arrangement of three horses pulling a carriage, one horse leading a pair. However, use of the word in pub names is always a heraldic reference. Two unicorns support the royal arms of Scotland. When James VI of Scotland became James I of England, one of these unicorns displaced the Welsh dragon on the English royal arms, the other supporter being the lion. (*See* Lion and Unicorn). A unicorn also features in the arms of the Worshipful Company of Wax Chandlers (1483), the Worshipful Company of Goldsmiths (1327) and the Worshipful Society of Apothecaries (1617). On the attractive inn sign at Abbot's Langley, near Watford part of the conversation between the unicorn and Alice from *Through the Looking Glass* is given: ' "Well, now that we have met," said the Unicorn, "if you'll believe in me I'll believe in you. Is that a bargain?" ' Our scout tells us that the sign has gone so we include the original picture from the book.

Union Child Okeford, Dors and elsewhere. This is often a reference to a political union, such as the Act of Union, 1707, which decreed that England and Scotland should be one kingdom with one parliament. An earlier Act of 1536 had incorporated Wales with England, and in 1800 an Act united Great Britain with Ireland, though that union ended in 1922. At Dorchester the pub name refers to the union of Dorchester with Fordington, 1835. At Newton Abbot a pair of modern newly-weds are leaving a church on the sign picture, and a wedding is also shown at Leek, though here Henry VII is seen marrying Elizabeth of York. That marriage union also united the House of Lancaster with that of York. The Union of Hearts was once in Derby.

Union Jack Stretton-under-Fosse, near Rugby. The name of the national flag, which makes a conveniently patriotic sign. The 'Union Jack' was originally a small flag flown on a ship, on the part of the mast known as the 'jack'. It has been the name of what was previously called the 'union flag'

since the beginning of the nineteenth century. It consists of three united crosses, those of St George for England, St Andrew for Scotland and St Patrick for Ireland.

Union Rose *See* Rose.

United Manchester. Another at Torquay. Both for the local football teams, Manchester United and Torquay United.

United Brethren New Writtle, near Chelmsford. This is another term for the Moravians, a Protestant sect who were formerly the Bohemian Brethren. They were driven out of Moravia and Bohemia in the seventeenth century but are currently found in Europe and the USA.

United Friends Ninfield, E. Ssx. Another at Deptford. Thought to be a reference to an early Friendly Society, the members of which insured themselves against sickness, old age and death.

United Kingdom Methley, near Leeds and elsewhere, (all in northern counties). This phrase formally came into use in 1800, after the union of Great Britain and Ireland. It was certainly used before then in an informal way and could refer, for instance, to the 1707 Act of Union between England and Scotland.

Unspoilt by Progress Five Ways, Birmingham. The pub was opened in 1983. The name comes from an advertising slogan used by the Wolverhampton and Dudley Brewery.

Up and Under Cwmbran, Gwent. A phrase associated with rugby, when the ball is 'hoisted' into the air and the forwards follow up and try to collect it.

Upper Bell Burham, near Rochester. A reference to the bell rung as a warning that a stagecoach was about to descend the hill, the road at that time being too narrow for two vehicles to pass.

Upper Welsh Harp London NW9. The pub is close to the Welsh Harp Reservoir, which takes its name from an inn called the Old Welsh Harp that was formerly nearby.

Upstairs Downstairs Londonderry and elsewhere. A name made famous by a long-running and popular television series, referring to the contrast between the well-to-do who lived in large houses and the servants who worked for them. The servants remained downstairs in the kitchen and lower rooms unless their duties took them up into the family living rooms.

Up the Garden Path Manton Hollow, near Marlborough. Presumably thought to be a suitable name for a 'leading' pub.

V

Vacuna Heath Hall, near Dumfries. The name of a Sabine goddess of victory, who presided over the works of the garden and field, also of the woods and hunting.

Vaga Hunderton, near Hereford. This appears to be for Perino del Vaga (1500–47), an Italian painter who was pupil of and assistant to Raphael. He painted chiefly historical amd mythological subjects.

Valentine and Orson London SE1. A reference to the twin sons of Bellisant and Alexander in a fifteenth-century French romance. Orson, whose name means 'little bear', is carried off by a bear and brought up as one of its cubs. He then becomes a Wild Man and the terror of France. The story seems to have appealed to writers of children's stories in the nineteenth century, since Dickens expects his readers to recognise his allusion to 'the most astonishing picture books: all about blue-beards and beanstalks and riches and caverns and forests and Valentines and Orsons' (*The Child's Story*).

Vale of Aeron Felinfach, near Lampeter, Dyfed. Several pub names refer to the vales or valleys in which they are situated. This one refers to the river Aeron; others include Vale of Glamorgan, Cowbridge, S Glam; Vale of Neath, Llanelli and Vale of Neath Arms, Port Tennant, near Swansea; Vale of Teify, Llanbbydder, Dyfed – the river Teify flows into Cardigan Bay. There was once a Vale of Health at London NW3.

Vale of White Horse Minety Station near Malmesbury. A reference to the white horse on the hill at Uffington, Berks, revealed by the underlying chalk. This representation of a horse, which measures 350 feet from nose to tail, is said to commemorate the victory of Alfred the Great over the Danes in 871.

Valiant Healing, near Grimsby. The pub was opened in 1972. It is in Wingate Road, and is surrounded by other roads named for valiant men, such as Hillary, Cheshire, Sir Donald Campbell and Cromwell. There is another pub of this name at Leek. (There was a British bomber of the 1950s called the *Valiant*, designed to carry a nuclear load. The name has also frequently been used by the Royal Navy, and in modern times describes its nuclear-powered submarines. They take their name from HMS *Valiant*, the first all–British nuclear submarine, commissioned in 1966.)

Valiant Soldier Exeter. This pub was rebuilt in 1670 and given a name that was current in the years following the Civil War. There are other pubs of the name at Roadwater, Som and Folkestone. Folkestone also has a Valiant Sailor.

Valiant Trooper *See* **Trooper**.

Van Gogh Ramsgate and elsewhere. Vincent van Gogh (1853–90), the post-Impressionist painter, was a tormented Dutch genius now known for his brilliantly-coloured and dynamic works that are very popular. He suffered from bouts of insanity and committed suicide during one of them. As a young man he spent one term teaching at a private school in Ramsgate.

Vansittart Arms Windsor. Nicholas Vansittart, Baron Bexley (1766–1851) was an English politician, chancellor of the Exchequer under Lord Liverpool. He was later chancellor of the duchy of Lancaster.

Van Tromp London E2. Marten Harpertzoon Tromp (1597–1653) was a celebrated Dutch naval commander, Admiral of Holland in 1639. He is said to have emerged as the victor in more than thirty battles, but was killed in a final encounter with Admiral Blake. His son, Cornelis van Tromp (1629–91) was also a distinguished seaman who gained victories over the English. After the death of De Ruyter he became lieutenant-admiral-general of the United Provinces.

Vaults Bath and elsewhere. A name which indicates that the premises were once used to store wines and other liquors. The word is frequently added to other names.

Vauxhall Cheltenham. The sign here shows an early Vauxhall car. At Evesham the sign shows Londoners enjoying Vauxhall Gardens.

Vauxhall Gardens Great Yarmouth. The name of a pleasure resort at Vauxhall, London, between the mid-seventeenth century and mid-nineteenth century. References to them by Thackeray and others show that the gardens had become decidedly unsavoury before they closed. There is an old tradition that Vauxhall derives from a 'hall belonging to Guy Fawkes'. The manor here was indeed held by a Falkes, but he was a supporter of King John in the thirteenth century.

Vectis Cowes. *Vectis* was the Roman name for the Isle of Wight.

Velindra Bristol. *Velindra* was the name of a paddle-steamer which once used the New Cut, a by-pass channel on the river Avon.

Vermuyden Goole, Humb. Sir Cornelius Vermuyden (1595–1683) was a Dutch engineer but came to England to do work for Charles I. He was concerned with draining low–lying areas.

Vernon *See* Admiral Vernon.

Verulam Arms St Albans. *Verulam* was the Roman name for St Albans. The pub of this name at Watford in is St Albans Road.

Vesper Bell Birmingham. The vesper bell is rung at sunset in monasteries and other religious establishments to summon worshippers to Vespers, or evensong, the evening service. 'Vesper' literally refers to Hesperus, the evening star.

Viaduct London W7. There is a viaduct nearby. Other pub named for proximity to viaducts are at

Birmingham and Kidderminster. The inn sign at Monkton Combe, near Bath shows an open-top vintage car driving alongside the viaduct.

Vicar of Wakefield London EC1 and elsewhere. The novel of this name is the best-known work of Oliver Goldsmith (1728–74). It was published in 1766 and was subsequently dramatised several times and turned into an opera. The vicar is Dr Primrose, who has a good fortune, a handsome house, wealthy friends and six fine children as the story begins. He is a pious but rather simple-minded man, and various misfortunes come his way. He loses his fortune, his daughter elopes, his house and all its contents are burnt, he is thrown into jail, as is his son. Things then get better and all ends fairly happily. The appeal of the vicar lies in the kind of serene dignity that comes from his basic goodness, even though he has very little worldly wisdom.

Victoria Chard, Som and elsewhere. Also Victoria Arms, Binfield, Berks. Usually after Queen Victoria. The sign at Banstead shows the carriage named after her. It is a four-wheeler with a collapsible hood, seating two passengers plus a driver on an elevated seat in front. The Victoria and Albert is also found at Edinburgh and elsewhere, but is by no means as frequent as signs honouring the queen and her consort individually. Other indirect references to the queen occur in Victoria Bridge, Framwellgate Moor, near Durham, Victoria Coach, Truro, Victoria Jubilee, Felling, near Gateshead and Leicester. There is a Victoria, British Queen at Bolton.

Victoria Cross London E12 and elsewhere. The London pub is in Jack Cornwell Street, named for the boy aged sixteen whose bravery on board the cruiser *Chester* at Jutland earned him a posthumous Victoria Cross. This is the highest British award for bravery in the presence of the enemy, and was instituted in 1856. The Scouting movement have their own award for gallantry named after this young hero, the Cornwell Badge. The London pub also displays records of fifteen-year-old Arthur Fitzgibbon, an army medical orderly who won the VC in 1860, and John Hannah of the RAF, aged nineteen, who won the award in 1940. Other pubs of this name no doubt have stirring tales to tell of local heroes.

Victoria Stakes London N10. This race was formerly run at the Alexandra Park racecourse, now no longer in use.

Victory Pinner, GL and elsewhere. The name of Nelson's flagship at Trafalgar, (now in permanent dry dock at Portsmouth) and a pub name meant to honour all those who served on her, some 700 officers and crew members in all. At Towan Cross, near Truro, the pub of this name is said to be named for a rather more trivial victory. In 1903 one of two pubs, local magistrates decided, would have to close: this one remained open.

Victualling Office Stonehouse, near Devonport. The pub is close to the naval victualling yard, which supplies ships with stores. Latin *victus* is 'food, sustenance', and victual is correctly pronounced 'vittle'.

Vigo Fairseat, near Sevenoaks. Named by a man who had served with the British fleet at the battle of Vigo Bay, northern Spain, in 1702. The British and Dutch destroyed the Spanish fleet.

Viking Middlesbrough and elsewhere. Also Vikings Tun, Aberdeen and Wigston, near Leicester. These names are not confined to the areas invaded by the Vikings, the Scandinavian ruffians of the eighth to the eleventh centuries who were pirates at sea and pillagers on land until they eventually settled in various places. The Vikings were not 'kings' but took their name, probably, from Old English *wick*, which meant a temporary camp of the type commonly established by these raiders.

Village Inn Twyning, near Tewkesbury and elsewhere. Village Pub, Barnsley, Glos; Also Village Home, Gosport; Village Maid, Birmingham; Village Tavern, Radwinter, Esx, and Lound, Sflk. 'Village' occurs in quite a few pub names besides these three, not surprisingly given that it is rather a prestige word in modern times, suggesting – to town-dwellers at least – a kind of ideal rural existence. Thus we find a Village Bells at Eling Hill, near Southampton; Village Blacksmith, Woolwich – title of a famous poem by Longfellow, 1841; Village Gate, Baginton, near Coventry; Village Green, Northall, Bucks; Village Home, Gosport, Hants; Village Maid Birmingham; Villager, Crossgar, Down; Villagers, Blackheath, Guildford.

Vine Frome, Som and elsewhere. This was formerly far more common as a pub name than it is today, though it is still well represented. It is sometimes a heraldic reference to the Worshipful Company of Distillers (1638), whose arms show a vine bearing grapes, but the sign

was already being used in the fourteenth century. Vines do in fact grow quite readily in England and can be trained to cover buildings. The Frome pub is one which has the plant itself growing on the wall. Associated names include Vine Tap, Ledbury; Vine Tree, Randwick, near Stroud and Ross-on-Wye; Vine Vaults, Newport, Salop; Vineyard, Rochester and Bristol; Vines, Liverpool. All of these refer ultimately to Latin *vinum* 'wine'. An earlier term for 'vineyard' was 'wineyard'.

Vintage Wellington, Som and elsewhere. A word which manages to suggest wine of excellent quality, though strictly speaking it refers to the wine crop of any season. The Wellington pub illustrates the name by showing an old car.

Vintners Arms Guildford. More usually interpreted as Three Tuns. *See also* Swan with Two Necks.

Viper Mill Green, Inglestone. Esx. The pub overlooks a common where until recently, it is said, vipers were to be found. The viper is the only venomous snake found in the wilds in Britain.

Virginia Ash Henstridge, Som. The sign shows Sir Walter Raleigh, credited with the introduction of tobacco to England, puffing on a clay pipe. Behind him a waiter hovers with a bucket of water, perhaps believing that Sir Walter is on fire. The sign serves as a useful reminder that smoking must have seemed very strange to those who first saw it being done.

Virginia Tavern Thornbury, Bradford. There was a small tobacco factory next door at one time. There is a Virginian at Maldon, Esx.

Virgins and Castle Kenilworth. This inn once had a passageway which connected it to the castle. It was used by the royal ladies-in-waiting who stayed here.

Virgin Tavern Worcester. This pub was formerly a presbytery which was converted and called the *Virgin Mary Tavern*. The name incensed local Roman Catholics and the name was changed. The sign shows a red-haired girl holding a bunch of daffodils.

Virtuous Lady Tavistock. This was the name of the former local copper mine. There is a polite explanation offered that it referred in turn to Elizabeth I, the Virgin Queen, but there may well have been a miner's joke inherent in the name.

Viscount Renfrew and elsewhere. Originally a vice-count was one acting in place of an earl or count. 'Viscount' now refers to a nobleman who ranks between a baron and an earl.

Viscount Hardinge Gillingham, Kent. Viscount Henry Hardinge (1785–1856) was born at Wrotham, Kent. He joined the army and served under Wellington with credit, though he was wounded two days before the Battle of Waterloo and was unable to take part in it. He was elected to parliament and became secretary of war. By 1844 he was governor-general of India, where he was obliged to defend British interests against the Sikhs. He did this successfully and was raised to the peerage. He succeeded Wellington as commander-in-chief of the British army and was himself made a field-marshal. The Hardinge Arms is also found, at Kings Newton, Derbys.

Vital Spark Glasgow. A phrase which refers to the basic signs of a person's being alive. The poet Alexander Pope referred to it finely as 'vital spark of heaven's flame'. The phrase is often used negatively: the vital spark is said to be missing when a person is dead. It is also used of fictional characters in that sense – they lack the vital spark when they fail to come to life on the page. The suggestion of the pub name is that wherever else the vital spark may be missing, it is not here.

Voltigeur Spennymoor, Dur. A horse of this name won the Derby in 1850.

Volunteer London NW1 and elsewhere. Also Volunteers, Sittingbourne and Weybridge; Volunteers' Canteen, Liverpool. Names which refer to various volunteer regiments, especially those in the eighteenth century during the wars with France, when Napoleon was threatening to invade. These threats continued well into the nineteenth century. There was a Volunteer Training Corps in World War One, and in World War Two the Home Guard and Local Defence Volunteers represented a fine tradition.

Von Alten Chatham. Count Karl August von Alten (1764–1840) was born in Hanover. He commanded the German Legion and fought with the British army in the Peninsular Wars and at Waterloo.

Vulcan Bolton. Another at Millwall. Also Vulcan Arms, Derby and Llanwrthwl, Pwys. Vulcan was the Roman god of natural fire, as represented by the volcano, to which he gave his name. Using such natural fire he forged thunderbolts for Jove. His name is therefore sometimes used in areas where there are blast furnaces and forges. The Vulcan bomber appeared in 1953. It was the world's largest delta-winged aircraft at that time, built to carry a nuclear load over 2000 miles.

W

Wadsley Jack Wadsley, Sheffield. This was the name of a book by B Hallam, published in 1866. It related the adventures of a local cutler who travelled around the area with his pedal-operated grinding machine, sharpening knives and scissors.

Wag(g)on and Horses Glastonbury and elsewhere. Goods were carried all over the country by horse-drawn waggons before the advent of the railways. Many inns acted as agents, and goods could be left there for sending on their way or for collection by the local people to whom they were addressed. This apart, waggons and horses continued to be a familiar sight in most areas as they carried goods or farm produce for short distances. The *Oxford Dictionary* prefers the spelling waggon, but wagon has long been used and is still to be seen in many pub names. Some of these are: Waggon Team, Dunston, near Gateshead; Waggoners Arms, Darwen and elsewhere; Waggonmakers Arms, Chorley, Lancs; Waggoners Rest, Witnesham, near Ipswich; Wagon Wheel, Grimley near Worcester and Armscote near Stratford-on-Avon; Wait for the Wagon, Wyboston, near Bedford. Needless to say there is no pub called 'On the Waggon', a fairly modern phrase for being teetotal which began as 'on the water waggon'.

Waggon-load of Lime *See* Limeburners Arms.

Wainhouse Corner Jacobstow, near Bude, Corn. The wain referred to here is the open kind of farm waggon used for carrying farm produce short distances. It is kept in a wainhouse or wainshed.

Wakeman Ripon. This term normally means 'watchman', but in Ripon it has two special meanings. In the fifteenth and sixteenth centuries it was the name of a municipal officer whose duties included attendance on the shrine of St Wilfrid. It was also the title of the chief magistrate of the borough until 1604, when it was exchanged for the title of mayor. A list of all the wakemen from 1400 to 1604 is still in existence, a certain Hugh Ripley being described then as 'the last wakeman and first mayor'. The Wakeman's House is in the town's market square.

Wakes Hindley, near Wigan. A reference to the annual festival of a parish, originally held on the feast day of a church's patron saint. Wakes is usually treated as a singular noun, and is a term heard in the North rather than the South of England.

Walk Inn Edinburgh. The Irish equivalent of this invitation is the Wander Inn at Kenmare, Londy.

Wallace Arms St Ninians, Stirling. This was formerly the Scots Wha Hae (a reference to the Burns' poem which begins: 'Scots, wha hae wi' Wallace bled, / Scots wham Bruce has aften led, / Welcome to your gory bed, / Or to victorie'. It is sung to the traditional tune of *Hey, tutti tatti* or to *Land o' the Leal*). Sir William Wallace (1270–1305) carried on a partisan war against the English forces as a young man, He led the Scots to victory at Stirling Bridge in 1297 and ravaged northern England afterwards. He was defeated in 1298 by the English under Edward I. After several years of border warfare he was betrayed into the hands of the English, condemned as a traitor and executed. His life has been much celebrated by Scottish writers and poets. There is a Wallace at Keresley, near Coventry; Wallace Head, London W1; Wallace Tower, Aberdeen; Wallace Tree, Elderslie, near Paisley.

Wally Dug Edinburgh. Mrs Elizabeth Inglis, of Edinburgh, tells us that this name relates to the ornamental china dog often kept on the mantelpiece in Scottish homes.

Walnut Tree Weston-super-Mare. Another at Gloucester. Also Walnut Tree Shades, Norwich. The pub at Weston-super-Mare has a walnut tree on the lawn outside. Bannut Tree is a variant of this name.

Walmesley Arms Also Walmesley Tavern. *See* Judge Walmesley.

Walpole Blackburn. Also Walpole Arms, Woolwich: Walpole Tavern, London SE14. Sir Robert Walpole (1676–1745) entered parliament in 1700. His successful handling of the financial wreckage caused by the South Sea Bubble led to his dominance in political life from 1721 to 1742 as prime minister. He was a prudent and safe minister, if unexciting. The war with Spain in 1739 came about because of popular demand, but Walpole himself was against it. Bells were rung to announce declaration of war, and Walpole is said to have remarked: 'Before long people will be wringing their hands'. Walpole resigned in 1742 and went to the House of Lords as Earl of Orford. His son, Horace Walpole, 4th Earl of Orford (1717–97) was a famous literary gossip and wit who settled at Strawberry Hill, Twickenham and became a publisher. He wrote a popular 'Gothic' novel, *The Castle of Otranto*.

Walrus Plymouth. A director of the brewery who had commanded a squadron of Walruses during World War Two suggested this name. The Walrus was a ship-borne seaplane, built in the 1930s for air-sea rescue work, and known to the flying fraternity as 'Pusser's Puddleduck' or 'Shagbat'. The inn sign shows both the seaplane and the marine mammal with its distinctive pair of tusks.

Walrus and Carpenter London EC3. Tweedledee recites a poem called *The Walrus and the Carpenter* in chapter four of *Through the Looking Glass*, by Lewis Carroll. It begins: ' "The time has come," the Walrus said,/"To talk of many things;/Of shoes – and ships – and sealing wax – /Of cabbages – and kings – / And why the sea is boiling hot – / And whether pigs have wings." '

Waltzing Weasel Birch Vale, Hayfield, near Stockport.

Manchester has a Dancing Weasel. The weasel dances around its intended prey (eg frogs or mice) and appears to hypnotise its victim by its gyrations. It then pounces. The weasel is also known for its habit of sucking out the contents of an egg. This has led to the modern term 'weasel word', meaning one which is used to evade or retreat from a direct statement.

Wanderer St Paul's Cray, Kent. A dreamier, more poetic version of Travelling Man.

Wandering Minstrel Birmingham. The minstrel, a singer of songs and teller of tales, did not originally wander. He was the servant in a castle or great manor house who 'ministered' to guests and the like by entertaining them. The wandering minstrel, an early kind of itinerant busker, came later. Later still came the minstrels who blacked their faces and sang Negro songs.

Wander Inn *See* Walk Inn.

Wansdyke Odd Down, near Bath. After the ancient defensive earthwork which runs from Inkpen, Berks, to Maesbury, Som. The name means 'Woden's dyke, or ditch'.

Wansfell Seascale, near Whitehaven, Cumb. The name of a nearby 'dark hill'.

Wanted Inn Sparrowpit, near Buxton. The Devonshire Arms until 1955, owned by successive dukes of Devonshire. It was put up for auction but failed to sell for two years, acquiring a reputation during that time as 'the pub nobody wanted'. The new owners gave it the present name in 1957 as a statement of their own feelings about the matter.

War-Bill-in-Tun Warbleton, near Heathfield, E Ssx. A rebus name based on the place name, 'Bill' was used to describe various kinds of sword-like weapons in ancient times, so a 'war-bill' can be translated as 'sword'. The tun is the usual large barrel. The place name Warbleton actually means 'farm belonging to a woman named Waerburh'.

Ward Jackson West Hartlepool. Ward Jackson (1806–80) was member of parliament for this area 1868–74. He was also chairman of the Hartlepool and Stockton Railway Company, builder of the harbour and dock, and a local philanthropist.

Wardroom Wallasea Island, Burnham-on-Crouch, Esx. A reference to the Mess set aside in warships where meals are taken by officers of all ranks. The name implies that the pub has a slightly 'superior' clientele.

Warren Romney, Kent. Another at Torquay. Also Warrens, Southampton; Warren House, Postridge, near Yelverton, Devon and Milnsbridge, near Huddersfield. All references to rabbit warrens which had to be filled in before the pub was built or which were to be seen near the pub.

Warrior London SE6. After HMS *Warrior*, the navy's first iron-clad warship. It was built at nearby Deptford in 1860. There is a more general reference to fighting men in Warriors Arms, Chester-le-Street and Warriors Gate, St Leonards-on-Sea.

Warwick Arms Worthing and elsewhere. Also Warwick Tavern, Paddington. The various earls of Warwick have owned land in different places. *See also* Neville.

Warwick Castle London W9. The pub is in Warwick Place, which in turn was named because the landowner had an estate in Warwickshire. There are other pubs of this name at London W10 and Birmingham.

Wash and Tope Hunstanton, Nflk. The pub was formerly the Railway, but this name won a competition to find something more interesting. The sign shows a map of the area which includes the Wash – the shallow bay of the North Sea into the coasts of Norfolk and Lincolnshire. The sign also shows the species of small shark called the tope, which has been caught in the Wash.

Wasp's Nest Mirfield, W Yorks. Presumably Wasps' Nest is meant. The pub may be for White Anglo-Saxon Protestants, otherwise a decidedly off-putting name.

Waste Dealers Arms Bottom o' th' Moor, Oldham. A companion name for Steptoe's.

Wastwater Wasdale Head, near St Bees, Cumb. Wastwater is a lake to the west of Ambleside, three miles long and at 260 feet, the deepest lake in England.

Watch House Bungay, Sflk. Another at Ropley, Hants. In a general sense this name refers to a house in which a watch or guard is stationed. In the eighteenth and nineteenth centuries the term was applied specifically to a house used by municipal night watchmen. Disorderly people arrested by the watchmen would be kept in custody there over night, then taken before the magistrates in the morning.

Watercress Harry Kettering. This was the Gaiety Tavern until 1984, when it was renamed in favour of a local 'character'. The man concerned was rumoured to be the disowned son of a parson who became a prizefighter for a time in Leicester. He was known in and around Kettering as a seller of baskets of watercress, or oranges and home-made wreaths in the winter. He was unkempt but well-spoken and always polite.

Water Gipsies Ham, near Richmond, Sry. The name of a novel by A P Herbert (Sir Alan Patrick Herbert, 1890–1971) about the people who live on Thames barges. It was published in 1930.

Watering Hole Dunfermline. 'Watering house' was the more usual term in the past, used of an inn where coachmen could get water for their horses. This variation seems to imply that the customers are wild animals who come to drink at a water hole.

Watering Trough Preston. Another at Walsall. This would have been an essential feature outside the coaching inns and others where riders or drivers of horses were likely to stop.

Water Lily *See* Flowers.

Waterloo Gravesend and elsewhere. Also Battle of Waterloo, Brighton; Waterloo Hero, London E14; Waterloo Arms, Abermule, near Montgomery, Pwys; Waterloo House, Bridgwater. The place where this famous battle was fought in 1815 is a small town in Brabant, twelve miles south of Brussels, in Belgium. The British and Prussian forces, under the Duke of Wellington and Blücher, together with some Dutch and Belgian troops, defeated Napoleon's French army. Napoleon abdicated four days after the battle. This was a British victory on land to match Nelson's superb achievement at Trafalgar ten years earlier, and led to a great many Duke of Wellington signs.

Waterman Norwich. Also Watermans Arms, Richmond, Sry and elsewhere; Waterman's Pub,

Edinburgh; Waterman's Tavern, Hendon, near Sunderland. There is a Worshipful Company of Watermen and Lightermen (1827). A waterman is one who makes his livelihood working on or with boats or barges.

Watermill Pateley Bridge, near Harrogate. This pub was formerly a mill which had produced rope for naval use, having earlier been a flax mill.

Water Rat London SW10. Members of the theatrical profession are proud to be members of the Grand Order of Water Rats, which was founded by music-hall artistes in 1890. They do a great deal of work for charity and helped found the Variety Artists' Benevolent Fund. Noone now seems able to explain why they called themselves 'water rats' in the beginning, with the society's officials receiving names like King Rat, Scribe Rat.

Waterside London N1. The pub is by the Bartlesbridge canal basin.

Waterside Meadery *See* Meadery.

Water Witch Didcot, Oxon and elsewhere. This is a provincial term for the storm petrel (*see* Stormy Petrel). In the USA the term is also applied to a water-finder, or dowser.

Watt Birmingham. James Watt (1736–1819) was the Scottish inventor who developed a new high-pressure steam engine in 1769. The unit of power or activity, the watt, was named after him. Many believe that it was Watt who first discovered the composition of water, though Cavendish is usually given the credit for that. Watt made a great impression on his contemporaries because of his remarkable memory and quick grasp of new information.

Wat Tyler Dartford, Kent and elsewhere. Wat Tyler (died 1381) was the leader of the Peasants' Revolt of 1381. The revolt appeared to be going well for the peasants, Richard II having made various promises in their favour, until Tyler was killed by Sir William Walworth, Lord Mayor of London. The rebels returned after that event in disarray to the Rose and Crown in Dartford, their meeting-place. That pub is now the Wat Tyler officially, though it was unofficially renamed in that way 500 years ago. After Tyler's death the king's promises were retracted and the Revolt crushed with force.

Waveney Ipswich. Another at Burgh St Peter, near Beccles. This river forms the boundary between Norfolk and Suffolk. It rises near Redgrave and flows to the Yare at Burgh Castle.

Waverley Ilfracombe. This name is closely associated with Sir Walter Scott, being the title of his first novel in 1814. From then on his novels were credited to 'the author of Waverley'. More recently it was the name of Sir John Anderson, Viscount Waverley, the wartime home secretary who introduced the Anderson shelter. This pub, however, took its name from a pleasure-steamer which used to operate locally, though that in turn may have been named for Scott's novel.

Wayfarer Southmead, Bristol. This was the name by which the Bristol Freighter was also known. It was used to transport cars and passengers across the Channel in the post-war period. The pub of this name at Hockley Heath, Warks, shows a Land-Rover on safari. Kettering has a Wayfarers.

Wayout Westmarsh, near Canterbury. This name is

presumably used in its hippy slang sense of 'extremely good' or 'original, unusual'. The expression was more easily adopted in the USA since 'Way Out' signs are not used as they are in Britain, 'Exit' being preferred. Way Inn does not seem to exist as a pub name, though for a roadside pub it would seem to have everything in its favour. Bickington, near Barnstaple, does have an Inn Place.

Weald Burgess Hill, W Ssx. The name of the region between the North and South Downs in Kent, Surrey and Sussex, once forrested but now used for grazing and cultivation.

We Anchor in Hope Welling, Kent. The sign shows the Pilgrim Fathers arriving in the New World in the *Mayflower*.

Wear Wear Chare, Bishop Auckland. Also Wear Valley, Bishop Auckland; Wearmouth Bridge, Claypath, near Durham. The Wear rises at Wear Head on the Cumbrian border and runs into the North Sea at Sunderland.

Weary Friar Inn Pillaton, near St Germans, Corn. The pub was once a religious house which offered hospitality to travelling friars. The ploughman who 'homeward plods his weary way' is accommodated in the Weary Ploughman, Cherston, Devon. There is a Weary Sportsman at Castle Carrock, Cumb, and Kidderminster has a Weary Traveller.

Weathercock Woburn Sands, Bucks. Also Weathervane, Cambridge. The figure of a cockerel has been used on weathervanes since the Middle Ages. The Catholic Church has given a Christian interpretation of this usage, relating it symbolically to St Peter's denial of Christ before the cock crew. This is a fairly modern explanation, or justification, of a weathercock being in that form.

Weaver Northwich, Ches. The river Weaver rises in south Cheshire and runs to the Mersey below Runcorn. The Weaver Arms at Winsford is named after this pub.

Weavers Arms Banbury and elsewhere. Also Weave, Moffat, D and G; Weavers Green, Crofton, near Wakefield; Weavers Knowe, Currie, Loth. The Worshipful Company of Weavers (1155) has the longest documented history of any City guild. Weaving played a vital part in the country's economy from the Middle Ages onwards, and cloth made in various parts of Britain has long been renowned for its quality.

Webbs *See* Hendras.

Wedgwood Cobridge, near Stoke-on-Trent. Josiah Wedgwood (1730–95) was born into a family of potters from Staffordshire but became the most famous of them. He transformed pottery making into an industry, building a village, Etruria, for his workmen. He invented Jasper ware, delicate blue with white Greek figures embossed on it, cream-coloured earthenware, veined ware in imitation of granite, and so on. He was appointed by Queen Charlotte to be her potter, and was a Fellow of the Royal Society.

Wedlocks Bristol. Wedlock was the name of the former licensee. Fred Wedlock was apparently well known in the area as a singer, songwriter and comedian.

Wee Dram Hamilton. Literally the 'small drink' of whisky that a Scotsman can sometimes be persuaded to accept. Associated names are Wee, Glasgow; Wee Man's, Musselburgh, Loth; Wee Manns, Glasgow; Wee Train,

Galston, Strath; Wee Waif, Twyford, near Reading.

Wee Thack Kilmarnock. Also Wee Thacket, Carluke, Strath. These names refer to small thatched premises.

Wee Willie Winkie Middlesbrough and elsewhere. Apparently a reference to the poem by William Miller (1810–72): 'Wee Willie Winkie runs through the town,/ Upstairs and downstairs in his nicht-gown,/Tirling at the window, crying at the lock,/"Are the weans in the bed, for it's now ten o'clock?"' Wark-on-Tyne and Dinnington, near Newcastle both have a Wee Willie.

Weighbridge Longford, Glos. Technically a platform scale, flush with the road, for weighing vehicles, cattle, etc. The sign here shows a very fat lady being weighed and turning the scales at four and a half hundredweight. At Kelso, Bdrs, there is a Weigh House. There is a Weighing Machine at Liverpool.

Welcome All Stone, near Dartford. Other welcoming pub names include Welcome Hand, Rainham, Esx; Welcome Home, Newport, Gwent; Welcome Inn, Accrington and Winchester; Welcome Return, Mossley, near Manchester; Welcome Sailor, Fullbridge, near Maldon, Esx; Welcome Tavern, Belper, Derbs; Welcome Traveller, Tyldesley, near Manchester; Welcome to All, Horns Cross, near Greenhithe, Kent; Welcome to Gower, Gowerton, near Swansea; Welcome to Town, Bridgend and elsewhere. The Welcome Stranger at Liverton, near Newton Abbot, shows a stork carrying a baby in a wicker basket. The reference is to a baby girl who was left on the steps of the New Inn locally in 1772. She was baptised Mary Ann, married at twenty-one and lived to be eighty-four. There are other pubs of this name at Court-at-Street, near Hythe, Kent and Crowborough, E Ssx.

Welland Spalding, Lincs. Also Welland Cottage, Stamford. The river Welland rises near Sibbertoft in Northamptonshire and flows to the Wash.

Well and Bucket London E2. The present pub name perpetuates that of a fifteenth-century pub, when the well and bucket would have been in daily use. The place where water emerged from the ground was the Well Head, Wendover, Bucks, also Wellhead Tavern, Perry Barr, near Birmingham. The well itself was sometimes enclosed in a Well House, Chipstead, Sry. Rumblingwell, near Dunfermline has a Well, and Wells is at Sunninghill, near Ascot. London NW3 has a Wells Tavern, Clitheroe, Lancs, a Wellsprings. There is an unusual Welldiggers at Low Heath, Petworth, W Ssx.

Wellesley Arms Also Wellesley Tavern. *See* Duke of Wellington.

Wellington Barnet and elsewhere. Normally a variant of Duke of Wellington, but at Hastings the sign shows the Wellington bomber of World War Two. The pilots attached to the RAF's Initial Training Wing were stationed locally at that time. At Chard, Som, the sign shows a stagecoach of this name which ran between Minehead and Taunton.

Wellington Heifer *See* Craven Heifer.

Wellington Shambles *See* Shambles.

Wellwishers Arms Bank Top, Blackburn. 'Well-wisher' is recorded from 1590 and seems to have been used almost as a synonym for 'friend', though not frequently. The pub name could therefore be 'translated' as Friendly Arms.

Welsh Harp Cheltenham and elsewhere. Also Welch Harp, Oswestry, Salop. An early form of harp with three rows of strings, used on signboards for its distinctive shape and as a symbol of the innkeeper's connection with Wales. The harp has long been used as a solo instrument in Wales, far more so than in other parts of Britain. 'Welch' is one of the many early spellings of the word before it became standardised, and has been retained especially in military circles, as with the Welch Fusilier, Holyhead, though Welsh Fusilier is also found, at Wrexham. Other names in the Welsh group include Welsh Arms, Whitehaven, Cumb; Welsh Bard, Neath; Welsh Guardsman, Tanerdy, Carmarthen; Welsh Oak, Swansea and Rogerstone, near Newport, Gwent; Welsh Star, Llanelli; Welsh Princess, Rayne, near Braintree, Esx – the latter more normally found as Princess of Wales as at Aldershot, Hants. The Welsh Pony at Oxford is near a former cattle market where such ponies were sold.

West India House Bridgwater. This was once the home of a merchant whose ships traded with the West Indies. There is a West India at Stonehouse, near Davenport.

West Meon Hut West Meon, near Petersfield, Hants. The reference here is to a hut that was built in the 1890s for the workmen who were building the railway. The hut was behind the inn and was licensed as a saloon. When the railway opened in 1903 the hut lost its licence, but the pub changed its name from the George, as it had been until then, to commemorate its use.

Welsh Prince *See* Prince Llewellyn.

Wensleydale Heifer *See* Craven Heifer.

West Bull *See* Bull.

West End Saxlingham Nethergate, near Norwich. This pub, opened in 1969, stands at the west end of the village. Its sign shows the statue of Eros at Piccadilly, in London's West End.

Westgate *See* Northgate.

West Kent Yeoman *See* Yeoman.

Westminster Abbey Nottingham. The original pub here was built at the end of the nineteenth century when royal weddings were taking place fairly regularly at the Abbey. That may have influenced the choice of name.

Westminster Arms London SW1 and elsewhere. The pub of this name near the House of Commons, like St Stephens Tavern, London SW1, has a division bell to recall members of parliament when it is time to vote. The other pubs of this name are also in London and are named after the district.

West Riding Huddersfield. The West Riding is now West Yorkshire. The 'riding' was originally a 'thriding' – a third part of the county.

West Somerset Watchet. The name of a local railway branch line, used to carry minerals.

West Wales Llanelli. Similarly West of England, Torrington, Devon and Newport, Gwent; West of Fife, Newmills, Dunfermline. The Irish are slightly more poetic with their West Winds, Newtonwards, Down.

Westward Ho! Edinburgh. Another in Birmingham. The village and small resort of this name in Devon, north of Bideford, was named for the novel by Charles Kingsley (1819–75), published in 1855. This is not the only pub name in the country with an exclamation mark, though the place name is probably unique in that respect. It is also decidedly unusual in having a literary origin. Kingsley began writing the novel in Torquay and completed it at Bideford. It was his most successful novel, though children are often more familiar with his *Water Babies*. Westward Ho! before being used by Kingsley was a seaman's cry meaning 'To the West!'

We Three Loggerheads *See* Loggerheads.

Whalebone Woodham Ferrers, Esx and elsewhere. The substance known as whalebone is not actually bone but a horny material properly called baleen. Pubs of this name, however, refer to the blade, or shoulder bones of whales, brought back by skippers of whaling boats. They would often tie such a bone, or a jawbone, to the mast of the ship if they had had a prosperous trip. This association with prosperity may well have encouraged use of the name, while the bones themselves would have made an easy sign to hang outside.

Wharf and Flyboat Aspley, near Huddersfield. For 'flyboat' *see* Shroppie Fly. Welford, near Market Harborough has a Wharf House, a 'wharf' being a built-up section of a bank where boats may be unloaded.

What Cheer! Birmingham. This was formerly a common phrase which meant simply 'How are you?' Its literal meaning was 'What mood are you in?' but it was not felt to be as specific as that by those to whom it was addressed. Here it is turned into an exclamation instead of a greeting, and implies that a cheerful time will be had within.

Whateley Hall Banbury. William Whateley (1583–1639) was an eminent Puritan preacher. He was born in Banbury and became its vicar about 1610.

Wheal Cury, near Helston. In Cornwall this means a mine.

Wheatland Fox *See* **Fox**.

Wheatsheaf South Petherton, Som and elsewhere. This has been a common sign since the seventeenth century and appears in several coats of arms, including those of the Worshipful Company of Bakers (1486). It is also one of the devices on the arms of the Brewers' Company. The South Petherton sign shows an attractive scene of a reaper gathering his harvest.

Wheel Truro and elsewhere. This was a wheelwright's shop in former times, carrying out repairs to the wheels of coaches and carts. The sign is a huge straw waggon-wheel incorporated into the thatched roof. There is a Wheel and Compass at Weston-by-Welland, Leics, a Wheel o' Worfield at Bridgnorth (Worfield also being in Salop), and Wheels of Pewsey at Pewsey, Wilts.

Wheelbarrow Southsea Common, Hants. The name may be ordinary, but the explanation given locally is fairly colourful. It is supposed to commemorate the garrison commander of Southsea Castle during the Civil War who was fond of his drink. He had to be taken home in a wheelbarrow every night.

Wheelbarrow and Castle Radford, near Pershore, H and W. A pub name influenced by another in the neighbourhood, as pub names sometimes are. The other name was Castle in the Air. The sign here shows a castle perched on a wheelbarrow, surrounded by clouds. The *Castle in the Air* sign is no more, though it was probably making a joke about a castle painted on a pub sign and therefore swinging in the air, as well as referring to a daydream. This pub has since been renamed. It is now called simply Wheelies.

Wheelers *See* Hendras.

Wheelhouse Hull. Another at Nottingham. This name is normally for the structure on board a ship which contains the ship's wheel – the pilot house as it is also known. The expression can also be used of a barn where wheels are stored.

Wheel of Fortune Holyport, near Maidenhead. Another at Alpington, near Norwich. Fortuna, goddess of fortune in both Greece and Italy in ancient times, was usually shown holding a ball or globe. It was meant to remind everyone that a ball revolves and that the whole world is subject to chance. In later representations this ball became a wheel. Poets and other writers have alluded to the wheel of fortune for centuries, optimistically thinking that times will inevitably get better, or pessimistically refusing to rejoice over much when things are going well, knowing that the situation may change.

Wheeltapper Taunton. The pub is in Station Road, and is for the railway employee who by tapping the wheels of carriages and other rolling stock could tell whether they had developed any faults. At Coatbridge, Strath there is a Wheeltappers and Shunters.

Wheelwrights Arms Havant, Hants. Another at Kingston–on–Thames, Sry. The Worshipful Company of Wheelwrights dates as a livery company from 1669. North Walsham, Nflk has a Wheelwright Arms.

Whiffler Norwich. Whifflers formed a regular part of Corporation processions at Norwich until 1835. They were attendants armed with a 'wifel' originally (a kind of battle–axe or javelin), which they used to clear the crowds away so that the procession might proceed. This word has often been explained erroneously as a 'piper', but early forms make it clear that it was not connected with the verb 'to whiffle', to blow in light gusts. The sign here says it all, showing the Whiffler in his truly splendid costume.

Whip Lacey Green, Bucks. The sign shows a horseman using the whip to urge his mount to clear a hedge. There is another pub of the same name at Dundee. Other horsey names are the Whip and Collar, Mill End, near Rickmansworth; Whip and Saddle, Duns, Bdrs.

Whippet Hare Hatch, Reading. Also Joyful Whippet, Sompting, near Worthing. The whippet is a small dog, a cross between a greyhound and a terrier, used for coursing, or hare-chasing. The place name Hare Hatch presumably influenced the choice of pub name.

Whipping Post Folkingham, near Sleaford, Lincs. Also Whipping Stocks, Holmes Chapel, near Knutsford, Ches. Offenders in former times, until the beginning of the nineteenth century, were either tied to a post in a public place and whipped or endured that punishment while they were secured in the stocks. We still talk of someone being a 'laughing-stock'. There was once an expression 'whipping-stock', used of a person who was frequently whipped.

Whistle Stop Sutton, Sry and elsewhere. This phrase originally referred to a small station at which a train stopped only when signalled to do so. It later came to mean the brief personal appearance of a political candidate, usually on the rear platform of a train, while making a tour. No doubt the 'brief personal appearance' idea inspired the pub name.

Whistling Duck Banwell, near Weston-super-Mare. This name won the prize in a local newspaper competition in 1967, having been submitted by a young lady named Lisa, who was then eight years old. It is another name for the coot. Other wild fowl are said to seek the company of coots because they act as sentries on their behalf. 'Whistling duck' is also applied locally to other birds, such as the golden-eye and the widgeon.

Whitbread Tavern Brighton. After the national brewery, with over 7,000 pubs.

White Admiral Harlow, Esx. One of the butterfly pub names in this town.

White Bear Bedale, N Yorks and elsewhere, mainly in London. A heraldic reference to the earls of Kent, and perhaps for that reason the name of a galleon built in 1563 which formed part of Drake's squadron when he attacked Cadiz in 1587. The Royal Navy sold it in 1629, but it is still to be seen on the inn sign at Bedale.

White Boar Bury, Lancs. A heraldic reference to Richard III.

White Buck *See* Buck.

White Bull *See* Bull.

White Cockade Aberdeen. Another at Edinburgh. This was the badge worn by the followers of Charles Edward, the Young Pretender or Bonnie Prince Charlie. A cockade is a knot of ribbons or a rosette worn in the hat. There was a popular Jacobite song which had

the line: 'He's ta'en the field wi' his white cockade'.

White Cross Askett, near Aylesbury. There is a cross cut in the turf nearby, revealing the underlying chalk. The pub of this name at Sidcup, Kent, is thought to relate to the Knights of St John, whose badge this was.

White Elephant Diss, Nflk and elsewhere. The kings of Siam are said to have given a white elephant to any courtier they disliked. The courtier was obliged to pay the heavy expenses of its upkeep, and could get nothing in return, the animal being sacred and not allowed to work. The figurative meaning of 'white elephant' is therefore anything that drains one's financial resources rather than contributing to one's income.

White Elm *See* Elm.

White Hart Spalding, Lincs, and elsewhere. The earliest instances of this very common sign coincide with the beginning of Richard II's reign in 1377, and it was that monarch's heraldic symbol. He ensured that all members of his household wore the device, and it would have been a sound move on the part of tavern keepers to show their allegiance by displaying it. It had the advantage in any case of being a highly distinctive visual symbol at a time when the hart, the male deer, was possibly more familiar to the average person than it is today. The continued use of *White Hart* signs in later centuries is explained by its having become a generic term for a tavern. In a similar way people often speak of 'hoovering' a carpet even though their vacuum-cleaner might not be made by the Hoover company. Later users of the *White Hart* name, in other words, were not thinking of Richard II or any other user of this heraldic symbol, they were simply aware that there were many very well-known pubs in existence bearing the name. The Spalding *White Hart* dates from the fourteenth century, while the sign at Old Lenton, Nottingham, is perhaps the finest wall sign in the country, showing the animal in parkland, a gold collar and chain around its neck and the ramparts of the medieval Nottingham Castle in the background. Historical associations with pubs of this name are many, as are the literary associations. Dickens gives a fine description of the inn at Southwark, London SE1, for instance, where Sam Weller first met Mr Pickwick. Bletchingley, Sry, has a Whyte Harte, and there is a White Hart Royal at Moreton-in-Marsh, Glos. There is also a White Heart at Headless Cross, near Redditch, H and W.

White Heather *See* Flowers.

White Heifer *See* Craven Heifer.

White Hind *See* Hind.

White Horse Alton, Hants and elsewhere. The Alton sign refers to a truly white horse, Mont Blank II, most horses described in this way being greys. The true white horse is an albino, foaled with pink skin and often blue eyes. This sign has been in use since the fifteenth century and remains very frequent because of its widespread heraldic usage. It was adopted by the kings of Wessex and is the traditional emblem of Kent. A galloping white horse refers heraldically to the House of Hanover, and dates from the accession of George I in 1714. The forty or so *White Horse* signs that remain in the Greater London area reflect the occurrence of such an animal in the arms of several Guilds, namely those of the Carmen, Coachmen, Farriers, Innholders, Saddlers, and Wheelwrights. One of the best-known *White Horse* signs is in Oxford's Broad Street, where a mounted policeman on a white horse is seen holding back part of the crowd which broke through the safety barrier at the opening of Wembley Stadium in 1923.

White House Bladon, near Woodstock. The inn sign shows the White House, the official residence and offices of the American president. The flagpole also flies the Stars and Stripes. All this connects with Sir Winston Churchill, who is buried in the village churchyard. He was himself an honorary citizen of the United States, and his mother was of American birth.

White Knight Pound Hill, Crawley, W Ssx. The name of a chess piece, but more specifically the name of the incompetent horseman and crazy inventor in Lewis Carroll's *Alice Through the Looking Glass*.

White Ladies Bristol. This term was applied to various orders of nuns who dressed in white, such as the Cistercians, the Magdalenes and the Sisters of the Presentation of Mary.

White Lion Cray, near Skipton, N Yorks and elsewhere. The Cray sign interprets this name unusually as relating to the roar of the nearby waterfall, which throws up a white foam. The normal reference is a heraldic one to Edward IV, or the earls of March or the Duke of Norfolk. (The sign is especially frequent in East Anglia.) The Whyte Lyon is found at Hartford Bridge, Hants, and there is a White Lyon at Worplesdon, near Guildford and Ramsey St Mary's, near Huntingdon.

White Pyramid Trewoon, near St Austell. A reference to the nearby china-clay tip, a local landmark which can be seen for many miles.

White Rock Penygraig, Glam. The sign shows a harpist seated on a boulder. He is presumably singing the favourite Welsh folksong 'David of the White Rock'. There is another pub of this name at Underriver, near Sevenoaks.

White Rose Sheffield. The white rose was the badge of the Duke of York (1411–60). A red rose was similarly a badge of the house of Lancaster, and the conflict between these noble houses is now usually known as the War of the Roses.

Whitesmiths Arms Gloucester and elsewhere. Whitesmiths were either tinsmiths, or were those who polished and finished metal goods as distinct from those who forged them – the term was applied to both kinds of workmen. The Gloucester sign shows a polisher at work.

White Star Liverpool. The White Star Line was a once–famous shipping company. The *Titanic* was a White Star liner. It sank on its maiden voyage in 1912, with the loss of 1517 lives.

White Swan Southall, GL and elsewhere. This sign is a relatively late variant of the more common Swan, and was perhaps inspired by the existence of Black Swan signs. Swans occur in various coats of

arms, such as those of the Vintners' Company, the Poulters' Company, the Musicians' Company, the earls of Essex and Edward III.

White Thorn Shaugh Prior, near Plymouth. This is another name for the common hawthorn, which has a lighter bark than blackthorn.

White Tun Wittin Gilbert, near Durham. A rebus name based on the place name.

Whittington Also Whittington and Cat, Whittington Arms, Whittington Cat, Whittington Stone. *See* Dick Whittington.

Whitworth Darley Dale, near Matlock. Sir Joseph Whitworth (1803–87) was an engineer who invented a rifle which bore his name, as well as the Whitworth thread, a standard screw thread for use in metal. He also found a way to manufacture ductile steel, for use in guns. There is a Whitworth Arms at Alverstoke, Hants. The Darley Dale pub recalls his local residence for many years and the interest he took in local affairs.

Who'd have Thought It? Milton Combe, near Plymouth and elsewhere. Also Who'd a Thought It? Egerton, Kent and elsewhere; Who'd a Thowt It? Middleton, near Manchester; Who'd ha' Tho't It? Rochester; Who'd a Tho't It? Wokingham. The sign at Milton Combe shows the landlord standing at the door of the pub flourishing his new licence before the villagers. The unexpected granting of the licence (as also at St Dominic, Corn) is one reason for this name: it has also been explained as the reaction of travellers at finding an inn in that place. Yet another possibility, probably not to be taken seriously, is that there is a reference to a certain brewer-baronet and the couplet: 'Who'd ha' thought it:/ Hops had bought it?' The Wokingham sign shows two astronauts on the moon, where they are slightly surprised to find a bottle of Morland's ale perched on a moonrock.

Whoop Hall Nether Burrow, near Settle, N Yorks. The pub is on the site of a former manor house, Upp Hall. This was adapted to *Whoop Hall* to link with the squire's pack of hounds and love of hunting.

Why Not Redditch and elsewhere. The name of a famous racehorse which won the Grand National in 1889 and again in 1894. The sign is especially popular in the West Midlands.

Wicked Lady No Man's Land, near Wheathampstead, Herts. Lady Kathleen Ferrers (1634–59) chose to become a highwaywoman at the age of eighteen. She was shot dead seven years later as she attempted to rob customers leaving the Park Inn. Her story was made into a film, *The Wicked Lady*, released in 1945 and starring Margaret Lockwood as Lady Kathleen. The licensee in 1967, Douglas Payne, asked the brewers to change to this name. The sign shows this adventurous lady holding up a stagecoach.

Wickets *See* Cricket.

Wicor Mill Portchester, near Fareham. Wicor is also in Hampshire, and its windmill is shown here on the sign in all its splendour.

Widow's Son London E3. The pub was named in 1824 and recalls a widow whose son disappeared for ever on his first voyage, though the widow prepared a hot cross bun for him every year on Good Friday. She strung these on a cord until she died. When her cottage was demolished the 'memorial collection' was passed to this pub. They hang from the ceiling, a new bun being added each year on Good Friday.

Wife of Bath Sittingbourne. The name of a much-married pilgrim in Chaucer's *Canterbury Tales*. Her own tale is about a knight who has to discover what women love most in order to save his own life. He discovers the answer with the help of an old witch, who insists that he marry her as a reward. Fortunately she then turns into a beautiful girl. What women do love most, according to the wife of Bath, is to control their husbands completely.

Wig and Fidgett Boxted, near Colchester. This curious combination name derives from the fact that the pub stands on the site of a former Circuit court house. The meaning of 'wig' then becomes self-evident. The 'fidgett', according to the licensee, is a wooden wigstand as shown on the sign, which also portrays a courtroom scene. One recorded meaning of fidget is the rustling sound made by a silk gown, which would be appropriate here as referring to a QC (Queen's Counsel) or Silk.

Wig and Gown Maidstone. This was the New Inn until 1952. The name-change was meant to attract legal patrons during the Kent Assizes or Quarter Sessions.

Wig and Mitre Lincoln. The pub is near the cathedral, which accounts for the 'mitre' (*see* Mitre). The 'wig' refers to the lawyers who have offices in the area. There are old prints of legal men and clerics inside, together with more witty up-to-date illustrations.

Wig and Pen Southsea and elsewhere. This name usually indicates that law courts or solicitors' offices are nearby.

Wild Boar Congleton, Ches. The boar on the sign is anything but wild. He is shown with his forelegs over the door of his sty, idly sucking a straw. He also wears a Panama hat.

Wild Boy *See* Wild Man.

Wild Bull *See* Bull.

Wild Duck Ewen, near Cirencester. The Wildfowl Trust's sanctuary is nearby. There are several other pubs of this name in England and Ireland in areas where wild duck are seen.

Wild Man Norwich and elsewhere. Also Wild Boy, St Albans. In 1724 a boy was found living wild in the woods near Hanover, Germany. He was taken to George I who brought him to England. What exactly happened after that is very difficult to determine, as accounts vary greatly. It is generally agreed that he never learned to speak properly, and that he eventually died in 1785.

Wilkes Head *See* North Briton.

Wild Life Skellingthorpe, Lincoln. The interior of the pub lives up to the exotic name, the African Lounge, for instance, having a bar canopy depicting a thatched kraal and stuffed heads of jungle animals behind it. There is another pub of this name at Creswell, near Worksop.

Wild Goose Combe-in-Teignhead, Devon. Others at Llanbethery, near Barry and Redditch. The Devonshire pub is named after the wild geese that assemble in the nearby estuary before their annual migration. When Shakespeare referred to a 'wild goose chase' in *Romeo and Juliet* he used the phrase in its earlier sense of an erratic course. This original meaning was forgotten, and the expression has come to mean an undertaking that is foolish, risky, and above all hopeless and fruitless, as if wild geese were impossible to catch.

William Butler Ettingshall, near Wolverhampton. This pub was opened in 1965 on the site of a former brewhouse. It was given the name of the founder of the Wolverhampton and Dudley Brewery Company.

William Camden *See* Camden.

William Caxton West Cross, Tenterden, Kent. William Caxton (1422–91) learned his trade as a printer in Cologne, then printed the first book in English in 1475. The sign of this pub, in the area where he was born, shows *The Game and Playe of Chesse*, his second book. The pub was formerly the Black Horse but changed its name when a Caxton Exhibition was held at Tenterden in 1951, during the Festival of Britain. Brighton has a Caxton Arms.

William Cobbett Farnham, Sry. This used to be the Jolly Farmer, but William Cobbett (1762–1835) was born here and is rightly remembered. Cobbett was the son of a farmer and self-educated. After serving in the army he emigrated to America for some time, then returned in 1800 to found the *Weekly Political Register*, a kind of early *Private Eye*. He was frequently fined for his libels and satirical comments and in 1810 was sent to prison for two years. He became a member of parliament in 1832, representing Oldham. Of his many writings, his *Rural Rides* are probably best remembered. He was a good observer and descriptive writer, and had great common sense, though he could not resist being sarcastic.

William Cowper *See* Cowper Arms.

William Harvey Willesborough, Kent. William Harvey (1578–1657) was born in Folkestone. He entered the medical profession and was chosen by the College of Physicians in 1615 to deliver lectures on anatomy and surgery. Soon afterwards he discovered the circulation of the blood, though physicians of the time refused to believe him. He became physician to Charles I about 1630 and attended him during the Civil War.

William Mitchell Morecambe. The pub was named in 1971 after the founder of Mitchells Brewery, Lancaster's surviving family brewery. It owns some fifty pubs.

William Murrell Barnham, near Bognor Regis. William Murrell (1725–99) lived here when it was still a farmhouse. He owned Barnham Mill.

Williamson's Tavern London EC4. This is said to have been the town house owned by Sir John Falstaff (1377–1459). It was turned into a tavern in the eighteenth century by a Mr Williamson.

William the Conqueror Rye Harbour and elsewhere. William I (1027?–87) was the illegitimate son of Robert I, duke of Normandy. He was probably promised the throne of England by his cousin Edward the Confessor, but when Edward died in January, 1066, the Saxon Prince Harold was crowned. William assembled a powerful army and invaded England in September of that year, over-coming Harold at Senlac, near Hastings, in October. Harold was killed in the battle, and William, though victor, is estimated to have lost 15,000 men. William was at first a mild ruler of England, but various rebellions and conspiracies against him gave him an excuse to be more ruthless. In the latter part of his reign he ordered the general survey of all the lands in the kingdom known as the Domesday Book, a historical document of immense importance. William had married Matilda, a daughter of the Earl of Flanders. They had three sons, Robert, William and Henry. Given his importance in English history, William the Conqueror is remembered on surprisingly few inn signs. The sign at Rye Harbour is based on a silver penny of the period.

William Twigg Great Hollands, near Bracknell, Berks. A plaque on the wall of the Public Bar shows a labourer at work and says: 'William Twigg, labourer and hard worker, whose parcel of land granted by the Lord of the Manor in 1553 is thought to be where this house now stands'.

William Webb Ellis Rugby. William Webb Ellis was the sixteen-year-old boy who picked up the ball during a game of football on the Close, at Rugby, and ran with it, thereby giving birth to the new game of Rugby football. This remarkable event occurred in 1823, and Webb Ellis was probably given a hearty kicking by his seniors for behaving so stupidly, yet twenty years later the rules had been changed at Rugby to make 'running in' legal. The 'rules' had until that time been very flexible in any case, and had varied from public school to public school, village to village. It is interesting to note that the brewery wanted to call this pub the Flashman, after the school bully at Rugby described by Thomas Hughes in *Tom Brown's Schooldays* and given new life in modern times by the novelist George MacDonald Fraser. Protests from the headmaster of Rugby caused Webb Ellis to be commemorated instead in 1983.

William Wilberforce East Farleigh, near Maidstone. William Wilberforce (1759–1833) was a noted campaigner in parliament for the abolition of slavery. His bill to that effect was defeated four times, but he succeeded in getting it through in 1807, after a twenty-year battle. He is also commemorated in Wilberforce University, Ohio, which is for co-ed black students. The inn sign here shows him holding a broken chain of fetters.

Will o' Nats Meltham, near Huddersfield. This pub was owned by a William who was a son of a Nathaniel.

Willow Beauty Harlow, Esx. The name of an insect which infests the willow tree.

Will Ritson's Bar Wasdale Head, Cumb. This is officially the Wasdale Head, but the nineteenth-century innkeeper is still remembered for his out-rageously tall stories. Liar competitions are held annually to see if anyone can match him as the world's biggest liar.

Will Scarlet Hucknall, near Nottingham. The pub is named after the companion of Robin Hood, also commemorated in a local pub name together with other pubs named after Maid Marian, Little John and Friar Tuck.

Wiltshire Brewery Cheltenham. Also Wiltshire Lamb, Alverstoke and Portsmouth, both Hampshire, while Cheltenham is in Gloucestershire. Wiltshire does at least have one of its own pubs, as it were: the Wiltshire Yeoman is at Chirton, near Devizes. *See* Yeoman.

Wiltshire Yeoman *See* Yeoman.

Willy Fox *See* Fox.

Windjammer Canvey Island, Esx. Another in Glasgow. This American slang term for a sailing vessel, one which the wind jams, or pushes forcibly, was first used at the end of the nineteenth century. The British adopted the term almost immediately.

Windmill Ruislip and elsewhere. There are still nine pubs of this name in central London, but most of them mark the sites where windmills formerly stood. There was one on Hampstead Hill until the early eighteenth century, and Windmill Street is named for another that was there until two centuries ago.

Windrush Near Witney, Oxon. The name of a river which rises near Cutsdean and flows into the Thames near Standlake.

Windsock Dunstable. The tubelike piece of material which is used to assess the direction in which the wind is blowing and its strength. Gliders take off from the nearby downs.

Windsor Castle Windsor and elsewhere. Also Windsor, Bedford; Windsor Arms, Esher, Sry; Windsor Bridge, Manchester; Windsor Tavern, Eastbourne. The distinctive shape and special royal associations of Windsor Castle make it a popular sign, with seventeen pubs bearing it in the London area. It was George V who by Royal Proclamation in 1917 changed the name of the royal house to the House of Windsor, it having previously been the House of Saxe-Coburg and Gotha.

Windsor Lad Windsor. The name of a racehorse which won the St Leger and the Derby in 1935.

Windwhistle Cricket St Thomas, Som. Another at Weston-Super-Mare. This name poses something of a problem for the sign-painter, but at Cricket St Thomas (where the 'Cricket' means 'little hill') he has managed to illustrate a gust of wind whistling through the tree tops.

Wine Barrel Rugby. 'Wine' is mentioned in various names, most of which speak for themselves. They include: Wine Cask, Sidcup; Wine Cellar, Wolstanton, Staffs; Wine Glass, Edinburgh; Wine Keg, Blackheath, Staffs; Wine Lodge, Ware and elsewhere; Wine Pipe, Bristol – where 'pipe' is similar to a butt, a large cask containing 106 imperial gallons; Wine Shades, Barnsley and Old Wine Shades, London EC4 – where 'shades' refers to a wine vault with a drinking bar, shaded either by being below ground or protected from the sun by an arcade; Wine Stores, Evesham; Wine Vaults, Ruthin, Clwyd and Yeovil; Wine and Spirit Vaults, Shepton Mallet, Som.

Winged Horse *See* Pegasus.

Winger Fenton, near Stoke-on-Trent. This name honours locally-born Sir Stanley Matthews, who played as outside right for Stoke City, then Blackpool. He was regarded by many as one of the finest forwards the game of football has ever produced. He was also a fine ambassador when he represented England in inter-national matches, having an enviable reputation for fair play and impeccable behaviour on and off the pitch.

Winking Frog Wedges Mills, near Cannock. A name that may be compared more easily with the Blinking Owl at Boroughbridge and Cwmbran than with the Winking Man at Blackshaw, near Leek.

Winkle Basingstoke. The pub is on the Winklebury Estate, which clearly suggested the name. The

sign shows the periwinkle, the edible gastropod, on one side. The other side shows Sir Winston Churchill for reasons which are not immediately apparent.

Winnall *See* Wulstan.

Winner Brighton. The pub is opposite the racecourse.

Winning Post Wolverhampton and elsewhere. This makes a highly convenient sign for pubs near a racecourse. The 'winning' theme is maintained in Winning Horse at Claygate, Sry and elsewhere, and Winnings, Ushaw Moor, near Durham.

Winston Also Winston Churchill *See* Sir Winston Churchill.

Winter Gardens Bournemouth. Another at Uttoxeter. The original Winter Gardens were in a glass pavilion at Bournemouth, opened in 1874, though the equable climate in this town makes outside winter gardens a possibility. The pavilion was filled with palms and ornamental trees.

Wise Alderman Kidlington, near Oxford. The sign here shows Alderman Frank Wise (died 1966), who was chairman of the local parish council and vice-chairman of Oxfordshire County Council. The pub was formerly the Railway Inn.

Wise Man West Stafford, near Dorchester. A trio of seventeenth century stone cottages were converted into this pub. The sign shows an 'honest lawyer' and is accompanied by a verse: 'I trust no wise man will condemn/A cup of genuine now and then;/When you are faint, your spirits low,/Your string relaxed: 'twill bend your bow . . . ' This has been curiously attributed to Thomas Hardy, who is said to have frequented the inn. Since it was converted in 1937 and Hardy died in 1928, he must have been present in spirit rather than bodily. He was also a fine poet, quite incapable of writing a verse of that kind.

Wise Owl Deighton, near Huddersfield. Another at Leeds. This name should not be interpreted literally, since the owl does not have a reputation for being intelligent. What it does have is a reputation for looking pompous and solemn, but when men were referred to as 'owls' in the past, the implication was always that beneath that outward appearance they were actually rather stupid – they were wiseacres, in other words, not truly wisemen. In folklore the owl is considered to be rather a bad omen.

Wishing Tree Hollington, near Hastings. Another at Cherry Willingham, near Lincoln. This name provides a reminder that in many villages an individual tree is named. Sidney refers in his *Arcadia* to a wishing tree, where it seems to be similar to a wishing well. Wishing Well is itself found as a pub name at St Ann's, Nottingham and elsewhere. There is a Wish Towers at Eastbourne and a Wishes at Wishaw, Strath, the last-named punning on its location.

Witch Lindfield, W Ssx. The local story is that two sisters ran this pub at one time and brewed their own ale, considered to be a real 'witch's brew'.

Witch and the Wardrobe Lincoln. The name is derived from the title of one of C S Lewis's books for children, *The Lion, the Witch and the Wardrobe*, published in 1950.

Witham Boston, Lincs. This river rises near Market Overton and flows past Grantham, Lincoln and Boston to the Wash.

Withens Ben Rhydding, Ilkley. 'Withen' is a dialectal word for a willow.

Withy Cutter Bridgwater. A 'withy' here is a pliable branch of a willow tree, used locally in basket making. The sign shows ancient and modern methods of cutting withies on nearby Sedgemoor. 'Withy' can also refer to the entire willow tree, as in Withies, Compton, near Guildford; Withy Trees, Fulwood, near Preston; Withywood, Four Acres, near Bristol.

Witness Box London EC4. This modern theme pub displays newspaper-cutting mementoes of celebrated criminal cases and awards a plaque annually to the reporter whose crime story is voted best of the year.

Wizard Nether Alderley, near Macclesfield. Another at Westcott, near Dorking. A long and complicated story attaches to the Nether Alderley pub name. It has to do with a wizard who revealed the whereabouts of King Arthur's knights to a local farmer. It seems that they are waiting in a secret cave to deliver the townsfolk of Macclesfield from some sad but unspecified fate. A 'wizard' is so-called because he is 'wise'.

Woad Man Boston. Woad is a blue dye prepared from the powdered and fermented leaves of *Isatis tinctoria*, a plant once grown in this area. The Ancient Britons dyed themselves with it. For modern uses indigo has replaced it.

Wobbly Wheel Alfrick Pound, near Worcester. Another at Warmington, near Banbury. These are no doubt straight-forward buckled wheels which serve usefully as inn signs. 'Wobble' has other connections with drinking. In nautical slang a ship that steered an erratic course was said to 'wobble like a drunken sailor with two left legs', while a 'wobble-shop', in the low slang of the nineteenth century, was a shop where liquor was sold though the proprietor had no licence.

Woden Church Hill, Wednesbury, W Mids. The place name Wednesbury means 'the borough belonging to Woden' (just as Wednesday is Woden's day). Woden, also known as Odin, is the chief Germanic god, identified with Mercury because of his wisdom and magical powers. His consort is Frigg, their son is Thor, god of thunder, commemorated in Friday and Thursday respectively.

Wolds Huggate, near Pocklington, N Yorks. The Wolds are a range of chalk hills in east Yorkshire and Lincolnshire. They run roughly parallel to the coast. The Yorkshire wolds in the north are separated from the Lincolnshire Wolds by the Humber estuary.

Wolsey Tavern *See* Cardinal Wolsey.

WOMEN IN PUB NAMES We can find reference to only about fifty women in British pub names, apart from queens, princesses and the like. Perhaps we should exclude George Eliot, who is remembered in that way and not as Mary Ann Evans. Only a handful of the ladies are nationally known, such as Lady Godiva, Florence Nightingale, Edith Cavell, Jean Harlow, Jenny Lind, Lancashire Lass, Lillie Langtry, Sarah Siddons, though many younger readers may exclaim 'Who is she?' at a few of those names. Almost as popular as these heroines are Lady Hamilton or Emma Hamilton mistress of Lord Nelson, and Nell Gwynn(e), mistress of Charles II. Of lesser fame is the Wicked Lady, Lady Kathleen Ferrers. Many of the women mentioned in pub names are in fact of rather local significance. Often they are former landladies who had strong personalities. It seems that pub customers prefer to find pretty girls behind the bars instead of on the inn signs. One such attraction of the past was Molly Millar, 'Sweet Molly Mog', daughter of an eighteenth-century landlord. She must have many modern counterparts, but how many of them will be remembered on inn signs of the future?

Wonder Chase Side, Enfield. Another at Tividale, W Mids. The name of an early nineteenth century stagecoach which did the London-Shrewsbury journey in just under sixteen hours.

Woodbine Bushbury, near Wolverhampton and elsewhere. This name is applied to several climbing plants. In early times it was used for the convulvulus and ivy, it is now mostly used of the common honeysuckle. Coventry has a Rose and Woodbine.

Woodcock Beacon Hill, Hindhead, Sry. A bird allied to the snipe, with a long bill and multicoloured plumage. Considered to be a delicacy when cooked.

Wood Colliers Arms Bewdley, H and W. The original meaning of 'collier' was a maker of wood charcoal. Making charcoal was formerly a common occupation in the Wyre Forest, which stretches from Bewdley to Cleobury Mortimer. Charcoal Burner is a similar name.

Woodcutter Shrewsbury and elsewhere. Also Woodcutters Arms, Leigh-on-Sea and else-where. After the men who pursued their trade in spite of poetic pleas such as that from Thomas Campbell: 'O leave this barren spot to me! Spare, woodman, spare the beechen tree' and George Pope Morris's: 'Woodman, spare that tree/Touch not a single bough/In youth it sheltered me,/And I'll protect it now.'

Wooden Bridge Woodbridge Hill, Guildford. The local people seem to be obsessed with crossing rivers in this area.

Wooden Fender Ardleigh, near Colchester. The fender, or defender, in this instance protected the sides of the pond opposite the pub.

Wooden Last *See* Last.

Wooden Spoon Downton, near Southampton. Perhaps a literal reference here, but this expression is now more frequently used to allude to an individual or team which finishes last in a competition, the wooden spoon being their imaginary prize. It derives in this sense from the custom at Cambridge University of presenting a wooden spoon to whoever comes lowest of those taking honours in the Mathematical Tripos. There is an 1803 reference to 'wooden spoons for wooden heads', referring to this examination tradition. This custom was transferred to Yale University in the US, where at first the wooden spoon was presented for the same reason. Later it was given annually to the most popular student, presumably because those students who were extremely sociable often did rather poorly in their exams.

Wooden Walls of Old England Collingtree, Northants. The reference here is to ships as a defensive force. Themistocles referred to the wooden walls of Athens, and the phrase was applied to English ships from the sixteenth century. Baron Coventry, in a speech made in 1635 to the judges, said: 'The wooden walls are the best walls of this kingdom'.

Woodin's Shades London EC2. William Woodin was a beer–retailer who took over these premises in 1863. For 'shades' *see* Wine Shades under Wine Barrel.

Woodlark Lambley, near Nottingham. The name of a species of lark which perches on trees.

Woodley Yeoman *See* Yeoman.

Woodman Ruislip and elsewhere. There are still about twenty-five pubs bearing this name in the greater London area alone, a reminder of the woodman's former importance. He looked after the forests as well as felling trees. *See also* Woodcutter. Associated names are Jolly Woodman, Littleworth Common, Bucks; Woodman Cottage, Gorefield, near Wisbech, Cambs; Woodman's, Ramsgate; Woodmans Arms, Hammerpot, near Angmering, W Ssx; Woodmans Hall, Boughton, near Faversham, Kent; Woodmans Rest, Shirley, near Solihull; Woodsman, Walderslade, near Chatham.

Woodpecker Mackworth Estate, Derby. This bird pecks the trunks and branches of trees in search of insects. It is known also as the woodchuck and the woodpie (because of its pied plumage). One early writer called it a hewhole.

Wood Pigeon Witley, near Godalming, Sry. This bird is also known as the ringdove. It was the subject of a curious superstition when pillows were stuffed with feathers in former times. If the feathers of this pigeon were used it was thought that someone who was dying would go slowly and painfully instead of quietly in his sleep.

Wookey Hole Wookey, near Wells, Som. The Wookey Hole is a large natural cave formed by the river Axe emerging from the Mendip Hills. There is a museum which contains objects proving that the cave was occupied in pre-historic times.

Woolcomber Hinckley, Leics. Another at Kettering. Also Woolcombers Arms, Leicester. The job of disentangling wool by combing it out was originally done by hand. This was a necessary process before the wool could be spun. Combing, or carding, is now done by machine.

Woolpack Slad, Glos and elsewhere. Also Woolpacks, Heckmondwike, W Yorks Woolsack, Derby and elsewhere, is a similar name. Both words originally meant large packs of wool, bales prepared for carriage or sale. The woolpack is said to have had a definite weight of 240 pounds, while a woolsack was of indeterminate weight. Woolsack has taken on a specific meaning because the lord chancellor in the House of Lords traditionally sits on a large square bag of wool covered with cloth. The law lords also sit on such woolsacks at the official opening of parliament. The tradition had symbolic origins as well as practical considerations of comfort – the woolsacks were a reminder of how much of the national wealth at one time depended on the wool trade.

Woolstaplers Bradford. The woolstaplers are merchants who buy wool from the producers, grade it, and sell it to the manu-facturers. The 'staplers' refers to the fact that they operate in a 'staple', in its sense of market or commercial centre, especially one dealing in a single product. The word derives from Latin *stapula*, and has nothing to do with the staples used in a stapling machine.

Woolwich Infant London SE18. The pub is near the main gate of the Woolwich Royal Arsenal, closed in 1966. The 'Infant' was the ironic name given to a gun manufactured there, the largest ever made in England at that time (the 1870s), weighing thirty-five tons.

Wordsworth Sheffield. William Wordsworth (1770–1850) was an English romantic poet, a friend and collaborator of Samuel Taylor Coleridge. Wordsworth moved with his sister Dorothy in 1799 to the Lake District. He married soon afterwards, and in 1813 went to live at Rydal Mount on Lake Windermere, where he remained until his death. He succeeded Southey as poet-laureate in 1843. Wordsworth deliberately used simple language, that 'of common men', and this often brought him into ridicule. He was certainly not commercially successful as a poet, and did perhaps tend to conceal some of his finest work within passages of great banality. Some of his shorter poems are nevertheless very widely known and admired, his 'Daffodils' being probably the best known of all.

Workman's Inn Talke Pits, Kidsgrove, near Stoke-on-Trent. There is a similar Workpeople's Inn at Huthwaite, Notts. Both names have a curiously humble flavour.

World Inn Edinburgh.
The customers are no doubt men and women of the world. 'Women of the world' in Shakespeare's time meant 'married women' as well as those who were socially aware.

World's End Almer, Dors and elsewhere. A name in use since the seventeenth century and used of an isolated inn. The name provides something of a challenge for the sign–painters. At Ecton, near Northampton, the horse of a medieval traveller is seen rearing in fright at the edge of a precipice. At Knaresborough, N Yorks, a motor coach is seen falling with the town bridge into the river Nidd. The allusion is to a prediction by Old Mother Shipton that when Knaresborough Bridge should fall for the third time, it would be the end of the world.

World's Wonder Warehorne, near Ashford, Kent. The name is interpreted on the sign as a cockerel surveying a square egg he has just laid. It contains a bottle of ale.

World Turned Upside Down London SE1. Others at Reading and Raunds, near Wellingborough, Northants. This dramatic phrase occurs in the Bible. Acts 17:6 has a reference to 'These men who have turned the world upside down', alluding to Paul and Silas who were preaching that 'This Jesus, whom I proclaim to you, is the Christ'. There is an earlier occurrence in the Old Testament. Isaiah 24:1. 'Behold the Lord maketh the earth empty, and maketh it waste, and turneth it upside down.' More recent translations refer instead to the Lord 'twisting its surface' instead of turning the earth upside down. It seems likely that there was therefore a Christian allusion in this name when it was first used, though the London pub had a sign at one time showing a man walking at the South Pole. This became a sign showing on one side an enormous fish which had just caught a man, and on the other side a football with legs about to boot a human between two goalposts.

Wormelow Tump Wormelow Tump, near Hereford. The 'tump' here is a small hill.

Wounded Soldier Wrangaton, Devon. The owner's husband was badly wounded in World War Two. The sign shows an old soldier with his arm in a sling, together with the motto: 'To serve is noble'. The pub has a reputation for giving practical support to military charities.

Wrecker Higher Blackley, Manchester. This was formerly the Lion and Lamb. It took on a new image in 1971, becoming in the words of the brewery a 'unique fun-and-fantasy recreation of Polynesia', complete with live alligators in their own pool. The pub seems to be named for those who designed its new image, since the word can mean 'one who wrecks an institution or structure'. The more usual meaning is one who causes a shipwreck by lighting false signals, etc, so that he can plunder the wrecked vessel. This is certainly the meaning in Cornwall, where pubs called the **Wreckers** are found at Truro and elsewhere.

Wrekendike Low Fell, near Gateshead. The name of a Roman road that ran through part of the county of Durham, ending at South Shields. The name possibly meant 'fugitives' dyke'.

Wrekin Wellington, Salop. The name of an isolated hill three miles south-west of Wellington. It rises to 1,335 feet. At Dawley Bank nearby there is a Wrekin View.

Wren's Nest Dudley and elsewhere, though only in the West Midlands. There is a well-known nature reserve called Wren's Nest Hill a mile to the north of Dudley Castle.

Wrestlers Cambridge and Great Yarmouth. Also Ye Olde

Wrestlers, London N6. Wrestling has been a popular sport in Britain since medieval times. Pepys mentions that he went to see the wrestling matches between the north and westcountrymen at Moorfields. The Water Poet, John Taylor, offered the following thought: 'Wrastling is held a Manly exercise,/A Game Olympick, both for Praise and Prize:/But hee that is most Skilfull, Strong or Tall/And wrastles with the wine, shall surely Fall.'

Wulstan Wolstanton, near Stoke-on-Trent. The name of an English monk, Bishop of Worcester in 1062 and patronised by William the Conqueror. The choice of name here, however, has more to do with local pronunciation of the place name, as has the Winnall at Willenhall, near Coventry.

Wuthering Heights Stanbury, near Haworth, W Yorks. Emily Brontë, the author of *Wuthering Heights* (1847) lived locally. The novel concerns a gipsy waif, Heathcliff, brought home and reared as one of his own children by Mr Earnshaw. He is badly treated by Earnshaw's son when young but revenges himself later. He falls passionately in love with Catherine, Earnshaw's daughter, but they are destined not to live in happily married bliss. The book made a great impact with its emotional intensity, illustrated by Catherine's remark: 'I *am* Heathcliff. The story has been filmed several times but is remembered in its 1939 version with Laurence Olivier and Merle Oberon as the passionate lovers. 'Wuthering' is a dialect word referring to sharp gusts of wind.

Wyandotte Kenilworth. This pub was built by a John Boddington, who then wrote to his eldest son, who had emigrated to the USA, and asked him to name it. The son suggested the name of the township in Michigan where he was now living. The township in its turn had 'borrowed' the name of an Indian tribe. The naming of the pub is said to have occurred in 1867. The sign now shows the handsome breed of domestic fowl known by this name since the 1880s.

Wych Elm Kingston-on-Thames, in Elm Road. Also Wych Tree, Morriston, near Swansea: Wych Way, Bridgemary, near Gosport, in Wych Lane. 'Wych' is applied especially to the elm but can describe other trees which are especially pliant. The word can also be spelt 'witch', but is not connected etymologically with the sorceress. The Bridgemary sign nevertheless puns on that meaning by showing three witches converging towards the centre of a circular maze, just as it puns simultaneously on 'which way'.

Wye Knot Ross-on-Wye. A punning link with Why Not, the name of a famous racehorse.

Wyken Pippin Wyken, near Coventry. A variety of apple said to have been raised by Lord Craven from the seed of a continental apple and planted at Wyken, about 1700. It has been known by other names, including *Gerkin Pippin* and *Pheasant's Eye*.

Wyvern Church Crookham, Hants and elsewhere. In heraldry this imaginary animal is a winged dragon which has feet like those of an eagle and a serpent-like, barbed tail. Two wyverns support the shield of the dukes of Rutland, and it occurs in various coats-of-arms.

X

X Westcott, near Cullompton, Devon. The pub of this name became the Merrie Harriers in 1983. Until then it had been shown in the *Guinness Book of Records* as having the shortest name in Britain.

XL Garstang, near Preston, Lancs. These letters appear on the pub sign here and are said to be suggestive of excellence. It was common practice in the seventeenth century for Excisemen to indicate the strength of ale by marking it X or XX. Several breweries still follow this convention and use a number of Xs to indicate a strong ale. Gales, for instance, has a cask light mild called XXXL. Clark of Wakefield has a strong winter ale called XS, presumably an unintentional pun on 'excess'.

Yacht Greenwich and elsewhere.
Also Yachtsman, Hamworthy,
near Poole and elsewhere.
Yachtsmans Arms, Brightlingsea,
Esx; Yacht Tavern, Northam and
Woolston, both near
Southampton. This vessel is now
used for racing and cruising, but
takes its name from a 'hunting'
ship, used for piratical purposes.
The *Yacht* near Ledsham, South
Wirral is said to be shown on old
maps as 'Yatch', for 'Ye Hatch', a
reference to the half-door known
as a hatch. The *Yacht* at Greenwich
has the world-famous Meridian
line running through its premises.

Yarborough Gainsborough. Also
Yarborough Arms, Ulceby, near
Immingham; Yarborough Hunt,
Brigg; Yarborough Vaults,
Grimsby. Yarborough is the name
of a parish in Lincolnshire, where
these pub names mostly occur. An
earl of Yarborough managed to get
the name entered into the
dictionary as a word, meaning a
'thirteen card hand at whist or
bridge containing no card higher
than a nine'. It seems that the earl
regularly used to offer odds of a
thousand to one against the
occurrence of such a hand. The
theoretical chance of such a hand
occurring is said to be 1827 to 1.

Yardarm Aberdeen. The yardarm is
technically either of the two ends
of a yard, though often used for
the yard itself, ie the spar which is
attached at its centre to the mast
and is used to support a square sail.
Offenders on board ship were
often hung or ducked from the
yardarm.

Yard of Ale Stratford-on-Avon and
elsewhere. This expression refers
to a special glass in the shape of an
old coaching horn, about a yard
long and with a bulb at one end. It
contains between two and four
pints, and is meant to be drained at
a single draught. Those unused to
it are likely to pour its contents
down themselves. The *Guinness
Book of Records* says that a two and a
half pints 'yard' was emptied in
five seconds in 1975.

Yare Great Yarmouth. The river
Yare rises near Shipdham and falls
into the sea at Yarmouth.

Yarn Spinner Spondon, near Derby.
Another at Bradford. Also Yarn
Spinners, Werneth, near Oldham.
These names refer literally to
spinning yarn, though no doubt
some of the customers also spin a
yarn, in the sense that they tell
long and complicated stories of a
slightly incredible kind. 'To yarn'
in the sense of to tell a story comes
from this expression, said to
originate in the stories told by
sailors as they engaged in the long
process of spinning yarn in order
to make ropes.

Y Bodel Talybont, near Conwy,
Gynd. Welsh for
'The Horseshoes'.

Y Ceffyl Du Carmarthen. This was
the **Black Horse** until 1968, when it

changed to the Welsh form of that name.

YE There was a word 'ye' in earlier forms of English: it was a plural form of 'you'. At no time did the word 'ye' mean 'the', and in a name like Ye Old Bull, the first word should properly be pronounced as if written 'The', for the 'y' in this instance is simply a graphic representation of 'th'. The important word in that sentence is *graphic*. When the graphic sign & is seen in a name, everyone knows that 'and' is to be pronounced, just as + and _ are to be spoken as plus and minus. The 'y' in 'ye' (when it stands for 'the') should be thought of in a similar way. What it actually represents is a letter that no longer exists in English, being one which died out in the sixteenth century. It was a letter which in its written form looked something like a 'y' or 'p', though by tacit agreement printers setting up texts which used the letter seem to have decided to use 'y' to represent it. The letter was called 'thorn', because its sound was the initial sound of that word, 'th'. In modern times some speakers deliberately refer to 'Yee oldee worldee' or whatever to indicate that a spurious kind of spelling has been used in order to suggest great age. In such cases the pronunciation *yee* for 'ye' is quite legitimate; in other cases *thee* is always the correct pronunciation of 'ye' when used for the definite article. Having said all that, we have in this book ignored its occurrence in pub names, just as we have ignored 'the' at the beginning of names.

Yeats Sligo. William Butler Yeats (1865–1939) was a poet and Irish nationalist. He also spent much time on the creation of an Irish theatre, writing plays himself which were performed by the Irish National Theatre Company at the Abbey Theatre, Dublin. He published many volumes of poetry, often on traditional Irish themes. He also served as a senator of the Irish Free State from 1922 to 1928, and was awarded the Nobel Prize for Literature in 1923.

Yellow Carvel Edinburgh. Carvel is another form of caravel, referring to a small, light and fast sailing ship, especially of Spain and Portugal. The pub has a sailing theme.

Yellow Lion Chesterfield and elsewhere. The lion in its relatively natural colour is not frequently mentioned in pub names, where it sometimes appears as green and blue, though usually red. *See* Lion.

Yellow Rose Middlesbrough. A name associated with Texas because of a once popular song, and with jealousy according to the language of flowers.

Yellow Wagtail Yeovil. Wadsworths, the Wiltshire brewers, have been pursuing a policy of naming their houses after birds since the 1960s. The wagtail does actually wag its tail constantly.

Yeoman Nuneaton and elsewhere. The origin of this word has given scholars much to think about. The *Oxford English Dictionary* derives it from 'young man'; Skeat seems to have been the first to make a case for 'country man, villager'. The yeoman became a trusted servant who was less than a squire and more than a knave. He probably owned and cultivated a small estate. Such respectable farmers who served in the army kept their name, becoming the Yeomanry, a volunteer cavalry force. Some yeomen were also foot soldiers. 'Yeoman' in a pub name may therefore refer to a farmer, or to a military man, the sign usually making it clear which is meant. At Gloucester, for instance, the *Yeoman* sign shows a soldier surveying the scene through binoculars from the turret of a tank. 'County' signs occur as follows: Bedfordshire Yeoman, Luton; Buckinghamshire Yeoman, Aylesbury; Cheshire Yeoman, Ledsham, near South Wirral; City of London Yeoman, London EC3; Derbyshire Yeoman, Derby; Devon Yeoman, Exeter; Essex Yeoman, Upminster; Hampshire Yeoman, Blackfield Cross, near Romsey; Kentish Yeoman, Seal, near Sevenoaks; Leicestershire Yeoman, Leicester; Oxfordshire Yeoman, Freeland, near Witney; Staffordshire Yeoman, Stafford; Surrey Yeoman, Burgh Heath, near Sutton; Sussex Yeoman, Worthing and Brighton; West Kent Yeoman, Deptford; Wiltshire Yeoman, Chirton, near Devizes and Trowbridge; Woodley Yeoman (for Berkshire), Woodley, near Reading. Wales has a Denbigh pub called the Denbigh Yeoman and a Pembroke Yeoman at Haverfordwest. At Grimstone, near Dorchester there is a Royal Yeoman, and at Wootton, near Northampton a Yeoman of England.

Yew Tree Colwall, near Malvern and elsewhere. The yew was of particular significance to our ancestors, who used them to make bows. An Act was therefore passed in the reign of Henry V to protect the tree. It is commonly seen in churchyards, being planted there as an evergreen symbol of immortality, and therefore has rather dismal associations.

York London SW11 and elsewhere. Normally a variant of Duke of York. Gloucester has a York House, Wakefield a York Street, Hastings a York and Crypt, London NW1 a York and Albany.

Yorke Arms Ramsgill, N Yorks. This pub was once the lodge of Gouthwaite Hall, the home of the Yorke family. The Hall now lies buried beneath the waters of Gouthwaite Reservoir nearby.

Yorker London W1. A 'yorker' is a cricketing term which refers to a ball which pitches directly under the bat. It is associated especially with the Australian cricketer Frederick Spofforth, who is seen on the inn sign here. It was the bowler's routing of the English team in 1882 which led to an advertisement regretting the death of English cricket in the *Sporting Times*. That same advertisement made the first reference to the mythical Ashes which England and Australia constantly strive to retain or regain, as the case may be. The other side of this inn sign features Doctor W G Grace. There is another *Yorker* pub in Nottingham.

York Minster London W1. The official name of this pub reflects the fact that it was once church property. The pub's unofficial name is the French House, having been run at one time by the first Frenchman to be granted a licence for this purpose. The pub was the centre for the Free French during World War Two, including amongst its customers at that time General de Gaulle.

Yorkshire Brewer Morecambe. A surprising name to find in Lancashire.

Yorkshire Bridge Bamford, Derbs. The nearby bridge over the Derwent was built in 1695 and is on a former packhorse route leading to Sheffield.

Yorkshire Coble *See* Coble.

Yorkshire Grey Biggleswade and elsewhere. The name of a famous breed of shire horse.

Yorkshireman Doncaster and elsewhere. Also Yorkshire Lass, Marske-by-the-Sea, near Redcar. The nickname for a Yorkshire-man, Tyke, is also found.

Yorkshire Rose Boroughbridge. Another at Guisley. The name is a variant of White Rose.

Yorkshire Terrier Brinsworth, near Rotherham. The sign here shows a Yorkshire terrier fielding on the boundary during a cricket match.

Young Pretender *See* Bonnie Prince Charlie.

Young Vanish Glapwell, near Chesterfield. The name of a steeplechaser which won many races 1823–32. It is thought that the horse was owned by the licensee here.

Ypres Castle Rye, E Ssx. This pub is below the Ypres Tower (twelfth century). Sittingbourne, Kent, has Ypres Tavern. Ypres is a town in the Flanders province of Belgium. It was an important textile centre in the Middle Ages, when it no doubt traded with Rye. In World War One three battles were fought there at great cost to the British. The Menin Gate was later erected there as a memorial to the British dead. In Belgium this name is pronounced as something like Eepr: the British soldiers called it Wipers.

Yutick's Nest Blackburn. 'Yutick' is an old Lancashire name for the whinchat, derived from its monotonous *u–tick* note. The landlord here in 1875 had worked in a weaving mill as a drawer-in, a job that involved him in much crouching over a low stool. The whinchat spends much time in what appears to be a crouching position on its ground-level nest, so men who were drawers-in were also called yuticks.

Z

Zach Willsher Thundersley, Esx. Named after a local boathouse proprietor, Zachary Willsher, who also ran an alehouse in the 1840s for the benefit of local farm-workers.

Zante Arms Liverpool. This pub appears to be named for one of the Ionian Islands, off the coast of Greece. Also the name of the capital of the Zante *nome* (a territorial division). The island produces wine, though its main exports are currants and olive oil.

Zanzibar Blackburn. Zanzibar, now part of Tanzania, is an island in the Indian ocean off the east coast of Africa. In 1890 it became a British protectorate, later it was briefly (1963–64) an independent territory within the British Commonwealth. This pub was perhaps owned by a retired British official.

Zebra Cambridge. The name of a Royal Navy destroyer in 1895, another in 1944. The pub name may have come from this source, though it is also used of anything which has a black and white striped appearance.

Zetland Middlesbrough. Also Zetland Arms in London SW7. Zetland is often used as an alternative name for the Shetland Islands. It is also the name of the county formed by the islands of Mainland, Yell and Unst.

Zoar Forfar, Tays. Zoar is a biblical place-name. Lot found refuge there following the destruction of Sodom (Genesis 19). Such names were established in Scotland as new villages were created and named by the pious. Padanaram (Genesis 25) and Jericho (*passim*) also became Scottish place names in the eighteenth century. In Hebrew *zoar* means 'little'.

Zodiac Ashford, Kent and elsewhere. An imaginary zone in space, conventionally divided into twelve parts. These in turn are normally shown as segments of a circle, with the signs of the zodiac contained in them, providing scope for a richly illustrated pub sign. Modern instances may refer to HMS *Zodiac*, a destroyer of 1944.

Zulu Ipswich. A native of Zululand, South Africa. The Zulus became powerful in the early nineteenth century. They were at war with both the Boers and the British, but were defeated by British forces in 1879. For a short time afterwards Zululand was a British protec-torate. HMS *Zulu* was a destroyer launched in 1909. It was severely damaged in 1916, whereupon its fore half was joined to the after part of another damaged destroyer, HMS *Nubian*. The resulting ship was named the *Zubian*.

Appendix

The publishers would like to thank Kenneth L. Whippy, of Harold Wood, Essex, for the following additions which he kindly compiled and sent to us.

Alexandra, Great Warley, Brentwood, Essex. Named after Edward VII's queen

Alfred Herring, Palmers Green, London. Named after local Victoria Cross hero

Argyll Arms, Argyll Street, London W1

Barrowboy and Banker, London SE1

Barking Dog, Barking, Essex

Ben Crouch, London W. Gothic theme pub

Beauchamp Arms, Buckenham, Norfolk

Blakesley Arms, London E12

Buckingham Arms, London SW1

Boy's Home (The boy is home), Abbots Langley, Herts. Formerly Rose & Crown, renamed after the First World War

Butcher's Hook and Cleaver, West Smithfield. Owes its name to its proximity to London's premier meat market

Cadogan Arms, Chelsea. Famous watering hole for sloane rangers

Captain Kidd, Wapping High Street, London E1. Named after famous pirate hanged at nearby Execution Dock in 1701

Carpenters Arms, Loughton, Essex

Chadwell Arms, Chadwell Heath, Romford, Essex

Cock and Woolpack, London EC3

College Arms, London E17

Collie Rowe, Collier Row, Romford, Essex

Colville Arms, Carlton Colville, Suffolk

Coopers Arms, Romford, Essex

Cottage Loaf, Loughton, Essex

Counting House, Cornhill, London EC3 and George Square, Glasgow

Crab, Shanklin, Isle of Wight

Crutched Friar, London EC3

Cutters Inn, Ely, Cambridgeshire

Dog and Partridge, Bury St Edmunds, Suffolk

Dolphin and Anchor, Chichester, West Sussex

Duckwood Inn, Harold Hill, Essex

Durham Arms, Romford, Essex

Eva Hart, Chadwell Heath, Romford, Essex. Named in honour of local *Titanic* survivor

Fine Line, Monument Street, London EC3

Fitzrovia, London W1. Pub sign indicates a Victorian army officer

Forester, Chigwell, Essex

Gardeners Arms, Loughton, Essex

General Redvers Buller, Crediton, Devon. Named in honour of local Victoria Cross hero

Golden Crane, Upminster, Essex. Only pub of this name?

Goose, Romford, Essex. Formerly the Morland Arms

Grasshopper on the Green, Westerham, Kent

Headley Arms, Great Warley, Essex

Henry Addington, London E14

Horniman at Hays, London SE1

Horse and Groom, Great Warley, Essex

Jerusalem, Clerkenwell, London. Georgian pub with original fireplace and tiling

Jobbers Rest, Upminster, Essex

John Fielding, Cwn Bran, Wales. Named in honour of local Victoria Cross hero

John Wallace Linton, Newport. Named in honour of local Victoria Cross hero

King Harold, Harold Wood, Essex. Only pub of this name?

Liberty Bell, Romford, Essex

Locomotive, Halstead, Essex

Lord Aberconway, London EC2

Magpie and Punchbowl, London EC2

Malt Shovel, Eynsford, Kent

Market Porter, London SE1

Marlborough Arms, Romford, Essex

Matchmaker, London EC3

Maybush, Waldringfield, Suffolk

Mawney Arms, Romford, Essex

Paper Mill, Apsley, Hertfordshire. Built on the site of the old John Dickinson printing works

Pitcher and Piano, London EC3

Porters Lodge, London EC3. Replaced the Ticket Porter, previously sited nearby

Princess Louise, Holborn, London EC1. Noted for its Victorian tiling in the gentlemen's toilet

Old Thameside Inn, Clink Street, London SE1

Optimist, Upminster, Essex

Rabbits, Stapleford Tawney, Essex

Rushcutters, Thorpe St Andrew, Norfolk

Sandmartin, Grays Thurrock, Essex

Shepherd and Dog, Harold Wood, Essex

Ship and Shovell, Charing Cross, London, Named in honour of Sir Cloudsley Shovell – English admiral who drowned when shipwrecked in the Scillies in 1707

Spa, Hockley, Essex. Named in honour of Victorian spa in town – closed 1838

Spencers Arms, Hornchurch, Essex

Squirrels, Romford, Essex

Still and Star, London E1. Associated with Jack the Ripper. Only two pubs bear this name

Theobald Arms, Grays Thurrock, Essex

Three Bishops, Brighstone, Isle of Wight. Honours three local rectors who became bishops

Three Colts, Ilford, Essex

Three Greyhounds, London W1

Three Travellers, Dagenham, Essex

Traitors Gate, Grays Thurrock, Essex

Treacle Mine, Grays Thurrock, Essex

Wentworth Arms, London EC3

Wharf, Grays Thurrock, Essex

Whitmore Arms, Grays Thurrock, Essex

Wilford Bridge, Melton Woodbridge, Suffolk. Contains many references to nearby Sutton Hoo, Saxon ship burial

Woodland Edge, South Ockendon, Essex

Wykeham Arms, Winchester, Hants. Arms of a noted Bishop of Winchester – William Wykeham

Ye Olde London, London EC4. Formerly Bell, Book and Candle

Ye Olde Valentine, Ilford, Essex